FINANCIAL ACCOUNTING

FINANCIAL ACCOUNTING ONLINE

A wide range of supporting resources are available at:

MyAccountingLab

Register to create your own personal account using the access code supplied with your copy of the book*, and access the following **student** learning resources:

- **A dynamic eText** of the book that you can search, bookmark, annotate and highlight as you please
- **Self-assessment questions** that identify your strengths before recommending a personalised study plan that points you to the resources which can help you achieve a better grade
- **Flashcards** to test your understanding of key terms

*If you don't have an access code, you can still access the resources. Visit **www.myaccountinglab.com** for details.

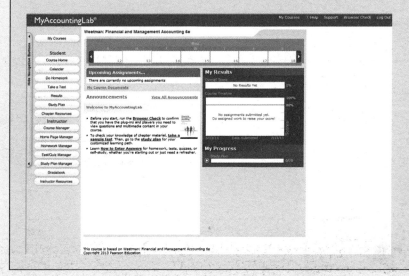

PEARSON

At Pearson, we take learning personally. Our courses and resources are available as books, online and via multi-lingual packages, helping people learn whatever, wherever and however they choose.

We work with leading authors to develop the strongest learning experiences, bringing cutting-edge thinking and best learning practice to a global market. We craft our print and digital resources to do more to help learners not only understand their content, but to see it in action and apply what they learn, whether studying or at work.

Pearson is the world's leading learning company. Our portfolio includes Penguin, Dorling Kindersley, the Financial Times and our educational business, Pearson International. We are also a leading provider of electronic learning programmes and of test development, processing and scoring services to educational institutions, corporations and professional bodies around the world.

Every day our work helps learning flourish, and wherever learning flourishes, so do people.

To learn more please visit us at: **www.pearson.com/uk**

Sixth Edition

FINANCIAL ACCOUNTING

Pauline Weetman

Professor of Accounting
University of Edinburgh

PEARSON

Harlow, England • London • New York • Boston • San Francisco • Toronto • Sydney • Auckland • Singapore • Hong Kong
Tokyo • Seoul • Taipei • New Delhi • Cape Town • São Paulo • Mexico City • Madrid • Amsterdam • Munich • Paris • Milan

PEARSON EDUCATION LIMITED
Edinburgh Gate
Harlow CM20 2JE
United Kingdom
Tel: +44 (0)1279 623623
Fax: +44 (0)1279 431059
Web: www.pearson.com/uk

———————————

First published under the Financial Times Pitman Publishing imprint in 1996 (print)
Second edition 1999 (print)
Third edition 2003 (print)
Fourth edition 2006 (print)
Fifth edition 2011 (print)
Sixth edition published 2013 (print and electronic)

The Financial Times. With a worldwide network of highly respected journalists, *The Financial Times* provides global business news, insightful opinion and expert analysis of business, finance and politics. With over 500 journalists reporting from 50 countries worldwide, our in-depth coverage of international news is objectively reported and analysed from an independent, global perspective. To find out more, visit www.ft.com/pearsonoffer.

ISBN: 978-0-273-78925-3 (print)
       978-0-273-78958-1 (PDF)
       978-0-273-778964-2 (eText)

British Library Cataloguing-in-Publication Data
A catalogue record for the print edition is available from the British Library

Library of Congress Cataloging-in-Publication Data
A catalog record for the print edition is available from the Library of Congress

10 9 8 7 6 5 4 3 2
16 15 14 13

Print edition typeset in 9.5/12pt Palatino by 35
Print edition printed and bound by L.E.G.O. S.p.A., Italy

NOTE THAT ANY PAGE CROSS REFERENCES REFER TO THE PRINT EDITION

Contents in brief

Contents

FINANCIAL ACCOUNTING

Part 1 A conceptual framework: setting the scene

Chapter 1 Who needs accounting?

Chapter 2 A systematic approach to financial reporting: the accounting equation

Chapter 3 Financial statements from the accounting equation

Chapter 4 Ensuring the quality of financial statements

Part 2 Reporting the transactions of a business

Part 3 Recognition in financial statements

Chapter 9   Current assets

Chapter 10   Current liabilities

Part 4 Analysis and issues in reporting

FINANCIAL ACCOUNTING ONLINE

A wide range of supporting resources are available at:

MyAccountingLab

Register to create your own personal account using the access code supplied with your copy of the book,* and access the following teaching and learning resources:

Resources for students

- **A dynamic eText** of the book that you can search, bookmark, annotate and highlight as you please
- **Self-assessment questions** that identify your strengths before recommending a personalised study plan that points you to the resources which can help you achieve a better grade
- **Flashcards** to test your understanding of key terms

Resources for instructors

- **Instructor's manual**, with additional questions, complete and fully worked solutions, as well as case study debriefs
- **PowerPoint slides**, containing figures from the book

For more information, please contact your local Pearson Education sales representative or visit **www.myaccountinglab.com**.

*If you don't have an access code, you can still access the resources. Visit **www.myaccountinglab.com** for details.

Preface to the sixth edition

Introduction

This book uses the international framework and International Financial Reporting Standards (IFRS) as its primary focus. It enables students in their early stages of study to understand and analyse the published annual reports and financial statements of our largest businesses and public sector institutions. IFRS are now applied in many aspects of government, local authority and other public sector accounting. Where relevant it also refers to the approach used in small and medium-sized businesses where the traditions of UK GAAP continue to be applied.

The book is written for the first level of undergraduate degree study in accounting and business studies, or equivalent introductory accounting courses for any professional training where an understanding of accounting is a basic requirement. While UK listed companies apply IFRS in their published financial statements, the remainder of the annual report is governed by UK-based regulations and codes. All UK companies operate under the Companies Act 2006. Their annual reports are influenced by the regulatory process applied to listed companies in the UK. This sixth edition is thoroughly revised to reflect these regulatory changes, particularly the restructuring of the Financial Reporting Council to take responsibility for the standards previously issued by the UK Accounting Standards Board.

All 'Real World' case studies at the start of each chapter have been updated to reflect changing conditions and particularly the note of caution over financial statements that has resulted from the banking and credit crisis of 2008–09. The underlying pedagogy of previous editions has been retained in response to encouraging comments from reviewers and from users of the book.

As institutions come under increasing scrutiny for the quality of the teaching and learning experience offered, a textbook must do more than present the knowledge and skills of the chosen subject. It must make explicit to the students what targets are to be achieved and it must help them to assess realistically their own achievements of those targets. It must help the class lecturer prepare, deliver, explain and assess the knowledge and skills expected for the relevant level of study. This is achieved by stating learning outcomes at the start of each chapter and by ensuring that the chapter headings and the end-of-chapter questions address the stated outcomes.

An accompanying website at **www.pearsoned.co.uk/weetman** provides the lecturer with a complete resource pack for each chapter. Student handouts containing a skeleton outline of each chapter, leaving slots for students to complete; overhead-projector masters that match the lecture handouts; additional multiple-choice questions and further graded questions in application of knowledge and in problem solving; all are features for this sixth edition.

End-of-chapter questions are graded according to the skills being assessed. There are tests of retained knowledge, tests of application of knowledge in straightforward situations and tests of problem solving and evaluation using the acquired knowledge in less familiar situations.

Overall the aim of the sixth edition is to provide an introduction to financial accounting which engages the interest of students and encourages a desire for further study.

It also contributes to developing the generic skills of application, problem solving, evaluation and communication, all emphasised by employers.

Subject coverage

Financial reporting is an essential component in the process of communication between a business and its stakeholders. The importance of communication increases as organisations become larger and more complex. Reporting financial information to external stakeholders not involved in the day-to-day management of the business requires a carefully balanced process of extracting the key features while preserving the essential core of information. The participants in the communication process cover a wide range of expertise and educational background, so far as accounting is concerned. The range begins with those who prepare financial statements, who may have a special training in accounting techniques, but it ends with those who may be professional investors, private investors, investment advisers, bankers, employee representatives, customers, suppliers and journalists.

First-level degree courses in accounting are increasingly addressed to this broad base of potential interest and this book seeks to provide such a broad base of understanding while also supplying a sound technical base for those intending to pursue specialised study of the subject further. In particular it makes use of the *Conceptual Framework* which is used by the International Accounting Standards Board in developing and reviewing accounting standards. That *Conceptual Framework* is intended to help preparers, users and auditors of financial statements to understand better the general nature and function of information reported in financial statements.

Aim of the book

The sixth edition has been updated throughout. It aims to provide a full understanding of the key aspects of the annual report, concentrating in particular on companies in the private sector but presenting principles of wider application which are relevant also to organisations operating in the public sector.

In the management accounting section, the book aims to establish a firm understanding of the basic techniques, while recognising that more recent developments in management accounting are becoming widespread. A contingency approach is adopted which emphasises that the selection of management accounting techniques is conditional on management's purpose. To meet this purpose, the management accountant performs the roles of directing attention, keeping the score and solving problems. Strategic management accounting is emphasised from the outset so that students are aware that management accounting must take an outward-looking approach. These themes are reiterated throughout, concluding with an explanation of the role of management accounting in business strategy, particularly e-business in the new economy. A student who has completed this first-level study of management accounting will be aware of many of the day-to-day practices of management accounting in business and the relevance of those practices. It also provides a self-contained, broad introduction to management accounting for business students who do not need to develop specialist knowledge.

In particular

An international perspective reflects the convergence in accounting standards across the European Union for listed companies. *Features specific to the UK* are retained where these continue to be relevant to other enterprises.

Concepts of financial accounting are identified by applying the principles enunciated by the International Accounting Standards Board in its *Conceptual Framework*. The

Conceptual Framework emphasises the desirability of meeting the needs of users of financial statements and it takes a balance sheet-oriented approach. That approach is applied consistently throughout the book, with some indication of the problems which may arise when it is clear that the established emphasis on the matching of revenues and costs may give a more rational explanation of existing practice.

User needs are explained in every chapter and illustrated by including first-person commentary from a professional fund manager, holding a conversation with an audit manager. The conversations are based on the author's research in the area of communication through the annual report.

The *accounting equation* is used throughout the financial accounting section for analysis and processing of transactions. It is possible for students who do not seek a technical specialism to complete the text without any reference to debit and credit bookkeeping. It is, however, recognised that particular groups of students may wish to understand the basic aspects of debit and credit bookkeeping and for this purpose the end-of-chapter supplements revisit, on a debit and credit recording basis, material already explored in the chapter. Debit and credit aspects of management accounting are not covered since these are regarded as best reserved for later specialist courses if the student so chooses.

Practical illustration is achieved by drawing on the financial information of a fictitious major listed company, taking an overview in early chapters and then developing the detailed disclosures as more specific matters are explored.

Interpretation of financial statements is a feature of all financial reporting chapters, formally brought together in Chapters 13 and 14. The importance of the wider range of corporate communication is reinforced in Chapter 14. This chapter also includes a discussion of some *current developments* that are under debate in the context of international convergence.

A *running case study example* of the fictitious company Safe and Sure plc provides illustration and interpretation throughout the chapters. Safe and Sure plc is in the service sector. The Instructors' Manual contains a parallel example, Craigielaw plc, in the manufacturing sector. On the website there are questions on Craigielaw to accompany most of the chapters.

Self-evaluation is encouraged by setting learning outcomes at the start of each chapter and reviewing these in the chapter summaries. Activity questions are placed at various stages throughout each chapter. Self-testing questions at the end of the chapter may be answered by referring again to the text. Further end-of-chapter questions provide a range of practical applications. Group activities are suggested at the end of each chapter with the particular aim of encouraging participation and interaction. Answers are available to all computational questions, either at the end of the book or on the website.

A *sense of achievement* is engendered in the reader of the financial accounting section by providing a general understanding of the entire annual report by the end of Chapter 7. Thereafter specific aspects of the annual report are explored in Chapters 8–12. Lecturers who wish to truncate a first-level course or leave specific aspects to a later level will find Chapters 8–12 may be used on a selective basis.

A *spreadsheet* approach to financial accounting transactions is used in the body of the relevant chapters to show processing of transactions using the accounting equation. The author is firmly convinced, after years of trying every conceivable approach, that the spreadsheet encourages students to apply the accounting equation analytically, rather than trying to memorise T-account entries. Furthermore students now use spreadsheets as a tool of analysis on a regular basis and will have little difficulty in applying suitable software in preparing spreadsheets. In the bookkeeping supplementary sections, the three-column ledger account has been adopted in the knowledge that school teaching is moving increasingly to adopt this approach which cuts out much of the bewilderment of balancing T-accounts. Computerised accounting systems also favour the three-column presentation with continuous updating of the balance.

Flexible course design

There was once a time when the academic year comprised three terms and we all knew the length of a typical course unit over those three terms. Now there are semesters, trimesters, modules and half-modules so that planning a course of study becomes an exercise in critical path analysis. This text is written for one academic year comprising two semesters of 12 weeks each but may need selective guidance to students for a module of lesser duration.

In financial accounting, Chapters 1–4 provide an essential conceptual framework which sets the scene. For a general appreciation course, Chapters 5 and 6 are practical so that one or both could be omitted, leading directly to Chapter 7 as a guide to published accounts. Chapters 8–12 are structured so that the explanation of principles is contained early in each chapter, but the practical implementation is later in each chapter. For a general appreciation course, it would be particularly important to refer to the section of each chapter which analyses users' needs for information and discusses information provided in the financial statements. However, the practical sections of these chapters could be omitted or used on a selective basis rather than attempting full coverage. Chapters 13 and 14 are important to all readers for a sense of interpretation and awareness of the range of material within corporate reports. Chapter 15 takes the reader through a cash flow statement item-by-item with the emphasis on understanding and interpretation.

Approaches to teaching and learning

Learning outcomes

Targets for student achievement in relation to knowledge and understanding of the subject are specified in learning outcomes at the head of each chapter. The achievements represented by these learning outcomes are confirmed against graded questions at the end of each chapter. The achievement of some learning outcomes may be confirmed by Activities set out at the appropriate stage within the chapter.

Skills outcomes

The end-of-chapter questions test not only subject-specific knowledge and technical skills but also the broader general skills that are transferable to subsequent employment or further training.

Graded questions

End-of-chapter questions are graded and each is matched to one or more learning outcomes. Where a solution is provided to a question this is shown by an [S] after the question number.

A series questions: test your understanding

The A series questions confirm the application of technical skills. These are skills specific to the subject of accounting which add to the specialist expertise of the student. More generally they show the student's capacity to acquire and apply a technical skill of this type.

The answers to these questions can be found in relevant sections of the chapter, as indicated at the end of each question.

B series questions: application

The B series questions apply the knowledge gained from reading and practising the material of the chapter. They resemble closely in style and content the technical material of the chapter. Confidence is gained in applying knowledge in a situation that is very similar to that illustrated. Answers are given in Appendix II or on the website. These questions test skills of problem solving and evaluation that are relevant to many subjects and many activities in life, especially in subsequent employment. Some initiative is required in deciding how to apply relevant knowledge and in solving problems.

C series questions: problem solving and evaluation

The C series questions apply the knowledge gained from reading the chapter, but in a varied style of question. Problem solving skills are required in selecting relevant data or in using knowledge to work out what further effort is needed to solve the problem. Evaluation means giving an opinion or explanation of the results of the problem-solving exercise. Some answers are given in Appendix II but others are on the website so that they can be used in tutorial preparation or class work.

Group and individual cases

Cases apply knowledge gained from the chapter but they also test communication skills. Communication may involve writing or speaking, or both. It may require, for example, explanation of a technical matter to a non-technical person, or discussion with other students to explore a controversial issue, or presentation of a report to a business audience.

S series questions in supplementary sections

The S series questions test knowledge of the accounting records system (bookkeeping entries) to confirm understanding by those who have chosen to study the supplementary bookkeeping sections.

Website

A website is available at **www.pearsoned.co.uk/weetman** by password access to lecturers adopting this book. It contains additional problem questions for each chapter, with full solutions to these additional questions as well as any solutions not provided in the book. The website includes basic tutorial instructions and overhead-projector masters to support each chapter.

Target readership

This book is targeted at a broad-ranging business studies type of first-level degree course. It is intended to support the equivalent of one semester of 12 teaching weeks. There is sufficient basic bookkeeping (ledger accounts) in the end-of-chapter supplements to make the book suitable for those intending to pursue a specialised study of accounting beyond the first level but the bookkeeping material is optional for those who do not have such special intentions. The book has been written with undergraduate students particularly in mind, but may also be suitable for professional and postgraduate business courses where financial reporting is taught at an introductory level.

Acknowledgements

I am grateful to academic colleagues and to reviewers of the text for helpful comments and suggestions. I am also grateful to undergraduate students of five universities who have taken my courses and thereby helped in developing an approach to teaching and learning the subject. Professor Graham Peirson and Mr Alan Ramsay of Monash University provided a first draft of their text based on the conceptual framework in Australia which gave valuable assistance in designing the structure of this book, which was also guided from the publishing side by Pat Bond and Ron Harper. Professor Ken Shackleton of the University of Glasgow helped plan the structure of the management accounting chapters. The Institute of Chartered Accountants of Scotland gave permission for use of some of the end-of-chapter questions.

Subsequently I have received valuable support in successive editions from the editorial staff at Pearson Education. For this latest edition I am grateful to colleagues and students who have used the book in their teaching and learning. I have also been helped by constructive comments from reviewers and by guidance from Katie Rowland, Acquisitions Editor, and Joy Cash, Senior Project Editor.

Guided tour of the book

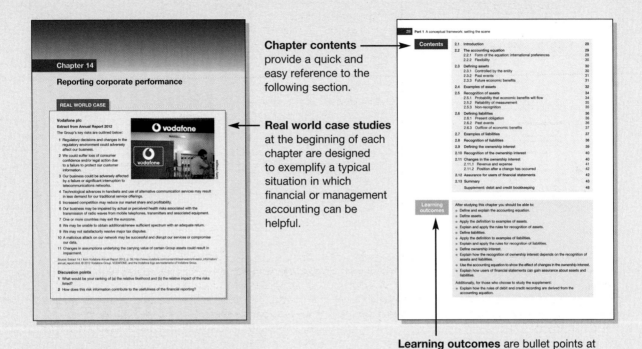

Chapter contents provide a quick and easy reference to the following section.

Real world case studies at the beginning of each chapter are designed to exemplify a typical situation in which financial or management accounting can be helpful.

Learning outcomes are bullet points at the start of each chapter to show what you can expect to learn from that chapter, highlighting the core coverage.

Key terms and **definitions** are emboldened where they are first introduced, with a definition box to provide a concise explanation where required.

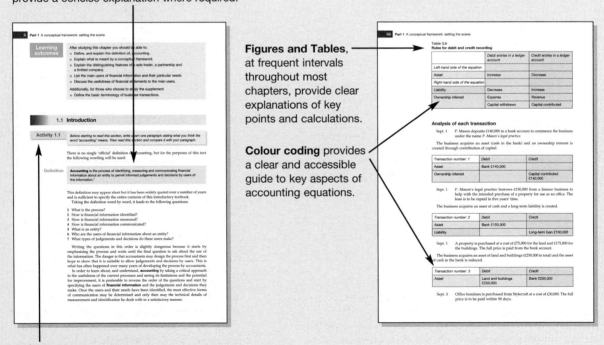

Figures and Tables, at frequent intervals throughout most chapters, provide clear explanations of key points and calculations.

Colour coding provides a clear and accessible guide to key aspects of accounting equations.

Activities appear throughout each chapter to encourage self-evaluation and help you to think about the application of the subject in everyday life.

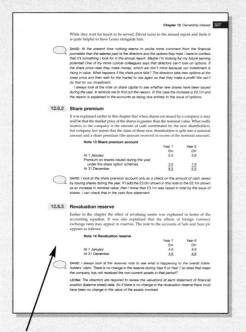

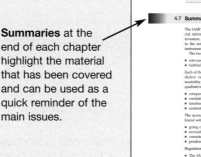

Summaries at the end of each chapter highlight the material that has been covered and can be used as a quick reminder of the main issues.

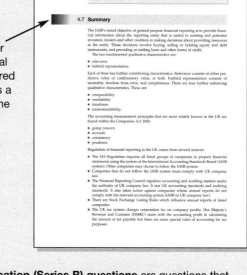

A conversation between two managers (**consultants**) appears at intervals throughout the text to provide a valuable insight into the type of interpretative comment which you may find more taxing. These conversations allow a more candid discussion of issues and problems within the subject.

Application (Series B) questions are questions that ask you to apply the knowledge gained from reading and practising the material in the chapter, and closely resemble the style and content of the technical material. Answers are given at the end of the book or in the Resources for Tutors on the Instructor Resource Centre at **www.pearsoned.co.uk/weetman**.

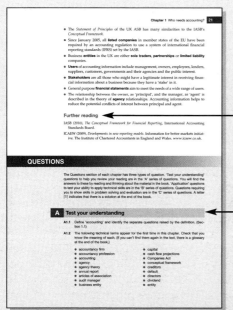

Further reading sections provide full details of sources of information referred to in the chapter.

Test your understanding (Series A) questions are short questions to encourage you to review your understanding of the main topics covered in each chapter.

Problem solving and evaluation (Series C) questions require problem solving skills to select relevant data in order to work out what further effort is needed to solve the problem. Evaluation questions ask for your opinion surrounding the results of the problem solving exercise. Some solutions are found at the end of the book but others are in the Resources for Tutors section on the Instructor Resource Centre at **www.pearsoned.co.uk/weetman**, for use in tutorial preparation or class work.

Activities for study groups at the end of most chapters are designed to help you apply the accounting skills and knowledge you have acquired from the chapter to the real world.

Publisher's acknowledgements

We are grateful to the following for permission to reproduce copyright material:

Figures

Figure UNF 3.1 from http://annualreport2012.j-sainsbury.co.uk/financial-review/summary-balance-sheet/, J Sainsbury plc, Reproduced by kind permission of J Sainsbury plc; Figure 4.1 from http://frc.org.uk/About-the-FRC/FRC-structure.aspx, '© Financial Reporting Council (FRC). Adapted and reproduced with the kind permission of the Financial Reporting Council. All rights reserved. For further information, please visit www.frc.org.uk or call +44 (0)20 7492 2300.'

Text

Extract 1.1 from *Transport for London Annual Report 2012*, pp. 70, 80, 92, 206. www.tfl.gov.uk/assets/downloads/corporate/tfl-annualreport-2012.pdf; Extract UNF 2.1 from http://www.btplc.com/Sharesandperformance/Annualreportandreview/pdf/BT_SFS_NOM_2012.pdf, BT Group plc, pp. 4, 9, with the permission of British Telecommunications plc; Extract 4.1a from *Rejected Accounts: Common reasons for accounts being rejected by Companies House & how to avoid them.* Financial Reporting Faculty, Institute of Chartered Accountants in England and Wales. (ICAEW 2010), Extract from Rejected Accounts: Common reasons for accounts being rejected by Companies House and how to avoid them. ICAEW, Financial Reporting Faculty 2010; Extract 4.1b from *The Sharman Inquiry. Going concern and liquidity risks: lessons for companies and auditors. Final report* (Sharman 2012) Financial Reporting Council, '© Financial Reporting Council (FRC). Adapted and reproduced with the kind permission of the Financial Reporting Council. All rights reserved. For further information, please visit www.frc.org.uk or call +44 (0)20 7492 2300.'; Extract 5.1 from Annual report 2011, Croda International plc, p. 14. http://www.croda.com; Extract 8.1 from http://www.itvplc.com/sites/itvplc/files/ITV%202011%20Annual%20Report%20and%20Accounts.pdf, with the permission of ITV plc; Extract 10.1 from Customers products and suppliers Extract from Business Review (p. 20); Payments to suppliers Extract from Directors' Report (p. 30); Figure – Extract from notes to the financial statements (p. 63) John Lewis Partnership, Annual Report 2012; Extract 11.1 from Extract from Significant Accounting Policies (p. 106); Source: SSE plc, Annual Report 2012; Figure: Extract from Notes to the Accounts (pp. 140–1), with the permission of SSE plc; Extract 12.1 from BAE signals high-liability results season, *Financial Times Lombard*, 16/02/2012 (Guthrie, J.), © The Financial Times Limited. All Rights Reserved.; Extract 13.1 from Tesco plc Annual Report 2012 pp. 29–30; Extract 13.2 from http://www.ft.com/cms/s/0/8588d422-b6ca-11e1-8c96-00144feabdc0.html#ixzz21tpdndrN, © The Financial Times Limited. All Rights Reserved.; Extract 14.1 from Vodafone Annual Report 2012, p. 39; http://www.vodafone.com/content/index/investors/investor_information/annual_report.html, © 2012 Vodafone Group. VODAFONE, and the Vodafone logo are trademarks of Vodafone Group.; Extract 15.1 from Amazon, *Financial Times*, 12/07/2012, p. 13 (Armstrong, R. and Kirk, S.), www.ft.com/cms/s/0/f3a02a44-cb53-11e1-b896-00144feabdc0.html#axzz21o2gR2kd, © The Financial Times Limited. All Rights Reserved.

In some instances we have been unable to trace the owners of copyright material, and we would appreciate any information that would enable us to do so.

FINANCIAL ACCOUNTING

Part 1

A conceptual framework: setting the scene

Chapter 1

Who needs accounting?

Meeting users' needs

Transport for London: extracts from Annual Report 2012

Transport for London (TfL) is a statutory corporation established by section 154 of the Greater London Authority Act 1999 (GLA Act 1999). It is a functional body of the Greater London Authority (GLA) and reports to the Mayor of London.

Accounting policies (p. 92)

TfL is required to prepare an annual Statement of Accounts by the Accounts and Audit (England) Regulations 2011 (the 2011 Regulations), which those Regulations require to be prepared in accordance with proper accounting practices.

Shutterstock.com/Stuart Monk

Highlights (p. 70)

In 2011/12, passenger demand again increased from the previous year. London Underground (LU) passenger journey growth continued, with passenger journeys up 5.7 per cent on 2010/11. Service demand on the bus network rose by 2.4 per cent and Docklands Light Railway (DLR) passenger journeys increased by 10.0 per cent reflecting the opening of the Stratford International Extension and Westfield Stratford City. Fares increased by an average 5.6 per cent in January 2012, resulting in an increase in gross fares income to £3,547m.

Gross expenditure before write off of goodwill increased by 5.2 per cent to £6,124m, reflecting the increased level of activity offset to a degree by the impact of efficiency savings. An exceptional goodwill impairment of £106m was recognised in relation to the acquisition of the CARE and WARE groups of companies (former PFI partners of DLR).

The level of capital works being undertaken during 2011/12 remained high reflecting the ongoing investment in Crossrail and Tube infrastructure required to increase capacity on the network. Capital expenditure during the year was £2,652m.

Statement of responsibilities (p. 80)

The Corporation is required to:

- Make arrangements for the proper administration of its financial affairs and to secure that one of its officers (its Chief Finance Officer) has responsibility for the administration of those affairs;

- Manage its affairs to secure economic, efficient and effective use of resources and safeguard its assets;
- Approve the Statement of Accounts.

Annual Governance Statement (p. 206)

TfL establishes clear channels of communication with all sections of the community and other stakeholders, ensuring accountability and encouraging open consultation by:

. . .

- Making clear to staff and the public what it is accountable for and to whom
- Publishing, publicising and making generally available an annual report as soon as practicable after the end of the financial year
- The annual report presenting an objective and understandable account of its activities and achievements and its financial position and performance

. . .

Discussion points

1 Who might be included in the stakeholders to whom TfL is accountable?
2 To what extent do the 'Highlights' meet the needs of users of the financial statements?

Contents

Learning outcomes

After studying this chapter you should be able to:

● Define, and explain the definition of, accounting.

● Explain what is meant by a *conceptual framework*.

● Explain the distinguishing features of a sole trader, a partnership and a limited company.

● List the main users of financial information and their particular needs.

● Discuss the usefulness of financial statements to the main users.

Additionally, for those who choose to study the supplement:

● Define the basic terminology of business transactions.

1.1 Introduction

Activity 1.1

Before starting to read this section, write down one paragraph stating what you think the word 'accounting' means. Then read this section and compare it with your paragraph.

There is no single 'official' definition of accounting, but for the purposes of this text the following wording will be used:

Definition

Accounting is the process of identifying, measuring and communicating financial information about an entity to permit informed judgements and decisions by users of the information.[1]

This definition may appear short but it has been widely quoted over a number of years and is sufficient to specify the entire contents of this introductory textbook.

Taking the definition word by word, it leads to the following questions:

1 What is the process?
2 How is financial information identified?
3 How is financial information measured?
4 How is financial information communicated?
5 What is an entity?
6 Who are the users of financial information about an entity?
7 What types of judgements and decisions do these users make?

Writing the questions in this order is slightly dangerous because it starts by emphasising the process and waits until the final question to ask about the use of the information. The danger is that accountants may design the process first and then hope to show that it is suitable to allow judgements and decisions by users. This is what has often happened over many years of developing the process by accountants.

In order to learn about, and understand, **accounting** by taking a critical approach to the usefulness of the current processes and seeing its limitations and the potential for improvement, it is preferable to reverse the order of the questions and start by specifying the users of **financial information** and the judgements and decisions they make. Once the users and their needs have been identified, the most effective forms of communication may be determined and only then may the technical details of measurement and identification be dealt with in a satisfactory manner.

Reversing the order of the questions arising from the definition of accounting is the approach used in this book, because it is the one which has been taken by those seeking to develop a **conceptual framework** of accounting.

This chapter outlines in particular the Conceptual Framework of the International Accounting Standards Board which has been developed for international use in accounting practice. The chapter explains the nature of three common types of business **entity** and concludes by drawing on various views relating to the users of accounting information and their information needs.

Because the understanding of users' needs is essential throughout the entire text, the chapter introduces David Wilson, a **fund manager** working for a large insurance company. In order to balance the demands of users with the restrictions and constraints on preparers of financial information, the chapter also introduces Leona Rees who works as an **audit manager** with an **accountancy firm**. Both of them will offer comments and explanations as you progress through the text.

Activity 1.2	*How does this section compare with your initial notions of what accounting means? If they are similar, then it is likely that the rest of this book will meet your expectations. If they are different, then it may be that you are hoping for more than this book can achieve. If that is the case, this may be a useful point at which to consult your lecturer, tutor or some other expert in the subject to be sure that you are satisfied that this book will meet your personal learning outcomes.*

1.2 The development of a conceptual framework

A **conceptual framework** for accounting is a statement of principles which provides generally accepted guidance for the development of new reporting practices and for challenging and evaluating the existing practices. Conceptual frameworks have been developed in several countries around the world, with the UK arriving a little late on the scene. However, arriving late does give the advantage of learning from what has gone before. It is possible to see a pattern emerging in the various approaches to developing a conceptual framework.

The conceptual frameworks developed for practical use by the **accountancy profession** in various countries all start with the common assumption that **financial statements** must be useful. The structure of most conceptual frameworks is along the following lines:

- Who are the users of financial statements?
- What are the information needs of users?
- What types of financial statements will best satisfy their needs?
- What are the characteristics of financial statements which meet these needs?
- What are the principles for defining and recognising items in financial statements?
- What are the principles for measuring items in financial statements?

The most widely applicable conceptual framework originated as the *Framework for the Preparation and Presentation of Financial Statements* produced by the International Accounting Standards Board (IASB). This *Framework* was issued in 1989 and either reflects, or is reflected in, national conceptual frameworks of the USA, Canada, Australia and the UK. In 2010 the *Framework* was partially updated but it seems unlikely that a fully revised version will be issued until after some challenging accounting issues have been addressed. The thinking in all those documents can be traced to two discussion papers of the 1970s in the UK and the USA. In the UK, *The Corporate Report*[2] was a slim but highly influential document setting out the needs of users and how these might be met. Two years earlier the *Trueblood Report*[3] in the USA had taken a similar approach of identifying the needs of users, although perhaps coming out more strongly in support of the needs of shareholders and creditors than of other user groups. In the UK, various documents on the needs of users have been prepared by individuals invited to help the process[4] or those who took it on themselves to propose radical new ideas.[5]

Since January 2005, all **listed companies** in member states of the European Union (EU) have been required by an accounting regulation called the IAS Regulation[6] to use a system of international financial reporting standards set by the International Accounting Standards Board. The UK ASB has been influential in the development of these international reporting standards and, over a period of years, has been moving UK accounting practice closely into line with the international standards. For **unlisted** companies and other organisations not covered by the IAS Regulation of the EU, the UK ASB has a conceptual framework of its own, called the *Statement of Principles*.[7] This document has many similarities to the IASB's *Conceptual Framework*.

Activity 1.3	*Most conceptual frameworks start with the question: Who are the users of financial statements? Write down a list of the persons or organisations you think would be interested in making use of financial statements, and their possible reasons for being interested. Have you included yourself in that list? Keep your list available for comparing with a later section of this chapter.*

1.3 The conceptual framework for financial reporting

The *Conceptual Framework* is under a process of gradual revision and updating, as a joint project of the IASB and the Financial Accounting Standards Board (FASB) of the USA. In 2010 a partial revision was published with the following structure:

Chapters
  1 The objective of general purpose financial reporting
  2 The reporting entity (to be added later)
  3 Qualitative characteristics of useful financial information
  4 Remaining text based on the **Framework** (1989):
        Underlying assumption 4.1
        The elements of financial statements 4.2–4.36
        Recognition of the elements of financial statements 4.37–4.53
        Measurement of the elements of financial statements 4.54–4.56
        Concepts of capital and capital maintenance 4.57–4.65

Chapters 1 and 3 of the *Conceptual Framework* are written at a general level and a reader would find no difficulty in reviewing these at an early stage of study, to gain a flavour of what is expected of financial statements. The remaining sections are a mixture of general principles, which are appropriate to first-level study of the subject, and some quite specific principles which deal with more advanced problems. Some of those problems need an understanding of accounting which is beyond a first level of study. This book will refer to aspects of the various sections of the *Conceptual Framework*, as appropriate, when particular issues are dealt with. You should be aware, however, that this book concentrates on the basic aspects of the *Conceptual Framework* and does not explore every complexity.

A conceptual framework is particularly important when practices are being developed for reporting to those who are not part of the day-to-day running of the business. This is called **external reporting** or **financial accounting** and is the focus of the *Financial Accounting* studied in this book. For those who are managing the business on a day-to-day basis, special techniques have been developed and are referred to generally as **internal reporting** or **management accounting**.

Before continuing with the theme of the conceptual framework, it is useful to pause and consider the types of business for which accounting information may be required.

Activity 1.4

Visit the website of the International Accounting Standards Board at ***www.ifrs.org*** *and find the link to the* Conceptual Framework. *What does the IASB say about the purpose of the* Conceptual Framework? *How is it being developed?*

web activity

Visit the UK website of the Financial Reporting Council at ***www.frc.org.uk*** *and find the link to the* Statement of Principles. *What is the stated purpose of the* Statement of Principles? *How was it developed?*

1.4 Types of business entity

The word **entity** means 'something that exists independently'. A business entity is a business that exists independently of those who own the business. There are three main categories of business which will be found in all countries, although with different titles in different ones. This chapter uses the terminology common to the UK. The three main categories are: **sole trader**, **partnership** and **limited liability company**. This list is by no means exhaustive but provides sufficient variety to allow explanation of the usefulness of most accounting practices and their application.

Activity 1.5

Before reading the next sections, take out a newspaper with business advertisements or a business telephone directory, or take a walk down your local high street or drive round the trading estate. Write down the names of five businesses, shops or other organisations. Then read the sections and attempt to match your list against the information provided in each.

1.4.1 Sole trader

An individual may enter into business alone, either selling goods or providing a service. Such a person is described as a **sole trader**. The business may be started because the sole trader has a good idea which appears likely to make a profit, and has some cash to buy the equipment and other resources to start the business. If cash is not available, the sole trader may borrow from a bank to enable the business to start up. Although this is the form in which many businesses have started, it is one which is difficult to expand because the sole trader will find it difficult to arrange additional finance for expansion. If the business is not successful and the sole trader is unable to meet obligations to pay money to others, then those persons may ask a court of law to authorise the sale of the personal possessions, and even the family home, of the sole trader. Being a sole trader can be a risky matter and the cost of bank borrowing may be at a relatively unfavourable rate of interest because the bank fears losing its money.

From this description it will be seen that the sole trader's business is very much intertwined with the sole trader's personal life. However, for accounting purposes, the business is regarded as a separate economic entity, of which the sole trader is the owner who takes the risk of the bad times and the benefit of the good times. Take as an example the person who decides to start working as an electrician and advertises their services in a newspaper. The electrician travels to jobs from home and has no business premises. Tools are stored in the loft at home and the business records are in a cupboard in the kitchen. Telephone calls from customers are received on the domestic phone and there are no clearly defined working hours. The work is inextricably intertwined with family life.

For accounting purposes that person is seen as the owner of a business which provides electrical services and the business is seen as being separate from the person's other interests and private life. The owner may hardly feel any great need for accounting information because they know the business very closely, but accounting information will be needed by other persons or entities, mainly the government (in the form of **HM Revenue and Customs**) for tax collecting purposes. It may also be required by a bank for the purposes of lending money to the business or by another sole trader who is intending to buy the business when the existing owner retires.

1.4.2 Partnership

One method by which the business of a sole trader may expand is to enter into **partnership** with one or more people. This may permit a pooling of skills to allow more efficient working, or may allow one person with ideas to work with another who has the money to provide the resources needed to turn the ideas into a profit. There is thus more potential for being successful. If the business is unsuccessful, then the consequences are similar to those for the sole trader. Persons to whom money is owed by the business may ask a court of law to authorise the sale of the personal property of the partners in order to meet the obligation. Even more seriously, one partner may be required to meet all the obligations of the partnership if the other partner does not have sufficient personal property, possessions and cash. This is described in law as **joint and several liability** and the risks have to be considered very carefully by those entering into partnership.

Partnership may be established as a matter of fact by two persons starting to work together with the intention of making a profit and sharing it between them. More often there is a legal agreement, called a **partnership deed**, which sets out the rights and duties of each partner and specifies how they will share the profits. There is also **partnership law**, which governs the basic relationships between partners and which they may use to resolve their disputes in a court of law if there is no partnership deed, or if the partnership deed has not covered some aspect of the partnership.

For accounting purposes the partnership is seen as a separate economic entity, owned by the partners. The owners may have the same intimate knowledge of the business as does the sole trader and may therefore feel that accounting information is not very important for them. On the other hand, each partner may wish to be sure that they are receiving a fair share of the partnership profits. There will also be other persons requesting accounting information, such as HM Revenue and Customs, banks who provide finance and individuals who may be invited to join the partnership so that it can expand even further.

1.4.3 Limited liability company

The main risk attached to either a sole trader or a partnership is that of losing personal property and possessions, including the family home, if the business fails. That risk would inhibit many persons from starting or expanding a business. Historically, as the

UK changed from a predominantly agricultural to a predominantly industrial economy in the nineteenth century, it became apparent that owners needed the protection of **limited liability**. This meant that if the business failed, the owners might lose all the money they had put into the business but their personal wealth would be safe.

There are two forms of limited liability company. The **private limited company** has the word 'Limited' (abbreviated to 'Ltd') in its title. The **public limited company** has the abbreviation 'plc' in its title. The private limited company is prohibited by law from offering its **shares** to the public, so it is a form of limited liability appropriate to a family-controlled business. The public limited company is permitted to offer its shares to the public. In return it has to satisfy more onerous regulations. Where the shares of a public limited company are bought and sold on a **stock exchange**, the public limited company is called a **listed company** because the shares of the company are on a list of share prices.

In either type of company, the owners are called **shareholders** because they share the ownership and share the profits of the good times and the losses of the bad times (to the defined limit of liability). Once they have paid in full for their shares, the owners face no further risk of being asked to contribute to meeting any obligations of the business. Hopefully, the business will prosper and the owners may be able to receive a share of that prosperity in the form of a cash **dividend**. A cash dividend returns to the owners, on a regular basis and in the form of cash, a part of the profit created by the business.

If the company is very small, the owners may run the business themselves. If it is larger, then they may prefer to pay someone else to run the business. In either case, the persons running the business on a day-to-day basis are called the **directors**.

Because limited liability is a great privilege for the owners, the company must meet regulations set out by Parliament in the form of a **Companies Act**. At present the relevant law is the Companies Act 2006.

For accounting purposes the company is an entity with an existence separate from the owners. In the very smallest companies the owners may not feel a great need for accounting information, but in medium- or large-sized companies, accounting information will be very important for the shareholders as it forms a report on how well the directors have run the company. As with other forms of business accounting information must be supplied to HM Revenue and Customs for tax-collecting purposes. The list of other users will expand considerably because there will be a greater variety of sources of finance, the company may be seeking to attract more **investors**, employees will be concerned about the well-being of the business and even the customers and suppliers may want to know more about the financial strength of the company.

Although the law provides the protection of limited liability, this has little practical meaning for many small family-controlled companies because a bank lending money to the business will ask for personal guarantees from the shareholder directors. Those personal guarantees could involve a mortgage over the family home, or an interest in life assurance policies. The potential consequences of such personal guarantees, when a company fails, are such that the owners may suffer as much as the sole trader whose business fails.

1.4.4 Limited liability partnership

A limited liability partnership (LLP) is a corporate body, which means it has a legal personality separate from that of its members. It is formed by being incorporated under the Limited Liability Partnerships Act 2000. Any new or existing partnership firm of two or more persons can incorporate as an LLP. There is no limit on the number of members. There must be at least two designated members who take responsibility for compliance with statutory requirements. The minimum capital requirement is only £2. An LLP structure may be used by any business seeking to make a profit. It has been used in particular by professional firms such as accountants, solicitors and architects.

The LLP may be managed like a normal partnership. All members may participate actively in the management of the business. However the LLP is responsible for the debts of the business. The individual members do not have the unlimited liability that they would have in a normal partnership. Taxation procedures are those that apply to a partnership.

From an accounting perspective in the UK the disclosure requirements are similar to those of a company. LLPs are required to provide financial information equivalent to that of companies, including the filing of annual accounts with the Registrar of Companies.

1.4.5 Comparing partnership and limited liability company

Table 1.1 summarises the differences between a partnership and a limited liability company that are relevant for accounting purposes.

Table 1.2 identifies the differences between the public limited company and the private limited company that are relevant for accounting purposes.

Table 1.1
Differences between a partnership and a limited liability company

	Partnership	Limited liability company
Formation	Formed by two or more persons, usually with written agreement but not necessarily in writing.	Formed by a number of persons registering the company under the Companies Act, following legal formalities. In particular there must be a written **memorandum** and **articles of association** setting out the powers allowed to the company.
Running the business	All partners are entitled to share in the running of the business.	Shareholders must appoint **directors** to run the business (although shareholders may appoint themselves as directors).
Accounting information	Partnerships are not obliged to make accounting information available to the wider public.	Companies must make accounting information available to the public through the **Registrar of Companies**.
Meeting obligations	All members of a general partnership are jointly and severally liable for money owed by the firm.	The personal liability of the owners is limited to the amount they have agreed to pay for shares.
Powers to carry out activities	Partnerships may carry out any legal business activities agreed by the partners.	The company may only carry out the activities set out in its **memorandum** and **articles of association**.
Status in law	The partnership is not a separate legal entity (under English law), the partnership property being owned by the partners. (Under Scots law the partnership is a separate legal entity.)	The company is seen in law as a separate person, distinct from its members. This means that the company can own property, make contracts and take legal action or be the subject of legal action.

Table 1.2
Brief comparison of private and public companies

	Public company	**Private company**
Running the business	Minimum of two directors.	Minimum of one director.
	Must have a company secretary who holds a relevant qualification (responsible for ensuring the company complies with the requirements of company law).	The sole director may also act as the company secretary and is not required to have a formal qualification.
Ownership	Shares may be offered to the public, inviting subscription.	Shares must not be offered to the public. May only be sold by private arrangements.
	Minimum **share capital** £50,000.	No minimum share capital.
Accounting information	Extensive information required on transactions between directors and the company.	Less need for disclosure of transactions between directors and the company.
	Information must be made public through the Registrar of Companies.	
	Provision of financial information to the public is determined by size of company, more information being required of medium- and large-sized companies.	
	Accounting information must be sent to all shareholders.	

Activity 1.6

Look at the list of five organisations which you prepared before reading this section. Did the list match what you have just read? If not, there are several possible explanations. One is that you have written down organisations which are not covered by this book. That would apply if you have written down 'museum', 'town hall' or 'college'. These are examples of public sector bodies that require specialised financial statements not covered by this text. Another is that you did not discover the name of the business enterprise. Perhaps you wrote down 'Northern Hotel' but did not find the name of the company owning the hotel. If your list does not match the section, ask for help from your lecturer, tutor or other expert in the subject so that you are satisfied that this book will continue to meet your personal learning outcomes.

1.5 Users and their information needs

Who are the users of the information provided by these reporting entities? This section shows that there is one group, namely the **management** of an organisation, whose information needs are so specialised that a separate type of accounting has evolved called **management accounting**. However, there are other groups, each of which may believe it has a reasonable right to obtain information about an organisation, that do not enjoy unrestricted access to the business and so have to rely on management to supply suitable information. These groups include the owners, where the owners are not also the managers, but extend further to employees, lenders, suppliers, customers, government and its branches and the public interest. Those in the wider interest groups are sometimes referred to as **stakeholders**.

> **Stakeholder** A general term to indicate all those who might have a legitimate interest in receiving financial information about a business because they have a 'stake' in it.

1.5.1 Management

Many would argue that the foremost users of accounting information about an organisation must be those who manage the business on a day-to-day basis. This group is referred to in broad terms as **management**, which is a collective term for all those persons who have responsibilities for making judgements and decisions within an organisation. Because they have close involvement with the business, they have access to a wide range of information (much of which may be confidential within the organisation) and will seek those aspects of the information which are most relevant to their particular judgements and decisions. Because this group of users is so broad, and because of the vast amount of information potentially available, a specialist branch of accounting has developed, called management accounting, to serve the particular needs of management.

It is management's responsibility to employ the resources of the business in an efficient way and to meet the objectives of the business. The information needed by management to carry out this responsibility ought to be of high quality and in an understandable form so far as the management is concerned. If that is the case, it would not be unreasonable to think that a similar quality (although not necessarily quantity) of information should be made available more widely to those stakeholders who do not have the access available to management.[8] Such an idea would be regarded as somewhat revolutionary in nature by some of those who manage companies, but more and more are beginning to realise that sharing information with investors and other stakeholders adds to the general atmosphere of confidence in the enterprise.

1.5.2 Owners as investors

Where the owners are the managers, as is the case for a sole trader or a partnership, they have no problem in gaining access to information and will select information appropriate to their own needs. They may be asked to provide information for other users, such as HM Revenue and Customs or a bank which has been approached to provide finance, but that information will be designed to meet the needs of those particular users rather than the owners.

Where the ownership is separate from the management of the business, as is the case with a limited liability company, the owners are more appropriately viewed as investors who entrust their money to the company and expect something in return, usually a **dividend** and a growth in the value of their investment as the company prospers. Providing money to fund a business is a risky act and investors are concerned with the **risk** inherent in, and **return** provided by, their investments. They need information to help them decide whether they should buy, hold or sell.[9] They are also interested in information on the entity's financial performance and financial position that helps them to assess both its cash-generation abilities and how management discharges its responsibilities.[10]

Much of the investment in shares through the Stock Exchange in the UK is carried out by **institutional investors**, such as pension funds, insurance companies, unit trusts and investment trusts. The day-to-day business of buying and selling shares is carried out by a **fund manager** employed by the institutional investor. Private investors are in the minority as a group of investors in the UK. They will often take the advice of an **equities analyst** who investigates and reports on share investment. The fund managers and the equities analysts are also regarded as users of accounting information.

The kinds of judgements and decisions made by investors could include any or all of the following:

(a) Evaluating the performance of the entity.

(b) Assessing the effectiveness of the entity in achieving objectives (including compliance with **stewardship** obligations) established previously by its management, its members or owners.

(c) Evaluating managerial performance, efficiency and objectives, including investment and dividend distribution plans.

(d) Ascertaining the experience and background of company directors and officials including details of other directorships or official positions held.

(e) Ascertaining the economic stability and vulnerability of the reporting entity.

(f) Assessing the **liquidity** of the entity, its present or future requirements for additional **working capital**, and its ability to raise long-term and short-term finance.

(g) Assessing the capacity of the entity to make future reallocations of its resources for economic purposes.

(h) Estimating the future prospects of the entity, including its capacity to pay **dividends**, and predicting future levels of investment.

(i) Making economic comparisons, either for the given entity over a period of time or with other entities at one point in time.

(j) Estimating the value of present or prospective interests in or claims on the entity.

(k) Ascertaining the ownership and control of the entity.[11]

That list was prepared in 1975 and, while it is a valid representation of the needs of investors, carries an undertone which implies that the investors have to do quite a lot of the work themselves in making estimates of the prospects of the entity. Today there is a stronger view that the management of a business should share more of its thinking and planning with the investors. The list may therefore be expanded by suggesting that it would be helpful for investors (and all external users) to know:

(a) the entity's actual performance for the most recent accounting period and how this compares with its previous plan for that period;

(b) management's explanations of any significant variances between the two; and

(c) management's financial plan for the current and forward accounting periods, and explanations of the major assumptions used in preparing it.[12]

If you look through some **annual reports** of major listed companies you will see that this is more a 'wish list' than a statement of current practice, but it is indicative of the need for a more progressive approach. In the annual reports of large companies you will find a section called the Operating and Financial Review (or Business Review). This is where the more progressive companies will include forward-looking statements which stop short of making a forecast but give help in understanding which of the trends observed in the past are likely to continue into the future.

1.5.3 Lenders

Lenders are interested in information that enables them to determine whether their loans, and the related interest, will be paid when due.[13]

Loan **creditors** provide finance on a longer-term basis. They will wish to assess the economic stability and vulnerability of the borrower. They are particularly concerned with the risk of **default** and its consequences. They may impose conditions (called **loan covenants**) which require the business to keep its overall borrowing within acceptable limits. The financial statements may provide evidence that the loan covenant conditions are being met.

Some lenders will ask for special reports as well as the general financial statements. Banks in particular will ask for **cash flow projections** showing how the business plans to repay, with interest, the money borrowed.

1.5.4   Suppliers and other trade creditors

Suppliers of goods and services (also called trade creditors) are interested in information that enables them to decide whether to sell to the entity and to determine whether amounts owing to them will be paid when due. The IASB mentions 'other lenders' as users of financial statements.[14] Suppliers (trade creditors) are likely to be interested in an entity over a shorter period than lenders unless they are dependent upon the continuation of the entity as a major customer. The amount due to be paid to the supplier is called a trade payable or an account payable.

Trade creditors supply goods and services to an entity and have very little protection if the entity fails because there are insufficient assets to meet all **liabilities**. They are usually classed as **unsecured creditors**, which means they are a long way down the queue for payment. So they have to exercise caution in finding out whether the business is able to pay and how much risk of non-payment exists. This information need not necessarily come from accounting statements; it could be obtained by reading the local press and trade journals, joining the Chamber of Trade, and generally listening in to the stories and gossip circulating in the geographic area or the industry. However, the financial statements of an entity may confirm the stories gained from other sources.

In recent years there has been a move for companies to work more closely with their suppliers and to establish 'partnership' arrangements where the operational and financial plans of both may be dovetailed by specifying the amount and the timing of goods and services required. Such arrangements depend heavily on confidence, which in turn may be derived partly from the strength of financial statements.

1.5.5   Employees

Employees and their representatives are interested in information about the stability and profitability of their employers. They are also interested in information that helps them to assess the ability of the entity to provide remuneration, retirement benefits and employment opportunities. Employees continue to be interested in their employer after they have retired from work because in many cases the employer provides a pension fund.

The matters which are likely to be of interest to past, present and prospective employees include: the ability of the employer to meet wage agreements; management's intentions regarding employment levels, locations and working conditions; the pay, conditions and terms of employment of various groups of employees; job security; and the contribution made by employees in other divisions of the organisation. Much of this is quite specialised and detailed information. It may be preferable to supply this to employees by means of special purpose reports on a frequent basis rather than waiting for the annual report, which is slow to arrive and more general in nature. However, employees may look to financial statements to confirm information provided previously in other forms. The IASB regards employees as persons who might find the general purpose financial statements useful. However, the IASB says that such financial statements are not primarily directed to these groups.[15]

1.5.6   Customers

Customers have an interest in information about the continuance of an entity, especially when they have a long-term involvement with, or are dependent upon, its prosperity. In particular, customers need information concerning the current and future supply of goods and services offered, price and other product details, and conditions of sale. Much of this information may be obtained from sales literature or from sales staff of the enterprise, or from trade and consumer journals.

The financial statements provide useful confirmation of the reliability of the enterprise itself as a continuing source of supply, especially when the customer is making payments in advance. They also confirm the capacity of the entity in terms of **non-current assets** (also called **fixed assets**) and working **capital** and give some indication of the strength of the entity to meet any obligations under guarantees or warranties.

1.5.7 Governments and their agencies

Governments and their agencies are interested in the allocation of resources and, therefore, in the activities of entities. They also require information in order to regulate the activities of entities, assess taxation and provide a basis for national income and economic statistics.

Acting on behalf of the UK government's Treasury Department, HM Revenue and Customs collects taxes from businesses based on profit calculated according to commercial accounting practices (although there are some specific rules in the taxation legislation which modify the normal accounting practices). HM Revenue and Customs has the power to demand more information than appears in published financial statements, but will take these as a starting point.

Other agencies include the regulators of the various utility companies. Examples are Ofcom[16] (the Office of Communications) and Ofgem[17] (the Office of Gas and Electricity Markets). They use accounting information as part of the package by which they monitor the prices charged by these organisations to consumers of their services. They also demand additional information designed especially to meet their needs.

1.5.8 Public interest

Enterprises affect members of the public in a variety of ways. For example, enterprises may make a substantial contribution to the local economy by providing employment and using local suppliers. Financial statements may assist the public by providing information about the trends and recent developments in the prosperity of the entity and the range of its activities.

A strong element of public interest has been aroused in recent years by environmental issues and the impact of companies on the environment. There are costs imposed on others when a company pollutes a river or discharges harmful gases into the air. It may be perceived that a company is cutting corners to prune its own reported costs at the expense of other people. Furthermore, there are activities of companies today which will impose costs in the future. Where an oil company has installed a drilling rig in the North Sea, it will be expected one day to remove and destroy the rig safely. There is a question as to whether the company will be able to meet that cost. These costs and future liabilities may be difficult to identify and quantify, but that does not mean that companies should not attempt to do so. More companies are now including descriptions of environmental policy in their annual reports, but regular accounting procedures for including environmental costs and obligations in the financial statements have not yet been developed.

| Activity 1.7 | *Look back to the list of users of financial statements which you prepared earlier in this chapter. How closely does your list compare with the users described in this section? Did you have any in your list which are not included here? Have you used names which differ from those used in the chapter? Are there users in the chapter which are not in your list? If your list does not match the section, ask for help from your lecturer, tutor or other expert in the subject so that you are satisfied that this book will continue to meet your personal learning outcomes.* |

1.6 General purpose or specific purpose financial statements?

Some experts who have analysed the needs of users in the manner set out in the previous section have come to the conclusion that no single set of **general purpose financial statements** could meet all these needs. It has been explained in the previous section that some users already turn to special reports to meet specific needs. Other experts hold that there could be a form of general purpose financial statements which would meet all the needs of some user groups and some of the needs of others.

This book is written on the assumption that it *is* possible to prepare a set of general purpose financial statements which will have some interest for all users. The existence of such reports is particularly important for those who cannot prescribe the information they would like to receive from an organisation. That is perhaps because they have no bargaining power, or because they are many in number but not significant in economic influence.

Preparers of general purpose financial statements tend to regard the owners and long-term lenders as the primary users of the information provided. There is an expectation or hope that the interests of these groups will overlap to some extent with the interests of a wider user group and that any improvements in financial statements will be sufficient that fewer needs will be left unmet.[18]

The primary focus of the *Conceptual Framework* is on general purpose financial statements.[19] It takes the view that many users have to rely on the financial statements as their major source of financial information. Financial statements should be prepared with their needs in mind. The *Conceptual Framework* assumes that if financial statements meet the needs of investors, they will also meet the needs of most other users.[20]

1.7 Stewards and agents

In an earlier section, the needs of investors as users were listed and the word 'stewardship' appeared. In the days before an industrial society existed, stewards were the people who looked after the manor house and lands while the lord of the manor enjoyed the profits earned. Traditionally, accounting has been regarded as having a particular role to play in confirming that those who manage a business on behalf of the owner take good care of the resources entrusted to them and earn a satisfactory profit for the owner by using those resources.

As the idea of a wider range of users emerged, this idea of the 'stewardship' objective of accounting was mentioned less often (although its influence remains strong in legislation governing accounting practice). In the academic literature it has been reborn under a new heading – that of **agency**. Theories have been developed about the relationship between the owner, as 'principal', and the manager, as 'agent'. A conscientious manager, acting as an agent, will carry out their duties in the best interest of the owners, and is required by the law of agency to do so. However, not all agents will be perfect in carrying out this role and some principals will not trust the agent entirely. The principal will incur costs in monitoring (enquiring into) the activities of the agent and may lose some wealth if the interests of the agent and the interests of the principal diverge. The view taken in **agency theory** is that there is an inherent conflict between the two parties and so they spend time agreeing contracts which will minimise that conflict. The contracts will include arrangements for the agent to supply information on a regular basis to the principal.

While the study of agency theory in all its aspects could occupy a book in itself, the idea of conflicts and the need for compromise in dealing with pressures of demand for, and supply of, accounting information may be helpful in later chapters in understanding why it takes so long to find answers to some accounting issues.

1.8 Who needs financial statements?

In order to keep the flavour of debate on accounting issues running through this text, two people will give their comments from time to time. The first of these is David Wilson, a fund manager of seven years' experience working for an insurance company. He manages a UK equity **portfolio** (a collection of company shares) and part of his work requires him to be an equities analyst. At university he took a degree in history and has subsequently passed examinations to qualify as a chartered financial analyst (CFA).[21]

The second is Leona Rees, an audit manager with a major accountancy firm. She has five years' experience as a qualified accountant and had previously spent three years in training with the same firm. Her university degree is in accounting and economics and she has passed the examinations to qualify for membership of one of the major accountancy bodies.

David and Leona had been at school together but then went to different universities. More recently they have met again at workout sessions at a health club, relaxing afterwards at a nearby bar. David is very enthusiastic about his work, which demands long hours and a flexible attitude. He has absorbed a little of the general scepticism of audit which is expressed by some of his fund manager colleagues.

Leona's main role at present is in company audit and she is now sufficiently experienced to be working on the audit of one listed company as well as several private companies of varying size. For two years she worked in the corporate recovery department of the accountancy firm, preparing information to help companies find sources of finance to overcome difficult times. She feels that a great deal of accounting work is carried out behind the scenes and the careful procedures are not always appreciated by those who concentrate only on the relatively few well-publicised problems.

We join them in the bar at the end of a hectic working week.

DAVID: *This week I've made three visits to companies, attended four presentations of preliminary announcements of results, received copies of the projector slides used for five others that I couldn't attend, and collected around 20 annual reports. I have a small mound of brokers' reports, all of which say much the same thing but in different ways. I've had to read all those while preparing my monthly report to the head of Equities Section on the performance of my fund and setting out my strategy for three months ahead consistent with in-house policy. I think I'm suffering from information overload and I have reservations about the reliability of any single item of information I receive about a company.*

LEONA: *If I had to give scores for reliability to the information crossing your desk, I would give top marks to the 20 annual reports. They have been through a very rigorous process and they have been audited by reputable audit firms using established standards of auditing practice.*

DAVID: *That's all very well, but it takes so long for annual reports to arrive after the financial year-end that they don't contain any new information. I need to get information at the first available opportunity if I'm to keep up the value of the share portfolio I manage. The meetings that present the preliminary announcements are held less than two months after the accounting year-end. It can take another six weeks before the printed annual report appears. If I don't manage to get to the meeting I take a careful look at what the company sends me in the way of copies of projector slides used.*

LEONA: *Where does accounting information fit in with the picture you want of a company?*

DAVID: *It has some importance, but accounting information is backward-looking and I invest in the future. We visit every company in the portfolio once a year and I'm looking for a confident management team, a cheerful-looking workforce and a general feeling that things are moving ahead. I'll also ask questions about prospects: how is the order book; which overseas markets are expanding; have prices been increased to match the increase in raw materials?*

LEONA: *Isn't that close to gaining insider information?*

DAVID: *No – I see it as clarification of information which is already published. Companies are very careful not to give an advantage to one investor over another – they would be in trouble with the Stock Exchange and perhaps with the Financial Services Authority if they did give price-sensitive information. There are times of the year (running up to the year-end and to the half-yearly results) when they declare a 'close season' and won't even speak to an investor.*

LEONA: *So are you telling me that I spend vast amounts of time auditing financial state-ments which no one bothers to read?*

DAVID: *Some people would say that, but I wouldn't. It's fairly clear that share prices are unmoved by the issue of the annual report, probably because investors already have that information from the preliminary announcement. Nevertheless, we like to know that there is a regulated document behind the information we receive – it allows us to check that we're not being led astray. Also I find the annual report very useful when I want to find out about a company I don't know. For the companies I understand well, the annual report tells me little that I don't already know.*

LEONA: *I'll take that as a very small vote of confidence for now. If your offer to help me redecorate the flat still stands, I might try to persuade you over a few cans of emulsion that you rely on audited accounts more than you realise.*

Activity 1.8	As a final activity for this chapter, go back to the start of the chapter and make a note of every word you have encountered for the first time. Look at the glossary at the end of the book for the definition of each technical word. If the word is not in the glossary it is probably in sufficiently general use to be found in a standard dictionary.

1.9 Summary

This chapter has explained that accounting is intended to provide information that is useful to a wide range of interested parties (stakeholders).

Key points are:

- **Accounting** is the process of identifying, measuring and communicating financial information about an entity to permit informed judgements and decisions by users of the information.

- A **conceptual framework** for accounting is a statement of principles which provides generally accepted guidance for the development of new reporting practices and for challenging and evaluating the existing practices.

- The *Conceptual Framework* of the IASB provides broad principles that guide account-ing practice in many countries.

- The *Statement of Principles* of the UK ~~~~ ...~~ many similarities to the IASB's *Conceptual Framework*.

- Since January 2005, all **listed companies** in member states of the EU have been required by an accounting regulation to use a system of international financial reporting standards (IFRS) set by the IASB.

- Business **entities** in the UK are either **sole traders**, **partnerships** or **limited liability** companies.

- **Users** of accounting information include management, owners, employees, lenders, suppliers, customers, governments and their agencies and the public interest.

- **Stakeholders** are all those who might have a legitimate interest in receiving financial information about a business because they have a 'stake' in it.

- General purpose **financial statements** aim to meet the needs of a wide range of users.

- The relationship between the owner, as 'principal', and the manager, as 'agent' is described in the theory of **agency** relationships. Accounting information helps to reduce the potential conflicts of interest between principal and agent.

Further reading

IASB (2010), *The Conceptual Framework for Financial Reporting*, International Accounting Standards Board.

ICAEW (2009), *Developments in new reporting models*. Information for better markets initiative. The Institute of Chartered Accountants in England and Wales. www.icaew.co.uk.

QUESTIONS

The Questions section of each chapter has three types of question. 'Test your understanding' questions to help you review your reading are in the 'A' series of questions. You will find the answers to these by reading and thinking about the material in the book. 'Application' questions to test your ability to apply technical skills are in the 'B' series of questions. Questions requiring you to show skills in problem solving and evaluation are in the 'C' series of questions. A letter [S] indicates that there is a solution at the end of the book.

A   Test your understanding

A1.1   Define 'accounting' and identify the separate questions raised by the definition. (Section 1.1)

A1.2   The following technical terms appear for the first time in this chapter. Check that you know the meaning of each. (If you can't find them again in the text, there is a glossary at the end of the book.)

- accountancy firm
- accountancy profession
- accounting
- agency
- agency theory
- annual report
- articles of association
- audit manager
- business entity

- capital
- cash flow projections
- Companies Act
- conceptual framework
- creditors
- default
- directors
- dividend
- entity

- equities analyst
- external reporting
- financial accounting
- financial information
- financial reporting standards
- financial statements
- fixed assets
- fund manager
- general purpose financial statements
- HM Revenue and Customs
- institutional investors
- internal reporting
- investors
- joint and several liability
- limited liability
- limited liability company
- liquidity
- listed companies
- loan covenants
- management
- management accounting
- memorandum

- non-current assets
- partnership
- partnership deed
- partnership law
- portfolio
- private listed company
- public listed company
- Registrar of Companies
- return
- risk
- share capital
- shareholders
- shares
- sole trader
- specific purpose financial statements
- stakeholders
- stewardship
- stock exchange
- unlisted companies
- unsecured creditors
- working capital

B   Application

B1.1
Brian and Jane are planning to work in partnership as software consultants. Write a note (100–200 words) to explain their responsibilities for running the business and producing accounting information about the financial position and performance of the business.

B1.2
Jennifer has inherited some shares in a public company which has a share listing on the Stock Exchange. She has asked you to explain how she can find out more about the financial position and performance of the company. Write a note (100–200 words) answering her question.

B1.3
Martin is planning to buy shares in the company that employs him. He knows that the directors of the company are his employers but he wonders what relationship exists between the directors and the shareholders of the company. Write a note (100–200 words) answering his question.

C   Problem solving and evaluation

C1.1
The following extracts are typical of the annual reports of large listed companies. Which of these extracts satisfy the definition of 'accounting'? What are the user needs that are most closely met by each extract?

(a) Suggestions for improvements were made by many employees, alone or in teams. Annual savings which have been achieved total £15m. The best suggestion for improvement will save around £0.3m per year for the next five years.

(b) As of 31 December, 3,000 young people were learning a trade or profession with the company. This represents a studentship rate of 3.9%. During the reporting period we hired 1,300 young people into training places. This is more than we need to satisfy our employment needs in the longer term and so we are contributing to improvement of the quality of labour supplied to the market generally.

(c) During the year to 31 December our turnover (sales) grew to £4,000 million compared to £2,800 million last year. Our new subsidiary contributed £1,000 million to this increase.

(d) It is our target to pay our suppliers within 30 days. During the year we achieved an average payment period of 33 days.

(e) The treasury focus during the year was on further refinancing of the group's borrowings to minimise interest payments and reduce risk.

(f) Our plants have emission rates that are 70% below the national average for sulphur dioxide and 20% below the average for oxides of nitrogen. We will tighten emissions significantly over the next ten years.

C1.2

Explain how you would class each of the following – as a sole trader, partnership or limited company. List any further questions you might ask for clarification about the nature of the business.

(a) Miss Jones works as an interior decorating adviser under the business name 'U-decide'. She rents an office and employs an administrative assistant to answer the phone, keep files and make appointments.

(b) George and Jim work together as painters and decorators under the business name 'Painting Partners Ltd'. They started the business ten years ago and work from a rented business unit on a trading estate.

(c) Jenny and Chris own a hotel jointly. They operate under the business name 'Antler Hotel Company' and both participate in the running of the business. They have agreed to share profits equally.

Activities for study groups (4 or 5 per group)

Obtain the annual report of a listed company. Each member of the group should choose a different company. Most large companies will provide a copy of the annual report at no charge in response to a polite request – or you may know someone who is a shareholder and receives a copy automatically. Many companies have websites with a section for 'Investor Relations' where you will find a document file containing the annual report.

1 Look at the contents page. What information does the company provide?

2 Find the financial highlights page. What are the items of accounting information which the company wants you to note? Which users might be interested in this highlighted information, and why?

3 Is there any information in the annual report which would be of interest to employees?

4 Is there any information in the annual report which would be of interest to customers?

5 Is there any information in the annual report which would be of interest to suppliers?

6 Find the auditors' report. To whom is it addressed? What does that tell you about the intended readership of the annual report?

7 Note the pages to which the auditors' report refers. These are the pages which are regulated by company law, accounting standards and Stock Exchange rules. Compare these pages with the other pages (those which are not regulated). Which do you find more interesting? Why?

8 Each member of the group should now make a five-minute presentation evaluating the usefulness of the annual report examined. When the presentations are complete the group should decide on five criteria for judging the reports and produce a score for each. Does the final score match the initial impressions of the person reviewing it?

9 Finally, as a group, write a short note of guidance on what makes an annual report useful to the reader.

Notes and references

1. AAA (1966), *A Statement of Basic Accounting Theory*, American Accounting Association, p. 1.
2. ASSC (1975), *The Corporate Report*, Accounting Standards Steering Committee.
3. AICPA (1973), *Report of a Study Group on the Objectives of Financial Statements* (The Trueblood Committee), American Institute of Certified Public Accountants.
4. Solomons, D. (1989), *Guidelines for Financial Reporting Standards*, Research Board of The Institute of Chartered Accountants in England and Wales.
5. ICAS (1988), *Making Corporate Reports Valuable*, Research Committee of The Institute of Chartered Accountants of Scotland.
6. The IAS Regulation (2002), see Chapter 4.
7. ASB (1999), *Statement of Principles for Financial Reporting*, Accounting Standards Board.
8. ICAS (1988), para. 3.3.
9. IASB (2010), para. OB 2.
10. IASB (2010), para. OB 4.
11. ASSC (1975), para. 2.8.
12. ICAS (1988), para. 3.12.
13. IASB (2010), para. OB 3.
14. *Ibid.*, para. OB 10.
15. *Ibid.*, para. OB 10.
16. www.ofcom.org.uk
17. www.ofgem.gov.uk
18. ICAS (1988), para. 3.7.
19. IASB (2010), para. OB 1.
20. IASB (2010), para. OB 10.
21. www.cfainstitute.org

Introduction to the terminology of business transactions

The following description explains the business terminology which will be encountered fre-quently in describing transactions in this textbook. The relevant words are highlighted in bold lettering. These technical accounting terms are explained in the Financial accounting terms defined *section at the end of the book.*

Most businesses are established with the intention of earning a **profit**. Some do so by selling goods at a price greater than that paid to buy or manufacture the goods. Others make a profit by providing a service and charging a price greater than the cost to them of providing the service. By selling the goods or services the business is said to earn *sales revenue*.

Profit arising from transactions relating to the operation of the business is measured by deducting from sales revenue the expenses of earning that revenue.

Revenue from sales (often abbreviated to 'sales' and sometimes referred to as 'turn-over') means the value of all goods or services provided to customers, whether for *cash* or for *credit*. In a *cash sale* the customer pays immediately on receipt of goods or services. In a *credit sale* the customer takes the goods or service and agrees to pay at a future date. By agreeing to pay in the future the customer becomes a **debtor** of the business. The amount due to be collected from the debtor is called a **trade receivable** or an **account receivable**. The business will send a document called a **sales invoice** to the credit customer, stating the goods or services provided by the business, the price charged for these and the amount owing to the business.

Eventually the credit customer will pay cash to settle the amount shown on the invoice. If they pay promptly the business may allow a deduction of discount for prompt payment. This deduction is called *discount allowed* by the business. As an example, if the customer owes £100 but is allowed a 5% discount by the business, he will pay £95. The business will record cash received of £95 and discount allowed of £5.

The business itself must buy goods in order to manufacture a product or provide a service. When the business buys goods it *purchases* them and holds them as an **inventory** of goods (also described as a 'stock' of goods) until they are used or sold. The goods will be purchased from a supplier, either for **cash** or for **credit**. In a **credit purchase** the business takes the goods and agrees to pay at a future date. By allowing the busi-ness time to pay, the supplier becomes a **creditor** of the business. The name creditor is given to anyone who is owed money by the business. The amount due to be paid to a creditor is called a **trade payable** or an **account payable**. The business will receive a purchase invoice from the supplier describing the goods supplied, stating the price of the goods and showing the amount owed by the business.

Eventually the business will pay cash to settle the amount shown on the purchase invoice. If the business pays promptly the supplier may permit the business to deduct a discount for prompt payment. This is called **discount received** by the business. As an example, if the business owes an amount of £200 as a **trade payable** but is permitted a 10% discount by the supplier, the business will pay £180 and record the remaining £20 as **discount received** from the supplier.

The purchase price of goods sold is one of the **expenses** of the business, to be deducted from sales revenue in calculating profit. Other expenses might include wages, salaries, rent, rates, insurance and cleaning. In each case there will be a document providing evidence of the expense, such as a wages or salaries slip, a landlord's bill for rent, a local authority's demand for rates, an insurance renewal note or a cleaner's time sheet. There will also be a record of the cash paid in each case.

Sometimes an expense is incurred but is not paid for until some time later. For example, electricity is consumed during a quarter but the electricity bill does not arrive until after the end of the quarter. An employee may have worked for a week but not yet have received a cash payment for that work. The unpaid expense of the business is called an *accrued expense* and must be recorded as part of the accounting information relevant to the period of time in which the expense was incurred.

On other occasions an expense may be paid for in advance of being used by the business. For example, a fire insurance premium covering the business premises is paid annually in advance. Such expenditure of cash will benefit a future time period and must be excluded from any profit calculation until that time. In the meantime it is recorded as a **prepaid expense** or a **prepayment**.

Dissatisfaction may be expressed by a customer with the quantity or quality of goods or service provided. If the business accepts that the complaint is justified it may replace goods or give a cash refund. If the customer is a credit customer who has not yet paid, then a cash refund is clearly inappropriate. Instead the customer would be sent a **credit note** for sales returned, cancelling the customer's debt to the business for the amount in dispute. The credit note would record the quantity of goods or type of service and the amount of the cancelled debt.

In a similar way the business would expect to receive a credit note from a supplier for *purchases returned* where goods have been bought on credit terms and later returned to the supplier because of some defect.

S | Test your understanding

S1.1 The following technical terms appear in this supplement. Check that you know the meaning of each.

- Profit
- Sales revenue
- Cash sale
- Credit sale
- Debtor
- Trade receivable
- Discount allowed
- Purchases
- Credit purchase
- Inventory

- Creditor
- Trade payable
- Discount received
- Expense
- Accrued expense
- Prepaid expense
- Credit note for sales returned
- Credit note for purchases returned
- Account receivable
- Sales invoice
- Account payable

Chapter 2

A systematic approach to financial reporting: the accounting equation

REAL WORLD CASE

BT Group plc

Summary group balance sheet

Year ended 31 March

	2012 £m	2011 £m
Property, plant and equipment	**14,388**	14,623
Other non-current assets	**5,029**	4,986
Current assets	**4,531**	3,931
Current liabilities	**(9,255)**	(7,031)
	14,693	16,509
Non-current liabilities	**13,385**	14,558
Parent shareholders' equity	**1,297**	1,925
Non-controlling interests	**11**	26
	14,693	16,509

Shutterstock.com/Madarakis

Who we are and what we do

- We are one of the world's leading communications services companies
- We are the leading provider of consumer voice and broadband services in the UK
- We are Europe's largest telecoms services wholesaler by revenue
- We provide networked IT services for some of the largest companies in the world
- In the UK we are delivering one of the fastest privately funded roll-outs of fibre broadband in the world
- Every day we touch the lives of millions of people, helping them communicate, do business and be entertained and informed

Source: http://www.btplc.com/Sharesandperformance/Annualreportandreview/pdf/BT_SFS_NOM_2012.pdf, BT Group plc, pp. 4, 9, with permission of British Telecommunications plc.

Discussion points

1 How does the summary statement of financial position (balance sheet) reflect the accounting equation?

2 To what extent is the statement of financial position reflected in 'Who we are and what we do'?

Contents

Learning outcomes

After studying this chapter you should be able to:

- Define and explain the accounting equation.
- Define assets.
- Apply the definition to examples of assets.
- Explain and apply the rules for recognition of assets.
- Define liabilities.
- Apply the definition to examples of liabilities.
- Explain and apply the rules for recognition of liabilities.
- Define ownership interest.
- Explain how the recognition of ownership interest depends on the recognition of assets and liabilities.
- Use the accounting equation to show the effect of changes in the ownership interest.
- Explain how users of financial statements can gain assurance about assets and liabilities.

Additionally, for those who choose to study the supplement:

- Explain how the rules of debit and credit recording are derived from the accounting equation.

2.1 Introduction

Chapter 1 considered the needs of a range of users of financial information and summarised by suggesting that they would all have an interest in the resources available to the business and the obligations of the business to those outside it. Many of these users will also want to be reassured that the business has an adequate flow of cash to support its continuation. The owners of the business have a claim to the resources of the business after all other obligations have been satisfied. This is called the **ownership interest** or the **equity interest**. They will be particularly interested in how that ownership interest grows from one year to the next and whether the resources of the business are being applied to the best advantage.

Accounting has traditionally applied the term **assets** to the resources available to the business and has applied the term **liabilities** to the obligations of the business to persons other than the owner. Assets and liabilities are reported in a financial statement called a **statement of financial position** (also called a **balance sheet**). The statement of the financial position of the entity represents a particular point in time. It may be described by a very simple equation.

2.2 The accounting equation

The **accounting equation** as a statement of financial position may be expressed as:

Assets minus **Liabilities**	equals	**Ownership interest**

The ownership interest is the residual claim after liabilities to third parties have been satisfied. The equation expressed in this form emphasises that residual aspect.

Another way of thinking about an equation is to imagine a balance with a bucket on each end. In one bucket are the assets (A) minus liabilities (L). In the other is the ownership interest (OI).

If anything happens to disturb the assets then the balance will tip unevenly unless some matching disturbance is applied to the ownership interest. If anything happens to disturb the liabilities then the balance will tip unevenly unless some matching disturbance is applied to the ownership interest. If a disturbance applied to an asset is applied equally to a liability, then the balance will remain level.

2.2.1 Form of the equation: international preferences

If you have studied simple equations in a maths course you will be aware that there are other ways of expressing this equation. Those other ways cannot change the magnitudes of each item in the equation but can reflect a different emphasis being placed on the various constituents. The form of the equation used in this chapter is the sequence which has, for many years, been applied in most statements of financial position (balance sheets) reported to external users of accounting information in the UK. The statements of financial position that have been reported to external users in some Continental European countries and in the USA are better represented by another form of the equation:

The 'balance' analogy remains applicable here but the contents of the buckets have been rearranged.

A disturbance on one side of the balance will require a corresponding disturbance on the other side if the balance is to be maintained.

2.2.2 Flexibility

The International Accounting Standards Board (IASB) has developed a set of accounting standards which together create an accounting system which in this book is described as the **IASB system**. The IASB offers no indication as to which of the above forms of the accounting equation is preferred. That is because of the different traditions in different countries. Consequently, for companies reporting under the IASB system, the form of the equation used in any particular situation is a matter of preference related to the choice of presentation of the statement of financial position (balance sheet). That is a communication issue which will be discussed later. This chapter will concentrate on the nature of the various elements of the equation, namely assets, liabilities and ownership interest. You should be prepared to find different variations of the accounting equation in different companies' financial statements.

Activity 2.1

Make a simple balance from a ruler balanced on a pencil and put coins on each side. Satisfy yourself that the ruler only remains in balance if any action on one side of the balance is matched by an equivalent action on the other side of the balance. Note also that rearranging the coins on one side will not disturb the balance. Some aspects of accounting are concerned with taking actions on each side of the balance. Other aspects are concerned with rearranging one side of the balance.

2.3 Defining assets

An **asset** is defined as: *'a resource controlled by the entity as a result of past events and from which future economic benefits are expected to flow to the entity'*.[1]

To understand this definition fully, each phrase must be considered separately.

2.3.1 Controlled by the entity

Control means the ability to obtain the economic benefits and to restrict the access of others. The items which everyone enjoys, such as the benefit of a good motorway giving access to the business or the presence of a highly skilled workforce in a nearby town, provide benefits to the business which are not reported in financial statements because there would be considerable problems in identifying the entity's share of the benefits. If there is no control, the item is omitted.

The condition of control is also included to prevent businesses from leaving out of the statement of financial position (balance sheet) some items which ought to be in there. In past years, practices emerged of omitting an asset and a corresponding liability from a statement of financial position on the grounds that there was no effective obligation remaining in respect of the liability. At the same time, the business carefully retained effective control of the asset by suitable legal agreements. This practice of omitting items from the statement of financial position was felt to be unhelpful to users because it was concealing some of the resources used by the business and concealing the related obligations.

The strongest form of control over an asset is the right of ownership. Sometimes, however, the entity does not have ownership but does have the right to use an item. This right may be very similar to the right of ownership. So far as the user of accounting information is concerned, what really matters is the availability of the item to the entity and how well the item is being used to earn profits for the business. Forms of **control** may include an agreement to lease or rent a resource, and a licence allowing exclusive use of a resource.

2.3.2 Past events

Accounting depends on finding some reasonably objective way of confirming that the entity has gained control of the resource. The evidence provided by a past transaction is an objective starting point. A transaction is an agreement between two parties which usually involves exchanging goods or services for cash or a promise to pay cash. (The supplement to Chapter 1 explains basic business transactions in more detail.) Sometimes there is no transaction but there is an event which is sufficient to give this objective evidence. The event could be the performance of a service which, once completed, gives the right to demand payment.

2.3.3 Future economic benefits

Most businesses use resources in the expectation that they will eventually generate cash. Some resources generate cash more quickly than others. If the business manufactures goods in order to sell them to customers, those goods carry a future economic benefit in terms of the expectation of sale. That benefit comes to the entity relatively quickly. The business may own a warehouse in which it stores the goods before they are sold. There is a future economic benefit associated with the warehouse because it helps create the cash flow from sale of the goods (by keeping them safe from damage and theft) and also because at some time in the future the warehouse could itself be sold for cash.

The example of the warehouse is relatively easy to understand, but in other cases there may be some uncertainty about the amount of the future economic benefit. When goods are sold to a customer who is allowed time to pay, the customer becomes a **debtor** of the business (a person who owes money to the business) and the amount of the **trade receivable** is regarded as an asset. There may be some uncertainty as to whether the customer will eventually pay for the goods. That uncertainty does not prevent the trade receivable being regarded as an asset but may require some caution as to how the asset is measured in money terms.

Activity 2.2

Write down five items in your personal possession which you regard as assets. Use the definition given in this section to explain why each item is an asset from your point of view. Then read the next section and compare your list with the examples of business assets. If you are having difficulty in understanding why any item is, or is not, an asset you should consult your lecturer, tutor or other expert in the subject area for a discussion on how to apply the definition in identifying assets.

2.4 Examples of assets

The following items are commonly found in the assets section of the statement of financial position (balance sheet) of a company:

- land and buildings (property) owned by the company
- buildings leased by the company on a 50-year lease
- plant and equipment owned by the company
- equipment leased (rented) by the company under a finance lease
- vehicles
- raw materials
- goods for resale
- finished goods
- work in progress
- trade receivables (amounts due from customers who have promised to pay for goods sold on credit)
- prepaid insurance and rentals
- investments in shares of other companies
- cash held in a bank account.

Do all these items meet the definition of an asset? Tables 2.1 and 2.2 test each item against the aspects of the definition which have already been discussed. Two tables have been used because it is conventional practice to separate assets into current assets and non-current assets. **Current assets** are held with the intention of converting them into cash within the business cycle. **Non-current assets**, also called **fixed assets**, are held for continuing use in the business. The business cycle is the period (usually 12 months) during which the peaks and troughs of activity of a business form

Table 2.1

Analysis of some frequently occurring non-current assets (fixed assets)

	Controlled by the entity by means of	Past event	Future economic benefits
Land and buildings owned by the company	Ownership.	Signing the contract as evidence of purchase of land and buildings.	Used in continuing operations of the business; potential for sale of the item.
Buildings leased (rented) by the company on a 50-year lease	Contract for exclusive use as a tenant.	Signing a lease agreeing the rental terms.	Used in continuing operations of the business.
Plant and equipment owned by the company	Ownership.	Purchase of plant and equipment, evidenced by receiving the goods and a supplier's invoice.	Used in continuing operations of the business.
Equipment used under a finance lease	Contract for exclusive use.	Signing lease agreeing rental terms.	Used in continuing operations of the business.
Vehicles owned by the company	Ownership.	Purchase of vehicles, evidenced by taking delivery and receiving a supplier's invoice.	Used in continuing operations of the business.

Table 2.2
Analysis of some frequently occurring current assets

	Controlled by the entity by means of	Past event	Future economic benefits
Raw materials	Ownership.	Receiving raw materials into the company's store, evidenced by goods received note.	Used to manufacture goods for sale.
Goods purchased from supplier for resale	Ownership.	Receiving goods from supplier into the company's store, evidenced by the goods received note.	Expectation of sale.
Finished goods (manufactured by the entity)	Ownership.	Transfer from production line to finished goods store, evidenced by internal transfer form.	Expectation of sale.
Work in progress (partly finished goods)	Ownership.	Evaluation of the state of completion of the work, evidenced by work records.	Expectation of completion and sale.
Trade receivables (amounts due from customers)	Contract for payment.	Delivery of goods to the customer, obliging customer to pay for goods at a future date.	Expectation that the customer will pay cash.
Prepaid insurance premiums	Contract for continuing benefit of insurance cover.	Paying insurance premiums in advance, evidenced by cheque payment.	Expectation of continuing insurance cover.
Investments in shares of other companies	Ownership.	Buying the shares, evidenced by broker's contract note.	Expectation of dividend income and growth in value of investment, for future sale.
Cash held in a bank account	Ownership.	Depositing cash with the bank, evidenced by bank statement or certificate.	Expectation of using the cash to buy resources which will create further cash.

a pattern which is repeated on a regular basis. For a business selling swimwear, production will take place all winter in preparation for a rush of sales in the summer. Painters and decorators work indoors in the winter and carry out exterior work in the summer. Because many businesses are affected by the seasons of the year, the business cycle is normally 12 months. Some of the answers are fairly obvious but a few require a little further comment here.

First, there are the items of buildings and equipment which are rented under a lease agreement. The benefits of such leases are felt to be so similar to the benefits of ownership that the items are included in the statement of financial position (balance sheet) as assets. Suitable wording is used to describe the different nature of these items so that users, particularly **creditors**, are not misled into believing that the items belong to the business.

Second, it is useful to note at this stage that partly finished items of output may be recorded as assets. The term 'work in progress' is used to describe work of the business which is not yet completed. Examples of such work in progress might be: partly finished items in a manufacturing company; a partly completed motorway being built by a construction company; or a continuing legal case being undertaken by a firm of lawyers. Such items are included as assets because there has been an event in the partial completion of the work and there is an expectation of completion and eventual payment by a customer for the finished item.

Finally, it is clear that the relative future economic benefits of these assets have a wide variation in potential risk. This risk is a matter of great interest to those who use accounting information, but there are generally no accounting techniques for reporting this risk directly in financial statements. Consequently, it is very important to have adequate descriptions of assets. Accounting information is concerned with the words used to describe items in financial statements, as well as the numbers attributed to them. (The narrative description of business risks is explained in Chapter 14, Section 14.10.)

Definitions

An **asset** is a resource controlled by the entity as a result of past events and from which future economic benefits are expected to flow to the entity.[2]

A **current asset** is an asset that satisfies any of the following criteria:

(a) it is expected to be realised in, or is intended for sale or consumption in, the entity's normal operating cycle;
(b) it is held primarily for the purpose of being traded;
(c) it is expected to be realised within 12 months after the reporting period;
(d) it is cash or a cash equivalent.[3]

A **non-current asset** is any asset that does not meet the definition of a current asset.[4] Non-current assets include tangible, intangible and financial assets of a long-term nature. These are also described as **fixed assets**.[5]

2.5 Recognition of assets

When an item has passed the tests of definition of an asset, it has still not acquired the right to a place in the statement of financial position (balance sheet). To do so it must meet further tests of recognition. **Recognition** means reporting an item by means of words and amounts within the main financial statements in such a way that the item is included in the arithmetic totals. An item which is reported in the notes to the accounts is said to be **disclosed** but *not* **recognised**.

The conditions for recognition have been expressed as in the following definition.

Definition

An **asset** is **recognised** in the statement of financial position (balance sheet) when:

it is probable that any future economic benefit associated with the asset will flow to the entity and the asset has a cost or value that can be measured reliably.[6]

2.5.1 Probability that economic benefits will flow

To establish probability needs evidence. What evidence is sufficient? Usually more than one item of evidence is looked for. In the case of non-current assets (fixed assets) which have a physical existence, looking at them to make sure they do exist is a useful precaution which some auditors have in the past regretted not taking. Checking on physical existence is not sufficient, however, because the enterprise may have no control over the future economic benefit associated with the item. Evidence of the benefit from non-current assets may lie in: title deeds of property; registration documents for vehicles plus the purchase invoice from the supplier; invoices from suppliers of plant and equipment or office furniture; a written lease agreement for a computer or other type of equipment; and also the enterprise's internal forecasts of the profits it will make by using these non-current assets. This is the kind of evidence which the auditor seeks in forming an opinion on the financial statements.

For current assets the evidence of future benefit comes when the assets are used within the trading cycle. A satisfactory sales record will suggest that the present **inventory (stock)** of finished goods is also likely to sell. Analysis of the time that credit customers have taken to pay will give some indication of whether the **trade receivables** should be recognised as an asset. Cash can be counted, while amounts deposited in banks may be confirmed by a bank statement or bank letter. Internal projections of profit and cash flow provide supporting evidence of the expected benefit from using current assets in trading activities.

2.5.2   Reliability of measurement

Reliable measurement of assets can be quite a problem. For the most part, this book will accept the well-tried practice of measuring an asset at the cost of acquiring it, allowing for any reduction in value through use of the asset (depreciation) or through it falling out of fashion (obsolescence). The suitability of this approach to measurement will be discussed in Chapter 14 as one of the main unresolved problems of accounting.

2.5.3   Non-recognition

Consider some items which pass the definition test but do not appear in a statement of financial position (balance sheet):

- the workforce of a business (a human resource)
- the strength of the management team (another human resource)
- the reputation established for the quality of the product
- the quality of the regular customers
- a tax refund which will be claimable against profits in two years' time.

These items all meet the conditions of rights or other access, future economic benefits, control and a past transaction or event. However, they all have associated with them a high level of uncertainty and it could be embarrassing to include them in a statement of financial position (balance sheet) of one year, only to remove them the following year because something unexpected had happened.

All these items fail one of the recognition tests and some fail both. The workforce as a whole may be reliable and predictable, but unexpected circumstances can come to all and the illness or death of a member of the management team in particular can have a serious impact on the perceived value of the business. A crucial member of the workforce might give notice and leave. In relation to the product, a reputation for quality may become well established and those who would like to include brand names in the statement of financial position (balance sheet) argue for the permanence of the reputation. Others illustrate the relative transience of such a reputation by bringing out a list of well-known biscuits or sweets of 30 years ago and asking who has heard of them today. Reliable customers of good quality are valuable to a business, but they are also fickle and may change their allegiance at a moment's notice. The tax refund may be measurable in amount, but will there be taxable profits in two years' time against which the refund may be claimed?

It could be argued that the assets which are not recognised in the financial statements should be reported by way of a general description in a note to the accounts. In practice, this rarely happens because accounting tries to avoid raising hopes which might subsequently be dashed. This cautious approach is part of what is referred to more generally as **prudence** in accounting practice.

2.6 Defining liabilities

A **liability** is defined as: 'a present obligation of the entity arising from past events, the settlement of which is expected to result in an outflow from the entity of resources embodying economic benefits'.[7] This wording reads somewhat tortuously but has been designed to mirror the definition of an asset.

The most familiar types of liabilities arise in those situations where specific amounts of money are owed by an entity to specific persons called creditors. There is usually no doubt about the amount of money owed and the date on which payment is due. Such persons may be **trade creditors**, the general name for those suppliers who have provided goods or services in return for a promise of payment later. Amounts due to **trade creditors** are described as **trade payables**. Other types of creditors include bankers or other lenders who have lent money to the entity.

There are also situations where an obligation is known to exist but the amount due is uncertain. That might be the case where a court of law has found an entity negligent in failing to meet some duty of care to a customer. The company will have to pay compensation to the customer but the amount has yet to be determined.

Even more difficult is the case where an obligation might exist if some future event happens. Neither the existence nor the amount of the obligation is known with certainty at the date of the financial statements. An example would arise where one company has guaranteed the overdraft borrowing of another in the event of that other company defaulting on repayment. At the present time there is no reason to suppose a default will occur, but it remains a possibility for the future.

The definition of a liability tries to encompass all these degrees of variation and uncertainty. It has to be analysed for each separate word or phrase in order to understand the full implications.

2.6.1 Present obligation

A legal obligation is evidence that a liability exists because there is another person or entity having a legal claim to payment. Most liabilities arise because a legal obligation exists, either by contract or by statute law.

However, a legal obligation is not a necessary condition. There may be a commercial penalty faced by the business if it takes a certain action. For example, a decision to close a line of business will lead to the knowledge of likely redundancy costs long before the employees are actually made redundant and the legal obligation becomes due. There may be an obligation imposed by custom and practice, such as a condition of the trade that a penalty operates for those who pay bills late. There may be a future obligation caused by actions and events of the current period where, for example, a profit taken by a company now may lead to a taxation liability at a later date which does not arise at this time because of the wording of the tax laws.

2.6.2 Past events

A decision to buy supplies or to acquire a new non-current asset is not sufficient to create a liability. It could be argued that the decision is an event creating an obligation, but it is such a difficult type of event to verify that accounting prefers not to rely too much on the point at which a decision is made.

Most liabilities are related to a transaction. Normally the transaction involves receiving goods or services, receiving delivery of new non-current assets such as vehicles and equipment, or borrowing money from a lender. In all these cases there is documentary evidence that the transaction has taken place.

Where the existence of a liability is somewhat in doubt, subsequent events may help to confirm its existence at the date of the financial statements. For example, when a company offers to repair goods under a warranty arrangement, the liability exists from the moment the warranty is offered. It may, however, be unclear as to the extent of the liability until a pattern of customer complaints is established. Until that time there will have to be an estimate of the liability. In accounting this estimate is called a **provision**. Amounts referred to as **provisions** are included under the general heading of liabilities.

2.6.3   Outflow of economic benefits

The resource of cash is the economic benefit transferable in respect of most obligations. The transfer of property in settlement of an obligation would also constitute a transfer of economic benefits. More rarely, economic benefits could be transferred by offering a resource such as labour in settlement of an obligation.

Activity 2.3	*Write down five items in your personal experience which you regard as liabilities. Use the definition given in this section to explain why each item is a liability from your point of view. Then read the next section and compare your list with the examples of business liabilities. If you are having difficulty in understanding why any item is, or is not, a liability you should consult your lecturer, tutor or other expert in the subject area for a discussion on how to apply the definition in identifying liabilities.*

2.7   Examples of liabilities

Here is a list of items commonly found in the liabilities section of the statements of financial position (balance sheets) of companies:

- bank loans and overdrafts
- trade payables (amounts due to suppliers of goods and services on credit terms)
- taxation payable
- accruals (amounts owing, such as unpaid expenses)
- provision for deferred taxation
- long-term loans.

The first five items in this list would be classified as **current liabilities** because they will become due for payment within one year of the date of the financial statements. The last item would be classified as **non-current liabilities** because they will remain due by the business for longer than one year.

| Definitions | A **liability** is a present obligation of the entity arising from past events, the settlement of which is expected to result in an outflow from the entity of resources embodying economic benefits.[8]

A **current liability** is a liability which satisfies any of the following criteria:

(a) it is expected to be settled in the entity's normal operating cycle;
(b) it is held primarily for the purpose of being traded;
(c) it is due to be settled within 12 months after the reporting period.[9]

A **non-current liability** is any liability that does not meet the definition of a current liability.[10] Non-current liabilities are also described as **long-term liabilities**. |
|---|---|

2.8 Recognition of liabilities

As with an asset, when an item has passed the tests of definition of a liability it may still fail the test of recognition. In practice, because of the concern for prudence, it is much more difficult for a liability to escape the statement of financial position (balance sheet).

The condition for recognition of a liability uses wording which mirrors that used for recognition of the asset. The only difference is that the economic benefits are now expected to flow *from* the enterprise. The conditions for recognition have been expressed in the following way:

Definition

A **liability** is **recognised** in the statement of financial position (balance sheet) when:

- it is probable that any future economic benefit associated with the liability will flow from the entity and
- the amount of the liability can be measured reliably.[11]

What kind of evidence is acceptable? For current liabilities there will be a payment soon after the date of the financial statements and a past record of making such payments on time. For non-current liabilities (long-term liabilities) there will be a written agreement stating the terms and dates of repayment required. The enterprise will produce internal forecasts of cash flows which will indicate whether the cash resources will be adequate to allow that future benefit to flow from the enterprise.

Reliable measurement will normally be based on the amount owing to the claimant. If goods or services have been supplied there will be an invoice from the supplier stating the amount due. If money has been borrowed there will be a bank statement or some other document of a similar type, showing the lender's record of how much the enterprise owes.

In cases which fail the recognition test, the documentary evidence is likely to be lacking, probably because there is not sufficient evidence of the existence or the measurable amount. Examples of liabilities which are not recognised in the statement of financial position (balance sheet) are:

- a commitment to purchase new machinery next year (but not a firm contract)
- a remote, but potential, liability for a defective product, where no court action has yet commenced
- a guarantee given to support the bank overdraft of another company, where there is very little likelihood of being called upon to meet the guarantee.

Because of the prudent nature of accounting, the liabilities which are not recognised in the statement of financial position (balance sheet) may well be reported in note form under the heading **contingent liabilities**. This is referred to as **disclosure** by way of a note to the accounts.

Looking more closely at the list of liabilities which are not recognised, we see that the commitment to purchase is not legally binding and therefore the outflow of resources may not occur. The claim based on a product defect appears to be uncertain as to occurrence and as to amount. If there has been a court case or a settlement out of court then there should be a provision for further claims of a similar nature. In the case of the guarantee the facts as presented make it appear that an outflow of resources is unlikely. However, such appearances have in the past been deceiving to all concerned and there is often interesting reading in the note to the financial statements which describes the contingent liabilities.

An analysis of some common types of liability is given in Table 2.3.

Table 2.3
Analysis of some common types of liability

Type of liability	Obligation	Transfer of economic benefits	Past transaction or event
Bank loans and overdrafts (repayable on demand or in the very short term)	The entity must repay the loans on the due date or on demand.	Cash, potentially within a short space of time.	Receiving the borrowed funds.
Trade payables (amounts due to suppliers of goods and services)	Suppliers must be paid for the goods and services supplied, usually about one month after the supplier's invoice is received.	Cash within a short space of time.	Taking delivery of the goods or service and receiving the supplier's invoice.
Taxation payable (tax due on company profits after the financial year-end date)	Cash payable to HMRC. Penalties are charged if tax is not paid on the due date.	Cash.	Making profits in the accounting year and submitting an assessment of tax payable.
Accruals (a term meaning 'other amounts owing', such as unpaid bills)	Any expense incurred must be reported as an accrued liability (e.g. electricity used, gas used, unpaid wages), if it has not been paid at the financial year-end date.	Cash.	Consuming electricity or gas, using employees' services, receiving bills from suppliers (note that it is not necessary to receive a gas bill in order to know that you owe money for gas used).
Provision for deferred taxation (tax due in respect of present profits but having a delayed payment date allowed by tax law)	Legislation allows companies to defer payment of tax in some cases. The date of future payment may not be known as yet.	Cash eventually, but could be in the longer term.	Making profits or incurring expenditure now which meets conditions of legislation allowing deferral.
Long-term loans (sometimes called debenture loans)	Statement of financial position will show repayment dates of long-term loans and any repayment conditions attached.	Cash.	Received borrowed funds.

2.9 Defining the ownership interest

The ownership interest is defined in the *Conceptual Framework* as equity. **Equity** is the residual interest in the assets of the entity after deducting all its liabilities.[12]

The term **net assets** is used as a shorter way of saying 'total assets less total liabilities'. Because the ownership interest is the residual item, it will be the owners of the business who benefit from any increase in assets after liabilities have been met. Conversely it will be the owners who bear the loss of any decrease in assets after liabilities have been met. The ownership interest applies to the entire net assets. It is sometimes described as the owners' wealth, although economists would take a view that the owners' wealth extends beyond the items recorded in a statement of financial position (balance sheet).

If there is only one owner, as in the sole trader's business, then there is no problem as to how the ownership interest is shared. In a partnership, the partnership agreement will usually state the profit-sharing ratio, which may also be applied to the net assets shown in the statement of financial position (balance sheet). If nothing is said in the partnership agreement, the profit sharing must be based on equal shares for each partner.

In a company the arrangements for sharing the net assets depend on the type of ownership chosen. The owners may hold **ordinary shares** in the company, which entitle them to a share of any dividend declared and a share in net assets on closing down the business. The ownership interest is in direct proportion to the number of shares held.

Some investors like to hold **preference shares**, which give them a preference (although not an automatic right) to receive a dividend before any ordinary share dividend is declared. The rights of preference shareholders are set out in the articles of association of the company. Some will have the right to share in a surplus of net assets on winding up, but others will only be entitled to the amount of capital originally contributed.

Definitions

The **ownership interest** is called **equity** in the IASB *Conceptual Framework*.

Equity is the residual interest in the assets of the entity after deducting all its liabilities.

Net assets means the difference between the total assets and the total liabilities of the business: it represents the amount of the ownership interest in the entity.

2.10 Recognition of the ownership interest

There can be no separate recognition criteria for the ownership interest because it is the result of recognising assets and recognising liabilities. Having made those decisions on assets and liabilities the enterprise has used up its freedom of choice.

2.11 Changes in the ownership interest

It has already been explained that the owner will become better off where the net assets are increasing. The owner will become worse off where the net assets are decreasing. To measure the increase or decrease in net assets, two accounting equations are needed:

At time $t = 0$	**Assets$_{(t0)}$ – Liabilities$_{(t0)}$**	equals	**Ownership interest$_{(t0)}$**
At time $t = 1$	**Assets$_{(t1)}$ – Liabilities$_{(t1)}$**	equals	**Ownership interest$_{(t1)}$**

Taking one equation away from the other may be expressed in words as:

Change in (assets – liabilities)	equals	Change in ownership interest

or, using the term 'net assets' instead of 'assets – liabilities':

Change in net assets	equals	Change in ownership interest

The change in the ownership interest between these two points in time is a measure of how much better or worse off the owner has become, through the activities of the business. The owner is better off when the ownership interest at time t = 1 is higher than that at time t = 0. To calculate the ownership interest at each point in time requires knowledge of all assets and all liabilities at each point in time. It is particularly interesting to know about the changes in assets and liabilities which have arisen from the day-to-day operations of the business.

The term **revenue** is given to any increase in the ownership interest arising from the operations of the business and caused by an increase in an asset which is greater than any decrease in another asset (or increase in a liability). The term **expense** is given to any reduction in the ownership interest arising from the operations of the business and caused by a reduction in an asset to the extent that it is not replaced by a corresponding increase in another asset (or reduction in a liability).

The owner or owners of the business may also change the amount of the ownership interest by deciding to contribute more cash or other resources in order to finance the business, or deciding to withdraw some of the cash and other resources previously contributed or accumulated. The amount contributed to the business by the owner is usually referred to as **capital**. Decisions about the level of capital to invest in the business are financing decisions. These financing decisions are normally distinguished separately from the results of operations.

So another equation may now be derived as a subdivision of the basic accounting equation, showing analysis of the changes in the ownership interest.

Change in ownership interest	equals	Capital contributed/withdrawn by the ownership plus **Revenue** minus **Expenses**

The difference between revenue and expenses is more familiarly known as profit. So a further subdivision of the basic equation is:

Profit	equals	**Revenue** minus **Expenses**

2.11.1   Revenue and expense

Revenue is created by a transaction or event arising during the operations of the business which causes an increase in the ownership interest. It could be due to an increase in cash or trade receivables, received in exchange for goods or services. Depending on the nature of the business, revenue may be described as sales, turnover, fees, commission, royalties or rent.

An **expense** is caused by a transaction or event arising during the operations of the business which causes a decrease in the ownership interest. It could be due to an outflow or depletion of assets such as cash, inventory (stock) or non-current assets (fixed assets). It could be due to a liability being incurred without a matching asset being acquired.

Definitions

> **Revenue** is created by a transaction or event arising during the ordinary activities of the entity which causes an increase in the ownership interest. It is referred to by a variety of different names including sales, fees, interest, dividends, royalties and rent.[13]
>
> An **expense** is caused by a transaction or event arising during the ordinary activities of the business which causes a decrease in the ownership interest.[14]

2.11.2 Position after a change has occurred

At the end of the accounting period there will be a new level of assets and liabilities recorded. These assets and liabilities will have resulted from the activities of the business during the period, creating revenue and incurring expenses. The owner may also have made voluntary contributions or withdrawals of capital as a financing decision. The equation in the following form reflects that story:

Assets minus **Liabilities** at the end of the period	equals	**Ownership interest at the start of the period** plus **Capital contributed/withdrawn in the period** plus **Revenue of the period** minus **Expenses of the period**

2.12 Assurance for users of financial statements

The definitions of assets and liabilities refer to expected flows into or out of the business. The recognition conditions refer to the evidence that the expected flows in or out will occur. The directors of a company are responsible for ensuring that the financial statements presented by them are a faithful representation of the assets and liabilities of the business and of the transactions and events relating to those assets and liabilities. Shareholders need reassurance that the directors, as their agents, have carried out this responsibility with sufficient care. To give themselves this reassurance, the shareholders appoint a firm of auditors to examine the records of the business and give an opinion as to whether the financial statements correspond to the accounting records and present a true and fair view. (Chapter 1 explained the position of directors as agents of the shareholders. Chapter 4 explains the regulations relating to company financial statements and the appointment of auditors.)

Meet David and Leona again as they continue their conversation on the work of the auditor and its value to the shareholder as a user of accounting information provided by a company.

DAVID: *I've now coated your ceiling with apple green emulsion. In return you promised to convince me that I rely on audited accounting information more than I realise. Here is your chance to do that. I was looking today at the annual report of a company which is a manufacturing business. There is a production centre in the UK but most of the production work is carried out in Spain where the operating costs are lower. The distribution operation is carried out from Swindon, selling to retail stores all over the UK. There is an export market, mainly in France, but the company has only scratched the surface of that market. Let's start with something easy – the inventories (stocks) of finished goods which are held at the factory in Spain and the distribution depot in Swindon.*

LEONA: *You've shown right away how limited your understanding is, by choosing the asset where you need the auditor's help the most. Everything can go wrong with inventories (stocks)! Think of the accounting equation:*

Assets − Liabilities = Ownership interest

If an asset is overstated, the ownership interest will be overstated. That means the profit for the period, as reported, is higher than it should be. But you won't know that because everything will appear to be in order from the accounts. You have told me repeatedly that you buy the future, not the past, but I know you look to the current profit and loss account as an indicator of future trends of profit. And so do all your friends.

DAVID: *How can the asset of finished goods inventories be overstated? It's quite a solid item.*

LEONA: *There are two types of potential error – the physical counting of the inventory and the valuation placed on it. There are two main causes of error, one being carelessness and the other an intention to deceive. I've seen situations where the stocktakers count the same stack of goods twice because they don't have a marker pen to put a cross on the items counted. I've also heard of situations where items are counted twice deliberately. We always attend the end-of-year counting of the inventory and observe the process carefully. I wish there weren't so many companies with December year-ends. Counting inventory on 2 January is never a good start to the new year.*

DAVID: *I suppose I can believe that people lose count but how does the valuation go wrong? All companies say that they value inventories at cost as the usual rule. How can the cost of an item be open to doubt?*

LEONA: *Answering that question needs a textbook in itself. The subject comes under the heading of 'management accounting'. Take the goods that you know are manufactured in Spain. There are costs of materials to make the goods, and labour to convert raw materials into finished goods. There are also the running costs of the production unit, which are called the overheads. There is an unbelievable variety of ways of bringing those costs together into one item of product. How much does the company tell you about all that? I know the answer – nothing.*

DAVID: *Well, I could always ask them at a briefing meeting. I usually ask about the profit margin on the goods sold, rather than the value of the goods unsold. But I can see that if the inventories figure is wrong then so is the profit margin. Do you have a systematic procedure for checking each kind of asset?*

LEONA: *Our magic word is **CEAVOP**. That stands for:*

> **C**ompleteness of information presented.
> **E**xistence of the asset or liability at a given date.
> **A**mount of the transaction is correctly recorded.
> **V**aluation reported for assets and liabilities is appropriate.
> **O**ccurrence of the transaction or event took place in the period.
> **P**resentation and disclosure is in accordance with regulations and accounting standards or other comparable regulations.

> *Every aspect of that list has to be checked for each of the assets and liabilities you see in the statement of financial position. We need good-quality evidence of each aspect before we sign off the audit report.*

DAVID: *I probably believe that you do a great deal of work with your CEAVOP. But next time I come round to paint your kitchen I'll bring a list of the situations where the auditors don't appear to have asked all the questions in that list.*

2.13 Summary

This chapter has set out the accounting equation for a situation at any one point in time:

Assets	minus	**Liabilities**	equals	**Ownership interest**

Key points are:

- An **asset** is a resource controlled by the entity as a result of past events and from which future economic benefits are expected to flow.
- A **current asset** is an asset that satisfies any of the following criteria:
  (a) it is expected to be realised in, or is intended for sale or consumption in, the entity's normal operating cycle;
  (b) it is held primarily for the purpose of being traded;
  (c) it is expected to be realised within 12 months after the date of the financial year-end;
  (d) it is cash or a cash equivalent.[15]
- A **non-current asset** is any asset that does not meet the definition of a current asset. Non-current assets include tangible, intangible and financial assets of a long-term nature. These are also described as **fixed assets**.
- A **liability** is a present obligation of the entity arising from past events, the settlement of which is expected to result in an outflow from the entity of resources embodying economic benefits.
- A **current liability** is a liability which satisfies any of the following criteria:
  (a) it is expected to be settled in the entity's normal operating cycle;
  (b) it is held primarily for the purpose of being traded;
  (c) it is due to be settled within 12 months after the date of the financial year-end.
- A **non-current liability** is any liability that does not meet the definition of a current liability. Non-current liabilities are also described as **long-term liabilities**.
- The **ownership interest** is called **equity** in the *Conceptual Framework*.
- **Equity** is the residual interest in the assets of the entity after deducting all its liabilities.
- **Net assets** means the difference between the total assets and the total liabilities of the business: it represents the amount of the ownership interest in the entity.
- **Recognition** means reporting an item in the financial statements, in words and in amounts, so that the amounts are included in the arithmetic totals of the financial statements. Any other form of reporting by way of note is called disclosure. The conditions for recognition of assets and liabilities are similar in wording.
- At the end of an accounting period the assets and liabilities are reported in a statement of financial position (balance sheet). Changes in the assets and liabilities during the period have caused changes in the ownership interest through revenue and expenses of operations. The owner may also have voluntarily added or withdrawn capital. The final position is explained on the left-hand side of the equation and the movement to that position is explained on the right-hand side:

Assets minus **Liabilities** at the end of the period	equals	**Ownership interest at the start of the period** plus **Capital contributed/ withdrawn in the period** plus **Revenue of the period** minus **Expenses of the period**

- As with any equation, it is possible to make this version more complex by adding further details. That is not necessary for the purpose of explaining the basic processes, but the equation will be revisited later in the book when some of the problems of accounting are opened up. The helpful aspect of the accounting equation is that it can always be used as a basis for arguing a feasible answer. The limitation is that it cannot give an opinion on the most appropriate answer when more than one option is feasible.

In Chapter 3 there is an explanation of how the information represented by the accounting equation is displayed in a form which is useful to the user groups identified in Chapter 1.

Further reading

IASB (2010), *The Conceptual Framework for Financial Reporting*, 'The Elements of Financial Statements' and 'Recognition of the Elements of Financial Statements', International Accounting Standards Board.

QUESTIONS

The Questions section of each chapter has three types of question. 'Test your understanding' questions to help you review your reading are in the 'A' series of questions. You will find the answers to these by reading and thinking about the material in the book. 'Application' questions to test your ability to apply technical skills are in the 'B' series of questions. Questions requiring you to show skills in problem solving and evaluation are in the 'C' series of questions. A letter [S] indicates that there is a solution at the end of the book.

A   Test your understanding

A2.1   Write out the basic form of the accounting equation. (Section 2.2)

A2.2   Define an asset and explain each part of the definition. (Section 2.3)

A2.3   Give five examples of items which are assets. (Section 2.4)

A2.4   Use the definition to explain why each of the items in your answer to A.2.3 is an asset. (Section 2.4)

A2.5   Explain what 'recognition' means in accounting. (Section 2.5)

A2.6   State the conditions for recognition of an asset. (Section 2.5)

A2.7   Explain why an item may pass the definition test but fail the recognition test for an asset. (Section 2.5)

A2.8   Give three examples of items which pass the definition test for an asset but fail the recognition test. (Section 2.5)

A2.9   Some football clubs include the players in the statement of financial position (balance sheet) as an asset. Others do not. Give the arguments to support each approach. (Section 2.5)

A2.10   Define a liability and explain each part of the definition. (Section 2.6)

A2.11   Give five examples of items which are liabilities. (Section 2.7)

A2.12   Use the definition to explain why each of the items in your answer to A2.11 is a liability. (Section 2.7)

A2.13   State the conditions for recognition of a liability. (Section 2.8)

A2.14   Explain why an item may pass the definition test but fail the recognition test for a liability. (Section 2.8)

A2.15   Define the term 'equity'. (Section 2.9)

A2.16   Explain what is meant by 'net assets'. (Section 2.9)

A2.17   Set out the accounting equation for a change in the ownership interest. (Section 2.11)

A2.18 Define 'revenue' and 'expenses'. (Section 2.11.1)

A2.19 Set out the accounting equation which represents the position after a change has occurred. (Section 2.11.2)

A2.20 Explain the auditor's approach to giving assurance about assets and liabilities. (Section 2.12)

B Application

B2.1 [S]

Classify each of the items in the following list as: asset; liability; neither an asset nor a liability.

(a) cash at bank
(b) loan from the bank
(c) letter from the bank promising an overdraft facility at any time in the next three months
(d) trade receivable (an amount due from a customer who has promised to pay later)
(e) trade receivable (an amount due from a customer who has promised to pay later but has apparently disappeared without leaving a forwarding address)
(f) trade payable (an amount due to a supplier of goods who has not yet received payment from the business)
(g) inventory of finished goods (fashion clothing stored ahead of the spring sales)
(h) inventory of finished goods (fashion clothing left over after the spring sales)
(i) investment in shares of another company where the share price is rising
(j) investment in shares of another company where the share price is falling
(k) lender of five-year loan to the business
(l) customer to whom the business has offered a 12-month warranty to repair goods free of charge
(m) a motor vehicle owned by the business
(n) a motor vehicle rented by the business for one year
(o) an office building owned by the business
(p) an office building rented by the business on a 99-year lease, with 60 years' lease period remaining.

B2.2 [S]

Explain whether each of the items from question B.2.1 above which you have identified as assets and liabilities would also meet the conditions for recognition of the item in the statement of financial position (balance sheet).

B2.3 [S]

Explain why each of the following items would not meet *either* the definition *or* the recognition conditions of an asset of the business:

(a) a letter from the owner of the business, addressed to the bank manager, promising to guarantee the bank overdraft of the business
(b) a list of the customers of the business
(c) an order received from a customer
(d) the benefit of employing a development engineer with a high level of 'know-how' specifically relevant to the business
(e) money spent on an advertising campaign to boost sales
(f) structural repairs to a building.

C Problem solving and evaluation

C2.1

The following information has been gathered from the accounting records of Pets Parlour:

Assets and liabilities at 31 December Year 4

	£
Cash at bank	500
Borrowings	6,000
Trade receivables (debtors)	5,000
Property, plant and equipment	29,000

Revenue and expenses for the year ended 31 December Year 4

	£
Fees charged for work done	20,000
Interest paid on borrowings	1,000
Administration costs incurred	1,500
Salaries paid to employees	14,000

Required

Using the accounting equation, calculate:

(a) The amount of ownership interest at 31 December Year 4.
(b) The amount of net profit for the year.
(c) The amount of the ownership interest at 1 January Year 4.

Activities for study groups

Obtain the annual report of a listed company. From the statement of financial position (balance sheet) list the items shown as assets and liabilities. (This will require you to look in detail at the notes to the accounts using the references on the face of the statement of financial position (balance sheet). Share out the list of assets and liabilities so that each person has four or five assets and four or five liability items.

1 Separately, using the definitions and recognition criteria, prepare a short statement explaining why each item on your list passes the tests of definition and recognition. State the evidence you would expect to see, as auditor, to confirm the expected future inflow of economic benefit from any asset and the expected future outflow of benefit from any liability.

2 Present your explanations to the group and together prepare a list of assets and a separate list of liabilities in order of the uncertainty which attaches to the expected future benefit.

3 Read the 'contingent liability' note, if there is one, to find examples of liabilities which have not been recognised but have been disclosed. Why will you not find a 'contingent asset' note?

Notes and references

1. IASB (2010), *Conceptual Framework*, para. 4.4(a).
2. *Ibid.*
3. IAS 1 (2009), para. 66.
4. *Ibid.*
5. IAS 1 para. 67 permits the use of alternative descriptions for non-current assets provided the meaning is clear.
6. IASB (2010), para. 4.38.
7. IASB (2010), para. 4.4(b).
8. *Ibid.*
9. IAS 1 (2012), para. 69.
10. *Ibid.*
11. IASB (2010), para. 4.38.
12. IASB (2010), para. 4.4(c).
13. IASB (2010), para. 4.29.
14. IASB (2010), para. 4.33.
15. IAS 1 (2012), para. 66.

Debit and credit bookkeeping

You do not have to read this supplement to be able to progress through the rest of the textbook. In the main body of each chapter the explanations are all given in terms of changes in elements of the accounting equation. However, for those who would like to know how debits and credits work, each chapter will have a supplement putting into debit and credit form the material contained in the chapter.

Recording in ledger accounts

The double-entry system of bookkeeping records business transactions in ledger accounts. It makes use of the fact that there are two aspects to every transaction when analysed in terms of the accounting equation.

A ledger account accumulates the increases and reductions either in a category of business activities such as sales or in dealings with individual customers and suppliers.

Ledger accounts may be subdivided. Sales could be subdivided into home sales and export sales. Separate ledger accounts might be kept for each type of non-current asset, e.g. buildings and machinery. The ledger account for machinery might be subdivided as office machinery and production machinery.

Ledger accounts for rent, business rates and property insurance might be kept separately or the business might instead choose to keep one ledger account to record transactions in all of these items, giving them the collective name administrative expenses. The decision would depend on the number of transactions in an accounting period and on whether it was useful to have separate records.

The managers of the business have discretion to combine or subdivide ledger accounts to suit the information requirements of the business concerned.

Using the accounting equation

Before entries are made in ledger accounts, the double entry system of bookkeeping assigns to each aspect of a business transaction a debit or a **credit** notation, based on the analysis of the transaction using the accounting equation.

In its simplest form the accounting equation is stated as:

Assets	minus	**Liabilities**	equals	**Ownership interest**

To derive the debit and credit rules it is preferable to rearrange the equation so that there is no minus sign.

Assets	equals	**Liabilities**	plus	**Ownership interest**

There are three elements to the equation and each one of these elements may either *increase* or *decrease* as a result of a transaction or event. The six possibilities are set out in Table 2.4.

Table 2.4
Combinations of increases and decreases of the main elements of transactions

Left-hand side of the equation		
Assets	Increase	Decrease

Right-hand side of the equation		
Liabilities	Decrease	Increase
Ownership interest	Decrease	Increase

The double-entry bookkeeping system uses this classification (which preserves the symmetry of the equation) to distinguish debit and credit entries as shown in Table 2.5.

Table 2.5
Rules of debit and credit for ledger entries, basic accounting equation

	Debit entries in a ledger account	Credit entries in a ledger account
Left-hand side of the equation		
Asset	Increase	Decrease
Right-hand side of the equation		
Liability	Decrease	Increase
Ownership interest	Decrease	Increase

It was shown in the main body of the chapter that the ownership interest may be increased by:

● earning revenue; and
● new capital contributed by the owner;

and that the ownership interest may be decreased by:

● incurring expenses; and
● capital withdrawn by the owner.

So the 'ownership interest' section of Table 2.5 may be expanded as shown in Table 2.6.

That is all you ever have to know about the rules of bookkeeping. All the rest can be reasoned from this table. For any transaction there will be two aspects. (If you find there are more than two, the transaction needs breaking down into simpler steps.) For each aspect there will be a ledger account. Taking each aspect in turn you ask yourself: *Is this an asset, a liability, or an aspect of the ownership interest?* Then you ask yourself: *Is it an increase or a decrease?* From Table 2.6 you then know immediately whether to make a debit or a credit entry.

Examples of the application of the rules of debit and credit recording are given in the supplement to Chapter 5 for a service business and in the supplement to Chapter 6 for a manufacturing business. They will also be used in later chapters to explain how particular transactions are reported.

Table 2.6
Rules of debit and credit for ledge **distinguishing different aspects of ownership interest**

	Debit entries in a ledger account	Credit entries in a ledger account
Left-hand side of the equation		
Asset	Increase	Decrease
Right-hand side of the equation		
Liability	Decrease	Increase
Ownership interest	Expense	Revenue
	Capital withdrawn	Capital contributed

S   Test your understanding

(The answer to each of the following questions is either **debit** or **credit**)

S2.1   What is the bookkeeping entry for an increase in an asset?

S2.2   What is the bookkeeping entry for a decrease in a liability?

S2.3   What is the bookkeeping entry for an increase in an expense?

S2.4   What is the bookkeeping entry for a withdrawal of owner's capital?

S2.5   What is the bookkeeping entry for an increase in revenue?

Chapter 3

Financial statements from the accounting equation

J Sainsbury plc

Summary balance sheet

Shareholders' funds as at 17 March 2012 were £5,629 million (19 March 2011: £5,424 million), an increase of £205 million. This is mainly attributable to the continued profitable growth of the underlying business, continued investment in space to support future growth, offset by an increase in the net retirement benefit obligations and net debt.

Alex Segre

Property, plant and equipment assets have increased by £545 million, as a result of increased space growth.

Summary balance sheet at 17 March 2012	2012 £m	2011 £m	Movement £m
Land and buildings (freehold and long leasehold)	6,802	6,440	362
Land and buildings (short leasehold)	648	622	26
Fixtures and fittings	1,879	1,722	157
Property, plant and equipment	9,329	8,784	545
Other non-current assets	911	842	69
Inventories	938	812	126
Trade and other receivables	286	303	(17)
Cash and cash equivalents	739	501	238
Debt	(2,719)	(2,315)	(404)
Trade and other payables and provisions	(3,400)	(3,262)	(138)
Retirement benefit obligations, net of deferred tax	(455)	(241)	(214)
Net assets	5,629	5,424	205

http://annualreport2012.j-sainsbury.co.uk/financial-review/summary-balance-sheet/, J Sainsbury plc, Reproduced by kind permission of J Sainsbury plc.

Discussion points

1 Explain how the balance sheet satisfies the accounting equation.

2 How does the description in words help users to understand the financial statement?

Contents

Learning outcomes

After studying this chapter you should be able to:

- Explain the benefits and problems of producing annual financial statements.
- Explain the purpose and structure of the statement of financial position (balance sheet).
- Explain the purpose and structure of the income statement (profit and loss account).
- Explain the purpose and structure of the statement of cash flows.
- Comment on the usefulness to users of the financial statements prepared.

Additionally for those who choose to study the supplement:

- Apply the debit and credit form of analysis to the transactions of a short period of time, summarising them in a list which may be used for preparation of simple financial statements.

3.1 Introduction

In the previous chapter the accounting equation was developed as a representation of the relationships among key items of accounting information: assets, liabilities and the ownership interest. An understanding of the accounting equation and the various elements of the equation provides a systematic approach to analysing transactions and events, but it gives no guidance as to how the results should be communicated in a manner which will be helpful and meaningful to users. The accounting equation is used in this chapter as a basis for explaining the structure of financial statements. Ideas beyond the accounting equation are required as to what qualities are expected of financial statements.

The various financial statements produced by enterprises for the owners and other external users are derived from the accounting equation. The *Conceptual Framework* identifies the purposes of financial reporting as producing information about the financial position, performance and financial adaptability of the enterprise. The three most familiar **primary financial statements**, and their respective purposes, are:

Primary financial statement	Purpose is to report
Statement of financial position (balance sheet)	Financial position
Income statement (Profit and loss account)	Financial performance
Statement of cash flows	Financial adaptability

This chapter explains the general shape and content of each of these financial statements.

3.2 Who is in charge of the accounting system?

Since 2005 two different accounting systems have existed for companies in the UK, depending on the type of company. When you look at the name of a company listed on the Stock Exchange, such as Vodaphone, BskyB, Burberry and Marks and Spencer, you are really looking at a family group of companies all owned by one parent company. One set of financial statements represents all the companies in the group. Under the law of the European Union (EU), these group financial statements for listed companies must apply the International Financial Reporting Standards (IFRS) accounting system set out by the International Accounting Standards Board (**IASB system**). Other companies in the UK may choose to follow the IASB system of standards but there is no requirement to do so. All companies in the UK that do not apply the IASB system must apply the accounting system set out by the UK Accounting Standards Board (ASB). Many public bodies in the UK, including central government and local authorities, now use the IASB system of IFRS.

Fortunately for those studying the subject, the ASB and the IASB have been working closely together for many years and there are relatively few differences between the two systems. However, there is a potential difference in the appearance and the wording of financial statements. Companies applying the UK ASB's accounting system must use specifications of the sequence and content of items (called **formats** of financial statements) set out in UK company law which is based on EU directives. Companies applying the IASB's system to their listed group reporting have a choice in how they present their financial statements. As a consequence we are now seeing variety in the content and sequence of financial statements published in the annual reports of groups listed on the Stock Exchange. This chapter gives you a flavour of the formats that you might see in financial statements. Where there are differences in words used, this chapter gives the wording of the IASB system first, followed by the wording of UK company law and ASB standards in brackets. As an example, the description:

> income statement (profit and loss account)

means that the IASB system uses **income statement** in its illustrations of a profit statement, while UK law and ASB standards use **profit and loss account** in their illustrations of a profit statement.

3.3 The accounting period

In the far-away days of traders sailing out of Italian ports on three-year voyages, the **accounting period** was determined by the date of return of the ship, when the accounts could be prepared for the whole voyage. That rather leisurely view of the scale of time would not be tolerated in an industrial and commercial society where there is always someone demanding information. The convention is that businesses should prepare financial statements at least once in every calendar year. That convention is a requirement of law expressed in the Companies Act 2006 in the case of limited liability companies. Where companies have a Stock Exchange listing they are required to produce an interim report six months into the accounting year. Some companies voluntarily produce quarterly reports to shareholders, reflecting the practice of listed companies in the USA. For internal management accounting purposes, a business may produce reports more frequently (e.g. on a monthly or a weekly basis).

Businesses may choose their accounting date as a time convenient to their activities. Many companies choose 31 December for the year-end, but others (including many of the utility companies which were formerly owned by the government) use 31 March. Some prefer a September or October date after the peak of the summer sales has passed. Whatever the choice, companies are expected to keep the same date from one year to the next unless there is a strong reason for changing.

The use of a 12-month accounting period should not be too much of a problem where the trading cycle fits neatly into a year. If the business is seasonal, there will be a peak of production to match the seasonal peak of sales and the pattern will be repeated every year. There could be a few technical problems of deciding exactly how to close the door on 31 December and whether transactions towards the end of the year are to be included in that year or carried to the next period. These problems can be dealt with by having systematic 'cut-off' rules. There is a bigger problem for those companies whose trading cycle is much longer. It could take two years to build a section of a motorway or three years to build a bridge over a wide river estuary. Such a company will have to subdivide the work on the main contract so that some can be reported each year.

The use of the 12-month accounting period also causes problems for recognition of assets and liabilities. Waiting for the ship to arrive was much safer evidence for the Venetian traders than hoping it was still afloat or relying on reported sightings. For today's business the equivalent situation would be waiting for a property to be sold or for a large customer to pay the amount due as a debt. However, in practice the statement of financial position (balance sheet) cannot wait. Notes to the accounts give additional explanations to help users of financial statements evaluate the risk, but it is all quite tentative. Narrative descriptions of risk are explained further in Chapter 14, section 14.10.

3.4 The statement of financial position (balance sheet)

The **statement of financial position (balance sheet)** reflects the accounting equation. Both descriptions are used in this textbook because you will find both in use. The International Accounting Standards Board prefers the term 'statement of financial position' while company law in the UK uses the term 'balance sheet'. You saw in Chapter 2 that there is more than one way to write the accounting equation. That means there is more than one way to present a statement of financial position (balance sheet). You will find throughout your study of accounting that there is often more than one approach to dealing with an activity or solving a problem. This is the first time but there will be more. It means that you need to be flexible in your approach to reading and using financial statements.

3.4.1 Focus on the ownership interest

One form of the accounting equation focuses on the ownership interest as the result of subtracting liabilities from assets. The equation is as follows:

Assets	minus	**Liabilities**	equals	**Ownership interest**

UK companies who apply this form of the equation will present the statement of financial position (balance sheet) in a narrative form, reading down the page, as follows:

Assets
minus
Liabilities
equals
Ownership interest

The assets are subdivided into current assets and non-current assets (defined in Chapter 2), while the liabilities are subdivided into current liabilities and non-current liabilities (also defined in Chapter 2). The ownership interest may also be subdivided to show separately the capital contributed or withdrawn and the profit of the period. Because current assets and current liabilities are closely intertwined in the day-to-day operations of the business, they are often grouped close to each other in the statement of financial position (balance sheet) (Table 3.1).

Table 3.1
Structure of a statement of financial position (balance sheet)

Non-current assets
plus
Current assets
minus
Current liabilities
minus
Non-current liabilities
equals
Capital at start of year
plus/minus
Capital contributed or withdrawn
plus
Profit of the period

Table 3.1 represents a typical sequence used by UK public companies. Most companies will try to confine the statement of financial position (balance sheet) to a single side of A4 paper but there is not much space on one sheet of A4 paper to fit in all the assets and liabilities of a company. Consequently a great deal of use is made of notes to the accounts which explain the detail. The statement of financial position (balance sheet) shows only the main categories of assets and liabilities.

3.4.2 Balancing assets and claims on assets

Another form of the accounting equation focuses on balancing the assets against the claims on assets. The claims on assets come from the ownership interest and from liabilities of all types. The equation is:

Assets	equals	Liabilities	plus	Ownership interest

UK companies who apply this form of the equation will present the statement of financial position (balance sheet) vertically on one sheet of paper but the sequence will be different:

Assets
equals
Liabilities
plus
Ownership interest

In some countries there is a preference for lining up the statement of financial position (balance sheet) horizontally to match the accounting equation even more closely.

	Liabilities
Assets	plus
	Ownership interest

Activity 3.1

Before reading further, make sure that you can explain why each item in the accounting records is an asset or a liability, as shown in the foregoing list. If you have any doubts, read Chapter 2 again before proceeding with this chapter.

3.4.3 Example of presentation

The following list of assets and liabilities of P. Mason's legal practice was prepared from the accounting records of transactions summarised at 30 September Year 5:

	£
Land and buildings	250,000
Office furniture	30,000
Receivables (debtors) for fees	1,200
Prepayment of insurance premium	540
Cash at bank	15,280
Total assets (A)	**297,020**
Trade payables (creditors)	2,800
Long-term loan	150,000
Total liabilities (L)	**152,800**
Ownership interest (A – L)	**144,220**

Table 3.2 shows how this would appear in a statement of financial position (balance sheet) based on the 'ownership interest' form of the equation. Table 3.3 shows how the same information would appear in a statement of financial position (balance sheet) based on the 'claims on assets' form of the equation.

The statement of financial position (balance sheet) in Table 3.2 is more informative than the list of assets and liabilities from which it was prepared because it has been arranged in a helpful format. The first helpful feature is the use of headings (shown in Table 3.2 in bold) for similar items grouped together, such as non-current assets, current assets, current liabilities and non-current liabilities. The second helpful feature is the use of **subtotals** (identified in Table 3.2 by descriptions in italics and shaded) for similar items grouped together. The subtotals used in this example are those for: total non-current assets; total current assets; total assets; and total liabilities. There are no standard rules on use of subtotals. They should be chosen in a manner most appropriate to the situation. Brackets round figures show the 'minus' in the accounting equation.

A person using this statement of financial position (balance sheet) can see at a glance that there is no problem for the business in meeting its current liabilities from its resources of current assets. The financing of the business is split almost equally between the non-current liabilities and the ownership interest, a split which would not be regarded as excessively risky by those who lend to businesses. The non-current assets used as a basis for generating profits from one year to the next are collected together as a group, although the statement of financial position (balance sheet) alone cannot show how effectively those assets are being used. For that, an income statement (profit and loss account) is needed.

The statement of financial position (balance sheet) in Table 3.3 is again more informative than the list of assets and liabilities from which it was prepared because it has been arranged in a helpful format. It offers a helpful feature in the use of headings (in bold) for similar items grouped together. It is also helpful in providing subtotals

Table 3.2

Statement of financial position (balance sheet): Assets minus liabilities equals ownership interest

P. Mason's legal practice Statement of financial position (balance sheet) at 30 September Year 5	
	£
Non-current assets	
Land and buildings	250,000
Office furniture	30,000
Total non-current assets	280,000
Current assets	
Receivables (debtors) for fees	1,200
Prepayment of insurance premium	540
Cash at bank	15,280
Total current assets	17,020
Total assets	**297,020**
Current liabilities	
Trade payables (creditors)	(2,800)
Non-current liabilities	
Long-term loan	(150,000)
Total liabilities	**(152,800)**
Net assets	144,220
Ownership interest	144,220

Table 3.3

Statement of financial position (balance sheet): Assets equal liabilities plus ownership interest

P. Mason's legal practice Statement of financial position (balance sheet) at 30 September Year 5	
	£
Non-current assets	
Land and buildings	250,000
Office furniture	30,000
Total non-current assets	280,000
Current assets	
Receivables for fees	1,200
Prepayment of insurance premium	540
Cash at bank	15,280
Total current assets	17,020
Total assets	**297,020**
Current liabilities	
Trade payables	2,800
Non-current liabilities	
Long-term loan	150,000
Total liabilities	**152,800**
Ownership interest	144,220
Total liabilities plus ownership interest	297,020

(identified by descriptions in italics and shaded) for similar items grouped together. The subtotals used in this example are those for: total non-current assets and total current assets. Some financial statements include a subtotal for the current assets less current liabilities (not current assets). There are no standard rules on use of subtotals. They should be chosen in a manner most appropriate to the situation.

A person using this statement of financial position (balance sheet) can again see at a glance that there is no problem for the business in meeting its current liabilities from its resources of current assets. The financing of the business is split almost equally between the non-current liabilities and the ownership interest, a split which would not be regarded as excessively risky by those who lend to businesses. The non-current assets used as a basis for generating profits from one year to the next are collected together as a group, although the statement of financial position (balance sheet) alone cannot show how effectively those assets are being used.

3.5 The income statement (profit and loss account)

For many years in the UK, **profit and loss account** was the only title used for the financial statement reporting profit of the period. From 2005 many of those listed groups following the IASB's system have chosen to follow an example given by the IASB which uses the heading **income statement**, found more commonly in US company reports. It is not compulsory for listed group companies to use 'income statement' and some retain the 'profit and loss account' heading. The income statement (profit and loss account) reflects that part of the accounting equation which defines profit:

Profit	equals	**Revenue** minus **Expenses**

The expenses of a period are matched against the revenue earned in that period. This is described as the application of the **matching** concept in accounting.

As with the statement of financial position (balance sheet), it is presented in a vertical form so that it can be read down the page as a narrative (Table 3.4).

Table 3.4
**Structure of an income statement
(profit and loss account)**

Revenue
minus
Expenses
equals
Profit

3.5.1   Example of presentation

The accounting records of P. Mason's legal practice at 30 September Year 5 showed that the ownership interest could be explained as follows (using brackets to show negative items):

	£
Increases in ownership interest	
Capital contributed at start of month	140,000
Fees	8,820
Decreases in ownership interest	
Computer rental and online searches	(1,500)
Gas	(100)
Electricity	(200)
Telephone/fax	(1,000)
Salary of assistant	(1,800)
Ownership interest at end of month	144,220

The statement of profit is quite simple, as shown in Table 3.5.

Table 3.5
Financial statement of profit, in a useful format

P. Mason's legal practice Income statement (profit and loss account) for the month of September		
	£	£
Revenues		
Fees		8,820
Expenses		
Computer rental and online searches	(1,500)	
Gas	(100)	
Electricity	(200)	
Telephone/fax	(1,000)	
Salary of assistant	(1,800)	
Total expenses		(4,600)
Net profit of the month		4,220

3.5.2 Comment

The income statement (profit and loss account) improves on the mere list of constituent items by providing headings (shown in bold) for each main category. As this is a very simple example, only two headings and one subtotal are required. Headings and subtotals are most useful where there are groups of items of a similar nature. The resulting net profit shows how the revenues and expenses have contributed overall to increasing the ownership interest during the month.

Activity 3.2	Taking each item of the income statement (profit and loss account) in turn, explain to an imaginary friend why each item of revenue and expense is regarded as increasing or decreasing the ownership interest. If necessary, look back to the definitions of revenue and expense in Chapter 2. Make sure that you feel confident about the income statement (profit and loss account) before you move on.

3.6 The statement of cash flows

It was shown in Chapter 1 that liquidity is of interest to more than one user group, but of particular interest to creditors of the business.

Liquidity is measured by the cash and near-cash assets and the change in those assets, so a financial statement which explains cash flows should be of general interest to user groups:

Cash flow	equals	**Cash inflows to the enterprise** minus **Cash outflows from the enterprise**

The **statement of cash flows** will appear in a vertical form:

Cash inflows
minus
Cash outflows
equals
Change in cash assets

In a business there will be different factors causing the inflows and outflows of cash. The enterprise will try to make clear what the different causes are. Subdivisions are commonly used for operating activities, investing activities and financing activities:

- *Operating activities* are the actions of buying and selling goods, or manufacturing goods for resale, or providing a service to customers.
- *Investing activities* are the actions of buying and selling non-current assets for long-term purposes.
- *Financing activities* are the actions of raising and repaying the long-term finance of the business.

Table 3.6 sets out the basic structure of a basic statement of cash flows.

Table 3.6
Structure of a statement of cash flows

Operating activities **Cash inflows** minus
Cash outflows
plus
Investing activities **Cash inflows** minus **Cash outflows**
plus
Financing activities **Cash inflows** minus **Cash outflows**
equals
Change in cash assets

3.6.1   Example of presentation

The cash transactions of P. Mason's legal practice for the month of September were recorded as follows:

Accounting records

Year 5		£
Cash received		
Sept. 1	Capital contributed by P. Mason	140,000
Sept. 1	Loan from bank	150,000
Sept. 19	Fees received from clients	7,620
	Total cash received	297,620
Cash paid		
Sept. 1	Land and buildings	250,000
Sept. 5	Prepayment of insurance premium	540
Sept. 26	Supplier for office furniture	30,000
Sept. 30	Salaries	1,800
	Total cash paid	282,340
	Cash remaining at 30 September	15,280

The statement of cash flows would be presented as shown in Table 3.7.

3.6.2   Comment

The cash flows, listed at the start of section 3.6.1 in the accounting records for the legal practice, relate to three different types of activity which are brought out more clearly in the statement of cash flows by the use of headings and subtotals. The headings are shown in bold and the subtotals are highlighted by italics and shading. The story emerging from the statement of cash flows is that the owner put in £140,000 and the bank lent £150,000, providing a total of £290,000 in start-up finance. Of this amount, £280,000 was used during the month to pay for non-current assets. That left £10,000 which, when added to the positive cash flow from operations, explains why the cash resources increased by £15,280 over the month.

Table 3.7

Financial statement showing cash flows of an enterprise

P. Mason's legal practice
Statement of cash flows for the month of September Year 5

	£
Operating activities	
Inflow from fees	7,620
Outflow to insurance premium	(540)
Outflows to salaries	(1,800)
Net inflow from operations	5,280
Investing activities	
Payment for land and building	(250,000)
Payment for office furniture	(30,000)
Net outflow for investing activities	(280,000)
Financing activities	
Capital contributed by owner	140,000
Five-year loan from bank	150,000
Net inflow from financing activities	290,000
Increase in cash at bank over period	15,280

Table 3.8

Comparison of profit and operating cash flow for the month of September

P. Mason's legal practice

	Profit £	Operating cash flow £
Revenues		
Fees/cash received	8,820	7,620
Expenses		
Computer rental and online searches	(1,500)	nil
Gas	(100)	nil
Electricity	(200)	nil
Telephone/fax	(1,000)	nil
Salary of assistant	(1,800)	(1,800)
Payment for insurance premium	nil	(540)
Total expenses/total cash paid	4,600	(2,340)
Net profit of the month	4,220	
Increase in cash in the month		5,280

It is quite common to compare the increase in ownership claim caused by making a profit with the increase in the cash resources of a business caused by operations. In this case the profit is £4,220 (Table 3.5) but the operations have added £15,280 to the cash assets of the business.

To make the comparison, Table 3.8 takes the income statement (profit and loss account) of Table 3.5 and sets alongside it the cash flows relating to operations.

Table 3.8 shows that the cash flow from fees was £1,200 less than the fee revenue earned because some customers had not paid at the month end. This is the amount shown in the statement of financial position (balance sheet) (Table 3.2) as receivables for fees. Table 3.8 also shows that expenses of rental, gas, electricity and telephone amounting to £2,800 in total had not been paid at the month end. These are shown as **trade payables** in the statement of financial position (balance sheet). The cash flow from operations is reduced by the payment for the insurance premium which does not affect the income statement (profit and loss account) for the month.

Users of financial statements regard both the profit and the cash flow as interesting items of information. The profit shows the overall increase in ownership claim which contributes to the overall wealth of the business. The cash flow shows the ability of the business to survive financially through planning the timing and amount of inflows and outflows of cash.

3.7 Usefulness of financial statements

Here are Leona and David, still working on Leona's flat, discussing the usefulness of financial statements.

LEONA: *Which financial statement is the most important for you?*

DAVID: *It has to be the income statement (profit and loss account). Profit creates wealth. Future profit creates future wealth. I have to make a forecast of each company's profit as part of my planning to meet our overall investment strategy. Maybe I should qualify that by adding that cash flow is also important, especially where there is high uncertainty about future prospects. We talk about 'quality of profits' and regard some types of profit as of higher quality than others. Cash flow support is one aspect of that quality. We have doubts about some accounting amounts which don't have a close relationship to cash. A business cannot survive if it can't pay its way.*

LEONA: *Where does that leave the statement of financial position?*

DAVID: *I'm not sure. It is a list of resources and claims on those resources. We are share-holders and so we have a claim on those resources but we don't think about it to any great extent because we are concentrating on the going concern aspects of the business, rather than closing down and selling the assets. The numbers in the statement of financial position don't mean very much because they are out of date.*

LEONA: *We studied research at university which suggested that cash flow is the answer and income statements (profit and loss accounts) are too difficult to understand. It was suggested that the statement of financial position (balance sheet) should show what the assets could be sold for. I don't think the ideas had caught on in practice, but they seemed to have some merits.*

DAVID: *I like to know the dynamics of the business. I like to see the movements of different aspects and the interactions. I think I would feel that cash flow alone is concentrating on only one aspect of the wealth of the business. I suppose the statement of financial position is a useful check on the position which has been reached as a result of making profits for the period. One thing we do look at in the statement of financial position is how much has been borrowed for use in the business. We don't like to see that become too high in comparison with the ownership interest.*

LEONA: *At least you are admitting to seeing something in the financial statements. I still have to persuade you that the auditors are important in giving you the reassurance you obviously obtain.*

Activity 3.3   *Analyse your own view of wealth and changes in wealth. Which items would you include in your personal statement of financial position (balance sheet) today? Which items would you include in your personal 'profit or loss' calculation for the past year? Which items would you include in your personal statement of cash flows? Has your view of 'wealth' been modified as a result of reading these first three chapters? If so, how have your views changed?*

3.8 Summary

This chapter has explained the structure of the main financial statements produced by business and non-business entities.

Key points are:

- An **accounting period** of 12 months is common for financial reporting.

- The **primary financial statements** produced by a wide range of entities are the statement of financial position (balance sheet), the income statement (profit and loss account) and the statement of cash flows.

- A **statement of financial position (balance sheet)** presents financial position at a point in time. The **format** of the statement of financial position (balance sheet) will vary depending on which version of the accounting equation is preferred by the entity preparing the statement.

- An **income statement** (profit and loss account) presents the performance over a period of time. The income statement (profit and loss account) presents financial performance by **matching** revenue and expenses to arrive at a profit of the period.

- A **statement of cash flows** presents the financial adaptability over a period of time. It explains changes in the cash position over a period caused by operating cash flows, investing cash flows and financing cash flows.

- Since 2005 two different accounting systems (consisting of **accounting standards** and legislation) have existed for companies in the UK, depending on the type of company. The **IASB system** applies to the group financial statements of listed companies. Other companies may choose voluntarily to follow the IASB system. The **UK ASB system**, based on UK law and the standards of the UK ASB, applies to all companies that do not follow the IASB system.

- The **accounting standards** of the UK ASB are very similar to those of the IASB.

QUESTIONS

The Questions section of each chapter has three types of question. 'Test your understanding' questions to help you review your reading are in the 'A' series of questions. You will find the answers to these by reading and thinking about the material in the book. 'Application' questions to test your ability to apply technical skills are in the 'B' series of questions. Questions requiring you to show skills in problem solving and evaluation are in the 'C' series of questions. A letter [S] indicates that there is a solution at the end of the book.

A Test your understanding

A3.1 Explain why an accounting period of 12 months is used as the basis for reporting to external users of financial statements. (Section 3.3)

A3.2 Explain how the structure of the statement of financial position (balance sheet) corresponds to the accounting equation. (Section 3.4)

A3.3 Explain how the structure of the income statement (profit and loss account) represents a subsection of the accounting equation. (Section 3.5)

A3.4 Explain how the structure of the statement of cash flows represents another subsection of the accounting equation. (Section 3.6)

A3.5 List three features of a statement of financial position (balance sheet) which are particularly useful in making the format helpful to readers. (Section 3.4.3)

A3.6 List three features of an income statement (profit and loss account) format which are particularly useful in making the format helpful to readers. (Section 3.5.1)

A3.7 List three features of a statement of cash flows which are particularly useful in making the format helpful to readers. (Section 3.6.1)

B   Application

B3.1 [S]

John Timms is the sole owner of Sunshine Wholesale Traders, a company which buys fruit from farmers and sells it to supermarkets. All goods are collected from farms and delivered to supermarkets on the same day, so no inventories (stocks) of fruit are held. The accounting records of Sunshine Traders at 30 June Year 2, relating to the year then ended, have been summarised by John Timms as follows:

	£
Fleet of delivery vehicles, after deducting depreciation	35,880
Furniture and fittings, after deducting depreciation	18,800
Trade receivables	34,000
Bank deposit	19,000
Trade payables (creditors)	8,300
Sales	294,500
Cost of goods sold	188,520
Wages and salaries	46,000
Transport costs	14,200
Administration costs	1,300
Depreciation of vehicles, furniture and fittings	1,100

Required

(a) Identify each item in the accounting records as either an asset, a liability, or ownership interest (identifying separately the expenses and revenues which contribute to the change in the ownership interest).

(b) Prepare a statement of financial position (balance sheet) at 30 June Year 2.

(c) Prepare an income statement (profit and loss statement) for the year ended 30 June Year 2.

B3.2 [S]

Prepare a statement of financial position (balance sheet) from the following list of assets and liabilities, regarding the ownership interest as the missing item.

	£
Trade payables (creditors)	43,000
Cash at bank	9,000
Inventories (stocks) of goods for resale	35,000
Land and buildings	95,000
Wages due to employees but not paid	2,000
Vehicles	8,000
Five-year loan from a bank	20,000

Explain how the statement of financial position (balance sheet) will change for each of the following transactions:

(a) The wages due to the employees are paid at £2,000.

(b) One-quarter of the inventory (stock) of goods held for resale is destroyed by fire and there is no insurance to cover the loss.

(c) Goods for resale are bought on credit at a cost of £5,000.

There are no questions in the C series for this chapter.

Activities for study groups

Return to the annual reports your group obtained for the exercise in Chapter 1. Find the statement of financial position (balance sheet), income statement (profit and loss account) and statement of cash flows. Use the outline formats contained in this chapter to identify the main areas of each of the published statements. Work together in preparing a list of features which make the formats useful to the reader. Note also any aspects of the presentation which you find unhelpful at this stage. (It may be useful to look back on this note at the end of the course as a collective check on whether your understanding and awareness of annual report items has improved.)

Using the accounting equation to analyse transactions

In the main body of the chapter the transactions of P. Mason's legal practice are set out in summary form and are then presented in financial statements. This supplement goes back one stage and looks at the transactions and events for the month of September which resulted in the summary and financial statements shown in the chapter.

The list of transactions and events is as follows:

Sept. 1	P. Mason deposits £140,000 in a bank account to commence the business under the name *P. Mason's legal practice*.
Sept. 1	P. Mason's legal practice borrows £150,000 from a finance business to help with the intended purchase of a property for use as an office. The loan is to be repaid in five years' time.
Sept. 1	A property is purchased at a cost of £75,000 for the land and £175,000 for the buildings. The full price is paid from the bank account.
Sept. 3	Office furniture is purchased from Stylecraft at a cost of £30,000. The full price is to be paid within 90 days.
Sept. 5	An insurance premium of £540 is paid in advance. The insurance cover will commence on 1 October.
Sept. 8	An applicant is interviewed for a post of legal assistant. She agrees to start work on 10 September for a salary of £24,000 per annum.
Sept. 11	Invoices are sent to some clients for work done in preparing contracts for them. The total of the invoiced amounts is £8,820. Clients are allowed up to 30 days to pay.
Sept. 19	Cheques received from clients in payment of invoices amount to £7,620.
Sept. 26	Payment is made to Stylecraft for the amount due for office furniture, £30,000.
Sept. 28	Bills are received as follows: for computer rental and online searches, £1,500; gas, £100; electricity, £200; and telephone/fax, £1,000.
Sept. 30	Legal assistant is paid salary of £1,800 for period to end of month.

In the supplement to Chapter 2 a table was prepared, based on the accounting equation, showing the classification used for debit and credit bookkeeping entries. As a reminder, the form of the equation used to derive the debit and credit rules is:

Assets	equals	Liabilities	plus	Ownership interest

As a further reminder, the rules are set out again in Table 3.9. Each of the transactions of P. Mason's legal practice for the month of September is now analysed in terms of the effect on the accounting equation and the resulting debit and credit entries which would be made in the accounting records.

Table 3.9
Rules for debit and credit recording

	Debit entries in a ledger account	Credit entries in a ledger account
Left-hand side of the equation		
Asset	Increase	Decrease
Right-hand side of the equation		
Liability	Decrease	Increase
Ownership interest	Expense	Revenue
	Capital withdrawn	Capital contributed

Analysis of each transaction

Sept. 1   P. Mason deposits £140,000 in a bank account to commence the business under the name *P. Mason's legal practice*.

The business acquires an asset (cash in the bank) and an ownership interest is created through contribution of capital.

Transaction number: 1	Debit	Credit
Asset	Bank £140,000	
Ownership interest		Capital contributed £140,000

Sept. 1   P. Mason's legal practice borrows £150,000 from a finance business to help with the intended purchase of a property for use as an office. The loan is to be repaid in five years' time.

The business acquires an asset of cash and a long-term liability is created.

Transaction number: 2	Debit	Credit
Asset	Bank £150,000	
Liability		Long-term loan £150,000

Sept. 1   A property is purchased at a cost of £75,000 for the land and £175,000 for the buildings. The full price is paid from the bank account.

The business acquires an asset of land and buildings (£250,000 in total) and the asset of cash in the bank is reduced.

Transaction number: 3	Debit	Credit
Asset	Land and buildings £250,000	Bank £250,000

Sept. 3   Office furniture is purchased from Stylecraft at a cost of £30,000. The full price is to be paid within 90 days.

The business acquires an asset of furniture and also acquires a liability to pay the supplier, Stylecraft. The liability is called a trade payable (creditor).

Transaction number: 4	Debit	Credit
Asset	Furniture £30,000	
Liability		Trade payable (Stylecraft) £30,000

Sept. 5   An insurance premium of £540 is paid in advance. The insurance cover will commence on 1 October.

The business acquires an asset of prepaid insurance (the benefit of cover exists in the future) and the asset of cash at bank is reduced.

Transaction number: 5	Debit	Credit
Asset	Prepayment £540	Bank £540

Sept. 8   An applicant is interviewed for a post of legal assistant. She agrees to start work on 10 September for a salary of £24,000 per annum.

The successful outcome of the interview is an *event* and there is an expected future benefit from employing the new legal assistant. The employee will be controlled by the organisation through a contract of employment. The organisation has a commitment to pay her the agreed salary. It could be argued that the offer of employment, and acceptance of that offer, create an asset of the human resource and a liability equal to the future salary. That does not happen because the *recognition* conditions are applied and it is felt too risky to recognise an asset when there is insufficient evidence of the future benefit. Commercial prudence dictates that it is preferable to wait until the employee has done some work and pay her at the end of the month for work done during the month. The accounting process is similarly prudent and no accounting recognition takes place until the payment has occurred. Even then it is the expense of the past which is recognised, rather than the asset of benefit for the future.

Sept. 11   Invoices are sent to some clients showing fees due for work done in preparing contracts for them. The total of the invoiced amounts is £8,820. Clients are allowed up to 30 days to pay.

Earning fees is the main activity of the legal practice. Earning fees makes the owner better off and is an example of the more general activity *of increasing the ownership interest* by creating revenue. The clients have not yet paid and therefore the business has an asset called a **trade receivable (debtor)**.

Transaction number: 6	Debit	Credit
Asset	Trade receivables £8,820	
Ownership interest (revenue)		Fees for work done £8,820

Sept. 19   Cheques received from clients in payment of invoices amount to £7,620.

When the customers pay, the amount due to the business from debtors will be decreased. So the asset of trade receivables decreases and the asset of cash in the bank increases.

Transaction number: 7	Debit	Credit
Asset	Bank £7,620	Trade receivables £7,620

Sept. 26   Payment is made to Stylecraft for the amount due for office furniture, £30,000.

The asset of cash in the bank decreases and the liability to Stylecraft decreases to nil.

Transaction number: 8	Debit	Credit
Asset		Bank £30,000
Liability	Trade payable (Stylecraft) £30,000	

Sept. 28   Bills are received as follows: for computer rental and online searches, £1,500; gas, £100; electricity, £200; and telephone/fax £1,000 (total £2,800).

The computer rental, online searches, gas, electricity and telephone have been used up during the period and are all expenses which reduce the ownership interest. They are unpaid and, therefore, a liability is recorded.

Transaction number: 9	Debit	Credit
Liability		Trade payables £2,800
Ownership interest	Expenses £2,800	

Sept. 30   Legal assistant is paid salary of £1,800 for period to end of month.

The asset of cash at bank decreases and the salary paid to the legal assistant is an expense of the month.

Transaction number: 10	Debit	Credit
Asset		Bank £1,800
Ownership interest	Expense £1,800	

Summarising the debit and credit entries

The formal system of bringing together debit and credit entries is based on ledger accounts. These are explained in the supplement to Chapter 5. For the present it will be sufficient to use a spreadsheet (Table 3.10) to show how the separate debit and credit entries analysed in this supplement lead to the list of items used in the main part of the chapter as the basis for the financial statements presented there.

In the spreadsheet there are dates which correspond to the dates of the foregoing ten separate analyses of transactions. The debit and credit entries are shown with Dr or Cr alongside to distinguish them. For each column all the debit entries are totalled

Table 3.10
Spreadsheet of transactions for P. Mason's legal practice, during the month of September

Date	Assets					Liabilities		Ownership interest		
	Land and buildings £	Office furniture £	Trade receivables £	Pre-payments £	Cash at bank £	Trade payables £	Bank loan £	Revenue £	Expenses £	Owner's capital contributed £
1 Sept.					140,000 Dr					140,000 Cr
1 Sept.					150,000 Dr		150,000 Cr			
1 Sept.	250,000 Dr				250,000 Cr					
3 Sept.		30,000 Dr				30,000 Cr				
5 Sept.				540 Dr	540 Cr					
11 Sept.			8,820 Dr					8,820 Cr		
19 Sept.			7,620 Cr		7,620 Dr					
26 Sept.					30,000 Cr	30,000 Dr				
28 Sept.						2,800 Cr			2,800 Dr	
30 Sept.					1,800 Cr				1,800 Dr	
Total debit entries in each column										
	250,000 Dr	30,000 Dr	8,820 Dr	540 Dr	297,620 Dr	30,000 Dr	nil	nil	4,600 Dr	nil
Total credit entries in each column										
	nil	nil	7,620 Cr	nil	282,340 Cr	32,800 Cr	150,000 Cr	8,820 Cr	nil	140,000 Cr
Surplus of debits over credits (or credits over debits)										
	250,000 Dr	30,000 Dr	1,200 Dr	540 Dr	15,280 Dr	2,800 Cr	150,000 Cr	8,820 Cr	4,600 Dr	140,000 Cr

and all the credit entries are totalled separately. The surplus of debits over credits (or credits over debits) is calculated and shown in the final line. This allows a summarised list to be prepared as shown in Table 3.11.

A spreadsheet is useful where there are not too many entries, but ledger accounts become essential when the volume of information increases.

Table 3.11
Summary of debit and credit entries for each category of asset, liability and ownership interest

	Debit	Credit
	£	£
Assets		
Land and buildings	250,000	
Office furniture	30,000	
Trade receivables (debtors)	1,200	
Prepayment	540	
Cash at bank	15,280	
Liabilities		
Trade payables (creditors)		2,800
Long-term loan		150,000
Ownership interest		
Revenue		8,820
Expenses	4,600	
Capital contributed		140,000
Totals	301,620	301,620

Note: The totals of each column have no particular meaning, but they should always be equal because of the symmetry of the debit and credit records, and so are useful as an arithmetic check that no item has been omitted or recorded incorrectly.

Turning the spreadsheet back to a vertical listing, using the debit column for items where the debits exceed the credits, and using the credit column for items where the credits exceed the debits, the list becomes as in Table 3.11. You will see that this list is the basis of the information provided about P. Mason's legal practice in the main body of the chapter, except that the debit and credit notation was not used there.

Activity 3.4

The most serious problem faced by most students, once they have understood the basic approach, is that of making errors. Look back through this Supplement and think about the errors which might have been made. What type of error would be detected by finding totals in Table 3.11 which were not in agreement? What type of error would not be detected in this way because the totals would be in agreement despite the error? Types of error will be dealt with in the supplement to Chapter 5.

S | Test your understanding

S3.1 [S] Analyse the debit and credit aspect of each transaction listed at (a), (b) and (c) of question B3.2.

S3.2 Prepare a spreadsheet similar to that presented in Table 3.10, setting out on the first line the items contained in the list of assets and liabilities of question B3.2 and then on lines 2, 3 and 4 adding in the transactions (a), (b) and (c). Calculate the totals of each column of the spreadsheet and show that the accounting equation remains equal on both sides.

Chapter 4

Ensuring the quality of financial statements

Main reasons accounts are rejected by Companies House

The extracts provided in this case indicate different ways in which the quality of financial statements is ensured.

Common errors

The main reasons given for rejection of accounts by Companies House are:

- incorrect or missing statements, i.e. wrongly stating that the accounts have been prepared according to the relevant legislation;
- audit exemption statements missing or incorrect;
- duplicate made up date i.e., accounts show same date as previously filed accounts;
- signatory name missing off balance sheet or balance sheet signature omitted; and
- accounting reference date/made up date absent or incorrect.

Source: Extract from *Rejected Accounts: Common reasons for accounts being rejected by Companies House & how to avoid them.* Financial Reporting Faculty, Institute of Chartered Accountants in England and Wales (ICAEW 2010). Financial Reporting Faculty 2010.

Going concern

In June 2012 the Sharman Panel of Inquiry published its final report and recommendations on *Going concern and liquidity risks; lessons for companies and auditors*. Its recommendations include the reporting of going concern status:

Recommendation 4
The Panel recommends that, in taking forward its work on reporting under the ECS [Engaging Company Stewardship initiative], the FRC should move away from a model where disclosures about going concern risks are only highlighted when there are significant doubts about the entity's survival, to one which integrates going concern reporting with the ECS proposals through seeking to ensure that:

a) the discussion of strategy and principal risks always includes, in the context of that discussion, the directors' going concern statement and how they arrived at it; and
b) the audit committee report illustrates the effectiveness of the process undertaken by the directors to evaluate going concern by:

i. *confirming that a robust risk assessment has been made; and*

ii. *commenting on or cross-referring to information on the material risks to going concern which have been considered and, where applicable, how they have been addressed;*

and recommends that the FRC should amend the standards and guidance for directors and auditors accordingly when the ECS proposals have been finalised.

Source: Extract from *The Sharman Inquiry Group. Going concern and liquidity risks: lessons for companies and auditors.* Final report (Sharman 2012) Financial Reporting Council, '© Financial Reporting Council (FRC). Adapted and Reproduced with the kind permission of the Financial Reporting Council. All rights reserved. For further information please visit www.frc.org.uk or call +44(0)207 492 2300.'

Discussion points

1 Which regulatory bodies and processes are mentioned in these extracts?

2 Would you expect to be assured about the going concern status of any company accounts that are accepted for filing at Companies House?

Contents

After studying this chapter you should be able to:

● List and explain the qualitative characteristics desirable in financial statements.

● Explain the approach to measurement used in financial statements.

● Explain why there is more than one view on the role of prudence in accounting.

● Understand and explain how and why financial reporting is regulated or influenced by external authorities.

● Be aware of the process by which financial statements are reviewed by an investor.

4.1 Introduction

The previous chapter used the accounting equation as a basis for explaining the structure of financial statements. It showed that design of formats for financial statements is an important first step in creating an understandable story from a list of accounting data.

The IASB's stated objective of general purpose financial reporting is to provide financial information about the reporting entity that is useful to existing and potential investors, lenders and other creditors in making decisions about providing resources to the entity. Those decisions involve buying, selling or holding equity and debt instruments, and providing or settling loans and other forms of credit. Critics of this objective argue for information being useful to a wide range of users in making economic decisions. The IASB's response is that meeting the needs of investors and lenders is likely to meet the needs of other users also.[1]

Information about financial position is provided in a **statement of financial position (balance sheet)**. Information about performance is provided in an **income statement** (profit and loss account).[2] Information about changes in the cash position is provided in a **statement of cash flows**. These three statements were explained in outline in Chapter 3. Information about changes in equity is also provided in a separate statement, described in Chapter 12. Notes to the financial statements provide additional information relevant to the needs of users. These notes may include information about risks and uncertainties relating to assets, liabilities, revenue and expenses.[3]

4.2 Qualitative characteristics of financial statements

The IASB *Conceptual Framework* sets out qualitative characteristics that make the information provided in financial statements useful to users. The two fundamental qualitative characteristics are:

● relevance
● faithful representation.[4]

The fundamental qualitative characteristics of relevance and faithful representation have further component characteristics:

● relevance
  – predictive value
  – confirmatory value

- faithful representation
  - neutrality
  - freedom from error
  - completeness.

A general quality of materiality applies across these fundamental characteristics.

There are four further characteristics which are described as 'enhancing qualitative characteristics'. These are:

- comparability
- verifiability
- timeliness
- understandability.

Each of these characteristics is now described.

4.2.1   Relevance[5]

Financial information is **relevant** if it is capable of making a difference in the decisions made by users. Even when users already know the information, or they receive the information but choose not to use it, it is still *capable* of making a difference. Preparers do not have to show that the information actually did make a difference. The information is capable of making a difference if it has predictive value, or confirmatory value, or both.

Predictive value[6]

Financial information has predictive value if it can be used as an input to processes employed by users to predict future outcomes. The information could be a forecast provided by the user. Alternatively it could be information that others, such as investors or financial analysts, use as input data for their own predictions.

Confirmatory value[7]

Financial information has confirmatory value if it provides feedback about (confirms or changes) previous evaluations.

Example

A company provides information about revenue (sales) in its income statement. Investors use this information to predict future trends of revenue for that company. Based on these predictions the investors buy shares in the company. In subsequent years the company provides further information about revenue. The investors are able to confirm the predictions they made previously. Information about revenue (sales) is therefore **relevant** information.

4.2.2   Faithful representation[8]

To be useful, financial information must faithfully represent the economic phenomena that it purports to represent. The use of the words 'economic phenomena' sounds scary – a single phenomenon is worrying enough but several pheonomena together sound worse. The easiest way to think of this is to substitute for 'economic phenomena' the wording 'economic events that can be observed'. An economic event could be a transaction, such as where an asset is purchased for cash. An economic event could be a change in value, such as where a plot of land falls in value through contamination being discovered. Financial information can be used to report both of those economic events.

Faithful representation ideally requires the financial information to have three characteristics. It will be complete, neutral and free from error. The IASB acknowledges that perfection is seldom, if ever, achievable.

Complete[9]

A complete depiction includes all information necessary for a user to understand what is being reported. This includes the words used to describe the item, and any notes of explanation that help the reader to understand. We will see in later chapters that words and numbers in financial statements are often supported by explanations and notes.

Neutral[10]

Financial information that is neutral has no bias in the selection or presentation of that information. The *Conceptual Framework* says that a neutral depiction of financial information is not slanted, weighted, emphasised, de-emphasised or otherwise manipulated to increase the probability that such formation will be received favourably or unfavourably by users. It uses the word 'depiction' to cover words as well as numbers and also the location and prominence of information. Preparers who want to give a favourable information might consistently choose the upper end of range of estimated values. Even if there was no bias in the valuation, preparers might use confusing words, or different sized fonts, or different colours, to distract users away from bad news information. Actions of these kinds could lead to bias and non-neutral depiction.

Free from error[11]

'Free from error' means there are no errors or omissions in the description of the phenomenon, and the process used to produce the reported information has been selected and applied with no errors in the process. It does not mean the financial statements are totally accurate. Preparers should make their best efforts but they will not have certainty about all economic events. There may be a list of accounts receivable (customers given credit who have not yet paid). It is likely that some of the accounts receivable will not be received but all the preparer can do is make an estimate for non-recovery. Equipment depreciates in value but the preparer can only estimate depreciation. It cannot be measured with total accuracy.

4.2.3 Materiality[12]

Information is material if omitting it or misstating it could influence decisions that users make on the basis of financial formation about a specific reporting entity. The measure of materiality is specific to the entity and is linked to **relevance**. The IASB does not specify a quantitative threshold for materiality and does not provide any specific guidance. It is for preparers of financial information to decide what is material when they prepare that information.

For example, it might be the case that in the statement of financial position (balance sheet) a company gives separate headings for inventory of raw materials and inventory of work-in-progress. This is because the company knows that investors and lenders are interested in the materially different types of risk attached to these two types of inventory. However the inventory of finished goods is given as a single item with no separation into the types of finished goods. That is because the company knows that investors see no material differences of risk in the types of finished goods; it is the overall amount that is of material interest.

4.2.4 Enhancing qualitative characteristics

The enhancing qualitative characteristics are: comparability; verifiability; timeliness; and understandability.

Comparability[13]

Comparability enables users to identify and understand similarities in, and differences among, items. Consistency refers to the use of the same methods for the same items, either from period to period within a reporting entity or in a single period across entities. Comparability is the goal; consistency helps to achieve that goal. Does this mean that everything has to be treated in exactly the same way? The *Conceptual Framework* notes that comparability is not uniformity. For information to be comparable, like things must look alike and different things must look different. Comparability is not enhanced by making unlike things look alike any more than it is enhanced by making like things look different.

To test this idea, find statements of financial position for two companies. Compare the way in which non-current assets are reported. Can you see similarities? Can you see differences? Do you think the financial statements meet the test of comparability?

Verifiability[14]

Verifiability means that different knowledgeable and independent observers could reach consensus (broad agreement), although not necessarily complete agreement, that a particular depiction is a faithful representation. Direct verification is usually carried out by auditors on behalf of investors. Auditors have access to information underlying the financial statements. Other users might verify information by reference to other external sources or by comparisons. Preparers can help users by disclosing the assumptions on which financial information is based.

Timeliness[15]

Timeliness means having information available to decision-makers in time to be capable of influencing their decisions. Generally, the older the information is the less useful it is. However, some information may continue to be timely long after the end of a reporting period because, for example, some users may need to identify and assess trends. You will see in company annual reports that there are tables of 5-year trends as well as the most recent financial information. National regulators know that timeliness is important and often impose time deadlines for reporting, particularly where companies have a stock market listing.

Understandability[16]

Financial information is understandable if it is presented clearly and concisely, using recognisable classification and descriptions. That seems obvious but the *Conceptual Framework* makes it explicit. There is also a warning that complex transactions may be difficult to understand because they are complex. Financial information cannot take away that type of complexity. All it can do is try to make the complexity understandable by clear descriptions. One very significant assumption in the *Conceptual Framework* is that users have a reasonable knowledge of business and economic activities and will review and analyse the information diligently. Even then such persons may sometimes need to take advice on complex matters.

4.2.5   Cost constraint on useful financial reporting[17]

Reporting financial information imposes costs, and it is important that those costs are justified by the benefits of reporting that information. The cost to preparers is eventually born by investors in reduced profits. The benefits are seen in more efficient operation of the capital markets. The standard setter has to balance such costs and benefits in developing accounting standards.

4.2.6 Other characteristics of financial information

When the IASB revised its *Conceptual Framework* in 2010 it omitted some characteristics that appeared in the original 1989 version. However you may still find these terms used in discussion of accounting. In particular you may hear about **prudence**, **reliability** and **substance over form**. In all three cases, during the discussion stage leading to the 2010 *Conceptual Framework* there were some strong objections to the omission. The reasons given for omission are explained in the following sections.

Prudence[18]

The preparers of financial statements have to contend with uncertainty surrounding many events and circumstances. The existence of uncertainties is recognised by the disclosure of their nature and extent and by the exercise of prudence in the preparation of the financial statements. Prudence is the inclusion of a degree of caution in the exercise of the judgements needed in making the estimates required under conditions of uncertainty, such that gains and assets are not overstated and losses and liabilities are not understated.

This guidance was provided in the 1989 version of the IASB *Framework*. It has been removed from the 2010 version because the standard setters concluded that describing *prudence* or *conservatism* as a qualitative characteristic or a desirable response to uncertainty would conflict with the quality of *neutrality*. They felt that encouraging preparers to be prudent was likely to lead to a bias in the reported financial position and financial performance. Introducing biased understatement of assets (or overstatement of liabilities) in one period frequently leads to overstating financial performance in later periods – a result that cannot be described as prudent.[19]

Reliability[20]

In the IASB *Framework* (1989) reliability was defined as:

> *Information has the quality of reliability when it is free from material error and bias and can be depended upon by users to represent faithfully that which it either purports to represent or could reasonably be expected to represent.*

This characteristic sat alongside reliability as a principal characteristic. It has been replaced in the 2010 version by 'faithful representation'. The standard setters explained that when they consulted on the changes they found different respondents had different interpretations of 'reliability'. Some thought it meant freedom from error, others thought it meant verifiability. The standard setters tried to clarify the meaning of reliability but eventually concluded that 'faithful representation' gave the clearest understanding of what reliability is intended to mean.[21]

Substance over form[22]

The IASB *Framework* (1989) made clear that if information is to meet the test of faithful representation, then the method of accounting must reflect the **substance** of the economic reality of the transaction and not merely its **legal form**.

For example, a company has sold its buildings to a bank to raise cash and then pays rent for the same buildings for the purpose of continued occupation. The company carries all the risks and problems (such as repairs and insurance) that an owner would carry. One view is that the commercial substance of that sequence of transactions is comparable to retaining ownership. Another view is that the legal form of the transaction is a sale. The characteristic of substance over form requires that the information in the financial statements should show the commercial substance of the situation.

This characteristic is omitted in the 2010 *Conceptual Framework* because the standard setters think that any attempt to represent legal form in a way that differs from the economic substance of the underlying economic phenomenon could not result in a faithful representation. Accordingly, it is not necessary to be explicit. To state that *substance over form* is a component of faithful representation would be like repeating the same idea.[23]

4.3 Measurement in financial statements

You have seen in Chapter 2, sections 2.5 and 2.8, that the recognition of assets and liability requires reliability of measurement. You have seen in Chapter 3 the methods of presentation of accounting information containing numbers that represent measurement. We now need to know more about the accounting measurement principles that establish reliability and about the disclosure of information that allows users of financial statements to understand the measurement process.

The accounting measurement principles that are most widely known in the UK are found within the Companies Act 2006:[24]

- going concern
- accruals
- consistency
- prudence.

The IASB *Conceptual Framework* refers to the accrual basis as a means of reflecting financial performance and to going concern as an 'underlying assumption' in the preparation of financial statements. Prudence is not discussed. Consistency is an aspect of comparability.

4.3.1 Going concern

Definition

> The financial statements are normally prepared on the assumption that an entity is a **going concern** and will continue in operation for the foreseeable future. Hence, it is assumed that the entity has neither the intention nor the need to liquidate or curtail materially the scale of its operations; if such an intention or need exists the financial statements may have to be prepared on a different basis and, if so, the basis used is disclosed.[25]

The UK Companies Act statement on **going concern** is rather like a crossword clue, in being short and enigmatic. It states: 'The company shall be presumed to be carrying on business as a going concern.'

The Financial Reporting Council provides a practical guide for directors in *Going Concern and Liquidity Risk: Guidance for Directors of UK Companies 2009*, published in October 2009. It took effect for accounting periods ending on or after 31 December 2009. The guidance is based on three principles covering: the process which directors should follow when assessing going concern; the period covered by the assessment; and the disclosures on going concern and liquidity risk. The guidance applies to all companies and in particular addresses the statement about going concern that must be made by directors of listed companies in their annual report and accounts.

Directors should plan their assessment of going concern as early as practicable including deciding on the processes, procedures, information, analyses and board papers that will be needed. These plans should also address the evidence to be obtained, including identifying any potential remedial actions that may need to be addressed, to support their conclusion prior to their approval of the annual or half-yearly financial statements.

The practical effect will usually be that directors of UK companies will adopt a review period of not less than 12 months from the date of approval of annual and half-yearly financial statements but, in rare cases, when they do not they should explain why.

Directors of listed companies incorporated in the UK are required by the Listing Rules to include in their annual financial report a statement that the business is a going concern, together with supporting assumptions or qualifications as necessary, that has been prepared in accordance with the Guidance.

The auditor is required to consider the disclosures about going concern and liquidity risk made in the financial statements. If the auditor concludes that the disclosures are not adequate to meet the requirements of accounting standards and CA 2006, including the need for financial statements to give a true and fair view, the auditor is required to qualify its opinion and to provide its reasons for doing so.

A major inquiry into going concern issues produced its final report in 2012 (the Sharman Report). It recommends greater prominence of discussions of business risk considered in the going concern evaluation.

4.3.2   Accruals (also called 'matching')

Definition

> Accrual accounting depicts the effects of transactions and other events and circumstances on a reporting entity's economic resources and claims in the periods in which those effects occur, even if the resulting cash receipts and payments occur in a different period. This is important because information about a reporting entity's economic resources and claims and changes in its economic resources and claims during a period provides a better basis for assessing the entity's past and future performance than information solely about cash receipts and payments during that period.[26]

Financial statements prepared on the accruals basis are useful for stewardship purposes because they report past transactions and events but are also helpful to users for forward-looking information because they show obligations to pay cash in the future and resources that represent cash to be received in the future.

The UK Companies Act explains the accruals concept as a requirement that all income and charges (i.e. expenses) relating to the financial year shall be taken into account, without regard to the date of receipt or payment.

The word 'accrue' means 'to fall due' or 'to come as a natural result'. If, during a year, a company sells £100m of goods but collects only £80m from customers, it records sales as £100m in the profit and loss account. The cash yet to be collected from customers is reported as an asset called 'debtor' in the statement of financial position (balance sheet). If, during the year, it uses electricity costing £50m but has only paid £40m so far, it records the expense of £50m in the profit and loss account. The unpaid electricity bill is reported as a liability called 'accruals' in the statement of financial position (balance sheet).

The idea of matching is also used in applying the idea of accruals. Matching has two forms, matching losses or gains against time and matching expenses against revenue. Time matching occurs when a gain or loss is spread over the relevant period of time, such as receiving interest on a loan or paying rent on a property. Matching of revenues and expenses occurs when costs such as labour are matched against the revenue earned from providing goods or services.

4.3.3   Consistency

Consistency is described in the IASB *Conceptual Framework* as an aspect of comparability (see section 4.2.4). The UK Companies Act requires that accounting policies shall be applied consistently within the same accounts and from one period to the next.

4.3.4   Prudence

The Companies Act does not define prudence but uses the word prudent in relation to measurement. It requires that the amount of any item shall be determined on a prudent basis, and in particular:

(a) only profits realised at the date of the financial year-end shall be included in the profit and loss account; and

(b) all liabilities and losses which have arisen or are likely to arise in respect of the financial year shall be taken into account, including those which only become apparent between the date of the financial year-end and the date on which it is signed by the board of directors.

The UK ASB has said that decisions about recognition of income or assets and of expenses or liabilities require evidence of existence and reliability of measurement. Stronger evidence and greater reliability of measurement are required for assets and gains than for liabilities and losses.[27]

4.3.5   Realisation

There is no clear statement of the conditions that will make a profit **realised**. It is not specifically defined in the IASB system. It is an example of an idea that is so widely used that it appears to be almost impossible to explain. If you turn to a dictionary you will find 'realise' equated to 'convert into cash'. The accounting standard FRS 18[28] confirms that it is the general view that profits shall be treated as realised when evidenced in the form of cash or other assets whose cash **realisation** is reasonably certain. However, the standard avoids linking realisation to 'prudence', explaining that a focus on cash does not reflect more recent developments in financial markets. Evidence of 'reasonable certainty' in such markets does not necessarily require cash. It is based on confidence in the reliable operation of the market.

Activity 4.1

Take a piece of paper having two wide columns. Head the left-hand column 'My thoughts on measurement in accounting' and head the right-hand column 'What the book tells me about measurement'. Fill in both columns and then exchange your paper with a fellow student. Discuss with each other any similarities and differences in the left-hand column and relate these to your personal views and prior experience. Discuss with each other any similarities and differences in the right-hand column and evaluate the extent to which different people see books differently. Finally, discuss with each other the extent to which reading this section has changed your views on measurement as a subject in accounting.

4.4   Views on prudence

The Companies Act 2006 makes an explicit link between prudence and realisation that reflects UK accounting practice when the previous Companies Act 1985 was written. The IASB's *Conceptual Framework* avoids mentioning realisation. From the UK ASB, the standard FRS 18 acknowledges the meaning of realisation but breaks the link between realisation and prudence.[29] It appears that FRS 18 has not changed the entrenched conservatism of accounting practice which tends towards understatement on grounds of caution. Where does that leave the student of accounting who wants to understand the meaning of prudence?

The most important message for students of accounting (and for many practitioners) has been expressed as follows:

the exercise of prudence does not allow . . . the deliberate understatement of assets or income, or the deliberate overstatement of liabilities or expenses, because the financial statements would not be neutral and, therefore, not have the quality of reliability.[30]

Why are there different views on understatement and overstatement, depending on the item being reported? Here is your first chance to use the accounting equation to solve a problem:

Assets minus Liabilities	equals	Capital contributed/withdrawn plus Profit

Profit	equals	Revenue minus Expenses

Activity 4.2	*Ask yourself what will happen to profit in the accounting equation if the amount of an asset is increased while the liabilities and the capital contributed remain the same. Then ask yourself what will happen to profit in the accounting equation if the amount of a liability is decreased while the assets and the capital contributed remain the same. Next ask yourself what will happen to profit if revenue is overstated. Finally ask yourself what will happen to profit if expenses are understated.*

Assuming that capital contributed/withdrawn remains constant, overstating assets will overstate profit. Understating liabilities will overstate profit. Overstating revenue will overstate profit. Understating expenses will overstate profit.

Examples

A market trader buys £100 of stock on credit, promising to pay the supplier at the end of the day. The trader sells three-quarters of the stock at a price of £90 and takes the rest home to keep for next week's market. At the end of the day the trader has £90 in cash, one-quarter of the stock which cost £25, and owes £100 to the supplier. How much profit has the trader made? The answer is that the profit is £15 (£90 received for the sale of stock less the cost of the items sold, £75, being three-quarters of the stock purchased). The accounting equation is:

Assets minus Liabilities at the end of the period	equals	Ownership interest at the start of the period plus Capital contributed/ withdrawn plus Revenue of the period minus Expenses of the period
stock £25 + cash £90 – liability £100	equals	nil + nil + revenue £90 – expenses £75
£15	equals	£15

1 Supposing the trader 'forgets' part of the liability and thinks it is only £84 owing, rather than £100. The assets remain at stock £25 + cash £90, which equals £115. The liability is now thought to be £84 and therefore the equation becomes:

£25 + £90 – £84	equals	nil + nil + revenue £90 – expenses £75 + [?] £16 [?]
£31	equals	£31

For the equation to be satisfied there must be a total of £31 on both sides. The total of £31 is therefore written in. The recorded profit is still only £15, calculated as revenue £90 minus expenses £75, so there is a 'hole' amounting to £16 on the right-hand side of the equation. The accounting equation has to balance so the extra £16 is written in, surrounded by question marks, on the right-hand side. It is assumed on the right-hand side that the trader has either forgotten to record revenue of £16 or has recorded too much expense, so that the amount appears to represent an unexplained profit. Thus *understating a liability will overstate profit*. That favourable news might mislead a competitor or investor. It might be bad news when HMRC demands tax on profit of £31. Also there is the unpaid supplier who may not be entirely patient when offered £84 rather than £100.

2 Supposing instead that the trader 'forgets' there is some unsold inventory left. The only recorded asset would be the cash at £90 and there would be a liability of £100. This gives negative net assets of (£10) and, because the accounting equation has to balance, suggests that there is a 'forgotten' expense of £25 on the right-hand side. The equation then becomes:

£90 – £100	equals	nil + nil + £90 – £75 – [?] £25 [?]
(£10)	equals	(£10)

This would cause HMRC to ask a lot of questions as to why there was no record of stock remaining, because they know that omitting inventory from the record is a well-tried means of fraudulently reducing profits and therefore reducing tax bills. *Understating an asset will understate profit*.

These two examples have illustrated the meaning of the warning that deliberate understatement or overstatement is not acceptable. The general message of prudence is: *avoid overstating profit*. In down-to-earth terms, don't raise the readers' hopes too high, only to have to tell them later that it was all in the imagination.

4.5 Regulation of financial reporting

Because the external users of accounting information do not have day-to-day access to the records of the business, they rely on the integrity and judgement of management to provide suitable information of a high quality. But will the management be honest, conscientious and careful in providing information? In an ideal world there should be no problem for investors in a company because, as shareholders, they appoint the directors and may dismiss them if dissatisfied with the service provided. However, the world is not ideal. Some companies are very large and they have many shareholders whose identity changes as shares are bought and sold. Over the years it has been found that regulation is needed, particularly for financial reporting by companies. The general regulation of companies in the UK is provided by parliamentary legislation, through the Companies Act 2006.

However, since 2005 the regulation of financial reporting by UK companies has taken two separate routes depending on the type of company.

The group financial statements of listed companies must comply with the IAS Regulation set by the European Commission. The IAS Regulation takes precedence over the relevant sections of the Companies Act. The IAS Regulation was issued in 2002, requiring listed group financial statements from 2005 to apply approved International Financial Reporting Standards (IFRS) (previously called International Accounting Standards, IAS). The UK government subsequently permitted individual companies and non-listed groups to choose to apply IFRS. Any companies not taking up this choice must continue to apply the relevant sections of the Companies Act and follow the accounting standards set by the UK Accounting Council (previously called the Accounting Standards Board (ASB)). Other organisations that are not companies (such as sole traders, partnership, public sector bodies) have to look to the regulations that govern their operations to decide which accounting guidance to follow.

So how can we tell which accounting system has been applied in any situation? Look first for the audit report, if there is one. That will include a paragraph starting 'In our opinion'. In that paragraph the auditors will specify the accounting system on which their opinion is based. If there is no auditors' report, look for the Note on Accounting Policies. There will usually be a paragraph stating the accounting system that has been applied.

4.5.1   The IAS Regulation

In 2002 the European Commission issued the *IAS Regulation* which took effect from 1 January 2005. Its purpose is to harmonise the financial information presented by public listed companies in order to ensure a high degree of transparency and comparability of financial statements. The Regulation is relatively short but has been extended and clarified by a trail of subsequent documents. The European Commission publishes all documents on its website[31] in the languages of all member states but that is more detail than is necessary for a first-year course.

A Regulation is directly applicable in member states. It has a higher status than a Directive, which is an instruction to member states on the content of their national laws. Before the Regulation was issued, the company law of member states was harmonised by following the Fourth and Seventh Directives on company law. Companies in member states did not need to know the Directives because the national company law applied the Directives. Now that the IAS Regulation is directly applicable, member states must ensure that they do not seek to apply to a company any additional elements of national law that are contrary to, conflict with or restrict a company's compliance with IASs.

The Commission decides on the applicability of IFRS within the Community. It is assisted by an Accounting Regulatory Committee and is advised by a technical group called the European Financial Reporting and Accounting Group (EFRAG).[32] The tests for adoption of IFRS are that the standards:

(a) do not contradict specific principles of the Fourth and Seventh Directive,
(b) are conducive to the European public good, and
(c) meet the criteria of understandability, relevance, reliability and comparability required of financial information needed for making economic decisions and assessing the stewardship of management.

A standard that is adopted is said to be **endorsed**. If a standard is awaiting endorsement, or is rejected, it may be used as guidance if it is not inconsistent with endorsed standards. If a rejected standard is in conflict with adopted standards, it may not be used. When the European Commission first announced the endorsement process there were fears expressed that this would be used to create 'European IFRS' by selecting some IFRS and rejecting others. The Commission's reply was that the EU cannot give its powers to a body (the IASB) that is not subject to EU jurisdiction, and it is necessary for the EU to endorse standards as part of its duty in setting laws for member states.

4.5.2   UK company law

Companies Act 2006

The Companies Act 2006 sets many rules to protect those investing in companies and to guide those operating companies. Parts of the Act cover the information presented in financial statements. For companies and other organisations that do not follow the IAS Regulation, the Companies Act 2006, by means of Statutory Instruments, prescribes formats of presentation of the statement of financial position (balance sheet) and profit and loss account. Companies must select one of the permitted formats. It also prescribes methods of valuation of the assets and liabilities contained in the statement of financial position (balance sheet), broadly expecting that normally these items will be recorded at their cost at the date of acquisition, subject to diminutions in value since that date. Some other approaches to valuation are permitted, but these are carefully regulated and are subject to requirements for prudence, consistency and an expectation that the business is a going concern (i.e. will continue for some time into the future). The UK legislation places strong emphasis on the requirement to present a **true and fair view** in financial statements.

Since the early 1980s company law on financial reporting has been harmonised with that of other Member States in the EU through the Fourth and Seventh Directives of the EU (see Chapter 7).

The directors are responsible for the preparation of company accounts. Exhibit 4.1 (see p. 90) sets out the statement made by directors of one major public company regarding their responsibilities in these matters. This type of statement will be found in the annual reports of most of the large listed companies. It is regarded as an important aspect of giving reassurance to investors and others that there is a strong system of corporate governance within the company. It is also intended to clarify any misunderstandings the shareholders may have about the work of directors as distinct from the work of the auditors (see below).

The Companies (Audit, Investigations and Community Enterprise) Act, 2004 made changes intended to improve the reliability of financial reporting, the independence of auditors and disclosure to auditors. In particular it required a statement to be inserted in the directors' report confirming that there is no relevant information that has not been disclosed to the auditors. The role of the Financial Reporting Review Panel was strengthened by giving it new powers to require documents. HM Revenue and Customs was authorised to pass information about companies to the FRRP.

4.5.3   The Financial Reporting Council[33]

The Financial Reporting Council (FRC) describes itself as the UK's independent regulator responsible for promoting high quality corporate governance and reporting to foster investment. It is recognised in its regulatory role by the UK government's Department for Business, Innovation and Skills. The government effectively delegates responsibility to an independent body but maintains close interest in the strategy and operations of the FRC.

There was a major restructuring of the FRC in July 2012. This section describes the new structure but also refers to the previous structure to explain terms that you may still encounter.

The FRC carries out a range of roles. Most relevant to this textbook is that it monitors and enforces accounting and auditing standards. It promotes high standards of corporate governance through the UK Corporate Governance Code. It sets standards for corporate reporting and actuarial practice. It also oversees the regulatory activities of the professional accountancy bodies and the actuarial profession and operates independent disciplinary arrangements for public interest cases involving accountants and actuaries.

The FRC is an independent body governed by a Board whose members are drawn from a wide range of business expertise.

The structure is summarised in Figure 4.1. Aspects of the FRC's work relevant to financial reporting are then described in this section.

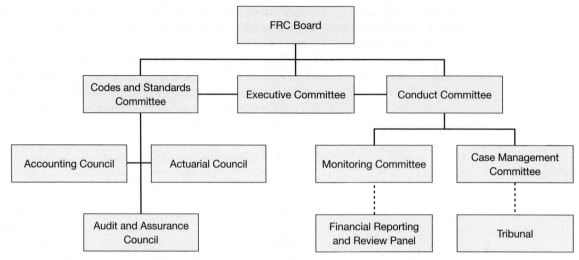

Figure 4.1
Structure of the Financial Reporting Council

Source: http://frc.org.uk/About the FRC/FRC Structure.aspx '© Financial Reporting Council (FRC)'. Adapted and reproduced with the kind permission of the Financial Reporting Council. All rights reserved. For further information, please visit frc.org.uk or call +44(0)207 492 2300.

Accounting role

One role of the FRC is to issue UK accounting standards. UK Accounting standards apply to all companies, and other entities that prepare accounts that are intended to provide a true and fair view, unless International Financial Reporting standards apply. IFRS apply to companies listed on a Stock Exchange.

The FRC took over this standard-setting role in July 2012. Until then it was carried out by the Accounting Standards Board (ASB) as a subsidiary of the FRC. The ASB had previously taken over the task of setting accounting standards from the Accounting Standards Committee (ASC) in 1990. Accounting standards formerly developed by the Accounting Standards Board are contained in 'Financial Reporting Standards' (FRSs). The ASB adopted the standards issued by the ASC, which are designated 'Statements of Standard Accounting Practice' (SSAPs). Whilst some of the SSAPs have been superseded by FRSs, some remain in force.

The FRC also collaborates with accounting standard-setters from other countries and with the International Accounting Standards Board (IASB). In this way the FRC seeks to influence the development of international standards and to ensure that its own standards are developed with due regard to international developments.

Codes and Standards Committee

The Codes and Standards Committee is responsible for advising the FRC Board on maintaining an effective framework of UK codes and standards for Corporate Governance, Stewardship, Accounting, Auditing and Assurance, and Actuarial technical standards. For this textbook the most important functions of this committee relate to accounting standards and audit and assurance standards.

Accounting Council

As explained above, in July 2012, the Accounting Council replaced the UK's Accounting Standards Board, which had been in place since 1990. It does not have the standard-setting power of the previous ASB but instead takes on more of an advisory role. The detailed remit uses 'consult and advise' or 'consult and comment' to describe the activities of the Accounting Council. It could be argued that the standard-setting role of the previous ASB has now largely been taken on by the IASB. Consequently a

Council which provides strategic input and thought leadership, within widespread consultation and research, is more valuable in maintaining UK influence on the international standard setting process.

The Council consists of up to twelve members, at least half of which are practising members of the relevant profession and the remainder will be other stakeholders. Members of the Councils are appointed through an open process overseen by the Chair of the Codes and Standards Committee (CSC) subject to the overall guidance of the Nominations Committee of the FRC.

Audit and Assurance Council

The Audit and Assurance Council has remit of similar type to that of the Accounting Council. The words are 'considers and comments' or 'considers and advises'. The FRC's Codes and Standards Committee develops and maintains standards and guidance for Audit and Assurance engagements that are performed in the public interest within the United Kingdom and Republic of Ireland. It also seeks to influence the development of international auditing and assurance standards and policy, issues that are relevant to its remit.

Conduct Committee

The Conduct Committee operates as a Conduct Division which encompasses the FRC's monitoring, oversight, investigative and disciplinary functions. It covers audit quality review, corporate reporting review, professional discipline and professional oversight, and supervisory enquiries.

Of particular relevance to this chapter, the work of the Conduct Division includes direct monitoring of financial reports and audits of public interest entities.

Under the Companies Act 2006 ('the Act') the Conduct Committee has been authorised and appointed by the Secretary of State for the Department of Business, Innovation and Skills (BIS) to exercise functions with a view to ensuring that accounts and financial and other reports, including annual reports, and directors' reports (Reports) of companies and other entities comply with the law and relevant reporting requirements.

The Conduct Committee's policy is to select Reports for review (a) by methods which take into account the Conduct Committee's assessment of the risk of non-compliance and the consequence of non-compliance, and (b) as a result of complaints.

The Conduct Committee maintains a Financial Reporting Review Panel (FRRP) comprising individuals who have the appropriate qualifications and experience to sit on a Review Group including the Chairman and Deputy Chairman or Chairmen who are also members of the Conduct Committee and the Monitoring Committee. Review Groups will be appointed from the FRRP by the Monitoring Committee.

The legal powers and duties described above for the Conduct Committee were, prior to July 2011, allocated to the FRRP. Consequently this type of monitoring work has been in place for many years and previous reports will be found under the authorship of the Financial Reporting Review Panel.

The Conduct Committee can ask directors to explain apparent departures from the requirements. If it is not satisfied by the directors' explanations it aims to persuade them to adopt a more appropriate accounting treatment. The directors may then voluntarily withdraw their accounts and replace them with revised accounts that correct the matters in error. Depending on the circumstances, the Conduct Committee may accept another form of remedial action – for example, correction of the comparative figures in the next set of annual financial statements. Failing voluntary correction, the Conduct Committee can exercise its powers to secure the necessary revision of the original accounts through a court order. The FRC maintains a legal costs fund of £2m for this purpose. The Conduct Committee's predecessor, the FRRP, enjoyed a long and successful record in resolving all cases brought to its attention without having to apply

Exhibit 4.1
Statement of directors' responsibilities as expressed in the annual report of a public limited company

The Directors are responsible for preparing the Annual Report, the Directors' Remuneration Report and the Group and the Parent Company financial statements in accordance with applicable law and regulations.

Company law requires the Directors to prepare financial statements for each financial year. Under that law the Directors have prepared the Group financial statements in accordance with International Financial Reporting Standards (IFRSs) as adopted by the European Union, and the Parent Company financial statements in accordance with United Kingdom Generally Accepted Accounting Practice (United Kingdom Accounting Standards and applicable law). Under Company law the Directors must not approve the financial statements unless they are satisfied that they give a true and fair view of the state of affairs of the Company and the Group and of the profit or loss of the Group for that period.

In preparing those financial statements, the Directors are required to:

- select suitable accounting policies and then apply them consistently;
- make judgements and estimates that are reasonable and prudent;
- state whether IFRSs as adopted by the European Union and applicable UK Accounting Standards have been followed, subject to any material departures disclosed and explained in the Group and Parent Company financial statements respectively; and
- prepare the Group and Parent Company financial statements on the going concern basis unless it is inappropriate to presume that the Group will continue in business.

The Directors are responsible for keeping adequate accounting records that are sufficient to show and explain the Company's and Group's transactions and disclose with reasonable accuracy at any time the financial position of the Company and the Group and to enable them to ensure that the financial statements and the Directors' Remuneration Report comply with the Companies Act 2006 and, as regards the Group financial statements, Article 4 of the IAS Regulation. They are also responsible for safeguarding the assets of the Company and the Group and hence for taking reasonable steps for the prevention and detection of fraud and other irregularities.

Each of the Directors, whose names and functions are listed on pages nn and nn, confirms that, to the best of their knowledge:

- the Group financial statements, which have been prepared in accordance with IFRSs as adopted by the EU, give a true and fair view of the assets, liabilities, financial position and profit of the Group; and
- the Directors' Report includes a fair review of the development and performance of the business and the position of the Group, together with a description of the principal risks and uncertainties that it faces.

The Directors are responsible for the maintenance and integrity of the Group website www.xxxname.com. Legislation in the UK governing the preparation and dissemination of financial statements may differ from legislation in other jurisdictions.

By order of the Board

(signed) Chief Executive,   Finance Director
(date)

for a court order. The Conduct Committee does not offer advice on the application of accounting standards or on the accounting requirements of the Companies Act 2006.

4.5.4 Corporate governance[34]

UK listed companies are required by the Stock Exchange to apply the Corporate Governance Code. Institutional investors are encouraged to recognise their responsibilities by adhering to the Stewardship Code. Both are explained in this section.

Corporate governance code

Corporate governance is a term applied to the way in which a company is managed by its directors to show a high level of responsibility to shareholders and the wider capital market. The UK has a tradition of codes of corporate governance dating from

1992. Initially the codes were written by committees and given the names of the chairs of the committees. Thus during the 1990s we saw in succession the Cadbury Code, the Greenbury Code and the Hampel Code (explained further in Chapter 14 section 14.7.1). These were consolidated as the *UK Corporate Governance Code*. Responsibility for maintaining the *UK Corporate Governance Code* now rests with the Financial Reporting Council.

The Code sets out good practice covering issues such as board composition and effectiveness, the role of board committees, risk management, remuneration and relations with shareholders. It operates on the principle of 'comply or explain'. If companies comply with the recommendations of the Code they do not need to describe compliance at great length. If they do not comply with any specific aspect, they must provide an explanation in the annual report.

The main recommendations of the Code include:

- separate Chairman and Chief Executive;
- a balance of executive and independent non-executive directors;
- strong, independent audit and remuneration committees;
- annual evaluation by the board of its performance;
- transparency on appointments and remuneration;
- effective rights for shareholders, who are encouraged to engage with the companies in which they invest.

Stewardship code

Experience with the Corporate Governance Code, particularly in the period of financial crisis around 2007 and 2008, indicated that something more was needed to enhance the quality of engagement between institutional investors and companies. The Stewardship Code was introduced to meet this need and to complement the Corporate Governance Code. It is written with the aim of helping to improve long-term returns to shareholders and the efficient exercise of governance responsibilities.

The word 'engagement' is used to emphasise the idea of all parties meeting and talking to each other. It expects purposeful dialogue on strategy, performance and the management of risk, as well as on issues that are the immediate subject of votes at general meetings.

Institutional shareholders are free to choose whether or not to engage as recommended by the Code but once the institution has agreed, their employees and agents are expected to follow the agreed procedures.

The main principles are that institutional investors should:

- publicly disclose their policy on how they will discharge their stewardship responsibilities;
- have a robust policy on managing conflicts of interest in relation to stewardship and this policy should be publicly disclosed;
- monitor their investee companies;
- establish clear guidelines on when and how they will escalate their activities as a method of protecting and enhancing shareholder value;
- be willing to act collectively with other investors where appropriate;
- have a clear policy on voting and disclosure of voting activity;
- report periodically on their stewardship and voting activities.

4.5.5 Stock Exchange regulation

Under the Financial Services and Markets Act 2000, the Financial Services Authority (FSA) was established as a single regulator with responsibility across a wide range of financial market activity. In particular the FSA has, for more than 10 years, regulated listing of companies' shares on the UK Stock Exchange. The work has been carried out by a division called the UK Listing Authority (UKLA). When a company first has its shares listed, it must produce a prospectus, which is normally much more detailed than the annual report. The regulations covering the content of a prospectus have been set by the UKLA. Once a company has achieved a listing, it must keep up with on-going obligations under the Listing Rules. This ongoing obligation includes providing accounting information to the market in the annual report and making press releases. Details of the Listing Rules are not necessary for first-level study but you should be aware that these have an influence on the content of a company's annual report. There are also Disclosure and Transparency rules which affect the content and timing of annual reports published by companies.

Following the financial crisis of 2007 and 2008 it became apparent that the loss of confidence in financial markets and financial systems required a new form of regu-lation in the UK. From 2013 the FSA splits into a Prudential Regulation Authority (PRA) and a Financial Conduct Authority (FCA). The Listing Rules become part of the remit of the FCA. The FCA regulates compliance of issuers (listed companies) and major shareholders with the disclosures required under the Disclosure and Transparency and Listing Rules.

There are three kinds of listing on the UK Stock Exchange: Premium (previously called Primary); Standard (previously called Secondary); and AIM (The Alternative Investment Market). Different levels of regulation and disclosure apply to each. A Premium Listing means the company is expected to meet the UK's highest standards of regulation and corporate governance – and as a consequence may enjoy a lower cost of capital through greater transparency and through building investor confidence. Issuers with a Premium Listing are required to meet the UK's 'super-equivalent' rules which are higher than the EU minimum requirement. Such companies are eligible for inclusion in the FTSE indices. A Standard Listing is more commonly used by overseas companies, as it allows issuers to access the main market by meeting EU harmonised standards only rather than the UK 'super-equivalent' requirements. AIM companies are usually newer and smaller companies making their initial entry to market trading for their shares. AIM listed companies are regulated but not as strongly as the Premium listed companies. Consequently the annual reports of AIM listed companies are less detailed.

4.5.6 Auditors

The shareholders of companies do not have a right of access to the records of the day-to-day running of the business, and so they need someone to act on their behalf to ensure that the directors are presenting a true and fair view of the company's position at a point in time and of the profits generated during a period of time. To achieve this reassurance, the shareholders appoint a firm of auditors to investigate the com-pany's financial records and give an opinion on the truth and fairness of the financial information presented. Exhibit 4.2 sets out the wording of a typical audit report to the

Exhibit 4.2
Sample audit report

Independent Auditors' Report to the Members of XYZ plc

We have audited the Group financial statements of XYZ plc for the year ended 31 December 2011 which comprise the Group Income Statement, the Group Statement of Comprehensive Income, the Group Balance Sheet, the Group Cash Flow Statement, the Group Statement of Changes in Equity, Reconciliation of net cash flow to movement in net debt and the related notes to the Group financial statements. The financial reporting framework that has been applied in their preparation is applicable law and International Financial Reporting Standards (IFRSs) as adopted by the European Union.

Exhibit 4.2 continued

Respective responsibilities of Directors and auditors

As explained more fully in the Statement of Directors' Responsibilities (set out on page nn), the Directors are responsible for the preparation of the Group financial statements and for being satisfied that they give a true and fair view. Our responsibility is to audit and express an opinion on the Group financial statements in accordance with applicable law and International Standards on Auditing (UK and Ireland). Those standards require us to comply with the Auditing Practices Board's Ethical Standards for Auditors.

This report, including the opinions, has been prepared for and only for the Company's members as a body in accordance with Chapter 3 of Part 16 of the Companies Act 2006 and for no other purpose. We do not, in giving these opinions, accept or assume responsibility for any other purpose or to any other person to whom this report is shown or into whose hands it may come save where expressly agreed by our prior consent in writing.

Scope of the audit of the financial statements

An audit involves obtaining evidence about the amounts and disclosures in the financial statements sufficient to give reasonable assurance that the financial statements are free from material misstatement, whether caused by fraud or error. This includes an assessment of: whether the accounting policies are appropriate to the Group's circumstances and have been consistently applied and adequately disclosed; the reasonableness of significant accounting estimates made by the Directors; and the overall presentation of the financial statements. In addition, we read all the financial and non-financial information in the Annual Report and Accounts to identify material inconsistencies with the audited financial statements. If we become aware of any apparent material misstatements or inconsistencies we consider the implications for our report.

Opinion on financial statements

In our opinion the Group financial statements:

- give a true and fair view of the state of the Group's affairs as at 31 December 2011 and of its profit and cash flows for the year then ended;
- have been properly prepared in accordance with IFRSs as adopted by the European Union; and
- have been prepared in accordance with the requirements of the Companies Act 2006 and Article 4 of the IAS Regulation.

Opinion on other matters prescribed by the Companies Act 2006

In our opinion the information given in the Directors' Report for the financial year for which the Group financial statements are prepared is consistent with the Group financial statements.

Matters on which we are required to report by exception

We have nothing to report in respect of the following:

Under the Companies Act 2006 we are required to report to you if, in our opinion:

- certain disclosures of Directors' remuneration specified by law are not made; or
- we have not received all the information and explanations we require for our audit.

Under the Listing Rules we are required to review:

- the Directors' statement (set out on page 90), in relation to going concern;
- the part of the Corporate Governance Statement relating to the Company's compliance with the nine provisions of the UK Corporate Governance Code specified for our review; and
- certain elements of the report to shareholders by the Board on Directors' remuneration.

Other matter

We have reported separately on the parent company financial statements of XYZ plc for the year ended 31 December 2011 and on the information in the Remuneration Report that is described as having been audited.

A B Name (Senior Statutory Auditor)
for and on behalf of DEF LLP
Chartered Accountants and Statutory Auditors
London
Date

shareholders of a public company. You will see that there are separate opinions on the financial statements and on other aspects of the accounting information recorded or provided by the company.

You will note that the auditors do not look at all the pages of the annual report. The earlier part of the annual report is important to the companies in setting the scene and explaining their businesses. These earlier pages are reviewed by the auditors to ensure that anything said there is consistent with the information presented in the audited financial statements. You will also note that the auditors have their own code of practice, referred to as International Standards for Auditing (ISAs). The ISAs are prepared by the International Auditing and Assurance Standards Board (IAASB) which operates under a body called the International Financial Accounting Committee (IFAC). The standards are then adopted by national standard-setters. In the UK the national standard-setter is the Financial Reporting Council.

What surprises some readers is the phrase 'reasonable assurance that the accounts are free from material misstatement'. The auditors are not expected to be totally certain in their opinion and they are only looking for errors or fraud which is material. The meaning of the word 'material' has proved difficult to define and it tends to be a matter left to the judgement of the auditor. The best guidance available is that an item is material if its misstatement or omission would cause the reader of the annual report (shareholder or creditor) to take a different decision or view based on the financial statements.

4.5.7 The tax system

Businesses pay tax to HM Revenue and Customs (HMRC) (as the tax-collecting agent of the government) based on the profits they make. Sole traders and partnerships pay income tax on their profits while companies pay corporation tax. There are differences in detail of the law governing these two types of taxes but broadly they both require as a starting point a calculation of profit using commercial accounting practices. The law governing taxation is quite separate from the law and regulations governing financial reporting, so in principle the preparation of financial statements is not affected by tax matters. That is very different from some other countries in the EU where the tax law stipulates that an item must be in the financial accounting statements if it is to be considered for tax purposes. Those countries have an approach to financial reporting which is more closely driven by taxation matters.

In the UK the distinction may be blurred in practice in the case of sole traders because HMRC is the main user of the financial statements of the sole trader. Similarly, tax factors may influence partnership accounts, although here the fairness of sharing among the partners is also important. The very smallest companies, where the owners also run the business, may in practice have the same attitude to tax matters as does the sole trader or partnership. For larger companies with a wider spread of ownership, the needs of shareholders will take priority.

4.5.8 Is regulation necessary?

There are those who would argue that all this regulatory mechanism is unnecessary. They take the view that in a market-based economy, competitive forces will ensure that those providing information will meet the needs of users. It is argued that investors will not entrust their funds to a business which provides inadequate information. Banks will not lend money unless they are provided with sufficient information to answer their questions about the likelihood of receiving interest and eventual repayment of the loan. Employee morale may be lowered if a business appears non-communicative regarding its present position and past record of performance. Suppliers may not wish to give credit to a business which appears secretive or has a reputation for producing poor-quality information. Customers may be similarly doubtful.

Against that quite attractive argument for the abolition of all regulations stand some well-documented financial scandals where businesses have failed. Employees have lost their jobs, with little prospect of finding comparable employment elsewhere; suppliers have not been paid and have found themselves in financial difficulties as a result. Customers have lost a source of supply and have been unable to meet the requirements of their own customers until a new source is found. Those who have provided long-term finance for the business, as lenders and investors, have lost their investment. Investigation shows that the signs and warnings had existed for those who were sufficiently experienced to see them, but these signs and warnings did not emerge in the published accounting information for external use.

Such financial scandals may be few in number but the large-scale examples cause widespread misery and lead to calls for action. Governments experience pressure from the electorate and lobby groups; professional bodies and business interest groups decide they ought to be seen to react; and new regulations are developed which ensure that the particular problem cannot recur. All parties are then reasonably satisfied that they have done their best to protect those who need protection against the imbalance of business life, and the new practices are used until the next scandal occurs and the process starts over again.

There is no clear answer to the question 'Is regulation necessary?' Researchers have not found any strong evidence that the forces of supply and demand in the market fail to work and have suggested that the need for regulation must be justified by showing that the benefits exceed the costs. That is quite a difficult challenge but is worth keeping in mind as you explore some of the more intricate aspects of accounting regulation.

Activity 4.3	*Look back through this section and, for each subheading, make a note of whether you were previously aware that such regulation existed. In each case, irrespective of your previous state of knowledge, do you now feel a greater or a lesser sense of confidence in accounting information? How strong is your confidence in published accounting information? If not 100%, what further reassurance would you require?*

4.6 Reviewing published financial statements

If you look at the annual report of any large listed company you will find that it has two main sections. The first part contains a variety of diagrams and photographs, a statement by the chairman, a report by the chief executive and, in many cases, a Business Review or an Operating and Financial Review which may extend to a considerable number of pages. Other aspects of the business, such as its corporate governance and environmental policy, may also be explained. This first part is a mixture of unregulated and broadly regulated material. There are many sources of influence on its contents, some of which will be explained in later chapters of this book.

The second part contains the financial statements, which are heavily regulated. As if to emphasise this change of status, the second part of the annual report will often have a different appearance, perhaps being printed on a different colour or grade of paper, or possibly having a smaller print size. Appendix I to this book contains extracts from the financial statements of a fictitious company, Safe and Sure plc, which will be used for illustration in this and subsequent chapters.

Relaxing after a hard workout at the health club, David Wilson took the opportunity to buy Leona a drink and tell her something about Safe and Sure prior to a visit to the company's headquarters to meet the finance director.

DAVID: *This is a major listed company, registered in the UK but operating around the world selling its services in disposal and recycling, cleaning and security. Its name is well known and its services command high prices because of the company's reputation gained over many years. Basically it is a very simple business to understand. It sells services by making contracts with customers and collects cash when the service is performed.*

In preparation for my visit I looked first at the performance of the period. This company promises to deliver growth of at least 20% in revenue and in profit before tax so first of all I checked that the promise had been delivered. Sure enough, at the front of the annual report under 'Highlights of the year' there was a table showing revenue had increased by 22.4% and profit before tax had increased by 20.4%. I knew I would need to look through the profit and loss account in more detail to find out how the increases had come about, but first of all I read the operating review (written by the chief executive) and the financial review (written by the finance director). The chief executive gave more details on which areas had the greatest increase in revenue and operating profit and which areas had been disappointing. That all helps me in making my forecast of profit for next year.

The chief executive made reference to acquisitions during the year, so I knew I would also need to think whether the increase in revenue and profits was due to an improvement in sales and marketing as compared with last year or whether it reflected the inclusion of new business for the first time.

In the financial review, the finance director explained that the business tries to use as little working capital as possible (that means they try to keep down the current assets and match them as far as possible with current liabilities). I guessed I would need to look at the statement of financial position to confirm that, so I headed next for the financial statements at the back of the annual report, pausing to glance at the auditors' report to make sure there was nothing highlighted by them as being amiss.

The financial statements are quite detailed and I wanted a broad picture so I noted down the main items from each in a summary format which leaves out some of the detail but which I find quite useful.

4.6.1 Income statement (profit and loss account)

Safe and Sure plc
Summary income statement (profit and loss account) with comparative figures

	Notes	Year 7 £m	Year 6 £m
Continuing operations			
Revenue		714.6	589.3
Cost of sales		(491.0)	(406.3)
Gross profit		223.6	183.0
Expenses and interest		(26.1)	(26.0)
Profit before tax		197.5	157.0
Tax on profit		(62.2)	(52.4)
Profit for the period from continuing operations		135.3	104.6
Discontinued operations			
Loss for the period from discontinued operations		(20.5)	(10.0)
Profit for the period attributable to ordinary shareholders		114.8	94.6

DAVID: *It is part of my job to make forecasts of what the next reported profit of the company is likely to be (i.e. the profit of Year 8). This is March Year 8 now so there are plenty of current signs I can pick up, but I also want to think about how far Year 7 will be repeated or improve during Year 8. A few years ago I would have made a rough guess and then phoned the finance director for some guidance on whether I was in the right area. That's no longer allowed because the Financial Services Authority tightened up the rules on companies giving information to some investors which is not available to others, especially where that information could affect the share price.*

One easy way out is for me to collect the reports which come in from our stockbrokers. Their analysts have specialist knowledge of the industry and can sometimes work out what is happening in a business faster than some of the management. However, I like to form my own opinion using other sources, such as trade journals, and I read the annual report to give me the background structure for my forecast. The company has helpfully separated out the effect of continuing and discontinued operations, which helps me in making a forecast.

When I meet the finance director next week I'll have with me a spreadsheet analysing revenue and profit before tax – so far as I can find the data – by product line and for each of the countries in which the company trades. I'll also ask the following questions:

1 *Although the revenue has increased, the ratio of gross profit to revenue on continuing operations has increased only very slightly, from 31.1% in Year 6 to 31.3% in Year 7. That suggests that the company has increased revenue by holding price rises at a level matching the increase in operating costs. I would like to see the company pushing ahead with price rises but does the company expect to see a fall in demand when its prices eventually rise?*

2 *The tax charge on continuing operations has decreased from approximately 33% to 31.5%, slightly higher than the rate which would be expected of UK companies. I know that this company is trading overseas. You say in your financial review that the tax charge is 30% in the UK and rates on overseas profits will reduce, so am I safe in assuming that 30% is a good working guide for the future in respect of this company?*

3 *With all this overseas business there must be an element of foreign exchange risk. You say in your financial review that all material foreign currency transactions are matched back into the currency of the group company undertaking the transaction. You don't hedge the translation of overseas profits back into sterling. You also say that using Year 6 exchange rates the Year 7 profit, including the effect of the discontinued operations, would have been £180.5m rather than the £177.0m reported. That seems a fairly minimal effect but are these amounts hiding any swings in major currencies where large downward movements are offset by correspondingly large upward movements?*

4 *Your increase in revenue, comparing £714.6m to £589.9m, is 21.1% which is meeting the 20% target you set yourself. However, elsewhere in the financial statements I see that the acquisitions in Year 7 contributed £13.5m to revenue. If I strip that amount out of the total revenue I'm left with an increase in respect of activities continuing from Year 6 which is only 19%. When the scope for acquisitions is exhausted, will you be able to sustain the 20% target by organic growth alone?*

4.6.2   Statement of financial position (balance sheet)

DAVID: *Looking at the statement of financial position, this is a fairly simple type of business. It is financed almost entirely by equity capital (shareholders' funds), so there are none of the risks associated with high levels of borrowings which might be found in other companies.*

Again, I have summarised and left out some of the details which aren't significant in financial terms.

Safe and Sure plc
Summarised statement of financial position (balance sheet)
(with comparative amounts)

	Notes	Year 7 £m	Year 6 £m
Non-current assets			
Property, plant and equipment		137.5	121.9
Intangible assets		260.3	237.6
Investments		2.8	2.0
Taxation recoverable		5.9	4.9
Total non-current assets		406.5	366.4
Current assets			
Inventories (stocks)		26.6	24.3
Amounts receivable (debtors)		146.9	134.7
Six-month deposits		2.0	–
Cash and cash equivalents		105.3	90.5
Total current assets		280.8	249.5
Total assets		687.3	615.9
Current liabilities			
Amounts payable (creditors)		(159.8)	(157.5)
Bank overdraft		(40.1)	(62.6)
Total current liabilities		(199.9)	(220.1)
Non-current liabilities			
Amounts payable (creditors)	9	(2.7)	(2.6)
Bank and other borrowings	10	(0.2)	(0.6)
Provisions	11	(20.2)	(22.2)
Total non-current liabilities		(23.1)	(25.4)
Total liabilities		(223.0)	(245.5)
Net assets		464.3	370.4
Capital and reserves			
Shareholders' funds		464.3	370.4

DAVID: *By far the largest non-current (fixed) asset is the intangible asset of goodwill arising on acquisition. It reflects the fact that the group has had to pay a price for the future prospects of companies it has acquired. Although the company reports this in the group's statement of financial position, and I like to see whether the asset is holding its value from the group's point of view, I have some reservations about the quality of the asset because I know it would vanish overnight if the group found itself in difficulties.*

The other non-current assets are mainly equipment for carrying out the cleaning operations and vehicles in which to transport the equipment. I've checked in the notes to the accounts that vehicles are being depreciated over four to five years and plant and equipment over five to ten years, all of which sounds about right. Also, they haven't changed the depreciation period, or the method of calculation, since last year so the amounts are comparable. Estimated useful lives for depreciation are something I watch closely. There is a great temptation for companies which have underperformed to cut back on the depreciation by deciding the useful life has extended. (Depreciation is explained more fully in Chapter 8.)

I think I might ask a few questions about working capital (the current assets minus the current liabilities of the business). Normally I like to see current assets somewhat greater than current liabilities – a ratio of 1.5 to 1 could be about right – as a cushion to ensure the liabilities are met as they fall due. However, in this company the finance director makes a point of saying that they like to utilise as little working capital as possible, so I'm wondering why it increased from £29.4m in Year 6 to more than £80m in Year 7. There appear to be two effects working together: current assets went up and current liabilities went down. Amounts receivable (trade debtors) increased in Year 7 in absolute terms but that isn't as bad as it looks when allowance is made for the increase in revenue. Amounts receivable in

Year 7 are 20.6% of continuing revenue, which shows some control has been achieved when it is compared with the Year 6 amount at 22.8% of revenue. My questions will be:

1 *Mostly, the increase in the working capital (net current assets) appears to be due to the decrease in bank borrowing. Was this a voluntary action by the company or did the bank insist?*

2 *The second major cause of the increase in the working capital is the increase in the balance held in the bank account. Is that being held for a planned purpose and, if so, what?*

3 *The ratio of current assets to current liabilities has increased from last year. What target ratio are you aiming for?*

I always shudder when I see 'provisions' in a statement of financial position. The notes to the financial statements show that these are broadly:

	£m
For treating a contaminated site	12.0
For restructuring part of the business	4.2
For tax payable some way into the future	4.0
Total	20.2

I shall want to ask whether the estimated liability in relation to the contaminated site is adequate in the light of any changes in legislation. I know the auditors will have asked this question in relation to existing legislation but I want to think also about forthcoming legislation.

I am always wary of provisions for restructuring. I shall be asking more about why the restructuring is necessary and when it will take place. I want to know that the provision is sufficient to cover the problem, but not excessive.

The provision for tax payable some way into the future is an aspect of prudence in accounting. I don't pay much attention unless the amount is very large or suddenly changes dramatically. (An explanation of deferred taxation is contained in Chapter 10.)

4.6.3   Statement of cash flows

DAVID: *Cash is an important factor for any business. It is only one of the resources available but it is the key to survival. I've summarised the totals of the various main sections of the cash flow statement. 'Net cash' means the cash less the bank borrowings.*

Safe and Sure plc
Summary statement of cash flows (with comparative amounts)
Consolidated statement of cash flows for the years ended 31 December

	Notes	Year 7	Year 6
		£m	£m
Net cash from operating activities		143.0	116.3
Net cash used in investing activities		(98.3)	(85.3)
Net cash used in financing activities		(10.2)	(46.4)
Net increase/(decrease) in cash and cash equivalents*		34.5	(15.4)

What I'm basically looking for in the cash flow statement is how well the company is balancing various sources of finance. It generated £143m from operating activities and that was more than sufficient to cover its investing activities in new fixed assets and acquisitions. There was also enough to cover the dividend of £29.5m, which is a financing activity but that was partly covered by raising new loan finance. This is why the cash used in financing activities is only £10.2m. I come back to my earlier question of why they are holding so much cash.

Activity 4.4	*Read David's explanation again and compare it carefully with the financial statements. It is quite likely that you will not understand everything immediately because the purpose of this book as a whole is to help you understand published financial statements and we are, as yet, only at the end of Chapter 4. Make a note of the items you don't fully understand and keep that note safe in a file. As you progress through the rest of the book, look back to that note and tick off the points which subsequently become clear. The aim is to have a page full of ticks by the end of the book.*

4.7 Summary

The IASB's stated objective of general purpose financial reporting is to provide financial information about the reporting entity that is useful to existing and potential investors, lenders and other creditors in making decisions about providing resources to the entity. Those decisions involve buying, selling or holding equity and debt instruments, and providing or settling loans and other forms of credit.

The two fundamental qualitative characteristics are:

- relevance
- faithful representation.

Each of these has further contributing characteristics. Relevance consists of either predictive value or confirmatory value, or both. Faithful representation consists of neutrality, freedom from error, and completeness. There are four further enhancing qualitative characteristics. These are:

- comparability
- verifiability
- timeliness
- understandability.

The accounting measurement principles that are most widely known in the UK are found within the Companies Act 2006:

- going concern
- accruals
- consistency
- prudence.

Regulation of financial reporting in the UK comes from several sources:

- The IAS Regulation requires all listed groups of companies to prepare financial statements using the system of the International Accounting Standards Board (IASB system). Other companies may choose to follow the IASB system.
- Companies that do not follow the IASB system must comply with UK company law.
- The Financial Reporting Council regulates accounting and auditing matters under the authority of UK company law. It sets UK accounting standards and auditing standards. It also takes action against companies whose annual reports do not comply with the relevant accounting system (IASB or UK company law).
- There are Stock Exchange Listing Rules which influence annual reports of listed companies.
- The UK tax system charges corporation tax on company profits. Her Majesty's Revenue and Customs (HMRC) starts with the accounting profit in calculating the amount of tax payable but there are some special rules of accounting for tax purposes.

- Auditors give an opinion on whether financial statements present a true and fair view of the profit or loss of the period and the state of affairs at the end of the period. They are professionally qualified accountants with auditing experience who are members of a recognised professional body.

Further reading

FRC (2010), *The UK Corporate Governance Code*, Financial Reporting Council.

FRC (2010), *The UK Stewardship Code*, Financial Reporting Council.

FRC (2011), *The Impact and Implementation of the UK Corporate Governance and Stewardship Codes*. Financial Reporting Council.

IASB (2010), *The Conceptual Framework for Financial Reporting*. International Accounting Standards Board.

ICAEW (2010), *Rejected Accounts: Common reasons for accounts being rejected by Companies House & how to avoid them*. Financial Reporting Faculty, Institute of Chartered Accountants in England and Wales.

Sharman (2012), *The Sharman Inquiry. Going concern and liquidity risks: lessons for companies and auditors*. Final report. Financial Reporting Council.

QUESTIONS

The Questions section of each chapter has three types of question. 'Test your understanding' questions to help you review your reading are in the 'A' series of questions. You will find the answers to these by reading and thinking about the material in the book. 'Application' questions to test your ability to apply technical skills are in the 'B' series of questions. Questions requiring you to show skills in problem solving and evaluation are in the 'C' series of questions. A letter [S] indicates that there is a solution at the end of the book.

A   Test your understanding

A4.1   Explain what is meant by each of the following: (Section 4.2)

(a) relevance;
(b) faithful representation;
(c) freedom from error
(d) neutrality;
(e) predictive value;
(f) completeness;
(g) comparability;
(h) understandability; and
(i) materiality.

A4.2   Explain the accounting measurement principles of each of the following: (Section 4.3)

(a) going concern;
(b) accruals;
(c) consistency;
(d) the concept of prudence.

A4.3   Explain why companies should avoid overstatement of assets or understatement of liabilities. (Section 4.4)

A4.4   Explain the responsibilities of directors of a company towards shareholders in relation to the financial statements of a company. (Section 4.5.2)

A4.5 Explain the impact on financial statements of each of the following: (Section 4.5)

(a) company law;
(b) the International Accounting Standards Board; and
(c) the UK tax law.

A4.6 Explain how the monitoring of financial statements is carried out by each of the following: (Section 4.5)

(a) the auditors; and
(b) the Conduct Committee of the FRC (previously FRRP).

B Application

B4.1 [S]
Explain each of the following:

(a) The IAS Regulation
(b) The Financial Reporting Council
(c) Stock Exchange Listing Rules

B4.2 [S]
Explain any two accounting measurement principles, explaining how each affects current accounting practice.

B4.3 [S]
Discuss the extent to which the regulatory bodies explained in this chapter have, or ought to have, a particular concern for the needs of the following groups of users of financial statements:

(a) shareholders;
(b) employees;
(c) customers; and
(d) suppliers.

C Problem solving and evaluation

C4.1
Choose one or more characteristics from the following list that you could use to discuss the accounting aspects of each of the statements 1 to 5 and explain your ideas:

- Relevance
- verifiability
- comparability

- understandability
- materiality
- neutrality

- completeness
- predictive value
- faithful representation

1 Director: 'We do not need to tell shareholders about a loss of £2,000 on damaged stock when our operating profit for the year is £60m.'
2 Shareholder: 'I would prefer the statement of financial position (balance sheet) to tell me the current market value of land is £20m than to tell me that the historical cost is £5m, although I know that market values fluctuate.'
3 Analyst: 'If the company changes its stock valuation from average cost to FIFO, I want to hear a good reason and I want to know what last year's profit would have been on the same basis.'
4 Regulator: 'If the company reports that it has paid "*commission on overseas sales*", I don't expect to discover later that it really meant bribes to local officials.'
5 Director: 'We have made a profit on our drinks sales but a loss on food sales. In the Notes to the Accounts on segmental results I suggest we combine them as "food and drink". It will mean the annual report is less detailed for our shareholders but it will keep competitors in the dark for a while.'

C4.2

Choose one or more accounting measurement principles from the following list that you could use to discuss the accounting aspects of each of the problems 1–5 and explain your ideas.

- going concern
- accruals
- consistency
- prudence.

1 Director: 'The fixed assets of the business are reported at depreciated historical cost because we expect the company to continue in existence for the foreseeable future. The market value is much higher but that is not relevant because we don't intend to sell them.'

2 Auditor: 'We are insisting that the company raises the provision for doubtful debts from 2% to 2.5% of debtor amount. There has been recession among the customer base and the financial statements should reflect that.'

3 Analyst: 'I have great problems in tracking the depreciation policy of this company. It owns several airports. Over the past three years the expected useful life of runways has risen from 30 years to 50 years and now it is 100 years. I find it hard to believe that the technology of tarmacadam has improved so much in three years.'

4 Auditor: 'We have serious doubts about the ability of this company to renew its bank overdraft at next month's review meeting with the bank. The company ought to put shareholders on warning about the implications for the financial statements.'

5 Shareholder: 'I don't understand why the company gives a profit and loss account and a cash flow statement in the annual report. Is there any difference between profit and cash flow?'

Activities for study groups

Continuing to use the annual reports of a company that you obtained for Chapter 1, look for the evidence in each report of the existence of the directors, the auditors and the various regulatory bodies.

In your group, draw up a list of the evidence presented by companies to show that the annual report has been the subject of regulation. Discuss whether the annual report gives sufficient reassurance of its relevance and faithful representation to the non-expert reader.

Notes and references

1. IASB (2010), *Conceptual Framework*, para. OB 2.
2. IAS 1 (2011), para. 10.
3. IAS 1 (2011), paras 10–12.
4. IASB (2010), *Conceptual Framework*, para. QC 5.
5. *Ibid.*, para. QC 6.
6. *Ibid.*, para. QC 8.
7. *Ibid.*, para. QC 9.
8. *Ibid.*, para. QC 12.
9. *Ibid.*, para. QC 13.
10. *Ibid.*, para. QC 14.
11. *Ibid.*, para. QC 15.
12. *Ibid.*, para. QC 11.
13. *Ibid.*, paras QC 20–25.
14. *Ibid.*, paras QC 26–28.
15. *Ibid.*, para. QC 29.
16. *Ibid.*, paras QC 30–32.
17. *Ibid.*, paras QC 35–39.
18. IASB *Framework* (1989), para. 37.
19. IASB (2008), Exposure Draft on Conceptual Framework, para. BC 2.21.
20. IASB *Framework* (1989), para. 31.
21. IASB (2008), Exposure Draft on Conceptual Framework, para. BC 2.15.
22. IASB *Framework* (1989), para. 35.
23. IASB (2008), Exposure Draft on Conceptual Framework, para. BC 2.19.
24. Under the Companies Act 2006, detailed accounting requirements are contained in Statutory Instruments. The accounting principles are specified in paras 11–15 of Schedule 1 of SI 2008/410

The Large and Medium-sized Companies and Groups (Accounts and Reports) Regulations 2008. Listed groups in the UK follow the International Financial Reporting Standards, where the same accounting measurement principles apply. www.legislation.gov.uk/uksi/2008/410/contents/made.

25. IASB (2010), *Conceptual Framework*, para. 4.1.
26. *Ibid.*, para. OB 17.
27. ASB (1999), *Statement of Principles*, Appendix III, paras 21–3.
28. ASB (2000), Financial Reporting Standard 18 (FRS 18) *Accounting Policies*, Accounting Standards Board, para. 28.
29. ASB (2000), Appendix IV, paras 12 to 20.
30. IASB (1989), *Framework*, para. 27.
31. http://europa.eu.int/comm/internal_market/accounting/index_en.htm.
32. www.efrag.org/.
33. www.frc.org.uk/.
34. FRC (2010), The UK Approach to corporate governance.

Part 2

Reporting the transactions of a business

Chapter 5

Accounting information for service businesses

Croda International plc is a global leader in speciality chemicals, sold to a wide range of markets – from personal care to health care; from crop care to coatings and polymers. In its annual report it describes its investment in employees:

Alamy Images/Stock Connection

Employees

1. Recruitment & retention

Like all successful businesses, we recognise that our future depends on our ability to attract and retain individuals who are passionate about personal and business growth and want to make a significant contribution to the future of our business. Recruiting individuals that fit this description and the culture of the business is always hard, but within the chemical industry it is increasingly a problem with a high level of competition for a decreasing number of graduates. As our business is focused on innovation and growth in emerging markets and developing countries, this challenge increases further.

2. Compensation & benefits

In a competitive recruitment marketplace we are conscious that we should not lose critical staff because of issues relating to pay or additional benefits. We realise that the remuneration package we offer plays a key part in attracting and retaining employees.

3. HR policies & systems

Information and knowledge sharing are at the heart of making better business decisions. Streamlined systems and policies not only provide the data and trends on which to base decisions, but will in turn drive employee engagement. We believe that well defined policies and procedures allow our employees to operate without constant management intervention. It is this autonomy and freedom to act that has made our business what it is today.

4. Talent management and employee development

The key to the future success of any business lies in the skills and abilities of its workforce. It is only through the continual development of our workforce that we will be able to meet the future demands of our customers in relation to enhanced creativity, innovation and customer service. Being a business dependent upon a large number of specialists including engineers and scientists as well as finance, IT, HR, marketing, purchasing, sales, regulatory and legal professionals we have to place great focus on continuous development.

5. Performance management

A strong, efficient performance management culture is not only important to employees' professional development, but also to meet the Company's objectives and so ultimately contributing to its bottom line. In addition, a clear, robust process will lead to enhanced communications and an opportunity to address performance problems effectively, thus delivering improvements in employee morale.

Source: Annual report 2011, Croda International plc, p. 14. http://www.croda.com.

Discussion points

1 The 'people' asset does not appear in the balance sheet of a company. What are the costs to the company of maintaining the 'people' asset?

2 What are the risks to a service business of strong reliance on a 'people' asset?

Contents

Learning outcomes

After studying this chapter you should be able to:

- Explain how the accounting equation is applied to transactions of a service business.
- Analyse the transactions of a service business during a specific period of time, using the accounting equation.
- Prepare a spreadsheet analysing the transactions and show that the results of the spreadsheet are consistent with the financial statements provided by the organisation.
- Explain the main aspects of the statement of cash flows, income statement (profit and loss account) and statement of financial position (balance sheet) of a service business.

Additionally, for those who read the supplement:

- Analyse the transactions of a service business using the rules of debit and credit bookkeeping.
- Prepare, from a list of transactions of an organisation, ledger accounts and a trial balance which could be used to prepare the financial statements provided by the organisation.

5.1 Introduction

A person who starts a service business intends to offer a service based on personal skills for which other people will be willing to pay a fee. The most important asset of the service business is the person or people providing the service. Despite that, the workforce as an asset never appears in an accounting statement of financial position (balance sheet). That is because, although it satisfies all the conditions of the definition, it is too difficult to measure objectively and so does not meet the conditions for recognition. (See Chapter 2 for the definition of an asset and the conditions for recognition of an asset.)

The service business will have other assets which accounting is able to record: for example, the taxi driver may own a taxi; the electrician will have electrical tools; the joiner will have a workbench and joinery tools; the car mechanic will have a repair garage and equipment; the lawyer will have an office and a word-processor. The service business will also buy materials for use in any particular job and the customer will be asked to pay for these materials as well as for the labour time involved. Moreover, it will have liabilities to suppliers of goods and services used by the business itself.

There will be an owner or owners having an ownership interest in the business. The service business will make profits for the owner (and thus increase the ownership interest) by charging a price for services which is greater than the cost of labour and materials used in providing the service.

All these aspects of the service business may be analysed and recorded on the basis of the accounting equation as specified in Chapter 2. This chapter will discuss the analysis of transactions using the accounting equation and will then apply that analysis to the transactions of a doctor providing a service of medical health screening for managerial and secretarial staff.

Activity 5.1	*Choose a service business and write down the main activity of that business. Then write down the types of expense you would expect to find in the income statement (profit and loss account) of such a business. Write down the types of asset you would expect to find in the statement of financial position (balance sheet). Exchange your list with a fellow student. What are the similarities and what are the differences? Keep your list safe and when you have finished the chapter compare your list with the example in the chapter. Ask yourself, at that point, whether you would be able to apply what you have learned to the business you have chosen.*

5.2 Analysing transactions using the accounting equation

Three main categories of accounting elements in the accounting equation have been defined in Chapter 2: **asset**, **liability** and **ownership interest**. Any one of these elements may increase or decrease during a period of time but the ownership interest may conveniently be subdivided. There will be increases and decreases caused by the decision of the owner(s) to make further contributions of capital or to withdraw capital. There will be increases and decreases due to the activity of the business, with **revenues** increasing the ownership claim and **expenses** decreasing it.

Decrease in ownership interest	*Increase in ownership interest*
Withdrawals of capital by the owner	Contributions of capital by the owner
Expenses	Revenues

Consequently there are several aspects to consider when transactions are analysed according to the accounting equation.

The accounting equation will be used in this chapter in the form:

Assets	minus	**Liabilities**	equals	**Ownership interest**

When one item in the equation increases, an upward arrow will be used and when one item decreases a downward arrow will be used:

Assets ↓	denotes a decrease in an asset.

Liabilities ↑	denotes an increase in a liability.

For further emphasis, **bold** highlighting will be used for the elements of the equation which are changed as a result of the transaction or event.

Each business transaction has two aspects in terms of the accounting equation. These aspects must be considered from the viewpoint of the *business*. Table 5.1 sets out a list of some common types of transaction encountered in a service business. Each transaction is then analysed using the accounting equation.

Table 5.1
List of transactions for a service business

	Transaction
1	Receive cash from the owner.
2	Buy a vehicle for cash.
3	Receive a bill for gas consumed.
4	Pay the gas bill in cash.
5	Buy materials for cash.
6	Buy materials on credit terms.
7	Sell services for cash.
8	Sell services on credit terms.
9	Pay wages to an employee.
10	Pay cash to the owner for personal use.

Transaction 1: receive cash from the owner

In this transaction the business *acquires* an **asset** (cash) and must note the **ownership interest** *created* by this contribution of capital from the owner:

Assets ↑ – Liabilities	equals	**Ownership interest** ↑

The equation remains in balance because an increase to the left-hand side is exactly matched by an increase to the right-hand side.

Transaction 2: buy a vehicle for cash

In this transaction the business *acquires* a new **asset** (the vehicle) but gives up another **asset** (cash):

Assets ↑↓ – Liabilities	equals	Ownership interest

Transaction 3: receive a bill for gas consumed

The business becomes aware that it has a **liability** to pay for gas consumed and also knows that the **ownership interest** has been *reduced* by the expense of using up gas in earning revenue for the business:

Assets – **Liabilities** ↑	equals	**Ownership interest** ↓ **(expense)**

Transaction 4: pay the gas bill in cash

The **asset** of cash is *reduced* and the **liability** to the gas supplier is *reduced*:

Assets ↓ – **Liabilities** ↓	equals	Ownership interest

Transaction 5: buy materials for cash

When the materials are acquired they will create an asset of inventory (stock), for future use. The **asset** of inventory (stock) will therefore *increase* and the **asset** of cash will *decrease*:

Assets ↓↑ – Liabilities	Equals	Ownership interest

Transaction 6: buy materials on credit terms

Again, materials are acquired which cause an *increase* in the **asset** of inventory (stock). Obtaining goods on credit means that there is a **liability** *created* for amounts owing to the supplier:

Assets ↑ – Liabilities ↑	equals	Ownership interest

Transaction 7: sell services for cash

The cash received from the customer causes an *increase* in the **asset** of cash, while the act of selling services *increases* the **ownership interest** through earning revenue:

Assets ↑ – Liabilities	equals	Ownership interest ↑ (revenue)

Transaction 8: sell services on credit terms

The sale of services creates an *increase* in the **ownership interest** through earning revenue, but also creates an *increase* in the **asset** of trade receivables (debtors):

Assets ↑ – Liabilities	equals	Ownership interest ↑ (revenue)

Transaction 9: pay wages to an employee

The **asset** of cash *decreases* when the wage is paid and there is a *decrease* in the **ownership interest** because the business has used up the service provided by the employee (an expense has been incurred):

Assets ↓ – Liabilities	equals	Ownership interest ↓ (expense)

This is a transaction which often causes problems to those new to accounting. They would like to argue that paying wages creates an asset, rather than an expense, because there is an expected future benefit to be gained from the services of the employee. The answer to that argument is that, while there is no disputing the expected future benefit from the services of most employees, the wages paid are for work *already done* and so there can be no future expectations about that particular week's or month's work. The question of whether the workforce as a whole should be recognised as an asset of the business is one of the unresolved problems of accounting.

Transaction 10: pay cash to the owner for personal use

The **asset** of cash *decreases* and the **ownership interest** *decreases* because the owner has made a voluntary withdrawal of capital:

Assets ↓ – Liabilities	equals	Ownership interest ↓ (voluntary withdrawal)

Activity 5.2	*Write down the transactions of Table 5.1 in a different order and put the piece of paper away for two days. Then take it out and practise the analysis of each transaction without looking at the answers in the book. If your answers are all correct, is it the result of memory or of genuine understanding? If your answers are not entirely correct, can you decide where the problem lies? It is very important that you can analyse transactions correctly using the accounting equation. It is also important that you use your powers of reasoning and not your powers of memory. You cannot possibly memorise the accounting treatment of every transaction you will meet.*

5.3 Illustration of accounting for a service business

We now move on to an example which considers the private medical practice of Dr Lee. At the start of October Dr Lee commenced a new medical practice offering a general health screening service to managerial and secretarial staff at a standard fee of £500 per examination. Where patients make personal arrangements they will be asked to pay cash on the day of the examination. If the patient's employer has agreed to pay for the screening, Dr Lee will send an invoice to the employer, requiring payment within 30 days.

In Table 5.2 there is a list of transactions for Dr Lee's medical practice during the month of October. Try to work out the effect on the accounting equation of each transaction listed. Do this before you read the rest of this section. Then compare your answers and your reasoning with that in the rest of this section. Being able to reason correctly at this stage will reduce the likelihood of error later.

Oct. 1   When Dr Lee provides the practice with cash in a bank account to allow the business to start, the business *acquires* an **asset** of cash at bank and the transaction *creates* an **ownership interest** by Dr Lee in the assets of the business. This means that the business now has the use of £50,000, but, if the business ceases immediately, that £50,000 must be returned to Dr Lee. The accounting equation is satisfied because an increase in an asset is matched by an increase in the ownership interest:

Assets ↓ – Liabilities	equals	**Ownership interest ↓**

Oct. 2   The medical practice now becomes the business entity so far as accounting is concerned (although it is fairly clear that Dr Lee is making all the decisions as the manager of the business as well as being the owner). The entity *acquires* an **asset** of medical equipment in exchange for an equal *decrease* in the amount of an **asset** of cash. The accounting equation is satisfied because the increase in one asset is exactly equal to the decrease in another.

Assets ↑↓ – Liabilities	equals	Ownership interest

Oct. 2   The medical practice pays one month's rent in advance. At the moment of paying the rent, an asset is acquired representing the benefit to be gained from the use of the consulting rooms for the month ahead. However, this benefit only lasts for a short time and will have expired at the end of the accounting period (which has been chosen as one month for the purpose of this example). Once the benefit of an asset has expired, the business

becomes worse off and the ownership interest decreases. That decrease is called an expense of the business. To save the time and trouble of recording such transactions as assets and then re-naming them as expenses at the end of the accounting period, the short-cut is taken of calling them expenses from the outset. There needs to be a check on such items at the end of the accounting period to ensure that there is no part of the benefit remaining which could still be an asset.

Table 5.2
Transactions of Dr Lee's medical practice for the month of October

Date	Business transactions of the entity (nature of the entity: medical practice)	Amount
		£
Oct. 1	Dr Lee provides the practice with cash to allow business to start.	50,000
Oct. 2	The entity acquires medical equipment for cash.	30,000
Oct. 2	One month's rent is paid in advance for consulting rooms.	1,900
Oct. 2	Office furniture is purchased on two months' credit from Office Supplies Company.	6,500
Oct. 7	The practice purchases medical supplies on credit from P. Jones and receives an invoice.	1,200
Oct. 8	Dr Lee pays the medical receptionist for one week's work, 2 to 8 October.	300
Oct. 10	Four patients are examined, each paying £500 cash.	2,000
Oct. 11	The business pays P. Jones in cash for the goods it acquired on credit.	1,200
Oct. 14	The business pays an electricity bill in cash.	100
Oct. 15	Dr Lee pays the medical receptionist for one week's work, 9 to 15 October.	300
Oct. 17	Three patients are examined, their employer (Mrs West) being sent an invoice requesting payment of £500 for each.	1,500
Oct. 22	Dr Lee pays the medical receptionist for one week's work, 16 to 22 October.	300
Oct. 23	The employer (Mrs West) pays in cash for the examination of three patients.	1,500
Oct. 24	Four patients are examined, their employer (Mr East) being sent an invoice requesting payment of £500 for each.	2,000
Oct. 28	Dr Lee draws cash from the business for personal use.	1,000
Oct. 29	Dr Lee pays the medical receptionist for one week's work, 23 to 29 October.	300
Oct. 31	The medical equipment and office furniture is estimated by Dr Lee to have fallen in value over the month.	250
Oct. 31	Dr Lee checks the inventory (stock) of medical supplies and finds that items costing £350 have been used during the month.	350

In terms of the accounting equation there is a *decrease* in the **ownership interest** due to an expense of the business. There is a corresponding *decrease* in the **asset** of cash.

Assets ↑ – Liabilities	equals	**Ownership interest ↓ (expense)**

Oct. 2   The entity acquires an asset of office furniture. It does not pay cash on this occasion, having been given two months to pay. Looking over the rest of the transactions for October it is clear that there has been no payment by the end of the month. At the moment of taking delivery of the asset, the business incurs a liability to the supplier, Office Supplies Company. The accounting equation is satisfied because the *increase* in an **asset** is exactly equal to the *increase* in a **liability**.

Assets ↑ – Liabilities ↑	equals	Ownership interest

Oct. 7   The practice purchases medical supplies on credit from P. Jones and receives an invoice. This is very similar to the previous transaction. An **asset** *is acquired* and a **liability** to a supplier is *created*. The liability is recognised when the practice accepts delivery of the goods because that is the moment of accepting legal liability. For convenience, accounting procedures normally use the arrival of the invoice as the occasion for recording the liability but, even if the invoice failed to arrive, the liability must be recognised in relation to accepting the goods.

Assets ↑ – Liabilities ↑	equals	Ownership interest

Oct. 8   The medical receptionist has worked for one week and is paid for the work done. The amount paid in wages is an expense of the business which *decreases* the **ownership interest** because the benefit of that work has been used up in providing support for the medical practice. There is a *decrease* in the **asset** of cash.

Assets ↓ – Liabilities	equals	**Ownership interest ↓ (expense)**

Oct. 10   The medical practice now begins to carry out the activities which increase the wealth of the owner by earning revenue. The patients pay cash, so there is an *increase* in the **asset** of cash, and the owner becomes better off so there is an *increase* in the **ownership interest**.

Assets ↑ – Liabilities	equals	**Ownership interest ↑ (revenue)**

Oct. 11   The business pays P. Jones in cash for the goods it acquired on credit. Payment of cash *decreases* the **asset** of cash and *decreases* the **liability** to the supplier. Because the supplier is paid in full, the liability is extinguished.

Assets ↓ – Liabilities ↓	equals	Ownership interest

Oct. 14 The business pays an electricity bill in full. The business has enjoyed the use of the electricity but there is no benefit remaining. This is an **expense** of the business which causes a *decrease* in the **ownership interest**. There is a *decrease* in the **asset** of cash.

Assets ↓ – Liabilities	equals	Ownership interest ↓ (expense)

Oct. 15 The payment to the medical receptionist is similar in effect to the payment made on 8 October, causing a further **expense** which *decreases* the **ownership interest** and causes a *decrease* in the **asset** of cash.

Assets ↓ – Liabilities	equals	**Ownership interest** ↓ **(expense)**

Oct. 17 There is an increase in the **ownership interest** which arises from the operations of the business and so is termed **revenue**. On this occasion the business *acquires* an **asset** of a trade receivable (debtor), showing that an amount of money is owed by the employer of these patients.

Assets ↑ – Liabilities	equals	**Ownership interest** ↑ **(revenue)**

Oct. 22 The payment to the medical receptionist causes a further **expense** and a *decrease* in the **asset** of cash.

Assets ↓ – Liabilities	equals	**Ownership interest** ↓ **(expense)**

Oct. 23 The cash received from the employer of the three patients examined on 17 October causes an *increase* in the **asset** of cash and a *decrease* in the **asset** of the trade receivable (debtor). Because the amount is paid in full, the asset of the trade receivable (debtor) is reduced to nil.

Assets ↑↓ – Liabilities	equals	Ownership interest

Oct. 24 Again the business carries out the activities intended to make the owner better off. The accounting effect is similar to that of 17 October, with an *increase* in the **ownership interest** and an *increase* in the **asset** of cash.

Assets ↑ – Liabilities	equals	**Ownership interest** ↑ **(revenue)**

Oct. 28 The owner of a sole trader business does not take a salary or wage as an employee would, but nevertheless needs cash for personal purposes. Taking cash for personal use is called taking 'drawings' and is recorded in terms of the accounting equation as a *decrease* in the **ownership interest** and a *decrease* in the **asset** of cash.

Assets ↓ – Liabilities	equals	**Ownership interest** ↓ **(drawings)**

Oct. 29 Paying wages causes an **expense** and a *decrease* in the **asset** of cash.

Assets ↓ – Liabilities	equals	**Ownership interest** ↓ **(expense)**

Oct. 31   The medical equipment and the office furniture are non-current (fixed) assets of the business. They are expected to have some years' useful life in the business but they will eventually be used up. In accounting, the term 'depreciation' is applied to this gradual using up and there are various ways of deciding how much of the fixed asset has been 'used up' in any period. (Chapter 8 gives more information on depreciation.) For this example the owner's estimate of depreciation is sufficient. There is a *decrease* in the non-current (fixed) **assets** which is not matched by an increase in any other asset and so there is a *decrease* in the **ownership interest** due to the operations of the business. **Depreciation** is an **expense** of the business.

Assets ↓ – Liabilities	equals	Ownership interest ↓ (expense)

Oct. 31   Dr Lee checks the inventory (stock) of medical supplies and finds that items costing £350 have been used during the month. When these medical supplies were received on 7 October, they were all treated as an asset of the business. It appears now that the asset has been reduced from £1,200 to £850 and that the items used up have caused a decrease of £350 in the ownership interest. This decrease is the expense of medical supplies which will appear in the income statement (profit and loss account) of the month. The two aspects of this event are therefore a *decrease* in the **ownership interest** and a *decrease* in the **asset** of inventory (stock) of medical supplies.

Assets ↓ – Liabilities	equals	Ownership interest ↓ (expense)

This analysis has been set out in some detail to show that each transaction must first of all be considered, in order to establish the nature of the two aspects of the transaction, before any attempt is made to deal with the monetary amounts. The next section uses the analysis based on the accounting equation to produce a spreadsheet which can be totalled to give a summary picture of the transactions of the month in terms of the accounting equation.

5.4   A process for summarising the transactions: a spreadsheet

In Table 5.3 the transactions are repeated in the left-hand column but the relevant money amounts are shown in columns which correspond to the assets, liabilities and ownership interest, using brackets to show a negative amount. (It would be equally acceptable to use a minus sign but minus signs tend to disappear or be confused with unintentional blobs on the paper, so brackets are frequently used in accounting in order to ensure clarity.)

Taking the first line as an example, the analysis of the transaction showed that there was an increase in the asset of cash and an increase in the ownership interest. Thus the amount of £50,000 is written in the spreadsheet column for cash and again in the spreadsheet column for ownership interest. In the second line, the asset of cash decreases by £30,000 and the asset of medical equipment increases by £30,000. A similar pattern follows down the spreadsheet for each transaction.

It may be seen that where there are more than a few transactions during the month, a spreadsheet of the type shown in Table 5.3 would need to be much larger and use more columns.

Table 5.3

Spreadsheet analysing transactions into the elements of the accounting equation

Date	Business transactions of the entity (nature of the entity: medical practice)	Assets				Liabilities	Ownership interest		
		Cash and bank £	Trade rec'ble (debtor) £	Inventory (stock) £	Fixed assets £	Liabilities £	Capital contributed or withdrawn £	Revenue + £	Expenses – £
Oct. 1	Dr Lee provides the practice with cash to allow business to start	50,000					50,000		
Oct. 2	The entity acquires medical equipment for cash	(30,000)			30,000				
Oct. 2	One month's rent is paid in advance for consulting rooms	(1,900)							1,900
Oct. 2	Office furniture is purchased on two months' credit from Office Supplies Company				6,500	6,500			
Oct. 7	The practice purchases medical supplies on credit from P. Jones and receives an invoice			1,200		1,200			
Oct. 8	Dr Lee pays the medical receptionist for one week's work, 2 to 8 October	(300)							300
Oct. 10	Four patients are examined, each paying £500 cash	2,000						2,000	
Oct. 11	The business pays P. Jones in cash for the goods it acquired on credit	(1,200)				(1,200)			
Oct. 14	The business pays an electricity bill in cash	(100)							100
Oct. 15	Dr Lee pays the medical receptionist for one week's work, 9 to 15 October	(300)							300
Oct. 17	Three patients are examined, their employer (Mrs West) being sent an invoice requesting payment of £500 for each		1,500					1,500	
Oct. 22	Dr Lee pays the medical receptionist for one week's work, 16 to 22 October	(300)							300
Oct. 23	The employer (Mrs West) pays in cash for the examination of three patients	1,500	(1,500)						
Oct. 24	Four patients are examined, their employer (Mr East) being sent an invoice requesting payment of £500 for each		2,000					2,000	
Oct. 28	Dr Lee draws cash from the business for personal use	(1,000)					(1,000)		
Oct. 29	Dr Lee pays the medical receptionist for one week's work, 23 to 29 October	(300)							300
Oct. 31	The medical equipment and office furniture is estimated by Dr Lee to have fallen in value over the month				(250)				250
Oct. 31	Dr Lee checks the inventory (stock) of medical supplies and finds that items costing £350 have been used during the month			(350)					350
	Totals	18,100	2,000	850	36,250	6,500	49,000	5,500	3,800

57,200 ————— 50,700

At the foot of the spreadsheet in Table 5.3 there is a total for each column. Those totals from Table 5.3 are used in Table 5.4, which represents the accounting equation, to show the state of the accounting equation at the end of the month. It may be used to explain to Dr Lee how the ownership interest has changed over the month. The owner contributed £50,000 at the start of the month and has a claim of £50,700 at the end of the month. The ownership interest was increased by earning revenue of £5,500 but reduced by incurring expenses of £3,800 and withdrawing £1,000 for personal use.

Table 5.4
Summary of transactions analysed into the elements of the accounting equation

Assets	minus	Liabilities	=	Ownership interest at start of period	plus	Capital contributed/ withdrawn	plus	Revenue	minus	Expenses
£57,200	–	£6,500		nil	+	£49,000	+	£5,500	–	£3,800
└──── £50,700 ────┘				└──────────────── £50,700 ────────────────┘						

5.5 Financial statements as a means of communication

This chapter has established the approach taken in accounting towards analysing and classifying transactions in such a way that Dr Lee as the owner of a business knows how much better or worse off she has become during a period. There is sufficient information contained in Table 5.3 and it is possible to write an interpretation based on Table 5.4. However, this presentation is not particularly informative or easy on the eye.

The process of communication requires some attention to a clear style of presentation. Accounting practice has evolved the statement of cash flows, the income statement (profit and loss account) and the statement of financial position (balance sheet) to give the owner a more informative presentation of the information contained in Tables 5.3 and 5.4.

Chapter 3 set out the structure of the financial statements of a business. These ideas are now applied to Dr Lee's medical practice. Don't worry too much about how the information is transferred from Table 5.3 to these financial statements, but look back to the table and satisfy yourself that you can find the corresponding pieces of information.

5.5.1 Statement of cash flows

Medical Practice of Dr Lee
Statement of cash flows for the month of October Year 20xx

	£
Operating activities	
Inflow from fees	3,500
Outflow: rent paid	(1,900)
payment to supplier (P. Jones)	(1,200)
wages	(1,200)
electricity	(100)
Net outflow from operations	(900)
Investing activities	
Payment for equipment	(30,000)
Net outflow for investing activities	(30,000)
Financing activities	£
Capital contributed by owner	50,000
Capital withdrawn as drawings	(1,000)
Net inflow from financing activities	49,000
Increase in cash at bank over period	18,100

Comment. All the amounts for this statement are taken from the 'Cash at bank' column of Table 5.3 but are regrouped for the three headings of operating activities, investing activities and financing activities. The statement shows that the business had a net outflow of cash of £900 due to operations and an outflow of cash amounting to £30,000 due to purchase of medical equipment. The owner contributed £50,000 at the start of the month but took drawings of £1,000 at the end, resulting in a net inflow of £49,000 from financing. The overall effect was an increase in cash over the period amounting to £18,100.

5.5.2   Income statement (profit and loss account)

Medical Practice of Dr Lee
Income statement (profit and loss account)
for the month of October Year 20xx

	£	£
Fees charged		5,500
Medical supplies used	(350)	
Wages	(1,200)	
Rent	(1,900)	
Electricity	(100)	
Depreciation	(250)	
		(3,800)
Profit		1,700

Comment. The total fees charged constitute the total revenue of the period as may be seen in the column in Table 5.3 headed 'revenue'. The expenses of the period amount to £3,800 and are taken from the final column of Table 5.3. The difference between revenue and expenses is the profit of £1,700. This is the amount by which the owner-ship interest has increased to make the owner of the business better off.

Some students ask at this point why the owner's drawings are not included in the income statement (profit and loss account). The answer is that making drawings of cash has nothing to do with the operations of the business. It is a voluntary action taken by the owner, who is also the manager, balancing the owner's personal need for cash against the needs of the business for cash to ensure continued smooth running. Where the owner is the only person working in the business, the owner may regard the drawings as being closer to wages. The amount taken may represent wages in economic terms. However, accounting ignores this economic reality and reports all amounts withdrawn by the owner as drawings.

Activity 5.3	The medical practice of Dr Lee has made a profit of £1,700 over the month but the cash flow caused by operations is an outflow of £900. How can a business make a profit and yet see an outflow of cash caused by operations? This question is asked all too often in reality. You can provide the answer by comparing the cash flow due to operating activities and the calculation of net profit. If you are not sure how to make the comparison, look back to Chapter 3 where the financial statements of P. Mason's legal practice were analysed (Table 3.7).

5.5.3   Statement of financial position (balance sheet)

Medical Practice of Dr Lee
Statement of financial position (balance sheet)
at 31 October Year 20xx

	£
Non-current (fixed) assets	
Medical equipment at cost	30,000
Office furniture	6,500
	36,500
Depreciation	(250)
Depreciated cost of fixed assets	36,250
Current assets	
Medical supplies	850
Trade receivables (debtors)	2,000
Cash at bank	18,100
Total current assets	20,950
Total assets	57,200
Current liabilities	
Trade payables (creditors)	(6,500)
Net assets	50,700
Capital at start	50,000
Add: profit	1,700
Less: drawings	(1,000)
Total ownership interest	50,700

Comment. The statement of financial position (balance sheet) follows the pattern of the accounting equation. The non-current (fixed assets) are presented first of all, showing the resources available to the business over a longer period of time. The depreciation is deducted to leave an amount remaining which is probably best described as the 'depreciated cost' but is often labelled 'net book value' or 'written down value'. Chapter 8 contains more information on the procedures for measuring and recording depreciation and the limitations of using the word 'value' in relation to those procedures.

The next section contains the **current assets** which are expected to be converted into cash within a 12-month period. The medical supplies shown are those which have not yet been used and therefore remain as a benefit for the next month. Trade receivables (debtors) are those customers who are expected to pay in the near future. The other current asset is the cash held at the bank, which is very accessible in the short term.

The only liability is the amount of £6,500 owing to the Office Supplies Company, due for payment at the start of December. This is a **current liability** because it is due for payment within 12 months.

It is felt to be helpful in the statement of financial position (balance sheet) to set out subtotals which may guide the reader. These have been shaded in the statement of financial position (balance sheet). The total of non-current (fixed) assets is interesting as the long-term asset base used to generate profits. The difference between the **current assets** and the **current liabilities** is sometimes identified separately as the **working capital**. At the moment the current assets look rather high in relation to the need to cover current liabilities. This is because the amount of cash held is quite high in relation to the apparent needs of the business. It is possible that Dr Lee has plans to use the cash for business purposes quite soon but, in the absence of such plans, Dr Lee ought to consider investing it to earn interest or else withdrawing it for other uses.

The amount for total assets less total liabilities (A – L) is usually called the **net assets** of the business. (The word 'net' means 'after taking something away' – in this case, after taking away the liabilities.) There is not much to say here except to note that it equals the ownership interest as would be expected from the accounting equation. The ownership interest has increased over the period through making a profit of £1,700 but decreased by £1,000 through making drawings, so that the resulting increase is £700 overall.

Activity 5.4	*Compare the financial statements of Dr Lee's medical practice with the information collected in the spreadsheet of Table 5.3. Take a pencil and, very lightly, place a tick against each amount in the financial statements and a tick against each amount in the spreadsheet, as you match them together. If you are able to work backwards in this way from the financial statements to the spreadsheet then you will be well on the way to understanding how the financial statements are related to the original list of transactions.*

5.6 Summary

The first stage in recording a transaction is to think about its effect on the accounting equation.

Assets minus **Liabilities**	equals	**Ownership interest**

A transaction must have at least two effects on the accounting equation. For example, when cash is contributed by the owner there is an *increase* in the **asset** of cash and an *increase* in the **ownership interest**:

Assets ↑ – Liabilities	equals	**Ownership interest** ↑

Accounting transactions may be recorded in a spreadsheet where the columns record the assets and liabilities and the rows record each transaction. The totals at the foot of all columns contain the information for the statement of financial position (balance sheet) at the end of the period. The columns for revenue and expenditure allow the profit or loss to be calculated. The bank or cash column provides information for the statement of cash flows.

QUESTIONS

The Questions section of each chapter has three types of question. 'Test your understanding' questions to help you review your reading are in the 'A' series of questions. You will find the answers to these by reading and thinking about the material in the book. 'Application' questions to test your ability to apply technical skills are in the 'B' series of questions. Questions requiring you to show skills in problem solving and evaluation are in the 'C' series of questions. A letter [S] indicates that there is a solution at the end of the book.

A   Test your understanding

A5.1   [S] The following list of transactions relates to a television repair business during the first month of business. Explain how each transaction affects the accounting equation: (Section 5.2)

(a)   Owner puts cash into the business.

(b)   Buy a vehicle for cash.

(c) Receive a bill for electricity consumed.
(d) Purchase stationery for office use, paying cash.
(e) Pay the electricity bill in cash.
(f) Pay rental for a computer, used to keep customer records.
(g) Buy spare parts for cash, to use in repairs.
(h) Buy spare parts on credit terms.
(i) Pay garage service bills for van, using cash.
(j) Fill van with petrol, using credit account at local garage, to be paid at the start of next month.
(k) Carry out repairs for cash.
(l) Carry out repairs on credit terms.
(m) Pay wages to an employee.
(n) Owner takes cash for personal use.

A5.2 [S] Which of the items in the list of transactions in question A5.1 will have an effect on an income statement (profit and loss account)?

A5.3 [S] Which of the items in the list of transactions in question A5.1 will have an effect on a statement of cash flows?

A5.4 [S] Which of the items in the list of transactions in question A5.1 will have an effect on a statement of financial position (balance sheet)?

A5.5 [S] Analyse each of the following transactions to show the two aspects of the transaction: (Section 5.3)

Apr. 1	Jane Gate commenced her dental practice on 1 April by depositing £60,000 in a business bank account.
Apr. 1	Rent for a surgery was paid, £800, for the month of April.
Apr. 2	Dental equipment was purchased for £35,000, paying in cash.
Apr. 3	Dental supplies were purchased for £5,000, taking 30 days' credit from a supplier.
Apr. 4	Fees of £1,200 were collected in cash from patients and paid into the bank account.
Apr. 15	Dental assistant was paid wages for two weeks, £700.
Apr. 20	Jane Gate withdrew £500 cash for personal use.
Apr. 21	Fees of £2,400 were collected in cash from patients and paid into the bank.
Apr. 29	Dental assistant was paid wages for two weeks, £700.
Apr. 29	Invoices were sent to patients who are allowed 20 days' credit, for work done during April amounting to £1,900.
Apr. 30	Telephone bill for April was paid, £80.
Apr. 30	Dental supplies unused were counted and found to be worth £3,500, measured at cost price.

B Application

B5.1 [S]
(a) Using the list of transactions at question A5.5 prepare a spreadsheet similar to that presented in Table 5.3.
(b) Show that the spreadsheet totals satisfy the accounting equation.

B5.2 [S]
Using the totals from the columns of the spreadsheet of question B5.1, prepare for the dental practice in the month of April:

(a) a statement of cash flows;
(b) a statement of financial position (balance sheet); and
(c) an income statement (profit and loss account).

There are no questions in the C series for this chapter.

Recording transactions in ledger accounts – a service business

In the supplement to Chapter 2 it was shown that the rules for debit and credit bookkeeping may be summarised in terms of the elements of the accounting equation as shown in Table 5.5.

Table 5.5
Rules for debit and credit entries in ledger accounts

	Debit entries in a ledger account	Credit entries in a ledger account
Left-hand side of the equation		
Asset	Increase	Decrease
Right-hand side of the equation		
Liability	Decrease	Increase
Ownership interest	Expense	Revenue
	Capital withdrawn	Capital contributed

In the supplement to Chapter 3 a spreadsheet was used to show that a series of transactions could be analysed and summarised in tabular form. That spreadsheet format is becoming increasingly used as the basis for computer-based recording of transactions but the more conventional approach to analysing transactions is to collect them together in ledger accounts. This supplement takes the transactions of Chapter 5 and analyses them in debit and credit form in order to produce a trial balance as a basis for the preparation of financial statements.

In Table 5.1 some common transactions of a service business were listed and then analysed using the accounting equation. They will now be analysed in terms of where the debit and credit entries would be made in a ledger account. Test yourself by trying out the answer before you look at the answer in Table 5.6 below. Once you are satisfied that you could produce the correct answer for the transactions in Table 5.1, you are ready to deal with Dr Lee's medical practice.

Illustration: Dr Lee's medical practice

The first transaction in Table 5.2 reads:

> Oct. 1   Dr Lee provides the practice with cash, £50,000.

The two aspects of this transaction were identified as:

1 Acquisition of an asset (cash).
2 Increasing the ownership interest (voluntary contribution).

The bookkeeping system requires two ledger accounts in which to record this transaction. One ledger account is called Cash and the other is called Ownership interest.

Table 5.6
Analysis of service business transactions (from Table 5.1) to identify two aspects of each

Transaction	Aspects of the transaction	Debit entry in	Credit entry in
Receive cash from the owner	Acquisition of an asset (cash)	Cash	
	Acceptance of ownership interest		Ownership interest
Buy a vehicle for cash	Acquisition of an asset (vehicle)	Vehicle	
	Reduction in an asset (cash)		Cash
Receive a bill for gas consumed	Incur an expense (gas consumed)	Gas expense	
	Incur a liability (to the gas supplier)		Supplier
Pay the gas bill in cash	Decrease a liability (to the gas supplier)	Supplier	
	Reduction in an asset (cash)		Cash
Buy materials for cash	Increase in an asset (inventory of materials)	Inventory (stock)	
	Decrease in an asset (cash)		Cash
Buy materials on credit	Acquisition of an asset (inventory of materials)	Inventory (stock)	
	Incur a liability (to the supplier)		Supplier
Sell services for cash	Acquisition of an asset (cash)	Cash	
	Earn revenue		Sales
Sell services on credit	Acquisition of an asset (trade receivables)	Trade receivables (debtors)	
	Earn revenue		Sales
Pay wages to an employee	Incur an expense (cost of wages)	Wages expense	
	Decrease in asset (cash)		Cash
Pay cash to the owner for personal use	Reduction in the ownership interest	Ownership interest	
	Reduction in an asset (cash)		Cash

There will be a *debit* entry of £50,000 in the Cash ledger account showing that the business has acquired an asset of £50,000 cash. There will be a *credit* entry of £50,000 in the Ownership interest ledger account showing that the business acknowledges the claim of the owner for eventual return of the amount contributed.

The second transaction in Table 5.2 reads:

> Oct. 2   The entity acquires medical equipment for cash, £30,000.

The two aspects of this transaction were identified as:

1 Acquisition of an asset (medical equipment).
2 Decrease of an asset (cash).

Table 5.7

Analysis of debit and credit aspect of each transaction of the medical practice

Date	Business transactions of medical practice	Amount	Debit	Credit
		£		
Oct. 1	Dr Lee provides the practice with cash to allow business to start.	50,000	Cash	Owner
Oct. 2	The entity acquires medical equipment for cash.	30,000	Equipment	Cash
Oct. 2	One month's rent is paid in advance for consulting rooms.	1,900	Rent	Cash
Oct. 2	Office furniture is purchased on two months' credit from Office Supplies Company.	6,500	Furniture	Office Supplies Company
Oct. 7	The practice purchases medical supplies on credit from P. Jones and receives an invoice.	1,200	Inventory (stock)	P. Jones
Oct. 8	Dr Lee pays the medical receptionist for one week's work, 2 to 8 October.	300	Wages	Cash
Oct. 10	Four patients are examined, each paying £500 cash.	2,000	Cash	Patients' fees
Oct. 11	The business pays P. Jones in cash for the goods it acquired on credit.	1,200	P. Jones	Cash
Oct. 14	The business pays an electricity bill in cash.	100	Electricity	Cash
Oct. 15	Dr Lee pays the medical receptionist for one week's work, 9 to 15 October.	300	Wages	Cash
Oct. 17	Three patients are examined, their employer (Mrs West) being sent an invoice requesting payment of £500 for each.	1,500	Mrs West	Fees
Oct. 22	Dr Lee pays the medical receptionist for one week's work, 16 to 22 October.	300	Wages	Cash
Oct. 23	The employer (Mrs West) pays in cash an invoice requesting payment of £500 for each.	1,500	Cash	Mrs West
Oct. 24	Four patients are examined, their employer (Mr East) being sent an invoice requesting payment of £500 for each.	2,000	Mr East	Fees
Oct. 28	Dr Lee draws cash from the business for personal use.	1,000	Owner	Cash
Oct. 29	Dr Lee pays the medical receptionist for one week's work, 23 to 29 October.	300	Wages	Cash
Oct. 31	The medical equipment and office furniture is estimated by Dr Lee to have fallen in value over the month.	250	Depreciation	Equipment and furniture
Oct. 31	Dr Lee checks the inventory (stock) of medical supplies and finds that items costing £350 have been used during the month.	350	Medical supplies expense	Inventory (stock)

The bookkeeping system requires two ledger accounts in which to record this transaction. One ledger account is called Medical equipment and the other is called Cash.

There will be a *debit* entry of £30,000 in the Medical equipment ledger account showing that the business has acquired an asset of £30,000 medical equipment.

There will be a *credit* entry of £30,000 in the Cash ledger account showing that the business has reduced its asset of cash by £30,000 to pay for the medical equipment.

Analysing the debit and credit entries for each transaction

Table 5.7 takes the information contained in Table 5.2 and analyses it under debit and credit headings showing the ledger accounts in which each entry will be made.

Ledger accounts required to record these transactions are:

L1 Cash	L8 Inventory (stock) of medical supplies
L2 Ownership interest	L9 P. Jones
L3 Medical equipment and office furniture	L10 Electricity
L4 Office Supplies Company	L11 Mrs West
L5 Rent	L12 Mr East
L6 Wages	L13 Depreciation
L7 Patients' fees	L14 Expense of medical supplies

Form of ledger accounts

There is no single standard form of ledger account rulings in which to record debit and credit transactions. Historically, ledger accounts were recorded in what were called 'T' accounts where all the debit entries were on the left-hand side and all the credit entries on the right-hand side. This was designed to minimise arithmetic errors by avoiding subtractions in systems which were dealt with manually.

Form of a 'T' ledger account

Page number and name of the account

Debit entries				Credit entries			
Date	*Particulars*	*Page*	*£ p*	*Date*	*Particulars*	*Page*	*£ p*

This type of layout requires a wide page if it is to be read clearly. In recent years ledger accounts have more frequently been prepared in a 'three-column' ruling which keeps a running total. This book will use the three-column ruling throughout. You will see by comparison of the column headings that the different types of rulings use the same information. If you have an opportunity to look at business ledgers you will probably come across yet more varieties, but they will all require the inclusion of this basic set of information.

Three-column ruling

Date	Particulars	Page	Debit		Credit		Balance	
			£	p	£	p	£	p

Features are:

- The left-hand column will show the date of the transaction.
- The 'particulars' column will show essential narrative, usually confined to the name of the ledger account which records the other aspect of the transaction.
- The 'page' column will show the ledger account page number of the ledger account where the other aspect of the transaction is recorded.
- The amount of the transaction will be entered in the debit or credit column as appropriate.
- The 'balance' column will keep a running total by treating all debit entries as positive and all credit entries as negative. A credit balance will be shown in brackets as a reminder that it is negative. Some ledger systems print the letters 'dr' or 'cr' against the balance.

Illustration

The first transaction of Table 5.7 may now be shown in the appropriate ledger accounts. It will require a *debit* entry in a cash account to indicate an increase in the asset of cash and a *credit* entry in the ownership interest account to indicate an increase in the owner's claim.

L1 Cash

Date	Particulars	Page	Debit	Credit	Balance
			£	£	£
Oct. 1	Ownership interest	L2	50,000		50,000

L2 Ownership interest

Date	Particulars	Page	Debit	Credit	Balance
			£	£	£
Oct. 1	Cash	L1		50,000	(50,000)

Ledger accounts for Dr Lee's medical practice

The full ledger account record for the transactions in Table 5.7 is now set out. Leona Rees comments on each ledger account, showing how she interprets ledger accounts in her work of auditing and accounting.

L1 Cash

Date	Particulars	Page	Debit	Credit	Balance
			£	£	£
Oct. 1	Ownership interest	L2	50,000		50,000
Oct. 2	Medical equipment	L3		30,000	20,000
Oct. 2	Rent	L5		1,900	18,100
Oct. 8	Wages	L6		300	17,800
Oct. 10	Patients' fees	L7	2,000		19,800
Oct. 11	P. Jones	L9		1,200	18,600
Oct. 14	Electricity	L10		100	18,500
Oct. 15	Wages	L6		300	18,200
Oct. 22	Wages	L6		300	17,900
Oct. 23	Mrs West	L11	1,500		19,400
Oct. 28	Ownership interest taken as	L2		1,000	18,400
Oct. 29	Wages	L6		300	18,100

LEONA's comment: *The amount of £50,000 put into the business at the start is quickly eaten into by spending cash on medical equipment and paying rent in advance. Further items such as paying a supplier, paying the electricity account and the assistant's wages took the cash balance down further but it remained quite high throughout the month. With the benefit of hindsight the owner might not have needed to put so much cash into the business at the outset. Up to £18,000 could have been invested on a short-term basis to earn interest, either for the business or for Dr Lee.*

L2 Ownership interest

Date	Particulars	Page	Debit	Credit	Balance
			£	£	£
Oct. 1	Cash contributed	L1		50,000	(50,000)
Oct. 28	Cash drawn	L1	1,000		(49,000)

LEONA's comment: *The ownership interest is created when the owner contributes cash or resources to the business. In this case it was cash. The sole trader in business may withdraw cash for personal use at any time – it is called owner's drawings – but the desirability of that action depends on how useful cash is to the owner when compared to how useful it might have been if left in the business. The owner of this business has a claim remaining equal to £49,000 after making the drawing.*

L3 Medical equipment and office furniture

Date	Particulars	Page	Debit	Credit	Balance
			£	£	£
Oct. 2	Cash	L1	30,000		30,000
Oct. 2	Office Supplies Company	L4	6,500		36,500
Oct. 31	Depreciation	L13		250	36,250

LEONA's comment: *This ledger account is particularly useful as a reminder that some very valuable assets are owned by the business. Having a record in the ledger account encourages the owner to think about continuing care for the medical equipment and office furniture and also to review their value against the amount recorded. If Dr Lee intended to have a large number of fixed asset items it is possible to have a separate ledger account for each, but that seems a long-distant prospect at the moment.*

Depreciation is a way of showing that the original cost of the asset has to be spread over its useful life. If the estimate of depreciation is correct, this ledger account should reduce to nil on the day the equipment and furniture ceases to be of use. In reality, things usually are not quite so straightforward. (Depreciation of non-current (fixed) assets is dealt with in more detail in Chapter 8.)

L4 Office Supplies Company

Date	Particulars	Page	Debit	Credit	Balance
			£	£	£
Oct. 2	Office furniture	L3		6,500	(6,500)

LEONA's comment: *When the office furniture was purchased from the Office Supplies Company, an invoice was received from that company showing the amount due. That invoice was used to make the credit entry on 2 October showing that the business had a liability. The liability remained owing at 31 October, but that is acceptable because the supplier allowed two months' credit.*

L5 Rent

Date	Particulars	Page	Debit	Credit	Balance
			£	£	£
Oct. 2	Cash	L1	1,900		1,900

LEONA's comment: *This payment in advance starts by being an asset and gradually turns into an expense as the benefit is used up. For bookkeeping purposes, a debit entry records both an asset and an expense so it is only at the end of the month that some care is needed in thinking about the nature of the debit balance. In this case it is clear that the benefit is used up but there could be a situation where part of the benefit remained to be reported as an asset.*

L6 Wages

Date	Particulars	Page	Debit	Credit	Balance
			£	£	£
Oct. 8	Cash	L1	300		300
Oct. 15	Cash	L1	300		600
Oct. 22	Cash	L1	300		900
Oct. 29	Cash	L1	300		1,200

LEONA's comment: *This is a straightforward account in which to accumulate all wages expenses. A very enthusiastic accountant would estimate the liability for the final two days of the month and add these on, but there is a very useful idea in accounting called 'materiality' which, broadly interpreted, means the extra information provided would not justify the extra amount of work involved.*

L7 Patients' fees

Date	Particulars	Page	Debit	Credit	Balance
			£	£	£
Oct. 10	Cash	L1		2,000	(2,000)
Oct. 17	Credit: Mrs West (as employer)	L11		1,500	(3,500)
Oct. 24	Credit: Mr East (as employer)	L12		2,000	(5,500)

LEONA's comment: *This is a revenue account so credit entries are expected. The balance column shows the total patients' fees earned in the month were £5,500. This could be described as 'turnover' or 'sales' but both of those words sound rather out of place when a professional service is being described.*

L8 Inventory (stock) of medical supplies

Date	Particulars	Page	Debit	Credit	Balance
			£	£	£
Oct. 7	P. Jones	L9	1,200		1,200
Oct. 31	Expense of medical supplies	L14		350	850

LEONA's comment: *This is an asset account so when the medical supplies were acquired on credit from P. Jones the entire amount was recorded as an asset. These medical supplies will be quite small items and it would not be appropriate for Dr Lee to have to count every cotton wool swab, hypodermic needle or sample bottle used in each examination. It is sufficient for accounting purposes to count up what is left at the end of the period (we call it 'taking stock') and assume that the difference represents the amount used during the period. As an auditor, I might start to ask questions about possible errors, fraud or theft if the amounts of supplies used did not look sensible when compared with the number of examinations carried out on patients.*

L9 P. Jones

Date	Particulars	Page	Debit	Credit	Balance
			£	£	£
Oct. 7	Inventory (stock) of medical supplies	L8		1,200	(1,200)
Oct. 11	Cash	L1	1,200		nil

LEONA's comment: *When the medical supplies were delivered to Dr Lee, the business took on a liability to pay P. Jones. That liability was recorded by a credit entry in the ledger account for P. Jones and was extinguished on 11 October when the medical practice paid £1,200 to P. Jones.*

L10 Electricity

Date	Particulars	Page	Debit	Credit	Balance
			£	£	£
Oct. 14	Cash	L1	100		100

LEONA's comment: *This is a very straightforward expense account. The balance on this account will show the total expense of electricity consumed during the period.*

L11 Mrs West

Date	Particulars	Page	Debit	Credit	Balance
			£	£	£
Oct. 17	Patients' fees	L7	1,500		1,500
Oct. 23	Cash	L1		1,500	nil

L12 Mr East

Date	Particulars	Page	Debit	Credit	Balance
			£	£	£
Oct. 24	Patients' fees	L7	2,000		2,000

LEONA's comment: *The credit sale to the employees of Mrs West and Mr East made them trade receivables (debtors) of the business and so there is a debit entry. By the end of October Mr East had not paid, so remains a debtor, denoted by a debit balance. Mrs West has paid during October and a nil balance is the result.*

L13 Depreciation

Date	Particulars	Page	Debit	Credit	Balance
			£	£	£
Oct. 31	Medical equipment and office furniture	L3	250		250

LEONA's comment: *This is another expense account showing an item which has decreased the ownership interest through a decrease in the recorded amount of some assets. This is where accounting begins to look slightly complicated because no cash has changed hands. Recording depreciation is the accounting way of expressing caution as to the expected future benefits from an asset. These will be eroded as the asset is used up. Depreciation is a way of acknowledging that erosion.*

L14 Expense of medical supplies

Date	Particulars	Page	Debit	Credit	Balance
			£	£	£
Oct. 31	Inventory (stock) of medical supplies	L8	350		350

LEONA's comment: *This account continues the story from L8 where the inventory (stock) of medical supplies was found to have dwindled through use in examining patients. It is assumed that the difference between the amount purchased and the amount held at the end of the month represents the expense of using the asset during the month.*

Checking the accuracy of double-entry records

At periodic intervals it may be considered necessary for a number of reasons to check the accuracy of the entries made in ledger accounts. For instance, the omission of an entry on the debit side of a customer's ledger account for goods sold on credit terms could result in a failure to issue reminders for payment of an amount owed to the business.

There are methods in double-entry bookkeeping of discovering these and other errors. One such method is the use of the *trial balance*.

If a debit entry and a credit entry have been made in the appropriate ledger accounts for each business transaction, then the total money amount of all the debit entries will equal the total money amount of all the credit entries. If a debit entry has been made without a corresponding credit entry (or vice versa), then the totals will not agree.

In the ledger accounts shown in this example, the balances have been kept as running totals. It would be possible to add up all the debit and all the credit entries in each ledger account but the same arithmetic proof will be obtained by listing all the debit balances and all the credit balances. It was explained earlier in this supplement that brackets are used in the ledger accounts to show credit balances. The list of balances on all the ledger accounts for Dr Lee's medical practice is set out in Table 5.8.

Error detection using the trial balance

The calculation of the totals of each column of the trial balance is a useful precaution which will reveal some, but not all, of the errors it is possible to make in a debit and credit recording system. Think first about the errors you might make and then check against the following list:

Table 5.8

Trial balance at 31 October for Dr Lee's medical practice

Ledger account title		Debit	Credit
		£	£
L1	Cash	18,100	
L2	Ownership interest		49,000
L3	Medical equipment and office furniture	36,250	
L4	Office Supplies Company		6,500
L5	Rent	1,900	
L6	Wages	1,200	
L7	Patients' fees		5,500
L8	Inventory (stock) of medical supplies	850	
L9	P. Jones		nil
L10	Electricity	100	
L11	Mrs West	nil	
L12	Mr East	2,000	
L13	Depreciation	250	
L14	Expense of medical supplies	350	
Totals		61,000	61,000

Errors which will be detected by unequal totals in the trial balance

- Omitting one aspect of a transaction (e.g. a debit entry but no credit entry).
- Writing incorrect amounts in one entry (e.g. debit £290 but credit £209).
- Writing both entries in one column (e.g. two debits, no credit).
- Incorrect calculation of ledger account balance.

Errors which will leave the trial balance totals equal

- Total omission of a transaction.
- Errors in both debit and credit entry of the same magnitude.
- Entering the correct amount in the wrong ledger account (e.g. debit for wages entered as debit for heat and light).

Preparing the financial statements

The main part of this chapter set out the statement of financial position (balance sheet) and income statement (profit and loss account) of Dr Lee's medical practice for the month of October. If you compare the amounts in the trial balance with the amounts in the financial statements you will see they are the same. The normal practice in accounting is to use the trial balance to prepare the statement of financial position (balance sheet) and income statement (profit and loss account).

In this case it would be a little easier to use the trial balance for this purpose if it were arranged so that all the statement of financial position (balance sheet) items are

Table 5.9
Rearranging the trial balance into statement of financial position (balance sheet) items and income statement (profit and loss account) items

Ledger account title	£	£
L3 Medical equipment and office furniture	36,250	
L8 Inventory (stock) of medical supplies	850	
L12 Mr East	2,000	
L11 Mrs West	nil	
L1 Cash at bank	18,100	
L4 Office Supplies Company		6,500
L9 P. Jones		nil
L2 Ownership interest		49,000
Subtotal X	57,200	55,500
Difference: profit of the month (57,200 – 55,000)		1,700
L7 Patients' fees		5,500
L14 Expense of medical supplies	350	
L6 Wages	1,200	
L5 Rent	1,900	
L10 Electricity	100	
L13 Depreciation	250	
Subtotal Y	3,800	5,500
Difference: profit of the month (5,500 – 3,800)	1,700	
Total of ledger balances in each column X + Y	61,000	61,000

together and all the income statement (profit and loss account) items are together. This is done in Table 5.9.

This form of trial balance will be used in later chapters as the starting point for the preparation of financial statements.

By way of providing further help in preparing the income statement (profit and loss account) and statement of financial position (balance sheet), subtotals are calculated for each part of the trial balance in Table 5.9. The difference between the subtotals in each section gives the profit amount. That is because the exhibit has been subdivided according to two equations, each of which leads to profit:

Assets	minus	Liabilities	minus	Capital contributed/withdrawn	equals	Profit

Revenue	minus	Expenses	equals	Profit

S   Test your understanding

S5.1   Prepare ledger accounts for the transactions of Jane Gate's dental practice, listed in question A5.5.

S5.2   Which of the following errors would be detected at the point of listing a trial balance?

   (a) The bookkeeper enters a cash sale as a debit of £49 in the cash book and as a credit of £94 in the sales account.
   (b) The bookkeeper omits a cash sale of £23 from the cash book and from the sales accounts.
   (c) The bookkeeper enters cash received of £50 from Peter Jones as a debit in the cashbook but enters the credit of £50 in the ledger account of Roger Jones.
   (d) The bookkeeper enters a cash sale as a credit of £40 in the cash book and as a debit of £40 in the sales account.

Chapter 6

Accounting information for trading businesses

REAL WORLD CASE

Sales and profit performance for the Group

Gross transaction value for the Group for the 53 weeks to 3 September 2011 of £2,679.3 million increased by 4.5% over the previous year. For the 52 weeks to 27 August 2011, Group gross transaction value grew by 2.9%. The primary drivers of gross transaction growth were the multi-channel business, Magasin du Nord, international sales and new UK space.

Revenue for the 53 week period was £2,209.8 million, 4.2% higher than last year. On a 52 week basis, revenue increased by 2.7%.

Like-for-like sales including VAT increased by 1.2% over the 52 week period. Excluding VAT, like-for-like sales for this period were slightly lower, down 0.3%. This was a good result given the difficult economic environment and the disruption to sales arising out of the adverse winter weather across the UK in November and December which alone adversely impacted like-for-like sales for the year by some 1%.

Group gross margin fell slightly by 20 basis points during the year. This was partly a result of a decision to maximise cash profit by driving sales during the second half of the year and partly some oneoff benefits in last year's figure as a result of the acquisition of the Faith footwear brand.

Gross profit before exceptional items for the year increased from £290.4 million to £296.7 million, an increase of 2.2% for the year.

Headline profit before tax for the year, which adds back amortisation of capitalised bank fees and exceptionals, for the 53 week year increased by 10.0% year-on-year from £151.0 million to £166.1 million.

Reported profit before tax and exceptionals rose by 10.3% to £160.3 million from £145.3 million for the same period last year.

Basic earnings per share for 2011 were 9.1 pence (2010: 7.5 pence) and diluted earnings per share were also 9.1 pence (2010: 7.5 pence).

Source: Debenhams 2011 Annual Report, p. 28; http://media.corporate-ir.net/media_files/IROL/19/196805/agm2011/ar2011.pdf.

Discussion points

1 How does the company describe its trading performance?

2 How does the company measure trends in operating performance?

Contents

Learning outcomes

After studying this chapter you should be able to:

- Explain the application of the accounting equation to transactions involving the buying and selling of inventory (trading stock).
- Explain the application of the accounting equation to transactions involving the manufacture and sale of products.
- Analyse transactions of a trading or manufacturing business during a specific period of time, using the accounting equation.
- Prepare a spreadsheet analysing the transactions, and show that the results of the spreadsheet analysis are consistent with financial statements provided by the organisation.
- Explain the main aspects of the statement of cash flows, profit and loss account and statement of financial position (balance sheet) of a trading or a manufacturing business.

Additionally, for those who choose to study the supplement:

- Analyse the transactions of a trading or a manufacturing business using the rules of debit and credit bookkeeping.
- Prepare, from a list of transactions of an organisation, ledger accounts and a trial balance which could be used to confirm the financial statements provided by the organisation.

6.1 Introduction

Chapter 5 has shown in detail the application of the accounting equation to the analysis of transactions in service businesses. The same approach applies in the case of trading businesses, but with one significant addition. Businesses which engage in trading have either purchased or manufactured a product with the intention of selling that product to customers. It is the purchase or manufacture of a product and the act of selling the product which must be analysed carefully in terms of the accounting equation. This chapter first analyses the transactions and events occurring when goods are purchased for resale and sold to a customer. Secondly, it analyses the transactions and events occurring when goods are manufactured and then sold to a customer. Finally, there is a worked example which takes one month's transactions of a trading business and shows the resulting financial statements.

6.2 Goods purchased for resale

A trading business which buys goods for resale (e.g. a wholesaler buying goods from a manufacturer for distribution to retailers) makes a profit by selling the goods at a price which is higher than the price paid. The difference between the selling price and the purchase price is called the **gross profit** of the business. The gross profit must be sufficient to cover all the costs of running the business (e.g. administration, marketing and distribution costs) and leave a net profit which will increase the ownership interest in the business.

6.2.1 Analysis of transactions

Consider the transactions of a trading company set out in Table 6.1, relating to buying and selling goods.

Table 6.1
Transactions of a trading company

		£
Apr. 1	Purchase goods from manufacturer, 100 items at £2 each, paying in cash, and store in warehouse.	200
Apr. 4	Remove 70 items from warehouse to meet a customer's request. Those 70 items cost £2 each on 1 April. They are delivered to the customer, who accepts the delivery.	140
Apr. 4	The customer pays in cash. Selling price is £2.50 per item.	175

What is the profit on the sale of 70 items? Each one cost £2.00 and is sold for £2.50, so there is a profit of 50 pence per item or £35 for 70 items. In accounting, that calculation might be set out as follows:

	£
Sale of goods (70 items)	175
Cost of goods sold (70 items)	(140)
Gross profit	35

There is an asset of unsold goods (30 items) which cost £2 each or £60 in total. Since that item is an asset, it will appear in the statement of financial position (balance sheet).

That is a statement of the gross profit and of the monetary amount of the asset of unsold goods, using common sense and intuition to arrive at an answer. Now look at how a systematic analysis is undertaken in accounting.

6.2.2 Analysis of transactions and events

Apr. 1	Purchase goods from manufacturer, 100 items at £2 each, paying in cash, and store in warehouse	£200

This transaction has two aspects in terms of the accounting equation. It *increases* the **asset** of inventory (stock of goods) and it *decreases* the **asset** of cash. One asset increases, another decreases by an equal amount and there is no effect on the ownership interest.

Assets ↑↓ – Liabilities	equals	Ownership interest

Apr. 4	Remove 70 items from warehouse to meet customer's request. Those 70 items cost £2 each on 1 April. They are delivered to the customer, who accepts the delivery.	£140

This is an event which is not a transaction. The goods which are in the store are removed to a more convenient place for sale to the customer. In this case they are removed to a delivery van and transported to the customer. The moment of delivery to, and acceptance by, the customer is the event which transforms the goods from an asset to an expense. By that event, ownership is transferred to the customer, who either pays cash immediately or agrees to pay in the future. The expense is called **cost of goods sold**.

It should be noted at this point that the acts of physical removal and transport are events which financial accounting does not record, because at that point there is not sufficient evidence for recognition that a sale has taken place. In management accounting you will find that quite a different attitude is taken to events which involve moving goods from one location to another. In management accounting, such movements are recorded in order to help the managerial process of control.

In terms of the accounting equation there is a *decrease* in the **asset** of inventory (stock) because it is no longer owned by the business and there can be no future benefit from the item. The benefit has occurred on this day, creating a sale by the act of delivery and acceptance.

If an asset has decreased then the **ownership interest** must also have *decreased* through an expense. The expense is called cost of goods sold.

Assets ↓ – Liabilities	equals	Ownership interest ↓ (expense: cost of goods sold)

Apr. 4	The customer pays in cash. Selling price is £2.50 per item.	£175

The final transaction is the payment of cash by the customer. In timing, it will occur almost simultaneously with the delivery and acceptance of the goods. In accounting it is nevertheless analysed separately. The business receives an *increase* in the **asset** of cash and the **ownership interest** *is increased* by an act which has earned **revenue** for the business.

Assets ↑ – Liabilities	equals	Ownership interest ↑ (revenue)

Activity 6.1

*Return to Table 6.1 and change the cost price to £3 and the selling price to £3.50.
Calculate the profit if the customer receives (a) 70 items, (b) 80 items, (c) 90 items and
(d) 100 items. How many items remain in inventory (stock) in each of these four cases?
What can you say about the pattern of profit which appears from the four calculations
you have carried out? Now write down the effect on the accounting equation for each of
these four separate situations. Doing this will help you to test your own understanding
before you proceed further.*

6.2.3 Spreadsheet summarising the transactions

It is possible to bring the analysis together in a spreadsheet similar to that used in
Chapter 5, but containing column headings which are appropriate to the assets
involved in these transactions. Table 6.2 shows the spreadsheet. Table 6.3 summarises
the impact of the accounting equation, showing that the assets remaining at the end
of the period, £35 in total, equal the sum of the opening capital at the start (nil in this
case) plus revenue, £175, minus expenses, £140.

Table 6.2
Spreadsheet analysing transactions and events into elements of the accounting equation

Date	Transaction or event	Assets		Ownership interest	
		Cash £	Inventory (stock) £	Revenue + £	Expense − £
Apr. 1	Purchase goods from manufacturer, paying in cash, 100 items at £2 each, and place in warehouse.	(200)	200		
Apr. 4	Remove 70 items from warehouse to meet customer's request. Those 70 items cost £2 each on Apr. 1. They are delivered to the customer, who accepts the delivery.		(140)		140
Apr. 4	The customer pays in cash. Selling price is £2.50 per item.	175		175	
	Totals at end of period	(25)	60	175	140

└─── 35 ───┘

Table 6.3
Summary of transactions analysed into the elements of the accounting equation

Assets	minus	Liabilities	=	Ownership interest at start of period	plus	Capital contributed/ withdrawn	plus	Revenue	minus	Expenses
£35	−	nil	=	nil	+	nil	+	£175	−	£140

6.3 Manufacturing goods for resale

The manufacture of goods for resale requires the purchase of raw materials which
are used in production of the finished goods. There are several stages here where the
business may hold an asset of one type or another. Any unused raw materials will

represent a benefit for the future and therefore be treated as an asset. Any finished goods which are not sold will also represent a benefit for the future and therefore be treated as an asset. Less obvious than these two items is the expected future benefit of partly completed goods that may be in the production process at the accounting date. That is also regarded as an asset, called work in progress. If the manufacturing process is rapid, then at any date there will be relatively little work in progress. If the manufacturing process is slow, there could be significant amounts of work in progress at an accounting date.

6.3.1 Analysis of transactions

Consider the transactions of a manufacturing company which are set out in Table 6.4. The company buys breakfast trays and customises them to designs requested by catering outlets.

Table 6.4
Transactions of a manufacturing company

		£
July 1	Purchase raw materials from supplier, 100 trays at £2 each, paying in cash, and place in raw materials store.	200
July 3	Remove 80 trays from raw materials store to meet production department's request (cost £2 each).	160
July 4	Carry out labour work and use production facilities to convert raw materials into finished goods. Additional costs incurred for labour and use of facilities were £1.50 per tray processed.	120
July 5	Finished goods are transferred to finished goods store. The job has cost £3.50 per tray in total (80 trays × £3.50 = £280).	280
July 10	60 trays, which cost £3.50 each to manufacture, are delivered to a customer.	210
July 10	The customer pays a price of £5 cash per tray immediately on delivery.	300

What is the profit on the sale of 60 trays? Each one cost £3.50 to manufacture and is sold for £5.00 so there is a profit of £1.50 per item or £90 for 60 items.

The business retains an inventory (stock) of 20 unsold finished trays which cost £3.50 each to manufacture (a cost of £70 in total) and an inventory (stock) of unused raw materials (20 basic trays costing £2 each which is a total cost of £40).

That is a statement of the position using common sense and intuition to arrive at an answer. Now look at how a systematic analysis is undertaken in accounting.

6.3.2 Analysis of transactions and events

July 1	Purchase raw materials from supplier, 100 trays at £2 each, paying in cash, and place in raw materials store.	£200

The business experiences an *increase* in the **asset** of inventory (stock) of raw materials and a *decrease* in the **asset** of cash. In terms of the accounting equation there is an increase in one asset matched by a decrease in another and there is no effect on the ownership interest.

Assets ↑↓ – Liabilities		equals	Ownership interest

July 3	Remove 80 trays from raw materials store to meet production department's request (cost £2 each).	£160

Next, some of the raw materials are removed for use in production. This is an event, rather than a transaction, but is recorded because it creates a possible asset of work in progress. The **asset** of work in progress *increases* and the **asset** of raw materials *decreases*. There is no effect on the ownership claim.

Assets ↑↓ – Liabilities		equals	Ownership interest

July 4	Carry out labour work and use production facilities to convert raw materials into finished goods. Additional costs incurred for labour and use of facilities were £1.50 per tray processed.	£120

The next stage is that some work is done to convert the raw materials into the product desired by customers. The work involves labour cost and other costs of using the production facilities. (You will find in management accounting that the other costs of using production facilities are usually described as **production overheads**.) This payment for labour and use of production facilities is adding to the value of the basic tray and so is adding to the value of the asset of work in progress (which will eventually become the asset of finished goods). So there is an *increase* in the **asset** of work in progress and a *decrease* in the **asset** of cash. There is no effect on the ownership interest.

Assets ↑↓ – Liabilities		equals	Ownership interest

July 5	Finished goods are transferred to finished goods store. The job has cost £3.50 per tray in total (80 trays × £3.50 = £280).	£280

When the work in progress is complete, it becomes finished goods and is transferred to the store. The **asset** of work in progress *decreases* and the **asset** of finished goods *increases*. A measure of the value of the asset is the cost of making it which, in this case, is £3.50 per item or £280 for 80 items. Again, there is no effect on the ownership interest.

Assets ↑↓ – Liabilities		equals	Ownership interest

July 10	60 trays, which cost £3.50 each to manufacture, are delivered to a customer.	£210

The customer now requests 60 trays and these are delivered from the store to the customer. At the moment of acceptance by the customer, the 60 trays cease to be an asset of the business. There is a *decrease* in an **asset** and a *decrease* in the **ownership interest** which is recorded as an **expense** of cost of goods sold.

Assets ↓ – Liabilities		equals	**Ownership interest** ↓ **(expense: cost of goods sold)**

The owner's disappointment is momentary because the act of acceptance by the customer results in immediate payment being received from the customer (or in some cases a promise of future payment).

July 10	The customer pays a price of £5 cash per tray immediately on delivery.	£300

When the customer pays immediately for the goods, there is an *increase* in the **asset** of cash and a corresponding *increase* in the **ownership interest**, recorded as **revenue** of the business.

Assets ↑ – Liabilities	equals	Ownership interest ↑ (revenue)

Activity 6.2

Return to Table 6.4. Without looking to the rest of the section, write down the effect of each transaction on the accounting equation. At what point in the sequence of events in Table 6.4 is the ownership interest affected? Why is it not affected before that point in the sequence? How would the ownership interest have been affected if, on 5 July, there had been a fire as the goods were being transferred to the finished goods store and one-quarter of the finished trays were destroyed?

6.3.3 Spreadsheet summarising the transactions

Table 6.5 brings the analysis together in a spreadsheet similar to that used in Table 6.2, showing the effect of each transaction separately and also the overall effect on the accounting equation. Table 6.6 sets out the accounting equation at the end of the period and shows that the assets remaining at the end of the period are equal to the ownership interest at the start (which is taken as nil in this example) plus the profit of the period.

Once you have understood the analysis up to this point, you are ready to embark on the financial statements of a trading business.

6.4 Illustration of accounting for a trading business

This example considers the business of M. Carter, wholesale trader. At the start of May, M. Carter commenced a trading business as a wholesaler, buying goods from manufacturers and storing them in a warehouse from which customers could be supplied. All the customers are small shopkeepers who need the services of the wholesaler because they are not sufficiently powerful in purchasing power to negotiate terms directly with the manufacturers.

In Table 6.7 there is a list of transactions for M. Carter's wholesaling business during the month of May. In section 6.4.1 each transaction is analysed using the accounting equation.

Activity 6.3

Before reading section 6.4.1, analyse each transaction in Table 6.7 using the accounting equation. (If necessary look back to Chapter 5 for a similar pattern of analysis.) Then compare your answer against the detail of section 6.4.1. If there is any item where you have a different answer, consult your lecturer, tutor or other expert before proceeding with the rest of the chapter.

Table 6.5
Spreadsheet analysing transactions and events into elements of the accounting equation

Date	Transaction or event	Assets				Ownership interest	
		Cash at bank £	Raw materials inventory (stock) £	Work in progress £	Finished goods £	Revenue + £	Expenses − £
July 1	Purchase raw materials from supplier, paying in cash, trays at £2 each, and place 100 in raw materials store.	(200)	200				
July 3	Remove 80 trays from raw materials store to meet production department's request (cost £2 each).		(160)	160			
July 4	Carry out labour work and use production facilities to convert raw materials into finished goods. Additional costs incurred for labour and use of facilities were £1.50 per tray processed.	(120)		120			
July 5	Finished goods are transferred to finished goods store. The job has cost £3.50 per tray in total (80 trays × £3.50 = £280).			(280)	280		
July 10	60 trays, which cost £3.50 each to manufacture, are delivered to a customer.				(210)		210
July 10	The customer pays a price of £5 cash per tray immediately on delivery.	300				300	
	Totals at the end of the period.	(20)	40	nil	70	300	210

⌞———— 90 ————⌟

Table 6.6
Summary of transactions analysed into the elements of the accounting equation

Assets	minus	Liabilities	=	Ownership interest at start of period	plus	Capital contributed/ withdrawn	plus	Revenue	minus	Expenses
£90	−	nil	=	nil	+	nil	+	£300	−	£210

Table 6.7

Transactions of the business of M. Carter, wholesaler, for the month of May

Date	Business transactions and events (nature of the entity: wholesale trader)	Amount £
May 1	The owner pays cash into a bank account for the business.	50,000
May 2	The business acquires buildings for cash.	30,000
May 4	The business acquires equipment for cash.	6,000
May 6	The business purchases an inventory (stock) of goods for cash.	6,500
May 7	The business purchases an inventory (stock) of goods on credit from R. Busby and receives an invoice.	5,000
May 11	The business pays R. Busby in cash for the goods it acquired on credit.	5,000
May 14	The business pays an electricity bill in cash.	100
May 17	Items costing £3,500 are removed from the store because sales have been agreed with customers for this date.	3,500
May 17	The business sells items costing £2,000 to customers for a cash price of £4,000.	4,000
May 17	The business sells items costing £1,500 on credit to R. Welsby and sends an invoice for the price of £3,000.	3,000
May 24	R. Welsby pays in cash for the goods obtained on credit.	3,000
May 28	The owner draws cash from the business for personal use.	1,000
May 30	The business pays wages to an employee for the month, in cash.	2,000
May 31	The business discovers that its equipment has fallen in value over the month.	250

6.4.1 Explanation of the analysis of each transaction

May 1   When M. Carter provides the business with cash in a bank account to allow the company to proceed, the business *acquires* an **asset** of cash and the transaction *creates* an **ownership interest** for M. Carter on the assets of the business. Using the symbols of the accounting equation:

Assets ↑ – Liabilities	equals	Ownership interest ↑ (contribution of capital)

May 2   The wholesale business now becomes the business entity so far as accounting is concerned (although M. Carter may still be making the decisions as an owner/manager of the business). The entity acquires an asset of buildings in exchange for an asset of cash. There is an *increase* in one **asset** and a *decrease* in another **asset**. There is no impact on the ownership interest.

Assets ↑↓ – Liabilities	equals	Ownership interest

May 4   The entity acquires an asset of equipment in exchange for an asset of cash. There is an *increase* in the **asset** of equipment and a *decrease* in the **asset** of cash. There is no impact on the ownership interest.

Assets ↑↓ – Liabilities	equals	Ownership interest

May 6   The entity acquires an asset of inventory (stock) of goods in exchange for an asset of cash. There is an *increase* in the **asset** of inventory (stock) and a *decrease* in the **asset** of cash. There is no impact on the ownership interest.

Assets ↑↓ – Liabilities	equals	Ownership interest

May 7   The entity again acquires an asset of inventory (stock) of goods but this time it is related to the acquisition of a liability to R. Busby. There is an *increase* in the **asset** of inventory (stock) and an *increase* in the **liability** of receivables (creditors). There is no impact on the ownership interest.

Assets ↑ – **Liabilities** ↑	equals	Ownership interest

May 11   When payment is made to R. Busby there is a *decrease* in the **asset** of cash and a *decrease* in the **liability** to R. Busby.

Assets ↓ – **Liabilities** ↓	equals	Ownership interest

May 14   When the electricity bill is paid, the benefit of using the electricity has been consumed. There is a *decrease* in the **asset** of cash and a *decrease* in the **ownership interest**, reported as an expense.

Assets ↓ – Liabilities	equals	**Ownership interest** ↓ **(expense)**

May 17   At the moment of acceptance by the customer, the goods cease to be an asset of the business. There is a *decrease* in the **ownership interest** (recorded as an **expense** of cost of goods sold) and a *decrease* in the **asset** of inventory (stock).

Assets ↓ – Liabilities	equals	**Ownership interest** ↓ **(cost of goods sold)**

May 17   The owner's wealth is then immediately restored or enhanced because some customers pay cash for the goods. There is an *increase* in the **asset** of cash and a corresponding *increase* in the **ownership interest**, recorded as revenue of the business. The information about cost of goods sold has been dealt with in the previous equation.

Assets ↑ – Liabilities	equals	**Ownership interest** ↑ **(revenue)**

May 17   The owner's wealth is similarly restored by a promise from the customer to pay at a future date. This creates the asset of a trade receivable (debtor) which, in accounting, is regarded as acceptable in the overall measure of shareholder wealth. There is an *increase* in the **asset** of trade receivable (debtor) and a corresponding *increase* in the **ownership interest**, recorded as

revenue of the business. The information about cost of goods sold has been dealt with in the earlier equation.

Assets ↑ – Liabilities	equals	Ownership interest ↑ (revenue)

May 24   R. Welsby is a credit customer of the business, called a 'trade receivable' or a 'debtor'. When a credit customer makes payment to the business there is an *increase* in the **asset** of cash and a *decrease* in the **asset** of trade receivable (debtor). There is no effect on the ownership interest.

Assets ↑↓ – Liabilities	equals	Ownership interest

May 28   As was explained in Chapter 5, the owner of a sole trader business does not take a salary or wage as an employee would, but needs cash for personal purposes. Taking cash for personal use is called **drawings** and is recorded in terms of the accounting equation as a *decrease* in the **ownership interest** and a *decrease* in the **asset** of cash.

Assets ↓ – Liabilities	equals	Ownership interest ↓ (withdrawal of capital)

May 30   Paying wages is similar in effect to paying the electricity bill. The benefit of the employee's work has been consumed. There is a *decrease* in the **asset** of cash and a *decrease* in the **ownership interest**, reported as an **expense**.

Assets ↓ – Liabilities	equals	Ownership interest ↓ (expense)

May 31   All fixed assets will eventually be used up by the business, after several years of useful life. Depreciation is a recognition of the *decrease* in the **asset** and the *decrease* in the **ownership interest**, reported as an **expense**. (There is more on **depreciation** in Chapter 8.)

Assets ↓ – Liabilities	equals	Ownership interest ↓ (expense)

6.5   A process for summarising the transactions: a spreadsheet

In Table 6.8 the transactions of Table 6.7 are repeated at the left-hand side and are analysed into columns headed for assets, liabilities and ownership interest using brackets to show a negative amount. It would be equally acceptable to use a minus sign but minus signs tend to disappear or be confused with unintentional blobs on the paper, so brackets are frequently used in accounting in order to ensure clarity.

At the foot of the spreadsheet in Table 6.8 there is a total for each column. Those totals are used in Table 6.9 to show the state of the accounting equation at the end of the month. It may be used to explain to M. Carter how the ownership interest has changed over the month. The owner contributed £50,000 at the start of the month and has a claim of £50,150 at the end of the month. The ownership interest was increased by earning revenue of £7,000 but reduced by incurring expenses of £5,850 and withdrawing £1,000 for personal use.

Table 6.8
Spreadsheet analysing transactions into the elements of the accounting equation

Date	Business transactions	Assets Cash at bank £	Assets Inventory (stock) of goods £	Assets Non-current (fixed) assets and trade receivables (debtors) £	Liabilities Trade payables (creditors) £	Ownership interest Capital contributed/ withdrawn £	Ownership interest Revenue + £	Ownership interest Expenses − £
May 1	The owner provides the business with cash.	50,000				50,000		
May 2	The business acquires buildings for cash.	(30,000)		30,000				
May 4	The business acquires equipment for cash.	(6,000)		6,000				
May 6	The business purchases an inventory (stock) of goods for cash.	(6,500)	6,500					
May 7	The business purchases an inventory (stock) of goods on credit from R. Busby and receives an invoice.		5,000		5,000			
May 11	The business pays R. Busby in cash for the goods it acquired on credit.	(5,000)			(5,000)			
May 14	The business pays an electricity bill in cash.	(100)						100
May 17	Some of the goods purchased for resale (items costing £3,500) are removed from the store because sales have been agreed with customers for this date.		(3,500)					3,500
May 17	The business sells some of the purchased goods for cash.	4,000					4,000	
May 17	The business sells the remaining purchased goods on credit to R. Welsby and sends an invoice.			3,000			3,000	
May 24	R. Welsby pays in cash for the goods obtained on credit.	3,000		(3,000)				
May 28	The owner draws cash from the business for personal use.	(1,000)				(1,000)		
May 30	The business pays wages to an employee for the past month, in cash.	(2,000)						2,000
May 31	The business discovers that its equipment has fallen in value over the month.			(250)				250
	Totals at the end of the period	6,400	8,000	35,750	nil	49,000	7,000	5,850

50,150

Table 6.9
Summary of transactions analysed into the elements of the accounting equation

Assets	minus	Liabilities	=	Capital contributed/ withdrawn	plus	Revenue	minus	Expenses
£50,150	–	nil	=	£49,000	+	£7,000	–	£5,850
	£50,150					£50,150		

How has the ownership interest changed over the month? The owner contributed £50,000 at the start of the month and has a claim of £50,150 at the end of the month. The ownership interest was increased by earning revenue of £7,000 but reduced by incurring expenses of £5,850 and withdrawing £1,000 for personal use.

6.6 Financial statements of M. Carter, wholesaler

The transactions in Table 6.8 may be summarised in financial statements for use by interested parties. The first user will be the owner, M. Carter, but others such as the Inland Revenue may ask for a copy. If the owner seeks to raise additional finance by borrowing from a bank, the bank manager may ask for a copy of the financial statements.

There are no regulations regarding the format of financial statements for a sole trader, but it is good practice to try to match, as far as possible, the more onerous requirements imposed on limited liability companies. The financial statements presented in this section follow the general formats set out in Chapter 3.

6.6.1 Statement of cash flows

M. Carter, wholesaler
Statement of cash flows for the month of May Year 20xx

	£
Operating activities	
Cash from customers	7,000
Outflow: payment for goods	(6,500)
payment to supplier (R. Busby)	(5,000)
wages	(2,000)
electricity	(100)
Net outflow from operations	(6,600)
Investing activities	
Payment for buildings	(30,000)
Payment for equipment	(6,000)
Net outflow for investing activities	(36,000)
Financing activities	
Capital contributed by owner	50,000
Capital withdrawn as drawings	(1,000)
Net inflow from financing activities	49,000
Increase in cash at bank over period	6,400

Comment. The operating activities caused a drain on cash with a net effect that £6,600 flowed out of the business. A further £36,000 cash flow was used for investing activities. The owner contributed £50,000 at the start of the month but withdrew £1,000 at the end of the month. Cash in the bank increased by £6,400 over the month.

6.6.2 Income statement (profit and loss account)

M. Carter, wholesaler
Income statement (profit and loss account)
for the month of May Year 20xx

	£	£
Sales		7,000
Cost of goods sold		(3,500)
Gross profit		3,500
Other expenses		
Wages	(2,000)	
Electricity	(100)	
Depreciation	(250)	
		(2,350)
Net profit		1,150

Comment. This profit and loss account differs slightly from that presented for the service business in Chapter 5. It has a subtotal for gross profit. The difference between sales and the cost of purchasing or manufacturing the goods sold is regarded as an important indicator of the success of the business in its particular product line. The gross profit is sometimes referred to as the **margin** or **gross margin** and is a piece of information which is much explored by professional investors and analysts.

Making a subtotal for **gross profit** means that the final line needs a different label and so is called **net profit**. The word 'net' means 'after taking everything away', so in this case the net profit is equal to sales minus all expenses of the operations of the business.

Activity 6.4

The business of M. Carter, wholesaler, has made a profit of £1,150 from operations during the month but the cash flow due to operating activities has been negative to the extent of £6,600. Make a comparison of the cash flow from operating activities and the profit from operations. From your comparison, explain how a business can make a profit and yet see its cash drain away. Then make some recommendations about reducing the outflow of cash without affecting profit.

6.6.3 Statement of financial position (balance sheet)

M. Carter, wholesaler
Statement of financial position (balance sheet)
at 31 May Year 20xx

	£
Non-current (fixed) assets	
Buildings	30,000
Equipment	6,000
	36,000
Depreciation	(250)
Total non-current (fixed) assets	35,750
Current assets	
Inventory (stocks)	8,000
Cash at bank	6,400
Total current assets	14,400
Total assets	50,150
Ownership interest	
Capital at start	50,000
add: profit	1,150
less: drawings	(1,000)
Total ownership interest	50,150

Comment. There are no liabilities at the end of the month and so the net assets are the same as the total of fixed assets and current assets. That somewhat artificial situation arises from keeping the example fairly simple and manageable. The depreciation has been recorded for the equipment but many businesses would also depreciate buildings. The useful life of a building is much longer than that of equipment and so the depreciation for any single month would be a negligible amount in relation to other information for the period. The amount of £35,750 has been described here as depreciated cost but could also be called the **net book value** or the **written down value**.

The statement of financial position (balance sheet) is a statement of position and, on its own, is of limited usefulness. Companies which publish accounting information will present the previous year's amounts alongside the current year's data so that comparisons may be made. Some companies provide, in addition, five- or ten-year summaries which allow comparison over a longer period.

6.7 Summary

The following sequence summarises the effect on the accounting equation of buying goods and then selling them to customers.

1 Inventory (stock) is acquired for cash.

Assets ↑↓ – Liabilities	equals	Ownership interest

2 When the inventory is sold an expense of cost of goods sold is recorded.

Assets ↓ – Liabilities	equals	**Ownership interest ↓** **(expense: cost of goods sold)**

3 At the same time the sale of the inventory increases an asset of cash or trade receivable (debtor) and creates revenue.

Assets ↑ – Liabilities	equals	**Ownership interest ↑ (revenue)**

The following sequence summarises the effect on the accounting equation of buying raw materials, converting them to finished products and then selling these to customers.

1 The asset of raw materials is converted to an asset of work in progress.

Assets ↑↓ – Liabilities	equals	Ownership interest

2 The asset of work in progress becomes an asset of finished goods.

Assets ↑↓ – Liabilities	equals	Ownership interest

3 When the finished goods are sold an expense of cost of goods sold is created.

Assets ↓ – Liabilities	equals	**Ownership interest ↓** **(expense: cost of goods sold)**

4 At the same time the sale of the inventory increases an asset of cash or trade receivable (debtor) and creates revenue.

Assets ↑ – Liabilities	equals	**Ownership interest** ↑ **(revenue)**

QUESTIONS

The Questions section of each chapter has three types of question. 'Test your understanding' questions to help you review your reading are in the 'A' series of questions. You will find the answers to these by reading and thinking about the material in the book. 'Application' questions to test your ability to apply technical skills are in the 'B' series of questions. Questions requiring you to show skills in problem solving and evaluation are in the 'C' series of questions. A letter [S] indicates that there is a solution at the end of the book.

A Test your understanding

A6.1 [S] On 1 May the Sea Traders Company purchased 200 spare parts for fishing boats, costing £20 each. On 5 May, 60 of these spare parts were sold to a customer at a price of £25 each. The customer paid in cash immediately.

(a) Calculate the profit made on this transaction.
(b) Explain the impact of each transaction on the accounting equation.

A6.2 [S] Summarise the transactions of question A6.1 in a spreadsheet and show that the totals of the spreadsheet satisfy the accounting equation.

A6.3 [S] The following transactions relate to Toy Manufacturers Company during the month of June.

Date	Business transactions	£
June 1	Purchase toy components from supplier, 100 items at £3 each, paying in cash, and place in raw materials store.	300
June 3	Remove 70 components from raw materials store to meet production department's request (cost £3 each).	210
June 5	Carry out labour work and use production facilities to convert components into finished goods. Additional costs incurred for labour and use of facilities were £2.50 per toy processed.	175
June 6	Finished goods are transferred to finished goods store. Each toy has cost £5.50 in total (70 toys × £5.50 = £385).	385
June 11	50 toys, which cost £5.50 each to manufacture, are delivered to a customer.	275
June 14	The customer pays a price of £8 cash per toy immediately on delivery.	400

(a) Calculate the profit on sale.
(b) Explain the effect of each transaction on the accounting equation.
(c) Prepare a spreadsheet summarising the transactions.

A6.4 [S] The following list of transactions relates to the business of Peter Gold, furniture supplier, during the month of April. Analyse each transaction to show the two aspects of the transaction.

Date	Business transactions and events (nature of the entity: wholesale trader)	Amount £
Apr. 1	The owner pays cash into a bank account for the business.	60,000
Apr. 2	The business acquires buildings for cash.	20,000
Apr. 4	The business acquires equipment for cash.	12,000
Apr. 6	The business purchases an inventory (stock) of goods for cash.	8,500
Apr. 7	The business purchases an inventory (stock) of goods on credit from R. Green and receives an invoice.	7,000
Apr. 11	The business pays R. Green in cash for the goods it acquired on credit.	7,000
Apr. 14	The business pays a gas bill in cash.	400
Apr. 17	Items costing £5,500 are removed from the store because sales have been agreed with customers for this date.	5,500
Apr. 17	The business sells some of the goods removed from store for cash of £6,000.	6,000
Apr. 17	The business sells the remainder of the goods removed from store on credit to P. Weatherall and sends an invoice.	4,200
Apr. 24	P. Weatherall pays in cash for the goods obtained on credit.	4,200
Apr. 28	The owner draws cash from the business for personal use.	2,700
Apr. 29	The business pays wages to employees for the past month, in cash.	2,800
Apr. 30	The business discovers that its equipment has fallen in value over the month.	550

B   Application

B6.1 [S]
(a) Using the list of transactions at question A6.4 above, prepare a spreadsheet similar to that presented in Table 6.8.
(b) Show the resulting impact on the accounting equation and demonstrate that it remains in balance.

B6.2 [S]
Using the total from the columns of the spreadsheet of question B6.1(a), prepare for the business in the month of April:

(a) a statement of cash flows;
(b) a statement of financial position (balance sheet); and
(c) a profit and loss account.

There are no questions in the C series for this chapter. These skills are tested in specific situations in Chapters 8 to 12.

Recording transactions in ledger accounts: a trading business

The supplement starts with a reminder of the rules of debit and credit bookkeeping, set out in Table 6.10.

Table 6.10
Rules of debit and credit

	Debit entries in a ledger account	Credit entries in a ledger account
Left-hand side of the equation		
Asset	Increase	Decrease
Right-hand side of the equation		
Liability	Decrease	Increase
Ownership interest	Expense	Revenue
	Capital withdrawn	Capital contributed

Activity 6.5

It might be a useful test of your understanding of the chapter if you try to write down the debit and credit entries before looking at Table 6.11. If you find your answers don't agree with that table then you should go back to the analysis contained in the chapter and think about the various aspects of the accounting equation. Debit and credit entries do nothing more than follow the analysis based on the accounting equation so you should not have a problem if you have followed the analysis.

Table 6.1 presented a short list of transactions for a trading company, relating to the purchase and sale of goods. That list of transactions is repeated in Table 6.11 but showing in the final two columns the ledger accounts in which debit and credit entries would be made. Compare Table 6.11 with Table 6.2 to see that the analysis of transactions and the analysis of debit and credit entries follow similar patterns.

Table 6.4 presented a short list of transactions for a manufacturing company. These are repeated in Table 6.12 with the ledger accounts for debit and credit entries being shown in the final two columns. Again, you should try this first and then check your answer against Table 6.12.

Table 6.11

Transactions of a trading company: debit and credit entries

		£	Debit	Credit
Apr. 1	Purchase goods from manufacturer, 100 items at £2 each, paying in cash, and store in warehouse.	200	Inventory (stock)	Cash
Apr. 4	Remove 70 items from warehouse to meet a customer's request. Those 70 items cost £2 each on 1 April. They are delivered to the customer who accepts the delivery.	140	Cost of goods sold	Inventory (stock)
Apr. 4	The customer pays in cash. Selling price is £2.50 per item.	175	Cash	Revenue

Table 6.12

Transactions of a manufacturing company: debit and credit entries

		£	Debit	Credit
July 1	Purchase raw materials from supplier, 100 trays at £2 each, paying in cash, and place in raw materials store.	200	Raw materials inventory (stock)	Cash
July 3	Remove 80 trays from raw materials store to meet production department's request (cost £2 each).	160	Work in progress	Raw materials inventory (stock)
July 4	Carry out labour work and use production facilities to convert raw materials into finished goods. Additional costs incurred for labour and use of facilities were £1.50 per tray processed.	120	Work in progress	Cash
July 5	Finished goods are transferred to finished goods store. The job has cost £3.50 per tray in total (80 trays × £3.50 = £280).	280	Finished goods	Work in progress
July 10	60 trays, which cost £3.50 each to manufacture, are delivered to a customer.	210	Cost of goods sold	Finished goods
July 10	The customer pays a price of £5 cash per tray immediately on delivery.	300	Cash	Revenue

M. Carter, wholesaler: analysing the debit and credit entries

Table 6.13 takes the information contained in Table 6.8 and analyses it under debit and credit headings showing the ledger accounts in which each entry will be made. Ledger accounts required to record these transactions are:

L1 Cash	L2 Owner	L3 Buildings	L4 Equipment
L5 Inventory (stock) of goods	L6 R. Busby	L7 Electricity	L8 Wages
L9 Cost of goods sold	L10 Sales	L11 R. Welsby	L12 Depreciation

The full ledger account records for the transactions in Table 6.13 are set out. Leona Rees has commented on each one, to show how she interprets them when she is carrying out work of audit or investigation.

L1 Cash

Date	Particulars	Page	Debit	Credit	Balance
			£	£	£
May 1	Owner's capital	L2	50,000		50,000
May 2	Buildings	L3		30,000	20,000
May 4	Equipment	L4		6,000	14,000
May 6	Inventory (stock) of goods	L5		6,500	7,500
May 11	R. Busby	L6		5,000	2,500
May 14	Electricity	L7		100	2,400
May 17	Sales	L10	4,000		6,400
May 24	R. Welsby	L11	3,000		9,400
May 28	Ownership interest drawn out	L2		1,000	8,400
May 30	Wages	L8		2,000	6,400

LEONA's comment: *The amount of £50,000 put into the business at the start is quickly swallowed up by spending cash on buildings, equipment, buying an inventory (stock) of goods and paying the supplier who gave credit. Paying the electricity account £100 took the cash balance down to £2,400 and it was only the sale of some goods which allowed the business to continue. If the sale of goods had not taken place, the owner might have needed to put more cash into the business at that point, or else ask the bank manager to make a loan to the business. With the benefit of hindsight, the owner might have waited a few days before paying R. Busby for goods supplied. It's not a good idea to delay paying the electricity bill in case there is a disconnection, and failing to pay wages usually means the employee does not return. It might have helped cash flow to have bought the buildings and equipment using a loan, but borrowing money has a cost in interest payments and perhaps the owner prefers not to start with a high level of borrowing.*

L2 Ownership interest

Date	Particulars	Page	Debit	Credit	Balance
			£	£	£
May 1	Cash contributed	L1		50,000	(50,000)
May 28	Cash drawn	L1	1,000		(49,000)

Table 6.13
Analysis of transactions for M. Carter, wholesaler

Date	Business transactions	Amount	Debit	Credit
		£		
May 1	The owner provides the business with cash.	50,000	Cash	Owner
May 2	The business acquires buildings for cash.	30,000	Buildings	Cash
May 4	The business acquires equipment for cash.	6,000	Equipment	Cash
May 6	The business purchases an inventory (stock) of goods for cash.	6,500	Inventory (stock)	Cash
May 7	The business purchases an inventory (stock) of goods on credit from R. Busby and receives an invoice.	5,000	Inventory (stock)	R. Busby
May 11	The business pays R. Busby in cash for the goods it acquired on credit.	5,000	R. Busby	Cash
May 14	The business pays an electricity bill in cash.	100	Electricity	Cash
May 17	Items costing £3,500 are removed from the store because sales have been agreed with customers for this date.	3,500	Cost of goods sold	Inventory (stock)
May 17	The business sells goods for cash.	4,000	Cash	Sales
May 17	The business sells goods on credit to R. Welsby and sends an invoice.	3,000	R. Welsby	Sales
May 24	R. Welsby pays in cash for the goods obtained on credit.	3,000	Cash	R. Welsby
May 28	The owner draws cash from the business for personal use.	1,000	Owner	Cash
May 30	The business pays wages to an employee for the past month, in cash.	2,000	Wages	Cash
May 31	The business discovers that its equipment has fallen in value over the month.	250	Depreciation	Equipment

LEONA's comment: *The ownership interest is created when the owner contributes cash or resources to the business. In this case, it was cash. The sole trader in business may withdraw cash for personal use at any time – it is called owner's drawings – but the desirability of that action depends on how useful it is to the owner when compared to how useful it might have been if left in the business. The owner of this business has a claim remaining equal to £49,000 after making the drawing.*

			L3 Buildings		
Date	Particulars	Page	Debit	Credit	Balance
			£	£	£
May 2	Cash	L1	30,000		30,000

LEONA's comment: *This ledger account is particularly useful as a reminder that a very valuable asset is owned by the business. Having a record in the ledger account encourages the owner to think about continuing care for the buildings and also to review their value against the amount recorded.*

L4 Equipment

Date	Particulars	Page	Debit	Credit	Balance
			£	£	£
May 4	Cash	L1	6,000		6,000
May 31	Depreciation	L12		250	5,750

LEONA's comment: *The equipment cost £6,000 but is being gradually used up over its life in the business. Depreciation is a way of showing that the original cost of the asset has to be spread over its useful life. If the estimate of depreciation is correct, this ledger account should reduce to nil on the day the equipment ceases to be of use. In reality things usually are not quite so straightforward. (Depreciation of fixed assets is dealt with in more detail in Chapter 8.)*

L5 Inventory (stock) of goods

Date	Particulars	Page	Debit	Credit	Balance
			£	£	£
May 6	Cash	L1	6,500		6,500
May 7	R. Busby	L6	5,000		11,500
May 17	Cost of goods sold	L9		3,500	8,000

LEONA's comment: *The balance on this ledger account at any point in time should equal the cost price of the goods held in the warehouse. So at the end of May, if the owner goes to the warehouse and carries out an inventory count (stock count), there should be goods to a total cost of £8,000. Checking the presence of an inventory (stock) of unsold goods which agrees with the ledger account is an important part of my work as an auditor. If they don't agree, I start to ask a lot of questions.*

L6 R. Busby

Date	Particulars	Page	Debit	Credit	Balance
			£	£	£
May 7	Inventory (stock) of goods	L5		5,000	(5,000)
May 11	Cash	L1	5,000		nil

LEONA's comment: *When the goods were purchased from R. Busby, the supplier, an invoice was received from that supplier showing the amount due. That invoice was used to make the credit entry on May 7 showing that the business had a liability. The liability was extinguished on May 11 by a payment to R. Busby, so at the end of May the business owes that supplier nothing.*

L7 Electricity

Date	Particulars	Page	Debit	Credit	Balance
			£	£	£
May 14	Cash	L1	100		100

LEONA's comment: *This is a very straightforward expense account. The balance on this account will show the total expense of electricity consumed during the period.*

L8 Wages

Date	Particulars	Page	Debit	Credit	Balance
			£	£	£
May 30	Cash	L1	2,000		2,000

LEONA's comment: *Another very straightforward account in which to accumulate all wages expenses.*

L9 Cost of goods sold

Date	Particulars	Page	Debit	Credit	Balance
			£	£	£
May 17	Inventory (stock) of goods	L5	3,500		3,500

LEONA's comment: *This is an expense account showing the cost of the goods sold during the month. The total sales are shown in ledger account L10 as £7,000 and the cost of goods sold is shown here as £3,500, so there is a profit ('margin') of 50% on sales before taking into account the expenses of electricity, wages and depreciation. As an auditor I have considerable interest in the profit margin on sales. It tells me a great deal about the business.*

L10 Sales

Date	Particulars	Page	Debit	Credit	Balance
			£	£	£
May 17	Cash	L1		4,000	(4,000)
May 17	R. Welsby	L11		3,000	(7,000)

LEONA's comment: *This is a revenue account, so credit entries are expected. The balance column shows the total sales of the month were £7,000.*

L11 R. Welsby

Date	Particulars	Page	Debit	Credit	Balance
			£	£	£
May 17	Sales	L10	3,000		3,000
May 24	Cash	L1		3,000	nil

LEONA's comment: *The credit sale to R. Welsby made him a trade receivable (debtor) of the business and so the first entry is a debit entry. When R. Welsby paid this extinguished the debt, by the end of the month R. Welsby owed nothing to the business.*

L12 Depreciation

Date	Particulars	Page	Debit	Credit	Balance
			£	£	£
May 31	Equipment	L4	250		250

LEONA's comment: *This is another expense account showing an item which has decreased the ownership interest through a decrease in the recorded amount of an asset. This is where accounting begins to look slightly complicated because no cash has changed hands. Recording depreciation is the accounting way of expressing caution as to the expected future benefits from the asset. These will be eroded as the asset is used up. Depreciation is a way of acknowledging that erosion.*

Checking the accuracy of double-entry records

In Chapter 5, the process of listing all ledger account balances in a trial balance was explained.

The trial balance for the accounting records of M. Carter, wholesaler, at 31 May year 1, is as shown in Table 6.14. This is a basic list summarising the transactions of the month. If you compare it with the financial statements in the main part of the chapter you will see that all the amounts correspond.

Table 6.14
Trial balance at 31 May for M. Carter, wholesaler

Ledger account title		£	£
L1	Cash	6,400	
L2	Ownership interest		49,000
L3	Buildings	30,000	
L4	Equipment	5,750	
L5	Inventory (stock) of goods	8,000	
L6	R. Busby		nil
L7	Electricity	100	
L8	Wages	2,000	
L9	Cost of goods sold	3,500	
L10	Sales		7,000
L11	R. Welsby	nil	
L12	Depreciation	250	
Totals		56,000	56,000

As was the case in the supplement to Chapter 5, it is rather easier to use the trial balance if it is arranged so that all the statement of financial position (balance sheet) items are together and all the profit and loss account items are together. This is done in Table 6.15. The unshaded lines are not part of the trial balance but take advantage of the various forms of the accounting equation to calculate profit in two different ways. In the first part of the table:

Profit	equals	Assets – Liabilities – Owner's capital at the start and any changes during the period

In the second part of the table:

Profit	equals	Revenue – Expenses

Table 6.15
Rearranging the trial balance into statement of financial position (balance sheet) items and profit and loss account items

Ledger account title		£	£
L3	Buildings	30,000	
L4	Equipment	5,750	
L5	Inventory (stock) of goods	8,000	
L11	R. Welsby	nil	
L1	Cash	6,400	
L6	R. Busby		nil
L2	Ownership interest		49,000
Subtotal X		50,150	49,000
Difference: profit of the month 50,150 – 49,000			1,150
L10	Sales		7,000
L9	Cost of goods sold	3,500	
L7	Electricity	100	
L8	Wages	2,000	
L12	Depreciation	250	
Subtotal Y		5,850	7,000
Difference: profit of the month 7,000 – 5,850		1,150	
Total of ledger balances in each column X + Y		56,000	56,000

The form of trial balance shown in Table 6.15 will be used in later chapters as the starting point for the preparation of financial statements.

S Test your understanding

S6.1   Prepare ledger accounts for the transactions of Peter Gold, furniture supplier, listed in question A6.4.

Part 3

Recognition in financial statements

Chapter 7

Published financial statements

Morgan Crucible plc: Operational and financial highlights

We produce a wide range of specialist, high-specification materials that have extraordinary attributes and properties. Engineered into products, they deliver enhanced performance, often under extreme conditions. Our dynamic, highly skilled people are continuously engaged in finding solutions for complex and technologically demanding applications, which are used all over the world. In short, we supply innovative, differentiated products made from highly technical advanced materials which enable our customers' products and processes to perform more efficiently, more reliably and for longer.

- A year of strong performance with record revenue and operating profit for the Group.

- Revenue for the year increased by 8.2% to £1,101.0 million.

- Underlying profit before taxation* increased by 58.1% to £119.7 million.

- Underlying earnings per share*** increased by 59.9% to 29.9 pence per share.

- Proposed final dividend increased by 20.0% to 6.0 pence, giving a full-year dividend of 9.25 pence.

Extract from Financial Review

Reference is made to 'Underlying operating profit' and 'Underlying earnings per share (EPS)'. EPS is defined in note 9 on page 98. These measures of earnings are shown because the Directors consider that they give a better indication of underlying performance.

Source: Morgan Crucible Annual Report 2011, pp. 1, 44.

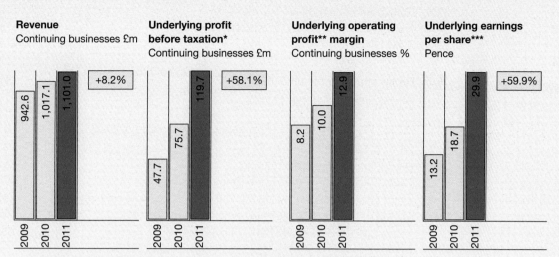

Revenue
Continuing businesses £m

Underlying profit before taxation*
Continuing businesses £m

Underlying operating profit margin**
Continuing businesses %

Underlying earnings per share**
Pence

* Defined as operating profit before amortisation of intangible assets less net financing costs.
** Defined as operating profit before amortisation of intangible assets.
*** Defined as basic earnings per share adjusted to exclude amortisation of intangible assets.

Discussion points

1 Why does the company provided a mixture of operational and financial higlights?

2 What are the arguments for and against a company defining its own measure of 'underlying' profits?

Contents

Learning outcomes	After reading this chapter you should be able to:
	● Explain the key international influences that affect accounting practice in the UK.
	● Explain the structure of company reporting as set out in the *Framework* and in UK guidance.
	● Explain the main contents of (a) the balance sheet, (b) the income statement (profit and loss account) and (c) the cash flow statement as presented by larger companies.
	● Define 'parent company' and 'subsidiary company' and explain how a group is structured.
	● Explain the main features of group financial statements.
	● Explain the nature of, and reason for, other forms of communication beyond the annual report.

7.1 Introduction

It is explained in Chapters 1 and 4 that in the case of sole traders and partnerships the groups of persons who have an interest in the financial statements are limited to the owners themselves, HM Revenue and Customs and organisations such as banks which are asked to provide finance for the company. For limited liability companies the list of potential users widens and the access to internal information becomes restricted. Even the owners of a limited liability company, called the equity holders (shareholders) are not permitted access to the day-to-day records of the company and are treated as being outsiders of (external to) the company they own. The quality and amount of information communicated to these users who are external to the company becomes a matter which is too important to be left entirely to the discretion of the directors running the company.

Chapter 4 outlined the various regulatory authorities which exist to establish the quality and quantity of information to be published by limited liability companies. There are over one million limited liability companies in the UK, although only a few thousand are listed on the Stock Exchange and of these only around 500 have their shares bought and sold regularly. The number of major listed companies, and their importance to the economy in terms of the funds invested in them, means it is appropriate to take them as the benchmark for current practice in external reporting. The practices applied by larger limited liability companies set a good example as a starting point for smaller ones and for organisations that are not limited liability companies, such as charitable trusts or public sector bodies.

In this chapter, and in Chapters 8 to 12, there is mention only of **limited liability companies** because the aim of this book is to provide an understanding of the accounting information published by companies. The more general word **enterprise** (meaning a business activity or commercial project) could be substituted throughout for limited liability company. Most of what is said in these chapters applies to all enterprises because the principles and practice described here have a wider application beyond companies, although modifications may be necessary when the needs of the users and the purposes of the enterprise are different from those relevant to a limited liability company.

7.2 International influences

Chapter 3 explained that, since January 2005, two different accounting systems have existed for companies in the UK, depending on the type of company. For the group financial statements of a listed company the accounting system set out by the International Accounting Standards Board (IASB) must be applied. All other companies, and the separate companies in the group, may choose to follow IASB standards but there is no requirement to do so. Companies that do not choose to follow the international accounting standards must continue to follow the rules of UK company law and the UK ASB's accounting standards.

For many years there has been a strong international influence on and from UK accounting practice so the change to international accounting standards in 2005 did not bring many surprises. The UK accounting standard-setting body was a founder member of the International Accounting Standards Committee (IASC), set up in 1973, and has been closely involved in its work since that date. In 2001, with an organisational change, the IASC became the IASB but the close similarity between international accounting standards and UK accounting standards continued. The UK ASB has worked continuously towards matching UK standards to IFRS.

Since 1980 the law regulating financial reporting in the UK (now contained in the Companies Act 2006 and related legislation) has reflected its membership of the European Union (EU) and the work of regulators across the EU to harmonise aspects of financial reporting. From 2005 the law governing financial reporting in the UK has been split into two routes. One route is the rule of UK company law influenced by the EU. The other route is the IASB system of accounting as endorsed by the EU.

7.2.1 The European Union

The UK is a member state of the EU and is required to develop its laws so as to harmonise with those of other member states of the EU. There are two procedures by which the EU influences the accounting practices of UK-based companies.

1 The European Commission, which is the permanent secretariat and staff of the EU, issues a Regulation which overrides national laws and applies to all companies specified in the Regulation.
2 The European Commission issues Directives which are incorporated in national laws of member states.

The IAS Regulation

In 2002 the European Commission issued the first IAS Regulation. The IAS Regulation is a direct instruction to companies in all member states. It required that, by 2005, all **listed companies** in the European Union would use IASB standards in preparing their **group** financial statements. This was intended to cause convergence ('bringing together') of accounting practices, and so improve the movement of capital across the stock markets of the EU. The Commission, which prepares and implements the legislation of the European Parliament, has established procedures for giving European approval to each of the IASB Standards. It takes advice from the European Financial Reporting Advisory Group (EFRAG), a team of experts that includes a UK member. The final recommendation to the Commission is made by the Accounting Regulatory Committee, which includes representatives of all member states. The process of approving IASB standards for use in the EU is called **endorsement**.

Harmonisation through Directives

For many aspects of regulation within the EU, the process of harmonisation starts when a **Directive** is issued by the European Commission, setting out the basic rules which should be followed in each member state's national laws. For limited liability companies in the UK, two such Directives have been particularly important. These are the Fourth Directive and the Seventh Directive. Together they specify the content of the Companies Act 2006. One important aspect of Directives is that they specify **formats** for the financial statements (see section 7.3.2) which ensure that all companies produce documents that are similar in appearance and present items in a systematic order. The idea of having standard formats was not a familiar concept in the UK before the Directives became effective in the 1980s, but became accepted during the 1980s and 1990. Having standard formats makes it easier for the reader to find the starting point in reading the financial statements. In later chapters we will see that having standard formats does not solve all the problems of comparability and understandability. For companies that do not apply IFRS these formats continue to apply. For companies using the IFRS there is potentially more flexibility of presentation.

Activity 7.1	*From your general interest reading, or perhaps from your study of law, make a list of other areas of activity in which the UK law is harmonised with that of other countries in the EU.*

7.2.2 IASB

The International Accounting Standards Board (IASB) is an independent body that sets International Financial Reporting Standards (IFRS). It was formed in 2000 as the successor to the International Accounting Standard Committee (IASC) which had been setting International Accounting Standards (IAS) since 1973. These IAS have been adopted by the IASB and will gradually be revised as IFRS. In the meantime the description 'IFRS' is used as a collective name for all forms of international accounting standard, whatever the precise title of the standard.

The IASB's objective is to bring about convergence of national accounting standards and international accounting standards to high-quality solutions. This will help participants in the world's capital markets and other users to make economic decisions.

There are many similarities between the UK accounting standards and the IASB Standards. There are also some differences where the UK standard-setter believes a particular approach is justified, or where historical developments have a strong influence. The UK Accounting Standards Board works on projects with the IASB, as do other countries' standard-setting bodies, all seeking to develop international convergence.

7.3 Accounting framework

Chapter 1, section 1.3 has explained that the IASB has developed a *Framework* of principles and definitions that are used in setting accounting standards. The UK ASB has also issued a *Statement of Principles*. There are many similarities between these documents because the UK ASB benefited from the earlier work of the IASB. The explanations in this chapter draw mainly on the IASB *Framework*, adding more information where this is needed to understand the separate ideas of the UK ASB.

7.3.1 The primary financial statements

The IASB requires a complete set of financial statements to comprise:[1]

- a statement of financial position (balance sheet) at the end of the period
- an income statement (showing the profit or loss for the period), as part of a larger statement of comprehensive income (see Chapter 12)
- a statement of changes in equity for the period
- a statement of cash flows, and
- notes that summarise the accounting policies and give other explanations.

The IASB also gives general guidance on how to prepare and present the financial statements but stops short of giving precise rules on presentation. There is discretion for companies to present information in a way that best suits the company and those who are likely to use the information.

The UK ASB requires the same four primary statements but with some differences of names. The income statement is called a profit and loss account. The statement of changes in equity is replaced by two items: a statement of total recognised gains and losses and a note of changes in share capital and reserves (explained in Chapter 12 of this book). The Companies Act 2006 sets out formats of financial statements (see section 7.3.2) which give detailed rules on the sequence of information. These formats apply to companies that do *not* follow the IFRS.

A comparison of the primary statements in the IASB and UK ASB systems is shown in Table 7.1.

Table 7.1
Primary statements – IASB and UK ASB compared

IASB system	UK ASB and company law
Statement of financial position	Balance sheet
Income statement	Profit and loss account
Statement of cash flows	Cash flow statement
Statement of changes in equity	
● Statement of recognised income and expense *plus*	● Statement of total recognised gains and losses *plus*
● *Transactions with equity holders (e.g. dividends paid) *plus*	● Reconciliation of movements in shareholders' funds[†]
● *Changes in the retained earnings (accumulated profit or loss) *plus*	
● *Changes in each class of equity and each reserve	

* May be shown on the face of the statement of changes in equity or in notes.
[†] Shown with primary statements or in notes.

The IASB's *Conceptual Framework* states that the objective of general purpose financial reporting is to provide financial information about the reporting entity that is useful to existing and potential investors, lenders and other creditors in making decisions about providing resources to the entity. Those decisions involve buying, selling or holding equity and debt instruments, and providing or settling loans and other forms of credit.[2]

Financial position

Information about financial position is reported primarily in a statement of financial position (balance sheet). It reports economic resources controlled by the company, its financial structure, its liquidity and its solvency. Information about economic resources held by the entity allows users of the information to estimate future cash flows from those resources. Information about financial structure is useful in predicting future needs for borrowing or for raising new equity finance. Liquidity refers to the availability of cash in the near future after taking account of commitments in the same period. Solvency refers to the availability of cash to meet financial commitments as they fall due. The balance sheet is not a statement of the value of the company because there are limitations in the measurement process and also because not all items which are of value to the company are included in the balance sheet.

Performance

Information about the performance of an entity is primarily provided in an income statement (profit and loss account). Performance is indicated by profitability and changes in profitability. Information about performance is useful in evaluating how well the resources of the entity have been used to generate profit. Statements of financial performance are seen as providing an account of the stewardship of management and also as helping readers to check the accuracy of previous estimates they may have made about the expected outcome of the period.

Changes in financial position

Information about changes in financial position of an entity is useful to help assess the operating, investing and financing activities of the period. It is usually found in a statement of cash flows.

7.3.2   Formats for financial statements

The word **format** means 'shape'. A format for a financial statement sets out the shape of the document. It sets out the items to be reported and the sequence in which they are reported. Section 7.2.1 explains that EU Directives have guided the formats used by UK companies for many years, as set out in company law and UK accounting standards. Since 2005 the group financial statements of listed companies have followed the IASB system of reporting. The IASB system does not specify formats. It does provide some lists of items to be included in financial statements but there is no requirement to present these items in any particular sequence. This means that companies have choices in the shape of their financial statements. This book describes the shapes of financial statements that you are likely to see in company reports but you will need to be flexible in understanding that companies do have choices.

7.3.3   Categories of financial information

The primary financial statements are the core of a much wider range of sources of financial information which users may obtain about a company. The relative position of the primary financial statements is shown in Figure 7.1.

Activity 7.2

Write down three items of accompanying information about a company which you feel would be useful in the annual report of a company. Exchange lists with other members of the group and establish the similarities and differences across the group. To what extent would one general set of financial statements with notes and accompanying information meet your collective expectations?

7.3.4   Notes and accompanying information

The annual report contains the primary financial statements, notes to the financial statements and accompanying information.

Notes to the financial statements

For listed companies, notes to the financial statements are based on required disclosures specified in the IFRS. For companies that do not follow the IFRS, many of the notes are required by regulations such as the Companies Act 2006 or relevant UK accounting standards. Where the annual report is audited, the full audit covers the notes to the financial statements.

The notes are essential in amplifying and explaining the primary financial statements. The notes and the primary financial statements form an integrated whole. The wording of the notes is as important as the numbers if ambiguity is to be avoided. Notes provide narrative descriptions or disaggregations of items presented in those statements and information about items that do not qualify for recognition in those statements. An entity cannot rectify the use of an inappropriate accounting policy merely by describing the accounting policy or by providing explanatory material.

Accompanying information

Accompanying information is any other information additional to the primary financial statements and notes. It could be information which is highly relevant but of lower reliability than the financial statements and notes. It could be information which will only interest a particular group of users. Such accompanying information may not be subject to the full audit process which is compulsory for the primary financial statements and notes. The IASB mandatory financial reporting standards relate only to the financial statements and the notes to the financial statements. There is non-mandatory

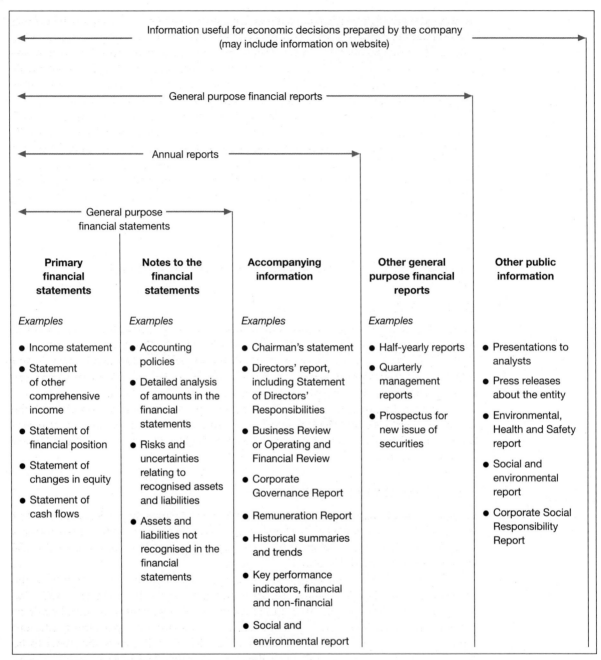

Figure 7.1
Categories of financial information

guidance on the management commentary (see Chapter 14). Accompanying information is more commonly regulated at national level or is encouraged as voluntary by organisations that encourage good practice. The range of accompanying information found in the annual report of a UK listed company is explained later (see Chapter 14).

Many annual reports include highlights pages showing amounts, ratios and other calculations that distil a great deal of information into a few key items. There is a risk that companies are selective in how they choose the items for specific attention. You cannot read about financial statements for long without meeting the phrase 'the bottom line'. That refers to the line in the income statement (profit and loss account) which reports the profit attributable to the equity holders (ordinary shareholders). It may be described as **earnings** for equity holders (ordinary shareholders). When this amount is divided by the number of shares which have been issued by the company it becomes the **earnings per share**. Investors, financial journalists and brokers' analysts have traditionally paid great attention to the earnings per share. The standard-setters would prefer to discourage this narrow focus and encourage instead a 'building block' approach where the company produces information in such a way that the user of the annual statement can create useful arrangements and combinations of information.

Companies also produce accompanying information for specialised needs. Regulated industries (such as gas, electricity, telecommunications and water) provide supplementary information about their regulated activities. Some companies give non-financial performance indicators (such as speed of answering customer enquiries, or level of customer satisfaction). Graphs, charts, diagrams and even photographs are all ways of providing accompanying information which adds to users' understanding of a document.

7.4 Statement of financial position (balance sheet)

7.4.1 What items must be reported?

Companies that follow the IASB system of accounting in presenting a statement of financial position (balance sheet) have choices in the way they present their balance sheet. There is no particular **format** required[3] but some items are listed in the relevant standard as a minimum set of disclosures (see Supplement 7.1 to this chapter). Companies choose the form of layout for items in the balance sheet.

Companies that do not follow the IASB system of accounting must comply with the Companies Act 2006 and the UK accounting standards. The Companies Act 2006 contains more detail of the format that must be used. The details are set out in Supplement 7.2 to this chapter.

7.4.2 What formats are used?

Companies applying the IASB system do not have to follow any particular format but it is likely that any balance sheet you see will resemble one of the three formats described in this section because they will retain some of the traditions of the UK system that has existed for more than 20 years.

Companies that do not apply the IASB system of accounting must follow the requirements of the Companies Act 2006 and the standards of the UK ASB. The Companies Act 2006 permits two different formats of statement of financial position (balance sheet), each conforming to the accounting equation but permitting different layouts on the page. The word format means 'shape' so it covers the items to be reported and the sequence in which they are reported. The most commonly used format in the UK is Format 1, which uses the accounting equation to create a vertical format as shown in Exhibit 7.1.

Exhibit 7.1
Vertical format of statement of financial position (balance sheet)

Assets
minus
Liabilities
equals
Ownership interest

Format 2 uses the accounting equation to create a horizontal format as shown in Exhibit 7.2.

Exhibit 7.2
Horizontal form of statement of financial position (balance sheet)

		Liabilities
Assets	equal	plus
		Ownership interest

Format 2 is observed more commonly in the financial statements of continental European countries where the horizontal format is preferred.

Some companies use a variation on Format 2 which stacks the assets on top and the ownership interest and liabilities underneath (see Exhibit 7.3).

Exhibit 7.3
Assets above, ownership interest plus liabilities below

Assets
equals
Liabilities
plus
Ownership interest

When you read a statement of financial position (balance sheet) you should first of all look at the overall structure to see where the main sections of **assets, liabilities** and **ownership interest** are placed. Then you can begin to look at each section in more detail. The process is something like seeing a landscape painting for the first time. You stand back to look at the overall impression of the landscape and the main features first. Then you step forward to look at some of the details in different parts of the painting. Finally if you are very enthusiastic you move in closer and start to examine the details of the texture, brush strokes and shading.

7.4.3 Descriptions in the statement of financial position (balance sheet)

You will see from the Supplement that the statement of financial position (balance sheet) formats contain some words you will recognise but also many new words. Non-current assets (fixed assets) are separated from current assets. Current liabilities (due in less than one year) are separated from non-current liabilities (due in more than one year). Some of the items under the Companies Act headings A to J may look rather strange at this stage (particularly A, D, I and J). Do not worry about that at present. If they are appropriate to first-level study they will be explained at some point in this text. If they are not explained, then they are relatively rare in occurrence and the time taken to explain them will outweigh the benefits you would gain from understanding.

The ownership interest is shown at heading K as **capital** and **reserves**. The word **capital** here means the claim which owners have because of the number of shares they own, and the word **reserves** means the claim which owners have because the company has created new wealth for them over the years. Various labels are used to describe the nature of that new wealth and how it is created. Some of the new wealth is created because new investors pay more than a specified amount for the shares. Paying more is referred to as paying a **premium**, so this kind of ownership interest is labelled the **share premium**. Some of the new wealth is created because the fixed assets held by the company increase in value and that new valuation is recorded. This kind of ownership interest is labelled the **revaluation reserve**. Some of the new wealth is created by making profits through operating activities. This kind of ownership interest is labelled the **retained earnings** reserve.

7.4.4 Subtotals

Subtotals in financial statements help to group information within financial statements into useful sections. There are no rules about the placing of subtotals in either the IASB lists or the Companies Acts formats. Companies have to decide for themselves where to place subtotals and totals in presentation of the list of items in the format. You will need to be flexible in reading statements of financial position (balance sheets) and using the subtotals provided.

Activity 7.3

Read again the format for the balance sheet. How many of the items there came as no surprise to you? How many looked unfamiliar? Make a note of these and check that you find out about them in later chapters.

7.4.5 Illustration

The remainder of this chapter explores the published financial statements of a hypothetical listed company, Safe and Sure plc, which operates in a service industry. There is a parent company called Safe and Sure plc and it owns some subsidiary companies that together make up a 'group'. The Safe and Sure Group sells recycling and cleaning services to customers based on the high reputation of the company's products and name. The Safe and Sure Group follows the IASB system of accounting and has chosen a format that is similar to Format 1 (see Exhibit 7.1).

The following illustration sets out the balance sheet of the Safe and Sure Group plc for Year 7 with comparative amounts alongside for the previous year. The balance sheet is followed by a comment on matters of particular interest.

Safe and Sure Group plc Consolidated statement of finacial position (balance sheet) at 31 December

	Notes	Year 7 £m	Year 6 £m
Non-current assets			
Property, plant and equipment	1	137.5	121.9
Intangible assets	2	260.3	237.6
Investments	3	2.8	2.0
Taxation recoverable	4	5.9	4.9
Total fixed assets		406.5	366.4
Current assets			
Inventories (stocks)	5	26.6	24.3
Amounts receivable (debtors)	6	146.9	134.7
Six-month deposits		2.0	–
Cash and cash equivalents		105.3	90.5
Total current assets		280.8	249.5
Total assets		687.3	615.9

	Notes	Year 7 £m	Year 6 £m
Current liabilities			
Amounts payable (creditors)	7	(159.8)	(157.5)
Bank overdraft	8	(40.1)	(62.6)
Total current liabilities		(199.9)	(220.1)
Non-current liabilities			
Amounts payable (creditors)	9	(2.7)	(2.6)
Bank and other borrowings	10	(0.2)	(0.6)
Provisions	11	(20.2)	(22.2)
Total non-current liabilities		(23.1)	(25.4)
Total liabilities		(223.0)	(245.5)
Net assets		464.3	370.4
Capital and reserves (ownership interest)			
Called-up share capital	12	19.6	19.5
Share premium account	13	8.5	5.5
Revaluation reserve	14	4.6	4.6
Retained earnings	15	431.6	340.8
Equity holders' funds		464.3	370.4

7.4.6 Discussion

The first feature to note is the title, *Consolidated statement of financial position (balance sheet)*. Companies listed on the Stock Exchange are generally using one name as an umbrella for a group of several companies linked together under one parent. It is thought to be more useful to the shareholders of the parent company to see all the assets controlled by that company within the single financial statement. The word **control** is important here. The parent company owns the other companies. They each own their separate assets. The parent company controls the use of those assets indirectly by controlling the companies it owns. The statement of financial position (balance sheet) as presented here represents a group where the parent company owns 100% of all the other companies in the group (called its subsidiary undertakings). A similar consolidated statement of financial position would be produced if the parent owned less than 100%, provided it had the same element of control. The only additional item would be a **non-controlling interest** in the ownership claim to indicate the proportion of the equity interest in subsidiaries held by shareholders outside the group. The non-controlling interest has previously been called the **minority interest**.

The second feature to note in the statement of financial position (balance sheet) as presented is that there are two columns of figures. Companies are required to present the figures for the previous year, in order to provide a basis for comparison.

The statement of financial position (balance sheet) follows the accounting equation and this company has helpfully set out in the left-hand margin the main elements of the equation. There are some phrases in the statement of financial position (balance sheet) which you are meeting for the first time but you should not feel intimidated by new titles when you can work out what they mean if you think about the ordinary meanings of words.

Intangible assets means assets which may not be touched – they have no physical existence. Examples are the goodwill of a business or the reputation of a branded product.

Property, plant and equipment is another phrase which you are seeing here for the first time, but again you can work out the meaning. It is also called tangible non-current assets. You know from Chapter 2 what **non-current assets** are and you know that tangible means 'something that may be touched'.

Investments here means shares in other companies which are not subsidiary undertakings within the group.

The *taxation recoverable* is an amount of tax which has been paid already but may be reclaimed in 18 months' time because of events that have occurred to reduce the tax due, after the tax was paid.

Current assets comprise inventories (stocks), receivables (debtors) and cash. They are set out in order of increasing liquidity. Inventories (stocks) are the least readily convertible into cash while amounts receivable (debtors) are closer to collection of cash. Cash itself is the most liquid asset. The notes to the accounts contain more detailed information. Take as an example note 4, relating to inventories (stocks). It appears as follows:

Note 4	Year 7	Year 6
Inventories (stocks)	*£m*	*£m*
Raw materials	6.2	5.4
Work in progress	1.9	1.0
Finished products	18.5	17.9
	26.6	24.3

The notes are shown in full in Appendix I at the end of this book. There is a note relating to amounts receivable (debtors), mainly relating to trade receivables (trade debtors). Amounts payable (creditors) has a similar type of note to the balance sheet.

The *non-current liabilities* include long-term borrowings, which are quite low in amount compared with those of many other companies of this size. The provisions relate to future obligations caused by: treating a contaminated site; reorganisation of part of the business; and future tax payable.

That stage of the statement of financial position (balance sheet) concludes with the net assets, defined as all assets minus all liabilities. Drawing a total at this point is not a requirement of any format, but is used by many companies as the point which creates a pause in the balance sheet before moving on to the ownership interest.

For a company the *ownership interest* is described as *capital and reserves*. The ownership interest in a company is specified in company law as comprising the claim created through the shares owned by the various equity holders (shareholders) and the claim representing additional reserves of wealth accumulated since the company began. That wealth is accumulated by making profits year after year. The claim is reduced when the owners take dividends from the company. (Further information on the reporting of share capital, reserves and dividends is contained in Chapter 12.)

The ownership interest is the part of the statement of financial position (balance sheet) which causes greatest confusion to most readers. It is purely a statement of a legal claim on the assets after all liabilities have been satisfied. The word *reserves* has no other significance. There is nothing to see, touch, count or hold. To add to the potential confusion, company law delights in finding names for various different kinds of ownership interest. If you are the kind of person who takes a broad-brush view of life you will not worry too much about share premium account, revaluation reserve and retained earnings. They are all part of accounting terminology which becomes important to a company lawyer when there is a dispute over how much dividend may be declared, but are less important to the investor who says 'How much is my total claim?'

7.5 Income statement (profit and loss account)

7.5.1 What items must be reported?

Companies that follow the IASB system of accounting in presenting an income statement must report the profit or loss for the period. There is no particular format required[4] but some items are listed in the relevant standard as a minimum set of disclosures (see Supplement 7.4 to this chapter). Companies choose the form of layout of the items in the income statement.

Companies that do not follow the IASB system of accounting must comply with the Companies Act 2006 and the UK accounting standards. The Companies Act 2006 contains more detail of the items to be reported and the format that must be used. The details are set out in Supplement 7.3 to this chapter.

7.5.2 What formats are used?

Companies applying the IASB system do not have to follow any particular format but it is likely that any income statement (profit and loss account) you see will resemble one of the formats described in this section because they will retain some of the traditions of the UK system that has existed for more than 20 years.

Companies that do not apply the IASB system of accounting must follow the requirements of the Companies Act 2006 and the standards of the UK ASB. The Companies Act 2006 permits four different formats of profit and loss account but the version most frequently observed in the UK is format 1 (see Supplement 7.4).

7.5.3 Illustration

The published income statements (profit and loss accounts) of most major companies are very similar to the illustration set out here for Safe and Sure plc.

Safe and Sure Group plc
Consolidated income statement (profit and loss account)
for the years ended 31 December

	Notes	Year 7 £m	Year 6 £m
Continuing operations			
Revenue	16	714.6	589.3
Cost of sales	16	(491.0)	(406.3)
Gross profit		223.6	183.0
Distribution costs		(2.2)	(2.5)
Administrative expenses	17	(26.2)	(26.5)
Profit from operations		195.2	154.0
Interest receivable (net)	18	2.3	3.0
Profit before tax	19	197.5	157.0
Tax	20	(62.2)	(52.4)
Profit for the period from continuing operations		135.3	104.6
Discontinued operations			
Loss for the period from discontinued operations	21	(20.5)	(10.0)
Profit for the period attributable to equity holders		114.8	94.6
Earnings per share	22	11.74	9.71

7.5.4 Discussion

The first point to note is the heading. This is a consolidated income statement (profit and loss account) bringing together the results of the activities of all the companies in the group during the year. The individual companies will also produce their own separate profit and loss accounts and these are added together to produce the consolidated picture. Where one company in the group sells items to another in the group, the sale and purchase are matched against each other on consolidation so that the results reported reflect only sales to persons outside the group.

The second point to note is that the income statement (profit and loss account) as presented by the company is more informative than the lists contained in Supplements 7.3 or 7.4 might suggest. That is partly because the company has used subtotals to break up the flow and make it digestible for the reader. One very common subtotal is the **gross profit** calculated as revenue minus the cost of the goods or services sold as revenue.

Starting at the top of the income statement we see that the word *revenue* is used to describe the sales of goods or services. **Revenue** is sometimes described as **turnover** or **sales**. Revenue (turnover) represents sales to third parties outside the group of companies. The **cost of sales** is the total of the costs of materials, labour and overheads which relate closely to earning the sales. The gross profit is sometimes referred to as the **gross margin** and is monitored closely by those who use the financial statements to make a judgement on the operations of the company. Within any industry the gross profit as a percentage of revenue (or turnover, or sales) is expected to be within known limits. If that percentage is low then the company is either underpricing its goods or else taking the market price but failing to control costs. If the percentage is high, then the company is perhaps a market leader which can command higher prices for its output because of its high reputation. However, it might also be seen by customers and competitors as charging too much for its goods or services.

The next item in the income statement (profit and loss account) is *distribution costs*, which would include the costs of delivering goods to customers. For this company the distribution costs are low because it provides services by contract and does not carry out much distribution work. For many users the trends in an amount are more interesting than the actual amount. They might ask why the amount has decreased. On the other hand, it is not a particularly significant component of the overall picture and the users might show little interest. They would pay more attention to the *administrative expenses*, a collective term for all those costs which have to be incurred in order to keep the business running but which are less closely related to the direct activity of creating revenue (making sales). The directors' salaries, head office costs and general maintenance of buildings and facilities are the kinds of details brought together under this heading. Directors' salaries are always a matter of some fascination and companies are expected to give considerable detail in the notes to the accounts about how much each director is paid and what other benefits are provided.

The *profit from operations* is the end of the first stage of the income statement (profit and loss account), where the story of the business operations is complete. The rest of the profit and loss account is concerned with the cost of financing the company.

As an example of finance costs, *interest* is paid on loans and received on investments, usually brought together in one net amount which shows, in this case, an excess of interest receivable over interest payable. That suggests a fairly cash-rich company with relatively low levels of borrowing. Next comes the *corporation tax*, which all companies must pay as a percentage of the profit before tax. The percentage is a standard percentage applied to the profit calculated according to the tax rules. Because the tax rules are not identical to the accounting rules, the percentage appears to vary when the reader looks at the income statement. Helpful companies will explain the tax charge in the Operating and Financial Review, as well as providing more detailed notes to the accounts on the tax charge.

That information ends with the profit for the period from continuing operations. Investors or analysts who want to make a forecast of future profits may decide to use this figure as a starting point because the activities will continue. Separately below this line the group shows the results in this period of operations that have been discontinued. Usually operations are discontinued because they are performing poorly so it is no great surprise to see a loss here. The loss is part of the performance of the period but investors can see that the bad news of this operation will not continue in future. Finally the equity holders (ordinary shareholders) see the profit for the period attributable to them.

They do not see here any mention of a reward in the form of a dividend which returns to them some of the wealth created by the company during the period. That information will appear in a statement of changes in equity which is explained in Chapter 12.

7.6 Statement of cash flows

The presentation of cash flow statements by companies is guided by IAS 7, *Statement of Cash Flows.* (There is a UK standard, FRS 1, which sets out a different form of cash flow statement,[5] but in this chapter the version required by IAS 7 is used because it is more likely that you will find this one in published financial statements.)

The benefits of cash flow information are explained in IAS 7.[6] A statement of cash flows, when used in conjunction with the rest of the financial statements, provides users with information on solvency and liquidity. It shows how cash is generated in the business and helps users to understand how much flexibility is available to adapt to changing circumstances and opportunities.

7.6.1 What items must be reported?

The statement of cash flows presents three classifications of cash flows.[7] These are:

- operating activities
- investing activities
- financing activities.

Definitions

Operating activities are the principal revenue-producing activities of the entity and other activities that are not investing or financing activities.

Investing activities are the acquisition and disposal of long-term assets and other investments not included in cash equivalents.

Financing activities are activities that result in changes in the size and composition of the contributed equity and borrowings of the entity.

Safe and Sure uses these classifications, as shown in the next section. We need two more definitions of terms in the cash flow statement. These are **cash** and **cash equivalents**.

Definitions

Cash comprises cash on hand and demand deposits.

Cash equivalents are short-term, highly liquid investments that are readily convertible to known amounts of cash and which are subject to an insignificant risk of changes in value.[8]

7.6.2 Illustration

Safe and Sure Group plc
Consolidated statement of cash flows for the years ended 31 December

	Notes	Year 7 £m	Year 6 £m
Cash flows from operating activities			
Cash generated from operations	23	196.7	163.5
Interest paid		(3.1)	(2.4)
UK corporation tax paid		(20.1)	(18.3)
Overseas tax paid		(30.5)	(26.5)
Net cash from operating activities		143.0	*116.3*

Cash flows from investing activities			
Purchase of tangible non-current assets		(60.0)	*(47.5)*
Sale of tangible non-current assets		12.0	*10.1*
Purchase of companies and businesses	25	(27.7)	*(90.1)*
Sale of a company		3.1	*–*
Movement in short-term deposits		(30.7)	*36.3*
Interest received		5.0	*5.9*
Net cash used in investing activities		(98.3)	*(85.3)*
Cash flows from financing activities			
Issue of ordinary share capital	27	3.1	*2.0*
Dividends paid to equity holders		(29.5)	*(24.4)*
Net loan movement (excluding overdraft)	26	16.2	*(24.0)*
Net cash used in financing activities		(10.2)	*(46.4)*
Net increase/(decrease) in cash and cash equivalents*		34.5	*(15.4)*
Cash and cash equivalents at the beginning of the year		27.9	*45.3*
Exchange adjustments		2.8	*(2.0)*
Cash and cash equivalents at the end of the year	29	65.2	*27.9*

* Cash on demand and deposits of maturity less than three months, net of overdrafts.

Note 23 Cash flow from operating activities
Reconciliation of operating profit to net cash flow from operating activities

	Year 7 £m	Year 6 £m
Profit before tax from continuing operations	195.2	*154.0*
Loss from discontinued operations	(20.5)	*(10.0)*
Profit from operations	174.7	*144.0*
Depreciation charge	33.2	*30.1*
Increase in inventories (stocks)*	(1.9)	*(1.1)*
Increase in trade receivables (debtors)*	(7.4)	*(5.3)*
Decrease in trade payables (creditors)*	(0.4)	*(3.6)*
Net cash inflow from continuing activities	198.2	*164.1*
Cash outflow in respect of discontinued item	(1.5)	*(0.6)*
Net cash inflow from operating activities	196.7	*163.5*

* *Note*: It is not possible to reconcile these figures with the information in the statement of financial position because of the effect of acquisitions during the year.

7.6.3 Discussion

The first line of the statement of cash flows is *cash flows from operating activities*, highlighted by the company as an important feature. Note 23 to the accounts explains why this is not the same as operating profit. When a company makes a profit it earns revenue which is greater than the expenses. Some of the revenue is collected as cash but some will be collected later when the credit customers pay. When expenses are incurred, some are paid for immediately but others relate to goods and services taken from suppliers. Note 23 to the accounts is set out above and shows that cash is generated by profits but is used when inventory (stock) levels increase and when trade receivables (debtors) increase. Allowing inventories (stocks) to increase will use up cash because more has to be paid for them. Allowing trade receivables (debtors) to increase means that credit customers are not paying the cash so fast and therefore the cash is not coming in. That will diminish cash flow. Allowing trade payables (creditors) to decrease is a further way of diminishing cash flow because it means that suppliers are being paid faster.

There is one other line in note 23 which gives pause for thought. That is the fourth line, *depreciation charge*. **Depreciation** is a measure of how much a non-current (fixed) asset has been used up. It is an amount which is deducted from profits as a measure of using up the cost of the non-current (fixed) asset in the accounting period. It does not of itself generate cash, but it stops the owners removing so much cash from the company that they are unable to replace a non-current (fixed asset) at the end of its useful life. Since it is not a cash item it has to be added back to the reported profit. By way of illustration, suppose a company pays £100 for goods and sells them for £150. It has generated £50 cash. In the income statement £10 is deducted for depreciation, so the reported profit becomes £40. The reconciliation of profit to cash flow from operations will be written as:

	£
Operating profit	40
add Depreciation	10
Cash inflow from operating activities	50

(There is more about depreciation in Chapter 8 and more about cash flow in Chapter 14.)

The cash generated from operations is used first of all to pay interest on loans, as a reward to lenders, and to pay taxation to the government. Deducting these items leaves the net cash from operating activities. This is the amount left over for long-term investment.

In the next section we find the cash flows from investing activities. The purchase of tangible non-current (fixed) assets is also called **capital expenditure**. Cash is paid to purchase new businesses and cash is received from selling companies or businesses no longer required. Safe and Sure has put some of its cash into short-term deposits to earn interest. In Year 6, Safe and Sure reduced the amount on short-term deposit, converting it back to cash that was available for spending, but in Year 7 it increased the amount on deposit, reducing the amount of cash available to spend in other ways. The final item in this investment section is interest received which is the reward for investment.

The third section shows the cash flows from financing activities. For some companies the cash inflow from operating activities may be insufficient to cover all the investment requirements for capital expenditure and acquisitions, so more finance has to be raised from external sources. Safe and Sure is not in such a difficult position because the cash generated from operations is greater than the cash paid out for investing activities. However, there is one further important outflow in the dividends paid to equity holders (shareholders). Dividend is the reward to equity holders (shareholders) for investing in the company. For the particular cash flow statement presented here, the broad story is that the company generated sufficient cash from its operations to cover loan interest, to pay the tax due, meet its investment needs and pay dividends. Despite that positive amount, the company has increased its loans by £16.2m and marginally increased its share capital by £3.1m, so that a total of £34.5m has been added to cash and deposits repayable on demand.

The company explained its cash flow management as follows in the Operating and Financial Review: 'The group's businesses are structured to use as little fixed and working capital as is consistent with the profit and earnings growth objective in order to produce a high cash flow.'

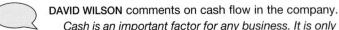

DAVID WILSON comments on cash flow in the company.

Cash is an important factor for any business. It is only one of the resources available but it is the key to survival.

What I'm basically looking for in the statement of cash flows is how well the company is balancing various sources of finance. It generated £196.7m from operating activities. The servicing of investment cost £3.1m in loan interest and the company paid taxes of £50.6m. That left net cash from operations amounting to £143.0m. That was used to cover its investing activities in new non-current (fixed) assets costing £48m (£60m less £12m) and acquisitions costing £24.6m after allowing for the sale of a company. Cash was used to increase short-term deposits by £30.7m. Interest received was £5m. The net cash used for investing activities amounted to £98.3m. If I deduct this from the £143m cash flow generated there is an increase in cash of £44.7m. The company had to pay a dividend of £29.5m, leaving £15.2m surplus cash. There was no immediate need for any long-term financing flows with a healthy cash flow like that. Nevertheless the company raised £3.1m in cash through an issue of shares to the employees' share option scheme and, perhaps surprisingly, there was an increase of £16.2m in short-term loans. Add the £15.2m to the £3.1m and £16.2m and you arrive at £34.5m which is the increase in cash and cash equivalents of the period. That brings me back to my earlier question of why they are holding so much cash and short-term deposits.

The company in this example has told me that it carries out its financial management by recognising that the tax bill has to be paid first of all. Then it plans its investment in non-current (fixed) assets and its programme of disposals. Once the investment has been decided the company aims to pay a dividend which will satisfy the expectations of investors. Surplus cash after that is available for acquisition of other companies and, because this company is always looking for good opportunities to expand, it will borrow ahead of time so that it is in a position to move quickly when a target presents itself. The company does not agree with IAS 7's requirement to separate out the bank deposits which had more than three months to run when they were made. The deposits are placed largely for six months, so that many have less than six months to run at the balance sheet date. It is all very accessible cash and the company sees it all as one pool.

In the Operating and Financial Review the finance director explains the company's view of cash flow as follows:

The Group's businesses are structured to utilise as little fixed and working capital as is consistent with the profit and earnings growth objective in order to produce a high cash flow. The impact of working capital on cash flow was held to an increase in Year 7 of £9.7m (Year 6: £10.0m).

A net cash flow of £196.7m was generated from operating activities. That was boosted by other amounts of cash from interest received. After paying interest and tax, the Group had £143.0m remaining. Fixed assets required £48.0m after allowing for the proceeds of selling some of our vehicle fleet in the routine replacement programme. That left £95m from which £24.6m was required to pay for acquisitions. The remaining £70.4m covered dividends of £29.5m leaving £40.9m. We received £5m interest on investments and raised £3.1m in ordinary share capital to give a net inflow of liquid funds in the year of £49.0m. Out of that amount, short-term deposits have increased by £14.5m, leaving an increase in cash of £34.5m.

You can see there are lots of different ways of interpreting the information in the cash flow statement. What is important is that the information is available.

7.7 Group structure of companies

Most major companies in the UK operate using a group structure. Within a group there is a **parent company** which controls **subsidiary companies** undertaking various different aspects of the operations of the business. It would in theory be possible to have all the operations located within one company but in practice, because company law draws very tight boundaries around a single company, there is some safety for the organisation in having different parts of the business packaged separately. If something goes seriously wrong with one subsidiary company, that company may be allowed to fail without irreparable damage to the total group. This approach has not always worked out in practice because very often the banks which lend money to a subsidiary will request guarantees from other companies in the group. So if one subsidiary fails in a spectacular way, it may drag the rest of the group with it.

Other reasons for retaining separate subsidiaries include: employee loyalty, product reputation, taxation legislation and overseas operations. When a new company is taken into the group, a sense of pride in the formerly independent company may be retained by continuing to use the traditional company name. The company name may be linked to a reputation for a high-quality product so that it is desirable to perpetuate the benefit of that reputation. Tax legislation applies to individual companies and not to the group as a whole. Efficient use of the tax laws may require different types of business to operate in different companies. Operations located in other countries will come under the legal systems of those countries and may be required to have a separate legal identity.

For accounting purposes the group as a whole is the economic entity for which financial statements are prepared. An entity should prepare and publish financial statements if financial information about the economic activities of that entity has the potential to be useful in making decisions about providing resources to the entity and in assessing whether the management and the governing board have made efficient and effective use of the resources provided.[9] The process of combining all the financial statements of the companies within a group is called **consolidation**. This chapter will explain sufficient aspects of the preparation of consolidated financial statements to allow an understanding of annual reports of groups of companies. The full complexities of consolidation and the wider aspects of group accounting may be found in advanced textbooks.

Definition

> **Consolidated** financial statements are the financial statements of a **group** in which the assets, liabilities, equity, income, expenses and cash flows of the **parent** and its **subsidiaries** are presented as those of a single economic entity.[10]

Consolidated financial statements recognise the parent's control of its subsidiaries. Consolidation is a process that aggregates the total assets, liabilities and results of all companies in the group. The consolidated balance sheet brings together all the assets controlled by the parent and shows all the liabilities to be satisfied from those assets. The consolidated income statement (profit and loss account) brings together all the revenues and costs of the companies in the group.

7.7.1 Defining a group

The smallest group consists of two companies. A group is created when one company (the **parent**) has **control** of another company (the **subsidiary**). There is no upper limit to the number of companies which may form a group.

The IASB has defined a group as a parent and all its subsidiaries.[11] A parent is an entity that controls one or more other entities.[12] A subsidiary is an entity, including an unincorporated entity such as a partnership, that is controlled by another entity (known as the **parent**).[13] **Consolidated** financial statements must include all **subsidiaries** of the parent, apart from some limited exemptions.[14]

Control is defined by the IASB. An investor controls an investee when it is exposed, or has rights, to variable returns from its involvement with the investee and has the ability to affect those returns through its power over the investee.[15] There are three elements to this definition of control. The investor must have all of the following:[16]

(a) power over the investee;

(b) exposure, or rights, to variable returns from its involvement with the investee; and

(c) the ability to use its power over the investee to affect the amount of the investor's returns.

7.7.2   The nature of control

The IASB has explained the reason for the definition of control used in IFRS 10. The need arose from the global financial crisis that started in 2007. Subsequent to the crisis it was found that some of the banks and other financial entities affected by the crisis had exposed investors to risk through using 'off balance sheet vehicles'. Political leaders of major economies across the world (the G20 leaders) asked the IASB to review the accounting and disclosure requirements for such 'off balance sheet vehicles'. The IASB found that the conditions applied were not always clear and consistent. IFRS 10 is the attempt to create that clarity and consistency.

Take each of the components of control in turn. Power over the investee is established by having rights that are capable of being exercised in practice. The most obvious right is a majority voting right as a shareholder in the investee. If the investor does not have a clear majority, there could nevertheless be control if other investors are passive. The investor might have control through agreements with other investors. The investor might have the right to appoint or remove the majority of the board of directors. It is important to consider the facts of the case in deciding whether there is control.

The second component is a variable return. Such a return could be a dividend, share repurchase, or a surplus on winding up. It could be a fee, tax benefit, or cost saving. The standard does not give an exhaustive list. Again all the facts must be considered.

Finally the investor must be able to exercise the power to influence the return. As examples: the investor might be able to vote for the amount of dividend payable; or the investor might be able to instruct the directors on the amount of dividend to be paid.

7.7.3   The parent company's statement of financial position

In some annual reports the parent company may choose to continue to produce its own statement of financial position (balance sheet), showing as an asset the cost of the investment in the subsidiary, but this information is not regarded as being particularly useful. The investment in the subsidiary is reported by the parent company as a single-line item but the consolidated statement of financial position shows all the assets and all the liabilities of the group under each separate heading. The group statement of financial position is more useful to readers. In previous chapters, where the financial statements of Safe and Sure plc have been discussed, the group accounts have been used.

7.7.4   Acquisition

The general term **business combination** may be applied to any transaction whereby one company becomes a subsidiary of another. The most common form of business combination is an **acquisition** where one party (the **acquirer**) is clearly the dominant entity and the other (the **acquiree**) is seen to be under new control. The method of accounting used to produce consolidated financial statements in an acquisition is called the **acquisition method**[17] (sometimes described as the **purchase method**). In this introductory text you do not need to worry about the details of the method of producing consolidated financial statements. All you need to do is recognise the descriptions used and be aware that when you see these words you are reading information about a group of companies combined.

Activity 7.4	*Check your understanding of the terms: parent, subsidiary, control, acquisition. Write down a definition of each and then look back through this section to test your definition against that in the text.*

7.8 Group financial statements

This section explains how the acquisition of a subsidiary affects the balance sheet of the parent company. It shows how the group's balance sheet and income statement (profit and loss account) are created. It also explains the nature of goodwill arising on acquisition and it outlines the nature and treatment of associated companies.

7.8.1 The parent company's balance sheet

When an acquisition takes place, the parent company acquires shares in the subsidiary in exchange for cash or for shares in the parent. The parent company will offer cash if it has adequate cash resources to make the offer and it appears that those selling the shares would prefer to take cash for investment elsewhere. The parent company will offer its own shares in exchange where it may not have sufficient cash resources available or where it thinks it can persuade those selling their shares in the target company of the desirability of acquiring shares in the new parent. Many deals offer a mixture of shares and cash.

For a cash purchase the effect on the parent company's balance sheet, in terms of the accounting equation, is:

For a share exchange, the effect on the parent company's balance sheet is to increase the assets and increase the ownership interest. In terms of the accounting equation:

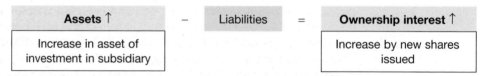

7.8.2 The group's consolidated statement of financial position

In the group's consolidated statement of financial position the parent company's assets and liabilities are added to the assets and liabilities of the subsidiary companies. The assets and liabilities of the subsidiary take the place of the parent company's investment in the subsidiary. Figure 7.2 shows the net assets of P and S separately. The arrows indicate the net assets of S moving in to take the place of P's investment in S. Removing

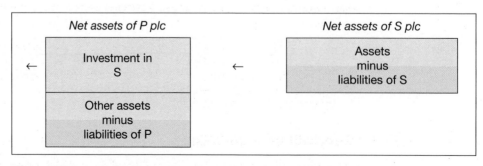

Figure 7.2
Separate net assets of parent and subsidiary

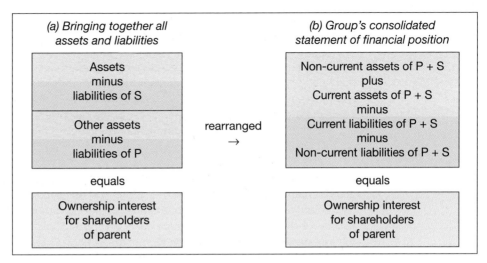

Figure 7.3
Completing the process of consolidation

the investment in S from the statement of financial position of P and replacing it with the net assets of S leads to the group's consolidated statement of financial position. Figure 7.3(a) shows the resulting amalgamation. The assets and liabilities in Figure 7.3(a) are then rearranged under each asset and liability category to result in Figure 7.3(b).

7.8.3 The group income statement (profit and loss account)

Investors and their advisers may wish to use the income statement (profit and loss account) of the group to make predictions of the future profitability of the group. To be able to do this, they must know how much of the current year's profit relates to continuing operations and how much relates to changes during the year. The illustration of the income statement of Safe and Sure plc in section 7.5.3 shows how the consolidated profit and loss is subdivided into continuing activities and discontinued activities.

One rule of acquisition accounting is that, where a subsidiary is acquired part-way through the year, only the profits earned after the date of acquisition may be included in the group income statement. The analyst seeking to make a forecast for the year ahead will be helped by a note to the accounts showing what the profit would have been from a full 12-month contribution.

Groups are not required to present separately the parent company's income statement (profit and loss account). It is not felt to be particularly interesting to users as, generally, the parent company's main income comprises the dividends received from its investments in subsidiaries. Usually it is the subsidiaries which carry out the operations generating profit. It is far more interesting to know about the underlying operating profits which allow those dividends to be paid to the parent.

Activity 7.5

P plc pays cash of £6m for an investment in net assets of S Ltd having a net book value (equal to fair value) of £6m. Explain how this transaction will affect the balance sheet of P plc as the parent company and explain how it will affect the group balance sheet of P Group plc, whose only subsidiary is S Ltd.

7.8.4 Goodwill on acquisition

In the illustration presented in Figure 7.2 and Figure 7.3 the net assets of the subsidiary were shown as being of the same magnitude as the amount of the investment in the subsidiary so that the substitution of the former for the latter was a neat replacement process. That situation is unlikely to apply in real life because the price paid for an investment will rarely depend solely on the net assets being acquired. The purchaser will be looking to the future expectations from the investment and the seller will be seeking a reward for all that has been built into the business which cannot readily be quantified in terms of tangible assets. The future expectations will rest upon the reputation of the product or service, the quality of the customers, the skills of the workforce and the state of the order book, amongst many other things. The price negotiated for the business will include some recognition of all these qualities under the global heading of **goodwill**.

In these circumstances the price paid for the investment in the subsidiary will be greater than the amount of the net assets of the subsidiary. When the consolidation into the group statement of financial position is attempted, a space will appear. Figure 7.4 shows the separate net assets of P plc and S plc. The amount of the cost of the investment in S is greater than the net assets of S plc.

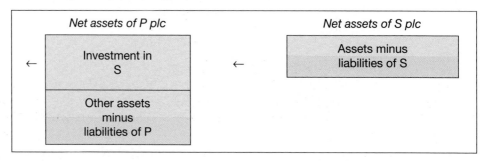

Figure 7.4
Net assets of the separate companies P plc and S plc

Figure 7.5 shows the resulting consolidation. The space shaded is equal to the difference between the amount of the investment in S and the net assets of S. This space is, in arithmetic terms, nothing more than a **difference on consolidation** but has traditionally been called **goodwill** because it is explained in terms of paying for something more than the underlying net assets.

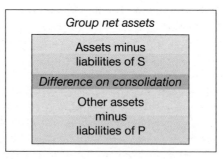

Figure 7.5
Group net assets of the P group

Definition

Goodwill is defined as an asset representing the future economic benefits arising from other assets acquired in a business combination that are not individually identified and separately recognised.[18]

Goodwill is recognised in the statement of financial position as an asset and is measured as the excess of the cost of the business combination over the fair value of the net assets acquired.[19]

The existence of a difference on consolidation is an inescapable consequence of the process of combining the statements of financial position of parent and subsidiary. For many years it caused one of the most difficult problems facing the accounting standard-setters. The questions asked were: 'How should this consolidation difference be reported in the balance sheets of succeeding years?' and 'Is it an asset?'

After a great deal of international debate and disagreement, the IASB has taken the view that acquisition goodwill is an asset that should be tested regularly by means of an **impairment test** which asks, 'Can the business expect to recover the carrying value of the intangible asset, through either using it or selling it?' If the answer is 'no' then the asset is impaired and its value must be reduced. An expense of impairment will appear in the income statement (profit and loss account). If the answer is 'yes' then the asset value should remain in the balance sheet.

Definition	**Impairment** means 'damaged' or 'spoiled'. Where the carrying value of goodwill cannot be recovered through sale or use, it is said to be 'impaired'. The asset value in the balance sheet must be reduced.

Activity 7.6	*P pays cash of £8m for an investment in net assets of S Ltd having a net book value (equal to fair value) of £6m. Explain how this transaction will affect the statement of financial position of P plc as the parent company and explain how it will affect the group statement of financial position of P Group plc, whose only subsidiary is S Ltd.*

7.8.5 Associated companies

Where company P holds less than a controlling interest in company A, it may nevertheless have a significant influence over company A. Such significant influence would involve the power to participate in the financial and operating policy decisions of company A. Significant influence is presumed to exist when one company or a group of companies holds 20% or more of the ordinary shareholders' voting rights of another company, unless the facts indicate that significant influence is not possible.[20]

Where significant influence over a company exists, that company is called an **associated company**. The group must show in its balance sheet the group's share of the net assets of the associated company as a single-line item, and must show in the income statement (profit and loss account) the group's share of the profits or losses of the associated company.

This treatment of an investment in an associated company is called **equity accounting** because it reports the parent's and the group's share of the investment in the ownership interest (also referred to as the equity).

For investments which do not meet the conditions of being reported as associated companies, the accounting treatment is to record the investment at cost in the balance sheet and to record in the income statement of the group only the dividend income received from the associate.

7.9 Small and medium-sized entities (SMEs)

7.9.1 Definitions

The amount of detail in the information presented by companies depends on their size. The Companies Act 2006 defines small and medium-sized companies. The definitions are based on turnover, balance sheet totals and average number of employees.

Currently the limits for a small company are satisfying two or more of the conditions: turnover not more than £5.6m, balance sheet total not more than £2.8m and employees not more than 50 (section 382). The limits for a medium-sized company are satisfying two or more of the conditions: turnover not more than £22.8m, balance sheet total not more than £11.4m and employees not more than 250 (section 465). The amounts for turnover and balance sheet totals are altered from time to time by Statutory Instrument to keep pace with inflation, so it is perhaps easiest to take as a 'rule of thumb' the employee limits of 50 for a small company and 250 for a medium-sized company. For these companies there are substantial exemptions from requirements to publish information (although they must still provide details to shareholders if asked to do so). Generally they are not listed companies and so are not required to meet the obligations placed on listed companies. Most of these small and medium-sized companies are currently presenting financial statements based on UK ASB standards and company law. Section 7.9.2 explains proposals for change that will affect these companies.

During the 1980s, concerns were expressed about the 'burden' of regulation for small companies. This burden was seen as falling from all directions, including tax laws, employment laws, product protection laws, health and safety laws and accounting regulation. The government of the time committed itself to reducing this burden. One consequence was that the UK Accounting Standards Board introduced a Financial Reporting Standard for Smaller Entities (FRSSE). This condenses into one standard the essential aspects of all the separate accounting standards for larger companies. It reduces disclosure requirements but maintains standards for measurement. Small companies may choose either to apply the FRSSE in full or to comply with the full range of separate standards.

The Companies Act 2006 permits small and medium-sized companies to file 'abbreviated' financial statements with the Registrar of Companies. The word 'abbreviated' can be explained as 'cutting down the detail' but views have been expressed that this has gone too far and that abbreviated financial statements do not provide useful information about small companies. It allows them, for example, to maintain confidentiality of profit margins. During discussions on law reform leading to the Companies Act 2006, the White Paper of 2005[21] acknowledged this concern but noted that the option was popular with many companies. It said that the Government intended to retain the option for abbreviated financial statements but would require small and medium-sized companies to disclose revenue (turnover).

7.9.2 IFRS for SMEs and the future of UK GAAP

After many years of discussion the IASB issued a shortened form of accounting standards called *International Financial Reporting Standards for Small and Medium-sized Entities* (IFRS for SMEs).[22]

It maintains measurement principles that are consistent with the full IFRS but is a considerably shorter document. It achieves this in several ways. Firstly, topics not relevant to SMEs are omitted. Secondly, where the full IFRSs allow accounting policy choices, the IFRS for SMEs specifies one choice only and selects the least difficult one. Thirdly, while the measurement principles are consistent with full IFRS, the SME version simplifies the principles for recognising and measuring assets, liabilities, income and expenses. Fourthly, the required disclosures are significantly reduced in number. Finally, the standard has been written in clear language that can be translated relatively easily.

After 2005 there was a continuing need for UK GAAP where standards were maintained by the UK ASB for those companies that do not use the full IFRS. The need for continuing UK GAAP seems less clear now there exists the IFRS for SMEs. However it is necessary for national regulators to decide whether their country will adopt the IFRS for SMEs.

Accordingly the UK ASB issued a discussion paper in 2009 asking whether, and how soon, UK SMEs could move to the IFRS for SMEs. The tentative target was 2012 but the proposals met some significant objections. This in turn led to a further consultation via an exposure draft, FRED 48, issued in January 2012 for comment, recommended:

(a) replacing all current financial reporting standards (FRS and SSAPs) in the UK and Republic of Ireland with a single FRS;

(b) introducing a reduced disclosure framework for the financial reporting of certain qualifying entities see now FRS 101 (November 2012) and

(c) retaining the FRSSE with a further consultation on how to update it following the European Commission proposals for the future of financial reporting for small and micro companies.

These recommendations are implemented in FRS 100, 101 and 102, issued in November 2012 and in 2013.[23]

7.10 Beyond the annual report

The annual report is a regulated base of information on which a reporting cycle is built. The cycle begins when the company makes its first announcement of the results of the financial year. This announcement is made in a manner dictated by the Disclosure and Transparency Rules of the FSA.

The cycle continues with reports being issued in the period between annual reports. These are called 'interim reports'. The FSA requires half-yearly reports. The regulators of the US stock exchanges require quarterly reports. All UK listed companies provide half-yearly reports and some voluntarily provide quarterly reports.

Other questions arising beyond the annual report are:

- What help exists for small and medium-sized companies to reduce the burden of communication for regulatory purposes?
- How do larger companies avoid information overload for their shareholders?
- Can users have confidence in additional information provided beyond the annual report?
- What developments is the UK government currently implementing or planning?

This section outlines developments on these issues.

7.10.1 Announcing the annual report

For many years the **preliminary announcement** was the first external communication of the financial performance and position of a company in relation to the financial year most recently completed. When the year-end results and half-yearly results were ready for publication, a preliminary announcement of key information was made in a manner set out by the Stock Exchange, consistent with the aim of fair and equal access for all investors. The preliminary announcement was usually accompanied by a press release, giving the information to the media, and by meetings with professional investors and brokers' analysts at which key personnel in the company (usually the chairman, chief executive and finance director) would make speeches and answer questions.

This traditional route has been modified since 2007 by the Disclosure and Transparency Rules (DTR) of the Financial Services Authority. The DTR set out the methods by which a company may announce that its annual report is available. Companies must make public their annual report within four months of the financial year end. A company cannot make an announcement until the full text of the annual report is available on the company's website.

Companies can announce their results in one of two ways. Either:

1. Disseminate the full annual report in unedited full text.

or

2. Disseminate 'components only' in unedited full text by providing those parts of the annual report that would be available in a half-yearly interim report.

In both cases there needs to be a link to the website where the full annual report can be found. 'Unedited full text' does not include pdf format.

There is no requirement for making a preliminary announcement, although the FSA expects that many companies will wish to continue this practice. For those who wish to do so, there is a defined process for making the preliminary announcement. If it is audited then there should be a link to the full annual report on the website. If it is unaudited there will be a dissemination announcement when the full audited report is published.

REAL WORLD CASE

BT Group plc

Thursday 24 May 2012

Annual Financial Report

Annual Report & Form 20-F 2012
Summary financial statement & notice of meeting 2012

Following release on 10 May 2012 of its final results for the fourth quarter and year to 31 March 2012 (the Results Announcement), BT announces that the above documents have been published today and are available on our website at www.bt.com/annualreport

Copies of these documents, together with the proxy forms for the BT Annual General Meeting, have been submitted to the National Storage Mechanism and will shortly be available for inspection at http://www.morningstar.co.uk/uk/NSM

Discussion point:

Compare the 'unedited full text' of the regulatory announcement with the pdf format of the full annual report. Which text format do you prefer?

7.10.2 Periodic reporting within the financial year

The Transparency Directive of the European Union seeks to enhance transparency in EU capital markets through a common framework which includes periodic financial reports.

Listed UK companies must produce two interim management statements (IMS) each financial year, with one in each six-month period, ten weeks after the beginning and six months before the end of the relevant six-month period. The IMS must provide information on any material events and transactions and their impact on the financial position of the company, along with a general description of the company's financial position and performance. IMS must contain up-to-date information from the beginning of the period until the date of publication.

Half-yearly reports must be produced within two months of the end of the first six months of the financial year. Half-yearly reports have previously been called 'interim reports'. The international accounting standard IAS 34[24] provides guidance on interim reporting which is acceptable to the FSA for the purpose of half-yearly reporting.

One interesting accounting question is how to measure the results of half a year. One view is that the results of half a year should represent the actual events of that half-year. This is called the 'discrete' method. A different view is that the result for six months should represent half of the results of the full year. This is called the 'integral' method. Why does this make a difference? Imagine a company which manufactures and sells fireworks. The costs will fall evenly through the year but most of the sales will arise in the months leading to 5 November. Using the discrete method, the first six months of the calendar year will show low profits or perhaps losses. The second six months will show relatively high profits. Using the integral method each half-year will show the same profit at 50% of the total figure of the year.

IAS 34 requires the discrete method to be used as far as possible. Some expense items, such as taxation, may have to be spread evenly over the year.

In matters of disclosure the IASB recommends that the interim report should include a balance sheet, income statement, statement of changes in equity and cash flow, together with explanatory notes and comments.

Activity 7.7

Obtain the half-yearly report and the annual report of a major listed company. Compare the half-yearly report with the annual report. What are the information items in the half-yearly report? How do they compare with the full year in the annual report? What statements of accounting policy are made in the half-yearly report?

7.10.3 Prospectus

When a major company wants to raise significant amounts of finance through selling shares on the Stock Market, it issues a **prospectus**. The contents of the prospectus are regulated by the UK Listing Authority, backed up on some items by the Companies Act 2006. The document is often several hundred pages in length and quite formidable in appearance. It contains more detail than the annual report. The prospectus is a public document but there is no central archive of prospectuses so it is useful in research projects to retain copies as they appear. Some business libraries retain copies.

7.10.4 Avoiding information overload

Even the very largest companies may take advantage of the rule which allows them to publish summary financial statements. These are usually very much shorter than the full annual report and are offered to shareholders as an alternative to the full report. There is a short form of the balance sheet, profit and loss account and cash flow statement, no notes to the accounts but usually an accompanying commentary by the company directors. Shareholders are reminded of the existence of the full report and invited to ask for a copy if desired.

7.10.5 Additional non-GAAP measures

A survey undertaken by the accountancy firm Deloitte[25] showed widespread use in 2010 and 2011 of additional non-GAAP measures of performance reported on the face of the income statement. Such additional measures are encouraged by IAS 1 when they are relevant to an understanding of the financial performance of the company. One criticism made by Deloitte is that some of the companies do not define their non-GAAP measures so that it is difficult for readers to understand why they are being used. The most common adjustments observed are the exclusion of the costs of fundamental reorganisation from non-GAAP performance measures. Other exclusions covered impairment, amortisation of intangibles and asset disposal and items relating to changes in value of financial assets and liabilities. A common form of presentation observed was the use of the word 'exceptional' to describe such costs, locating them in a separate column on the income statement or in a separate box that can be removed from the performance measures. In the Real World case study at the start of this chapter you can see additional non-GAAP measures illustrated.

Two different views may be taken of this flexible approach. One is that it allows a company to provide a better understanding of its financial performance. The other is that it allows a company to confuse investors by presenting performance in a way that favours the company and distracts the reader from the overall picture.

7.10.6 'Pro forma' financial statements

'Pro forma' financial statements represent a recent development in company reporting that is causing some confusion among users of accounting information, and some concern among the regulators. According to the dictionary, the phrase 'pro forma' means 'as a matter of form'. The underlying accounting meaning is 'outside the normal reporting regulations'. It usually involves selective editing from a larger body of information that has been prepared under accounting rules, or the inclusion of some items that would not be permitted under the accounting standards applied. The risk is that the selective information may not, by itself, represent a true and fair view. This does not necessarily mean that the information is bad or misleading, but it does mean that the investor is deprived of the full protection of regulation. As an example, a company was formed by a demerger from a larger group, changing the capital structure and changing the accounting year-end. To preserve comparability the company adjusted the figures for earlier years to be presented on a basis consistent with more recent years. This company also defined its own 'benchmark' profit measures which are not specified in accounting standards. It claimed the pro forma and benchmark information helps readers better to understand the performance of the group.

7.10.7 Electronic publication of documents

One conclusion of the Company Law Review, leading to the Companies Act 2006, was that the law allows financial reporting to be a slow process that could be speeded up by use of electronic delivery. The Companies Act now confirms that a document supplied in electronic form will be validly delivered if that form has been agreed by the intended recipient (or the intended recipient had not replied when asked for a preference). However, shareholders and others having a right to receive information are able to ask for a paper copy of a document.

7.11 Summary

- Company law in the UK includes sections that implement EU Directives. This means that UK company accounting has for many years been harmonised with company accounting in other member states of the EU, but mainly in matters of disclosure. Member states have continued to require or permit different measurement practices.

- From 2005 listed groups of companies in EU member states have been required to follow the IASB system of reporting. Individual companies and unlisted groups have the choice of the IASB system or UK company law and UK ASB standards.

- The primary financial statements under both systems include a statement of financial position, income statement (profit and loss account) and statement of cash flows. Under the IASB system a statement of changes in equity is required. Under the UK ASB standards a statement of recognised gains and losses is required and a note of movements on reserves.

- Formats set out the content and layout of financial statements. Under UK company law there are detailed formats required for the balance sheet and profit and loss account. The IASB system is more flexible on layout but provides lists of essential items.

- A group of companies consists of a parent and subsidiaries. All must be included. A subsidiary is defined by the control exercised by the parent. Control is commonly evidenced by the parent holding more than half of the voting power in the subsidiary. Control may be evidenced in other kinds of agreements relating to shareholdings or to the board of directors.

- A consolidated statement of financial position contains the total assets and liabilities of the group of companies, after eliminating any amounts receivable and payable between group companies.

- A consolidated income statement (profit and loss account) contains the total revenues and expenses of the group of companies, after eliminating any transactions and profits made between group companies.

- A consolidated statement of cash flows contains the total cash flows of the group of companies, after eliminating any cash flows between group companies.

- Goodwill arising on acquisition is calculated by comparing the fair value of the payment for the subsidiary with the fair value of net assets acquired. It represents future economic benefits arising from assets that are not capable of being individually identified and separately recognised.

- Goodwill is recognised as an asset in the balance sheet and is tested annually for impairment.

- Beyond the annual report there is a range of corporate communications – often found most readily by visiting a company's website.

- For small companies special disclosure rules apply to reduce the burden of providing information.

Further reading

Deloitte LLP provide regular surveys of the content of annual report, published on the website www.deloitte.com in the Audit Section.

IAS 1 (2012), *Presentation of Financial Statements*. International Accounting Standards Board. This is a detailed standard, some of which is beyond a first-level course, but the examples of financial statements given in the Appendix show the types of presentation that companies might use or adapt.

IFRS 3 (2012), *Business Combinations*. International Accounting Standards Board. (This is a very detailed standard which is beyond a first-level course but the definitions in the Appendix may be useful in explaining terms encountered in financial statements.)

FRS 102 The Financial Reporting Standard applicable in the UK and Republic of Ireland issued by the Financial Reporting Council (2013).

Useful websites

International Accounting Standards Board: www.ifrs.org

Financial Reporting Council: www.frc.org.uk

London Stock Exchange: www.londonstockexchange.com

Financial Services Authority: www.fsa.gov.uk

QUESTIONS

The Questions section of each chapter has three types of question. 'Test your understanding' questions to help you review your reading are in the 'A' series of questions. You will find the answers to these by reading and thinking about the material in the book. 'Application' questions to test your ability to apply technical skills are in the 'B' series of questions. Questions requiring you to show skills in problem solving and evaluation are in the 'C' series of questions. A letter [S] indicates that there is a solution at the end of the book.

A Test your understanding

A7.1 What is a Directive? (Section 7.2.1)

A7.2 What is the IAS Regulation? (Section 7.2.1)

A7.3 What is the role of the IASB? (Section 7.2.2)

A7.4 Name the primary financial statements and explain the purpose of each. (Section 7.3.1)

A7.5 The following technical terms appear in this chapter. Check that you know the meaning of each. (If you cannot find them again in the text, they are defined at the end of the book.)

(a) revenue
(b) capital
(c) non-current asset
(d) depreciation
(e) directors
(f) earnings for equity holders (ordinary shareholders)
(g) earnings per share
(h) external users (of financial statements)
(i) financial position
(j) gross
(k) gross margin
(l) gross profit
(m) net
(n) net assets
(o) primary financial statements
(p) reserves
(q) revaluation reserve
(r) share premium
(s) property, plant and equipment
(t) revenue

A7.6 How do companies report: (Section 7.3.1)

(a) financial position;
(b) performance; and
(c) changes in financial position?

A7.7 What are the main headings to be found in most company statements of financial position? (Section 7.4)

A7.8 In the Companies Act formats, what is the reason for the order of items under heading C: current assets? (Section 7.4)

A7.9 What are the main headings to be found in most company income statements (profit and loss accounts)? (Section 7.5)

A7.10 What are the main sections of a statement of cash flows prepared according to IAS 7? (Section 7.6)

A7.11   Why does depreciation appear as a line item in the reconciliation of operating profit with cash flow? (Section 7.6.3)

A7.12   Explain why groups of companies are formed. (Section 7.7)

A7.13   Explain the purpose of consolidated financial statements. (Section 7.7)

A7.14   Define the terms: (Section 7.7.1)

(a)   group;
(b)   parent company; and
(c)   subsidiary.

A7.15   Explain, using the accounting equation, the effect on the parent company's balance sheet of a cash payment for an investment in a subsidiary company. (Section 7.8.1)

A7.16   Explain, using the accounting equation, the effect on the parent company's balance sheet of a share issue in exchange for shares in the subsidiary company. (Section 7.8.1)

A7.17   Explain what is meant by goodwill on acquisition. (Section 7.8.4)

A7.18   What is an associated company? (Section 7.8.5)

A7.19   Apart from the annual report, what other documents do companies use to communicate financial statement information to investors, creditors and other users of financial statements? (Section 7.9)

B   Application

B7.1 [S]
Write a letter to the financial controller of a company advising on the factors which a company should take into consideration when deciding how to arrange information in financial statements.

B7.2 [S]
Write a note for financial analysts explaining how the published income statement (profit and loss account) provides a useful indication of the financial performance of a company.

B7.3 [S]
What features are likely to make a balance sheet helpful to users?

B7.4 [S]
Could a statement of cash flows be presented as the only financial statement reported by a company? Explain your view.

C   Problem solving and evaluation

C7.1 [S]
A listed company is of the view that shareholders might welcome a statement of highlights and supplementary information as a leaflet to be inserted in the annual report. Give advice on the principles to be followed in making such information useful to users.

Activities for study groups

Continuing to use the annual reports of companies which you obtained for Chapters 1 and 4, find the financial statements and the notes to the accounts.

1   Compare the financial statements with the formats and presentations shown in this chapter, and note any differences which you observe. Look at the notes to the accounts for items

which are required by the regulations but are included in the notes rather than the main financial statements.

2 Find the Operating and Financial Review (sometimes named the Business Review or the finance director's review) and compare the cash flow discussion there with the FRS 1 presentation. Form a view on how readily the discussion may be related to the financial statement.

3 In your group, take the list of qualitative characteristics listed at section 4.2 and use the financial statements as a means of illustrating how the company has met those characteristics. If you have a set of different annual reports, each member of the group should take the role of a finance director pointing out the qualitative characteristics of their own company's financial statements. The group together should then decide on a ranking with a view to nominating one of the annual reports for an award of 'Communicator of the Year'.

Notes and references

1. IAS 1 (2012), *Presentation of Financial Statements*, para. 10.
2. IASB *Conceptual Framework*, para. OB 2.
3. The Appendix to IAS 1 (2012) gives an illustration which is not compulsory.
4. The Appendix to IAS 1 (2012) gives an illustration which is not compulsory.
5. ASB (1996), Financial Reporting Standard (FRS 1), *Cash Flow Statements*, Accounting Standards Board (revised from 1991 version).
6. IASB (2012), IAS 7 *Statement of Cash Flows*, para. 4.
7. IAS 7 (2012), para. 6.
8. IAS 7 (2012), para. 6.
9. IASB (2010), Exposure Draft: The Reporting Entity, para. RE 3.
10. IFRS 10 (2012), *Consolidated financial statements*, Appendix A.
11. IFRS 10 (2012), Appendix A.
12. IFRS 10 (2012), Appendix A.
13. IFRS 10 (2012), Appendix A.
14. IFRS 10 (2012), para. 4.
15. IFRS 10 (2012), para. 6.
16. IFRS 10 (2012), para. 7.
17. IFRS 3 (2012), para. 4.
18. IFRS 3 (2012), Appendix A.
19. IFRS 3 (2012), para. 32. In this section it is assumed in the explanations that fair value equals book value of net assets of subsidiary.
20. IAS 28 (2012), *Investments in Associates and Joint Venture*, paras 2 and 5.
21. DTI Company Law Reform 2005, http://www.bis.gov.uk/files/file13958.pdf
22. IASB (2012), *International Financial Reporting Standard for Small and Medium-sized Entities*.
23. The Financial Reporting Council has issued the following:
    FRS 100 *Application of Financial Reporting Requirements* (Nov. 2012);
    FRS 101 *Reduced Disclosure Framework* (Nov. 2012);
    FRS 102 *The Financial Reporting Standard applicable in the UK and Republic of Ireland* (2013).
24. IASB (2012), IAS 34 *Interim Financial Reporting*.
25. *Gems and Jetsam: Surveying annual reports*. Deloitte LLP (2011), www.deloitte.com.

Information to be presented on the face of the statement of financial position, as required by IAS 1

Note that this is a list of items, not a format, so a company could choose to present the items in a different sequence.

There must be separate headings for current and non-current assets, and current and non-current liabilities.[1]

As a minimum the face of the statement of financial position must include the following line items:[2]

(a) Property, plant and equipment
(b) Investment property
(c) Intangible assets
(d) Financial assets
(e) Investments accounted for using the equity method
(f) Biological assets
(g) Inventories
(h) Trade and other receivables
(i) Cash and cash equivalents
(j) The total of assets classified as 'held for sale'
(k) Trade and other payables
(l) Provisions
(m) Financial liabilities (excluding items shown under (k) and (l))
(n) Liabilities and assets for current tax
(o) Deferred tax assets and deferred tax liabilities
(p) Liabilities included in disposal groups classified as held for sale
(q) Non-controlling (minority) interests within equity (ownership interest)
(r) Issued capital and reserves attributable to equity holders of the parent.

An entity must disclose further subclassifications of these line items, classified in a manner appropriate to the entity's operations. These further subclassifications may be presented either on the face of the statement of financial position or in notes.[3]

1. IAS 1 (2012), para. 60.
2. IAS 1 (2012), para. 54.
3. IAS 1 (2012), para. 77.

Balance sheet format 1, as prescribed by the Companies Act 2006

The details of the Companies Act 2006 are implemented in regulations called Statutory Instruments (SI). SI 2008/410 *The Large and Medium-sized Companies and Groups (Accounts and Reports) Regulations 2008* sets out formats that should be used by UK companies that are not reporting under IFRS. The formats are specified as lists of headings. The list attaches letters A to K to the main headings and uses roman numerals for subheadings of items which are important but slightly less important than the main headings. The headings labelled by letters A to K and the subheadings labelled by roman numerals must be shown in the main body of the balance sheet. There are further lists of detailed items which must be reported but which may be contained in additional pages of notes to the balance sheet. These lists are given arabic numerals to identify them. There is a general rule that where an item under any heading is not relevant to the company, or is of zero amount, it need not be disclosed. So if a company does not mention one of the items in the format, it has to be presumed that the particular item is not relevant to that company.

A **Called-up share capital not paid**

B **Fixed assets**
    I   *Intangible assets*
        1 Development costs
        2 Concessions, patents, licences, trade marks and similar rights and assets
        3 Goodwill
        4 Payments on account
    II   *Tangible assets*
        1 Land and buildings
        2 Plant and machinery
        3 Fixtures, fittings, tools and equipment
        4 Payments on account and assets in course of construction
    III *Investments*
        1 Shares in group undertakings
        2 Loans to group undertakings
        3 Participating interests (excluding group undertakings)
        4 Loans to undertakings in which the company has a participating interest
        5 Other investments other than loans
        6 Other loans
        7 Own shares

C **Current assets**
    I   *Stocks*
        1 Raw materials and consumables
        2 Work in progress
        3 Finished goods and goods for resale
        4 Payments on account
    II   *Debtors*
        1 Trade debtors
        2 Amounts owed by group undertakings

3 Amounts owed by undertakings in which the company has a participating interest

4 Other debtors

5 Called-up share capital not paid

6 Prepayments and accrued income

III *Investments*

1 Shares in group undertakings

2 Own shares

3 Other investments

IV *Cash at bank and in hand*

D Prepayments and accrued income

E Creditors: amounts falling due within one year

1 Debenture loans

2 Bank loans and overdrafts

3 Payments received on account

4 Trade creditors

5 Bills of exchange payable

6 Amounts owed to group undertakings

7 Amounts owed to undertakings in which the company has a participating interest

8 Other creditors including taxation and social security

9 Accruals and deferred income

F Net current assets (liabilities)

G Total assets less current liabilities

H Creditors: amounts falling due after more than one year

1 Debenture loans

2 Bank loans and overdrafts

3 Payments received on account

4 Trade creditors

5 Bills of exchange payable

6 Amounts owed to group undertakings

7 Amounts owed to undertakings in which the company has a participating interest

8 Other creditors including taxation and social security

9 Accruals and deferred income

I Provisions for liabilities and charges

1 Pensions and similar obligations

2 Taxation, including deferred taxation

3 Other provisions

J Accruals and deferred income

Minority interests*

K Capital and reserves

I *Called-up share capital*

II *Share premium account*

III *Revaluation reserve*

IV *Other reserves*

1 Capital redemption reserve

2 Reserve for own shares

3 Reserves provided by the articles of association

4 Other reserves

V *Profit and loss account*

Minority interests*

* *Note*: Where minority interests are relevant, they are to be treated as having a letter attached. Companies may choose one of the two permitted locations.

Information to be presented on the face of the Income Statement as required by IAS 1

The IASB sets out the contents of the full statement of comprehensive income and then explains how it may be separated into an income statement and a statement of other comprehensive income.

As a minimum, the statement of comprehensive income must include line items that present the following amounts for the period:[1]

(a) revenue;

(b) gains and losses arising from the derecognition of financial assets measured at amortised cost;

(c) finance costs;

(d) share of the profit or loss of associates and joint ventures accounted for using the equity method;

(e) if a financial asset is reclassified so that it is measured at fair value, any gain or loss arising from a difference between the previous carrying amount and its fair value at the reclassification date (as defined in IFRS 9);

(f) tax expense;

(g) a single amount comprising the total of:

    1. the post-tax profit or loss of discontinued operations; and

    2. the post-tax gain or loss recognised on the measurement to fair value less costs to sell or on the disposal of the assets or disposal group(s) constituting the discontinued operation;

(h) profit or loss;

(i) each component of other comprehensive income classified by nature (excluding amounts in (h));

(j) share of the other comprehensive income of associates and joint ventures accounted for using the equity method; and

(k) total comprehensive income.

An entity must disclose the following items in the statement of comprehensive income as allocations for the period:[2]

(a) profit or loss for the period attributable to:

    i. non-controlling interests, and

    ii. *owners* of the parent.

(b) total comprehensive income for the period attributable to:

    i. non-controlling interests, and

    ii. owners of the parent.

If the entity chooses to present a separate income statement then this must include the line items (a) to (f) from the first list above and the disclosures in paragraph (a)(i) and (ii) of the allocations for the period between non-controlling interests and owners of the parent.[3]

An entity must present additional line items, headings and subtotals in the statement of comprehensive income and the separate income statement (if presented), when such presentation is relevant to an understanding of the entity's financial performance.[4]

1. IAS 1 (2012), para. 82.
2. IAS 1 (2012), para. 83.
3. IAS 1 (2012), para. 84.
4. IAS 1 (2012), para. 85.

UK Companies Act profit and loss account format 1 – list of contents

1 Turnover
2 Cost of sales
3 Gross profit
4 Distribution costs
5 Administrative expenses
6 Other operating income
7 Income from shares in group undertakings
8 Income from participating interests (excluding group undertakings)
9 Income from other fixed asset investments
10 Other interest received and similar income
11 Amounts written off investments
12 Interest payable and similar charges
13 Tax on profit or loss of ordinary activities
14 Profit or loss on ordinary activities after taxation
15 Extraordinary income
16 Extraordinary charges
17 Extraordinary profit or loss
18 Tax on extraordinary profit or loss
19 Other taxes not shown under the above items
20 Profit or loss for the financial year

Chapter 8

Non-current (fixed) assets

ITV is the largest commercial television network in the UK. It operates a family of channels including ITV1 and delivers content across multiple platforms. Read the following extracts from the Accounting Policies section of the annual report.

Alamy Images/CB Signs

Keeping it simple . . .

The following section shows the physical assets used by the Group to generate revenues and profits. These assets include office buildings and studios, as well as equipment used in broadcast transmissions, programme production and support activities.

The cost of these assets is the amount initially paid for them. A depreciation expense is charged to the income statement to reflect annual wear and tear and the reduced value of the asset over time. Depreciation is calculated by estimating the number of years the Group expects the asset to be used (useful economic life). If there has been a technological change or decline in business performance the Directors review the value of assets to ensure they have not fallen below their depreciated value. If an asset's value falls below its depreciated value an additional one-off impairment change is made against profit.

This section also explains the accounting policies followed by ITV and the specific estimates made in arriving at the net book value of these assets.

Accounting policies
Property, plant and equipment

Property, plant and equipment are stated at cost less accumulated depreciation and impairment losses. Certain items of property, plant and equipment that were revalued to fair value prior to 1 January 2004, the date of transition to IFRS, are measured on the basis of deemed cost, being the revalued amount less depreciation up to the date of transition.

Depreciation

Depreciation is provided to write off the cost of property, plant and equipment, less estimated residual value, on a straight-line basis over their estimated useful lives. The annual depreciation charge is sensitive to the estimated useful life of each asset and the expected residual value at the end of its life. The major categories of property, plant and equipment are depreciated as follows:

Asset class	Depreciation policy
Freehold land	Not depreciated
Freehold buildings	Up to 60 years
Leaseholder properties	Shorter of residual lease term or 60 years
Leasehold improvements	Shorter of residual lease term or estimated useful life
Vehicles, equipment and fittings[1]	3 to 20 years

[1] Equipment includes studio production and technology assets.

Impairment of assets

Property, plant and equipment that is subject to depreciation is reviewed annually for impairment or whenever events or changes in circumstances indicate that the carrying amount may not be recoverable. Indicators of impairment may include changes in technology and business performance.

Source: Pages 103 and 104 Annual Report and Accounts 2011, ITV plc, http://www.itvplc.com/sites/itvplc/files/ITV%202011%20Annual%20Report%20and%20Accounts.pdf.

Discussion points

1 Compare the wording of the 'Keeping it simple' section and the descriptions of accounting policies that follow. Which version do you find more helpful?

2 What information is provided in the accounting policies that is not in the 'Keeping it simple' section. Which types of user would find this additional information useful for decision making?

Contents

After studying this chapter you should be able to:

● Define a non-current (fixed) asset and apply the definition.

● Explain the recognition conditions that are applied to tangible non-current (fixed) assets, intangible non-current (fixed) assets and non-current (fixed) asset investments.

● Explain users' needs for information about non-current (fixed) assets.

● Describe and explain the non-current (fixed) asset information provided in annual reports of companies.

● Evaluate the usefulness of published information about non-current (fixed) assets.

● Explain the nature of depreciation.

● Calculate depreciation, record the effect on the accounting equation and report the result in financial statements.

Additionally, for those who choose to study the supplement:

● Record non-current (fixed) assets and depreciation in ledger accounts.

8.1 Introduction

If you have progressed through Chapters 1 to 7 you are now familiar with the accounting equation and the analysis of transactions or events using that equation. You know what is meant by the terms asset, liability, revenue, expense and ownership interest. You are aware of the structure of the primary financial statements and the way in which they seek to provide information which is relevant and reliable.

This chapter starts a new phase of the text which will help you to develop a critical awareness of some of the component items in the financial statements. Chapters 8 to 12 progress through the main sections of the statement of financial position (balance sheet). Inevitably, they also cover relevant aspects of the income statement (profit and loss account) and the statement of cash flows because transactions involving the statement of financial position (balance sheet) will sometimes have an effect in the other financial statements.

It is important at this stage not to become so enthusiastic for the intricacies of accounting procedures as to lose sight of the importance of user needs, which were set out in Chapter 1. That chapter set out, in section 1.2, the structure of most conceptual frameworks, which provides a sequence for each of Chapters 8 to 12, as follows:

● What are the principles for defining and recognising these items?
● What are the information needs of users in respect of the particular items?
● What information is currently provided by companies to meet these needs?
● Does the information show the desirable qualitative characteristics of financial statements?
● What are the principles for measuring, and processes for recording, these items?

That analysis is applied to non-current (fixed) assets in this chapter.

8.2 Definitions

The following definition of an asset was provided in Chapter 2.

Definition

An **asset** is a resource controlled by the entity as a result of past events and from which future economic benefits are expected to flow to the entity.[1]

The following definitions explain the nature of tangible and non-tangible non-current assets. The word 'tangible' means 'able to be touched'. So 'intangible' means 'not able to be touched'.

Definitions

A **non-current asset** is any asset that does not meet the definition of a current asset.[2] Non-current assets include tangible, intangible and financial assets of a long-term nature. These are also described as **fixed assets**.[3]

Tangible non-current (fixed) assets, such as property, plant and equipment, are assets that have physical substance and are held for use in the production or supply of goods or services, for rental to others, or for administrative purposes and an expected to be used during more than one period.[4]

An **intangible** asset is an identifiable non-monetary asset without physical substance.[5]

These definitions are taken from different sources because the definitions have been developed and discussed at different times for different purposes. The IASB and the UK ASB have both spent many years in discussion over the subjects of accounting for tangible and intangible non-current assets because these are complex matters.

8.2.1 Examples of non-current (fixed) assets

The following is a sample of the non-current (fixed) assets found in a company's statement of financial position (balance sheet).

Tangible non-current (fixed) assets

Companies following the International Financial Reporting Standards (IFRS) will typically use a general heading of 'Property, plant and equipment'. This general heading might include:

- Land and buildings (property) owned by the entity
- Buildings leased by the entity
- Plant and equipment (owned or leased)
- Vehicles (owned or leased)
- Office equipment
- Assets under construction
- Telecommunications network
- Airport runways
- Water pipes and sewers
- Oil and mineral reserves.

Definition[6]

Property, plant and equipment includes intangible items that:

(a) are held for use in the production or supply of goods or services, for rental to others, or for administrative purposes; and

(b) are expected to be used during more than one period.

Intangible non-current (fixed) assets

- Newspaper titles and publishing rights
- Patents
- Trade marks
- Goodwill purchased
- Brand names purchased.

Investments

- Long-term investments in subsidiary companies
- Long-term investments in other companies.

That sample was taken from only 10 annual reports of leading companies. Looking at more companies would soon extend the list considerably. The potential variety and the likelihood of encountering something new is one reason why definitions are essential.

8.2.2 Cost of a non-current (fixed) asset

There is one issue which is not as straightforward as it seems. That is the question of measuring the cost of a non-current (fixed) asset. When a toffee manufacturer buys a new toffee-shaping machine, the purchase price will be known from the supplier's invoice and the manufacturer's catalogue, but should the costs of delivery and installation be added to the amount recorded as the asset cost? When an insurance company buys a new head office, the purchase price will be shown in the contract, but should the legal costs be added to the amount recorded as the asset cost? When a new head office building is under development and interest is being paid on the funds borrowed to finance the development, should the interest paid on the borrowed funds be added to the cost of the development as part of the asset value?

The answer in all three cases is 'yes', although the third example causes greatest discussion and debate. The general principle is that the cost of a non-current (fixed) asset is the purchase price or the amount spent on its production together with any other expenditure incurred in bringing the non-current (fixed) asset to working condition for its intended use at its intended location.

Definition

> The **cost** of a non-current (fixed) asset is the purchase price or the amount spent on its production together with any costs directly attributable to bringing the non-current (fixed) asset to working condition for its intended use at its intended location.

8.2.3 Repairs and improvements

There are sometimes problems in deciding whether a payment for a repair to a non-current (fixed) asset should be treated as an expense of the business or an asset. The key lies in the words of the definition of an asset and the phrase *future economic benefits*. If the payment relates to some act which merely preserves the existing life of the asset and the existing expectations of benefit from the asset, then the payment is treated as a repair and reported as an **expense**. The asset of cash decreases and there is a decrease in the ownership interest caused by the expense.

If the payment relates to some act which significantly extends the useful life of the asset, or increases the future economic benefit expected from the asset, then the payment is treated as an **improvement** and reported as an asset. It may be reported as a separate asset but, more usually, the amount will be added to the cost or value recorded for the asset which has been improved. The asset of cash decreases and is replaced by an asset of improvements. There is no effect on the ownership interest.

The following are examples of improvements and repairs.

Improvements

- Extensions to a building which increase the operating capacity of the business.
- A new roof which gives a building an extra ten years of life.
- A new engine for a delivery van which is more powerful than the existing engine and allows faster delivery in hilly districts.
- Renewing the fittings and interior decoration of a hotel to attract international visitors instead of the traditional local customers.

Repairs

- A new roof, required because of storm damage, which will keep the building weatherproof for the remainder of its estimated life.
- A new engine for a delivery van which replaces an existing damaged engine.
- Redecorating inside a building to preserve the existing standards of cleanliness and appearance.

Activity 8.1	*Imagine you are the owner of a big hotel in the centre of town. Make a list of the items you would expect to include in your business statement of financial position (balance sheet) as non-current (fixed) assets. Make a list of the types of repair which would be classed as 'improvements'. Use the definition of a non-current (fixed) asset to show that your list includes items which are correctly classified.*

8.3 Recognition

This section outlines the recognition issues faced in reporting non-current assets in the separate categories of tangible assets, intangible assets and investment assets.

8.3.1 Tangible non-current (fixed) assets

Tangible non-current (fixed) assets are those items which can be touched, seen or heard and meet the conditions set out in the definition of a non-current (fixed) asset. **Recognition** by reporting in the statement of financial position (balance sheet) presents no problem where the future benefit can be identified and the cost of the asset can be measured. (Look back to section 2.5 for an explanation of recognition.) The evidence of cost is usually a purchase invoice. Some tangible non-current (fixed) assets are recorded at a valuation made subsequent to the purchase. Revaluations are discussed in Chapter 12.

As the list in the previous section indicates, there is considerable variety in tangible non-current (fixed) assets. The common feature is that they all have a limited life expectancy. They may wear out, be used up, go out of fashion, break down or be sold for scrap. Whatever the reason, the effect is the same and is called **depreciation**. Users have many questions to ask about tangible non-current (fixed) assets, such as:

- What kinds of tangible fixed assets are in use?
- How old are they?
- How has the company measured the depreciation?
- Where is the depreciation recorded?

Answering those questions will take up most of the remainder of this chapter.

8.3.2 Intangible non-current (fixed) assets

An intangible non-current (fixed) asset is an item which meets the definition of a non-current (fixed) asset but has no physical substance. It cannot be touched, seen or heard.

The evidence of its existence is the benefit flowing from it. For many years, items such as patents, trademarks and licences to manufacture products have been bought and sold between companies. The purchase has been recorded as a non-current (fixed) asset and depreciated over the estimated life of the patent, trademark or licence. The estimated life is decided by law (for patents and trademarks) or by legal contract (for licences). The depreciation of intangible non-current (fixed) assets is usually referred to as **amortisation** (in which you may recognise the French word *mort* meaning *death*).

The intangible non-current (fixed) asset which has attracted most accounting-related comment in recent years has been the brand name of a company's product. When a company works over many years to develop the reputation of its product, that reputation creates an expected future benefit for the company and meets the definition of an **asset** as set out in Chapter 2. However, the generally held view is that it should not be recognised in the statement of financial position (balance sheet) because it fails the **recognition** test of Chapter 2. The conventional argument is that there is no measurable **cost** of the reputation gained by the brand name and the value cannot be measured with reliability.

That is the generally held view which was challenged in the mid-1980s by a number of leading companies. Some had bought other companies which had developed brand names. The new owners argued that they were buying the other company purely because of the quality of the brand name and they wanted to show that brand name in the new statement of financial position (balance sheet). They had a reasonable argument because they had paid a price in the market and could show the cost of the brand name acquired. Other companies who had developed their own brand names did not want to be left behind and so paid expert valuers to calculate a value for their home-grown brands. A new professional specialism of brand valuation gained prominence and the experts claimed they could measure the value of a home-grown brand with reliability.

The companies which reported brand names in the statement of financial position (balance sheet) argued that the brand had a long life and did not require amortisation. This argument gave them the advantage of expanding the statement of financial position (balance sheet) without the disadvantage of amortisation appearing in the income statement (profit and loss account).

The IASB has issued a standard, IAS 38, covering accounting for intangible assets. Internally generated brand names must *not* be recognised as intangible assets. This rule applies to similar assets such as publishing titles, customer lists, or newspaper titles. Purchased brand names or trademarks or patents may be reported in a statement of financial position (balance sheet) if they meet the conditions for recognition. Recognition requires that it is probable that the expected economic benefit will flow to the entity, and the cost of the asset can be measured reliably.

If the intangible asset has a finite life it must be amortised over its useful life. The method of amortisation must reflect the pattern of use of the asset.

Activity 8.2	*A company which has manufactured a well-known brand of brown bread for many years has decided that the brand name is so well known that it should appear in the statement of financial position (balance sheet). Write down two arguments in favour of this, to be made by the company's finance director, and two arguments against, which will appear in a newspaper article.*

8.3.3 Investments

Investments exist in many different forms but the essential feature is an ability to generate future economic benefits so that the wealth of the owner increases. This increase in wealth may arise because the value of the investment increases, or may arise because the investment creates income for the owner in the form of a distribution such as interest paid or dividends. Companies may hold investments for a variety of reasons. A non-current (fixed asset) investment is one which is held for long-term purposes, such as shares in another company which has close trading links with the investing company.

The number of shares held may be such as to give direct control of the investment or may be of a lesser amount which indicates a long-term relationship, without direct control, in a similar line of business.

Non-current (fixed) asset investments may be held so that resources are available to meet a long-term obligation, such as the payment of pensions. Such non-current (fixed) assets are normally found in the statements of financial position (balance sheets) of insurance companies or pension funds, rather than in the balance sheet of the company employing staff.

The features which make investments different as non-current (fixed) assets are the importance of the increase in value of the investment itself and the fact that they are not used in the production or service process. Both features require a different kind of accounting treatment from that given to other non-current (fixed) assets. Those special treatments are advanced accounting matters and will not be dealt with in any detail in this text. What you should look for in accounts is the existence of non-current (fixed) asset investments and the information provided about them. The questions users will ask are: 'How well is this investment keeping up its value?' and 'How important is the income from this investment to the overall profit of the company?'

8.4 Users' needs for information

Activity 8.3

Before you read this section, make a list of the information about non-current (fixed) assets which would be useful to you if you wished to learn more about a specific company. Then read the section and compare it with your list. How far-thinking are you in respect of accounting information?

Analysts who write reports for professional and private investors have a particular interest in the non-current (fixed) assets because these are the base from which profits are generated. They want to know what types of assets are held, how old they are and what plans the company has for future investment in non-current (fixed) assets.

The analysts also want to know about the impact of the depreciation charge on the profit of the year. They are aware that detailed aspects of calculations of depreciation may vary from one year to the next and this may affect the comparability of the profit amounts.

To estimate the remaining life of the assets, analysts compare the accumulated depreciation with the total cost (or value) of the non-current (fixed) assets. If the accumulated depreciation is relatively low, then the non-current (fixed) assets are relatively new. Other companies in the industry will be used for comparison. The analysts also compare the depreciation charge for the year with the total cost (or value) of the assets and expect to see a similar relationship from one year to the next. A sudden change will cause them to ask more questions about a change in the basis of calculation.

8.5 Information provided in the financial statements

In Chapter 7 the statement of financial position (balance sheet) of Safe and Sure plc was presented. The statement of financial position (balance sheet) showed a single line of information on property, plant and equipment. This section shows how that single line becomes understandable when read in conjunction with the notes to the accounts, the statement of accounting policy and the finance director's review.

8.5.1 Statement of financial position (balance sheet)

	Notes	Year 7 £m	Year 6 £m
Non-current assets			
Property, plant and equipment	1	137.5	121.9

8.5.2 Notes to the statement of financial position (balance sheet)

In the notes to the statement of financial position (balance sheet) there is considerably more information:

Note 1 Property, plant and equipment

	Land and buildings £m	Plant and equipment £m	Vehicles £m	Total £m
Cost or valuation				
At 1 January Year 7	28.3	96.4	104.8	229.5
Additions at cost	3.9	18.5	37.8	60.2
On acquisitions	0.3	1.0	0.7	2.0
Disposals	(0.6)	(3.1)	(24.7)	(28.4)
At 31 December Year 7	31.9	112.8	118.6	263.3
Aggregate depreciation				
At 1 January Year 7	2.2	58.8	46.6	107.6
Depreciation for the year	0.5	13.5	19.2	33.2
On acquisitions	0.1	0.7	0.6	1.4
Disposals	(0.2)	(2.8)	(13.4)	(16.4)
At 31 December Year 7	2.6	70.2	53.0	125.8
Net book value at 31 December Year 7	29.3	42.6	65.6	137.5
Net book value at 31 December Year 6	26.1	37.6	58.2	121.9

Analysis of land and buildings at cost or valuation

	Year 7 £m	Year 6 £m
At cost	10.4	7.1
At valuation	21.5	21.2
	31.9	28.3

The majority of the group's freehold and long-term leasehold properties were revalued during Year 5 by independent valuers. Valuations were made on the basis of the market value for existing use. The book values of the properties were adjusted to the revaluations and the resultant net surplus was credited to the revaluation reserve.

Analysis of net book value of land and buildings

	Year 7 £m	Year 6 £m
Freehold	24.5	21.0
Leasehold:		
Over 50 years unexpired	2.1	2.4
Under 50 years unexpired	2.7	2.7
	29.3	26.1

If the revalued assets were stated on the historical cost basis the amounts would be:

	Year 7 £m	Year 6 £m
Land and buildings at cost	15.7	14.5
Aggregate depreciation	(2.2)	(1.9)
	13.5	12.6

It is clear from the extensive nature of note 2 to the statement of financial position (balance sheet) that property, plant and equipment assets are regarded as important by those who regulate the information. All companies present a detailed note of this kind because the information is required by IAS 16, *Property, Plant and Equipment*.

8.5.3   Statement of accounting policy

In addition the company is required, by the accounting standard IAS 1, *Presentation of Financial Statements*, to disclose its significant accounting policies. For this company the wording of the accounting policy statement is as follows:

Freehold and leasehold property
Freehold and leasehold land and buildings are stated either at cost (Security and Cleaning) or at their revalued amounts less depreciation (Disposal and Recycling). Full revaluations are made at five-year intervals with interim valuations in the intervening years, the most recent full revaluation being in year 5.

Provision for depreciation of freehold land and buildings is made at the annual rate of 1% of cost or the revalued amounts. Leasehold land and buildings are amortised in equal annual instalments over the periods of the leases subject to a minimum annual provision of 1% of cost or the revalued amounts. When properties are sold the difference between sales proceeds and net book value is dealt with in the income statement (profit and loss account).

Plant and equipment
Plant and equipment are stated at cost less depreciation. Provision for depreciation is made mainly in equal annual instalments over the estimated useful lives of the assets as follows:

4 to 5 years   vehicles
5 to 10 years   plant, machinery and equipment

8.5.4   Operating and financial review

There is also a comment in the finance director's report, as a contribution to the operating and financial review:

Capital expenditure
The major items of capital expenditure are vehicles, equipment used on customers' premises and office equipment, particularly computers. Disposals during the year were mainly of vehicles being replaced on a rolling programme.

Activity 8.4

Find the annual report of a company of your choice. This may be through access to the website, or by requesting a printed copy of the annual report through the website www.ft.com, or by using the free annual reports offer on the London Stock Exchange page of the Financial Times.

In the annual report find the information that corresponds to the extracts from Safe & Sure given in section 8.5. What are the similarities and differences? What do you learn about the non-current (fixed) asset base of your chosen company?

8.6   Usefulness of published information

Here is David Wilson to explain how useful he sees the information provided by companies about their tangible non-current (fixed) assets. If you look back to Chapter 4 you will see that he was about to visit the company and had made a preliminary list of questions. He has now made the visit and has a better understanding of what is reported in the statement of financial position (balance sheet). He talks to Leona in a break at a workout session.

DAVID: *I told you that in making my review before visiting the company I looked closely at the type of tangible non-current (fixed) assets held and the estimated useful life. I also checked that the depreciation period and method of calculation had not changed from previous years.*

As I was making a site visit I took the opportunity to look at the various non-current (fixed) assets. This is a group of companies, expanding by acquisition of other companies, and each acquisition brings in more land and buildings. Some of these assets are recorded at valuation rather than original cost. The company has to review the valuation on a regular basis. That is quite a common practice and I have confidence in the firm of valuers used.

Plant and equipment has an aggregate depreciation of £70.2m which is 62% of the cost of the assets at £112.8m. It seems to me that must be saying that the plant and equipment is more than halfway through its estimated life. The finance director wasn't too enthusiastic about this interpretation. He pointed out that when another company is acquired the non-current (fixed) assets may be quite old and have to be brought into the group statement of financial position, but once they are in group control there is a strict policy of evaluation and replacement. He views the depreciation policy as being at the prudent end of the spectrum, so the realistic life remaining might be marginally over half, but discretion and the fast-moving nature of the industry requires an element of caution. He called in the plant manager who showed me the replacement schedules for plant and equipment for the next three years. It certainly reassured me that risk of obsolescence is probably not a serious worry. I also met the vehicle fleet supervisor who showed me similar replacement schedules for the vehicles.

I saw how the vehicle fleet is managed so that every vehicle is idle for the minimum time. Each vehicle is assigned to a group of cleaning operatives, whose shifts are scheduled so that the vehicle's use is maximised. Plant and equipment are the responsibility of area managers who have to look after security, maintenance and efficiency of usage. I thought it was all really quite impressive.

The depreciation charge for the plant and equipment in Year 7 is £13.5m which is 12% of the cost of £112.8m and suggests an estimated life of just over eight years is being applied. That is within the range of five to ten years stated as the company's accounting policy. I think the wording 'five to ten years' is too vague. Using five years would double the depreciation charge compared with ten. I tried to pin down the finance director so that I can get a good figure for my forecast but all he would say was that there is no reason to suppose there are any unusual features in the amount in the accounts. The depreciation charge for vehicles is £19.2m which is 16% of the cost of £118.6m. That suggests an estimated life of just over six years is being applied. I asked the finance director how that squared with the accounting policy statement of estimated useful lives of four to five years for vehicles. He did seem to sigh a little at that point but was quite patient in explaining that there are some fully depreciated vehicles still in use (because they are quite prudent in their estimates of depreciation) and so the depreciation charge is not the 20% to 25% I was looking for. I'll need to think about that one but I might move my estimate for next year closer to 20%.

You asked me how this company's information measures up to the qualitative characteristics (set out in Chapter 4). Relevance I would rate highly, because there is plenty of information in the notes which I can use to ask questions about the effective use of non-current (fixed) assets and the impact on income statement (profit and loss account) through the depreciation charge. Faithful representation and neutrality are qualities I leave to the auditors. Prudence is something which seems to come out strongly in conversation with the finance director. The detailed schedule of assets which I saw suggests that completeness is not a problem. Comparability is fine because there are amounts for the previous year and the standard format allows me to make comparison with other companies in the industry. Understandability is perhaps more of a problem than I thought. Those fully depreciated assets caught me out.

LEONA: *Well, I have now heard you admit that there is some value in having auditors. Shall I tell you how much you have missed? You could have asked more searching questions about the way in which they measure the cost of plant and equipment. Does it include delivery charges and installation costs? You could have asked whether a technical expert inside the company estimates and reviews the asset lives used, or whether the finance director makes a guess. Did you ask whether they are perhaps verging on being over-prudent so that surprises come later when the depreciation charge is less than expected? You could have asked how the interim valuations are carried out. These are all questions we ask as auditors so that you may treat the information as being reliable and a faithful representation.*

Hopefully you now have a feeling for the information provided by companies on tangible non-current (fixed) assets and how it is used by the professional investor. The nature and recording of depreciation is now explained.

8.7 Depreciation: an explanation of its nature

Activity 8.5

Before you read this section, write down what you think 'depreciation' means. Then read the section and compare it with your initial views. Depreciation is a very subjective matter and there are different views of its purpose, so your answer may be interesting even if it does not match the text. You should consult your lecturer, tutor or other expert in the area to understand why your perceptions may be different.

Definitions[7]

Depreciation is the systematic allocation of the depreciable amount of an asset over its useful life.

The **depreciable amount** is the cost of an asset, or other amount substituted for cost, less its residual value.

Residual value is the estimated amount that an entity would currently obtain from disposal of the asset, after deducting the estimated cost of disposal, if the asset were already of the age and in the condition expected at the end of its useful life.

The asset may be an item of plant or equipment which is wearing out through being used. It may be a payment made by a company for the right to become a tenant of a property. That payment purchases a lease which reduces in value through the passage of time. The asset may be a computer system which becomes out of date in a very short space of time because of obsolescence. It may be a machine which produces goods for which demand falls because of changing market conditions.

The definition shows that depreciation is a device used in accounting to allocate (spread) the cost of a non-current (fixed) asset over its useful life. The process of spreading cost over more than one accounting period is called **allocation**.

In terms of the accounting equation, the useful life of the non-current (fixed) asset is being reduced and this will reduce the ownership interest.

	Assets		Liabilities		**Ownership** interest
Year 1	↓	–		=	↓
2	↓				↓
3	↓				↓
etc.					

As the asset becomes older, the depreciation of one year is added to the depreciation of previous years. This is called the **accumulated depreciation** or **aggregate depreciation**. The accumulated depreciation at the end of any year is equal to the accumulated depreciation at the start of the year plus the depreciation charge for that year.

Deducting the accumulated depreciation from the original cost leaves the **net book value**. The net book value could also be described as the cost remaining as a benefit for future years.

Showing the effect of depreciation by use of arrows and the accounting equation is relatively easy. Deciding on the amount of depreciation each year is much more difficult because there are so many different views of how to calculate the amount of asset used up in each period.

8.7.1 Calculation of depreciation

Calculation of depreciation requires three pieces of information:

1 the cost of the asset;
2 the estimated useful life; and
3 the estimated residual value.

The total depreciation of the non-current (fixed) asset is equal to the cost of the non-current (fixed) asset minus the estimated residual value. The purpose of the depreciation calculation is to spread the total depreciation over the estimated useful life.

The first point at which differences of opinion arise is in the estimation of the useful life and residual value. These are matters of judgement which vary from one person to the next.

Unfortunately the differences do not stop at those estimates. There is also no agreement on the arithmetical approach to spreading the total depreciation over the useful life. Some people are of the opinion that a non-current (fixed) asset is used evenly over time and that the depreciation should reflect the benefit gained from its use. Others argue that the non-current (fixed) asset declines in value most in the early years and so the depreciation charge should be greater in earlier years.

8.7.2 Straight-line method

Those who are of the opinion that a non-current (fixed) asset is used evenly over time apply a method of calculation called straight-line depreciation. The formula is:

$$\frac{\text{Cost} - \text{Expected residual value}}{\text{Expected life}}$$

To illustrate the use of the formula, take a non-current (fixed) asset which has a cost of £1,000 and an estimated life of five years. The estimated residual value is nil. The calculation of the annual depreciation charge is:

$$\frac{£1,000 - \text{nil}}{5} = £200 \text{ per annum}$$

The depreciation rate is sometimes expressed as a percentage of the original cost. In this case the company would state its depreciation policy as follows:

Accounting policy:
Depreciation is charged on a straight-line basis at a rate of 20% of cost per annum.

Table 8.1
Pattern of depreciation and net book value over the life of an asset

End of year	Depreciation of the year (a) £	Total depreciation (b) £	Net book value of the asset (£1,000 – b) £
1	200	200	800
2	200	400	600
3	200	600	400
4	200	800	200
5	200	1,000	nil

The phrase 'straight-line' is used because a graph of the net book value of the asset at the end of each year produces a straight line. Table 8.1 sets out the five-year pattern of depreciation and net book value for the example used above.

Figure 8.1 shows a graph of the net book value at the end of each year. The graph starts at the cost figure of £1,000 when the asset is new (Year 0) and reduces by £200 each year until it is zero at the end of Year 5.

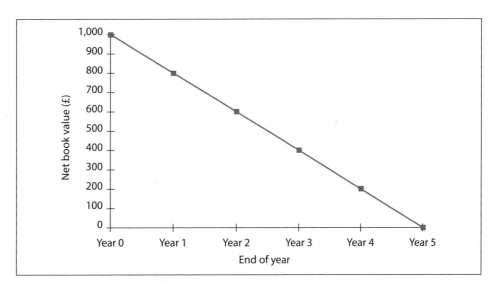

Figure 8.1
Graph of net book value over Years 1 to 5, for the straight-line method of depreciation

8.7.3   Reducing-balance method

Those who believe that the asset depreciates most in earlier years would calculate the depreciation using the formula:

Fixed percentage × Net book value at the start of the year

Take the example of the asset costing £1,000. The fixed percentage applied for the reducing-balance method might be as high as 50%. The calculations would be as shown in Table 8.2.

You will see from Table 8.2 that under the reducing-balance method there is always a small balance remaining. In this example, the rate of 50% is used to bring the net book value to a relatively small amount. The formula for calculating the exact rate requires a knowledge of compound interest and may be found at the end of the

Supplement to this chapter. For those whose main interest is in understanding and interpreting accounts it is not necessary to know the formula, but it is useful to be aware that a very much higher percentage rate is required on the reducing-balance method as compared with the straight-line method. As a useful guide, the reducing-balance rate must be at least twice the rate of the straight-line calculation if the major part of the asset is to be depreciated over its useful life.

Table 8.2
Calculation of reducing-balance depreciation

Year	Net book value at start of year (a) £	Annual depreciation (b) = 50% of (a) £	Net book value at end of year (a – b) £
1	1,000	500	500
2	500	250	250
3	250	125	125
4	125	63	62
5	62	31	31

A graph of the net book value at the end of each year under the reducing-balance method is shown in Figure 8.2. The steep slope at the start shows that the net book value declines rapidly in the early part of the asset's life and then less steeply towards the end when most of the benefit of the asset has been used up.

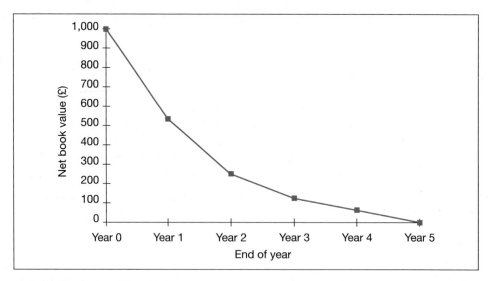

Figure 8.2
Graph of net book value over Years 1 to 5, for the reducing-balance method of depreciation

8.7.4 Which method to choose?

The separate recording of asset at cost and accumulated depreciation is accounting information provided in many countries. The UK practice at a general level is consistent with the IASB standard. Country-specific factors may lead to differences in matters of detail such as the choice of depreciation method or the estimated life of non-current (fixed) assets. In some countries, the depreciation expense in the accounting income statement (profit and loss account) must match that used for the purposes of calculating taxable profit. This may encourage the use of the reducing-balance method, giving a higher expense (and so a lower profit) in the early years of the asset's life. In the UK there are separate rules in tax law for calculating depreciation, and so this has no effect on accounting profit.

The choice of depreciation method should be based on the expected pattern of usage of the asset. If the usage is evenly spread then the straight-line method is appropriate. If the usage is heaviest in early years then the reducing-balance method is the best representation of the economic activity. In practice, it is found that most UK companies use straight-line depreciation. In some other countries, particularly those where tax rules and accounting laws are closely linked, the reducing-balance method is commonly observed. So it appears that there are different international practices that may reflect different conditions in the respective countries. David and Leona discuss the problem.

DAVID: *The choice of depreciation method may have a significant impact on reported profit. Companies that are actively investing in non-current (fixed) assets will do so in the expectation of increased profits. However, it may take some time for such profits to emerge. If, in the meantime, there is a relatively high charge to income statement (profit and loss account) through reducing-balance depreciation, profits may fall in the short term. In contrast the use of straight-line depreciation will have a less dramatic impact on reported profit immediately following the new investment, so the company avoids a dip in profits.*

LEONA: *I can't accept that as a valid argument to give to the auditor. I ask the company what the pattern of usage is. If the company tells me that the asset produces benefit evenly over its useful life, I can accept straight-line depreciation. If, on the other hand, I hear that the asset is more productive in its early years of life, I expect to see reducing-balance depreciation.*

DAVID: *Well let me try your social conscience. I came across a case of a UK company that had been taken over by a German parent company. The UK company had always used straight-line depreciation and was making small profits each year. The parent company had always used reducing-balance depreciation and so changed the accounting method of the UK subsidiary. Small profits turned into large losses and the parent company said that there would have to be a reduction in the workforce to cut costs. The employee representatives said that nothing had changed except that the accountants had redefined the game. They blamed the accountants for the resulting job losses and increased unemployment.*

LEONA: *My role is confined to giving an opinion on the accounting information. If a particular accounting process is detrimental to the public interest then it is the job of government to legislate.*

Activity 8.6

Consider the discussion between David and Leona. Do you share the concern of the employee representatives as described by David? Do you agree with Leona that the economic impact of accounting information is not a problem for the auditor? What is your view on the social responsibility attached to financial reporting?

8.7.5   Retaining cash in the business

Suppose that the policy of the owner is to take all the available profits as drawings for personal use. Take a company that has fee income of £120,000 and pays wages and other costs of £58,000. If the company did not recognise the expense of depreciation the owner's drawings could be as high as £62,000. Suppose now that depreciation of non-current (fixed) assets is calculated as £10,000. The net profit after depreciation becomes £52,000. The owner can still see £62,000 in the bank account but knows £10,000 of that amount represents using up non-current (fixed) assets. Leaving the £10,000 in the bank will allow the business to save cash for asset replacement. The owner should withdraw no more than £52,000.

It is often said that depreciation limits the amount of profits available for cash drawings by the owner and encourages saving for asset replacement. However, there is nothing to stop the business spending the £10,000 on some purpose other than replacement of non-current (fixed) assets. We can only say that cash withheld from shareholders *may* be used to replace assets at the end of the asset life.

8.8 Reporting non-current (fixed) assets and depreciation in financial statements

This section moves step by step through the recording process. First, it looks at a situation of straight-line depreciation with no residual value for the asset. Then it takes in the additional complication of an estimated residual value.

8.8.1 Straight-line depreciation, no residual value

When a retail company wants new premises, it must either buy a shop or rent one. Renting is referred to as **leasing**. When the rent agreement is signed, the tenant may pay an agreed price for the privilege of having the lease. This is called the initial payment for the lease. It is paid in addition to the annual rental payment. The initial payment to acquire the lease provides a benefit of occupation for the entire period of the lease and so is a non-current (fixed) asset. Because the lease has a known life, it must be depreciated.

On 1 January Year 2 Electrical Instruments purchased a three-year lease of a shop for a payment of £60,000. Using the straight-line method of depreciation the amount of depreciation each year will be calculated on a straight-line basis as £20,000 (one-third of the cost of the lease). The income statement (profit and loss account) will report this amount as an expense in each of the three years of the lease. The statement of financial position (balance sheet) will show on one line the original cost of £60,000 and, on a second line, the accumulated depreciation to be subtracted at the end of each year.

The financial statements over the period of three years will show the following information relating to this lease:

Income statement (profit and loss account) (extract)			
Year ended 31 December	*Year 2*	*Year 3*	*Year 4*
	£000s	*£000s*	*£000s*
Depreciation expense	(20)	(20)	(20)

Statement of financial position (balance sheet) (extract)			
At 31 December	*Year 2*	*Year 3*	*Year 4*
	£000s	*£000s*	*£000s*
Lease at cost	60	60	60
Less accumulated depreciation	20	40	60
Net book value	40	20	nil

8.8.2   Straight-line depreciation with a residual value

In the case of Electrical Instruments the lease had no residual value. Take now the example of The Removals Company which commences business on 1 January Year 2 by paying cash for a van costing £60,000. It is estimated to have a useful life of three years and is estimated to have a residual value of £6,000. On 31 December Year 2 the owner calculates annual depreciation of the van as £18,000, using the formula:

$$\frac{Cost - Estimated\ residual\ value}{Estimated\ life}$$

During each year of operating the van, the company collected £120,000 in cash from customers and paid £58,000 in cash for drivers' wages, fuel and other running costs.

These transactions and events may be summarised using the accounting equation and a spreadsheet similar to that used in Chapter 5 (Table 5.3). In Table 8.3 there is a spreadsheet for the first year of the use of the van by the company. The assets section of the spreadsheet has three columns, one of which is for cash but two of which are for the van. The two columns for the van keep a separate record of the original cost and the accumulated depreciation. The original cost is the positive part of the asset but the accumulated depreciation is the negative part of the asset. Taking the accumulated depreciation from the original cost leaves the net book value. That is the amount of cost not yet amortised which acts as a measure of the benefit remaining in the asset for the future. In Table 8.4 the information collected together by Table 8.3 is presented in the form of a statement of financial position (balance sheet) and an income statement (profit and loss account).

8.8.3   Continuing to use the non-current (fixed) asset

So far, the accounting entries have related to the first year of the business so that there was no need to ask any questions about the position at the start of the period. To show the full impact of the progressive depreciation of the asset, the spreadsheet and financial

Table 8.3
Spreadsheet analysing transactions and events of The Removals Company into the elements of the accounting equation

	Transaction or event	Assets			Ownership interest	
		Van at cost	Accumulated depreciation of van	Cash	Capital contributed or withdrawn	Profit = revenue minus (expenses)
Year 2		£	£	£	£	£
1 Jan.	Owner contributes cash			60,000	60,000	
1 Jan.	Purchase furniture van	60,000		(60,000)		
All year	Collected cash from customers			120,000		120,000
All year	Paid for wages, fuel, etc.			(58,000)		(58,000)
31 Dec.	Calculate annual depreciation		(18,000)			(18,000)
	Totals	60,000	(18,000)	62,000	60,000	44,000

———— 104,000 ————   ———— 104,000 ————

Table 8.4

The Removals Company: Statement of financial position (balance sheet) at end of Year 2 and Income statement (profit and loss account) for Year 2

The Removals Company
Statement of financial position (balance sheet) at 31 December Year 2

	£
Non-current (fixed) assets	
Furniture van at cost	60,000
Accumulated depreciation	(18,000)
Net book value	42,000
Current assets	
Cash	62,000
Total assets	104,000
Ownership interest	
Ownership interest at the start of the year	nil
Capital contributed during the year	60,000
Profit of the year	44,000
	104,000

The Removals Company
Income statement (profit and loss account)
for the year ended 31 December Year 2

	£	£
Revenue		
Fees for removal work		120,000
Expenses		
Wages, fuel and other running costs	(58,000)	
Depreciation	(18,000)	
		(76,000)
Net profit		44,000

Table 8.5

Spreadsheet analysis of transactions of The Removals Company, Year 3

	Transaction or event	Assets			Ownership interest		
		Van at cost	Accumulated depreciation of van	Cash	Ownership interest at start of year	Capital contributed or withdrawn	Profit = revenue minus (expenses)
Year 3		£	£	£	£	£	£
1 Jan.	Amounts brought forward at start of year	60,000	(18,000)	62,000	104,000		
All year	Collected cash from customers			120,000			120,000
All year	Paid for wages, fuel, etc.			(58,000)			(58,000)
31 Dec.	Calculate annual depreciation		(18,000)				(18,000)
	Totals	60,000	(36,000)	124,000	104,000		44,000

└──── 148,000 ────┘   └──── 148,000 ────┘

Table 8.6
The Removals Company statement of financial position (balance sheet) at end of Year 3 and Income statement (profit and loss account) for Year 3

The Removals Company Statement of financial position (balance sheet) at 31 December Year 3	£
Non-current (fixed) assets	
Furniture van at cost	60,000
Accumulated depreciation	(36,000)
Net book value	24,000
Current assets	
Cash	124,000
Total assets	148,000
Ownership interest	
Ownership interest at the start of the year	104,000
Profit of the year	44,000
	148,000

The Removals Company Income statement (profit and loss account) for the year ended 31 December Year 3	£	£
Revenue		
Fees for removal work		120,000
Expenses		
Wages, fuel and other running costs	(58,000)	
Depreciation	(18,000)	
		(76,000)
Net profit		44,000

statements are now presented for Year 3. Table 8.5 sets out the spreadsheet and Table 8.6 sets out the financial statements. It is assumed that for Year 3 the amounts of cash collected from customers and the amounts paid in cash for running costs are the same as for Year 2. No further capital is contributed by the owner and no new vans are acquired.

The first line of the spreadsheet in Table 8.5 shows the position at the start of the year. The asset columns show the amounts as they were at the end of the previous year. The ownership interest shows the amount resulting at the end of the previous year, as seen in the Year 2 statement of financial position (balance sheet). The columns for revenue and expenses are empty at the start of the year, awaiting the transactions and events of Year 3.

8.8.4 Disposing of the non-current (fixed) asset

During Year 4 the amounts of cash received from customers and cash paid for running costs are the same as they were in Year 3. Table 8.7 sets out the spreadsheet for the transactions and events.

Now suppose that the van is sold for £6,000 in cash on the final day of December Year 4. The spreadsheet contained in Table 8.7 requires further attention, the additional accounting impact of the sale being seen in Table 8.8.

The disposal of the van must be analysed in stages:

1 collecting cash;
2 transferring ownership of the vehicle;
3 removing the vehicle from the accounting records.

Table 8.7
Spreadsheet analysis of transactions of The Removals Company, Year 4

	Transaction or event	Assets			Ownership interest		
		Van at cost	Accumulated depreciation of van	Cash	Ownership interest at start of year	Capital contributed or withdrawn	Profit = revenue minus (expenses)
Year 4		£	£	£	£	£	£
1 Jan.	Amounts brought forward at start of year	60,000	(36,000)	124,000	148,000		
All year	Collected cash from customers			120,000			120,000
All year	Paid for wages, fuel, etc.			(58,000)			(58,000)
31 Dec.	Calculate annual depreciation		(18,000)				(18,000)
	Totals	60,000	(54,000)	186,000	148,000		44,000

└──────── 192,000 ────────┘ └──────── 192,000 ────────┘

Table 8.8
Spreadsheet analysis of transactions of The Removals Company, Year 4, including sale of non-current (fixed) asset

	Transaction or event	Assets			Ownership interest		
		Van at cost	Accumulated depreciation of van	Cash	Ownership interest at start of year	Capital contributed or withdrawn	Profit = revenue minus (expenses)
Year 4		£	£	£	£	£	£
1 Jan.	Amounts brought forward at start of year	60,000	(36,000)	124,000	148,000		
All year	Collected cash from customers			120,000			120,000
All year	Paid for wages, fuel, etc.			(58,000)			(58,000)
31 Dec.	Calculate annual depreciation		(18,000)				(18,000)
31 Dec.	Van disposal	(60,000)	54,000	6,000			
	Totals	nil	nil	192,000	148,000		44,000

└──────── 192,000 ────────┘ └──────── 192,000 ────────┘

When the vehicle is removed from the record, two columns must be reduced to zero. These are the *van at cost* column and the *accumulated depreciation* column. The van at cost column shows the original cost of £60,000 and the accumulated depreciation shows the amount of £54,000 which has to be deducted to show the amount of the net book value. The asset of cash increases by £6,000. In terms of the accounting equation:

Assets		−	Liabilities	=	Ownership interest
	£		no change		no change
Increase in cash	**6,000**				
Decrease van:					
At cost	**60,000**				
Accumulated depreciation	**(54,000)**				
	6,000				

The resulting statement of financial position (balance sheet) and income statement (profit and loss account) are shown in Table 8.9.

Table 8.9
The Removals Company: statement of financial position (balance sheet) at end of Year 4 and Income statement (profit and loss account) for Year 4

The Removals Company
Statement of financial position (balance sheet)
at 31 December Year 4

	£
Non-current (fixed) assets	Nil
Current assets	
Cash	192,000
Total assets	192,000
Ownership interest	
Ownership interest at the start of the year	148,000
Profit of the year	44,000
	192,000

The Removals Company
Income statement (profit and loss account)
for the year ended 31 December Year 4

	£	£
Revenue		
Fees for removal work		120,000
Expenses		
Wages, fuel and other running costs	(58,000)	
Depreciation	(18,000)	
		(76,000)
Net profit		44,000

8.8.5 Selling for a price which is not equal to the net book value

The previous illustration was based on selling the van for £6,000, an amount equal to the net book value. Suppose instead it was sold for £9,000. There is a gain on disposal of £3,000. This gain is reported in the income statement (profit and loss account).

Assets		−	Liabilities	=	Ownership interest
	£				
Increase cash	9,000				
Decrease van:			no change		**Increase by £3,000**
At cost	60,000				
Accumulated depreciation	(54,000)				
	6,000				

If the amount of the gain or loss on disposal is relatively small, it may be deducted from the depreciation charge. In that situation the income statement (profit and loss account) would appear as shown in Table 8.10 where bold printing highlights the difference when compared with the income statement (profit and loss account) in Table 8.9. If the gain or loss is **material** it will be reported separately.

Table 8.10
Income statement (profit and loss account) for Year 4 when proceeds of sale exceed net book value of non-current (fixed) asset

The Removals Company
Income statement (profit and loss account)
for the year ended 31 December Year 4

	£	£
Revenue		
Fees for removal work		120,000
Expenses		
Wages, fuel and other running costs	(58,000)	
Depreciation (18,000 − 3,000)	**(15,000)**	
		(73,000)
Net profit		47,000

8.8.6 A table of depreciation expense

To test your understanding of the impact of depreciation you may wish to use a table of the type shown in Table 8.11. It shows that, whatever the proceeds of sale of the asset, the total expense in the income statement (profit and loss account) will always be the same but the amount of expense each year will vary.

If you compare the two tables (a) and (b) you will see that:

- total depreciation over the three years is the same in both cases;
- total net profit after depreciation over the three years is the same in both cases;
- annual depreciation in Years 1 and 2 is lower in table (b);
- net profit after depreciation in Years 1 and 2 is higher in table (b);
- net book value of the asset at the end of Years 1 and 2 is higher in table (b);
- the depreciation charge in Year 3 is higher in table (b);
- the net profit after depreciation in Year 3 is lower in table (b).

This is an example of what is referred to in accounting as an **allocation** problem (a 'sharing' problem). The expense is the same in total but is allocated (shared) differently across the years of the asset's life. As a result, there are different amounts

Table 8.11
Table of depreciation charge

(a) A van cost £60,000, was estimated to have a useful life of three years and a residual value of £6,000. It was sold for £9,000 on the last day of Year 3. Net profit before depreciation is £62,000.

Year	Net profit before depreciation	Depreciation expense of the year	Net profit after depreciation	Cost less accumulated depreciation	Net book value
	£	£	£	£	£
1	62,000	18,000	44,000	60,000 – 18,000	42,000
2	62,000	18,000	44,000	60,000 – 36,000	24,000
3	62,000	15,000	47,000	60,000 – 54,000	6,000
Total depreciation charge		51,000			
Total reported net profit			135,000		

Proceeds of sale exceed net book value by £3,000. This gain is deducted from the depreciation expense of £18,000 leaving £15,000 as the expense of the year.

(b) A van cost £60,000, was estimated to have a useful life of three years and a residual value of £9,000. The annual depreciation was calculated as £17,000. The van was sold for £9,000 on the last day of Year 3. Net profit before depreciation is £62,000.

Year	Net profit before depreciation	Depreciation expense of the year	Net profit after depreciation	Cost less accumulated depreciation	Net book value
	£	£	£	£	£
1	62,000	17,000	45,000	60,000 – 17,000	43,000
2	62,000	17,000	45,000	60,000 – 34,000	26,000
3	62,000	17,000	45,000	60,000 – 51,000	9,000
Total depreciation charge		51,000			
Total reported net profit			135,000		

Net book value equals proceeds of sale so the depreciation charge of Year 3 is the same as that of previous years.

in the income statement (profit and loss account) for each year but the total profit over the longer period is the same.

8.8.7 Impairment

An asset is impaired when the business will not be able to recover the amount shown in the statement of financial position (balance sheet), either through use or through sale. If the enterprise believes that impairment may have taken place, it must carry out an **impairment review**. This requires comparison of the net book value with the cash-generating ability of the asset. If the comparison indicates that the recorded net book value is too high, the value of the asset is reduced and there is an expense in the income statement (profit and loss account).[8]

The impairment test may be applied to intangible non-current (fixed) assets such as goodwill, in order to justify non-amortisation. If no impairment is detected it may be argued that the asset has maintained its value and so amortisation is not necessary. If there has been impairment of the historical cost net book value, then the loss in asset value becomes an expense for the income statement (profit and loss account).

8.9 Summary

- A **non-current asset** is any asset that does not meet the definition of a current asset.[9] Non-current assets include tangible, intangible and financial assets of a long-term nature. These are also described as **fixed assets**.

- **Tangible non-current (fixed) assets** such as property, plant and equipment are assets that have physical substance and are held for use in the production or supply of goods or services, for rental to others, or for administrative purposes on a continuing basis in the reporting entity's activities.

- An **intangible asset** is an identifiable non-monetary asset without physical substance.

- Users need information about the cost of an asset and the aggregate (accumulated) depreciation as the separate components of net book value. Having this detail allows users to estimate the proportion of asset life remaining to be used. This information will be reported in the notes to the statement of financial position (balance sheet).

- Users also need information about the accounting policy on depreciation and its impact on the reported asset values. This information will be found in the notes to the accounts on accounting policies and the notes. There may also be a description and discussion in the Operating and Financial Review, including a forward-looking description of intended capital expenditure.

- **Depreciation** is estimated for the total life of the asset and then allocated to the reporting periods involved, usually annual reporting. No particular method of depreciation is required by law. Preparers of financial statements have to exercise choices. Companies in the UK commonly use straight-line depreciation. An alternative is reducing-balance depreciation. This is found more commonly in some other countries. Choice of depreciation method affects the comparability of profit.

Further reading

The following standards are too detailed for a first level course but the definitions sections may be helpful:

IASB (2012), IAS 38, *Intangible Assets*, International Accounting Standards Board.

IASB (2012), IAS 16, *Property, Plant and Equipment*, International Accounting Standards Board.

QUESTIONS

The Questions section of each chapter has three types of question. 'Test your understanding' questions to help you review your reading are in the 'A' series of questions. You will find the answers to these by reading and thinking about the material in the book. 'Application' questions to test your ability to apply technical skills are in the 'B' series of questions. Questions requiring you to show skills in problem solving and evaluation are in the 'C' series of questions. A letter [S] indicates that there is a solution at the end of the book.

A   Test your understanding

A8.1   State the definition of a non-current (fixed) asset and explain why each condition is required. (Section 8.2)

A8.2   Explain the categories: (Section 8.2.1)

(a) tangible non-current (fixed) assets;
(b) intangible non-current (fixed) assets; and
(c) non-current (fixed) asset investments;

and give an example of each.

A8.3   What do users of financial statements particularly want to know about non-current (fixed) assets? (Section 8.4)

A8.4   What type of information would you expect to find about non-current (fixed) assets in the financial statements and notes of a major UK listed company? (Section 8.4)

A8.5   State the definition of depreciation. (Section 8.7)

A8.6   What is meant by accumulated depreciation (also called aggregate depreciation)? (Section 8.7)

A8.7   What information is needed to calculate annual depreciation? (Section 8.7.1)

A8.8   What is the formula for calculating straight-line depreciation? (Section 8.7.2)

A8.9   How is reducing-balance depreciation calculated? (Section 8.7.3)

A8.10   How does depreciation help to retain cash in a business for asset replacement? (Section 8.7.5)

A8.11   Why does the net book value of a non-current (fixed) asset not always equal the proceeds of sale? (Section 8.8.5)

A8.12   Why is depreciation said to cause an **allocation** problem in accounting? (Section 8.8.6)

A8.13   How should the cost of a non-current (fixed) asset be decided? (Section 8.2.2)

A8.14   [S] What are the matters of judgement relating to non-current (fixed) assets which users of financial statements should think about carefully when evaluating financial statements?

A8.15   What is meant by **impairment**? (Section 8.8.7)

B   Application

B8.1 [S]

On reviewing the financial statements of a company, the company's accountant discovers that expenditure of £8,000 on repair to factory equipment has been incorrectly recorded as a part of the cost of the machinery. What will be the effect on the income statement (profit and loss account) and statement of financial position (balance sheet) when the error is corrected?

B8.2

On 1 January Year 1, Angela's Employment Agency was formed. The owner contributed £300,000 in cash which was immediately used to purchase a building. It is estimated to have a 20-year life and a residual value of £200,000. During Year 1 the agency collects £80,000 in fee income and pays £60,000 in wages and other costs. Record the transactions and events of Year 1 in an accounting equation spreadsheet. (See Table 8.3 for an illustration.) Prepare the statement of financial position (balance sheet) at the end of Year 1 and the income statement (profit and loss account) for Year 1.

B8.3

Assume that fee income and costs are the same in Year 2 as in Year 1. Record the transactions and events of Year 2 in an accounting equation spreadsheet. Prepare the statement of financial position (balance sheet) at the end of Year 2 and the income statement (profit and loss account) for Year 2.

B8.4

Angela's Employment Agency sells the building for £285,000 on the final day of December Year 3. Record the transactions and events of Year 3 in an accounting equation spreadsheet. (See Table 8.7 for an illustration.) Assume depreciation is calculated in full for Year 3.

B8.5

Explain how the accounting equation spreadsheet of your answer to question B8.4 would alter if the building had been sold for £250,000.

B8.6

On 1 January Year 1, Company A purchased a bus costing £70,000. It was estimated to have a useful life of three years and a residual value of £4,000. It was sold for £8,000 on the last day of Year 3.

On 1 January Year 1, Company B purchased a bus also costing £70,000. It was estimated to have a useful life of three years and a residual value of £7,000. It was sold for £8,000 on the last day of Year 3.

Both companies have a net profit of £50,000 before depreciation. Calculate the depreciation charge and net profit of each company for each of the three years. Show that over the three years the total depreciation charge for each company is the same. (See Table 8.11 for an example.)

C   Problem solving and evaluation

C8.1 [S]

The Biscuit Manufacturing Company commenced business on 1 January Year 1 with capital of £22,000 contributed by the owner. It immediately paid cash for a biscuit machine costing £22,000. It was estimated to have a useful life of four years and at the end of that time was estimated to have a residual value of £2,000. During each year of operation of the machine, the company collected £40,000 in cash from sale of biscuits and paid £17,000 in cash for wages, ingredients and running costs.

Required
(a) Prepare spreadsheets for each of the four years analysing the transactions and events of the company.
(b) Prepare a statement of financial position (balance sheet) at the end of Year 3 and an income statement (profit and loss account) for that year.
(c) Explain to a non-accountant how to read and understand the statement of financial position (balance sheet) and income statement (profit and loss account) you have prepared.

C8.2 [S]

The biscuit machine in question C8.1 was sold at the end of Year 4 for a price of £3,000.

Required
(a) Prepare the spreadsheet for Year 4 analysing the transactions and events of the year.
(b) Prepare the statement of financial position (balance sheet) at the end of Year 4 and the income statement (profit and loss account) for Year 4.
(c) Explain to a non-accountant the accounting problems of finding that the asset was sold for £3,000 when the original expectation was £2,000.

C8.3 [S]

The Souvenir Company purchased, on 1 January Year 1, a machine producing embossed souvenir badges. The machine cost £16,000 and was estimated to have a five-year life with a residual value of £1,000.

Required

(a) Prepare a table of depreciation charges and net book value over the five-year life using straight-line depreciation.

(b) Make a guess at the percentage rate to be used in the reducing-balance calculation, and prepare a table of depreciation charges and net book value over the five years using reducing-balance depreciation.

(c) Using the straight-line method of depreciation, demonstrate the effect on the accounting equation of selling the asset at the end of Year 5 for a price of £2,500.

(d) Using the straight-line method of depreciation, demonstrate the effect on the accounting equation of disposing of the asset at the end of Year 5 for a zero scrap value.

Activities for study groups

Turn to the annual report of a listed company which you have used for activities in previous chapters. Find every item of information about non-current (fixed) assets. (Start with the financial statements and notes but look also at the operating and financial review, chief executive's review and other non-regulated information about the company.)

As a group, imagine you are the team of fund managers in a fund management company. You are holding a briefing meeting at which each person explains to the others some feature of the companies in which your fund invests. Today's subject is *non-current (fixed) assets*. Each person should make a short presentation to the rest of the team covering:

1 the nature and significance of non-current (fixed) assets in the company;

2 the asset lives stated in the accounting policies for depreciation purposes;

3 the asset lives estimated by you from calculations of annual depreciation as a percentage of asset cost;

4 the remaining useful life of assets as indicated by comparing accumulated depreciation with asset cost;

5 the company's plans for future investment in non-current (fixed) assets.

Notes and references

1. IASB (2010), *Conceptual Framework*, para. 4.4(a).
2. IASB (2012), IAS 1 paras 66 and 67.
3. IASB (2012), IAS 1 para. 67 permits the use of alternative descriptions for non-current assets provided the meaning is clear.
4. IASB (2012), IAS 16, *Property, Plant and Equipment*, para. 6.
5. IASB (2012), IAS 38, *Intangible Assets*, para. 8.
6. IASB (2012), IAS 16, *Property, Plant and Equipment*, para. 6.
7. IASB (2012), IAS 16, *Property, Plant and Equipment*, para. 6.
8. There remain international differences on the precise method of estimating cash-generating ability. There are detailed rules in IAS 38 but these are beyond a first-level text.
9. IASB (2012), IAS 1 paras 66 and 67.

Recording non-current (fixed) assets and depreciation

The rules for debit and credit entries in a ledger account should by now be familiar but are set out again in Table 8.12 for convenience. If you still feel unsure about any aspect of Exhibit 8.14 you should revisit the supplements of earlier chapters before attempting this one.

In this supplement you will concentrate primarily on the ledger accounts for the non-current (fixed) assets. It takes The Removals Company of the main chapter as the example for illustration.

Table 8.12
Rules for debit and credit entries in ledger accounts

	Debit entries in a ledger account	Credit entries in a ledger account
Left-hand side of the equation		
Asset	Increase	Decrease
Right-hand side of the equation		
Liability	Decrease	Increase
Ownership interest	Expense	Revenue
	Capital withdrawn	Capital contributed

Information to be recorded

The Removals Company commences business on 1 January Year 2 by paying cash for a van costing £60,000. The cash was contributed by the owner. The van is estimated to have a useful life of three years and is estimated to have a residual value of £6,000. On 31 December Year 2 the owner calculates annual depreciation of the van as £18,000, using the formula:

$$\frac{\text{Cost} - \text{Estimated residual value}}{\text{Estimated life}}$$

During each year of operating the van, the company collected £120,000 in cash from customers and paid £58,000 in cash for drivers' wages, fuel and other running costs.

The transactions of Year 2 have been analysed in Table 8.3 for their impact on the accounting equation. That same list may be used to set out the debit and credit book-keeping entries, as shown in Table 8.13.

Table 8.13
Analysis of transactions for The Removals Company, Year 2

Date	Transaction or event	Amount	Dr	Cr
Year 2		£		
1 Jan.	Owner contributes cash	60,000	Cash	Ownership interest
1 Jan.	Purchase furniture van	60,000	Van at cost	Cash
All year	Collected cash from customers	120,000	Cash	Sales
All year	Paid for running costs	58,000	Running costs	Cash
31 Dec.	Calculate annual depreciation	18,000	Depreciation	Accumulated depreciation

Ledger accounts required to record transactions of Year 2 are as follows:

L1 Ownership interest		L4 Accumulated depreciation of van	
L2 Cash		L5 Sales	
L3 Van at cost		L6 Running costs	
		L7 Depreciation of the year	

L1 Ownership interest

Date	Particulars	Page	Debit	Credit	Balance
Year 2			£	£	£
Jan. 1	Cash	L2		60,000	(60,000)

LEONA's comment: *This ledger account shows the opening contribution to the start of the business which establishes the ownership interest.*

L2 Cash

Date	Particulars	Page	Debit	Credit	Balance
Year 2			£	£	£
Jan. 1	Ownership interest	L1	60,000		60,000
Jan. 1	Van	L3		60,000	nil
Jan.–Dec.	Sales	L5	120,000		120,000
Jan.–Dec.	Running costs	L6		58,000	62,000

LEONA's comment: *For convenience in this illustration all the sales and running costs have been brought together in one amount for the year. In reality there would be a large number of separate transactions recorded throughout the year. The balance at the end of the year shows that there is £62,000 remaining in the bank account.*

L3 Van at cost

Date	Particulars	Page	Debit	Credit	Balance
Year 2			£	£	£
Jan. 1	Cash	L2	60,000		60,000

LEONA's comment: *The van is recorded by a debit entry and this entry remains in the ledger account for as long as the van is in use by the company. A separate ledger account is maintained for the cost of the asset because it is regarded as a useful piece of information for purposes of financial statements.*

L4 Accumulated depreciation of van

Date	Particulars	Page	Debit	Credit	Balance
Year 2			£	£	£
Dec. 31	Depreciation of the year	L7		18,000	(18,000)

LEONA's comment: *The accumulated depreciation account completes the story about the van. It has an original cost of £60,000 and an accumulated depreciation at the end of Year 2 equal to £18,000. The accumulated depreciation account will always show a credit balance because it is the negative part of the asset. Deducting accumulated depreciation from cost gives a net book value of £42,000.*

L5 Sales

Date	Particulars	Page	Debit	Credit	Balance
Year 2			£	£	£
Jan.–Dec.	Cash	L2		120,000	(120,000)

LEONA's comment: *For convenience all the sales transactions of the year have been brought together in one single amount, but in reality there would be many pages of separate transactions.*

L6 Running costs

Date	Particulars	Page	Debit	Credit	Balance
Year 2			£	£	£
Jan.–Dec.	Cash	L2	58,000		58,000

LEONA's comment: *As with the sales transactions of the year, all running costs have been brought together in one single amount, but in reality there will be several pages of separate transactions recorded over the year.*

L7 Depreciation of the year

Date	Particulars	Page	Debit	Credit	Balance
Year 2			£	£	£
Dec. 31	Depreciation of year 2	L4	18,000		18,000

LEONA's comment: *The depreciation of the year is a debit entry because it is an expense. The process of depreciation is continuous but that is not convenient for ledger account recording, so companies prefer a single calculation at the end of the year.*

At this point a trial balance may be prepared, as explained in the supplement to Chapter 5, and shown in Table 8.14.

Table 8.14
Trial balance at the end of Year 2 for The Removals Company

Ledger account title	£	£
L1 Ownership interest		60,000
L2 Cash	62,000	
L3 Van at cost	60,000	
L4 Accumulated depreciation of van		18,000
L5 Sales		120,000
L6 Running costs	58,000	
L7 Depreciation	18,000	
Totals	198,000	198,000

Closing at the end of Year 2 and starting the ledger accounts for Year 3

At the end of the year the balances on asset and liability accounts are *carried forward* to the next year. The phrase 'carried forward' means that they are allowed to remain in the ledger account at the start of the new year. The balances on revenue and expense accounts are treated differently. After the trial balance has been prepared and checked, the amounts on each revenue account and expense account are *transferred to an income statement (profit and loss account)*. Transferring a balance requires an entry of the opposite type to the balance being transferred. A debit entry is made to transfer a credit balance. A credit entry is made to transfer a debit balance. Matching but opposite entries are made in the income statement (profit and loss account). This is called 'closing' the expense or revenue account.

L5 Sales

Date	Particulars	Page	Debit	Credit	Balance
Year 2			£	£	£
Jan.–Dec.	Cash	L2		120,000	(120,000)
Dec. 31	Transfer to profit and loss account	L8	120,000		nil

LEONA's comment: *The ledger account for sales shows a credit balance of £120,000 for the total transactions of the year. This is transferred to the income statement (profit and loss account) by making a debit entry of similar amount, so that the balance of the sales account is reduced to nil.*

L6 Running costs

Date	Particulars	Page	Debit	Credit	Balance
Year 2			£	£	£
Jan.–Dec.	Cash	L2	58,000		58,000
Dec. 31	Transfer to income statement (profit and loss account)	L8		58,000	nil

LEONA's comment: *The ledger account for running costs shows a debit balance of £58,000 for the total transactions of the year. This is transferred to the income statement (profit and loss account) by making a credit entry of similar amount, so that the balance of the running costs account is reduced to nil.*

L7 Depreciation of the year

Date	Particulars	Page	Debit	Credit	Balance
Year 2			£	£	£
Dec. 31	Depreciation of Year 2	L4	18,000		18,000
Dec. 31	Transfer to income statement (profit and loss account)	L8		18,000	nil

LEONA's comment: *The ledger account for depreciation expense shows a debit balance of £18,000 for the depreciation charge of the year. This is transferred to the income statement (profit and loss account) by making a credit entry of similar amount, so that the balance of the depreciation expense account of the year is reduced to nil.*

L8 Income statement (profit and loss account)

Date	Particulars	Page	Debit	Credit	Balance
Year 2			£	£	£
Dec. 31	Sales	L5		120,000	(120,000)
Dec. 31	Running costs	L6	58,000		(62,000)
Dec. 31	Depreciation of the year	L7	18,000		(44,000)

LEONA's comment: *The income statement (profit and loss account) in ledger form shows all items of revenue in the credit column and all items of expense in the debit column. The balance in the third column shows, at the end of the ledger account, the profit of £44,000 for the year. There is one final entry to be made, and that is to transfer the £44,000 balance of the income statement (profit and loss account) to the ownership interest account. That requires a debit entry in the income statement (profit and loss account) to remove the credit balance.*

L8 Income statement (profit and loss account)

Date	Particulars	Page	Debit	Credit	Balance
Year 2			£	£	£
Dec. 31	Sales	L5		120,000	(120,000)
Dec. 31	Running costs	L6	58,000		(62,000)
Dec. 31	Depreciation	L7	18,000		(44,000)
Dec. 31	Transfer to ownership interest	L1	44,000		nil

L1 Ownership interest

Date	Particulars	Page	Debit	Credit	Balance
Year 2			£	£	£
Jan. 1	Cash	L2		60,000	(60,000)
Dec. 31	Transfer from income statement (profit and loss account)	L8		44,000	(104,000)

LEONA's comment: *The transfer from the income statement (profit and loss account) is shown as a credit entry in the ledger account for the ownership interest. That credit entry matches the debit entry, removing the balance from the ledger account. As a check on the common sense of the credit entry, go back to the table at the start of this Supplement (Table 8.12), which shows that a credit entry records an increase in the ownership interest. In the ledger account the credit entry of £44,000 increases the ownership interest from £60,000 to £104,000.*

Subsequent years

The income statement (profit and loss account)s for Year 3 and Year 4 are identical to that for Year 2. The cash account flows on in a pattern similar to that of Year 2. These ledger accounts are therefore not repeated here for Years 3 and 4. Attention is concentrated on the asset at cost and the accumulated depreciation.

L3 Van at cost

Date	Particulars	Page	Debit	Credit	Balance
Year 2			£	£	£
Jan. 1	Cash	L2	60,000		60,000
Year 3	Balance	b/fwd			60,000
Year 4	Balance	b/fwd			60,000

LEONA's comment: *The asset continues in use from one year to the next and so the ledger account remains open with the balance of £60,000 remaining. At the start of each new year the balance on each asset account is brought forward (repeated) from the previous line to show clearly that this is the amount for the start of the new accounting year. Because this is merely a matter of convenience in tidying up at the start of the year, the abbreviation 'b/fwd' (for 'brought forward') is entered in the 'page' column to show that there are no debit or credit entries for transactions on this line.*

L4 Accumulated depreciation

Date	Particulars	Page	Debit	Credit	Balance
Year 2			£	£	£
Dec. 31	Depreciation of Year 2	L7		18,000	(18,000)
Year 3					
Dec. 31	Depreciation of Year 3	L7		18,000	(36,000)
Year 4					
Dec. 31	Depreciation of Year 4	L7		18,000	(54,000)

LEONA's comment: *The accumulated depreciation account is now showing more clearly what the word 'accumulated' means. Each year it is building in a further amount of £18,000 annual depreciation to build up the total shown in the 'balance' column. After three years the accumulated depreciation has built up to £54,000.*

L7 Depreciation of the year: Year 3

Date	Particulars	Page	Debit	Credit	Balance
Year 3			£	£	£
Dec. 31	Depreciation of Year 3	L4	18,000		18,000
Dec. 31	Transfer to income statement (profit and loss account)	L8		18,000	nil

L7 Depreciation of the year: Year 4

Date	Particulars	Page	Debit	Credit	Balance
Year 4			£	£	£
Dec. 31	Depreciation of Year 4	L4	18,000		18,000
Dec. 31	Transfer to income statement (profit and loss account)	L8		18,000	nil

LEONA's comment: *The depreciation of the year is an income statement (profit and loss account) item and so is transferred to the income statement (profit and loss account) each year in Years 3 and 4 in the manner explained earlier for Year 2.*

Disposal of the asset

At the end of Year 4 the asset is sold for a cash price of £6,000. To remove the asset requires entries in the 'Van at cost' account (L3), the 'Accumulated depreciation' account (L4) and the 'Cash' account (L2). The corresponding debit and credit entries are recorded in a 'Non-current (fixed) asset disposal' account (L9).

Table 8.15 shows the breakdown of the sale transaction into the removal of the asset at cost, the removal of the accumulated depreciation, and the collection of cash. The entry required to remove a balance on a ledger account is the opposite to the amount of the balance. So in the 'Van at cost' account (L3) a credit entry of £60,000 is required to remove a debit balance of £60,000. In the 'Accumulated depreciation' account (L4) a debit entry is required to remove a credit balance of £54,000. In the 'Cash' account (L2) there is a debit entry of £60,000 to show that the asset of cash has increased. In each case the 'Disposal' account (L9) collects the matching debit or credit.

Table 8.15
Analysis of debit and credit aspects of sale of a fixed asset

Date	Transaction or event	Amount	Dr	Cr
Year 4		£		
Dec. 31	Removal of asset at cost	60,000	Disposal	Van at cost
Dec. 31	Accumulated depreciation	54,000	Accumulated depreciation	Disposal
Dec. 31	Cash	6,000	Cash	Disposal

L3 Van at cost

Date	Particulars	Page	Debit	Credit	Balance
Year 2			£	£	£
Jan. 1	Cash	L2	60,000		60,000
Year 3	Balance	b/fwd			60,000
Year 4	Balance	b/fwd			60,000
Dec. 31	Disposal	L9		60,000	nil

L4 Accumulated depreciation

Date	Particulars	Page	Debit	Credit	Balance
Year 2			£	£	£
Dec. 31	Depreciation of Year 2	L7		18,000	(18,000)
Year 3					
Dec. 31	Depreciation of Year 3	L7		18,000	(36,000)
Year 4					
Dec. 31	Depreciation of Year 4	L7		18,000	(54,000)
Dec. 31	Disposal	L9	54,000		nil

L9 Non-current (fixed) asset disposal account

Date	Particulars	Page	Debit	Credit	Balance
Year 4			£	£	£
Dec. 31	Van at cost	L3	60,000		60,000
Dec. 31	Accumulated depreciation	L4		54,000	6,000
Dec. 31	Cash	L2		6,000	nil

LEONA's comment: *The disposal account is a very convenient way of bringing together all the information about the disposal of the van. The first two lines show the full cost and accumulated depreciation. The balance column, on the second line, shows that the difference between these two items is the net book value of £6,000. Collecting cash of £6,000 is seen to match exactly the net book value, which means that there is no depreciation adjustment on disposal.*

Sale for an amount greater than the net book value

In the main text of this chapter there is a discussion of the consequences of selling the van for £9,000 cash. There would be no problem in recording that in the bookkeeping system. Everything explained in the previous section would be unchanged except for the amount of the cash received. The Disposal account would now be recorded as:

L9 Non-current (fixed) asset disposal account

Date	Particulars	Page	Debit	Credit	Balance
Year 4			£	£	£
Dec. 31	Van at cost	L3	60,000		60,000
Dec. 31	Accumulated depreciation	L4		54,000	6,000
Dec. 31	Cash	L2		9,000	(3,000)
Dec. 31	Transfer to income statement (profit and loss account)	L8	3,000		nil

The income statement (profit and loss account) for Year 4 would be recorded as:

L8 Income statement (profit and loss account)

Date	Particulars	Page	Debit	Credit	Balance
Year 4			£	£	£
Dec. 31	Sales	L5		120,000	(120,000)
Dec. 31	Running costs	L6	58,000		(62,000)
Dec. 31	Depreciation of the year	L7	18,000		(44,000)
Dec. 31	Gain on disposal	L9		3,000	(47,000)

LEONA's comment: *This income statement (profit and loss account) in ledger form matches the income statement (profit and loss account) presented at Table 8.10 in the main text as a financial statement, although you will see that the latter is much more informative.*

Formula for calculating percentage rate for reducing-balance depreciation

The rate of depreciation to be applied under the reducing-balance method of depreciation may be calculated by the formula:

$$\text{rate} = (1 - \sqrt[n]{(R/C)}) \times 100\%$$

where: n = the number of years of useful life
         R = the estimated residual value
         C = the cost of the asset.

For the example given in the main chapter:

   $N = 5$ years
   $C = £1,000$
   $R = £30$ (The residual value must be of reasonable magnitude. To use an
       amount of nil for the residual value would result in a rate of 100%.)

$$\text{rate} = (1 - \sqrt[5]{(30/1,000)}) \times 100\%$$

To prove that the rate is 50% you will need a scientific calculator or a suitable computer package. You may know how to calculate a fifth root using logarithms. Otherwise, if you have a very basic calculator it may be easier to use trial-and-error methods.

S | Test your understanding

S8.1   Prepare ledger accounts to report the transactions and events of questions C8.1 and C8.2.

S8.2   Write a short commentary on each ledger account prepared in S1, to enable a non-accountant to understand their purpose and content.

Chapter 9

Current assets

Rexam plc

Rexam is a leading global consumer packaging group and a leading global beverage can maker. The company serves a number of markets including the beverage, personal care, healthcare and food markets. The following extracts are taken from the Directors' Report and the Principal Accounting Policies

Shutterstock.com/Celso Pupo

Extracts from Directors' Report

Across our beverage can sectors our vision is to keep the metal in a closed material loop: our aim is for zero cans ending up in landfill following consumers' use of the product. This makes good economic sense due to the high value of the materials, more than covering the cost of their collection, as well as environmental sense with up to 95% of the energy needed for primary production saved. As metal can be continually reused, every tonne of recycled material offsets the need to use a tonne of virgin raw material.

Recycling rates for beverage cans vary across countries, due to different operating environments, culture and lifestyles. We report these together with the targets set by industry associations of which we are a member.

Beverage can average recycling rates (%)

2015 targets	2010	2009	2008	2007
Europe 75	n/a[1]	68	68	66
USA 63	58	57	54	54
Brazil 98	98	98	91	96

[1] European 2010 recycling rates will be published mid 2012.

Source: Extracts from Directors' report. Page 46. Annual report 2011.

Extract from Principal Accounting Policies

Inventories are measured at the lower of cost and net realisable value. Cost is determined on a first in first out or a weighted average cost basis. Cost comprises directly attributable purchase and conversion costs and an allocation of production overheads based on normal operating capacity. Net realisable value is the estimated selling price less estimated costs to completion and selling costs.

Source: Extract from Principal Accounting Policies page 96, Annual report 2011 http://www.rexam.com/files/reports/2011ar/files/ 2011_annual_report.pdf.

Discussion points

1 What does the reader learn about inventory valuation from the accounting policy note?

2 What does the reader learn about the management of raw materials from the explanation in the directors' report?

3 How do these two sets of information help investors in their decision making?

Contents

After studying this chapter you should be able to:

- Define a current asset and apply the definition.
- Explain the operation of the working capital cycle.
- Explain the factors affecting recognition of inventories (stocks), receivables (debtors) and investments.
- Explain how the information presented in a company's statement of financial position (balance sheet) and notes, in relation to current assets, meets the needs of users.
- Explain the different approaches to measurement of inventories (stocks) and cost of goods sold.
- Analyse provisions for doubtful debts using a spreadsheet.
- Analyse prepayments using a spreadsheet.
- Explain the term 'revenue' and the application of principles of revenue recognition.

Additionally, for those who choose to study the supplement:

- Record receivables (debtors) and prepayments in ledger accounts.

9.1 Introduction

This chapter will continue the progress through the statement of financial position (balance sheet) which we began in Chapter 8. As in that chapter, the approach will be:

- What are the principles for defining and recognising these items?
- What are the information needs of users in respect of the particular items?
- What information is currently provided by companies to meet these needs?
- Does the information show the desirable qualitative characteristics of financial statements?
- What are the principles for measuring, and processes for recording, these items?

9.2 Definitions

Definitions were provided in Chapter 2. They are repeated here for convenience.

Definition

An **asset** is a resource controlled by the entity as a result of past events and from which future economic benefits are expected to flow to the entity.[1]

A **current asset** is an asset that satisfies any of the following criteria:

(a) it is expected to be realised in, or is intended for sale or consumption in, the entity's normal operating cycle;
(b) it is held primarily for the purpose of being traded;
(c) it is expected to be realised within twelve months after the reporting period;
(d) it is cash or a cash equivalent.[2]

The following list is a sample of the current assets found in most company statement of financial position (balance sheet)s:

- raw materials
- work in progress
- finished goods
- trade receivables (debtors)
- amounts owed by other companies in a group
- prepayments and accrued income
- investments held as current assets
- short-term bank deposits
- bank current account (also called 'cash at bank')
- cash in hand.

Activity 9.1   *Using the definition provided, explain why each item in the foregoing list may be classed as a current asset. Could a plot of land ever be treated as a current asset?*

The definition of a current asset refers to 'the entity's normal operating cycle'. The operating cycle experienced by many businesses lasts for 12 months, covering all the seasons of one year. One year is the reporting period most commonly used by most enterprises for reporting to external users of financial statements.

9.3 The working capital cycle

Working capital is the amount of long-term finance the business has to provide in order to keep **current assets** working for the business. Some short-term finance for current assets is provided by the suppliers who give credit by allowing time to pay, but that is not usually sufficient. Some short-term finance for current assets is provided by short-term bank loans but, in most cases, there still remains an excess of **current assets** over **current liabilities**.

The working capital cycle of a business is the sequence of transactions and events, involving current assets and current liabilities, through which the business makes a profit.

Figure 9.1 shows how the working capital cycle begins when suppliers allow the business to obtain goods on credit terms, but do not insist on immediate payment. While they are waiting for payment they are called **trade creditors**. The amounts owing to suppliers as creditors are called **trade payables** in the statement of financial position (balance sheet). The goods obtained by the business are used in production, held for resale or used in providing a service. While the goods acquired are held by the business they are called the **inventories (stocks)** of the business. Any products manufactured from these goods and held for resale are also part of the inventories (stocks) of the business. The resulting product or service is sold to customers who may pay immediately in cash, or may be allowed time to pay. If they are allowed time to pay they become **debtors** of the business. Debtors eventually pay and the business obtains cash. In the statement of financial position (balance sheet) the amount due from **trade debtors** is described as **trade receivables**. **Cash** is a general term used to cover money held in the bank, and money held in notes and coins on the business premises. Cash held in the bank will be in an account such as a current account which allows immediate access. Finally the cash may be used to pay the suppliers who, as creditors, have been waiting patiently for payment.

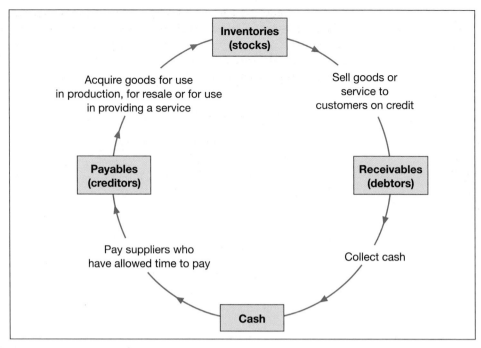

Figure 9.1
The working capital cycle for a manufacturing or service business

Inventories (stocks), receivables (debtors) and cash are all current assets of the business and will be dealt with in this chapter. Creditors who have supplied goods to the business are current liabilities and will be dealt with in the next chapter.

Working capital is calculated as **current assets** minus **current liabilities**. If the working capital is low, then the business has a close match between current assets and current liabilities but may risk not being able to pay its liabilities as they fall due. Not all the current assets are instantly available in cash. There may be some delay in selling the inventories (stocks) of unsold goods. An impatient supplier or bank manager may cause difficulties if cash is not available when payment of a liability is due. On the other hand, if current assets are very much greater than current liabilities, then the business has a large amount of finance tied up in the current assets when perhaps that finance would be better employed in the acquisition of more fixed assets to expand the profit-making capacity of the operations.

Definition	**Working capital** is the amount which a business must provide to finance the current assets of a business, to the extent that these are not covered by current liabilities. It is calculated by deducting current liabilities from current assets.

9.4 Recognition

The general conditions for recognition were set out in Chapter 2. An item that meets the definition of an asset should be recognised if there is sufficient evidence that the new asset has been created and the item can be measured at a monetary amount with sufficient reliability. There is no doubt that inventories (stocks), receivables (debtors), investments and cash are commonly recognised in a statement of financial position (balance sheet) but it is useful to be aware of the element of doubt which may be attached to the expectation of economic benefit which creates the asset and to the reliability of measurement. That awareness is essential to understanding the level of uncertainty which surrounds reported financial statements.

9.4.1 Inventories (stocks)

'Inventories' means lists of items. You might come across an inventory if you rent a flat and the owner has a list of the contents that is checked at the start and end of your tenancy. The pronunciation is *IN-ven-t'rees*, with stress on the first syllable 'IN' and not *INVENTOR-ees*, which sounds like a collection of inventors.

Definition

Inventories are assets:

(a) held for sale in the ordinary course of business;
(b) in the process of production for sale; or
(c) in the form of materials or supplies to be consumed in the production process or in the rendering of services.[3]

If a company is presenting its financial statements using the IASB's accounting system you will probably see the description 'inventories'. If the company is following UK company law and UK ASB standards then you will probably see the description 'stocks'. The remainder of this chapter explains the IASB's system for reporting inventories. The rules of UK law and standards are very similar. In business entities there are three main categories of inventories: raw materials, work in progress and finished goods. Consider these in reverse order.

Finished goods

The future economic benefit expected from finished goods is that they will be sold to customers for a price which exceeds the cost of purchase or manufacture. That makes a profit which increases the ownership interest. However, until the sale is agreed with the customer, this expected benefit is uncertain and the concept of **prudence** (explained in Chapter 4) dictates that it is safer not to anticipate that the profit will arise. The value of the inventories of finished goods is therefore measured at the **cost** of purchase or manufacture. In most cases that is a reliable measure because it is based on recorded costs and is not anticipating an uncertain selling price. Sometimes there may be a disappointment where goods are manufactured and then it is found there is a lack of demand. Where there is strong doubt about the expected selling price, such that it might be less than the cost of purchase or manufacture, the inventories (stock) of finished goods are valued at the net realisable value. This is defined as the estimated proceeds from sale of the items in question, less all costs to be incurred in marketing, selling and distributing these items.

The accounting policy note of most companies confirms this prudent approach. You will see in a later section of this chapter that Safe and Sure plc recognises inventories in its statement of financial position (balance sheet) at the lower of cost and net realisable value.

Work in progress

During the course of production the asset of finished goods is gradually being created. The expected future benefit of that activity is gradually building up as the work moves towards completion. A business could wait until the asset is totally finished, before recognising the asset in the statement of financial position (balance sheet). That would satisfy the concept of **prudence**, supported by the characteristic of **faithful representation**, but would run into problems with the characteristic of **relevance**. Where work in progress is a substantial aspect of the operations of the business, users need to know how much work in progress there is, whether it is increasing or decreasing, and what risks are attached. The risks attached to work in progress are often greater than those attached to finished goods because there is the risk of non-completion to add to all the risks faced when the goods are completed and awaiting sale. There is a reliable measurement, in the cost of work completed at the date of the financial year-end, but careful checking is required by the managers of the business to ensure that this is a reliable measure.

A particularly important type of **work in progress** is the construction contract (long-term contract) such as may be found in the engineering and building industries. A company building a bridge over three years will want to tell the shareholders about the progress being made in creating profit. Each year a portion of the total contract price will be reported as turnover and costs of the period will be matched against that turnover to calculate profit. The value of the work completed will be recognised as an asset in the statement of financial position (balance sheet), sometimes called work in progress. The reporting of profit on construction contracts (long-term contracts) is reviewed later in this chapter, in section 9.11.

Raw materials

The approach to recognition is the same as that for finished goods. Raw materials are expected to create a benefit by being used in the manufacture of goods for sale. On grounds of prudence the profit is not anticipated and the raw materials are measured at the lower of cost and net realisable value.

9.4.2 Receivables (debtors) and prepayments

Debtors are those persons who owe money to a business. Usually the largest amount shown under this heading relates to customers buying goods on credit. These are the **trade receivables (trade debtors)**. Additionally, the business may have lent money to another enterprise to help that enterprise in its activities. There may be loans to employees to cover removal and relocation expenses or advances on salaries. The business may be due to receive a refund of overpaid tax.

Trade receivables (debtors) meet the recognition conditions because there is an expectation of benefit when the customer pays. The profit on the sale of the goods is known because the customer has taken the goods or service and agreed the price. Trade receivables (debtors) are therefore measured at the selling price of the goods and the profit is recognised in the income statement (profit and loss account). There is a risk that the customer will not pay, but the view taken is that the risk of non-payment should be seen quite separately from the risk of not making a profit on a sale. The risk of non-payment is dealt with by reducing the reported value of the asset using an estimate for doubtful debts. That process is explained later in the chapter.

Prepayments are amounts of expenses paid in advance. Insurance premiums, rent of buildings, lease charges on a vehicle, road fund licences for the delivery vans and lorries, are all examples of items which have to be paid for in advance. At the date of the financial year-end some part of the future benefit may remain. This is recognised as the prepayment. Take the example of an insurance premium of £240 paid on 1 October to cover a 12-month period. At the company's year-end of 31 December, three months' benefit has expired but nine months' benefit remains. The statement of financial position (balance sheet) therefore reports a prepayment of £180.

Definition | **Prepayment** An amount paid for in advance for an benefit to the business, such as insurance premiums or rent in advance. Initially recognised as an asset, then transferred to expense in the period when the benefit is enjoyed.

9.4.3 Investments

Investments held as current assets are usually highly marketable and readily convertible into cash. The expectation of future economic benefit is therefore usually sufficient to meet the conditions of recognition. Measurement is more of a problem. There are two possible measures. One is the cost of the investment and the other is the market value. Recognising the investment at cost is prudent and reliable, but not as relevant as the current market value which is the amount of cash that could be released by sale of the investment. There is no agreed answer to this problem at the present time, although the issue has been debated in the standard-setting context. Most businesses report current asset investments at cost but a smaller number use the market value. Using the market value is called **marking to market**. It is a departure from the normal practice of recording assets at original cost but is justified in terms of the requirement of company law that financial statements should show a **true and fair view** (see Chapter 4). It is seen in companies whose business involves dealing in investments.

9.4.4 Cash

Recognising cash is no problem either in the expectation of benefit or in the measurement of the asset. The amount is known either by counting cash in hand or by looking at a statement from the bank which is holding the business bank account. The expectation of benefit lies in making use of the cash in future to buy fixed assets or to contribute to the working capital cycle so that the business earns a profit. In the meantime, cash which is surplus to immediate requirements should be deposited in such a way that it is earning interest. Where a company has substantial cash balances there should be indications in the income statement (profit and loss account) that investment income has been earned, to provide a benefit to the business.

Activity 9.2 | *This section has covered in some detail the characteristics of various groups of current assets. Before reading the next section, write down what information you would expect to see, in respect of these groups of assets, in the statement of financial position (balance sheet) and notes to the accounts. Then read the section and consider similarities to, or differences from, the views given there.*

9.5 Users' needs for information

Investors have an interest in knowing that current assets are not overstated. If the assets are overstated the profit of the business will be overstated (see the explanation in Chapter 4, using the accounting equation). They will want to know particularly whether there has been allowance for inventories of goods which may not lead to sales and whether there has been allowance for customers who may not be able to pay the debts shown as due to the business. They may also want the reassurance that the auditors have established the existence of all the current assets, particularly ensuring that a very portable asset such as cash is where it ought to be in the ownership of the company.

The needs of users do not stop with the investors. The trade creditors who supply goods and services to the business are strongly reliant on the working capital cycle for their eventual payment. Employees look for their salaries and wages from the cash generated during the working capital cycle. They want to know that the cash will be there on the day it is required, rather than being tied up in inventories or receivables (debtors) awaiting release as cash. Tax collecting authorities, such as HMRC, have definite dates on which payments are required. All these persons have an interest in the working capital of the business and how it is managed. The concern of creditors and employees is primarily with the flow of cash and its availability on the day required. That information will not appear in the statement of financial position (balance sheet) but there will be some indications of flow in the statement of cash flows (outlined in Chapter 3).

9.6 Information provided in the financial statements

In Chapter 7 the statement of financial position (balance sheet) of Safe and Sure plc contained three lines relating to current assets:

	Notes	Year 7 £m	Year 6 £m
Current assets			
Inventories (stocks)	5	26.6	24.3
Amounts receivable (debtors)	6	146.9	134.7
Six-month deposits		2.0	–
Cash and cash equivalents		105.3	90.5
Total current assets		280.8	249.5

There is more information provided in the notes to the statement of financial position (balance sheet).

9.6.1 Details in notes

There are two relevant notes, of which note 5 deals with inventories and note 6 with receivables (debtors):

Note 5	Year 7 £m	Year 6 £m
Inventories (stocks)		
Raw materials	6.2	5.4
Work in progress	1.9	1.0
Finished products	18.5	17.9
	26.6	24.3

This company is a service company so it is not surprising that stocks do not figure prominently in the overall collection of current assets. It is perhaps more surprising that there are inventories of finished products, but reading the description of the business shows that there is a Products Division which manufactures special cleaning chemicals under the company name.

The note on receivables (debtors) shows that the main category is trade receivables (debtors) with information to help assess the risks of the asset:

Note 6	Year 7	Year 6
Amounts receivable (debtors)	£m	£m
Trade receivables (trade debtors)	133.3	121.8
Less: provision for impairment of receivables	(5.2)	(4.8)
Trade receivables, net	128.1	117.0
Other receivables (debtors)	10.9	9.8
Prepayments and accrued income	7.9	7.9
	146.9	134.7

The ageing of the Group's year end overdue receivables, against which no provision has been made, is as follows:

	Year 7	Year 6
	£m	£m
Not impaired		
Less than 3 months	19.4	12.1
3 to 6 months	0.3	0.3
Over 6 months	0.1	–
	19.8	12.4

The individually impaired receivables relate to customers in unexpectedly difficult circumstances. The overdue receivables against which no provision has been made relate to a number of customers for whom there is no recent history of default and no other indication that settlement will not be forthcoming.

The carrying amounts of the Group's receivables are denominated in the following currencies:

	Year 7	Year 6
	£m	£m
Sterling	80.8	79.4
US Dollar	33.6	29.1
Euro	27.2	25.5
Other	5.3	3.4
	146.9	137.4

Movements in the Group's provision for impairment of trade receivables are as follows:

	Year 7	Year 6
	£m	£m
At 1 January	4.8	4.9
(Released)/charged to income statement	0.3	(0.1)
Net write off of uncollectible receivables	0.1	–
At 31 December	5.2	4.8

Amounts charged to the income statement are included within administrative expenses. The other classes of receivables do not contain impaired assets.

There is no indication of the nature of 'other receivables (debtors)'. It could indicate employees who have received loans or advances of salaries. It could indicate a loan to a company which has trading links with the group but is not a full subsidiary. Prepayments are expenses paid in advance of gaining the benefit, as explained in the previous section of this chapter.

9.6.2　Accounting policy

It will be shown later in this chapter that the valuation of inventories is a matter of potential variation from one person to the next, so it is important to know that the company has followed an acceptable policy in its valuation of inventories. The accounting policy note of Safe and Sure provides that confirmation (see Exhibit 9.1).

Exhibit 9.1
Accounting policy note

> **Safe and Sure plc Accounting policy**
>
> Inventories (stocks and work in progress) are stated at the lower of cost and net realisable value, using the first in first out principle. Cost includes all direct expenditure and related overheads incurred in bringing the inventories to their present condition and location.

For the moment you will have to accept that this form of wording represents standard practice, but each phrase will be explained later in the chapter.

9.6.3 Operating and financial review

The finance director of Safe and Sure commented as follows in his review:

> *The group's businesses are structured to utilise as little fixed and working capital as is consistent with the profit and earnings growth objective in order to produce a high cash flow.*

The focus on **working capital** is perhaps an indication of the importance seen in explaining how the company manages its current assets and current liabilities. It also shows that for this business the high cash flow is planned and is not an accident of events.

9.6.4 Analyst's view

DAVID WILSON comments: *This is a service business and so holds inventories of goods to be used in the service process. The note to the statement of financial position (balance sheet) does not actually say what the inventories are, so I asked when I made my visit. They tell me the raw materials are inventories of cleaning materials and chemicals for processes such as disinfecting. My main concern is to be assured that there is nothing in the inventories which could carry a risk of losing value through obsolescence or deterioration. There is not much problem of that with cleaning materials. The finished goods took me by surprise until I found out that there is a Products Division. It was actually the cleaning products that I knew best from years ago but I thought they had moved entirely into service contracts.*

In any event, inventories are not all that important for this company. The receivables (debtors) amount is much larger. I know they have a relatively low risk of bad debts because most customers pay in advance for their contracts.

When I started as an analyst I worked alongside someone who had 20 years' experience. He told me that he had always used what he called 'the 10% test' when looking at inventories (stocks) and receivables (debtors) in a statement of financial position (balance sheet). He worked out what effect a 10% error in the inventories or receivables would have on the profit before tax. In this case a 10% error in inventories would be £2.7m. The profit from operations is £195.2m. A difference of £2.7m on £195.2m is 1.4%. An error of 1.4% in profit would not have a significant impact on the view of most investors. So in this company inventories is not a matter which needs time taken for questions. On the other hand, a 10% error in receivables (debtors) would be £14.7m. That is 7.5% of profit from operations. So receivables (debtors) are worth more attention. The extended note explaining the areas of risk is useful. If this were a company I didn't know, I would ask about the quality of the asset and the type of customer who is given credit. In fact I do know the answer here. The finance director told me that when I met him. The receivables (debtors) are largely public sector bodies such as local authorities and hospitals who insist on paying after the work has been done to their satisfaction. There could be a risk of non-payment because of shoddy work but there is little risk of non-payment through default.

The final point to note in relation to current assets is that this company is a cash-generating business. I looked at the statement of cash flows for the past five years which shows that the group builds up cash balances, buys another company, and then generates even more cash. I suppose that can't go on for ever but there are no signs of problems at present.

LEONA: *I told you I would be looking for admissions of how much you rely on the auditor without knowing it. Your '10% test' is a very rough-and-ready example of the ratio analysis we carry out on a systematic basis as part of our analytical review of the financial statements. Maybe one day I'll tell you more about that. We have quite a long list of ratios which we calculate. We also look at interrelationships between ratios and relative changes in one compared with another.*

It is also an application of what we call 'materiality'. When we see an asset – in this case it is receivables (debtors) – where an error in estimation of the asset value could cause a serious impact on profit, we identify that as a matter for special attention. We would probably spend more time on receivables (debtors) than on inventories in our audit of this company but we would target the risk-related aspects of what is reported about each asset. For receivables (debtors) it is the risk of non-payment through either disputed debts or lack of funds. For inventories it is the risk of obsolescence or similar loss which is not covered by insurance.

Have you decided on how the company's information on current assets meets the list of desirable qualitative characteristics?

DAVID: *You're trying to get me to admit that I need the auditors. Reliability is in the auditors' hands as far as the numbers go, but I place a lot of reliance on my assessment of the qualities of senior management when I meet them. You can't audit that kind of feeling. It's all a matter of chemistry. Also, the main current asset is receivables (debtors) and I know they are reliable because the finance director told me what class of customer was involved. I didn't need the auditors for that. Relevance probably scores about eight out of ten because there aren't any complications here with unusual types of inventories. Faithful representation and neutrality are something I leave to the auditors for now but I'll be asking questions next year if the information in the financial statements turns out not to be neutral. Prudence, I know, is built into all aspects of accounting which uses historical cost measures. That sometimes works against relevance. Completeness is not a problem for current assets. The company is unlikely to leave anything out. They are more likely to include too much. I do expect the auditor to check that the assets are there. Comparability is a matter of presentation. This company has a five-year summary elsewhere in the annual report and gives the previous year's amounts in the financial statements. As for understandability, I like to think that I can see my way around figures for inventories, receivables (debtors) and cash. I usually get the answers I want when I phone the financial controller.*

LEONA: *But don't you see that by admitting that you have to ask more questions to help you understand the amounts, there must be some further explanations which the company could give in the annual report so that your understanding may be shared by others?*

DAVID: *My fund manager colleagues would say that only the professional investors have the expertise. Even if more information were reported by companies, only the professionals would know how to use it.*

9.7 Measurement and recording

The basic measurement rule applying to all current assets is that they should be measured at the *lower* of **cost** and **net realisable value**.[4] The exception is receivables (debtors) which are measured at selling price because the related profit is earned when the sale is made and not when the credit customer chooses to pay.

The next three sections look at issues of measurement and recording, in relation to inventories, receivables (debtors) and current asset investments, which are essential to an understanding of how much variability and uncertainty lies behind the apparent confidence of the numbers reported in financial statements.

9.8 Inventories (stocks) of raw materials and finished goods

The analysis of transactions involving inventories of raw materials, work in progress and finished goods has been explained in detail in Chapter 6 and will not be repeated here. This section examines the problems created by the general rule that inventories must be valued at the lower of cost and net realisable value. This rule is a consequence of the **prudence** concept, based on not anticipating a sale until the goods are delivered to the customer.

Net realisable value means the estimated selling price in the ordinary course of business less the estimated costs of completion and the estimated costs necessary to make the sale. For example, damaged inventories are sold at auction for £10,000. The auctioneer charges selling commission of 20% which is £2,000. The amount received by the seller is £8,000, called the net realisable value.

Definition

> **Net realisable value** is the estimated selling price in the ordinary course of business less the estimated costs of completion and the estimated costs necessary to make the sale.[5]

This section covers first of all the accounting equation in relation to the rule. It then looks at the meaning of cost and the allocation of overhead costs. Various specific models to deal with changing input prices are then discussed and the section concludes with the rules to be applied in financial reporting.

9.8.1 Lower of cost and net realisable value

Consider the example of a container of coffee beans purchased by a coffee manufacturer at a cost of £1,000. The beans are held for three months up to the date of the financial year-end. During that time there is a fall in the world price of coffee beans and the container of coffee beans would sell for only £800 in the market.

When the asset is acquired, the impact on the accounting equation is an increase of £1,000 in the asset of inventories and a decrease of £1,000 in the asset of cash.

Assets ↑↓	–	Liabilities	=	Ownership interest
+ £1,000 inventories – £1,000 cash				

At the end of the year the asset is found to be worth £800 and the ownership interest is reduced because the asset has fallen in value. The asset is reduced by £200 and an expense of loss of value in inventories value is reported in the income statement (profit and loss account).

Assets ↓	–	Liabilities	=	Ownership interest ↓
– £200 inventories				– £200 expense

If a business fails to report a fall in the value of the asset of inventories, the profit of the period will be overstated.

Where there are separate categories of inventories the rule of 'lower of cost and net realisable value' must be applied to each category separately. Suppose, for example, there is an inventory (stock) of paper at a cost of £2,000 with a net realisable value of £2,300 and an inventory (stock) of pens with a cost of £1,800 and a net realisable value of £1,400. The lower amount must be taken in each case, giving a value of £3,400 for inventories (calculated as £2,000 plus £1,400).

9.8.2 Meaning of cost

The **cost** of inventories comprises all costs of purchase, costs of conversion and other costs incurred in bringing the inventories to their present location and condition.[6] This expenditure will include not only the cost of purchase but also costs of converting raw materials into finished goods or services.

Costs of purchase include the price charged by the supplier, plus transport and handling costs, plus import duties and less discounts and subsidies.[7] Costs of conversion include items readily identifiable with the product, such as labour, expenses and subcontractors' costs directly related to the product. They also include production overheads and any other overheads directly related to bringing the product or service to its present condition and location. **Production overheads** are items such as depreciation of machines, service costs, rental paid for a factory, wages paid to supervisory and support staff, costs of stores control and insurance of production facilities.

Example

Take the example of a business which purchases 10 wooden furniture units for conversion to a customer's specification for installation in a hotel. The units cost £200 each and the labour cost of converting them is £100 each. Production overheads for the period are fixed at £3,500. Two units remain unsold at the end of the period. These two units will be recorded in the statement of financial position (balance sheet) at £1,300, calculated as £650 each (materials cost of £200 plus labour cost of £100 plus a share of the production overheads at £350 per item).

That was easy because there were 10 identical units to take equal shares of the production overheads. But suppose they had all been different and required different amounts of labour? Would it have been fair to share the overheads equally? Probably not. The problems of sharing out production overhead costs create a chapter in themselves and are studied further as part of management accounting. You need to be aware, in reading published accounting information, that there is considerable scope for discretion to be exercised by management in the allocation of overheads between completed goods and goods held in inventories. The general risk of overstatement of assets applies here. If the asset is overstated by having too much production overhead allocated, the profit of the period is also overstated because it is not bearing the share of production overheads which it should.

9.8.3 Costs when input prices are changing

One very tiresome problem faced by the accounts department in its record keeping is that suppliers change their prices from time to time. Goods held in store may have arrived at different times and at different unit prices. How does the accounts department decide on the unit price to be charged to each job when all the materials look the same once they are taken into store?

In some cases it may be possible to label the materials as they arrive so that they can be identified with the appropriate unit price. That is a very time-consuming process and would only be used for high-value low-volume items of materials. In other cases a convenient method is needed which gives an answer that is useful and approximately close to the true price of the units used. Some possibilities are shown in Table 9.1 using three options – first in first out (FIFO), last in first out (LIFO) and average cost. In each case, Table 9.1 takes a very simple approach, not complicated by having inventory at the start of the period. In real life the calculations can be even more tricky.

Table 9.1
Pricing the issue of goods to production

There are three parts to this illustration. Part (a) contains a table setting out the data to be used in the calculation. Part (b) defines the three bases of calculation. Part (c) uses the data from part (a) to illustrate each of the three bases.

(a) Data

Date	Received	Unit price	Price paid	Issued to production
	Units	£	£	Units
1 June	100	20	2,000	–
20 June	50	22	1,100	–
24 June	–	–	–	60
28 June	–	–	–	70
Total	150		3,100	130

(b) Bases of calculation
First in first out (FIFO)
Assume that the goods which arrived first are issued first.

Last in first out (LIFO)
Assume that the goods which arrived last are issued first.

Average cost
Assume that all goods are issued at the average price of the inventories held.

(c) Calculations

Basis	Date	Quantity and unit price	Issued to production	Held in inventories	Total
			£	£	£
FIFO					
	24 June	60 units at £20	1,200		
	28 June	40 units at £20			
		30 units at £22	1,460		
	30 June	20 units at £22		440	
Total			2,660	440	3,100

Table 9.1 continued

LIFO					
	24 June	50 units at £22			
		10 units at £20	1,300		
	28 June	70 units at £20	1,400		
	30 June	20 units at £20		400	
Total			2,700	400	3,100

Average					
	24 June	60 units at *£20.67	1,240		
	28 June	70 units at *£20.67	1,447		
	30 June	20 units at *£20.67		413	
Total			2,687	413	3,100

Note: * Weighted average [(100 × 20) + (50 × 22)]/150 = £20.67.

9.8.4 Approximation when dates are not recorded

In business there may not be time to keep the detailed records shown in the calculations in Table 9.1. In such cases the sales volume is known in total but the dates of sales are not recorded. The calculation then uses the best approximation available, which usually means working through the costs from the oldest date, for FIFO, or the most recent date, for LIFO, without attempting to match the various batches bought and sold during the year.

9.8.5 Choice of FIFO, LIFO or average cost

Look at table (c) of Table 9.1 and compare it with table (a) of that table. You will see from table (a) that the total amount spent on materials during the month was £3,100. You will see from table (c) that the total of the cost of goods issued to production, plus the cost of unsold goods, is always £3,100 irrespective of which approach is taken. All that differs is the allocation between goods used in production and goods remaining unsold. Cost can never be gained or lost in total because of a particular allocation process, provided the process is used consistently over time. The FIFO approach suffers the disadvantage of matching outdated costs against current revenue. The LIFO approach improves on FIFO by matching the most recent costs against revenue, but at the expense of an inventory value which becomes increasingly out of date. The average cost lies between the two and becomes more intricate to recalculate as more items come into inventory. In practice, the choice for internal reporting in management accounting is a matter of finding the best method for the purpose.

There is an effect on profit of the year which may influence management choice. When prices are rising and inventories volumes are steady or increasing, FIFO gives a lower cost of sales and so a higher profit than LIFO. If there were no regulations, companies that wished to show high profits (perhaps to impress investors buying shares in the company) might prefer FIFO. Companies that wished to show lower profits (perhaps to reduce tax bills) might prefer LIFO.

The IASB standard IAS 2 prohibits the use of LIFO. In the UK the tax authorities will not accept LIFO valuation. In the USA the LIFO method of valuation is permitted. Investors need to read the accounting policy note in the financial statements to find which approach a company has used.

Activity 9.3

Look back to Table 9.1 and write your own table of data for goods received, unit price, price paid and goods issued to production. Create calculations of cost of goods sold, using the various models in Table 9.1 (FIFO, LIFO and average price). Check that the value of goods issued to production, plus the value of goods held in stock, will always add up to the same answer in total.

9.9 Receivables (debtors)

The measurement of receivables (debtors) requires attention to bad and doubtful debts. A debt is described as a **bad debt** when there is no further hope of the customer paying the amount owed. This might be due to the customer being declared bankrupt or else disappearing without trace. If the customer is known to be in difficulties or there is some dispute over the amount owed, the debt is described as a **doubtful debt**. The company still hopes to recover the cash owed but realistically has some doubt. Evidence of doubtful debts may be seen in slow payment, partial payments, the need for several reminders or even rumours in the business community. A company will usually analyse the age of its debts to help identify those which may be doubtful.

Example

At the end of Year 1 the Garden Pond Company has a statement of financial position (balance sheet) comprising £2,000 receivables (debtors), £7,000 other assets and £9,000 ownership interest that consists of £1,800 ownership interest at the start of the period and £7,200 profit of the period. On the date of the financial year-end the manager of the company reviews the receivables (debtors) list and decides that debts amounting to £200 are doubtful because there are rumours of a customer not paying other suppliers in the trade. The statement of financial position (balance sheet) at the end of Year 1 is amended to show that the asset is of lower value than was thought and the ownership interest has consequently diminished.

Table 9.2 shows the spreadsheet for analysis set out to reflect the accounting equation. The new column is the one headed **provision for doubtful debts**. This is included

Table 9.2
Spreadsheet to analyse the effect of provision for doubtful debts at the end of Year 1, using the accounting equation

Date	Transaction or event	Assets			Ownership interest	
Year 1		Receivables (debtors)	Provision for doubtful debts	Other assets	Ownership interest at start	Profit of the period
		£	£	£	£	£
Dec. 31	Statement of financial position (balance sheet) first draft	2,000		7,000	1,800	7,200
Dec. 31	Recognition of doubtful debts		(200)			(200)
Dec. 31	Revised statement of financial position (balance sheet)	2,000	(200)	7,000	1,800	7,000

Table 9.3

Statement of financial position (balance sheet) of Garden Pond Company showing the presentation of information on doubtful debts

Garden Pond Company		
Statement of financial position (balance sheet) at 31 December Year 1		
	£	£
Other assets		7,000
Receivables (debtors)	2,000	
Less: provision for doubtful debts	(200)	
		1,800
		8,800
Ownership interest at the start of the year		1,800
Profit of the year		7,000
		8,800

in the assets section because it tells the user more about the asset of receivables (debtors), although it is the negative part of the asset. It causes some confusion to those who meet it for the first time because anything called a provision is usually reported under the heading of liabilities. However, on grounds of usefulness to readers and relevance to the provision of information about the asset, the provision for doubtful debts has special treatment in being included as a negative aspect within the asset section of the statement of financial position (balance sheet).

It is quite a difficult matter for a company to be prudent in expressing doubt about a debtor while still pursuing the non-payer with a view to collection of the debt. To remove the debt from the record would be to admit defeat. Even to show a separate provision among the liability headings might lead other customers to think, 'Why not me also?' However, companies are expected to provide information about impairment of assets, as indicated in the case study of Safe and Sure.

The statement of financial position (balance sheet) after incorporating a provision for the doubtful debt would appear as in Table 9.3.

There is no single method of calculating the provision for doubtful debts. Some companies consider separately the amount owed by each customer. To economise on time, most companies use previous experience to estimate a percentage of total receivables (debtors). A mixture of approaches could be used, with known problems being identified separately and a general percentage being applied to the rest.

9.9.1 Change in a provision

During Year 2 matters take an upward turn and in July the customer who was showing signs of financial distress manages to pay the amount of £200 owed. The effect on the accounting equation is that the asset of cash is increased and the asset of debtor is reduced by £200. The provision for doubtful debts is now no longer required and could be transferred back to the income statement (profit and loss account), but in practice it tends to be left for tidying up at the end of the year.

The business continues and at the end of Year 2 the receivables (debtors) amount to £2,500. A review of the list of receivables (debtors) causes considerable doubt regarding an amount of £350. It is decided to create a new provision of £350. The old provision of £200 related to last year's receivables (debtors) and is no longer required.

Table 9.4 shows the spreadsheet at the end of Year 2, before and after recording the new provision for doubtful debts. It is assumed that the other assets have grown to £10,000 and there is a profit of £3,500 before amending the provision for doubtful debts.

The income statement (profit and loss account) could show two separate entries, one being £200 increase in ownership interest and the other being £350 decrease in

Table 9.4
Spreadsheet to analyse the effect of provision for doubtful debts at the end of Year 2, using the accounting equation

Date	Transaction or event	Assets			Ownership	
Year 2		Receivables (debtors)	Provision for doubtful debts	Other assets	Ownership interest at start	Profit of the period
		£	£	£	£	£
Dec. 31	Statement of financial position (balance sheet) first draft	2,500	(200)	10,000	8,800	3,500
Dec. 31	Elimination of provision no longer required		200			200
Dec. 31	Creation of new provision		(350)			(350)
Dec. 31	Revised statement of financial position (balance sheet)	2,500	(350)	10,000	8,800	3,350

ownership interest. It is rather cumbersome in that form and most enterprises would report as an expense, in the income statement (profit and loss account), the single line:

Increase in provision for doubtful debts   £150

9.10 Prepayments

Prepayments arise when an item of expense is paid in advance of the benefit being received. A common example is the payment of an insurance premium. The payment is made in advance for the year ahead and the benefit is gradually used up as the year goes along. The statement of financial position (balance sheet) recognises the unexpired portion of the insurance premium as an asset, while the income statement (profit and loss account) reports the amount consumed during the period.

Example

On 1 October Year 1 a company paid £1,200 for one year's vehicle insurance. At the financial year-end date of 31 December there have been three months' benefit used up and there is a nine-month benefit yet to come. The transactions relating to insurance would be reported as in Table 9.5.

Table 9.5
Spreadsheet recording prepayment of insurance at the financial year-end date

Date	Transaction or event	Assets		Ownership interest
Year 2		Cash £	Prepayment £	Expense £
Oct. 1	Payment of premium	(1,200)		(1,200)
Dec. 31	Identification of asset remaining as prepayment		900	900
		(1,200)	900	(300)

The effect of identifying the asset is to reduce the expense of the period from £1,200 to £300 and to hold the remaining £900 as a benefit for the next accounting period. In Year 2 the amount of £900 will be transferred from the prepayment column to the expense column, so that the decrease in the ownership interest is reported in the period in which it occurs.

9.11 Revenue recognition

The sale of goods and services creates **revenue** for the business. Sometimes that revenue is referred to as **sales** or **turnover**. The term revenue may also be applied to rents received from letting out property, or interest received on investments made. In the conceptual frameworks of various countries, different views are held of the exact meaning and extent of the word *revenue*. The IASB defines revenue in terms of equity (ownership interest).

Definition

> **Revenue** is defined as the gross inflow of economic benefits during the period arising in the course of the ordinary activities of an enterprise when those inflows result in increases in equity, other than increases relating to contributions from equity participants.[8]

The main problem in recognition of revenue lies in the timing. Assets are recognised at a point in time but revenue is created over a period of time. What are the rules for deciding on the time period for which revenue should be reported? One suggestion has been that the **critical event** is the important factor.[9] When goods are produced or services are carried out, there is one part of the process which is critical to providing sufficient reassurance that the revenue has been earned by the efforts of the enterprise. For the sale of goods the point of delivery to the customer is the usual critical event which determines the date of revenue recognition. For a contract of service, the critical event is the production of the service.

9.11.1 Contract revenue

Where the service extends over more than one time period, the revenue may be split over the time periods involved. That may happen in a civil engineering or a building contract. In each year of the contract a portion of the revenue will be matched against costs of the period so as to report a portion of profit.

Take the example of a two-year bridge-building contract. The contract price is £60m. Two-thirds of the work has been completed in Year 1 and it is expected that the remainder will be completed in Year 2. The costs incurred in Year 1 are £34m and the costs expected for Year 2 are £17m.

The income statement (profit and loss account) of the business for Year 1 will report, in respect of this contract, turnover of £40m less costs of £34m giving profit of £6m. This gives a fair representation of the profit earned by the activity of the year (as two-thirds of the total). An independent expert, in this case an engineer, would confirm that the work had been completed satisfactorily to date. The effect on the accounting equation would be:

Assets ↑↓	−	Liabilities	=	Ownership interest ↑
+ £40m − £34m				+ £6m

Reporting contract revenue of £40m in Year 1 will increase the ownership interest by £40m. A matching asset will be reported, representing the value of the contract at that stage. The value of £40m shown for the construction contract represents the aggregate amount of costs incurred plus recognised profits to date.

In the income statement (profit and loss account) the expenses of £34m are reported in the usual way and a profit of £6m results. All being well, the income statement (profit and loss account) of Year 2 will report the remaining £20m of revenue minus £17m of expenses, leaving a profit of £3m. Over the two years the total profit of £9m will be reported.

Users of accounting information need to pay particular attention to contract revenue in a business and ask some careful questions. Has prudence been exercised in deciding what portion of revenue to report? Is there a risk that the future costs will escalate and there will be an overall loss? They should look carefully at the provisions section of the statement of financial position (balance sheet) (see Chapter 11).

Where the customer has paid money in advance as an instalment towards the final contract price, the effect on the accounting equation is to increase the asset of cash and create a liability towards the customer. These amounts received in advance from customers may be described as 'progress billings', 'payments on account', or 'payments in advance'. There is a liability because the business has an obligation to repay the customer if the contract is not completed on time or on specification. Although it might be expected that the liability towards the customer would appear in the current liabilities section of the statement of financial position (balance sheet), that does not happen. The liability in respect of payments made in advance is deducted from the value of the contract and the resulting net figure is reported as *construction contracts* in the current assets section of the statement of financial position (balance sheet). That may mean that, at first glance at the statement of financial position (balance sheet), the reader does not realise the true size of the contract being undertaken for the customer. There is no guarantee that any better information will be found anywhere else in the financial statements, because turnover is aggregated for all activities. For the analyst as an expert user, construction contracts (long-term contracts) require a great deal of careful questioning if the underlying details are to be understood.

9.11.2 A continuing debate

There are problems in revenue recognition that continue to be debated. Consider three examples. In the first, a film production company sells a programme to a television company which agrees to pay royalties every time the programme is broadcast. In the second, a farmer sells a cow to a neighbour in return for five sheep. In the third, a mobile phone company charges customers a start-up fee that is 24 times the monthly rental and service charge. There is no specific accounting standard to cover any of these situations. One approach to each is to ask, 'Has the revenue been earned?' The companies would all answer, 'Yes, we have completed our side of the transaction.' So perhaps revenue should be recognised in all three cases. Another approach is to ask, 'Are there any risks related to recognising revenue?' The answer is, 'Yes – the programme may never be broadcast; we are not sure about the exchange values between cows and sheep; and the telephone company may not be able to provide the service for the long period implied by the high initial charge.' So perhaps the revenue should not be reported until the risks are diminished. Both views are being applied, with the result that there has been some lack of clarity and comparability as new types of business have emerged. It is necessary to pay careful attention to the accounting policy on revenue recognition.

9.12 Summary

- A **current asset** is an asset that satisfies any of the following criteria:
  (a) it is expected to be realised in, or is intended for sale or consumption in, the entity's normal operating cycle;
  (b) it is held primarily for the purpose of being traded;
  (c) it is expected to be realised within 12 months after the date of the financial year-end;
  (d) it is cash or a cash equivalent.

- **Working capital** is the amount which a business must provide to finance the current assets of a business, to the extent that these are not covered by current liabilities. It is calculated by deducting current liabilities from current assets.

- Inventories (stocks), receivables (debtors), investments and cash are commonly **recognised** in a balance sheet. If there is doubt attached to the expectation of economic benefit which creates the asset and to the reliability of measurement, then this is recognised by making a **provision** such as the provision for doubtful debts.

- Users need information about the working capital of the business to judge whether it is suitable to support the activities of the business. Information provided to help users includes: detailed notes of current assets and current liabilities; notes of accounting policy describing the valuation of current assets; and a discussion of working capital management in the operating and financial review.

- **Inventories** (stocks) are measured at the lower of cost and net realisable value.

- Receivables (debtors) are measured at the amount receivable on settlement less any provision for doubtful debts.

- **Prepayments** are amounts paid in advance for benefits expected. Prepayments are assets until the benefit is used up. The amount is then transferred from an asset to an expense.

- **Revenue** is defined as the gross inflow of economic benefits during the period arising in the course of the ordinary activities of an enterprise when those inflows result in increases in equity, other than increases relating to contributions from equity participants.

- If revenues are earned over more than one time period (e.g. on long-term contracts) then the revenue is allocated across time periods in proportion to the amount of work completed.

QUESTIONS

The Questions section of each chapter has three types of question. 'Test your understanding' questions to help you review your reading are in the 'A' series of questions. You will find the answers to these by reading and thinking about the material in the book. 'Application' questions to test your ability to apply technical skills are in the 'B' series of questions. Questions requiring you to show skills in problem solving and evaluation are in the 'C' series of questions. A letter [S] indicates that there is a solution at the end of the book.

A   Test your understanding

A9.1   What is the definition of a current asset? (Section 9.2)

A9.2   What is the working capital cycle? (Section 9.3)

A9.3 What are the features of raw materials, work in progress and finished goods which justify their recognition in a balance sheet? (Section 9.4.1)

A9.4 What information do users need about current assets? (Section 9.5)

A9.5 What is meant by FIFO, LIFO and the average cost method of pricing issues of goods? (Section 9.8.3)

A9.6 How is a provision for doubtful debts decided upon? (Section 9.9)

A9.7 What is a prepayment? (Section 9.10)

A9.8 What is meant by 'revenue recognition'? (Section 9.11)

A9.9 Why are there problems with revenue recognition? (Section 9.11.2)

A9.10 [S] The Sycamore Company has inventories which include the following four items:

Description	Purchase cost £	Selling price £	Cost of selling £
Engine	6,500	8,250	350
Chassis	2,000	1,800	200
Frame	4,800	4,900	300

What amount should be reported as total inventory in respect of these three items?

A9.11 [S] On reviewing the company's financial statements, the company accountant discovers that items of year-end inventory of goods which cost £18,000 have been omitted from the record. What will be the effect on the income statement (profit and loss account) and the statement of financial position (balance sheet) when this omission is rectified?

A9.12 [S] On reviewing the financial statements, the company accountant discovers that an amount of £154,000 owed by a customer will be irrecoverable because the customer has fled the country. What will be the effect on the income statement (profit and loss account) and the statement of financial position (balance sheet) when this event is recognised?

B Application

B9.1 [S]
During its first month of operations, a business made purchases and sales as shown in the table below:

Date	Number of units purchased	Unit cost	Number of units sold
Jan. 5	100	£1.00	
Jan. 10			50
Jan. 15	200	£1.10	
Jan. 17			150
Jan. 24	300	£1.15	
Jan. 30			200

All sales were made at £2 each.

Required
Calculate the profit for the month and the stock value held at the end of the month using:

(a) the FIFO approach to the issue of units for sale, where:
  (i) the calculation is carried out at the date of sale; and
  (ii) the calculation is carried out at the end of the month without regard for the date of sale; and
(b) the LIFO approach to the issue of units for sale, where:
  (i) the calculation is carried out at the date of sale; and
  (ii) the calculation is carried out at the end of the month without regard for the date of sale; and
(c) the average-cost approach to the issue of units for sale, making the calculation at the end of the month without regard for the date of sale.

B9.2 [S]

A company has a stock of goods consisting of four different groups of items. The cost and net realisable value of each group is shown in the table below.

Group of items	Cost	Net realisable value
	£	£
A	1,000	1,400
B	1,000	800
C	2,100	1,900
D	3,000	3,100

Required

Calculate the amount to be shown as the value of the company's stock.

B9.3

At the end of Year 3 the Bed Company has a statement of financial position (balance sheet) comprising £3,000 receivables (debtors), £8,000 other assets and £11,000 ownership interest, consisting of £2,000 ownership interest at the start of the period and £9,000 profit of the period. On the date of the financial year-end the manager of the company reviews the receivables (debtors) list and decides that debts amounting to £450 are doubtful because the customers have not replied to repeated requests for payment.

Required

(a) Prepare an accounting equation spreadsheet to show the effect of the provision. (See Table 9.2 for an illustration.)

(b) Show the statement of financial position (balance sheet) information. (See Table 9.3 for an illustration.)

B9.4

The Bed Company continues trading during Year 4. The statement of financial position (balance sheet) at the end of Year 4, in its first draft, showed receivables (debtors) as £4,850 and the provision for doubtful debts unchanged from Year 3 at £450. Enquiry showed that during Year 4 some of the receivables (debtors) at the end of Year 3 had been confirmed as bad. They amounted to £250 but nothing had yet been recorded. The management wish to make the provision £550 at the end of Year 4. Other assets amount to £12,000, ownership interest at the start of Year 4 is £10,550 and the profit is £5,750.

Required

Prepare an accounting equation spreadsheet to show the effect of the bad debt being recognised and of the decision to make a provision at the end of Year 4. (See Table 9.4 for an illustration.)

B9.5

On 1 December Year 1 a company paid £2,400 as an insurance premium to give accident cover for the 12 months ahead. The accounting year-end is 31 December.

Required

Prepare an accounting equation spreadsheet to show the effect of the prepayment in the year ended 31 December Year 1.

C Problem solving and evaluation

C9.1

A fire destroyed a company's detailed stock records and much of the merchandise held in stock. The company accountant was able to discover that stock at the beginning of the period was £40,000, purchases up to the date of the fire were £250,000, and sales up to the date of the fire were £400,000. In past periods, the company has earned a gross profit of 35% of sales.

Required

Calculate the cost of the stock destroyed by the fire.

C9.2

It is the policy of Seaton Ltd to make provision for doubtful debts at a rate of 10% per annum on all debtor balances at the end of the year, after deducting any known bad debts at the same date. The following table sets out the total receivables (debtors) as shown by the accounting records and known bad debts to be deducted from that total. There is no provision at 31 December Year 0.

Year-end	Debtor balances	Known bad debts
	£	£
31 Dec. Year 1	30,000	2,000
31 Dec. Year 2	35,000	3,000
31 Dec. Year 3	32,000	1,500
31 Dec. Year 4	29,000	1,000

Required

(a) Calculate the total expense in the income statement (profit and loss account) in respect of bad and doubtful debts.

(b) Set out the statement of financial position (balance sheet) information in respect of receivables (debtors) and provision for doubtful debts at each year-end.

Activities for study groups

Turn to the annual report of a listed company which you have used for activities in previous chapters. Find every item of information about current assets. (Start with the financial statements and notes but look also at the operating and financial review, chief executive's review and other non-regulated information about the company.)

As a group, imagine you are the team of fund managers in a fund management company. You are holding a briefing meeting at which each person explains to the others some feature of the companies in which your fund invests. Today's subject is current assets. Each person should make a short presentation to the rest of the team covering:

1 The nature and significance of current assets in the company.

2 The effect on profit of a 10% error in estimation of any one of the major categories of current asset.

3 The company's comments, if any, on its present investment in working capital and its future intentions.

4 The risks which might attach to the inventories of the company.

5 The liquidity of the company.

6 The trends in current assets since last year (or over five years if a comparative table is provided).

7 The ratio of current assets to current liabilities.

Notes and references

1. IASB (2010), *Conceptual Framework*, para. 4.4(a).
2. IASB (2012), IAS 1, para. 66.
3. IASB (2012), IAS 2 *Inventories*, para. 6.
4. IASB (2012), IAS 2 *Inventories*, para. 9.
5. IASB (2012), IAS 2 *Inventories*, para. 6.
6. IASB (2012), IAS 2 *Inventories*, para. 10.
7. IASB (2012), IAS 2 *Inventories*, para. 11.
8. IASB (2012), IAS 18, *Revenue*, para. 7.
9. J. H. Myers (1959), 'The critical event and recognition of net profit', *Accounting Review*, 34: 528–32; and ASB (1999), *Statement of Principles for Financial Reporting*, ch. 5, paras 5.33–5.36.

Bookkeeping entries for (a) bad and doubtful debts; and (b) prepayments

The debit and credit recording aspects of inventories of raw materials and finished goods were explained in the supplement to Chapter 6. That leaves, for this supplement, the recording of bad and doubtful debts as a new area where potential care is needed. Prepayments are also illustrated here.

Provision for doubtful debts

The following ledger accounts illustrate the recording of the transactions analysed in section 9.9. Look back to that section for the description and analysis of the transactions. The debit and credit analysis is shown in Table 9.6. So that you will not be confused by additional information, the ledger accounts presented here show only sufficient information to illustrate the recording of transactions relating to doubtful debts. Leona comments on the main features.

Table 9.6
Analysis of debit and credit aspect of each transaction and event

Date		Debit	Credit
Year 1			
End of year	Manager identifies doubtful debts £200	Profit and loss account £200	Provision for doubtful debts £200
Year 2			
July	Customer who was doubtful pays £200 in full	Cash £200	Receivables (debtors) £200
End of year	Manager identifies new provision required £350	Profit and loss account £350	Provision for doubtful debts £350
End of year	Former provision no longer required	Provision for doubtful debts £200	Profit and loss account £200

The ledger accounts required are as follows:

L1 Receivables (debtors)   L3 Cash

L2 Provision for doubtful debts   L4 Profit and loss account

Also required to complete the double entry, but not shown here as a ledger account, is ledger account L5 Ownership interest.

The full list of transactions for the year would be too cumbersome to deal with here, so dots are used to show that the ledger account requires more information for completeness.

L1 Receivables (debtors)

Date	Particulars	Page	Debit	Credit	Balance
Year 1			£	£	£
	. . .		. . .		. . .
Dec. 31	Balance at end of year				2,000
Year 2					
	. . .		. . .		. . .
July	Cash from customer	L3		200	. . .
	. . .		. . .		. . .
Dec. 31	Balance at end of year				2,500

LEONA: *The ledger account for receivables (debtors) has no entries relating to doubtful debts. That is important because although there may be doubts from the viewpoint of the business, the customer still has a duty to pay and should be encouraged by all the usual means. Keeping the full record of amounts due is an important part of ensuring that all assets of the business are looked after.*

L2 Provision for doubtful debts

Date	Particulars	Page	Debit	Credit	Balance
Year 1			£	£	£
Dec. 31	Profit and loss account – new provision	L4		200	(200)
Year 2					
Dec. 31	Profit and loss account – old provision	L4	200		nil
Dec. 31	Profit and loss account – new provision	L4		350	(350)

LEONA: *The provision for doubtful debts is a credit balance because it is the negative part of an asset. It keeps a separate record of doubt about the full value of the asset. A credit entry in the ledger account increases the amount of the provision and a debit entry decreases the amount of the provision.*

L3 Cash

Date	Particulars	Page	Debit	Credit	Balance
Year 2			£	£	£
	. . .		. . .		. . .
July	Cash from debtor	L1	200		
	. . .		. . .		. . .

LEONA: *Receiving cash from the doubtful customer looks like any other transaction receiving cash. It is important that the cash is collected and the debt is removed by receiving the full amount due.*

L4 Profit and loss account

Date	Particulars	Page	Debit	Credit	Balance
Year 1			£	£	£
	. . .		. . .		. . .
Dec. 31	Balance before provision for doubtful debts				(7,200)
Dec. 31	Provision for doubtful debts	L2	200		(7,000)
Dec. 31	Transfer to ownership interest	L5	7,000		nil
Year 2					
	. . .		. . .		. . .
Dec. 31	Balance before provision for doubtful debts				(3,500)
Dec. 31	Removal of provision no longer required	L2		200	(3,700)
Dec. 31	New provision for doubtful debts	L2	350		(3,350)
Dec. 31	Transfer to ownership interest	L5	3,350		nil

LEONA: *In Year 1 of this example the provision is established for the first time so there is one debit entry to establish an expense which decreases the profit (as a part of the ownership interest). In Year 2 of this example the old provision is removed and a new provision created. The overall effect is that the provision increases by £150. Some people would take a shortcut and make one entry of £150 to increase the provision from £200 to £350 but I am not keen on shortcuts. They sometimes lead to disaster. Separate entries make me think carefully about the effect of each.*

Recording a doubtful debt which turns bad

Suppose that in July of Year 2 it was found that the doubtful debt turned totally bad because the customer was declared bankrupt. The effect on the accounting equation is that the asset of debtor is removed. That would normally reduce the ownership interest but on this occasion the impact on ownership interest was anticipated at the end of Year 1 and so the provision for doubtful debts is now used to match the decrease in the asset. The analysis of the transaction would be:

Date	Transaction or event	Debit	Credit
Year 2			
July	Doubtful debt becomes bad	Provision for doubtful debts £200	Receivables (debtors) £200

The consequence of using the provision for doubtful debts is that there is no impact on the income statement (profit and loss account) of Year 2 of a bad debt which was known to be likely at the end of Year 1. However, when the provision for doubtful debts is reviewed at the end of Year 2 there is no reversal of the £200 because that has already been used during the year. The charge of £350 for Year 2 relates solely to the provision for doubt in respect of receivables (debtors) owing money at the end of Year 2.

Prepayments

The prepayment transaction analysed in the chapter was as follows. On 1 October of Year 1 a company paid £1,200 for one year's vehicle insurance. At the financial year-end date of 31 December there have been three months' benefit used up and there is a nine-month benefit yet to come. (See Table 9.7.)

Table 9.7
Analysis of prepayment of insurance, Year 1

Date	Transaction or event	Debit	Credit
Year 2			
Oct. 1	Payment of premium £1,200	Expense (insurance)	Cash
Dec. 31	Identification of asset remaining as a prepayment £900	Asset (prepayment)	Expense (insurance)

Ledger accounts required to record the prepayment are:

L6 Expense of insurance
L7 Prepayment

Not shown, but necessary for completion of the debit and credit record, are:

L3 Cash
L4 Profit and loss account

L6 Expense of insurance					
Date	Particulars	Page	Debit	Credit	Balance
Year 1			£	£	£
Oct. 31	Cash	L3	1,200		1,200
Dec. 31	Prepayment	L7		900	300
Dec. 31	Transfer to profit and loss account	L4		300	nil

LEONA: *Although it is known in October that there will be a balance remaining at the end of the year, it is usually regarded as more convenient to debit the entire payment as an expense of the period initially. The expense is reviewed at the end of the year and £900 is found to be an asset which benefits the future. It is transferred to the asset account for pre-payments, leaving only the expense of £300 relating to this period, which is transferred to the income statement (profit and loss account).*

L7 Prepayment

Date	Particulars	Page	Debit	Credit	Balance
Year 1			£	£	£
Oct. 31	Insurance expense prepaid	L6	900		900

LEONA: *The prepayment account is an asset account and therefore the balance remains in the account until the benefit asset is used up. During Year 2 the benefit will disappear and the asset will become an expense. The bookkeeping treatment will be to credit the prepayment account and debit the insurance expense account.*

S   Test your understanding

S9.1   Record the transactions of question B9.3 in ledger accounts for L1 Receivables (debtors), L2 Provision for doubtful debts, L3 Cash and L4 Profit and loss account.

S9.2   Record the transactions of question B9.4 in ledger accounts for L1 Receivables (debtors), L2 Provision for doubtful debts, L3 Cash and L4 Profit and loss account.

S9.3   Record the transactions of question B9.5 in ledger accounts for L6 Expense of insurance and L7 Prepayment.

Chapter 10

Current liabilities

John Lewis Partnership

The following extracts relating to suppliers and accounts payable are taken from the annual report of the John Lewis Partnership.

Customers, products and suppliers (Extract from Business Review, p. 20)

The Partnership's vision is for long term sustainable trading. We are committed to selling responsibly sourced products, dealing fairly with suppliers, engaging with and acting in the interests of our customers and providing excellent value and unrivalled customer service.

In 2011 Waitrose came first in *Which?* magazine's supermarket survey of over 12,000 shoppers and John Lewis was voted Britain's favourite retailer for the fourth year running by retail analysts Verdict. The Partnership works with over 5,000 suppliers to sell quality products, supported by ethical and environmental standards and policies, paying them a fair price and helping them to reinvest in their businesses.

In June 2011, the Partnership joined the Ethical Trading Initiative (ETI), a collaborative arrangement between businesses, trade unions and NGOs which aims to improve the lives of workers internationally.

The Partnership has two supply chain foundations: the Waitrose Foundation established in 2005, which contributed £550,000 to projects supporting communities in Waitrose's supply chain in Africa in 2011/12; and the John Lewis Foundation which has invested £58,500 in 2011/12 in projects which support and service the communities where John Lewis products are sourced.

Payments to suppliers (Extract from Directors' Report, p. 30)

The group's policy on the payment of its suppliers is to agree terms of payment in advance and, provided a supplier fulfils the agreement, to pay promptly in accordance with those terms. The group's trade creditors at 28 January 2012 were equivalent to 27 days of average purchases (2011: 24 days).

Note 19 Extract from notes to the financial statements (p. 63)
19 Trade and other payables

Consolidated	2012 £m	2011 £m
Current:		
Trade payables	**530.1**	424.5
Amounts owed to parent undertaking	**74.2**	57.1
Other payables	**101.2**	95.2
Other taxation and social security	**143.1**	141.4
Accruals	**185.1**	167.5
Deferred income	**25.0**	25.7
Partnership bonus	**148.6**	176.1
	1,207.3	1,087.5

Source: John Lewis Partnership, Annual Report 2012.

Discussion points

1 How does the narrative information add insight into the nature of the liability for trade payables?

2 The total equity in the statement of financial position is £2008.9m. How significant are trade payables to the financing of the company?

Contents

After studying this chapter you should be able to:

● Define a liability and explain the distinguishing feature of current liabilities.

● Explain the conditions for recognition of liabilities.

● Explain how the information presented in a company's statement of financial position (balance sheet) and notes, in relation to liabilities, meets the needs of users.

● Explain the features of current liabilities and the approach to measurement and recording.

● Explain the terms 'accruals' and 'matching concept' and show how they are applied to expenses of the period.

● Explain how liabilities for taxation arise in companies.

Additionally, for those who choose to study the supplement:

● Prepare the ledger accounts to record accruals.

10.1 Introduction

The theme running through this textbook is the accounting equation:

Assets	minus	**Liabilities**	equals	**Ownership interest**

It was explained in Chapter 2 that the ownership interest is the residual amount found by deducting all liabilities of the company from total assets. Chapters 8 and 9 have taken you through aspects of non-current and current assets which are particularly significant to users of financial statements. Chapters 10 and 11 complete the left-hand side of the equation by providing a similar overview of current liabilities and non-current liabilities.

This chapter follows the approach established in Chapters 8 and 9:

● What are the principles for defining and recognising these items?
● What are the information needs of users in respect of the particular items?
● What information is currently provided by companies to meet these needs?
● Does the information show the desirable qualitative characteristics of financial statements?
● What are the principles for measuring, and processes for recording, these items?

10.2 Definitions

The definition of a liability, as provided in Chapter 2, is repeated here:

Definitions

A **liability** is a present obligation of the entity arising from past events, the settlement of which is expected to result in an outflow from the entity of resources embodying economic benefits.[1]

A **current liability** is a liability which satisfies any of the following criteria:

(a) it is expected to be settled in the entity's normal operating cycle;
(b) it is held primarily for the purpose of being traded;
(c) it is due to be settled within twelve months after the reporting period.[2]

Supplement 7.1 to Chapter 7 sets out the information to be presented on the face of the statement of financial position (balance sheet) of companies using the IASB system in their financial statements. The only current liabilities listed there are item (j) trade and other payables, item (l) financial liabilities (where these are short-term loans) and (m) liabilities for current tax.

Supplement 7.2 to Chapter 7 sets out the information to be presented in the financial statements of companies that are using the UK Companies Act and UK ASB standards. There is one heading for current liabilities and a detailed list below. The list is as follows:

E Creditors: amounts falling due within one year
1 Debenture loans
2 Bank loans and overdrafts
3 Payments received on account
4 Trade creditors
5 Bills of exchange payable
6 Amounts owed to group undertakings
7 Amounts owed to undertakings in which the company has a participating interest
8 Other creditors including taxation and social security
9 Accruals and deferred income

Activity 10.1

Look back to Table 2.3, which analyses some common types of liability. Set up on a blank sheet a similar table with four columns and headings for: type of liability; obligation; transfer of economic benefits; and past transaction or event. Then close the book and write down any ten liabilities you have come across during your study. Fill in all the columns as a check that, at this stage, you really understand what creates a liability.

10.3 Recognition

The general conditions for recognition were set out in Chapter 2. An item that meets the definition of a liability should be recognised if there is sufficient evidence that the liability has been created and that the item has a cost or value that can be measured with sufficient reliability. In practice, recognition problems related to liabilities centre on ensuring that none is omitted which ought to be included. This is in contrast to the case of assets where there is a need, in practice, to guard against over-enthusiastic inclusion of items which do not meet the recognition conditions.

10.3.1 Risk of understatement of liabilities

The risk related to liabilities is therefore the risk of understatement. This is explained in Chapter 4 under the heading of prudence. The risk of understatement of liabilities is that it will result in overstatement of the ownership interest.

In recent years the standard-setting bodies have devoted quite strenuous efforts to discouraging companies from keeping liabilities (and related assets) off the statement of financial position (balance sheet). This problem is called **off-balance sheet finance** and will be explained in Chapter 14.

10.3.2 Non-recognition: contingent liabilities

There are some obligations of the company which fail the recognition test because there is significant uncertainty about future events that may cause benefits to flow from the company. The uncertainty may be about the occurrence of the event or about the measurement of the consequences. These are called **contingent liabilities** because they are contingent upon (depend upon) some future event happening. Examples are:

- A company is involved in legal action where a customer is seeking damages for illness allegedly caused by the company's product. If the customer is successful, there will be more claims. The company does not believe that the customer will succeed.
- A parent company has given guarantees to a bank that it will meet the overdraft and loans of a subsidiary company if that company defaults on repayment. At the present time there is no reason to suppose that any default will take place.
- A company is under investigation by the Competition Commission for possible price-fixing within the industry in contravention of an order prohibiting restrictive practices. If there is found to be a restrictive practice, a penalty may be imposed.
- The company has acquired a subsidiary in Australia where the tax authorities have raised an action for tax due on a disputed transaction which occurred before the subsidiary was acquired. The action is being defended strenuously.

In each of these examples, the company is convinced that it will not have a liability at the end of the day, but the users of the financial statements may wish to have some indication of the upper bounds of the liability if the company's optimism proves unfounded. There may, however, be a problem for the company in publishing an estimate of the amount of the possible liability because it may be seen as admitting liability and furthermore may require disclosure of commercially sensitive confidential information.

Where a **contingent liability** is identified, the obligation is not recognised in the statement of financial position (balance sheet) but it may be important that users of the financial statements are aware of the problem. There will therefore be a note to the statement of financial position (balance sheet) reporting the circumstances of the contingent liability and sometimes giving an indication of the amount involved. Because of the confidentiality aspect, companies tend to give little information about the financial effect of a contingent liability, but some will try to set the outer limits of the liability.

Definition

> A **contingent liability** is either:
>
> (a) a possible obligation that arises from past events and whose existence will be confirmed only by the occurrence of one or more uncertain future events not wholly within the control of the entity; or
> (b) a present obligation that arises from past events but is not recognised because:
> (i) either it is not probable that a transfer of economic benefits will be required to settle the obligation;
> (ii) or the amount of the obligation cannot be measured with sufficient reliability.[3]

A company should disclose a brief description of the nature of the contingent liability and, where practicable:

(a) an estimate of its financial effect;
(b) an indication of the uncertainties relating to the amount or timing of any outflow; and
(c) the possibility of any reimbursement.[4]

Rules about measurement are given in detail in the accounting standard. The detail is not necessary for an introductory course.

10.3.3   Changing thoughts on contingencies

In 2005 the IASB issued a proposal to eliminate the term 'contingent liability' because if the item cannot be recognised in a statement of financial position (balance sheet) then it cannot be a true liability. The proposal of the IASB was that items carrying an unconditional obligation should be recognised as a liability and measured at the best estimate. Any uncertain event affecting the measurement of the obligation would be explained in a note. Items that do not carry an unconditional obligation are seen as business risks. Such business risks would be reported as a note to the financial statements because they may have a significant effect on the carrying amount of assets and liabilities in the near future. These changing thoughts on contingencies do not change the overall amount of information to be disclosed about contingencies but the method of disclosure may change. This development was not taken further because the financial crisis of 2007–08 brought other accounting problems to the fore. At some point the IASB will revisit contingent liabilities.

Activity 10.2	*Consider the four examples of contingent liability given at the start of this section. Based on the definition, explain why each is a contingent liability.*

10.4 Users' needs for information

There are two aspects of information in relation to liabilities. The first relates to the amount owed (sometimes called the **principal sum** or the **capital** amount) and the second relates to the cost of servicing the loan (usually the payment of **interest**).

In respect of current liabilities, other than a bank overdraft or bank loans repayable within the year, it is unlikely that interest will be payable, and so generally there will be no information about interest charges. The shareholders in the company will be concerned that there are adequate current assets to meet the current liabilities as they fall due. Those who supply goods and services will want to be reassured that payment will be made on the due date.

Owners of a company need to know how much the company owes to other parties because the owners are at the end of the queue when it comes to sharing out the assets of the company if it closes down. Many of those who supply goods and services are what is known as unsecured creditors, which means they come at the end of the list of creditors. They will also have an interest in the balance of long-term and current liabilities.

10.5 Information provided in the financial statements

The statement of financial position (balance sheet) of Safe and Sure plc, set out in Chapter 7, contains the following information in relation to current liabilities:

	Notes	Year 7 £m	Year 6 £m
Current liabilities			
Amounts payable (creditors)	7	(159.8)	(157.5)
Bank overdraft	8	(40.1)	(62.6)
		(199.9)	(220.1)

Notes to the statement of financial position (balance sheet) explain more about the statement of financial position (balance sheet) items. Note 7 lists the details of current liabilities.

Note 7 Current liabilities: amounts payable

	Year 7 £m	Year 6 £m
Deferred consideration on acquisition	1.1	4.3
Trade payables (trade creditors)	23.6	20.4
Corporation tax	31.5	26.5
Other tax and social security payable	24.5	21.2
Other payables (creditors)	30.7	23.8
Accruals and deferred income	48.4	61.3
	159.8	157.5

Trade payables (trade creditors) comprise amounts outstanding for trade purchases. The average credit period taken for trade purchases is 27 days. Most suppliers charge no interest on the trade payables for the first 30 days from the date of the invoice. Thereafter, interest is charged on the outstanding balances at various interest rates. The Group has financial risk management policies in place to ensure that all payables are paid within the agreed credit terms.

The note describing payment policy provides reassurance about avoiding the risk of additional costs through late payment. The company is complying with the financial reporting standard IFRS 7 *Financial Instruments: Disclosures*. Its general objective is to provide qualitative and quantitative information about exposure to risks arising from financial instruments. Any financial liability is an example of a financial instrument. You will therefore see descriptions of risk relating to financial liabilities in annual reports. The detail of that standard is beyond the scope of a first-level text.

Note 8 gives information on bank overdrafts due on demand and confirms that the interest charges incurred on these loans are payable at commercial rates:

Note 8 Bank borrowings: current liabilities

	Year 7 £m	Year 6 £m
Bank overdrafts due on demand:	40.1	62.6

Interest on overdrafts is payable at normal commercial rates appropriate to the country where the borrowing is made.

The report of the finance director provides further insight into the currency spread of the bank borrowings:

Foreign currency: £35.2m of foreign currency bank borrowings have been incurred to fund overseas acquisition. The main borrowings were £26.8m in US dollars and £8.4m in Japanese yen. The borrowings are mainly from banks on a short-term basis, with a maturity of up to one year, and we have fixed the interest rate on $20m of the US dollar loans through to November, Year 7, at an overall cost of 4.46%.

All material foreign currency transactions are matched back into the currency of the group company undertaking the transaction.

David Wilson has already commented in Chapters 4 and 7 on some aspects of the liabilities in the financial statements of Safe and Sure plc. Here he is explaining to Leona, in the coffee bar at the health club, his views on current liabilities in particular.

DAVID: *Current liabilities are relatively similar in total to last year so there are no particular questions to ask there.*

Then I start to think about the limits of risk. There is £40m due for repayment to the bank within the year. Will the company have any problem finding this amount? With £105m in cash and cash equivalents, it seems unlikely that there could be a problem. The entire current liabilities are £199.9m, all of which could be met from the cash and cash equivalents and receivables (debtors).

There is another risk that £40m shown as owing to the banks may be the wrong measure of the liability if exchange rates move against the company. Whenever I see foreign borrowings I want to know more about the currency of borrowings. You know from your economics class the theory of interest rates and currency exchange rates. It backs up my rule of thumb that borrowing in currencies which are weak means paying high rates of interest. Borrowing in currencies which are strong will mean paying lower rates of interest but runs a greater risk of having to use up additional pounds sterling to repay the loan if the foreign currency strengthens more. Information about the currency mix of loans is something I can probably get from the company if I need it. In this case, the finance director's report is sufficiently informative for my purposes. In past years, before finance directors started providing explanations in the annual report, we were asking these questions at face-to-face meetings.

LEONA: *What you have described is similar in many respects to the analytical review carried out by the auditors. We do much more than merely check the bookkeeping entries and the paperwork. We are looking at whether the statement of financial position (balance sheet) makes sense and whether any items have changed without sufficient explanation.*

10.6 Measurement and recording

Liabilities are measured at the amount originally received from the lender of finance or supplier of goods and services, plus any additional charges incurred such as rolled-up interest added to a loan. This is generally agreed to be a useful measure of the obligation to transfer economic benefits from the company.

From the accounting equation it may be seen that an increase in a liability must be related either to an increase in an asset or a decrease in the ownership interest. Usually any related decrease in the ownership interest will be reported in the statement of financial position (balance sheet) as an expense.

The most significant current liabilities for most companies are bank borrowing and trade creditors. Both of these are essential sources of finance for small companies and are an important aspect, if not essential, for larger companies.

Activity 10.3

Write down the documentation you would expect to see as evidence of the money amount of the following liabilities:

● *bank overdraft;*
● *amount owing to a trade supplier.*

Now read the next sections and find whether your answer matches the information in the text.

10.6.1 Bank overdraft finance

Banks provide short-term finance to companies in the form of an overdraft on a current account. The advantage of an overdraft is its flexibility. When the cash needs of the company increase with seasonal factors, the company can continue to write cheques and watch the overdraft increase. When the goods and services are sold and cash begins to flow in, the company should be able to watch the overdraft decrease again. The most obvious example of a business which operates in this pattern is farming. The farmer uses the overdraft to finance the acquisition of seed for arable farming, or feed through the winter for stock farming and to cover the period when the crops or animals are growing and maturing. The overdraft is reduced when the crops or the animals are sold.

The main disadvantage of an overdraft is that it is repayable on demand. The farmer whose crop fails because of bad weather knows the problem of being unable to repay the overdraft. Having overdraft financing increases the worries of those who manage the company. The other disadvantage is that the interest payable on overdrafts is variable. When interest rates increase, the cost of the overdraft increases. Furthermore, for small companies there are often complaints that the rate of interest charged is high compared with that available to larger companies. The banks answer that the rates charged reflect relative risk and it is their experience that small companies are more risky.

10.6.2 Trade payables (trade creditors)

It is a strong feature of many industries that one enterprise is willing to supply goods to another in advance of being paid. Most suppliers will state terms of payment (e.g. the invoice must be paid within 30 days) and some will offer a discount for prompt payment. In the UK it has not been traditional to charge interest on overdue accounts but this practice is growing as suppliers realise there is a high cost to themselves of not collecting cash in good time. A supplier who is waiting to be paid is called a **trade creditor**.

Trade creditors rarely have any security for payment of the amount due to them, so that if a customer fails to pay the supplier must wait in the queue with other suppliers and hope for a share of some distribution. They are described as **unsecured creditors**. Some suppliers will include in the contract a condition that the goods remain the property of the supplier should the customer fail to pay. This is called retention of title (ROT) and will be noted in the statement of financial position (balance sheet) of a company which has bought goods on these terms. Retention of title may offer some protection to the unpaid supplier but requires very prompt action to recover identifiable goods in the event of difficulty.

Some suppliers send goods to a customer on a sale-or-return basis. If there are no conditions to prevent return then the goods will not appear as stock in the statement of financial position (balance sheet) of the customer and there will be no indication of a liability. This practice is particularly common in the motor industry where manufacturers send cars to showrooms for sale or return within a specified period of time. Omitting the inventories and the related potential liability is referred to as **off-balance-sheet finance**, a topic explored further in Chapter 14.

Suppliers send **invoices** to the customer showing the amount due for payment. These invoices are used in the customer's accounts department as the source of information for liabilities. At the end of the month the suppliers send statements as a reminder of unpaid invoices. Statements are useful as additional evidence of liabilities to suppliers.

Measurement of trade creditors is relatively straightforward because the company will know how much it owes to short-term creditors. If it forgets the creditors, they will soon issue a reminder.

Recording requires some care because omission of any credit transaction will mean there is an understatement of a liability. In particular, the company has to take some care at the end of the year over what are called **cut-off procedures**. Take the example of raw materials provided by a supplier. The goods arrive at the company's store by delivery van but the invoice for their payment arrives a few days later by mail. The accounts department uses the supplier's invoice as the document which initiates the *recording* of the asset of stock and the liability to the supplier. In contrast, the event which *creates* the liability is the acceptance of the goods. (It is difficult for the accounts department to use the delivery note as a record of the liability because it shows the quantities but not the price of the goods delivered.) So, at the end of the accounting year the accounts department has to compare the most recent delivery notes signed by the storekeeper with the most recent invoices received from the supplier. If goods have been received by the company, the statement of financial position (balance sheet) must include the asset of stock and the related liability. Using a similar line of reasoning, if a supplier has sent an invoice ahead of delivery of the goods, it should not be recorded as a liability because there is no related asset.

The recording of purchases of goods for resale is shown in Chapter 6. In the illustration of the process for recording the transactions of M. Carter there is a purchase of goods from the supplier, R. Busby, on credit terms. Payment is made later in the month. The purchase of the goods creates the asset of stock and the liability to the supplier. Payment to the supplier reduces the asset of cash and eliminates the liability to the supplier. The liability is described as an 'account payable'.

10.7 Accruals and the matching concept

At the financial year-end date there will be obligations of the company to pay for goods or services which are not contained in the accounting records because no document has been received from the supplier of the goods or services. It is essential that all obligations are included at the financial year-end date because these obligations fall under the definition of liabilities even although the demand for payment has not been received. The process of including in the statement of financial position (balance sheet) all obligations at the end of the period is called the accrual of liabilities and is said to reflect the **accruals basis** or accruals concept (see Chapter 4).

Definition

> Accrual accounting depicts the effects of transactions and other events and circumstances on a reporting entity's economic resources and claims in the periods in which those effects occur, even if the resulting cash receipts and payments occur in a different period. This is important because information about a reporting entity's economic resources and claims and changes in its economic resources and claims during a period provides a better basis for assessing the entity's past and future performance than information solely about cash receipts and payments during that period.[5]

The argument contained in the previous paragraph is based on the definition of a liability, but some people prefer to arrive at the same conclusion using a different argument. They say that all expenses of the accounting period must be matched against the revenue earned in the period. If a benefit has been consumed, the effect must be recorded whether or not documentation has been received. This argument is referred to as the **matching concept**.

In the *Conceptual Framework*, the IASB explains that in the income statement there is a direct association between the costs incurred and the earning of specific items of income. This process is called the matching of costs with revenues. As an example, the expenses that make up the cost of goods sold are recognised at the same time as the revenue derived from the sale of the goods.[6]

The accruals concept and the matching concept are, for most practical purposes, different ways of arriving at the same conclusion. (There are exceptions but these are well beyond the scope of a first-level text.)

10.7.1 The distinction between the expense of the period and the cash paid

A company starts business on 1 January Year 1. It has a financial year-end of 31 December Year 1. During Year 1 it receives four accounts for electricity, all of which are paid ten days after receiving them. The dates of receiving and paying the accounts are as follows:

Date invoice received	Amount of invoice	Date paid
	£	
31 Mar. Year 1	350	10 Apr. Year 1
30 June Year 1	180	10 July Year 1
30 Sept. Year 1	280	10 Oct. Year 1
31 Dec. Year 1	340	10 Jan. Year 2
	1,150	

The company has used electricity for the entire year and therefore should match against revenue the full cost of £1,150. Only three invoices have been paid during the year, the final invoice not being paid until the start of Year 2. That is important for cash flow but is not relevant for the measurement of profit. The transactions during the year would be recorded as shown in Table 10.1. The arrival of the electricity invoice causes a record to be made of the increase in the liability and the increase in the expense (decreasing the ownership interest). The payment of the amount due requires a separate record to be made of the decrease in the liability and the decrease in the asset of cash.

The payment made to the electricity company in January Year 2 is not recorded in Table 10.1 because it is not a transaction of Year 1. It will appear in a spreadsheet for January Year 2. The totals at the foot of the spreadsheet show that the transactions of Year 1 have caused the cash of the company to decrease by £810. There remains a liability of £340 to the electricity company at the end of Year 1. The profit and loss account for the year will show an expense of £1,150. The spreadsheet satisfies the accounting equation because there is a decrease in an asset, amounting to £810, and an increase in a liability amounting to £340. These together equal the decrease of £1,150 in the ownership interest:

Asset ↓	–	Liability ↑	=	Ownership interest ↓
– £810		+ £340		– £1,150

Table 10.1
Spreadsheet analysis of transactions relating to the expense of electricity consumed, Year 1

Date	Transactions with electricity company	Asset	Liability	Ownership interest: profit of the period
		Cash	Electricity company	Electricity expense
Year 1		£	£	£
Mar. 31	Invoice received £350		350	(350)
Apr. 10	Pay electricity company £350	(350)	(350)	
June 30	Invoice received £180		180	(180)
July 10	Pay electricity company £180	(180)	(180)	
Sept. 30	Invoice received £280		280	(280)
Oct. 10	Pay electricity caompany £280	(280)	(280)	
Dec. 31	Invoice received £340		340	(340)
	Totals	(810)	340	(1,150)

That one needs a little careful thought because several things are happening at once. You might prefer to think about it one stage at a time. You know from earlier examples in Chapters 2, 5 and 6 that a decrease in an asset causes a decrease in the ownership interest. You also know that an increase in a liability causes a decrease in the ownership interest. Put them together and they are both working in the same direction to decrease the ownership interest.

10.7.2 Accrual where no invoice has been received

Now consider what might happen if the final electricity invoice for the year has not been received on 31 December Year 1. If no invoice has been received then there will be no entry in the accounting records. That, however, would fail to acknowledge that the electricity has been consumed and the company knows there is an obligation to pay for that electricity. In terms of the matching concept, only nine months' invoices are available to match against revenue when there has been twelve months' usage. The answer is that the company must make an *estimate* of the accrual of the liability for electricity consumed. Estimates will seldom give the true answer but they can be made reasonably close if some care is taken. If the company keeps a note of electricity meter readings and knows the unit charge, it can calculate what the account would have been.

The entries in the spreadsheet at the end of the month are shown in Table 10.2. They will be the same numerically as those in the final line of Table 10.1 but the item shown at 31 December will be described as an accrual.

Table 10.2
Spreadsheet entry for accrual at the end of the month

Date	Transactions with electricity company	Asset	Liability	Ownership interest: profit of the period
		Cash	Electricity company	Electricity expense
Year 1		£	£	£
Dec. 31	Accrual for three months		340	(340)

10.7.3 The nature of estimates in accounting

Making an accrual for a known obligation, where no invoice has been received, requires estimates. In the example given here it was a relatively straightforward matter to take a meter reading and calculate the expected liability. There will be other examples where the existence and amount of an expense are both known with reasonable certainty. There will be some cases where the amount has to be estimated and the estimate is later found to be incorrect. That is a normal feature of accounting, although not all users of financial statements realise there is an element of uncertainty about the information provided. If a liability is unintentionally understated at the end of a period, the profit will be overstated. In the next accounting period, when the full obligation becomes known, the expense incurred will be higher than was anticipated and the profit of that period will be lower than it should ideally be. If the error in the estimate is found to be such that it would change the views of the main users of financial statements, a prior year adjustment may be made by recalculating the profits of previous years and reporting the effect, but that is a relatively rare occurrence.

Activity 10.4

Write down five types of transaction where you might expect to see an accrual of expense at the year-end. Against each transaction type write down the method you would use to estimate the amount of the accrued expense.

10.8 Liabilities for taxation

In the statement of financial position (balance sheet) of a company there are two main categories of liability related directly to the company. The first is the **corporation tax** payable, based on the taxable profits of the period, the second is **deferred taxation**. Each of these will be discussed here. You will also see in the current liabilities section of a statement of financial position (balance sheet) the words 'other tax and social security payable'. This refers to the amounts deducted from employees' salaries and wages by the company on behalf of HMRC and paid over at regular intervals. In respect of such amounts the company is acting as a tax collecting agent of HMRC.

10.8.1 Corporation tax

Companies pay corporation tax based on the taxable profit of the accounting period (usually one year). The taxable profit is calculated according to the rules of tax law. That in itself is a subject for an entire textbook but one basic principle is that the taxable profit is based on profit calculated according to commercially accepted accounting practices. So, apart from some specific points of difference, the accounting profit is usually quite close to the taxable profit. Assume that the corporation tax rate is 30% of the taxable profit. (The tax rate each year is set by the Chancellor of the Exchequer.) Analysts will evaluate the tax charge in the income statement (profit and loss account) as a percentage of taxable profit and start to ask questions when the answer is very different from 30%. The explanation could be that there are profits earned abroad where the tax rate is different, but it could also be that there has been some use of provisions or adjustments for accounting purposes which are not allowed for tax purposes. That will lead to more probing by the analysts to establish whether they share the doubts of the tax authorities.

Large companies must pay corporation tax by four quarterly instalments. A company with a year-end of 31 December Year 1 will pay on 14 July Year 1, 14 October Year 1, 14 January Year 2 and 14 April Year 2. The amount of tax due is estimated by making a forecast of the profit for the year. As the year progresses the forecast is revised and the tax calculation is also revised. This means that at the end of the accounting year there is a liability for half that year's tax bill. A 'large' company is any company that pays corporation tax at the full rate. Small companies, which have a special, lower, rate of corporation tax, pay their tax bill nine months after the end of the accounting period. The precise limits for defining 'large' and 'small' companies change with tax legislation each year. (You will be given the necessary information in any exercise that you are asked to attempt.) Suppose the taxable profit is £10m and the tax payable at 30% is £3m. During the year £1.5m is paid in total on the first two instalment dates. At the statement of financial position (balance sheet) date there will remain a liability of £1.5m to be paid in total on the final two instalment dates.

10.8.2 Deferred taxation liability

It was explained earlier in this section that the taxable profit is based on the accounting profit unless there are taxation rules which indicate otherwise. There are taxation rules which allow companies to defer the payment of some taxation on the full accounting profit. ('Deferring' means paying much later than the normal period of nine months.) The deferral period might be for a few months or it might be for a few years. The obligation to pay tax eventually cannot be escaped but the liability becomes long term. This is reflected, in terms of the accounting equation, by reporting the decrease in ownership claim in the profit and loss account but showing the deferred liability as a separate item under **non-current liabilities**.

10.9 Summary

- A **current liability** is a liability which satisfies any of the following criteria:
  (a) it is expected to be settled in the entity's normal operating cycle;
  (b) it is held primarily for the purpose of being traded;
  (c) it is due to be settled within 12 months after the financial year-end date.

- The risk of understatement of liabilities is that it will result in overstatement of the ownership interest.

- **Off-balance sheet finance** means keeping liabilities (and related assets) off the statement of financial position (balance sheet).

- There are some obligations of the company which fail the recognition test because there is significant uncertainty about future events that may cause benefits to flow from the company. These are reported as **contingent liabilities** in the notes to the financial statements.

- Users need to know about the existence of liabilities, the amount and timing of expected repayments and interest charges payable on loans.

- Under the **accruals** basis, the effects of transactions and other events are recognised when they occur (and not as cash or its equivalent is received or paid) and they are recorded in the accounting records and reported in the financial statements of the periods to which they relate.

- Liabilities for unpaid expenses are often called **accruals**.

- The **matching concept** is the idea that all expenses of the accounting period must be matched against the revenue earned in the period. If a benefit has been consumed, the effect must be recorded whether or not documentation has been received.

- Companies pay corporation tax. The arrangements vary depending on the size of the company but there will usually be a liability for unpaid corporation tax in the current liabilities section of the statement of financial position (balance sheet). Where government policy allows payment to be delayed for more than 12 months the liability is described as **deferred taxation**.

QUESTIONS

The Questions section of each chapter has three types of question. 'Test your understanding' questions to help you review your reading are in the 'A' series of questions. You will find the answers to these by reading and thinking about the material in the book. 'Application' questions to test your ability to apply technical skills are in the 'B' series of questions. Questions requiring you to show skills in problem solving and evaluation are in the 'C' series of questions. A letter [S] indicates that there is a solution at the end of the book.

A | Test your understanding

A10.1 What is the definition of a liability? (Section 10.2)

A10.2 What is the distinction between a long-term liability and a current liability? (Section 10.2)

A10.3 What is the effect of understatement of liabilities? (Section 10.3.1)

A10.4 What is a contingent liability? (Section 10.3.2)

A10.5 What information do users of financial statements need to have concerning current liabilities of a company? (Section 10.4)

A10.6 How are the current liabilities for (a) bank overdraft and (b) trade creditors measured? (Section 10.6)

A10.7 What is meant by an accrual? How is it recorded? (Section 10.7)

A10.8 Explain what is meant by the matching concept. (Section 10.7)

A10.9 [S] On reviewing the financial statements, the company accountant discovers that a supplier's invoice for an amount of £10,000 has been omitted from the accounting records. The goods to which the invoice relates are held in the warehouse and are included in stock. What will be the effect on the profit and loss account and the statement of financial position (balance sheet) when this error is rectified?

A10.10 [S] On reviewing the financial statements, the company accountant discovers that a payment of £21,000 made to a supplier has been omitted from the cash book and other internal accounting records. What will be the effect on the profit and loss account and the statement of financial position (balance sheet) when this omission is rectified?

A10.11 [S] On reviewing the financial statements, the company accountant discovers that an invoice for the rent of £4,000 owed to its landlord has been recorded incorrectly as rent receivable of £4,000 in the company's accounting records. What will be the effect on the profit and loss account and the statement of financial position (balance sheet) when this error is rectified?

B | Application

B10.1 [S]

White Ltd commenced trading on 1 July Year 3 and draws up its accounts for the year ended 30 June Year 4. During its first year of trading the company pays total telephone expenses of £3,500. The three-month bill paid in May Year 4 includes calls of £800 for the quarter up to 30 April Year 4 and advance rental of £660 to 31 July Year 4. The bill received in August Year 4 includes calls of £900 for the quarter up to 31 July Year 4 and advance rental of £660 to 31 October Year 4.

Required
Show calculations of the telephone expense to be recorded in the profit and loss account of White Ltd for its first year of trading.

B10.2 [S]

Plastics Ltd pays rent for a warehouse used for storage. The quarterly charge for security guard services is £800. The security firm sends an invoice on 31 March, 30 June, 30 September and 31 December. Plastics Ltd always pays the rent five days after the invoice is received. The security services have been used for some years. Plastics Ltd has an accounting year-end of 31 December.

Required
Prepare a spreadsheet to show how the transactions of one year in respect of security services are recorded.

B10.3 [S]

The accountant of Brown Ltd has calculated that the company should report in its profit and loss account a tax charge of £8,000 based on the taxable profit of the period. Of this amount, £6,000 will be payable nine months after the accounting year-end but £2,000 may be deferred for payment in a period estimated at between three and five years after the accounting year-end. Using the accounting equation explain how this information will be reported in the financial statements of Brown Ltd.

C | Problem solving and evaluation

C10.1 [S]
The following file of papers was found in a cupboard of the general office of Green Ltd at the end of the accounting year. Explain how each would be treated in the financial statements and state the total amount to be reported as an accrued liability on the financial year-end date. The year-end is 31 December Year 1.

Item	Description	Amount £
1	Invoice dated 23 December for goods received 21 December.	260
2	Invoice dated 23 December for goods to be delivered on 3 January Year 2.	310
3	Foreman's note of electricity consumption for month of December – no invoice yet received from electricity supply company.	100
4	Letter from employee claiming overtime payment for work on 1 December and note from personnel office denying entitlement to payment.	58
5	Telephone bill dated 26 December showing calls for October to December.	290
6	Telephone bill dated 26 December showing rent due in advance for period January to March Year 2.	90
7	Note of payment due to cleaners for final week of December (to be paid in January under usual pattern of payment one week in arrears).	48
8	Invoice from supplier for promotional calendars received 1 December (only one-third have yet been sent to customers).	300
9	Letter dated 21 December Year 1 to customer promising a cheque to reimburse damage caused by faulty product – cheque to be sent on 4 January Year 2.	280
10	Letter dated 23 December promising donation to local charity – amount not yet paid.	60

Activities for study groups

Turn to the annual report of a listed company which you have used for activities in previous chapters. Find every item of information about current liabilities. (Start with the financial statements and notes but look also at the operating and financial review, chief executive's review and other non-regulated information about the company.)

Divide into two groups. One group should take on the role of the purchasing director and one should take on the role of a company which has been asked to supply goods or services to this company on credit terms.

- *Supplier group*: What questions would you ask to supplement what you have learned from the annual report?
- *Purchasing director*: What questions would you ask about the supplier? What might you learn about the supplier from the annual report of the supplier's company?

Notes and references

1. IASB (2010), *Conceptual Framework*, para. 4.4(b).
2. IASB (2012), IAS 1, para. 69.
3. IASB (2012), IAS 37, *Provisions, Contingent Liabilities and Contingent Assets*, para. 10.
4. *Ibid.*, para. 86.
5. IASB (2010), *Conceptual Framework*, para. OB 17.
6. IASB (2010), *Conceptual Framework*, para. 4.50.

Bookkeeping entries for accruals

In the main part of the chapter the accruals for electricity were analysed. Now consider the debit and credit recording. The following transactions are to be recorded.

A company starts business on 1 January Year 1. It has a financial year-end of 31 December Year 1. During Year 1 it receives three accounts for electricity, all of which are paid ten days after receiving them. The dates of receiving and paying the accounts are as follows:

Amount of invoice £	Date invoice received	Date paid
350	31 Mar. Year 1	10 Apr. Year 1
180	30 June Year 1	10 July Year 1
280	30 Sept. Year 1	10 Oct. Year 1

At 31 December the final invoice for the year has not arrived because of delays in the mail but the amount due for payment is estimated at £340.

Activity 10.5	*Before you read further, attempt to write down the debit and credit entries for: each of the three invoices received; the payments of those three invoices; and the estimated amount due for payment at the end of the year. You may find help in looking back to Tables 10.1 and 10.2.*

Table 10.3 sets out the debit and credit aspect of each transaction and event. The amount of the liability to the supplier cannot be recorded until the invoice is received. The credit entry for the estimate of the amount owing to the supplier is therefore shown in a separate account called *accruals* which will be the basis for the amount shown in the statement of financial position (balance sheet) under that heading.

The ledger accounts required here are:

L1 Expense (electricity)
L2 Liability to supplier
L3 Accrual

Also required to complete the double entry, but not shown here as a ledger account, are:

L4 Cash
L5 Profit and loss account

Table 10.3
Analysis of debit and credit aspect of each transaction and event

Date	Transaction	Debit	Credit
Year 1			
Mar. 31	Receive invoice for electricity £350	Expense (electricity)	Liability to supplier
Apr. 10	Pay supplier £350	Liability to supplier	Cash
June 30	Receive invoice for electricity £180	Expense (electricity)	Liability to supplier
July 10	Pay supplier £180	Liability to supplier	Cash
Sept. 30	Receive invoice for electricity £280	Expense (electricity)	Liability to supplier
Oct. 10	Pay supplier £280	Liability to supplier	Cash
Dec. 31	Estimate amount owing to supplier £340	Expense (electricity)	Accruals

L1 Expense (electricity)

Date	Particulars	Page	Debit	Credit	Balance
Year 1			£	£	£
Mar. 31	Invoice from supplier	L2	350		350
June 30	Invoice from supplier	L2	180		530
Sept. 30	Invoice from supplier	L2	280		810
Dec. 31	Estimated accrual	L3	340		1,150
Dec. 31	Transfer to profit and loss account	L5		1,150	nil

LEONA: *The electricity account for the year shows a full 12 months' expense which is transferred to the profit and loss account at the end of the year.*

L2 Liability to supplier

Date	Particulars	Page	Debit	Credit	Balance
Year 1			£	£	£
Mar. 31	Invoice for electricity expense	L1		350	(350)
Apr. 10	Cash paid	L4	350		nil
June 30	Invoice for electricity expense	L1		180	(180)
July 10	Cash paid	L4	180		nil
Sept. 30	Invoice for electricity expense	L1		280	(280)
Oct. 10	Cash paid	L4	280		nil

LEONA: *The supplier's account is showing a nil liability because all invoices received have been paid. We know there is another invoice on the way but the bookkeeping system is quite strict about only making entries in the ledger when the documentary evidence is obtained. The document in this case is the supplier's invoice. Until it arrives the liability has to be recognised as an accrual rather than in the supplier's account.*

L3 Accruals

Date	Particulars	Page	Debit	Credit	Balance
Year 1			£	£	£
Dec. 31	Estimate of electricity expense	L1	340	(340)	

LEONA: *The statement of financial position (balance sheet) will record a nil liability to the supplier but will show an accrual of £340 for electricity. When the supplier's invoice arrives in January of Year 2, the debit and credit entries will be:*

Date	Transaction	Debit	Credit
Year 2			
Jan. 4	Receive invoice for electricity £340	Accrual	Liability to supplier

In this way the liability remaining from Year 1 is recorded without affecting the expense account for Year 2. The credit balance on the accrual account at the end of Year 1 is eliminated by being matched against the debit entry at the start of Year 2.

S | Test your understanding

S10.1 Prepare bookkeeping records for the information in question B10.1.

S10.2 Prepare bookkeeping records for the information in question B10.2.

S10.3 Prepare bookkeeping records for the information in question B10.3.

S10.4 Prepare bookkeeping records for the information in question C10.1.

Chapter 11

Provisions and non-current (long-term) liabilities

SSE plc

Extract from Significant Accounting Policies (p. 106)

Provisions

A provision is recognised in the balance sheet when the Group has a present legal or constructive obligation as a result of a past event, and it is probable that an outflow of economic benefits will be required to settle the obligation. If the effect is material, provisions are determined by discounting the expected future cash flows at a pre-tax rate that reflects current market assessments of the time value of money and, where appropriate, the risks specific to the liability.

Shutterstock.com/Photo Roman

Extract from Notes to the Accounts (pp. 140–1)

25. Provisions

	Decommissioning	Contracting provisions	Onerous contracts	Other	Total
	(i)	(ii)	(iii)	(iv)	
	£m	£m	£m	£m	£m
Consolidated					
At 1 April 2011	148.8	9.7	1.3	19.3	179.1
Charged in the year	–	14.4	37.4	12.1	63.9
Unwind of discount	7.7	–	–	0.1	7.8
Released during the year	(3.7)	–	(1.3)	(2.3)	(7.3)
Utilised during the year	(0.9)	–	–	(5.0)	(5.9)
At 31 March 2012	**151.9**	**24.1**	**37.4**	**24.2**	**237.6**
At 31 March 2012					
Non-current	151.9	13.0	–	17.4	182.3
Current	–	11.1	37.4	6.8	55.3
	151.9	**24.1**	**37.4**	**24.2**	**237.6**
At 31 March 2011					
Non-current	148.8	1.2	–	19.2	169.2
Current	–	8.5	1.3	0.1	9.9
	148.8	9.7	1.3	19.3	179.1

Provision has been made for the estimated net present cost of decommissioning North Sea exploration and production assets and certain generation and gas storage assets.

Estimates are based on forecast clean-up costs at the time of decommissioning discounted for the time value of money. The timing of costs provided is dependent on the lives of the facilities.

(ii) The Group hold provisions in relation to long-term construction contracts including streetlighting PFIs. These relate to contract costs that are not guaranteed to being recovered under the respective contracts.

(iii) The Group has recognised provisions of £37.4m in relation to onerous contracts in the year. These have been treated as exceptional charges (note 5). These contracts will be settled in the next year.

(iv) Other provisions include balances held in relation to insurance and warranty claims. In addition, the Group has an employer financed retirement benefit provision for pensions for certain Directors and former Directors and employees, which is valued in accordance with IAS 19.

Source: Extract from Significant Accounting Policies (p. 106); Source SSE plc, Annual Report 2012; Extract from Notes to the Accounts (pp. 140–1), with the permission of SSE plc.

Discussion points

1 Why is there a provision for decommissioning when the decommissioning may take place many years into the future?

2 What are the significant uncertainties in estimating the amounts of the provisions?

Contents

Learning outcomes

After studying this chapter you should be able to:

- Define a non-current (long-term) liability.
- Explain the needs of users for information about non-current (long-term) liabilities.
- Explain the different types of non-current (long-term) loan finance which may be found in the statements of financial position (balance sheets) of major companies.
- Understand the purpose of provisions and explain how provisions are reported in financial statements.
- Understand the nature of deferred income and explain how it is reported in financial statements.
- Know the main types of loan finance and capital instruments used by companies and understand the principles of reporting information in the financial statements.

Additionally, for those who choose to study the supplement to this chapter:

- Prepare the ledger accounts to record provisions and deferred income.

11.1 Introduction

Supplement 7.1 to Chapter 7 sets out the information to be presented on the face of the statement of financial position (balance sheet) of companies using the IASB system in their financial statements. The non-current liabilities listed there are item (k) provisions, (l) financial liabilities (where these are loans due in more than one year's time) and (n) deferred tax liabilities.

Supplement 7.2 to Chapter 7 sets out the information to be presented in the financial statements of companies that are using the UK Companies Act and UK ASB standards. There is one heading for non-current liabilities, with a detailed list below, as follows:

H Creditors: amounts falling due after more than one year
1 Debenture loans
2 Bank loans and overdrafts

3 Payments received on account
4 Trade creditors
5 Bills of exchange payable
6 Amounts owed to group undertakings
7 Amounts owed to undertakings in which the company has a participating interest
8 Other creditors including taxation and social security
9 Accruals and deferred income

Comparing Supplements 7.1 and 7.2 it could appear that companies using the IASB system face fewer detailed rules. However, those companies still produce a great deal of detailed information in practice because the IASB has other standards that require more detail.

In this chapter we follow the pattern established in earlier chapters by asking:

● What are the principles for defining and recognising these items?
● What are the information needs of users in respect of the particular items?
● What information is currently provided by companies to meet these needs?
● Does the information show the desirable qualitative characteristics of financial statements?
● What are the principles for measuring, and processes for recording, these items?

This chapter looks first at provisions, then turns to non-current (long-term) liabilities and finally covers deferred income. General principles of definition and recognition of liabilities are dealt with in Chapter 10 and you should ensure you have read and understood that chapter before embarking on this one. For convenience the definitions from Chapter 2 are repeated here.

Definitions

A **liability** is a present obligation of the entity arising from past events, the settlement of which is expected to result in an outflow from the entity of resources embodying economic benefits.[1]

A **current liability** is a liability which satisfies any of the following criteria:

(a) it is expected to be settled in the entity's normal operating cycle;
(b) it is held primarily for the purpose of being traded;
(c) it is due to be settled within 12 months after the reporting period.[2]

A **non-current liability** is any liability that does not meet the definition of a current liability.[3] Non-current liabilities are also described as **long-term liabilities**.

11.2 Users' needs for information

There are two aspects of information needed in relation to liabilities. The first relates to the amount owed (sometimes called the **principal sum** or the **capital amount**) and the second relates to the cost of servicing the loan (usually the payment of **interest**).

Owners of a company need to know how much the company owes to other parties because the owners are at the end of the queue when it comes to sharing out the assets of the company if it closes down. Lenders to the company want to know how many other lenders will have a claim on assets if the company closes down and how much the total claim of lenders will be. They may want to take a **secured loan**, where the agreement with the company specifies particular assets which may be sold by the lender if the company defaults on payment.

Cash flow is important to a range of users. Interest payments are an expense to be reported in the income statement (profit and loss account), but paying interest is a drain on cash as well as affecting the ownership interest by a reduction in profit.

Owners of the company want to know if there will be sufficient cash left to allow them a **dividend** (or **drawings** for partnerships and sole traders) after interest has been paid. Lenders want to be reassured that the company is generating sufficient cash flow and profit to cover the interest expense.

Both owners and lenders want to see the impact of borrowing on future cash flows. They need to know the scheduled dates of repayments of loans (sometimes referred to as the **maturity profile of debt**), the currency in which the loan must be repaid and the structure of interest rates (e.g. whether the loan period is starting with low rates of interest which are then stepped up in future years).

Finally, owners and lenders are interested in the **gearing** of the company. This means the ratio of loan capital to ownership interest in the statement of financial position (balance sheet) or the ratio of interest payments to net profit in the income statement (profit and loss account). Chapter 13 will provide more detail on the calculation and interpretation of gearing.

Activity 11.1	*Imagine you are a shareholder in a company which is financed partly by long-term loans. Write down the information needed by users in the order of importance to you as a shareholder and explain your answer.*

11.3 Information provided in the financial statements

The statement of financial position (balance sheet) of Safe and Sure plc, set out in Chapter 7, contains the following information in relation to non-current (long-term) liabilities:

	Notes	Year 7 £m	Year 6 £m
Non-current liabilities			
Amounts payable (creditors)	9	(2.7)	(2.6)
Bank and other borrowings	10	(0.2)	(0.6)
Provisions	11	(20.2)	(22.2)
Net assets		464.3	370.4

Notes to the statement of financial position (balance sheet) explain more about each item. Note 9 gives some indication of the type of creditors due after more than one year.

Note 9 Non-current liabilities: payables (creditors)		
	Year 7 £m	Year 6 £m
Deferred consideration on acquisition	0.6	–
Other payables (creditors)	2.1	2.6
	2.7	2.6

Note 10 distinguishes secured and unsecured loans among the borrowings due after one year and also gives a schedule of repayment over the immediate and medium-term or longer-term future. For this company, bank borrowings all mature within five years. Note 10 also confirms that commercial rates of interest are payable.

Note 10 Non-current liabilities: bank and other borrowings

	Year 7 £m	Year 6 £m
Secured loans	–	0.3
Unsecured loans	0.2	0.3
	0.2	0.6
Loans are repayable by instalments:		
Between one and two years	0.1	0.2
Between two and five years	0.1	0.4
	0.2	0.6

Interest on long-term loans, which are denominated in a number of currencies, is payable at normal commercial rates appropriate to the country in which the borrowing is made. The last repayment falls due in Year 11.

Note 11 gives information on provisions for liabilities which will occur at a future date, as a result of past events or of definite plans made.

Note 11 Provisions

	Year 7 £m	Year 6 £m
Provisions for treating contaminated site:		
At 1 January	14.2	14.5
Utilised in the year	(2.2)	(0.3)
At 31 December	12.0	14.2
Provisions for restructuring costs:		
At 1 January	4.2	–
Created in year	1.0	4.3
Utilised in year	(1.0)	(0.1)
At 31 December	4.2	4.2
Provision for deferred tax:		
At 1 January	3.8	2.7
Transfer to income statement	0.5	1.2
Other movements	(0.3)	(0.1)
At 31 December	4.0	3.8
Total provision	20.2	22.2

Finally, note 33 sets out contingent liabilities. (Contingent liabilities are defined and explained in Chapter 10.) Two contingent items have the amount quantified. The impact of litigation (legal action) is not quantified. The company may think that to do so would be seen as an admission of legal liability.

Note 33 Contingent liabilities

The company has guaranteed bank and other borrowings of subsidiaries amounting to £3.0m (Year 6: £15.2m). The group has commitments, amounting to approximately £41.9m (Year 6: £28.5m), under forward exchange contracts entered into in the ordinary course of business.

Certain subsidiaries have given warranties for service work. These are explained in the statement on accounting policies. There are contingent liabilities in respect of litigation. None of the actions is expected to give rise to any material loss.

The accounting policy statement contains three items relevant to liabilities:

Accounting policies

Deferred tax
The provision for deferred tax recognises a future liability arising from past transactions and events. Tax legislation allows the company to defer settlement of the liability for several years.

Warranties
Some service work is carried out under warranty. The cost of claims under warranty is charged against the income statement (profit and loss account) of the year in which the claims are settled.

Deferred consideration
For acquisitions involving deferred consideration, estimated deferred payments are accrued in the statement of financial position (balance sheet). Interest due to vendors on deferred payments is charged to the income statement (profit and loss account) as it accrues.

In this extract the word 'charged' appears several times. In relation to interest or taxes, the use of the word **charge** describes the reduction in ownership interest reported in the income statement (profit and loss account) due to the cost of interest and tax payable.

Because the level of borrowing is low in this company, and therefore would not create any concern for investors or new lenders, the finance director has very little to say about it in his report. To some extent the chairman takes the initiative earlier in the annual report:

Finance
Once again, during Year 7 we had a strong operating cash flow, amounting to £196.7m (up from £163.5m in Year 6). This funded expenditure of £24.6m on acquisition of other companies and businesses (after allowing for £3.1m received from a disposal of a company) and the group still ended the year with an increase in its cash balances.

David Wilson has already commented in Chapters 4 and 7 on some aspects of the liabilities in the financial statements of Safe and Sure plc. Here he is explaining to Leona, in the coffee bar at the health club, his views on liabilities in particular.

DAVID: *Where do I start in explaining how I look at liabilities? Well, I always read the accounting policy notes before I look at any financial statements. This company provides three accounting policy notes relating to matters of liabilities. The policy on warranties is interesting because it confirms that the company does not record any expected liability on warranties. The first time I saw this in the annual report I was quite concerned about lack of prudence, but on my first visit to the company I was shown the warranty settlement file. There are very few claims under warranty because the company has lots of procedures which have to be followed by employees who carry out service work. Warranty claims are relatively unusual and unpredictable for this company so there is no previous pattern to justify setting up a liability in the form of a provision for future claims.*

The deferred consideration arises because this company has acquired another business and wants to look into all aspects of the newly acquired investment before making full payment.

Deferred tax provisions are common to many companies. They are an attempt to line up the accounting profit with the tax charge based on taxable profits, which are usually different. I don't understand the technical details but my test of importance is to look at the amount charged to the income statement (profit and loss account) for the year. It is less than 1% of the profit after tax, so I shan't be giving it much attention on this occasion.

Provisions for restructuring are my real headache. These are a measure of the costs expected when the company plans a restructuring such as changing the management structure with redefinition of the role of some employees and redundancy for others. It sounds reasonable to give warning of what all this will cost but the standard-setters have to be strict about the details because in the past the use of provisions has been linked to some creative accounting in the income statement (profit and loss account). Do you know anything about that?

LEONA: *Yes. On the one hand, you would like to know that a company is prudent in reporting in the income statement (profit and loss account) now the likely losses which will arise in future years because of a decision to reorganise. On the other hand, you would not like to think that a company has loaded the income statement with lots of bad news this year so that it can make next year look much better when the results are published. The accounting standard-setter has prevented companies from being excessively prudent. I could explain more but not at this time on a Friday night. What do you see in the statement of financial position (balance sheet) and the other information provided by the company?*

DAVID: *After reading and thinking about the items in the accounting policy notes I look to the breakdown between current liabilities and longer-term liabilities. I also look to the amount of long-term finance compared with the amount of the equity holders' funds. The borrowings in this company are relatively low in relation to equity-holders' funds, so there is not a high financial risk, but I still want to look for unexplained changes since the previous year. Again, there is nothing which springs to the eye.*

The contingent liability note is usually quite interesting. One of my senior colleagues says that you should start at the end of the annual report and read it backwards. Then you find the best parts first. The contingent liability note is always near the end. I would be asking lots of questions about the forward exchange contracts, if I had not already asked the financial controller. He confirmed in more detail what the finance director says rather briefly. The forward exchange contracts are used as part of prudent financial management to put a limit on any potential loss through adverse currency movements on transactions in different countries.

LEONA: *Much of what you say is reflected in what auditors carry out by way of analytical review. What we don't provide is a view to the future. What are your thoughts there?*

DAVID: *This is a cash-rich company and it has very little in the way of complicated financial structures. For a major company that is probably unusual, but it means I can concentrate on the operating aspects of the business and on whether it will continue to generate cash. It uses cash generated to buy other businesses and expand further, but I wonder what will happen when the scope for that expansion ceases. It is unlikely to be a problem in the near future because the company has a foothold in expanding markets in Asia. When that scope for expansion comes to an end the company may have to start borrowing to finance expansion rather than relying on internal cash flows.*

11.4 Provisions

Making a provision is an accounting process similar to that of making accrual for a known obligation.

Definition	A **provision** is a liability of uncertain timing or amount.[4]

The distinguishing feature of a provision often lies in the larger element of uncertainty which surrounds a provision. Such a provision will appear in the liabilities section of a statement of financial position (balance sheet). (This book has already considered in Chapter 8 the provision for depreciation and in Chapter 9 the provision for doubtful debts. These are examples of what is regarded as an adjustment to the reported value of an asset, rather than an adjustment for significant uncertainty. They are therefore reported as adjustments to the asset and do not appear in the liabilities section.) The following are examples of provisions which may be found in the liabilities sections of published accounts:

- losses on contracts
- obsolescence of stock
- costs related to closure of a division of the company
- costs of decommissioning an oil rig
- cost of landscaping a site at the end of the period of use
- warranties given for repair of goods.

Recording a **provision** is relatively straightforward. The ownership interest is reduced by an expense in the income statement (profit and loss account) and a liability is created under the name of the provision:

Assets – **Liabilities** ↑	equals	**Ownership interest ↓ (expense)**

When the provision is no longer required it is released to the income statement (profit and loss account) as an item of revenue which increases the ownership interest and the liability is reduced:

Assets – **Liabilities** ↓	equals	**Ownership interest ↑**

The provision may also be released to the income statement (profit and loss account) so as to match an expense which was anticipated when the provision was made. The effect on the accounting equation is an increase in the ownership interest – the same effect as results from regarding the release of the provision as an item of revenue.

Of the topics covered in this chapter, provisions give the greatest scope for international variation in accounting treatment. In countries where the accounting system and the tax system are linked, there may be specific rules about the level and nature of provisions allowed. In countries that have a strong culture of **conservatism** (strong **prudence**) the provisions may be used to understate profit. The problem with such an approach is that the unnecessary provision may then be released in a year when profits would otherwise be lower. This has the effect of 'smoothing out' the peaks and troughs of profit. The IASB believes that provisions should only be used under carefully defined conditions. This approach also applies in the USA.

The IASB has proposed[5] to change the description of provisions to become 'non-financial liabilities'. It has taken longer than expected to bring this proposal to practice. The IASB: 'Current projects'' web page will give updates. The IASB has proposed that any items satisfying the definition of a liability should be recognised unless they cannot be measured reliably. Any unconditional obligation would be recognised so there would no longer be a need to estimate the likelihood of the obligation being implemented. Uncertainty about the amount or timing of the economic benefits required to settle the non-financial liability would be recognised in the measurement of the liability.

Example of a provision

During the year ending 31 December Year 5, a company's sales of manufactured goods amounted to £1m. All goods carry a manufacturer's warranty to rectify any faults arising during the first 12 months of ownership. At the start of the year, based on previous experience, a provision of 2.5% of sales was made (estimating the sales to be £1m). During Year 5 repairs under warranty cost £14,000. There could be further repair costs incurred in Year 6 in respect of those items sold part-way through Year 5 whose warranty extends into Year 6.

Using the accounting equation, the effect of these events and transactions may be analysed. When the provision is established there is an increase in a liability and an expense to be charged to the income statement (profit and loss account):

Assets	–	Liabilities ↑	=	Ownership interest ↓ (expense)
		+ £25,000		– £25,000

As the repairs under warranty are carried out, they cause a decrease in the asset of cash and a decrease in the provision. They do not directly affect the income statement (profit and loss account) expense:

Assets ↓	–	Liabilities ↓	=	Ownership interest
– £14,000		– £14,000		

The overall effect is that the income statement (profit and loss account) will report an expense of £25,000 but the provision will only be used to the extent of £14,000, leaving £11,000 available to cover any further repairs in respect of Year 5 sales. The repairs, when paid for, decrease the asset of cash but are not seen as decreasing the ownership interest. They are seen as meeting a liability to the customer (rather like making a payment to meet a liability to a supplier). The creation of the provision establishes the full amount of the liability and the decrease in the ownership interest which is to be reported in the income statement (profit and loss account).

The spreadsheet for analysis is contained in Table 11.1.

Table 11.1
Spreadsheet for analysis of provision for warranty repairs

Date	Transaction or event	Asset	Liability	Ownership interest
		Cash	Provision	Profit and loss account
Year 5		£	£	£
Jan. 1	Provision for repairs		25,000	(25,000)
Jan.–Dec.	Repairs under warranty	(14,000)	(14,000)	
	Totals	(14,000)	11,000	(25,000)

Activity 11.2

Test your understanding of the previous section by analysing the following information and entering it in a spreadsheet to show analysis of the impact of the information on the accounting equation:

Jan. 1 Year 1   Make a provision for repairs, £50,000.
During Year 1   Spend £30,000 against the provision and carry the rest forward.
Jan. 1 Year 2   Make a further provision for repairs, £10,000.
During Year 2   Spend £25,000 against the provision and carry the rest forward.
Jan. 1 Year 3   Reduce the remaining provision to £3,000.

11.5 Deferred income

For companies located in areas of the country where there are particular problems of unemployment or a need to encourage redevelopment of the location, the government may award grants as a contribution to the operating costs of the company or to the cost of buying new fixed assets.

Consider the award of a government grant to a company, intended to help with the cost of training employees over the next three years. The asset of cash increases, but there is no corresponding effect on any other asset or liability. Consequently, the ownership interest is increased. The obvious label for this increase is **revenue**. However, the benefit of the grant will extend over three years and it would therefore seem appropriate to spread the revenue over three years to match the cost it is subsidising. The accounting device for producing this effect is to say that the cash received as an asset creates a liability called **deferred income**. This does not meet the definition of a liability stated at the start of this chapter because the practice of deferring income is dictated by the importance of **matching** revenues and costs in the income statement (profit and loss account). It is one of the cases where established custom and practice continues because it has been found to be useful although it does not fit neatly into the conceptual framework definitions.

Example

A company receives a grant of £30,000 towards the cost of employee retraining. The retraining programme will last for three years and the costs will be spread evenly over the three years.

The income statement (profit and loss account) will show revenue of £10,000 in each year. At the outset the deferred income will be recorded in the statement of financial position (balance sheet) as £30,000. By the end of Year 1 the deferred income will be reduced to £20,000. At the end of Year 2 the deferred income will be reduced to £10,000. At the end of Year 3 the deferred income is reduced to nil. The accounting records are shown in Table 11.2.

Where grants are received towards the acquisition of fixed assets there is a similar approach of spreading the grant over the period during which the company will

Table 11.2
Recording deferred income and transfer to profit or loss

Date	Transaction or event	Asset	Liability	Ownership interest
		Cash	Deferred income	Revenue
Year 1		£	£	£
Jan. 1	Receiving the grant	30,000	30,000	
Dec. 31	Transfer to profit and loss account of first year's revenue		(10,000)	10,000
Year 2				
Dec. 31	Transfer to profit and loss account of second year's revenue		(10,000)	10,000
Year 3				
Dec. 31	Transfer to profit and loss account of third year's revenue		(10,000)	10,000

benefit from use of the asset. Some companies show the revenue as a separate item in the income statement (profit and loss account) while others deduct it from the depreciation expense. This is a matter of presentation which makes no difference to the overall profit. The statement of financial position (balance sheet) treatment is more controversial. Some companies report separately the net book value of the asset and the deferred income. Others deduct the deferred income from the net book value of the asset. This does not affect the ownership interest but shows a lower amount in the fixed assets section of the statement of financial position (balance sheet). In consequence, the user who calculates profit as a percentage of non-current (fixed) assets or a percentage of total assets will obtain a higher answer where a company shows the lower amount for net assets. Most companies report the asset and deferred income separately, but some argue for the **net** approach which sets one against the other. (Both methods are permitted by the international accounting standard and by the UK national standard. There is a view that the net approach may not be complying with the Companies Act 2006 and so relatively few UK companies have taken the net approach.) The choice will be set out in the notes on accounting policies. This is a useful illustration of the importance of reading the note on accounting policies.

Activity 11.3	*Consider a grant received as a contribution to staff retraining costs over the next three years. Write down three arguments in favour of reporting the entire grant in the income statement (profit and loss account) in the year it is received and write down three arguments in favour of spreading the grant across the period of retraining. Which set of arguments do you find more persuasive?*

11.6 Non-current (long-term) liabilities

The statement of financial position (balance sheet) requires a separate heading for all liabilities payable after one year. Users of financial statements need information about when the liabilities will be due for repayment (the **maturity** pattern).

Users also need to know about the nature of the liability and any risks attaching to expected outflows of economic benefit from the liability. The risks lie in: the interest payable on the loan; the currency of the loan; and the eventual amount to be repaid to the lender. Interest payable may be at a fixed rate of interest or a variable rate of interest. The currency of borrowing is important when foreign exchange rates alter. Repayment amounts may equal the amount borrowed initially, in some cases. In other cases there may be a **premium** (an extra amount) payable in addition to the sum borrowed. There are some very complex accounting aspects to reporting non-current (long-term) liabilities, the technical aspects of which are well beyond the capacity of a first-level text, but they are all directed towards ensuring that liabilities are recorded in full and the matching concept is observed in relation to interest charges.

Users want to know about the risks of sacrificing particular assets if the loan is not repaid on the due date. A claim to a particular asset may be made by a creditor who has a loan **secured** on a particular asset or group of assets.

11.6.1 Recording and measurement

This section concentrates on the terminology of non-current (long-term) liabilities and the general issues of recording and measurement that they raise. The basic feature of non-current (long-term) loan finance is that it is:

- provided by a lender for a period longer than one year;
- who expects payment of interest at an agreed rate at agreed points in time; and
- expects repayment of the loan on an agreed date or dates.

The names given to loan capital vary depending on the type of lender, the possibility that the loan will be bought and sold like ordinary shares, the currency in which the loan has been provided and the legal form of the documents creating the loan. Some of the names you will see are: loan stock, debentures, bonds, commercial paper, loan notes and bank facility.

- **Loan stock**. If a company shows loan stock in its statement of financial position (balance sheet) this usually indicates that the stock is available for purchase and sale, in a manner similar to the purchase and sale of shares in a company.
- **Debenture**. The legal meaning of the term **debenture** is a written acknowledgement of a debt. This means there will be a contract, in writing, between the company and the lender. The contract is called the debenture deed and is held by a trustee who is required to look after the needs of the lenders. If the company does not pay interest, or repay capital, on the due date, the trustee must take action to recover what is owed to the lenders. Debentures may be secured or unsecured, depending on what is stated in the debenture deed.
- **Bond.** The term **bond** has been in common use in the USA for some time as a name for loan capital. It is now found increasingly frequently in the statements of financial position (balance sheets) of UK companies, particularly when they are raising finance in the international capital markets where the US terminology is more familiar.
- **Commercial paper**, **loan notes** and **bank facility**. These are all names of short- to medium-term financing provided by banks or similar organisations. The interest payable is usually variable and the loans are unsecured.

This is only a sample of the main variations of names given to loan finance. It is not exhaustive because the name does not matter greatly for the purposes of accounting records and interpretation. The essential information needed for the users of accounting information is the answer to five questions:

1 How much was borrowed (the **principal sum**)?
2 How much has to be repaid (the capital sum plus any additional interest charge)?
3 When is repayment required?
4 What are the interest payments required?
5 Has the lender sought any security for repayment of the interest and the principal sum?

You will find detailed notes to the statement of financial position (balance sheet) setting out the interest costs and repayment conditions for loans reported as liabilities.

11.6.2 Secured and unsecured loans

- **Unsecured loan**. An **unsecured loan** is one where the lender has no first claim on any particular assets of the company and, in the event of default, must wait for payment alongside all the other unsecured creditors. If there is no wording to indicate that the loan is secured, then the reader of financial statements must assume it is unsecured.
- **Secured loan**. Where any loan is described as **secured**, it means that the lender has first claim to named assets of the company. Where a debenture or loan stock is secured, and the company defaults on payment, the trustee for the debenture will take possession of the asset and use it to make the necessary repayment. In the event of the company not being able to pay all the amounts it owes, secured lenders come before unsecured lenders in the queue for repayment.

Activity 11.4

A financial weekly magazine contains the following sentence:

Telecoms plc this week raised cash by selling $1m bonds with five-year and ten-year maturities.

Explain each part of the sentence.

11.6.3 Loan having a range of repayment dates

When a loan is made to a business, conditions will be negotiated regarding the amount and date of repayment. Some banks are willing to offer a range of repayment dates, say any time between 10 and 15 years hence, with the company being allowed to choose when it will repay. If the company needs the money and the interest rate is favourable, the company will borrow for the longest period allowed under the contract. If the company finds it no longer needs the money, or else the interest rate is burdensome, the company will repay at the earliest possible opportunity. For statement of financial position (balance sheet) purposes the preparer of accounts has to decide which date to use as a basis for classification.

The general principle is that if there is an obligation to transfer economic benefits, there will be a liability in the statement of financial position (balance sheet). Where there is a range of possible dates for repayment, the maturity date will be taken as the earliest date on which the lender can require repayment.[6]

11.6.4 Change in the nature of finance source

Some types of finance provided to a business may be arranged so as to allow a change in the nature of the source during the period of financing. As an example, consider the case of convertible loans.

A **convertible loan** is a source of finance which starts its life as a loan but, at some point in the future, may be converted to ordinary shares in the company (e.g. the lender is promised five shares per £100 of loan capital). At the date of conversion, the lender becomes a **shareholder**. This kind of financial arrangement is attractive to those providing finance because it provides the reassurance of loan finance and a payment of interest in the early years of a new development, with the option of switching to shares if the project is successful. If the project is not successful and the share price does not perform as expected, then the lender will not convert and will look for repayment of the loan on the due date. For the company there are some tax advantages in issuing loan finance. Also, the rate of interest required by investors in a convertible loan is usually lower than that required for a straight (non-convertible) loan because investors see potential additional rewards in the convertible loan.

While a convertible loan remains unconverted it is reported as a loan. Companies are not allowed to say, 'We are almost certain there will be a conversion', and report the convertible loan as share finance from the outset. However, there is an awareness that the eventual conversion will dilute the existing shareholders' claim on future profits and so the company will report the earnings per share before and after taking into account the effect of this dilution. Consequently, you will see 'fully diluted earnings per share' at the foot of the income statement (profit and loss account).

11.6.5 Interest payable on the loan

Companies and their banks may negotiate a variety of patterns for interest payment on loans. The pattern of interest payment might be based on a low percentage charge in earlier years and a higher percentage charge in later years, because the company expects that profits will be low initially but will rise later to cover the higher interest payments. For many years the income statement (profit and loss account) would have reported the interest charge based on the amount paid in each year, but now the standard-setters require the interest charge to be reported as it would be if a compound interest rate were applied over the life of the loan. This is described as the **effective interest rate**.[7]

Definition	The **effective interest rate** is the rate that exactly discounts estimated future cash payments or receipts through the expected life of the financial instrument.

The reasoning behind this approach is that, for purposes of reporting profit, the flexibility of negotiation of interest payment patterns makes comparability difficult to achieve. The banks will, however, ensure that they receive the overall compound interest they require and this gives a commercially relevant basis for comparability in the matching of interest charges against the profits of the period.

The general principle is that the amount shown as the expense of interest payable in the income statement (profit and loss account) should be based on the compound rate of interest applying over the entire period of the loan. This will not always be the same as the amount of interest paid in cash during the period. The spreading of interest charges over the period of the loan is an application of the accruals or matching concept. As an example, consider stepped bonds and deep discount bonds.

Stepped bonds

A **stepped bond** is a form of lending where the interest rate increases over the period of the loan. Take as an example a loan of £5m which carries a rate of interest of 8% per annum for the first three years, 10% per annum for the next three years and 13% per annum for the final four years. The cash payment for interest starts at £400,000 and by the tenth year has risen to £650,000. The overall payments may be shown to be equivalent to a compound rate of 10.06% per annum. Table 11.3 shows that the income statement (profit and loss account) charge of £503,000 would start higher than the cash amount, £400,000. By the final year the income statement (profit and loss account) charge of £517,000 would be lower than the cash amount, £650,000. The pattern followed on each line of Table 11.3 is to start with the amount owing, add interest at 10.06% and deduct the amount of the cash payment, leaving the amount owing at the end of the period which becomes the amount owing at the start of the next period. By the end of the ten years the amount owing is exactly £5,000,000, the amount required by the lender.

It may be seen from Table 11.3 that the expense charged in the income statement (income statement (profit and loss account)) has a smoother pattern than that of the cash payments. Over the life of the loan the total expense charged must equal the total of the cash payments. The accounting processes for recording these amounts are too complex for a first-level course. The important point to note is that all companies are required to use this approach in calculating the expense charged in calculating profit. The cash flow implications of interest payments may be quite different and it will be necessary to look to the cash flow statement for evidence of the cash flow effect.

Deep discount bonds

A **deep discount bond** is issued at a price lower than (at a 'discount' to) its repayment amount. The interest rate (**coupon**) paid during the life of the loan may be very low (a 'low coupon' bond) or there may be no interest paid at all during the period of the loan (a 'zero coupon' bond). As an example, consider a zero coupon bond issued at £28m with a redemption value of £41m in four years' time. The cash payments of interest are zero but the income statement (profit and loss account) would show an annual charge of 10% per annum (starting at £2.8m in Year 1 and rising to £3.73m by Year 4). If there were no pattern of annual interest the entire discount of £13m would be shown as an expense of Year 4, distorting the underlying pattern of trading profit. Table 11.4 shows the pattern of interest charges for the income statement (profit and loss account).

Table 11.3
Calculation of expense charged in income statement (profit and loss account) for interest based on compound interest calculation

Year	Loan at start	Expense charged	Cash payment record	
		Interest at 10.06%	Cash paid	Loan at end
	(a)	(b)	(c)	(a) + (b) − (c)
	£000s	£000s	£000s	£000s
1	5,000	503	400	5,103
2	5,103	513	400	5,216
3	5,216	525	400	5,341
4	5,341	537	500	5,378
5	5,378	541	500	5,419
6	5,419	545	500	5,464
7	5,464	550	650	5,364
8	5,364	540	650	5,254
9	5,254	529	650	5,133
10	5,133	517	650	5,000
Total		5,300	5,300	

Table 11.4
Schedule of interest charges for zero coupon bond

Year	Loan at start £m	Interest £m	Loan at end £m
1	28.00	2.80	30.80
2	30.80	3.08	33.88
3	33.88	3.39	37.27
4	37.27	3.73	41.00
Total		13.00	

In the statement of financial position (balance sheet) the amount recorded for the liability will start at £28m and rise to £41m as shown in the final column of Table 11.4, so that the liability at the end represents the total amount due.

Activity 11.5

A three-year loan of £100,000 will be repaid at the end of three years as £133,100. No interest is payable during the three-year period. The interest included in the loan repayment arrangement is equivalent to a compound annual charge of 10% per annum. Explain how this transaction would appear in the income statement (profit and loss account) and statement of financial position (balance sheet) over the three-year period.

11.6.6 Complex capital instruments

It is impossible to read the statement of financial position (balance sheet) of most major listed companies without realising rapidly that there is a bewildering array of capital instruments being used to raise money for business. The reasons are complex but lie in the need to provide conditions which are attractive to both borrower and lender when they may be based in different countries and may have different perspectives on interest rates and currency exchange rates. This section explains the term 'interest rate swaps', which are increasingly used by companies, and takes an illustration from a major company to indicate the variety of capital instruments (sources of finance) in use. Detailed descriptions and discussion are beyond the scope of this text but would be found in a finance manual.

Interest rate swaps

Suppose there are two companies, A and B. Both have identical amounts of loan finance. Company A is paying fixed rates of interest, but would prefer to be paying variable rates, while Company B is paying variable rates of interest, but would prefer to be paying fixed rates. The reasons could be related to patterns of cash flow from trading, cash flow from investments or beliefs about future directions of interest rates. Whatever the reason, it would seem quite acceptable for them to swap (exchange) so that A pays the variable interest on behalf of B and B pays the fixed interest on behalf of A. This type of arrangement has to be explained carefully because neither company can escape from the legal obligation on the loans taken out initially. The explanation will usually be found in a note to the accounts which gives information on the legal obligation and on the actual impact on the income statement (profit and loss account) of implementing the swap.

Capital instruments of a listed company

The following illustration is based upon the statement of financial position (balance sheet) of a major UK listed company:

Note on borrowings:		Year 2	Year 1
		£m	£m
Unsecured borrowings:			
10½% euro-sterling bonds Year 17		100.0	100.0
Loan stocks			
13.625%	Year 16	25.0	25.0
5.675% – 9.3%	Year 3/Year 10	5.9	6.1
Zero coupon bonds Year 3		96.6	87.2
Variable rate multi-option bank facility		15.8	155.2
Bank loans, overdrafts, commercial paper, short- and			
medium-term notes		257.0	244.8
. . . the nominal value of the zero coupon bonds is £100m and the effective annual rate of interest is 10.85% . . .			

Comment. The euro-sterling bonds and the loan stocks are reported at the amount due for repayment at the end of the loan period. The euro-sterling bonds are loans raised in the eurobond market, repayable in sterling. Those loans which have fixed rates of interest are indicated in the table by a fixed percentage rate. Zero coupon means a zero percentage rate of annual interest payable. That does not mean the company escapes interest payment altogether. The liability on the zero coupon bonds increases by 10.85% each year as indicated in the extract note at the foot of the table. It is presumably due for repayment part-way through Year 3 since the liability shown at the end of Year 2 is quite close to the £100m amount due (called the **nominal value** in the note). The remaining loans are variable rate and so the annual interest charge depends on current rates of interest. Professional investors might want to know more about the nature of the bank facility and also the breakdown of the various components of the figure £257m.

11.7 Summary

- A **non-current liability** is any liability that does not meet the definition of a current liability. Non-current liabilities are also described as **long-term liabilities**.

- Users need information about the **principal sum** repayable and the **interest** payable during the lifetime of a liability. They also need to know the dates on which significant payments will be required (called the **maturity profile of debt**).

- Detailed information about **non-current liabilities** is found in the notes to the financial statements.

- A **provision** is a liability of uncertain timing or amount. The amount of a provision is reported in the liabilities section of a statement of financial position (balance sheet). Changes in provisions are reported in the income statement (profit and loss account).

- **Deferred income** arises where a business receives a government grant or receives cash for goods or services before these are provided. The cash received is reported as an increase in cash and an increase in a liability to represent the obligation to satisfy the conditions of the grant or provide the goods or services. When the conditions are satisfied the liability is reduced and the ownership interest is increased by recording the revenue.

QUESTIONS

The Questions section of each chapter has three types of question. 'Test your understanding' questions to help you review your reading are in the 'A' series of questions. You will find the answers to these by reading and thinking about the material in the book. 'Application' questions to test your ability to apply technical skills are in the 'B' series of questions. Questions requiring you to show skills in problem solving and evaluation are in the 'C' series of questions. A letter [S] indicates that there is a solution at the end of the book.

A   Test your understanding

Skills outcomes

A11.1 Explain why a provision may be required. (Section 11.4)

A11.2 Give three examples of situations which may lead to provisions. (Section 11.4)

A11.3 Explain how deferred income is recorded. (Section 11.5)

A11.4 Is it justifiable to report deferred income under the category of liability? (Section 11.5)

A11.5 Explain what is meant by each of the following terms: (Section 11.6)

  (a) loan stock;
  (b) debenture;
  (c) bond;
  (d) maturity date; and
  (e) convertible loan stock.

A11.6 [S] On reviewing the financial statements, the company accountant discovers that a grant of £60,000 towards expenditure of the current year plus two further years has been reported entirely as revenue of the period. What will be the effect on the income statement (profit and loss account) and the statement of financial position (balance sheet) when this error is rectified?

A11.7 [S] On reviewing the financial statements, the company accountant discovers that there has been no provision made for urgent repairs to external doors and window frames, already identified as being of high priority on grounds of health and safety. The amount of £50,000 should be provided. What will be the effect on the income statement (profit and loss account) and the statement of financial position (balance sheet) when this error is rectified?

B Application

B11.1 [S]

The Washing Machine Repair Company gives a warranty of no-cost rectification of unsatisfactory repairs. It has revenue from repair contracts recorded as:

Year	Amount of revenue
	£
1	80,000
2	90,000

Based on previous experience the manager makes a provision of 10% of revenue each year for warranty costs. In respect of the work done during Years 1 and 2, repairs under warranty are carried out as follows:

Date of repair work	Amount in respect of Year 1 revenue	Amount in respect of Year 2 revenue	Total
	£	£	£
1	4,500		4,500
2	3,200	4,800	8,000
3		5,000	5,000

Required
(a) Show how this information would be recorded in the financial statements of the Washing Machine Repair Company.
(b) Explain how the financial statements would appear if the company made no provision for warranty costs but charged them to income statement (profit and loss account) when incurred.

B11.2 [S]

General Engineering Ltd receives a government grant for £60,000 towards employee training costs to be incurred evenly over the next three years. Explain how this transaction will be reported in the financial statements.

C Problem solving and evaluation

C11.1

Explain why each of the following is recognised as a provision in the statement of financial position (balance sheet) of a telecommunications company:

(a) On 15 December Year 2, the Group announced a major redundancy programme. Provision has been made at 31 December Year 2 for the associated costs. The provision is expected to be utilised within 12 months.

(b) Because of the redundancy programme, some properties have become vacant. Provision has been made for lease payments that cannot be avoided where subletting is not possible. The provision will be utilised within 15 months.

(c) There is a legal claim against a subsidiary in respect of alleged breach of contract. Provision has been made for this claim. It is expected that the provision will be utilised within 12 months.

C11.2

(Refer also to Chapter 10, section 10.3.2, on Contingent liabilities.)

Explain why each of the following is reported as a contingent liability but not recognised as a provision in the statement of financial position (balance sheet).

(a) Some leasehold properties which the group no longer requires have been sublet to third parties. If the third parties default, the group remains responsible for future rent payments. The maximum liability is £200,000.

(b) Group companies are defendants in the USA in a number of product liability cases related to tobacco products. In a number of these cases, the amounts of compensatory and punitive damages sought are significant.

(c) The Department of Trade and Industry has appointed Inspectors to investigate the company's flotation ten years ago. The directors have been advised that it is possible that circumstances surrounding the flotation may give rise to claims against the company. At this stage it is not possible to quantify either the probability of success of such claims or of the amounts involved.

Activities for study groups

Turn to the annual report of a listed company which you have used for activities in previous chapters. Find every item of information about liabilities. (Start with the financial statements and notes but look also at the operating and financial review, chief executive's review and other non-regulated information about the company.)

As a group, imagine you are the team of fund managers in a fund management company. You are holding a briefing meeting at which each person explains to the others some feature of the companies in which your fund invests. Today's subject is liabilities. Each person should make a short presentation to the rest of the team covering:

(a) The nature and significance of liabilities in the company.

(b) The effect on profit of a 10% error in estimation of any one of the major categories of liability.

(c) The company's comments, if any, on its future obligations.

(d) The risks which might attach to the liabilities of the company.

(e) The liquidity of the company.

(f) The trends in liabilities since last year (or over five years if a comparative table is provided).

(g) The ratio of current assets to current liabilities.

Notes and references

1. IASB (2010), *Conceptual Framework*, para. 4.4(b).
2. IASB (2012), IAS 1, para. 69.
3. IASB (2012), IAS 1, para. 69.
4. IASB (2012), IAS 37, *Provisions, Contingent Liabilities and Contingent Assets*, para. 10.
5. IASB (2005), Exposure draft of proposed amendments to IAS 37 *Provisions, Contingent Liabilities and Contingent Assets*, para. 1.
6. IFRS 7 (2012), *Financial Instruments: Disclosures*, para. B11C.
7. IASB (2011), IAS 39 *Financial Instruments: Recognition and Measurement*. Definitions section.

Bookkeeping entries for provisions and deferred income

Provisions

In the main text of this chapter there is an example based on the recording of provision for repairs under warranty. The analysis of the transactions and events is set out in Table 11.1. The ledger account will appear as follows:

L3 Provision for warranty repairs

Date	Particulars	Page	Debit	Credit	Balance
Year 5			£	£	£
Jan. 1	Provision in respect of Year 5	L2		25,000	(25,000)
Jan.–Dec.	Repairs carried out	L1	14,000		(11,000)

LEONA: *At the start of the year (or possibly in practice at the end of each month) the provision is recorded by debiting the profit and loss account (L2) and crediting the provision. When the repairs are carried out there is a credit entry in the cash account (L1) and a debit entry in the provision account. Nothing is recorded as an income statement (profit and loss account) expense at that time. The overall effect is that the income statement (profit and loss account) carries an expense of £25,000 and the provision account shows a potential liability of £11,000 to cover any further repairs arising from work done during Year 5 (since some of the goods sold will remain under warranty into Year 6).*

Deferred income

In the main text of this chapter there is an example based on the recording of deferred income arising under a grant. The analysis of the transactions and events is set out in Table 11.2. The ledger account will appear as follows:

L3 Deferred income (statement of financial position/balance sheet)

Date	Particulars	Page	Debit	Credit	Balance
Year 1			£	£	£
Jan. 1	Grant received	L1		30,000	(30,000)
Dec. 31	Transfer to profit and loss account	L2	10,000		(20,000)
Year 2					
Dec. 31	Transfer to profit and loss account	L2	10,000		(10,000)
Year 3					
Dec. 31	Transfer to profit and loss account	L2	10,000		nil

LEONA: *The deferred income account is reported as a liability in the statement of financial position (balance sheet). It is established by a credit entry matched by a debit in the cash account (L1). Each year there is a transfer of one-third to the profit and loss account (L2) so that the revenue is spread evenly over the period.*

S | Test your understanding

S11.1 Prepare bookkeeping records for the information in question B11.1.

S11.2 Prepare bookkeeping records for the information in question B11.2.

Ownership interest

BAE signals high-liability results season

BAE Systems produces enough high-tech weaponry to overwhelm a confederacy of banana republics. But none of its missiles can neutralise a final salary scheme that on Thursday triggered a £1.52bn write-off larger than its 2011 pre-tax profits.

Getty Images

This prefigures a slew of writedowns and contributions increases for many companies about to report results. The reason is that gilt yields, the risk-free interest rates against which pensions liabilities are indirectly measured, are at rock bottom and unlikely to rise for years.

BAE illustrates the problem nicely. It discounts pension liabilities using corporate bond yields that fell about 10 per cent after inflation to 1.9 per cent last year in line with gilt yields depressed by investors' flight to safety. This has contributed to a £2bn increase in the liabilities of a scheme co-funded by Airbus to £23.3bn, against a £600m assets uptick.

The cost of dumping the final salary scheme would be far higher for BAE and other sponsors. According to Adrian Hartshorn of consultancy Mercer, no insurer would take on the risks without a steep premium to cover solvency reserves.

BAE pushed the scheme's write-off, including Airbus's portion, through the sanitiser of comprehensive income. This protected pre-tax profits, leaving the group with an absolute bottom line loss of £29m. Fair enough, perhaps, given that a deficit increase is a non-cash cost. But the extra £1.1bn in long-term contributions that BAE plans will be real, unless gilt yields rally.

So corporate pleas for twangier accounting standards will grow louder through the results season. But deficits result partly from contributions holidays that lifted profits in the 1990s. And most sponsors are cash rich. They should maintain down payments on promises to staff. The credibility of business needs bolstering, not eroding further.

Source: Jonathan Guthrie, *Financial Times Lombard*, 16 February 2012.

Extract from BAE Systems Annual Report 2011 (p. 119)

**Consolidated statement of comprehensive income
for the year ended 31 December**

	Notes	2011		
		Other reserves[1] £m	Retained earnings £m	Total £m
Profit for the year		–	1,256	1,256
Other comprehensive income				
Net actuarial (losses)/gains on defined benefit pension schemes		–	(1,522)	(1,522)
Currency translation on foreign currency net investments		(19)	–	(19)
Recycling of cumulative currency translation reserve on disposal	7	(14)	–	(14)
Amounts charged to hedging reserve		(56)	–	(56)
Recycling of cumulative net hedging reserve on disposal		–	–	–
Fair value movements on available-for-sale investments	15	–	5	5
Recycling of fair value movements on available-for-sale investments	5	–	(21)	(21)
Share of other comprehensive income of equity accounted investments	25	(17)	(45)	(62)
Tax on other comprehensive income	6	17	387	404
Total other comprehensive income for the year (net of tax)		(89)	(1,196)	(1,285)
Total comprehensive income for the year		(89)	60	(29)
Attributable to:				
Equity shareholders		(89)	44	(45)
Non-controlling interests		–	16	16
		(89)	60	(29)

[1] An analysis of other reserves is provided in note 25.

Source: Extract from BAE Systems Annual Report 2011 (p. 119).

Discussion points

1 Read the extract from the Statement of Comprehensive Income of BAE Systems.

2 Read the article from the *Financial Times*. Do you agree with the opinions of the author regarding the role of comprehensive income?

Contents

Learning outcomes

After reading this chapter you should be able to:

- Define ownership interest.
- Explain and demonstrate how the ownership interest is presented in company accounts.
- Understand the nature and purpose of the statement of changes in equity in the IASB system.
- Explain the needs of users for information about the ownership interest in a company.
- Read and interpret the information reported by companies in their annual reports, in respect of the ownership interest.
- Explain the accounting treatment of dividends.
- Understand the methods by which a company's shares may be issued when the company has a Stock Exchange listing.
- Show that you understand the impact of transactions and events on ownership interest in company accounts.

Additionally, for those who choose to study the supplement:

- Record end-of-period adjustments as debit and credit adjustments to a trial balance taken from the ledger accounts and produce figures for financial statements.

12.1 Introduction

The final element of the accounting equation has been reached. It was explained in Chapter 2 that the ownership interest is the residual amount found by deducting all liabilities of the entity from all of the entity's assets:

Assets	minus	**Liabilities**	equals	**Ownership interest**

The terminology was also explained in Chapter 2. The words equity and net assets both appear in the press and in commentaries in connection with the ownership interest. **Equity** is a word used to describe the ownership interest in the assets of the business after all liabilities are deducted. This is also referred to as the **net assets**, calculated as the assets minus the liabilities.

The structure which has been adopted for Chapters 8 to 12 is based on a series of questions:

- What are the principles for defining and recognising these items?
- What are the information needs of users in respect of the particular items?
- What information is currently provided by companies to meet these needs?
- Does the information show the desirable qualitative characteristics of financial statements?
- What are the principles for measuring, and processes for recording, these items?

Each of these questions will be addressed in turn.

12.2 Definition and recognition

The definition of **ownership interest** was presented in Chapter 2 as: 'the residual amount found by deducting all of the entity's liabilities from all of the entity's assets'.

Because the ownership interest is the residual item of the equation, it can only increase or decrease if something happens to an asset or to a liability. Recognition conditions are applied to assets and liabilities but there cannot be any additional recognition criteria applied to the ownership interest.

Events which change assets or liabilities include:

1 Making a profit (or loss) through the operations of the business – earning revenue and incurring expenses;
2 A contribution of cash by incoming shareholders purchasing new shares;
3 Holding an asset which increases or decreases in value;
4 Holding a liability which increases or decreases in value.

Each one of these events is important to the users of the financial statements and affects the claims of owners on the assets of the business. Since owners are the user group most interested in the ownership interest, this chapter will focus primarily on the information which is helpful to them. Item (1) of this list, reporting a profit or a loss in the income statement through the operations of the business, has been dealt with in some length in previous chapters. In this chapter we concentrate on item (2), the issue of new shares, and on items (3) and (4), the events which cause increases or decreases in assets and liabilities which are *not* reported in the income statement (profit and loss account). Items (3) and (4) are part of what is called comprehensive income (where 'comprehensive' means 'including everything that creates income for the owners').

12.3 Presentation of ownership interest

Chapters 7 to 11 have concentrated primarily on the limited liability company. For any limited liability company the **income statement (profit and loss account)** is the primary financial statement which reports the revenues and expenses of the business that arise through operations.

The change in value of an asset or liability while it is *held* by the company gives more cause for debate. If the asset has increased in value while still being held by the company, then there may be an increase in the valuation for financial reporting purposes. That is not a **realised** gain and so cannot be reported in the income statement (profit and loss account). There is another primary financial statement which companies must use to report **unrealised** gains. For companies using the IASB system in their financial statements, the unrealised gains are reported in a **statement of comprehensive income**. All changes in ownership interest, including contributions and withdrawals by owners, are reported in a **statement of changes in equity**.

Example of an unrealised gain

A business buys a building at a cost of £10m. One year later similar buildings are selling for £13m. The business does not intend to sell but would like to report the potential increase in the market value of the asset. Because there is no sale, the £3m estimate of the increase in value is unrealised. It is not reported in the income statement (profit and loss account) but is reported in the statement of comprehensive income.

The presentation of the ownership interest is therefore a potentially complex affair, using more than one financial statement. There is information about the current position of the ownership interest contained in the statement of financial position (balance sheet) and the related notes to the accounts. There is information about changes in the ownership interest in the income statement (profit and loss account) and the statement of comprehensive income (statement of total recognised gains and losses). The approach taken in this chapter is first of all to 'walk through' the early years of operating a limited liability company and the various types of ownership interest which arise.

12.3.1 Issue of shares at the date of incorporation

When the company first comes into existence it issues shares to the owners, who become **equity holders (shareholders)**. The date on which the company comes into existence is called the date of incorporation.

Each share has a *named value* which is called its **nominal value**. Sometimes it is referred to as the **par value**. This amount is written on the **share certificate** which is the document given to each owner as evidence of being a shareholder. Exhibit 12.1 shows the share certificate issued by a company which confirms that J. A. Smith is the owner of 100,000 ordinary shares of 25p nominal value each. This means that J. A. Smith has paid £25,000 to the company and that is the limit of this person's liability if the company fails.

All share certificates are recorded in the share register by the company secretary. The share certificate is a piece of paper which may be sold by the existing owner to another person who wishes to become a shareholder. The person who wishes to become a shareholder is often referred to as a **prospective investor**. That is not a legal term but is a useful way of indicating a person who has an interest in finding out more about the company, without having the legal rights of ownership. When the new owner has acquired the shares, the term 'investor' may continue to be used as a

Exhibit 12.1
Share certificate issued by a company

Certificate number 24516

Public Company plc

SHARE CERTIFICATE

This is to certify that

J. A. Smith

is the registered owner of 100,000 ordinary shares of 25 pence each.
Given under Seal of the Company the 15th day of August 20XX

Signed *P McDowall*
Company Secretary

J Jones
W Brown
Directors

---

description which emphasises that this person now has a financial interest in knowing that the company is performing well.

The issue of 100,000 shares at a price of 25 pence each will collect £25,000 cash for the company. The effect on the accounting equation is that the asset of cash increases by £25,000 and the ownership interest is increased by £25,000.

Assets ↑	–	Liabilities	=	**Ownership interest ↑**
Increase in cash £25,000				Increase in nominal value of shares £25,000

For a company, the ownership interest created by the issue of new shares at their nominal value is recorded as **share capital**.

Activity 12.1

Look at the financial pages of a newspaper. Find the daily list of share prices. What information does the newspaper provide about shares in each company? Which of these items of information would you expect to find in the annual report of the company? Give reasons for your answer.

12.3.2 Buying and selling shares

The company itself has no concern about the purchase and sale of shares from one owner to another, other than having to record the new owner's name in the share register. The purchase and sale may take place by private arrangement or may take place in an established **stock market** (also called a **stock exchange**) if the company is a public limited company. If the shares are traded in an established stock market they are called listed shares because the daily prices are listed on screens for buyers and sellers to see. If there is high demand for the shares, their price will rise. If there is little demand, the price will fall. The market price on any day will depend on investors' expectations about the future of the company. Those expectations will be influenced by announcements from the company, including financial information but also covering a much wider range of company news. The expectations may also be influenced by information about the industry in which the company operates. One of the main purposes of a well-regulated stock exchange is to ensure that all investors have access to the same information at the same time so that no one has an advantage.

12.3.3 Issue of further shares after incorporation

As time goes by, the company may wish to raise new finance and to issue new shares. This could be intended to buy new non-current (fixed) assets, or even to provide cash so that the company may purchase the shares of another company and create a larger group.

Although the **nominal value** remains the same, the **market value** may be quite different.

Example

Suppose a company has shares of nominal value 25 pence but finds that its shares are selling in the market at 80 pence each. If the company issues 200,000 new shares it will collect £160,000 in cash. That is the important piece of information for the company because it can use the cash to buy new assets and expand the activities of the business. The asset of cash has increased by £160,000 and the ownership interest has increased by £160,000.

The accounting records are required by company law to show separately the nominal value of the shares and any extra amount over the nominal value. The nominal value is 25 pence and the total amount collected per share is 80 pence. So the extra amount collected is 55 pence. This extra amount is called a **premium** (the word means 'something extra'). So the £160,000 increase in the ownership interest is recorded as two separate items, namely the **nominal value** of £50,000 and the **share premium** of £110,000.

12.3.4 Retained earnings

Once the business is in operation it starts to make profits. The income statement (profit and loss account) shows the profit earned in a time period. This profit increases the ownership interest. The accumulation of past profits in the statement of financial position (balance sheet) is called **retained earnings**. The retained earnings represent the ownership interest in the net assets of the business. It is one type of **reserve**. At any point in time someone could ask the owner 'How much would you expect to receive if this business were to close down today?' The owner would look at the statement of financial position (balance sheet) and reply with the total of the **ownership interest**, shown by **equity share capital** plus all **reserves**.

You should be aware that the reserves are given different names in different countries. In some there is a legally defined reserve with a tax-deductible transfer to the reserve from the income statement (profit and loss account). It requires careful reading of the ownership interest section of the statement of financial position (balance sheet). An understanding of the changes in retained profits is helped by reading the **statement of comprehensive income**, explained in section 12.3.5.

12.3.5 Statement of comprehensive income

Look back to the accounting equation explained in Chapter 3. Section 3.4.1 describes ownership interest as:

Capital at the start of the year
plus/minus
Capital contributed or withdrawn
plus
Profit of the period

That chapter gives the simplest possible definition of 'profit' as 'revenue minus expenses'. A broader definition of 'profit' would be to say 'any changes in assets and liabilities other than those caused by capital contributed or withdrawn'. Chapters 9 and 10 have shown that many changes in inventories, accounts receivable and accounts payable will lead to changes in revenue and expenses, reported in the income statement (profit and loss account). This section and section 12.3.6 of this chapter show that other factors may affect the values of assets and liabilities.

The IASB wants to encourage companies to report all changes in assets and liabilities, whatever the cause, in a **statement of comprehensive income**. The word 'comprehensive' means 'including everything'. However, many companies would like to retain the separate income statement as explained in Chapters 5 and 6. Consequently the IASB allows a two-part approach:

1 A separate income statement
2 A second statement beginning with profit or loss from the income statement and incorporating other components of comprehensive income.

This two-part approach is used by many UK companies which report using IFRS. It is used in this chapter to illustrate the comprehensive income approach. Two examples are provided in the following sections. The first is the revaluation of non-current assets and the second is the reporting of changes in exchange rates of foreign currency.

12.3.6 Revaluation of non-current (fixed) assets

Suppose a company buys a hotel costing £560,000. The hotel is run successfully for a period of three years and at the end of that period a professional valuer confirms that the hotel, if sold, would probably result in sale proceeds of £620,000 because of the change in property values and the reputation which the hotel has established. The directors of the company may wish to tell shareholders about this increased market value of the company's non-current (fixed) asset.

There are two ways of informing shareholders in the financial statements. One is to continue to record the value at £560,000 (the historical cost) in the statement of financial position (balance sheet) but to include also a note to the financial statements explaining that the market value has been confirmed as £620,000 by an expert. That information would allow the investor to think, 'That makes me feel better off by £60,000.'

This feeling of investor happiness is surrounded by a note of caution, because the gain in value is not **realised**. The asset has not in fact been sold in the market. It only needs a rumour of pollution on the local beach to depress the market value of all the hotels in the town. Some companies feel that this note of caution is conveyed by providing the information on the increase in value in the notes to the financial statements rather than the statement of financial position (balance sheet) itself.

Other companies take a bolder view and decide that, in the interests of providing information which is relevant to the needs of users, the company should apply the accounting equation on behalf of the readers of the financial statement. These companies then have a problem of deciding on the name to be given to describe this £60,000 increase in the ownership interest. It cannot be called revenue and included in the income statement (profit and loss account) because it has not been realised by the operations of the business. It represents a new ownership interest as a newly identified 'reserve' of wealth. The wealth lies in the asset, but the interest in that wealth is a claim which belongs to the owners. The increased wealth is caused by revaluation of the asset, and so the name chosen for this claim is **revaluation reserve**. In terms of the accounting equation there is an increase in the value of an asset and an increase in the ownership interest.

This section has explained the accounting processes for revaluing non-current (fixed) assets. You may see revaluation of non-current assets in some annual reports of UK companies. It is not compulsory but if companies choose to revalue then they must do so regularly as explained in Chapter 8. In contrast such revaluation is not allowed in the USA or Germany. In other countries, such as France, it is allowed but rarely used. Revaluation is permitted by the IASB but is not a requirement. So while the IASB system has brought standardisation of accounting practices across Europe it does not entirely take away the choices that may make comparisons less easy.

Example

A company, Office Owner Ltd, is formed on 1 January Year 1 by the issue of 4m ordinary shares of 25 pence nominal value each. The cash raised from the issue is used on 2 January to buy an office block which is rented to a customer for an annual rent of £50,000. The tenant carries all costs of repairs. The company's administration costs for the year are £10,000. At the end of the year the office block is valued by an expert at £1,015,000. On the last day of the year the company issues a further 2 million ordinary shares at a price of 40 pence each, to raise cash in Year 2 for expansion plans.

Activity 12.2

For the analysis of each transaction you should look back to the previous sections where each type of transaction is dealt with in detail. Write down the effect of each transaction on the accounting equation. Check your answer against Table 12.1. When you are satisfied that you understand Table 12.1 go to Table 12.2 where you will find the amounts entered in the spreadsheet.

Table 12.1

Office Owner Ltd – analysis of transactions for Year 1

Date	Transaction or event		Effect on assets	Effect on ownership interest
Year 1		£000s		
Jan. 1	Issue of shares at nominal value	1,000	Increase asset of cash	Increase share capital at nominal value
Jan. 2	Purchase of office block	1,000	Increase asset of property	Decrease asset of cash
Jan.–Dec.	Rent received	50	Increase asset of cash	Revenue of the period
Jan.–Dec.	Administration costs	10	Decrease asset of cash	Expense of the period
Dec. 31	Revaluation of asset	15	Increase asset of property	Increase ownership interest by revaluation
Dec. 31	Issue of further shares nominal value 500 share premium 300		Increase asset of cash	Increase share capital at nominal value and increase share premium

Table 12.2

Office Owner Ltd – spreadsheet of transactions for Year 1

Date	Transaction or event	Cash	Office block	Share capital	Share premium	Income statement (profit and loss account)	Revaluation reserve
Year 1		£000s	£000s	£000s	£000s	£000s	£000s
Jan. 1	Issue of shares	1,000		1,000			
Jan. 2	Purchase of office block	(1,000)	1,000				
Jan.–Dec.	Rent received	50				50	
Jan.–Dec.	Administration costs	(10)				(10)	
Dec. 31	Revaluation of asset		15				15
Dec. 31	Issue of further shares	800		500	300		
		840	1,015	1,500	300	40	15

|———— 1,855 ————| |———————— 1,855 ————————|

Entering the amounts in the spreadsheet of Table 12.2 shows, in the final line, that the accounting equation is satisfied and allows a statement of comprehensive income and a statement of financial position (balance sheet) to be prepared as in Table 12.3.

Table 12.3

Office Owner Ltd – income statement and statement of comprehensive income at end of Year 1

Income statement for Year 1	
	£000s
Revenue: rent received	50
Administration costs	(10)
Profit for the year	40
Statement of comprehensive income for Year 1	
Profit for the year	40
Revaluation of asset	15
Total comprehensive income for the year	55

Office Owner Ltd – statement of financial position (balance sheet) at end of Year 1

Office Owner Ltd Statement of financial position (balance sheet) at end of Year 1	
	£000s
Non-current (fixed) asset: Office block (at valuation)	1,015
Current asset: Cash	840
Net assets	1,855
Share capital	1,500
Share premium	300
Revaluation reserve	15
Retained earnings	40
	1,855

Activity 12.3

Suppose you note that a company has revalued its land and buildings as reported in the statement of financial position (balance sheet). What evidence would you expect to see as justification for the amount of the revaluation? What questions might you ask about the basis of revaluation?

12.3.7 Changes in exchange rates of foreign currency

All information in the financial statements of a UK company is shown in pounds (£) sterling. Where exchange rates alter, a company may lose or gain purely because of the exchange rate movement. That loss or gain must be reported.

The accounting process is called translation. Translation from one currency to another is particularly important when the financial statements of companies in a group are added together and so must all be restated in a common currency. The word 'translation' is used because the process is comparable to translating words from one language to another.

There are different methods of reporting depending on the type of transaction or event. Two different stories are considered here. The first is the purchase of an asset located in a foreign country. The second is the purchase, by a group of companies, of the share capital of a company in a foreign country.

Purchase of an asset

Take first of all the example of a UK company which buys a factory in Sweden. The factory is priced at Kr10,000,000. At the date of purchase of the factory the exchange rate is Kr10 = £0.70. The UK company has agreed to pay for the factory on the day of the transfer of legal title.

For accounting purposes the cost of the factory is recorded at the amount paid at the date of purchase. This is calculated as:

$$\frac{0.70}{10} \times \text{Kr}10,000,000 = \text{£}700,000$$

The effect of the transaction on the statement of financial position (balance sheet) of the UK company is:

That is the end of the story so far as the UK company is concerned. The exchange rate between the krona and the £ may fluctuate, and this may affect the company's view of the price for which the factory might eventually be sold, but that information will not appear in the financial statements of the UK company until such time as the factory is sold.

Purchase of shares in another company

Suppose now that a UK group of companies has decided to purchase the entire share capital of a Swedish company whose only asset is the same factory. The purchase price is Kr10,000,000. The Swedish company distributes its entire profit as dividend each year so that the only item remaining in its statement of financial position (balance sheet) is the factory at a cost of Kr10,000,000. (This is a very simplistic example but is sufficient to illustrate the exchange rate problem.)

At the date of purchase of the investment, the factory will be recorded in the group statement of financial position (balance sheet) at £700,000.

One year later the exchange rate has altered to Kr10 = £0.68. The factory is the only asset of the subsidiary. In the Swedish accounts it remains at Kr10,000,000 but, translated into £ sterling, this now represents only £680,000:

$$\frac{0.68}{10} \times Kr10{,}000{,}000 = £680{,}000$$

This represents a potential loss of £20,000 on the translated value of the asset at the start of the year. The loss is unrealised but as a matter of prudence the fall in the translated asset value should be reported. However, there have been strong feelings expressed by companies over many years that the unrealised loss should not affect the reported profit of the period. Consequently the relevant accounting standard[1] allows the effect on the ownership interest to be shown in the **statement of comprehensive income** as an increase or decrease for the period.

The reporting of the reduction in the asset value as a decrease in reserves is controversial because less attention is sometimes paid to reserves than is paid to the income statement (profit and loss account). This means that the impact on the ownership interest may pass unnoticed. The IASB is hoping that the use of the statement of comprehensive income will increase the transparency of such information.

This practice of translation is required by the accounting standard on the subject. In group accounting there is considerable complexity to the technical aspects of which exchange rate effects must pass through the income statement (profit and loss account) and which may pass through the reserves. The important message for the reader of the annual reports is to be alert to the possibility of exchange rate effects on the ownership interest being reported in reserves and to look carefully at the statement of comprehensive income.

12.4 Statement of changes in equity

In Chapter 7 it was noted that the IASB specifies four primary financial statements:[2]

1 a statement of financial position (balance sheet)
2 an income statement (showing the profit or loss for the period), as part of a larger statement of comprehensive income
3 a statement of changes in equity for the period, and
4 a statement of cash flows.

The statement of financial position (balance sheet), income statement and statement of cash flows were dealt with in Chapter 7. The statement of comprehensive income has been explained in section 12.3.5 of this chapter. The statement of changes in equity is now explained.

The IASB has decided that all owner changes in equity should be presented in the statement of changes in equity, separately from non-owner changes in equity. The detailed requirements are set out in IAS 1.

IAS 1 requires an entity to present, in a statement of changes in equity, all owner changes in equity. As explained in section 12.3.4, all non-owner changes in equity (i.e. comprehensive income) are required to be presented in one statement of comprehensive income or in two statements (a separate income statement and a statement of comprehensive income). Components of comprehensive income are not permitted to be presented in the statement of changes in equity.

Dividends are distributions to owners in their capacity as owners. Consequently dividends paid are reported in the statement of changes in equity. There will also be a separate note on the dividend per share paid during the year.

The statement of changes in equity includes the following information:

- total comprehensive income for the period, showing separately the total amounts attributable to owners of the parent and to non-controlling interests;
- for each component of equity, the effects of retrospective application or retrospective restatement recognised in accordance with IAS 8; and
- for each component of equity, a reconciliation between the carrying amount at the beginning and the end of the period, separately disclosing changes resulting from:
  - (i) profit or loss;
  - (ii) other comprehensive income; and
  - (iii) transactions with owners in their capacity as owners, showing separately contributions by and distributions to owners.

The term 'components of equity' includes, for example, each class of contributed equity, the accumulated balance of each class of other comprehensive income and retained earnings.

12.5 Users' needs for information

The owners of a company, and potential investors in a company, are primarily interested in whether the business will make them better off or worse off. They also want to be reassured that the business has taken care of the resources entrusted to it (carrying out the function of **stewardship**). The first source of an increase in the ownership interest is the **profit** generated by the company. Professional investors will use the phrase **quality of earnings** to refer to the different components of profit. They tend to regard profits generated by the main operating activity as being of higher quality than windfall gains such as profits on the sale of non-current (fixed) assets which are not a regular feature of the company's activity.

Owners of a company expect to receive a reward for ownership. One form of reward is to watch the business grow and to know that in the future a sale of shares will give them a satisfactory gain over the period of ownership. That requires a long-term horizon. Some investors prefer to see the reward more frequently in the form of a dividend. They want to know that the ownership interest is adequate to support the dividend and yet leave sufficient assets in the business to generate further profits and dividends.

Creditors of a company know that they rank ahead of the shareholders in the event of the company being wound up, but they want to know that the company is generating sufficient wealth for the owners to provide a cushion against any adverse events. Therefore creditors will also be concerned with the ownership interest and how it is being maintained or is growing.

Employees, suppliers and customers similarly look for reassurance as to the strength of the business to continue into the future. The ownership interest is a convenient focus which summarises the overall impact of the state of assets and liabilities, although what employees are really interested in is the preservation of the earnings capacity of the business.

12.6 Information provided in the financial statements

In Chapter 7 the statement of financial position (balance sheet) of Safe and Sure plc was presented. The final section of that statement of financial position (balance sheet) presented information on the capital and reserves representing the claim of the shareholders on the assets.

		Year 7 £m	Year 6 £m
Capital and reserves			
Called-up share capital	12	19.6	19.5
Share premium account	13	8.5	5.5
Revaluation reserve	14	4.6	4.6
Retained earnings	15	431.6	340.8
Equity holders' funds		464.3	370.4

In the discussion contained in Chapter 7 it was emphasised that the most important feature of this information is that, in total, it represents the shareholders' legal claim. There is nothing to see, touch, count or hold. If the company were to cease trading at the date of the financial statements, sell all its assets for the statement of financial position (balance sheet) amount and pay off all liabilities, the shareholders would be left with £464.3m to take away. The shareholders have the residual claim, which means that if the assets were to be sold for more than the statement of financial position (balance sheet) amount, the shareholders would share the windfall gain. If the assets were sold for less than the statement of financial position (balance sheet) amount, the shareholders would share the loss.

The total ownership interest is a claim which is described by this company as 'equity holders' funds'. It is equal to the **net assets** of the company. The total claim is subdivided so as to explain how the various parts of the claim have arisen. This section now considers each part of the claim in turn.

12.6.1 Share capital

The information shown by the company at note 12 is as follows:

Note 12 Share capital

	Year 7 £m	Year 6 £m
Ordinary shares of 2 pence each		
Authorised: 1,050,000,000 shares		
(Year 6: 1,000,000,000)	21.0	20.0
Issued and fully paid: 978,147,487 shares	19.6	19.5

Certain senior executives hold options to subscribe for shares in the company at prices ranging from 33.40p to 244.33p under schemes approved by equity holders at various dates. Options on 3,479,507 shares were exercised during Year 7 and 66,970 options lapsed. The number of shares subject to options, the years in which they were granted, the option price and the years in which they can be exercised are:

Options granted	Exercisable	Option price (pence)	Numbers
	Year 8	33.40	13,750
All granted	Year 9	53.55	110,000
10 years	Year 10	75.42	542,500
before	Year 11	100.22	1,429,000
exercisable	Year 12	120.33	2,826,600
	Year 13/14	150.45	3,539,942
	Year 15	195.20	3,690,950
	Year 16	201.50	2,279,270
	Year 17	244.33	3,279,363
			17,711,375

Called up means that the company has called upon the shareholders who first bought the shares to make payment in full. When a new company is brought to the stock market for the first time, investors may be invited to buy the shares by paying an instalment now and the rest later. That was quite common in the 1980s when former nationalised industries, such as electricity and water companies, were being sold to the private sector. The **prospectus**, which is issued to invite the purchase of shares, specifies the dates on which the company would make a call for the rest of the share price due. After all the cash has been received by the company, the shares are described as **fully paid**.

Ordinary shareholders are entitled to vote at meetings, usually in proportion to the number of shares held. That means that the power of the individual shareholder depends on the number of shares held. For most large companies there are relatively small numbers of shareholders who control relatively large proportions of the share capital. A company which is part of a larger group of companies is required to report in the notes to the accounts the name and country of the ultimate parent company. Companies that are listed on the Stock Exchange are required to disclose in the directors' report the name of any shareholder interested in 3% or more of the company's issued share capital.

Before the directors of a company may issue new shares, they must be authorised to do so by the existing shareholders. The existing shareholders need to be aware that their claim will be diluted by the incoming shareholders. (If there are 50 shares owned equally by two persons, each controls 50% of the company. If 25 new shares are issued to a third person, then all three have 33.3% each, which dilutes the voting power of the first two persons.)

One of the controversial aspects of share capital in recent years has been the privilege of share options taken by directors and other employees (usually senior employees of the business but sometimes spreading to the wider employee range). A share option allows the person holding the option to buy shares in the company, at any future date up to a specified limit in time, at an agreed fixed price. The argument in favour of such an arrangement is that it gives senior management an incentive to make the company prosperous because they want the share price to increase above the price they have agreed to pay. The argument against it is that they have no very strong incentive because the worst that can happen to directors and other employees is that they decide not to take up the option when the share price has not performed well. Until 1995 there were also some personal tax advantages in taking options rather than a normal portion of salary, but since then, the tax rules have limited such benefits.

Major companies now disclose, in the directors' report, the options held by each of the directors.

The analyst's view

David and Leona are on the plane flying from London to Aberdeen for a week's holiday in the Cairngorms. David has brought the annual report of Safe and Sure plc as a precaution against inclement weather disturbing their plans for outdoor activities.

While they wait for lunch to be served, David turns to the annual report and finds it is quite helpful to have Leona alongside him.

DAVID: *At the present time nothing seems to excite more comment from the financial journalists than the salaries paid to the directors and the options they hold. I have to confess that it's something I look for in the annual report. Maybe I'm looking for my future earning potential! One of my more cynical colleagues says that directors can't lose on options. If the share price rises they make money, which we don't mind because our investment is rising in value. What happens if the share price falls? The directors take new options at the lower price and then wait for the market to rise again so that they make a profit! We can't do that for our investment.*

I always look at the note on share capital to see whether new shares have been issued during the year. It reminds me to find out the reason. In this case the increase is £0.1m and the reason is explained in the accounts as being due entirely to the issue of options.

12.6.2 Share premium

It was explained earlier in this chapter that when shares are issued by a company it may well be that the market price of the shares is greater than the nominal value. What really matters to the company is the amount of cash contributed by the new shareholders, but company law insists that the claim of these new shareholders is split into a nominal amount and a share premium (the amount received in excess of the nominal amount).

Note 13 Share premium account

	Year 7 £m	Year 6 £m
At 1 January	5.5	3.6
Premium on shares issued during the year under the share option schemes	3.0	1.9
At 31 December	8.5	5.5

DAVID: *I look at the share premium account only as a check on the amount of cash raised by issuing shares during the year. If I add the £3.0m shown in this note to the £0.1m shown as an increase in nominal value, then I know that £3.1m was raised in total by the issue of shares. I can check that in the cash flow statement.*

12.6.3 Revaluation reserve

Earlier in the chapter the effect of revaluing assets was explained in terms of the accounting equation. It was also explained that the effects of foreign currency exchange rates may appear in reserves. The note to the accounts of Safe and Sure plc appears as follows:

Note 14 Revaluation reserve

	Year 7 £m	Year 6 £m
At 1 January	4.6	4.6
At 31 December	4.6	4.6

DAVID: *I always look at the reserves note to see what is happening to the overall share-holders' claim. There is no change in the reserve during Year 6 or Year 7 so does that mean the company has not revalued the non-current assets in that period?*

LEONA: *The directors are required to review the valuations at each statement of financial position (balance sheet) date. So if there is no change in the revaluation reserve there must have been no change in the value of the assets involved.*

12.6.4 Statement of comprehensive income

Safe and Sure plc
Consolidated statement of comprehensive income

	Year 7 £m	Year 6 £m
Profit for the period	114.8	94.6
Other comprehensive income:		
Exchange rate adjustments	5.5	(6.0)
Total comprehensive income for the year	120.3	88.6

LEONA: *Let me take you through the Statement of comprehensive income. It brings together the items which cause an overall decrease or increase in the ownership interest. On the first line you can see the profit for the period which comes from the income statement. On the next line there are the exchange rate adjustments that relate to translation of investments held in other currencies. In Year 6 the exchange rates worked against the interests of equity holders but in Year 7 there was a favourable effect.*

12.6.5 Statement of changes in equity

Consolidated statement of changes in equity for the year ended
31 December Year 7

	Share capital	Share premium	Revaluation reserve	Retained earnings (including exchange rate adjustments)	Total
	£m	£m	£m	£m	£m
Balance at 1 Jan Year 6	19.4	3.6	4.6	276.6	304.2
Share capital issued	0.1	1.9			2.0
Total comprehensive income				88.6	88.6
Less dividend				(24.4)	(24.4)
Balance at 1 Jan Year 7	19.5	5.5	4.6	340.8	370.4
Share capital issued	0.1	3.0			3.1
Total comprehensive income				120.3	120.3
Less dividend				(29.5)	(29.5)
Balance at 31 Dec Year 7	19.6	8.5	4.6	431.6	464.3

LEONA: *Now you really can start to tie things together. The statement of changes in equity shows changes during Year 7 in the lower part of the statement, with comparative figures for Year 6 in the upper part of the statement. Starting at the top of the table we see the amounts for the different components of equity at the start of Year 6. Share capital was issued, increasing the nominal value and the share premium reserve. The comprehensive income of the period increased the retained earnings. Dividends paid decreased the retained earnings. That takes us to the start of Year 7 with an overall total of £370.4m. On the next line we see that the new share capital issued is £3.1m which is a combination of the increase of £3.0m in share premium (Note 13) and the increase of £0.1m in nominal share capital (Note 12). That is really tricky to sort out from the Notes – it's very helpful to have the reconciliation give the information in one place. The comprehensive income is taken from the statement of comprehensive income and is shown as increasing retained earnings. The next line shows the dividend of £29.5m paid during Year 7. That dividend relates to the profits earned in Year 6. For the dividend recommended in respect of Year 7 we have to look at the Finance Director's review. Finally the statement shows all the separate components adding to the overall total of £464.3m.*

DAVID: *You have given me plenty to think about. I can see the drinks trolley on its way – what would you like?*

12.7 Dividends

Shareholders who invest in a company do so because they want the value of their shares to increase over time and return greater wealth when eventually sold. In the meantime the shareholders look for an income to spend each year. That comes to some of them by means of dividends.

Companies are not obliged to pay dividends and may decide not to do so if there is a shortage of cash or it is needed for other purposes. The directors make a recommendation to the shareholders in the annual general meeting. The shareholders may vote against taking the dividend but that happens only very rarely. Final dividend payments usually take place soon after the annual general meeting. Some companies also pay an interim dividend during the accounting year. Major UK companies have in past years ensured that a dividend was paid every year, however small, because it allowed the shares to be regarded as sufficiently 'safe' for investors such as trustees of charitable institutions.

When a company decides it wants to pay a dividend, there are two essential tests. The first is, 'Does the company have the cash resources to pay a dividend?' The second is, 'Has the company made sufficient profits, adding this year to previous years, to justify the dividend as being paid out of wealth created by the business?'

Even where the company has cash in the bank from which to pay the dividend, it must look forward and ensure that there are no other commitments in the near future which will also need cash. The company may decide to borrow short term to finance the dividend. In such a situation the company has to weigh the interest cost of borrowing against the risk of its shares being undervalued because of lack of interest from shareholders. These are all problems of cash management (more often called 'treasury management').

Company law imposes a different viewpoint. It takes the view that a company should not return to shareholders, during the life of the company, a part of the capital contributed by the shareholder body. Accordingly there is a requirement that dividends must be covered by accumulated reserves of past profit in excess of accumulated reserves of past losses. It is not required that the dividend is covered by the profit of the year. A company might choose to smooth things over by keeping the dividend reasonably constant even where profits are fluctuating.

The dividend declared by the company is usually expressed in pence per share. Shareholders receive dividend calculated by multiplying the dividend in pence per share by the number of shares held. For the company there is a reduction in the asset of cash and a reduction in the ownership claim. The management of the company may regard the dividend as an expense of the business but it is more properly regarded as a reduction in the claim which the owners have on the net assets as a whole. The reduction in the ownership interest is reported in the statement of changes in equity because it is a transaction with the owners.

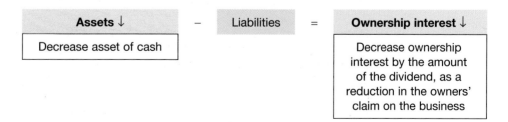

At the end of the accounting period the company will calculate profit and then declare a recommended dividend. The dividend is recommended by the directors to the shareholders. The shareholders, in the annual general meeting, may accept or decline but are not allowed to increase the amount. At the balance sheet date there is no legal liability because the shareholders' meeting has not been held. Therefore there is no information reported in the financial statements. The directors' report, which is required by company law, will contain a statement of the recommended dividend for the year. There will probably also be information in the chairman's statement or on a 'highlights' page.

12.8 Issue of further shares on the Stock Exchange

Once a company has a listing on the Stock Exchange it may decide to issue further shares. There are different methods by which this may be done, depending on the company's motive for the action. This section describes an offer for sale, a capitalisation issue and a rights issue.

12.8.1 Offer for sale

When a company seeks a listing of its shares for the first time, it must offer those shares to the public (using the services of a member firm of the Stock Exchange as a sponsor) and issue a **prospectus** setting out information about itself. Some of the information to be included in the prospectus is required by the Companies Act but this is expanded upon by the **Listing Rules**. The prospectus is a highly informative document, revealing far more about a company than would be found in the annual report. There is a requirement for an accountant's report which includes a three-year history of the financial statements. In particular, there must be a specific statement confirming the adequacy of working capital.

There may also be a forecast of the expected profits for the next accounting period. The reporting accountants will be asked to give an opinion on the forecast. Particularly interesting are the assumptions on which the forecast is based. The reporting accountants will confirm that the amounts in the forecast are consistent with the assumptions but the reader will have to decide how appropriate the assumptions themselves are.

Exhibit 12.2 contains an example of a statement of assumptions taken from a company prospectus.

Exhibit 12.2
Assumptions on which profit forecast is based

> The forecasts have been prepared on a basis consistent with the accounting policies normally accepted by the Group and on the following principal assumptions:
>
> (i) there will be no changes in taxation or other legislation or government regulations or policies which will have a significant effect on the Group; and
> (ii) the operations of the Group and its suppliers will not be significantly affected by weather conditions, industrial action or civil disturbances.

You may be surprised to learn that the wording in Exhibit 12.2 is extracted from the prospectus of a company retailing high-quality chocolates. You may be further surprised to learn that very similar wording appeared in the prospectus of a company offering dry cleaning services. There is no regulation which says that the statement of assumptions has to be helpful to the user of the annual report.

12.8.2 Capitalisation issue

After the shares have been listed for some time, the market value may have grown to the point where the shares are less marketable because the price of each is too large for convenient trading in small lots. The company may decide to increase the number of shares held by shareholders without making any change to the assets or liabilities of the company. One way of achieving this is to convert reserves into share capital. Take the simplified statement of financial position (balance sheet) in Table 12.4. The company decides to convert £1m of reserves into share capital. It writes to each shareholder saying, 'You will receive one new share for each share already held'. The statement of financial position (balance sheet) now becomes as shown in Table 12.5.

The shareholder now holds twice as many shares by number but is no better or worse off financially because the total value of the company has not changed. The shares will each be worth one-half of the market price of an old share at the moment of issue. This process is sometimes referred to as a bonus issue because the shareholders receive new share certificates, but in reality there is no bonus because no new wealth is created.

Table 12.4
Statement of financial position (balance sheet) of company prior to capitalisation

	£m
Assets	7
Liabilities	(4)
Net assets	3
Share capital, in shares of 25 pence each	1
Reserves	2
	3

Table 12.5
Statement of financial position (balance sheet) of company after capitalisation

	£m
Assets	7
Liabilities	(4)
Net assets	3
Share capital, in shares of 25 pence each	2
Reserves	1
	3

In terms of the accounting equation the effect on the statement of financial position (balance sheet) is:

Assets	−	Liabilities	=	**Ownership interest ↑↓**
				Increase in share capital £1m
				Decrease in reserves £1m

12.8.3 Rights issue

Once a company has a market listing it may decide that it needs to raise further finance on the stock market. The first people it would ask are the existing shareholders, who have already shown their commitment to the company by owning shares in it. Furthermore, it is desirable to offer them first chance because if strangers buy the shares the interests of the existing shareholders may be diluted. Suppose the company in Table 12.4 wishes to raise £3m new finance. It will offer existing shareholders the right to pay for, say, 2 million new shares at 150 pence each. There are already 4 million shares of 25p nominal value in issue, so the letter to the shareholders will say: 'The company is offering you the right to buy 1 new share at a price of 150p for every 2 existing shares you hold.' Existing shareholders will be attracted by this offer provided the market price stays above 150 pence for existing shares. They may take up the rights themselves or sell the right to someone else. In either event, the company will receive £3m cash, the company will issue 2 million new shares at 150 pence each and the statement of financial position (balance sheet) will appear as in Table 12.6.

Table 12.6
Statement of financial position (balance sheet) after rights issue

	£m
Assets	7.0
New cash	3.0
	10.0
Liabilities	(4.0)
Net assets	6.0
Share capital, in shares of 25 pence each	1.5
Share premium	2.5
Reserves	2.0
	6.0

The issue price of 150 pence is split for accounting purposes into the nominal value of 25 pence and the premium of 125 pence. In terms of the accounting equation the effect of the rights issue on the statement of financial position (balance sheet) is:

Assets ↑	–	Liabilities	=	**Ownership interest** ↑
Increase in cash £3m				Increase in share capital £0.5m Increase in share premium £2.5m

12.8.4 Buying back shares that have been issued

Companies are permitted to buy back shares that have been issued. The Companies Act sets limits on the proportion of shares that may be bought back from existing shareholders and sets conditions on the availability of retained earnings to support the buy-back. Two possible reasons for buying back shares are (1) to return surplus cash to shareholders and reduce the shareholding base, and (2) to stabilise share prices in the short term where investors want to sell but for some reason there is a temporary lack of demand in the market.

When companies buy back their own shares they may either cancel the shares or hold them as 'treasury shares'. Shares held as 'treasury shares' will be shown as a deduction from share capital in the equity section of the statement of financial position (balance sheet) and the transaction will be reported in the Statement of changes in equity.

Activity 12.4

Look in the financial section of a newspaper for the list of recent issues of new shares. Obtain the address of one company from a trade directory and write politely to ask for a copy of the prospectus. If you are sufficiently fortunate to obtain a copy of a prospectus, look at the accounting information and compare it with the amount and type of information published in the annual report. Why are they not the same?

12.9 Summary

- **Ownership interest** is the residual amount found by deducting all of the entity's liabilities from all of the entity's assets.

- Unrealised gains are reported in a **statement of comprehensive income** in the IASB system. They are reported in a **statement of total recognised gains and losses** in the UK ASB system.

- Each share has a named value when the company is formed. This is called its **nominal value**. It does not change unless the shareholders agree to split shares into smaller units.

- When the shares are sold on a stock market they have a **market value**. The market value of frequently traded shares changes daily with the forces of supply and demand.

- The difference between the nominal value and the market value is called the **share premium**. When the company issues further shares at market price the share premium is recorded separately from the nominal value.

- When non-current assets are revalued, the **unrealised** increase in value is added to the **revaluation reserve**.

- **Dividends** paid to shareholders reduce the ownership interest and are reported in the **statement of comprehensive income**. The effect on the accounting equation is reported when dividends are paid. Dividends proposed to be paid in future are described in the directors' report.

- When a company issues more shares after incorporation it may be through a capitalisation issue, an offer for sale or a rights issue. A **capitalisation issue** gives more shares to equity shareholders. It changes the relationship between share capital and reserves but brings no new resources into the business. An **offer for sale** increases the ownership interest and brings in new cash. A **rights issue** also increases the ownership interest and brings in new cash but it gives the existing shareholders the first choice of maintaining their proportionate interest in the company.

QUESTIONS

The Questions section of each chapter has three types of question. 'Test your understanding' questions to help you review your reading are in the 'A' series of questions. You will find the answers to these by reading and thinking about the material in the book. 'Application' questions to test your ability to apply technical skills are in the 'B' series of questions. Questions requiring you to show skills in problem solving and evaluation are in the 'C' series of questions. A letter [S] indicates that there is a solution at the end of the book.

A   Test your understanding

A12.1 Why may it be said that the ownership interest is the residual item in the accounting equation? (Section 12.1)

A12.2 What is the definition of ownership interest? (Section 12.2)

A12.3 What is the effect on the accounting equation where new shares are issued for cash? (Section 12.3.1)

A12.4 Why does the company not record the buying and selling of shares in its statement of financial position (balance sheet)? (Section 12.3.3)

A12.5 What is a share premium? How is it recorded? (Section 12.3.4)

A12.6 How is the revaluation of a non-current (fixed) asset reported? (Section 12.3.5)

A12.7 Why may the revaluation of a non-current (fixed) asset not be reported in the profit and loss account? (Section 12.3.5)

A12.8 Where may the reader of the annual report find out about the effect of movements in foreign exchange rates? (Section 12.3.6)

A12.9 What is the purpose of the statement of total recognised income and expenses? (Section 12.6.4)

A12.10 What is the purpose of the reconciliation of movements in equity? (Section 12.6.5)

A12.11 How do the directors report their recommended dividend for the financial period, to be agreed at the shareholders' meeting? (Section 12.7)

A12.12 What is meant by:

(a) offer for sale; (section 12.8.1)
(b) capitalisation issue; and (section 12.8.2)
(c) rights issue? (section 12.8.3)

Explain the effect of each of the above on the statement of financial position (balance sheet) of a company.

B Application

B12.1 [S]
Explain the effect on the accounting equation of each of the following transactions:

(a) At the start of Year 1, Bright Ltd issues 200,000 shares at nominal value 25 pence per share, receiving £50,000 in cash.
(b) At the end of Year 2, Bright Ltd issues a further 100,000 shares to an investor at an agreed price of 75 pence per share, receiving £75,000 in cash.
(c) At the end of Year 3 the directors of Bright Ltd obtain a market value of £90,000 for a company property which originally cost £70,000. They wish to record this in the statement of financial position (balance sheet).

B12.2 [S]
Explain the effect on the accounting equation of the following transactions and decisions regarding dividends:

(a) The company pays a dividend of £20,000 during the accounting period.
(b) The directors recommend a dividend of £30,000 at the end of the accounting year. It will be paid following shareholder approval at the Annual General Meeting, held two months after the accounting year-end.

B12.3 [S]
The following is a summarised statement of financial position (balance sheet) of Nithsdale Ltd.

	£000s
Cash	20
Other assets less liabilities	320
	340
Ordinary shares (400,000 of 25 pence each)	100
Share premium	40
Reserves of retained profit	200
	340

The company is considering three possible changes to its capital structure:

(a) issue for cash 50,000 additional ordinary shares at £1 per share, fully paid; or
(b) make a 1 for 4 capitalisation issue of ordinary shares; or
(c) make a 1 for 5 rights issue at £3 per share.

Show separately the impact of each change on the statement of financial position (balance sheet) of the company.

B12.4 [S]

Fragrance plc has owned a factory building for many years. The building is recorded in the statement of financial position (balance sheet) at £250,000, being historical cost of £300,000 less accumulated depreciation of £50,000. The recent report of a professional valuer indicated that the property is valued at £380,000 on an open market basis for its existing use. Explain the effect this information will have on the reported financial statements.

B12.5 [S]

Suppose the factory building in question B12.4 was valued by the professional expert at £240,000. What effect would this information have on the reported financial statements?

C Problem solving and evaluation

This question reviews your understanding of Chapters 8–12 and the effect of transactions on ownership interest.

C12.1

Set out below is a summary of the accounting records of Titan Ltd at 31 December Year 1:

	£000s	£000s
Assets		
Land and buildings	200	
Plant and machinery	550	
Investment in shares	150	
Stock	250	
Trade receivables (debtors)	180	
Cash	150	
Liabilities		
Trade payables (creditors)		365
Debenture loan 10% nominal rate of interest		250
Ownership interest		
Share capital		600
Retained earnings at 1 Jan. Year 1		125
Revenue		
Sales		1,815
Cost of goods sold	1,505	
Expenses		
Overhead expenses	145	
Debenture interest paid	25	
Totals	3,155	3,155

The summary of the accounting records includes all transactions which have been entered in the ledger accounts up to 31 December, but investigation reveals further adjustments which relate to the accounting period up to, and including, that date.

The adjustments required relate to the following matters:

(i) No depreciation has been charged for the year in respect of buildings, plant and machinery. The depreciation of the building has been calculated as £2,000 per annum and the depreciation of plant and machinery for the year has been calculated as £55,000.

(ii) The company is aware that electricity consumption during the months of November and December, Year 1, amounted to around £5,000 in total, but no electricity bill has yet been received.

(iii) Overhead expenses include insurance premiums of £36,000 which were paid at the start of December, Year 1, in respect of the 12-month period ahead.

(iv) The stock amount is as shown in the accounting records of items moving into and out of stock during the year. On 31 December a check of the physical stock was made. It was discovered that raw materials recorded as having a value of £3,000 were, in fact, unusable. It was also found that an employee had misappropriated stock worth £5,000.

(v) The company proposes to pay a dividend of £30,000.

(vi) The corporation tax payable in respect of the profits of the year is estimated at £45,000, due for payment on 30 September, Year 2.

Required

(a) Explain how each of the items (i) to (vi) will affect the ownership interest.

(b) Calculate the amount of the ownership interest after taking into account items (i) to (vi).

(*Hint*: first calculate the profit of the year.)

Activities for study groups

Turn to the annual report of a listed company which you have used for activities in earlier chapters. Find every item which relates to the ownership interest (including any discussion in the non-regulated part of the annual report).

As a group, imagine you are shareholders in this company. You are holding a meeting of the shareholders' action group calling for clarity of information about your total interest in the business. Make lists of the good points and weak points in the quality of information available to you and then arrange the weak points in descending order of importance. Then draft an action plan for improved communication with shareholders which you would propose sending to the company.

Notes and references

1. IASB (2012), IAS 21, *The Effects of Changes in Foreign Exchange Rates*, International Accounting Standards Board.

2. IASB (2012), IAS 1, *Presentation of Financial Statements*, para. 10.

A spreadsheet for adjustment to a trial balance at the end of the accounting period

End-of-period adjustments and the ownership interest

If you look back to Chapter 6 you will see that it finished with a trial balance and a promise that the trial balance would be used later as the starting point for preparation of financial statements. The moment has now arrived where the trial balance is used as a starting point for making end-of-period adjustments to show the change in the ownership interest during the period.

The accruals concept (or the parallel argument of matching in the income statement [profit and loss account]) requires all items relevant to the period to be included in the financial statements of the period. Most items will be included because they will have been recorded in the ledger and hence in the financial statements. However, there will be some items of information, emerging from enquiry at the end of the period, which have not yet resulted in a transaction but which are undoubtedly based on events relevant to the period.

The enquiry will take a routine form of:

- estimating the depreciation of non-current (fixed) assets where this has not already been recorded;
- examining non-current (fixed) assets for signs of obsolescence beyond the amount allowed for in the depreciation charge;
- counting the inventory (stock) of raw materials, work in progress and finished goods, for comparison with the accounting record;
- evaluating the doubtful debts;
- checking files for any purchase invoices received but not yet recorded;
- checking files for any sales invoices for goods sent out but not yet recorded;
- considering whether any resource has been consumed, or service received, for which a supplier has not yet sent an invoice.

Returning to the trial balance contained in Table 6.15 of Chapter 6, it may be noted that the depreciation for the month has been charged, there are no trade receivables (debtors) and therefore no concerns about doubtful debts, and it would appear from the list of transactions for the month that all sales and purchases have been recorded carefully. Suppose, however, that when M. Carter checks the inventory (stock) of goods at the end of the month it is found that the roof has been leaking and rainwater has damaged goods worth £500. Furthermore, the business uses gas to heat a water boiler and it is estimated that consumption for the month amounts to £80.

These items of information are called *end-of-period adjustments*. Both events could, and would, be recorded in the ledger accounts by the business. If you were presented with this information as a class exercise, or you were the auditor taking the trial balance and adjusting it for this further information, you would use a spreadsheet which set out the trial balance and then provided further columns for the end-of-period adjustments. The spreadsheet for this example is set out in Table 12.7 but before looking at that you should read through the next section which explains the recording of end-of-period adjustments. In this case a one-month period is covered and so the adjustments are referred to as month-end adjustments.

Analysis of the month-end adjustments

Before any entries may be made in the adjustments columns of the spreadsheet, the effect of each adjustment on the accounting equation must be considered so that the debit and credit entries may be identified.

(a) At the end of the month it is found that the roof has been leaking and rainwater has damaged goods worth £500

The loss of inventory (stock) causes the ownership interest to decrease and is recorded as a debit entry in the expense of cost of goods sold. The decrease in the inventory (stock) is recorded as a credit entry in the ledger account.

Dr	Cost of goods sold	£500
Cr	Inventory (stock) of goods		£500

(b) The business uses gas to heat a water boiler and it is estimated that consumption for the month amounts to £80

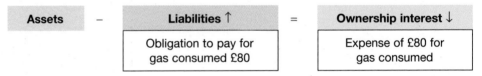

The event of consuming the gas causes the ownership interest to decrease and is recorded as a debit entry in an expense account for gas consumed. The obligation to pay for the gas at a future time is recorded as a credit entry in the ledger account for accruals.

Dr	Expense of gas	£80
Cr	Accruals		£80

The spreadsheet

Table 12.7 contains, in the left-hand pair of debit and credit columns, the trial balance of Table 6.15 from Chapter 6. The next pair of columns contains the debit and credit entries necessary for the end-of-period adjustments. The third pair of columns shows the resulting amounts on each line of income statement (profit and loss account) items. The final pair of columns shows the resulting amounts on each line of statement of financial position (balance sheet) items. The entire spreadsheet could be thought of as a series of ledger accounts stretched across the page, with one line for each ledger account.

The debit and credit entries identified by the foregoing analysis are shown in the adjustments columns of the spreadsheet with identifying letters in brackets alongside. Where no suitably named line exists, a new line may be inserted. The use of a new line is shown here for accruals and the expense of gas. If the exercise is being carried out using a computer spreadsheet package, the insertion of an extra line is not a problem. For a handwritten exercise it may be necessary to leave spaces at possible insertion points.

Once all adjustments have been entered, each of the adjusted amounts can be carried across to one of the final four columns, depending on whether the item belongs to the income statement (profit and loss account) or the statement of financial position

Table 12.7
Trial balance of M. Carter at the end of May, before month-end adjustments

Ledger account title	Trial balance		Adjustments		Income (profit) statement		Statement of financial position	
	Dr	Cr	Dr	Cr	Expense	Revenue	A	L + OI
	£	£	£	£	£	£	£	£
L3 Buildings	30,000						30,000	
L4 Equipment	5,750						5,750	
L5 Inventory (stock) of goods	8,000			500 (a)			7,500	
L11 R. Welsby	nil							
L1 Cash	6,400						6,400	
Accruals				80 (b)				80
L6 R. Busby		nil						
L2 Ownership interest		49,000						49,000
Subtotal	50,150	49,000					49,650	49,080
Difference: profit of the month								570
L10 Sales		7,000				7,000		
L9 Cost of goods sold	3,500		500 (a)		4,000			
L7 Electricity	100				100			
Gas			80 (b)		80			
L8 Wages	2,000				2,000			
L12 Depreciation	250				250			
Subtotal	5,850	7,000	580		6,430	7,000		
Difference: profit of the month					570			
Total of each column	56,000	56,000	580	580	7,000	7,000	49,650	49,650

(balance sheet). Each pair of columns is added and the difference between the totals in the income statement (profit and loss account) columns should equal the difference between the totals in the statement of financial position (balance sheet) columns. If that is not the case, it means that an error has taken place at some point in the spreadsheet and must be found.

Revised statement of profit

The statement of profit before adjustments is shown in section 6.6.2 of Chapter 6 and the statement of financial position (balance sheet) is in section 6.6.3. From the final four columns of the spreadsheet in Table 12.7, these could now be restated as follows:

M. Carter, Wholesaler
Income statement (profit and loss account) (adjusted)
for the month of May Year XX

	£	£
Revenue (sales)		7,000
Cost of goods sold		(4,000)
Gross profit		3,000
Other expenses		
Wages	(2,000)	
Electricity	(100)	
Gas	(80)	
Depreciation	(250)	
		(2,430)
Net profit		570

Statement of financial position (balance sheet)

M. Carter, Wholesaler
Statement of financial position (balance sheet) (adjusted) at 31 May Year XX

	£
Non-current (fixed) assets	
Buildings	30,000
Equipment	6,000
	36,000
Depreciation	(250)
Total non-current (fixed) assets	35,750
Current assets	
Inventory (stock)	7,500
Cash at bank	6,400
Total current assets	13,900
Total assets	49,650
Accruals	(80)
Net assets	49,570
Ownership interest	
Capital at start	50,000
Add profit	570
Less drawings	(1,000)
Total ownership interest	49,570

This completes the study of double-entry bookkeeping in this book. You are now in a position to be able to carry out the following tasks in relation to the business of a sole trader:

- record transactions in ledger accounts
- prepare a trial balance
- make end-of-period adjustments to the trial balance
- prepare an income statement (profit and loss account) and statement of financial position (balance sheet).

S | Test your understanding

S12.1 (a) Using the information provided in question C12.1, prepare a spreadsheet containing a trial balance, adjustment and resulting figures for income statement (profit and loss account) and statement of financial position (balance sheet) items. (Table 12.7 provides a pattern to follow.)

(b) Present the income statement (profit and loss account) for the year and the statement of financial position (balance sheet) at the end of the year in an informative and useful manner.

Part 4

Analysis and issues in reporting

Chapter 13

Ratio analysis

REAL WORLD CASE

Key performance indicators (Tesco plc Annual report 2012)

Our KPIs measure how we are doing across the Group in terms of both operational and financial performance in the context of the key elements of our strategy.

More detailed definitions for our Group performance and Group financial KPIs can be found in the glossary on the inside back cover.

All KPIs exclude the results from our operation in Japan for 2011/12 unless stated otherwise.

Alamy Images/Aardvark

Group performance

Growth in underlying profit before tax

1.6%

08/09	09/10	10/11	11/12
9.8%*	8.7%	12.3%	1.6%

Definition
Our underlying profit provides information on the underlying trend and performance of the business. It is adjusted for a number of (non-cash) accounting adjustments and one-off costs.

Performance
We saw modest progress in the year, with the rate of improvement impacted by two events: the Hungary crisis tax (£38 million) and the increase in provision for Payment Protection Insurance ('PPI') in Tesco Bank (£57 million). Growth before these impacts was 5.4%.

* Restated for IFRS 2 and IFRIC 13.

Return on Capital Employed ('ROCE')

13.3%

12.9% 13.3%

10/11 11/12

14.6%

14/15
TARGET

Definition
ROCE is a relative profit measurement that demonstrates the return the business is generating from its gross assets.

Performance
Although our UK performance was weaker than planned, ROCE improved by 40 basis points, benefiting from Japan now being classified as a discontinued operation.

Growth in underlying diluted earnings per share (at a constant tax rate)

2.1%

08/09	09/10	10/11	11/12
11.0%	7.7%	10.8%	2.1%

Definition
Underlying diluted earnings per share ('EPS') is the amount of underlying profit, adjusted for the number of shares in issue.

Performance
The growth in underlying diluted EPS reflects modest progress in earnings in the year. The proposed full year dividend per share grew by 2.1%, in line with this, to 14.76p, continuing our unrivalled record of consecutive years of dividend growth in the FTSE 100.

Group financial ratios

Total shareholder return ('TSR')

08/09	09/10	10/11	11/12
8.0%	9.5%	6.7%	(3.0)%

Definition
TSR is the notional annualised return from a share: the percentage change in the share price, plus the dividends paid and reinvested, over the last five years. For example, five-year TSR for 11/12 is the annualised growth in the share price from 06/07 and dividends paid and reinvested in Tesco shares, as a percentage of the 06/07 share price.

Performance
Returns reduced reflecting the effect on our share price of our decision to invest significantly in the customer offer in the UK.

Capital expenditure ('capex') % of sales

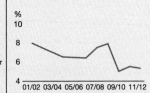
%
10

8

6

4
01/02 03/04 05/06 07/08 09/10 11/12

Definition
Capex is the investment in property, plant and equipment, investment property and intangible assets. This is divided by Group sales (inc. VAT, inc. petrol) to show a relative investment to sales.

Performance
This year we reduced our rate of capital investment to reflect the challenging trading environment and increased our focus on lower capital-intensive investments with high returns, such as online and convenience.

Last year we set a target of 5% to 5.5% of sales. We will reduce capex to £3.3 billion in 12/13 and, beyond that, comfortably less than 5.0% of sales.

Source: Tesco plc Annual Report 2012 (pp. 29–30).

Discussion points

1 What does the reader learn from the ratios and performance measures presented in the extract?

2 What other ratios could provide additional information about the company's performance?

Contents

Learning outcomes

After reading this chapter you should be able to:

- Define, calculate and interpret ratios that help analyse and understand (a) performance for investors, (b) management performance, (c) liquidity and working capital and (d) gearing.
- Explain investors' views of the balance of risk and return, and the risks of investing in a geared company when profits are fluctuating.
- Explain how the pyramid of ratios helps integrate interpretation.
- Describe the uses and limitations of ratio analysis.
- Carry out a practical exercise of calculating and interpreting ratios.

13.1 Introduction

Ratios are widely used as a tool in the interpretation of financial statements. The ratios selected and the use of the resulting information depend on the needs of the person using the information. What investors really want to do is choose the best moment to sell shares when the share price is at its highest. To choose that best moment, the investors will monitor the company's performance. Bankers lending to the company will also monitor performance, and look for indicators of solvency and ability to repay interest and capital.

Many users will rely on others to monitor ratios on their behalf. Employees will look to their advisers, perhaps union officials, to monitor performance. Small private investors with limited resources will rely heavily on articles in the financial sections of newspapers. Professional fund managers will look to their own research resources and may also make use of the analysts' reports prepared by the brokers who act for the fund managers in buying and selling shares. Each broker's analyst seeks as much information as possible about a company so that he or she can sell information which is of better quality than that of any other broker's analyst. There is fierce competition to be a highly rated analyst because that brings business to the broking firm and high rewards for the analyst.

In monitoring performance the expert analysts and fund managers will use ratios rather than absolute amounts. A figure of £100m for sales (revenue) means nothing in isolation. The reader who knows that last year's sales (revenue) amounted to £90m sees immediately an increase of 11.1%. The reader who knows that fixed (non-current) assets remained constant at £75m knows that the fixed (non-current) assets this year have earned their value in sales (revenue) 1.33 times (100/75 = 1.33) whereas last year they earned their value in sales (revenue) 1.2 times (90/75 = 1.2). Ratios show changes in relationships of figures which start to create a story and start to generate questions. They do not provide answers.

The fund managers and analysts all have their own systems for calculating ratios and some keep these a carefully guarded secret so that each may hopefully see an important clue before the next person does so. That means there is no standard system of ratio analysis. There are, however, several which are used frequently. A selection of these will be used here as a basic framework for analysis. As you start to read more about company accounts you will find other ratios used but you should discover that those are largely refinements of the structure presented here.

13.2 A note on terminology

Ratio analysis is not a standardised exercise. It is often taught in finance courses and management accounting courses as well as in financial accounting courses. Businesses use ratios to describe their own performance. There is a tendency towards creating ratios that suit the purpose and towards using descriptions that are personal choices of the presenter. This chapter gives commonly used names for ratios (such as 'gross profit percentage') and links these to the terminology of the IASB system of accounting by using additional descriptions in brackets. For example, the title 'gross profit percentage' is used as a name for a ratio and it is defined as follows:

$$\frac{\text{Gross profit}}{\text{Sales (revenue)}} \times 100\%$$

In the denominator of this ratio the word 'sales' describes the activity that creates gross profit; the additional word (revenue) in brackets reminds you that the information will be found in financial statements under 'revenue'. Similarly 'fixed assets (non-current assets)' uses the commonly established words 'fixed assets' with the addition of (non-current assets) in brackets to remind you of where the information will be found in the statement of financial position (balance sheet).

13.3 Systematic approach to ratio analysis

A systematic approach to ratio analysis seeks to establish a broad picture first of all, and then break that broad picture down until there are thumbnail sketches of interesting areas. Four key headings commonly encountered in ratio analysis are:

1 *Investor ratios*. Ratios in this category provide some measure of how the price of a share in the stock market compares to key indicators of the performance of the company.
2 *Analysis of management performance*. Ratios in this category indicate how well the company is being run in terms of using assets to generate sales (revenue) and how effective it is in controlling costs and producing profit based on goods and services sold.
3 *Liquidity and current assets*. The management of cash and current assets and the preservation of an adequate, but not excessive, level of liquidity is an essential feature of business survival especially in difficult economic circumstances.
4 *Gearing (referred to in American texts as 'leverage')*. Gearing is a measure of the extent to which there is financial risk indicated in the statement of financial position (balance sheet) and in the income statement (profit and loss account) (see section 13.4 on risk and return). Financial risk means the risk associated with having to pay interest and having an obligation to repay a loan.

In the following sections key ratios for each of these aspects of a systematic analysis are specified by the name of the ratio and the definition in words. Below each definition there is a brief discussion of the meaning and interpretation of the ratio.

13.3.1 Investor ratios

Investors who buy shares in a company want to be able to compare the benefit from the investment with the amount they have paid, or intend to pay, for their shares. There are two measures of benefit to the investors. One is the profit of the period (usually given the name **earnings** when referring to the profit available for equity holders (ordinary shareholders)). The other is the **dividend** which is an amount of cash that is paid to the shareholders. Profit indicates wealth created by the business. That wealth may be accumulated in the business or else paid out in the form of dividend. Four ratios are presented with a comment on each.

Earnings per share	$\dfrac{\text{Profit after tax for ordinary equity holders}}{\text{Number of issued ordinary shares}}$

Comment. **Earnings per share** is the most frequently quoted measure of company performance and progress. The percentage change from year to year should be monitored for the trend. Criticisms are that this strong focus on annual earnings may cause 'short-termism' among investors and among company managers. The IASB would like to turn the attention of preparers and users of accounts away from reliance on earnings per share as a single performance measure, but the earnings per share remains a strong feature of comments on company results.

You may also see 'fully diluted earnings per share'. This is explained in section 11.6.4.

Price–earnings ratio	$\dfrac{\text{Share price}}{\text{Earnings per share}}$

Comment. The **price–earnings ratio** (often abbreviated to 'p/e ratio') compares the amount invested in one share with the earnings per share. It may be interpreted as the number of years for which the currently reported profit is represented by the current share price. The p/e ratio reflects the market's confidence in future prospects of the company. The higher the ratio, the longer is the period for which the market believes the current level of earnings may be sustained.

In order to gain some feeling for the relative magnitude of the p/e ratio of any individual company, it should be compared with the average p/e ratio for the industry, given daily in the *Financial Times*. The p/e ratio is quite commonly used as a key item of input information in investment decisions or recommendations.

Dividend per share	$\dfrac{\text{Dividend of the period}}{\text{Number of issued ordinary shares}}$

Comment. The **dividend** per share is one of the key measures announced by the company at the end of the financial year (and sometimes as an interim dividend during the year as well). Shareholders immediately know how much to expect in total dividend, depending on the number of shares held. The figure of dividend per share is the cash amount paid by the company. It may or may not be subject to tax in the hands of the recipient, depending on whether or not the recipient is a taxpayer.

The dividend of the period is equal to any interim dividend paid plus the final recommended dividend (see section 12.7). To find the recommended dividend you will have to look beyond the financial statements. The Directors' Report will contain a note on the recommended dividend which is to be paid to shareholders following their agreement at the annual general meeting. There may also be a description of the recommended dividend in the Chairman's Statement, or a Highlights Statement, or the Operating and Financial Review (OFR).

Dividend cover (payout ratio)	$\dfrac{\text{Earnings per share}}{\text{Dividend per share}}$
Also calculated as	$\dfrac{\text{Profit after tax for ordinary equity holders}}{\text{Total dividend for ordinary equity holders}}$

Comment. Companies need cash to enable them to pay dividends. For most companies the profits of the business must generate that cash, so the dividend decision could be regarded as a two-stage question. The first part is, 'Have we made sufficient profits?' and the second stage is, 'Has that profit generated cash which is not needed for reinvestment in fixed or current assets?' The **dividend cover** helps in answering the first of these questions. It shows the number of times the dividend has been covered by the profits (earnings) of this year. It could be said that the higher the dividend cover, the 'safer' is the dividend. On the other hand, it could be argued that a high dividend cover means that the company is keeping new wealth to itself, perhaps to be used in buying new assets, rather than dividing it among the shareholders.

The dividend policy of the company is a major decision for the board of directors. Many companies like to keep to a 'target' dividend cover with only minor fluctuations from one year to the next. The evidence from finance research is that company managers have two targets, one being the stability of the dividend cover but the other being a desire to see the dividend per share increase, or at least remain stationary, rather than decrease. Dividends are thought to carry a signal to the market of the strength and stability of the company.

Dividend yield	$\dfrac{\text{Dividend per share}}{\text{Share price}} \times 100\%$

Comment. The **dividend yield** is a very simple ratio comparing dividend per share with the current market price of a share. It indicates the relationship between what the investor can expect to receive from the shares and the amount which is invested in the shares. Many investors need income from investments and the dividend yield is an important factor in their decision to invest in, or remain in, a company. It has to be noted that dividends are not the only benefit from share ownership. Section 13.4 on risk and return presents a formula for return (yield) which takes into account the growth in share price as well as the dividend paid. Investors buy shares in expectation of an increase in the share price. The directors of many companies would take the view that the dividend yield should be adequate to provide an investment income, but it is the wealth arising from retained profits that is used for investment in new assets which in turn generate growth in future profits.

13.3.2 Analysis of management performance

Management of a business is primarily a function requiring **stewardship**, meaning careful use of resources for the benefit of the owners. There are two central questions to test this use of resources:

1 How well did the management make use of the investment in assets to create sales (revenue)?
2 How carefully did the management control costs so as to maximise the profit derived from the sales (revenue)?

Return on shareholders' equity	$\dfrac{\text{Profit after tax for ordinary equity holders}}{\text{Share capital} + \text{Reserves}} \times 100\%$

Comment. A key measure of success, from the viewpoint of shareholders, is the success of the company in using the funds provided by shareholders to generate profit. That profit will provide new wealth to cover their **dividend** and to finance future expansion of the business. The **return on shareholders' equity** is therefore a measure of company performance from the shareholders' perspective. It is essential in this calculation to use the profit for ordinary equity holders, which is the profit after interest charges and after tax. The formula uses the phrase **equity** holders which will probably be the wording that you see in the financial statements. It has the same meaning as ordinary shareholders.

Return on capital employed	$\dfrac{\text{Operating profit (before interest and tax)}}{\text{Total assets} - \text{Current liabilities}} \times 100\%$

Return on capital employed	$\dfrac{\text{Operating profit (before interest and tax)}}{\text{Ordinary share capital} + \text{reserves} + \text{long-term loans}} \times 100\%$

Comment. **Return on capital employed** (ROCE) is a broader measure than return on shareholders' equity. ROCE measures the performance of a company as a whole in using all sources of long-term finance. Profit before interest and tax is used in the numerator as a measure of operating results. It is sometime called 'earnings before interest and tax' and is abbreviated to EBIT. Return on capital employed is often seen as a measure of management efficiency. The denominator can be written in two ways, as shown in the alternative formulae. Think about the accounting equation and rearrange it to read:

Total assets – current liabilities = Ordinary share capital plus
reserves plus long-term loans

The ratio is a measure of how well the long-term finance is being used to generate operating profits.

Return on total assets	$\dfrac{\text{Operating profit (before interest and tax)}}{\text{Total assets}} \times 100\%$

Comment. Calculating the **return on total assets** is another variation on measuring how well the assets of the business are used to generate operating profit before deducting interest and tax.

Operating profit as % of sales (revenue)	$\dfrac{\text{Operating profit (before interest and tax)}}{\text{Sales (revenue)}} \times 100\%$

Comment. The ratio of operating profit as a percentage of sales (revenue) is also referred to as the **operating margin**. The aim of many successful business managers is to make the margin as high as possible. The margin reflects the degree of competitiveness in the market, the economic situation, the ability to differentiate products and the ability to control expenses. At the end of this section it is shown that companies are not obliged to seek high **margins**. Some cannot, because of strong competitive factors. Yet they still make a satisfactory return on capital employed by making efficient use of the equipment held as fixed (non-current) assets.

Gross profit percentage	$\dfrac{\text{Gross profit}}{\text{Sales (revenue)}} \times 100\%$

Comment. The gross profit as a percentage of sales (revenue) is also referred to as the **gross margin**. It has been seen in earlier chapters that the gross profit is equal to sales (revenue) minus all cost of sales. That gross profit may be compared with sales (revenue) as shown above. The gross profit percentage concentrates on costs of making goods and services ready for sale. Small changes in this ratio can be highly significant. There tends to be a view that there is a 'normal' value for the industry or for the product that may be used as a benchmark against which to measure a company's performance.

Because it is such a sensitive measure, many companies try to keep secret from their competitors and customers the detailed breakdown of gross profit for each product line or area of activity. Companies do not want to give competitors any clues on how much to undercut prices and do not want to give customers a chance to complain about excessive profits.

Total assets usage	$\dfrac{\text{Sales (revenue)}}{\text{Total assets}}$

Comment. **Total assets usage** indicates how well a company has used its fixed and current assets to generate sales (revenue). Such a ratio is probably most useful as an indication of trends over a period of years. There is no particular value which is too high or too low but a sudden change would prompt the observer to ask questions.

Fixed assets (non-current assets) usage	$\dfrac{\text{Sales (revenue)}}{\text{Fixed assets (non-current assets)}}$

Comment. **Fixed assets usage** is a similar measure of usage, but one which concentrates on the productive capacity as measured by non-current (fixed) assets, indicates how successful the company is in generating sales (revenue) from fixed assets (non-current assets). The ratio may be interpreted as showing how many £s of sales (revenue) have been generated by each £ of fixed assets. The ratio is usually based on the amount of property, plant and equipment.

13.3.3 Liquidity and working capital

Liquidity is a word which refers to the availability of cash in the near future after taking account of immediate financial commitments. Cash in the near future will be available from bank deposits, cash released by sale of stocks and cash collected from customers. Immediate financial commitments are shown in current liabilities. The first ratio of liquidity is therefore a simple comparison of current assets with current liabilities.

Current ratio	Current assets:Current liabilities

Comment. If the current assets amount to £20m and the current liabilities amount to £10m the company is said, in words, to have 'a current ratio of 2 to 1'. Some commentators abbreviate this by saying 'the current ratio is 2'. Mathematically that is incorrect wording but the listener is expected to know that the words 'to 1' have been omitted from the end of the sentence.

The current ratio indicates the extent to which short-term assets are available to meet short-term liabilities. A current ratio of 2:1 is regarded, broadly speaking, as being a reasonable order of magnitude. As with other ratios, there is no 'best' answer for any particular company and it is the trend in this ratio which is more important. If the ratio is worsening over time, and especially if it falls to less than 1:1, the observer would look closely at the cash flow. A company can survive provided it can meet its obligations as they fall due. Some companies therefore operate on a very tight current ratio because they are able to plan the timing of inflows and outflows of cash quite precisely.

Companies which generate cash on a daily basis, such as retail stores, can therefore operate on a lower current ratio. Manufacturing businesses which have to hold substantial stocks would operate on a higher current ratio.

Acid test	Current assets minus inventories (stock):Current liabilities

Comment. In a crisis, where short-term creditors are demanding payment, the possibility of selling stocks (inventories) to raise cash may be unrealistic. The **acid test** takes a closer look at the liquid assets of the current ratio, omitting the stocks (inventories). For many companies this ratio is less than 1:1 because it is unlikely that all creditors will require payment at the same time. As with the current ratio, an understanding of the acid test has to be supported by an understanding of the pattern of cash flows. Analysts in particular will often ask companies about the peak borrowing requirements of the year and the timing of that peak in relation to cash inflows.

Stock holding period (inventories holding period)	$\dfrac{\text{Average inventories (stock) held}}{\text{Cost sales (revenue)}} \times 365$

Comment. The **stock holding period** (inventories holding period) measures the average period during which stocks (inventories) of goods are held before being sold or used in the operations of the business. It is usually expressed in days, which is why the figure of 365 appears in the formula. If months are preferred, then the figure 12 should be substituted for the figure 365. One point of view is that the shorter the period, the better. An opposite point of view is that too short a period may create a greater risk of finding that the business is short of a stock item.

In calculating the stock holding period it is preferable to use the average of the stock (inventories) held at the start of the year and the stock (inventories) held at the end of the year. Some analysts use only the year-end figure if the start-of-year figure is not available. Whatever variation is used, it is important to be consistent from one time period to the next.

Customers (trade debtors collection period)	$\dfrac{\text{Trade receivables (trade debtors)}}{\text{Credit sales (revenue)}} \times 365$

Comment. The **customers'** (trade debtors') **collection period** measures the average period of credit allowed to credit customers. An increase in this measure would indicate that a company is building up cash flow problems, although an attempt to decrease the period of credit allowed might deter customers and cause them to seek a competitor who gives a longer period of credit. It is important to be aware of the normal credit period for the industry. Some companies offer discount for prompt payment. Any offer of discount should weigh the cost of the discount against the benefit of earlier receipt of cash from customers. When you are looking for information in the annual report of companies using the IASB system you will probably have to start on the face of the statement of financial position (balance sheet) with the heading 'trade and other receivables' and then read the corresponding Note to the statement of financial position (balance sheet) to find the amount of trade receivables. If you are looking at the statement of financial position (balance sheet) of a company that does not use the IASB system you will have to find the Note to the statement of financial position (balance sheet) that gives detailed information about trade debtors.

Suppliers (trade creditors) payment period	$\dfrac{\text{Trade payables (trade creditors)}}{\text{Credit purchases}} \times 365$

Comment. The **suppliers'** (trade creditors') **payment period** measures the average period of credit taken from suppliers of goods and services. An increase in this measure could indicate that the supplier has allowed a longer period to pay. It could also indicate that the company is taking longer to pay, perhaps because of cash flow problems. If payment is delayed then the company may lose discounts available for prompt payments. A reputation for being a slow payer could make it more difficult to obtain supplies in future. Some large companies have gained a reputation for delaying payment to smaller suppliers. Company law now requires company directors to make a statement of policy in relation to creditor payment.

Companies do not usually report **purchases** directly, so the figure must be calculated as follows:

$$\text{Purchases} = \text{Cost of goods sold} + \text{Closing stock} - \text{Opening stock}$$

Analysts often use **cost of goods sold** rather than calculate purchases, arguing that stock levels are broadly similar at corresponding period-ends.

Working capital cycle	Stock (inventories) holding period PLUS Customers (trade debtors) collection period MINUS Suppliers (trade creditors) payment period

Comment. You saw in Chapter 9 (Figure 9.1) the **working capital cycle** whereby stocks (inventories) are purchased on credit, then sold to customers who eventually pay cash. The cash is used to pay suppliers and the cycle starts again. We can now put some timings into the diagram. The working capital represents the long-term finance needed to cover current assets that are not matched by current liabilities. The longer the total of the stock holding period and customer collection period, compared to the suppliers payment period, the greater the need for working capital to be financed long term.

13.3.4 Gearing

The term **gearing** is used to describe the mix of loan finance and equity finance in a company. It is more properly called **financial gearing** and in American texts is called **leverage**. There are two main approaches to measuring gearing. The first looks at the statement of financial position (balance sheet) and the second looks at the income statement (profit and loss account).

Debt/equity ratio	$\dfrac{\text{Long-term liabilities plus Preference share capital*}}{\text{Equity share capital + reserves}} \times 100\%$

* Where preference share capital is in existence.

Comment. From the statement of financial position (balance sheet) perspective the **gearing** measure considers the relative proportions of long-term (non-current) loans and equity in the long-term financing of the business. The precise meaning of long-term liabilities will vary from one company to the next. It is intended to cover the loans taken out with the aim of making them a permanent part of the company's financing policy. As they come due for repayment, they are replaced by further long-term finance. The starting point is the loans (but not the provisions) contained in the section headed *non-current liabilities*. However, the accounting rules require separate reporting of loans due for repayment within one year, reported as current liabilities. It is necessary to look in the *current liabilities* for bank loans that are becoming due for repayment. In some companies the bank overdraft is a semi-permanent feature and so is included in this ratio calculation.

Preference share capital is included in the numerator because it has the characteristics of debt finance even although it is not classed as debt in company law. The preference shareholders have the first right to dividend, before the ordinary shareholders receive any dividend. This is why they are called 'preference' shares. The amount of the dividend is usually fixed as a percentage of nominal value of shares. The amount repaid to preference shareholders on maturity is the amount of the share capital only. They do not normally take a share of accumulated profits.

Some companies say 'we have interest-bearing obligations such as bank overdrafts, long-term liabilities and preference shares but we also have cash and cash equivalents that are earning interest. We prefer to deduct the assets from the liabilities to calculate the **net debt**'. An alternative form of gearing ratio is therefore defined by calculating net debt as all interest-bearing liabilities minus cash and cash equivalents.

Debt/equity ratio	$\dfrac{\text{Net debt}}{\text{Equity share capital + reserves}} \times 100$

Different industries have different average levels, depending on the types of assets held and the stability or otherwise of the stream of profits. A low gearing percentage indicates a low exposure to financial risk because it means that there will be little difficulty in paying loan interest and repaying the loans as they fall due. A high gearing percentage indicates a high exposure to financial risk because it means that there are interest charges to be met and a requirement to repay the loans on the due date.

Interest cover	$\dfrac{\text{Operating profit (before interest and tax)}}{\text{Interest}}$

Comment. The importance of being able to meet interest payments on borrowed funds is emphasised by measuring gearing in terms of the income statement (profit and loss account). If the profit generated before interest and tax is sufficient to give high cover for the interest charges, then it is unlikely that the company is over-committing itself in its borrowing. If the interest cover is falling or is low, then there may be increasing cause for concern.

Activity 13.1	*Write down the name of each ratio given in this section. Close the book and test your knowledge by writing down the formula for each ratio. Then write one sentence for each ratio which explains its purpose. Be sure that you know each ratio and understand its purpose before you proceed with the rest of the chapter.*

13.4 Investors' views on risk and return

Uncertainty about the future means that all investments contain an element of risk. For investors who are averse to risk, there is a fear of income falling below an acceptable level and a fear of losing the capital invested in the company. Given a choice between two investments offering the same expected return, risk-averse investors will choose the least risky investment.

13.4.1 Return

The word **return** has many meanings but for an investor the basic question is, 'What have I gained from owning these shares?' One simple formula which answers that question is:

$$\frac{(Market\ price\ of\ share\ today - Price\ paid\ for\ share) + Dividends\ received}{Price\ paid\ for\ share} \times 100\%$$

Investors in a company which is in a low-risk industry may be willing to accept a low rate of return. Investors in a company which is in a high-risk industry will be seeking a higher rate of return to compensate for the additional risk they take.

Research has shown that share prices react very rapidly to any item of information which is sufficiently important to affect investors' decisions. This phenomenon is sometimes referred to as the **efficient markets hypothesis**, which is a statement that share prices react immediately to make allowance for each new item of information made available. The annual results of a listed company are announced through the Stock Exchange by means of a document called a **preliminary announcement**, issued approximately two months after the accounting year-end. The annual report then goes to the printers and is distributed to shareholders about three months after the related year-end.

When investors evaluate share price by calculating return, they take the most up-to-date price available.

13.4.2 Risk

There are two main types of risk: operating risk and financial risk.

Operating risk exists where there are factors which could cause sales (revenue) to fluctuate or cause costs to increase. Companies are particularly vulnerable to operating risk when they have a relatively high level of fixed operating costs. These fixed costs are incurred independently of the level of activity. If sales (revenue) fall, or the direct costs of sales increase, the fixed costs become a greater burden on profit.

Financial risk exists where the company has loan finance, especially long-term loan finance where the company cannot relinquish its commitment. Loan finance carries an obligation to pay interest charges and these create a problem similar to the fixed costs problem. If the sales (revenue) are strong and the direct costs of sales are well under control, then interest charges will not be a problem. If sales (revenue) fall, or the direct costs of sales rise, then a company may find that it does not have the cash resources to meet the interest payments as they fall due. Repaying the loan could become an even greater worry.

Both operating risk and financial risk are important to the company's shareholders because they have the residual claim on assets after all liabilities are met. If the company's assets are growing then these risks will not pose a problem but if the business becomes slack then the combination of high fixed operating costs and high interest charges could be disastrous. As a rule of thumb, investors look for low financial risk in companies which have high operating risk and, conversely, will tolerate a higher level of financial risk where there is relatively low operating risk.

The terms **operating gearing** and **financial gearing** are frequently used to describe the extent of operating risk and financial risk. (Financial gearing has been explained in the previous section.) In terms of the income statement (profit and loss account) they are defined as follows:

Operating gearing	$\dfrac{\text{Profit before fixed operating costs}}{\text{Fixed operating costs}}$

Financial gearing	$\dfrac{\text{Profit before interest charges}}{\text{Interest charges}}$

In analysis of published accounting information, it is not possible to estimate the operating gearing because detailed information on fixed costs is not provided. Thus the term **gearing** is applied only in measuring financial gearing. Despite the lack of published information, professional investors will be aware of the importance of operating gearing and will try to understand as much as possible about the cost structure of the company and of the industry. The next section illustrates the benefits to shareholders of having gearing present when operating profits are rising and the risks when operating profits are falling.

13.4.3 Impact of gearing when profits are fluctuating

In a situation of fluctuating profits the presence of a fixed charge, such as an interest payment, will cause the profit for ordinary shareholders to fluctuate by a greater percentage. Table 13.1 sets out data to illustrate this fluctuation. Company X has no gearing but company Y has loan finance in its capital structure.

Table 13.2 uses the data to ask 'what happens to earnings per share if there is an increase or a decrease in operating profit?'

The conclusion to be drawn from Table 13.2, panels (a) and (b), is that a 20% increase or decrease in operating profit causes a corresponding 20% increase or decrease in profit for ordinary shareholders in the ungeared company but a 40% increase or decrease in profit for ordinary shareholders in the geared company. It would appear preferable to be a shareholder in a geared company when profits are rising but to be a shareholder in an ungeared company when profits are falling.

13.5 Pyramid of ratios

The various ratios which contribute to the analysis of management performance may be thought of as forming a pyramid, as in Figure 13.1.

Table 13.1
Data to illustrate the effect of gearing on profits for ordinary shareholders

	X plc £m	Y plc £m
Summary statement of financial position (balance sheet)		
Total assets minus current liabilities	1,000	1,000
Ordinary shares (£1 nominal value per share)	1,000	500
Loan stock (10% per annum)	–	500
	1,000	1,000
Expected level of profit		
Operating profit	100	100
Interest	–	(50)
Net profit for ordinary shareholders (A)	100	50

Table 13.2
Fluctuations in profit

	X plc	Y plc
(a) Effect of 20% decrease in operating profit		
Operating profit	80	80
Interest		(50)
Net profit for ordinary shareholders (B)	80	30
Percentage decrease of (B) on (A)	20%	40%
(b) Effect of 20% increase in operating profit		
Operating profit	120	120
Interest	–	(50)
Net profit for ordinary shareholders (C)	120	70
Percentage increase of (C) on (A)	20%	40%

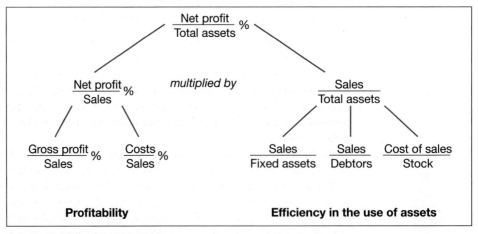

Figure 13.1
Pyramid of ratios for analysis of management performance

At the apex is the **return on capital employed** (measuring capital employed here as total assets). As the pyramid spreads out there are more detailed explanations of how the pyramid is built up. Net profit as a percentage of total assets has two components. One is the net profit as a percentage of sales (revenue) and the other is sales (revenue) as a multiple of total assets. Multiply these two together and you return to the net profit as a percentage of total assets. This relationship indicates that there could be two quite different types of business, both of which may be highly successful. One business trades on low margins, charging prices which look highly competitive, and succeeds by having a high level of sales (revenue) so that the assets are being used very effectively. The other business trades on high margins and sells goods or services less frequently. You could contrast the discount furniture store on the outskirts of town, where the car park is always full and the prices are unbeatable, with the old-world charm of the retail furnisher in the town centre whose prices look high but which attracts customers preferring extra service and attention. Both businesses are able to earn sufficient return on total assets to satisfy the owners.

The pyramid then spreads out into two areas: profitability and efficiency in the use of assets. The relationships here are additive – each component explains a little of the profitability of sales (revenue) or the efficiency in the use of assets. The pyramid is a useful tool of detective work to trace the cause of a change in return on capital employed.

13.6 Use and limitations of ratio analysis

The important feature of ratios is that they indicate trends and deviations from expected patterns. Ratios taken in isolation for a single company or a single period of time are of limited usefulness. The first requirement is to find a benchmark against which to compare ratios calculated for one period only.

13.6.1 Evaluating ratios by comparison

The comparison could be made with any or all of:

- the company's prior expectations of the outcome
- external observers' prior expectations of the outcome
- ratios based on previous years' figures for this company
- ratios calculated from this year's figures for other companies
- ratios calculated from previous years' figures for other companies
- industry averages published by commercial organisations.

The company's prior expectations are set out in a budget which is usually kept confidential. It is therefore unlikely that the user of the financial statements will have access to such a high-quality source of comparison. External observers may also have prior expectations. Professional analysts make forecasts of profits to help them or their clients in making investment decisions. The forecasts may be sent to clients of professional advisers, by way of investment advice bulletins. There are directories which publish such forecasts.

In the absence of information based on expectations, the user of the annual report may have to rely on the past as a possible predictor of the future, or on comparisons with other companies and industry norms. Professional investment advisers will collect data from annual reports and calculate ratios in their preferred manner. Advisory services will process the information and sell the results in the form of directories, online search facilities or CD-ROM with regular updates. One of the most widely used sources of ratio analysis of company accounts is Datastream, available in many colleges and universities and also used commercially. Organisations such as Reuters publish regular analyses of company information but usually charge a commercial fee. Newspapers and weekly journals such as the *Financial Times* and the *Investors Chronicle* are yet another source of information which will include ratios.

It could be argued that companies should themselves publish the norms against which their own particular results may be compared, but most would claim that their business is unique and no comparisons would be entirely valid.

13.6.2 Limitations

No two companies are exactly alike in the nature of their operations. Comparisons must make allowances for differences in the types of business or the relative weighting of different types of business. Many companies operate in more than one industry so that comparison with industry norms has to be treated with care.

Accounting numbers are used in ratio analysis and it has been a theme of the preceding chapters that accounting numbers may be affected by different accounting policies. The most common causes of variation due to accounting policy differences lie in depreciation and stock valuation, both of which are highly subjective.

Ratios are primarily a starting point from which to identify further questions to ask about the present position and future directions of the operations and the financing of a company. They do not provide answers in themselves.

13.7 Worked example of ratio analysis

In the following worked example, information is provided about a company buying and selling television and video equipment. Data are given for the current year in the first pair of columns and there are comparative figures for the previous year in the second pair of columns. Ratios are calculated for the two years as an indication of trends. Tentative comments are provided as to the possible interpretation of the resulting figures.

13.7.1 Financial statements to be analysed

Peter (Television) plc
Income statement (profit and loss account)
for the year ended 31 December Year 2

	Year 2		Year 1	
	£m	£m	£m	£m
Revenue		720		600
Cost of sales		(432)		(348)
Gross profit		288		252
Distribution costs	(72)		(54)	
Administrative expenses	(87)		(81)	
		(159)		(135)
Operating profit		129		117
Interest payable		(24)		(24)
Profit before taxation		105		93
Taxation		(42)		(37)
Profit for the period for ordinary equity holders		63		56

Statement of financial position (balance sheet)
as at 31 December Year 2

	£m	£m	£m	£m
Non-current (fixed) assets:				
Land and buildings		600		615
Plant and equipment		555		503
Total non-current assets		1,155		1,118
Current assets:				
Inventories (stock)		115		82
Trade receivables (debtors)		89		61
Prepayments		10		9
Bank		6		46
Total current assets		220		198
Total assets		1,375		1,316

Current liabilities		
Trade payables (creditors)	(45)	(30)
Taxation	(21)	(19)
Accruals	(29)	(25)
Total current liabilities	(95)	(74)
6% debentures	(400)	(400)
Total liabilities	(495)	(474)
Net assets	880	842
Ordinary shares of £1 each	500	500
Retained earnings	380	342
Share capital and reserves	880	842

Extract from directors' report

The directors propose a dividend of 6.0 pence per share in respect of Year 2 (Year 1: 5.0 pence), amounting to £30m in total (Year 1: £25m).

Notes to the financial statements: reconcilation of movements in equity

	£m
Share capital and reserves at the end of year 1	842
Less dividend paid in respect of year 1	(25)
Add profit for year 2	63
Share capital and reserves at the end of year 2	880

13.7.2 Share price information

When investors evaluate share price, they take the most up-to-date price available. However, for the exercise of comparing financial ratios it is useful to take the share prices immediately after the preliminary announcement at the end of February or beginning of March, representing the market's opinion when the accounting information has not become too much out of date.

Market price at 1 March Year 2	202 pence
Market price at 1 March Year 3	277 pence

13.7.3 Presenting the ratio calculations

Because there are so many variations on the methods of calculating ratios in accounting, it is extremely important to practise a useful and informative layout. That must include, at a minimum:

- the name of each ratio
- the formula in words
- the workings to show how the formula has been applied
- the value of the ratio
- a narrative comment.

Tables 13.3 to 13.6 present this information in a set of ratio calculations for Peter (Television) plc, each exhibit covering one of the main headings explained earlier. The calculations are given first for the more recent year, Year 2, followed by the comparative figures for Year 1. A commentary is provided for each table.

Activity 13.2

Use the ratios explained in section 13.6 to carry out a full analysis of the Year 2 column of the accounts of Peter (Television) plc. Prepare your analysis before you read Tables 13.3 to 13.6. When you have finished, compare your analysis with the ratios calculated. Where your answers differ, be sure that you understand whether it is due to an arithmetic error or a more fundamental point. Keep a note of your score of the number of items calculated correctly.

Then go back to Year 1 and repeat the exercise. Hopefully your score of correct items will have increased.

Table 13.3
Investor ratios

Ratio	Definition in words	Year 2		Year 1	
		Workings	Result	Workings	Result
Earnings per share	$\dfrac{\text{Profit after tax for ordinary equity holders}}{\text{Number of issued ordinary shares}}$	$\dfrac{63}{500}$	12.6p	$\dfrac{56}{500}$	11.2p
Price earnings ratio	$\dfrac{\text{Share price}}{\text{Earnings per share}}$	$\dfrac{277}{12.6}$	22	$\dfrac{202}{11.2}$	18
Dividend per share	$\dfrac{\text{Dividend of the period}}{\text{Number of issued ordinary shares}}$	$\dfrac{30}{500}$	6.0p	$\dfrac{25}{500}$	5.0p
Dividend cover (payout ratio)	$\dfrac{\text{Earnings per share}}{\text{Dividend per share}}$	$\dfrac{12.6}{6.0}$	2.1 times	$\dfrac{11.2}{5.0}$	2.24 times
Dividend yield	$\dfrac{\text{Dividend per share}}{\text{Share price}} \times 100$	$\dfrac{6.0}{277} \times 100\%$	2.17%	$\dfrac{5.0}{202} \times 100\%$	2.48%

Comment. Earnings per share increased over the period, indicating an improved profit performance for shareholders. The price earnings ratio rose, indicating greater confidence in the stock market about the sustainability of this new level of profit. The dividend cover has fallen marginally, but is still more than twice covered. This marginal decrease in dividend cover is caused by increasing the dividend per share from 5 pence to 6 pence. The dividend yield has fallen, despite the increased dividend per share, because the market price has risen. The fall in yield may not be significant if it reflects a general trend in the market where, possibly, all shares have risen in price over the year. To say anything more about these ratios requires comparative figures for the industry and for the market as a whole. Both types of data would be found in the *Financial Times*.

Table 13.4
Analysis of management performance

Ratio	Definition in words	Year 2			Year 1		
		Workings	Result		Workings	Result	
Return on shareholders' equity	$\dfrac{\text{Profit after tax for ordinary equity holders}}{\text{Share capital + Reserves}} \times 100\%$	$\dfrac{63}{880} \times 100\%$	7.2%		$\dfrac{56}{842} \times 100\%$	6.7%	
Return on capital employed	$\dfrac{\text{Operating profit (before interest and tax)}}{\text{(Total assets − Current liabilities)}} \times 100\%$	$\dfrac{129}{1,280} \times 100\%$	10.1%		$\dfrac{117}{1,242} \times 100\%$	9.4%	
Operating profit on sales (revenue)	$\dfrac{\text{Operating profit (before interest and tax)}}{\text{Sales (revenue)}} \times 100\%$	$\dfrac{129}{720} \times 100\%$	17.9%		$\dfrac{117}{600} \times 100\%$	19.5%	
Gross profit percentage	$\dfrac{\text{Gross profit}}{\text{Sales (revenue)}} \times 100\%$	$\dfrac{288}{720} \times 100\%$	40%		$\dfrac{252}{600} \times 100\%$	42%	
Total assets usage	$\dfrac{\text{Sales (revenue)}}{\text{Total assets}} \times 100\%$	$\dfrac{720}{(1,155 + 220)}$	0.52 times		$\dfrac{600}{(1,118 + 198)}$	0.46 times	
Fixed assets (non-current assets) usage	$\dfrac{\text{Sales (revenue)}}{\text{Fixed assets (non-current assets)}} \times 100\%$	$\dfrac{720}{1,155}$	0.62 times		$\dfrac{600}{1,118}$	0.54 times	

Comment. The return on shareholders' equity and the return on capital employed both show an improvement on the previous year. This is due to an improvement in the use of assets (total assets and fixed assets) which more than offsets a fall in the operating profit as a percentage of sales (revenue). The gross profit percentage fell by a similar amount, which suggests that the price charged for goods and services is not keeping pace with increases in costs. The company should look carefully at either increasing prices or attempting to control costs of goods sold more effectively.

Table 13.5
Liquidity and working capital

Ratio	Definition in words	Year 2		Year 1	
		Workings	Result	Workings	Result
Current ratio	Current assets:Current liabilities	220:95	2.3:1	198:74	2.7:1
Acid test	(Current assets – inventories):Current liabilities	(220 – 115):95	1.11:1	(198 – 82):74	1.11:1
Stock holding period (inventories holding period)	$\dfrac{\text{Average inventories (stock) held}}{\text{Cost of sales}} \times 365$	$\dfrac{(115 + 82)/2}{432} \times 365$	83.2 days	$\dfrac{(*82 + 82)/2}{348} \times 365$	86 days
Customers (trade debtors) collection period	$\dfrac{\text{Trade receivables (trade debtors)}}{\text{Credit sales (revenue)}} \times 365$	$\dfrac{89}{720} \times 365$	45.1 days	$\dfrac{61}{600} \times 365$	37.1 days
Suppliers (trade creditors) payment period	$\dfrac{\text{Trade payables (trade creditors)}}{\text{Credit purchases}} \times 365$	$\dfrac{45}{432 + 115 - 82} \times 365$	35.3 days	$\dfrac{30}{348 + 82 - *82} \times 365$	31.5 days

Note: * Assuming the opening inventories are the same as the closing inventories.

Comment. The current ratio has fallen over the period while the acid test ratio remains constant. The ratios appear relatively high and are probably still within acceptable ranges (although this needs to be confirmed by comparison with industry norms). One cause of the relatively high current ratio at the start and end of the period appears to be in the combination of stock holding period and customers collection period compared to the suppliers payment period. The period of credit taken by customers has increased and this should be investigated as a matter of urgency. There is a marginal decrease in the stock holding period but it remains relatively long, compared to the creditors payment period. The acid test remains similar because there is an increase in the number of customer days for payment and a similar increase in the number of supplier days for payment.

Table 13.6
Gearing (leverage)

Ratio	Definition in words	Year 2		Year 1	
		Workings	Result	Workings	Result
Debt/equity ratio	$\dfrac{\text{Long-term liabilities plus Preference share capital}}{\text{Equity share capital + reserves}} \times 100\%$	$\dfrac{400}{880} \times 100\%$	45.5%	$\dfrac{400}{842} \times 100\%$	47.5%
Interest cover	$\dfrac{\text{Operating profit (before interest and tax)}}{\text{Interest}} \times 100\%$	$\dfrac{129}{24}$	5.38 times	$\dfrac{117}{24}$	4.88 times

Comment. Gearing in the statement of financial position (balance sheet) has remained almost constant and the interest cover has increased marginally. The relative stability of the position indicates that there is probably no cause for concern but the ratios should be compared with those for similar companies in the industry.

13.8 Linking ratios to the statement of cash flows

In Chapter 7 the statement of cash flows of a company was illustrated and discussed. Any ratio analysis which seeks to interpret liquidity, management performance or financial structure should be related to the information provided by the statement of cash flows. Ratios give a measure of position at a particular point in time while the statement of cash flows gives some understanding of the movements in cash and cash-related items.

The operating cash flow will be explained by a note showing the movements in working capital and these may usefully be linked to changes in the rate of movement of stock or the period of credit allowed to customers and taken from suppliers. The ratio will give the change in terms of number of days, while the statement of cash flows will indicate the overall impact on liquid resources.

If the efficiency in the use of fixed assets appears to have fallen, it may be that new assets were acquired during the year which, at the statement of financial position (balance sheet) date, were not fully effective in generating sales. That acquisition will appear in the statement of cash flows. If the gearing has changed, the impact on cash flow will be revealed in the statement of cash flows.

Activity 13.3

Read again the sections of Chapters 3, 4 and 7 on statements of cash flows. What is the purpose of the statement of cash flows? What are the main headings? Which ratios may be used in conjunction with the statement of cash flows to help understand the financial position of the company?

13.8.1 Explanation of a statement of cash flows

The statement of cash flows in Table 13.7 is calculated from the statements of financial position (balance sheets) and income statement (profit and loss account) of Peter (Television) plc (see section 13.6). It is presented using headings similar to those of Safe and Sure in Chapter 7. The headings are taken from the international accounting standard IAS 7.

In Chapters 3, 5 and 6 you saw simple statements of cash flows prepared using the information entered in the cash column of a spreadsheet. Those were examples of what is called the **direct method** of preparing a statement of cash flows because the figures came directly from the cash column of the transaction spreadsheet. The statement of cash flows in Table 13.7 is said to be prepared using the **indirect method** because it takes an indirect route of starting with an accruals-based profit figure and then making adjustments to arrive at the cash figure. Consider each line in turn.

One purpose of the statement of cash flows is to answer the question, 'Why do we have a cash problem despite making an operating profit?' We saw in Table 3.7 of Chapter 3 that profit and cash flow can be different because the cash generated in making a profit is spent in various ways. The statement of cash flows emphasises ways in which cash has come into, or moved out of, the company. So we start with profit before taxation of £129m.

Depreciation is an expense in the income statement (profit and loss account) which represents cost being shared across accounting periods. There is no cash flow and so there should be no deduction for this item. To correct the position, depreciation of £50m is 'added back' as an adjustment to the accounting profit.

Next we consider how changes in working capital have affected cash flow. Looking first at current assets, we find that the inventories (stocks) have increased from £82m to £115m. Allowing inventories (stocks) to increase has reduced the cash available for other purposes. Trade receivables (debtors) have increased from £61 to £89. This

Table 13.7
Statement of Cash flows

Peter (Television) plc
Statement of cash flows
for the year ended 31 December Year 2

Notes: assume depreciation charge for year is £50m.
No non-current (fixed) assets were sold.

The words and figures printed in italics are not normally shown in published statements of cash flows – they are to help you with interpretation.

	£m	£m
Cash flows from operating activities		
Profit before taxation		129
Adjustment for items not involving a flow of cash:		
Depreciation		50
		179
Increase in inventories (stocks) *(115 – 82)*	33	
Increase in trade receivables (debtors) *(89 – 61)*	28	
Increase in prepayments *(10 – 9)*	1	
Reduction in cash due to increases in current assets	62	
Increase in trade payables (creditors) *(45 – 30)*	(15)	
Increase in accruals *(29 – 25)*	(4)	
Increase in cash due to increases in liabilities	(19)	
Reduction in cash due to working capital changes		(43)
Cash generated from operations		136
Interest paid		(24)
Taxes paid *(42 + 19 – 21)*		(40)
Net cash inflow from operating activities		72
Cash flows from investing activities		
Capital expenditure *(1,155 – 1,118 + 50)*		(87)
		(15)
Cash flows from financing activities		
Equity dividends paid (dividend proposed at end of Year 1)		(25)
Decrease in cash		(40)
Check in statement of financial position (balance sheet)		
Decrease in bank (46 – 6) = 40		

---

means the cash is flowing less fast and so cash is reducing. Prepayments have increased from £9m to £10m. This is also using up cash. In total the increases in current assets have used up £62m of the cash generated in making profit.

Looking next at current liabilities, we see that trade payables (creditors) have increased from £30m to £45m. If payables (creditors) are increasing, it means they are not being paid. This helps cash flow by not spending it. Accruals have increased by £4m, again helping cash flow by not making a payment. It is not a good idea to help cash flow indefinitely by not paying creditors, but where stocks and debtors are expanding to use up cash flow, it is helpful if current liabilities are expanding in a similar way to hold back cash flow.

Interest paid is taken from the income statement (profit and loss account) as £24m. There is no liability for unpaid interest at either the start or end of the period so the amount in the income statement (profit and loss account) must equal the amount paid.

The taxation payment involves more calculation. Cash has been required to meet the liability of £19m remaining in the Year 1 statement of financial position (balance sheet), and also to pay half of the tax expense of Year 2, which is £21m. The calculation is: tax expense of the year as shown in the income statement (profit and loss account), minus liability at the end of the year in the statement of financial position (balance sheet), plus liability at the start of the year in the statement of financial position (balance sheet).

Capital expenditure is calculated by comparing the book values at the beginning and end of the year and adjusting for changes during the year. We are told there were no sales of fixed assets so any increase must represent an addition. The balance started at £1,118m, fell by £50m for depreciation, increased by the unknown figure for additions, and finished at £1,155m. The missing figure is calculated as £87m.

The dividend paid during Year 2 was the dividend proposed at the end of Year 1. If you look back to section 13.7.1, you will see the dividend paid as an entry in the 'reconciliation of movements on equity'.

Finally the right-hand column of the statement of cash flows is added and produces a figure of £40m which is then checked against the statement of financial position (balance sheet) figures. This shows that cash has fallen from £46m to £6m and so the calculation is confirmed as being correct.

13.8.2 Analyst's commentary

Here is the comment made by one analyst in a briefing note to clients.

Despite making a profit before taxation of £129,000, the cash balances of the company have decreased by £40,000 during the year.

The cash generated by operating profit is calculated by adding back depreciation of £50,000 because this is an accounting expense which does not involve an outflow of cash. The resulting cash flow of £179,000 was eroded by allowing current assets to increase by more than the increase in current liabilities. This suggests that we should ask questions about the rate of usage of inventories (stocks) and the period of credit allowed to credit customers (debtors). Our analysis [see section 13.7] shows that the inventories (stocks) holding period reduced marginally from 86 to 83 days, which is not unexpected in the industry. The period of credit taken from suppliers increased by 4 days but the customers collection period increased by 8 days. Our attention should focus on the control of credit customers to look for any weaknesses of credit control and a potential risk of bad debts.

After paying interest charges and taxation the company was still in cash surplus at £72,000 but swung into cash deficit through capital expenditure of £87,000. Taking in the dividend payment of £25,000 the positive cash flow of £72,000 changed to a negative cash flow of £40,000.

We take the view that in the short run it is reasonable to run down cash balances in this way. The company probably had excessive liquidity at the end of Year 1. However, if there is to be a further major investment in fixed assets we would want to see long-term finance being raised, either through a share issue or through a new long-term loan.

13.8.3 EBITDA

EBITDA stands for earnings before interest, taxation, depreciation and amortisation. It is increasingly used by analysts as an approximate measure of cash flow because it removes the non-cash expenses of depreciation and amortisation from profit. Instead of a price–earnings multiple based on earnings per share, the analyst will relate share price to EBITDA. The reason appears to be a desire to get away from the subjectivity of accruals-based profit and closer to cash flow as something objectively measured.

13.8.4 Free cash flow

'Free cash flow' is a phrase that you may encounter in company reports, particularly in the narrative discussions by the chief executive and the finance director. It is a term that is used differently by different people and so you have to read it in the setting where it is used. A common theme is to say, 'We have calculated our operating cash flow and allowed for investment in working capital and we have deducted the amount of cash invested in capital expenditure.' How much cash does that leave free to pay dividends or to invest in new ideas for expansion?

Following this theme, the calculation of free cash flows generally starts with the net cash flow generated from operations (operating cash flow after tax) and then deducts the capital expenditure of the period. This leaves an amount of 'free' cash (in the sense of 'freely available' for future planning). The free cash is available to pay dividends to shareholders and to pay for further investment to expand the business. Directors have to decide their priorities and allocate the cash accordingly. If the free cash flow is a negative figure then the company will need to borrow to pay dividends or finance expansion.

13.9 Combining ratios for interpretation

Researchers have asked 'Can we find ways of combining ratios to predict types of management behaviour in companies?' There have been many answers published as academic research papers. This section explains two answers that have developed from academic research into commercial applications. The Z-score is used to predict the risk of bankruptcy. The M-score is used to predict overstatement of earnings.

13.9.1 Z-score

An American academic, Edward Altman, published in 1968 the results of statistical analysis of a large set of failed companies to establish a formula that could predict the likelihood of a company failing through becoming bankrupt.[1] This statistical analysis applied a combination of accounting ratios. Altman called the result a 'z-score'. A UK-based academic, Richard Taffler, developed a similar analysis for UK companies, publishing the results in 1983. The Altman and Taffler z-score calculations are frequently applied in practice by analysts, such as credit analysts working in banks, to assess the risk of an investment or a loan.

Taffler's model for analysing fully listed industrial firms is:

$$Z = 3.20 + 12.18{*}x_1 + 2.50{*}x_2 - 10.68{*}x_3 + 0.029{*}x_4$$

x_1 = profit before tax/current liabilities (measures profitability)
x_2 = current assets/total liabilities (measures working capital position)
x_3 = current liabilities/total assets (measures financial risk)
x_4 = no-credit interval (measures liquidity).

[No-credit interval = (quick assets – current liabilities)/daily operating expenses.
Daily operating expenses = (sales – pre-tax profit – depreciation)/365]

Firms with a computed z-score less than 0 are at risk of failure (in the 'at risk' region); those with z-score greater than 0 are financially solvent.

13.9.2 M-score

Messod Beneish, an academic based in the USA, published in 1999 a statistical analysis to be used in detecting overstatement of earnings.[2] He used a combination of financial ratios which he called an 'M-score'. He pointed out that such analysis should be used with caution in screening companies, to consider whether any distortions in the financial statement numbers result from earnings manipulation or have another root. For example the distortions could be the result of a material acquisition during the period examined, a material shift in the company's value maximising strategy, or a significant change in the company's economic environment. The formula does not detect under-statement of earnings.

The formula has been applied by Stockopedia, a stock-screening website. A dis-cussion of this approach is provided in the Real World Case at the end of this section.

The M score is based on a combination of the following eight different indices:

1 **DSRI = Days' Sales in Receivables Index**. This measures the ratio of days' sales in receivables versus prior year as an indicator of revenue inflation.
2 **GMI = Gross Margin Index**. This is measured as the ratio of gross margin versus prior year. A firm with poorer prospects is more likely to manipulate earnings.
3 **AQI = Asset Quality Index**. Asset quality is measured as the ratio of non-current assets other than plant, property and equipment to total assets, versus prior year.
4 **SGI = Sales Growth Index**. This measures the ratio of sales versus prior year. While sales growth is not itself a measure of manipulation, the evidence suggests that growth companies are likely to find themselves under pressure to manipulate in order to keep up appearances.
5 **DEPI = Depreciation Index**. This is measured as the ratio of the rate of depreciation versus prior year. A slower rate of depreciation may mean that the firm is revising useful asset life assumptions upwards, or adopting a new method that is income friendly.
6 **SGAI = Sales, General and Administrative expenses Index**. This measures the ratio of SGA expenses to the prior year. This is used on the assumption that analysts would interpret a disproportionate increase in sales as a negative signal about firms' future prospects.
7 **LVGI = Leverage Index**. This measures the ratio of total debt to total assets versus prior year. It is intended to capture debt covenants incentives for earnings manipulation.
8 **TATA – Total Accruals to Total Assets**. This assesses the extent to which managers make discretionary accounting choices to alter earnings. Total accruals are calcu-lated as the change in working capital accounts other than cash less depreciation.

The eight variables are then weighted together according to the following formula:

$$M = -4.84 + 0.92{*}DSRI + 0.528{*}GMI + 0.404{*}AQI + 0.892{*}SGI + 0.115{*}DEPI - 0.172{*}SGAI + 4.679{*}TATA - 0.327{*}LVGI$$

Beneish found that companies with a composite score greater than −1.78 had a higher probability of manipulating their earnings favourably.

REAL WORLD CASE

'M-Score' flags dubious company earnings

Shareholders seeking an early warning of when to sell up, and traders aiming to profit from falling prices, can now use an online indicator to spot companies with potentially unreliable earnings.

Stockopedia, the stock-screening website, has calculated the 'M-Score' for the 2,300 UK companies in its database, which aims to identify those that may have, in some way, 'manipulated' their earnings per share figures.

In early April, according to Stockopedia chief executive Edward Page-Croft, this M-Score correctly predicted problems at SuperGroup – the clothing company that was later forced to issue a profit warning, claiming 'arithmetic errors' in its most recent profit forecast. SuperGroup shares fell 38 per cent on the day.

Page-Croft says: 'We'd been discussing SuperGroup's appearance on our high-risk list just earlier in the week . . . the M-Score for SuperGroup was −1.19, well above the −1.78 threshold for high risk. It was showing the following risk factors: receivables increasing strongly as a proportion of sales, excessive sales growth and high accruals as a proportion of assets.'

More than a decade earlier, students at Cornell University had demonstrated the value of the M-Score, by using it to identify Enron as an 'earnings manipulator', before the company's collapse in 2001 – something equity analysts failed to do.

M-Scores were first devised in the late 1990s by Professor Messod Beneish of Indiana University, using a mathematical model of eight financial ratios that can help to detect signs of 'earnings manipulation' – which is not illegal. These signs include extending customer credit terms and reporting high sales growth.

Stockopedia believes M-Scores can now be used as a way of screening the market for shares to 'short-sell' – by borrowing stock, selling it and buying it back cheaper, or by simply trading derivatives on the stock.

When Beneish tested this strategy over the period 1993–2003, it generated a hedged return of nearly 14 per cent per annum.

However, Page-Croft says an M-Score should only be used as a starting point. 'You can't be sure without forensic accounting whether a company has genuinely been fiddling their numbers but, as an indicator to do further research, it's pretty useful,' he argues.

Professional investors suggest company accounts still need close scrutiny.

'When a company is having problems it normally first appears on the company's balance sheet before reaching the profit and loss figures,' says Richard Brown, investment specialist at Henderson Global Investors. 'For this reason, we spend a great deal of time looking at the debt level of a company. We also look for more subtle indicators, such as inventory levels or accounts receivable. An increase in either may suggest that a company is finding it difficult to reach its sales targets and are having to offer clients better terms.'

Nicolas Ziegelasch, analyst at broker Killik & Co, says stockpickers also need to check for: the capitalisation of expenses, to see if expenses from the current year are being shifted into the future; the use of 'accrual accounting or reserves' to smooth out earnings; the revaluation of assets or liabilities after an acquisition to release earnings; the classification of large expenses as 'one-off items'; and the recording of sales revenues in different financial years.

How and when revenue is recognised is 'the key manipulation', says James Butterfill, equity strategist at Coutts. 'Booking all in one year would make earnings very large for that year and consequently distort valuations,' he warns.

Ziegelasch recommends studying cash flow. 'Look at the ratio of operating earnings to operating cash flows,' he says. 'Often a company making profits but not generating any cash is a warning sign of manipulation.'

Source: Financial Times, http://www.ft.com/cms/s/0/8588d422-b6ca-11e1-8c96-00144feabdc0.html#ixzz21tpdndrN.

Discussion points

1 How should an investor interpret any given M-score?
2 Should companies be expected to report the M-score in their annual reports?

13.10 Summary

The main areas of ratio analysis explained in this chapter are:

- investor ratios (summarised in Table 13.3)
- analysis of management performance (summarised in Table 13.4)
- liquidity and working capital (summarised in Table 13.5)
- gearing (summarised in Table 13.6).

Section 13.8 explains how the interpretation of ratios may be linked to an understanding of cash flows. Section 13.9 explains how ratios may be combined to detect financial distress or overstatement of earnings.

It is essential to treat ratio analysis with great caution and to understand the basis of calculation and the nature of the data used. For that reason the illustrations have been set out in detail using a layout that allows you to demonstrate your knowledge of the formula, your ability to collect data for calculation, and the result of that calculation which can then be interpreted. In this chapter all the information has been made available to you as and when you required it. In Chapter 14 we move on to consider published financial statements where more exploration may be required to find the most useful information.

The general principles explained in this chapter can be applied to the annual report of any profit-seeking business. The precise formulae may require adaptation to suit particular national characteristics. However, international comparison requires great caution. Accounting policies and practices are not yet harmonised entirely. If the underlying data are not comparable then neither are the ratios.

The key is to ask first, 'What value do we expect for this ratio?' Then calculate the ratio and seek an interpretation of the similarity or difference.

QUESTIONS

The Questions section of each chapter has three types of question. 'Test your understanding' questions to help you review your reading are in the 'A' series of questions. You will find the answers to these by reading and thinking about the material in the book. 'Application' questions to test your ability to apply technical skills are in the 'B' series of questions. Questions requiring you to show skills in problem solving and evaluation are in the 'C' series of questions. A letter [S] indicates that there is a solution at the end of the book.

A Test your understanding

A13.1 Which ratios provide information on performance for investors? (Section 13.3.1)

A13.2 Which ratios provide information on management performance? (Section 13.3.2)

A13.3 Which ratios provide information on liquidity and working capital? (Section 13.3.3)

A13.4 Which ratios provide information on gearing? (Section 13.3.4)

A13.5 What is the view of investors on risk and return? (Section 13.4)

A13.6 Why is financial gearing riskier for a company which has fluctuating profits? (Section 13.4.3)

A13.7 Explain the use of the pyramid of ratios in analysis of performance. (Section 13.5)

A13.8 What are the limitations of ratio analysis? (Section 13.6)

B Application

B13.1 [S]

The following financial statements relate to Hope plc:

Income statement (profit and loss account)
for the year ended 30 June Year 4

	£000s	£000s
Revenue		6,200
Cost of sales		(2,750)
Gross profit		3,450
Administration and selling expenses		(2,194)
Operating profit		1,256
Debenture interest		(84)
Profit before taxation		1,172
Taxation		(480)
Profit for equity holder		692

The directors have recommended a dividend of 36.7 pence per share in respect of Year 4, to be paid following approval at the next annual general meeting.

Statement of financial position (balance sheet)
as at 30 June Year 4

	£000s	£000s
Non-current (fixed assets) net of depreciation		1,750
Current assets:		
Inventory		620
Trade receivables (debtors)		1,540
Cash		200
Total current assets		2,360
Total assets		4,110
Current liabilities:		
Trade payables (creditors)		(300)
Other creditors and accruals		(940)
Total current liabilities		(1,240)
Non-current liabilities		
6% debentures		(1,400)
Total liabilities		(2,640)
Net assets		1,470
Share capital and reserves		
Issued share capital:		
900,000 ordinary shares of 50p nominal value		450
Retained earnings		1,020
		1,470

Required

(a) Calculate ratios which measure:
  (i) liquidity and the use of working capital;
  (ii) management performance; and
  (iii) gearing.

(b) Explain how each ratio would help in understanding the financial position and results of the company.

(c) The market price is currently 1,100 pence per share. Calculate ratios which are useful to investors.

B13.2

The following financial statements relate to Charity plc:

Income statement (profit and loss account)
for year ended 30 September Year 4

	£000s	£000s
Revenue		2,480
Cost of sales		(1,100)
Gross profit		1,380
Administration and selling expenses		(678)
Operating profit		702
Debenture interest		(31)
Profit before taxation		671
Taxation		(154)
Profit for equity holders		517

Note: The directors have recommended a dividend of 11.4 pence per share in total in respect of Year 4, to be paid following approval at the next annual general meeting.

Statement of financial position (balance sheet)
as at 30 September Year 4

	£000s	£000s
Non-current assets, net of depreciation		785
Current assets:		
Inventories (stocks)		341
Trade receivables (debtors)		801
Cash		110
Total current assets		1,252
Total assets		2,037
less: Current liabilities		
Trade payables (creditors)		(90)
Other payable and accruals		(654)
Total current liabilities		(744)
Net current assets		508
Total assets less current liabilities		1,293
Non-current liabilities		
7% debentures		(440)
Total liabilities		(1,184)
Net assets		853
Share capital and reserves		
Issued share capital		
(1,360,000 ordinary shares of 25p nominal value)		340
Retained earnings		513
		853

Required

(a) Calculate ratios which measure:
 (i) liquidity and the use of working capital;
 (ii) management performance; and
 (iii) gearing.
(b) Explain how each ratio would help in understanding the financial position and results of the company.
(c) The market price of one share is 800 pence. Calculate ratios which will be of interest to investors.

C   Problem solving and evaluation

C13.1

Carry out a ratio analysis of Safe and Sure plc, using the financial statements set out in Appendix I (at the end of this book) and applying the method of analysis set out in section 13.6. Making a comparison of Year 7 with Year 6, write a short commentary on each ratio separately and then summarise the overall themes emerging from the ratios. Assume a share price of 260 pence is applicable at 31 December Year 7 and a share price of 210 pence is applicable at 31 December Year 6.

Notes and references

1. Agarwal, V. and Taffler, R. J. (2007), Twenty-five years of the Taffler z-score model: Does it really have predictive ability? *Accounting and Business Research*, 37(4): 285–300.
2. Beneish, Messod D. (1999), The Detection of Earnings Manipulation, *Financial Analysts Journal*, 55(5): 24–36.

Chapter 14

Reporting corporate performance

Vodafone plc

Extract from Annual Report 2012

The Group's key risks are outlined below:

1 Regulatory decisions and changes in the regulatory environment could adversely affect our business.

2 We could suffer loss of consumer confidence and/or legal action due to a failure to protect our customer information.

3 Our business could be adversely affected by a failure or significant interruption to telecommunications networks.

4 Technological advances in handsets and use of alternative communication services may result in less demand for our traditional service offerings.

5 Increased competition may reduce our market share and profitability.

6 Our business may be impaired by actual or perceived health risks associated with the transmission of radio waves from mobile telephones, transmitters and associated equipment.

7 One or more countries may exit the eurozone.

8 We may be unable to obtain additional/renew sufficient spectrum with an adequate return.

9 We may not satisfactorily resolve major tax disputes.

10 A malicious attack on our network may be successful and disrupt our services or compromise our data.

11 Changes in assumptions underlying the carrying value of certain Group assets could result in impairment.

Source: Extract 14.1 from Vodafone Annual Report 2012, p. 39; http://www.vodafone.com/content/indexinvestors/investor_information/annual_report.html. © 2012 Vodafone Group. VODAFONE, and the Vodafone logo are trademarks of Vodafone Group.

Discussion points

1 What would be your ranking of (a) the relative likelihood and (b) the relative impact of the risks listed?

2 How does this risk information contribute to the usefulness of the financial reporting?

Contents

<table>
<tr><td>Learning
outcomes</td><td>After reading this chapter you should be able to:</td></tr>
</table>

Learning outcomes

After reading this chapter you should be able to:

- Explain the importance of the operating and financial review as a component of the annual report of a company.

- Describe and explain other useful information in the annual report that is relevant to analysis of corporate performance.

- Relate the interpretation of ratios to the information in a statement of cash flows.

- Explain how segmental information is useful to the analysis of corporate performance.

14.1 Introduction

You have learned from Chapter 13 the basic techniques of ratio analysis that may help you to interpret the performance of a company relative to other companies or other periods of time. You have also learned how the ratios may be linked to the statement of cash flows to interpret the factors affecting cash flow. It might be helpful to users of annual reports if companies themselves would carry out some analysis and interpretation of this type. There was a time when it was felt that the role of the company should stop at the presentation of the financial statements. Today, however, there is an expectation that companies will recognise the need to give more information to users, such as an objective discussion. The title of the discussion that is included in the annual report may be the **business review** or it may be the **operating and financial review** (OFR). Companies may choose to provide other guidance such as highlights statements and trends of data. Most large companies report group accounts which, as explained in Chapter 7, are quite complex. Because of this complexity, analysts like to receive segmental information that breaks the total information into key areas of activity of the business. Some companies have sought to avoid disclosing all their activities in group accounts by use of 'off-balance-sheet finance'. Because this omission may distort the view of performance, the standard-setters have tried to restrict the use of off-balance-sheet finance and encourage full reporting of group activities.

Beyond the responsibility for financial performance, the managers of companies have a responsibility and accountability to society in terms of their social and environmental activities. They are expected to demonstrate accountability by reporting on social and environmental activity in the annual report. The managers are also expected to follow best practice in the way they operate their business and in their relations with shareholders. This is described as corporate governance and the compliance with good practice in corporate governance must also be explained in the annual report.

Finally this chapter gives a taste of three areas of debate that extend beyond a first-level course in accounting but which help the student to be aware that studying accounting should include a questioning and thoughtful approach to what is being learned. These three areas of debate are: the meaning of 'true and fair'; the nature of value; and the relevance of the stakeholder model.

14.2 Operating and financial review (OFR) and business review

14.2.1 Development of the OFR and the business review

The operating and financial review (OFR) has been a feature of the annual reports of many UK listed companies since 1993.[1] It was created by the UK ASB as a move towards providing shareholders with information on a company's performance and prospects. The ASB received encouragement from the Cadbury Committee in its 1992 report on the financial aspects of corporate governance. From 1993 to 2005 the provision of an OFR in an annual report was voluntary. The ASB hoped that giving companies wide discretion would encourage the development of best practice in reporting rather than a slavish adherence to rules which might result in a lacklustre document. Most larger listed companies published an OFR in the annual report.

In 2004 the European Commission issued its Modernisation Directive requiring all member states to incorporate a business review in the legislation governing annual reports. Initially the UK government intended to meet this requirement by making the OFR a legal requirement, because it felt that the OFR could cover all the requirements of the business review and achieve other useful purposes in communicating with shareholders. Very briefly, in 2005, the OFR became mandatory but by the start of 2006 the legislation had been repealed because the government decided that a mandatory OFR would be adding unnecessarily to the regulatory burden facing UK companies (referred to as 'gold plating' the regulation).

From comments made at that time it appeared that the OFR was a somewhat strange target for reducing regulation because users of annual reports found it useful and it was a location for reporting on the activities carried out by companies that harmonised with government policy on social issues. There is also a continuing strong movement towards more narrative discussion in annual reports, as explained later in this chapter.

UK companies are now faced with Company Law requiring a Business Review[2] and the UK ASB providing non-mandatory guidance on the OFR in *Reporting Statement 1 (RS 1): Operating and Financial Review.*[3] The ASB has indicated that following the recommendations of the OFR will cover the requirements of the business review. However, it seems that most companies prefer to use the 'business review' description.

14.2.2 Business review

The Companies Act 2006 explains that the purpose of the business review is to inform members of the company and help them assess how the directors have performed their duty to promote the success of the company. The business review must contain (a) a fair review of the company's business, and (b) a description of the principal risks and uncertainties facing the company.

The fair review is to be a balanced and comprehensive analysis of (a) the development and performance of the company's business during the financial year, and (b) the position of the company's business at the end of that year.

If the company is quoted on a stock exchange it must comply with further requirements that include:

(a) the main trends and factors likely to affect the future development, performance and position of the company's business; and
(b) information about:
    (i) environmental matters, including the impact of the company's business on the environment,
    (ii) the company's employees, and
    (iii) social and community issues
(c) information about persons with whom the company has contractual or other arrangements which are essential to the business of the company.

The review must also, to the extent necessary for an understanding of the development, performance or position of the company's business, include:

(a) analysis using financial key performance indicators, and
(b) where appropriate, analysis using other key performance indicators, including information relating to environmental matters and employee matters.

14.2.3 Key performance indicators (KPIs)[4]

There is no specific guidance in the Companies Act on how to define **key performance indicators** (KPIs) but there is some guidance provided by the UK ASB in its Reporting Statement RS 1 on the *Operating and Financial Review*. KPIs are quantified measures of factors that help to measure the performance of the business effectively. They reflect 'critical success factors' and show how the entity is progressing towards its objectives.

The Reporting Statement RS 1 encourages the entity to provide in its OFR sufficient information to enable members to understand each KPI disclosed in the OFR. These KPIs are expected to become an important help to shareholders in understanding the performance of the entity as seen by the directors. For each KPI the directors should give a definition and explain the calculation. They should explain the purpose of the KPIs and the sources of data used, together with any assumptions made. There should be a commentary on each KPI and future targets, with comparative figures for the previous year. Where there is a change in a KPI there should be an explanation and a calculation giving comparison to previous years.

Examples of KPIs are:

- Return on capital employed (see Chapter 13).
- Market share – the revenue of the entity as a percentage of the industry total (e.g. a market leader demonstrating dominant position).
- Average revenue per customer (e.g. in a pay-per-view television service).
- Sales per square foot of selling space (e.g. a chain of retail stores).
- Employee costs per £ of sales (any labour-intensive business).
- Environmental spillage (e.g. in a business using toxic chemicals).

The following extract from the annual report of Safe and Sure plc shows how Key Performance Indicators are reported.

Safe and Sure plc: Key Performance Indicators
The Board reviews the following indicators:
Non Financial Performance Indicators

	Year 6	Year 7
CO_2 emissions[i]	119	108
Water consumption[ii]	13	12
Colleague engagement	70%	70%
Colleague enablement	68%	68%
Sales colleague retention	64%	64%
Service colleague retention	74%	76%
Customer satisfaction[iii]	n/a	19%
State of Service	98%	97%
Number of Lost Time Accidents[iv]	1.53	1.72

(i)   Total CO_2 emissions in tonnes per £m turnover reported on a total company basis.
(ii) Water consumed – litres per kilogramme of textiles processed in continental European plants.
(iii) Customer satisfaction score, represents the net balance of those customers promoting our service compared with those neutral or not promoting.
(iv) LTA equals accidents per 100,000 hours worked.

14.2.4 Directors' and auditors' responsibilities for the business review

The directors of the company are responsible for the preparation of the business review. The auditors read the business review, along with other narrative sections of the annual report, to satisfy themselves that there are no inconsistencies between the information in the narrative report and that in the financial statements. If they find an inconsistency they will discuss it with the directors and attempt to resolve the problem. When the business review was being introduced the government wanted a stronger form of audit that would review the process by which the business review was prepared, but this stronger form of audit was resisted by both auditors and directors. Commentators felt that too strong a burden would be placed on auditors and directors if subsequent events did not correspond to expectations raised by the business review.

14.2.5 Objective and principles of the OFR

Although the business review is the requirement of the Companies Act 2006, the UK ASB has retained its Reporting Statement for the OFR, asserting that a company which applies the OFR will also meet the requirements of the business review.

The stated objective of the OFR is to provide a balanced and comprehensive analysis, consistent with the size and complexity of the business, of:[5]

(a) the development and performance of the business of the entity during the financial year;
(b) the position of the entity at the end of the financial year;
(c) the main trends and factors underlying the development, performance and position of the business of the entity during the financial year; and
(d) the main trends and factors which are likely to affect the entity's future development, performance and position, prepared so as to assist members to assess the strategies adopted by the entity and the potential for those strategies to succeed.

The objective mentions only 'members' of the company, which means the existing shareholders. Earlier drafts of the reporting standard attempted to widen the objective to include intending investors but this was criticised as being too wide-ranging. There is no mention of any other stakeholders. (Look back to Chapter 1 for the potential range of interested parties.)

The ASB sets out seven principles[6] followed by a disclosure framework.

1 The OFR should set out an analysis of the business through the eyes of the board of directors.
2 The OFR should focus on matters that are relevant to the interests of members.
3 The OFR should have a forward-looking orientation, identifying those trends and factors relevant to the members' assessment of the current and future performance of the business and the progress towards the achievement of long-term business objectives.
4 The OFR should complement as well as supplement the financial statements, in order to enhance the overall corporate disclosure.
5 The OFR should be comprehensive and understandable.
6 The OFR should be balanced and neutral, dealing even-handedly with both good and bad aspects.
7 The OFR should be comparable over time.

What are the significant aspects of these principles? The idea of looking through the eyes of the directors is an important feature. It carries the idea of taking shareholders inside the company to reduce the gap between directors, who manage the company, and shareholders, who own the company. The forward-looking orientation is another important feature because shareholders want to make estimates of the future of their investment. 'Forward-looking' does not mean that the company will be making a forecast. The idea of balancing good and bad aspects is important but in practice it may be difficult to persuade directors to say as much about bad aspects as they do about the good ones. One argument the directors put forward is that if they disclose bad aspects of performance there will be loss of confidence and the bad will become worse.

14.2.6 OFR disclosure framework

The Reporting Statement does not set out a format or a template. It does not specify headings that must be included in an OFR. However, the section of the Reporting Statement describing the disclosure framework runs from paragraphs 27 to 76 with headings and bold-lettered paragraphs and liberal sprinkling of the verb 'shall' (meaning 'must'), so it seems likely that companies will tend to use similar headings.

The framework is introduced by a statement that the OFR shall provide information to assist members to assess the strategies adopted by the entity and the potential for those strategies to succeed. Four key elements of the framework are then specified:[7]

(a) The nature of the business, including a description of the market, competitive and regulatory environment in which the entity operates and the entity's objectives and strategies.
(b) The development and performance of the business, both in the financial year under review and in the future.
(c) The resources, principal risks and uncertainties and relationships that may affect the entity's long-term value.
(d) The position of the business including a description of the capital structure, treasury policies and objectives and liquidity of the entity, both in the financial year under review and in the future.

14.2.7 International developments

The IASB has published guidance on a Management Commentary that may be included in annual reports. The guidance is called a Practice Statement and is not a mandatory standard. It provides the following definition:

> *A management commentary is a narrative report that relates to financial statements that have been prepared in accordance with IFRSs. Management commentary provides users with historical explanations of the amounts presented in the financial statements, specifically the entity's financial position, financial performance and cash flows. It also provides commentary on an entity's prospects and other information not presented in the financial statements. Management commentary also serves as a basis for understanding management's objectives and its strategies for achieving those objectives.*

The guidance explains that a management commentary should provide users of financial statements (existing and potential investors, lenders and other creditors) with integrated information providing a context for the related financial statements, including the entity's resources and the claims against the entity and its resources, and the transactions and other events that change them.

Management commentary should be consistent with the following principles:

● provide management's view of the entity's performance, position and progress (including forward looking information);
● supplement and complement information presented in the financial statements (and possess the qualitative characteristics described in the *Conceptual Framework for Financial Reporting*).

In presentation, a management commentary should be clear and straightforward and be presented with a focus on the most important information in a manner intended to address the principles described in the Practice Statement, specifically:

- being consistent with its related financial statements;
- avoiding duplicating disclosures made in the notes to the financial statements where practicable;
- avoiding generic and immaterial disclosures.

Companies based in Europe do not at present follow this guidance on a non-mandatory Management Commentary because national laws, under a directive of the European Commission, all require a management report or business review that covers similar ground.

In the US there is a requirement for a report called the Management's Discussion and Analysis (MD&A). This is required by the Securities and Exchange Commission (SEC) from all companies listed on one of the US stock exchanges (mainly the New York Stock Exchange or the NASDAQ over-the-counter market). The SEC has detailed regulations setting out the content of the MD&A. If you are studying or researching a US-listed company you may find the company's MD&A in its annual report or you may find it in the company's report to the SEC (called a 'form 10-K'). The company's web page for 'investors' is often the best place to search. Some UK companies have their shares listed on the New York Stock Exchange or NASDAQ. These companies also prepare an MD&A for the SEC but it is within a report called a 'form 20-F'. You will probably find this on the web page for 'investors' if you are studying or researching a UK company that has a listing in both London and New York.

Activity 14.1	*Read through the sections on the business review and the OFR again. How much of the information suggested for the business review or the OFR is extracted directly from the financial statements? How much of the information suggested for the business review or the OFR provides additional understanding which is not available from the financial statements?*

14.3 Other guidance in analysis

In Figure 7.1, there is a list of 'accompanying information' that may be found in the annual report. The first item listed there is the operating and financial review, explained in section 14.2. The second item is the Chairman's statement, which usually appears at the start of the annual report, as a short narrative lasting no more than a page and often preceded by a 'Highlights' statement of key financial measures. The Chairman sets out key features as an introduction to the detail that follows in later pages. The third item listed there is the Directors' report, which is usually found part-way through the annual report. Its contents are required partly by the Companies Act, partly by the Stock Exchange Listing Rules and partly by the Corporate Governance Code. The fourth item is the historical summaries that allow trends to be seen over several years, with some companies giving five-year trends and others giving ten-year trends. The final item is 'non-accounting and non-financial information'. This covers the rest of the annual report and often provides the most interesting aspects for the reader who wants to understand the company in its entirety.

In this section we will consider the highlights statement and the historical trend analysis.

14.3.1 Highlights statement

Safe and Sure plc presents Highlights of Year 7 as follows:

		Year 7	Increase %	Year 6
		£m		£m
Revenue	United Kingdom	323.4	31.1	246.7
	Europe	164.3	7.0	153.5
	North America	104.5	30.5	80.1
	Asia Pacific and Africa	122.4	12.3	109.0
	Total revenue	714.6	21.3	589.3
Profit	United Kingdom	97.4	28.8	69.7
	Europe	45.3	12.4	40.3
	North America	17.0	22.3	13.9
	Asia Pacific and Africa	35.5	17.9	30.1
	Net interest income	2.3		3.0
	Profit before tax	197.5	25.8	157.0
Earnings	Earnings per share	11.74p	20.9	9.71p
Dividends paid (pence per share)		3.02p	20.8	2.50p

The Highlights statement shows what the company regards as important information for investors as the primary users of the annual report. Turnover is a measure of the size of operations, with growth of turnover being an indicator of expansion. Profit is the reward for shareholders, with growth again being an important indicator. Segment figures are provided for both turnover and profit. This company has a target profit growth of 20% per annum and so is emphasising that it has more than met the target. Earnings per share and dividend per share are the key indicators from which investors can calculate yields based on the current market price. There is no regulation of highlights statements and so other companies may give different information. Together with the Chairman's statement, the Highlights present the key messages of the annual report.

14.3.2 Historical summaries and trend analysis

Listed companies usually provide a historical summary of the financial statements of previous years. The historical summary for Safe and Sure may be found in Appendix I. The analyst may use this table to establish trends of:

- year-on-year growth of turnover and operating profit
- growth rates adjusted for annual inflation
- key ratios.

The company does not usually carry out the ratio analysis; this is left to the analysts to calculate and interpret. On relatively rare occasions the company will provide ratios but it is not always clear which formula has been used.

14.3.3 Finance director's review

There are relatively few references to ratios in the annual reports of companies. Some finance directors claim that interpretation of ratios is a very complex matter. They say that if they provide ratio calculations in the annual report, then they will have to provide detailed explanation, which will make the report too lengthy. So in general they leave the ratios for others to calculate and interpret. Sometimes they will comment on a ratio where they know the expert users will ask questions.

In the operating and financial review of Safe and Sure plc the finance director states:

The pleasing return on our tangible net assets (42.4% per annum before tax on average net assets) reflects the high value of the intangible assets of the Safe and Sure brand and of businesses built up over the years. Such value is not reported in the statement of financial position (balance sheet).

Is it possible to check on the finance director's calculation? He has used pre-tax profit which is £177m (£197.5m from continuing and £20.5m from discontinued operations) and the average of the tangible net assets. The respective figures for Year 7 and Year 6 are £464.3m and £370.4m. The average net assets figure is therefore £417.4m. The calculation of the ratio is:

$$\frac{177}{417.4} \times 100\% = 42.4\%$$

which confirms the figure given by the finance director. (It should be noted that confirming ratios reported in annual reports is not always so straightforward, although it ought to be.) We need other evidence before we can agree that 42.4% is a 'pleasing' return.

In the next section, David aims to explain his approach to using ratios to pinpoint target areas for probing by way of questions to the company, while Leona explains how ratios are useful to the auditor.

14.3.4 The analyst and the auditor

DAVID: *We subscribe to the major online database sources of information about companies, so I don't very often sit down to calculate ratios. I'm more interested in the interpretation. There are a few key ratios that I look at for major clues as to strange goings-on and then I scan a more detailed ratio report for unusual changes. We can program in an instruction to set a warning flag against any ratio which has altered by more than a specified range since the previous figures, or over a given period of time.*

What do I look to first? Gross margins on turnover and net margins on turnover, with as much segmental detail as I can find. Segmental information is an area where often we do have to carry out our own analysis using our skills, experience and specialist sources of information. Not many databases break down the company's results by segment. Then I'll check the tax charge as a percentage of the taxable profit. It should be around 30% if the company's accounts have been accepted for tax purposes, but if there are items which the tax authorities don't allow, then the percentage will be different. I'm always interested in what appears in the income statement (profit and loss account) but is not accepted by the tax rules. Depreciation is a notoriously variable figure and is difficult to spot because the accounting rules say that a change in depreciation rate or useful asset life is not a change in policy. Companies have to draw attention to a change in policy and explain the impact. Depreciation escapes that rule. So I calculate the depreciation charge as a percentage of total asset value. If that percentage changes then I start asking questions.

Common-size statements are very useful. That means turning all items in the financial statements to percentages with the total assets represented by 100% in the statement of financial position (balance sheet) and the turnover represented by 100% in the income statement (profit and loss account). It is also useful to have percentage changes from one year to the next. That is all relatively easy when you are using spreadsheets.

Over a period of time I monitor the variability of a ratio for a particular company. I calculate this as:

$$\frac{\text{Maximum value} - \text{Minimum value}}{\text{Mean value of ratio}}$$

Again I am looking for unusual movements outside an expected range.

LEONA: *The auditors don't rely on anyone else's calculations. We carry out our own ratio analysis as part of our analytical review. For commercial, manufacturing and service companies we monitor a standard list of ratios which is:*

- *acid test ratio*
- *current ratio*
- *customers collection period*
- *inventories (stocks) holding period*
- *gearing*
- *interest cover*
- *return on capital employed*
- *return on total assets*
- *gross profit margin.*

We are looking at these with a focus on the particular concerns of the auditor. Possible liquidity crises or working capital shortages could raise a question as to whether the company is a going concern. Customer collection period provides a clue to whether the doubtful debt provision is adequate. Inventories holding period may indicate a need for provision for slow-moving inventories. Gearing and interest cover are further indicators of financial stability or otherwise in relation to the going concern issue. Return on capital employed and on total assets may show inefficient use of assets and perhaps point to assets which have no future benefit. Gross margins may cause us to ask questions about incorrect records of sales or stocks if the margins are different from the norms.

For listed companies we also look at the dividend cover and the Altman Z-score. The Z-score is a model developed for use in predicting insolvency. You need to read a finance textbook to get the details, but basically it is a combined score based on a list of key variables all pointing to potential insolvency problems. We have to be able to say that the business is a going concern, so that kind of information is important to us.

DAVID: *That's OK for the current year. What about trends?*

LEONA: *Yes, trends are an important part of our review. We try to use a predictive approach and estimate the current year's figure from the previous data rather than merely compare this year with last. Taking a predictive approach encourages us to challenge fluctuations and to seek persuasive explanations. We use all the familiar forms of trend analysis – graphical representation, moving averages and simple regression analysis.*

DAVID: *How much reliance do you place on these analytical procedures?*

LEONA: *It can range from conclusive reliance to no reliance at all. It depends very much on the nature of the assertions being tested, the plausibility and predictability of the relationships involved, and the extent to which data is available and reliable.*

DAVID: *Maybe I have underestimated auditors in the past. None of the activities you describe is really apparent from the audit report. Perhaps you undersell your work.*

LEONA: *I probably have to admit that our work stops when we have gained sufficient assurance to write the audit report. We don't give information to the reader – that is not the function of the audit.*

DAVID: *You and I need to spend more time together on this question of analysis in depth. Analysts with insight command top ratings and that's what I'm looking for. And I think the benefit would not all be one-way – I can help you with broader awareness of the strategies used by management in giving the markets the messages they want to convey.*

LEONA: *Sounds fine to me.*

14.4 Segmental information

In Sections 7.7 and 7.8, you read about the group structure used by many companies, and saw the method of construction of consolidated financial statements. Safe and Sure presents consolidated financial statements, which are discussed in section 7.4. The process of consolidation of financial information in group accounts is intended to be an improvement on sending the parent company shareholders a bundle of the separate financial statements of each member of the group. It lets them see, in one set of financial statements, the full picture of the group. On the negative side, the process of aggregation causes a loss of information about the various different activities of the group. In order to balance the benefits of aggregation with the need for detail, accounting provides additional information about the various segments of the group on a year-by-year basis.

14.4.1 Users' needs for information

Consolidated financial statements are a very convenient means of bringing together a large volume of data, but they suffer a major defect in losing much of the rich detail available from seeing each constituent company separately. It is particularly important for users of financial statements to know how the results of various activities compare, where the group of companies is involved in more than one product line and more than one type of market.

Segmental reporting has developed as a means of supplementing the consolidated financial statements by providing more insight into the activities of the group. In particular it reports information about the different types of products and services that an entity produces and the different geographical areas in which it operates.

The accounting standard which deals with segmental reporting[8] requires the entity to disclose information to enable users of its financial statements to evaluate the nature and financial effects of the business activities in which it engages and the economic environments in which it operates. To achieve this objective the managers start by identifying the operating segments from which it earns revenues and incurs expenses. These operating segments will be regularly reviewed by the entity's 'chief operating decision maker'. The information provided about each segment will correspond to that provided to the chief operating decision maker. In this way the standard seeks to help the user of financial statements view the business in the way it is seen by its managers.

The entity must disclose some general information about how the reportable segments have been identified and the types of products and services from which each reportable segment derives its revenues. It must also report a measure of profit or loss and total assets for each reportable segment and a measure of liabilities for each segment if that information is regularly provided to the chief operating officer.

The entity must also disclose specific accounting information as set out in the following list, if these items are reported to the chief operating decision maker:

(a) revenues from external customers
(b) revenues from transactions with other operating segments of the same entity
(c) interest revenue
(d) interest expense
(e) depreciation and amortisation
(f) material items of income and expense
(g) the entity's interest in the profit or loss of associates and joint ventures
(h) income tax expense or income
(i) material non-cash items other than depreciation and amortisation.

The accounting standard containing these requirements took effect from 1 January 2009, with a review promised in 2012. Those commentators who were concerned about this standard felt that it gave too much discretion to the company management and could even be damaging to the quality of corporate governance. The IASB supported the standard by referring to research showing that when a similar standard was introduced in the US no detrimental effects were observed.

Research[9] has shown that under IFRS 8 the number of segments has increased and the extent of the segmental note disclosure has increased. Interviews with users of reports have welcomed the management-based approach but have expressed some concern that the flexibility of the standard could allow managerial manipulation of disclosures. There is not always consistency between the narrative sections of the annual report and the IFRS 8 segmental note disclosure.

14.4.2   Information provided in the financial statements

The group statement of financial position (balance sheet) and income statement (profit and loss account) of Safe and Sure plc are presented in full in Chapter 7 and have been explored in more detail in subsequent chapters. Consequently you are already familiar with much of the information about the assets and liabilities of the group.

Parent company

Some companies publish the statement of financial position (balance sheet) of the parent company alongside or near to the group statement of financial position (balance sheet). This is a requirement for groups that continue to report under UK rules, but is not compulsory for group accounts prepared under the IASB system. In most cases the parent company statement of financial position (balance sheet) confirms that the parent is primarily a holding company whose main asset is the investment in its subsidiaries. It owns some of the group's land and buildings and a small portion of the vehicle fleet. Its current assets consist mainly of amounts owed by subsidiaries and dividends due from subsidiaries. Its current liabilities consist mainly of amounts owed to subsidiaries and dividends payable to its own shareholders. The parent company has some long-term liabilities for money borrowed to purchase subsidiaries. Most of the cash used for purchase of new subsidiaries is provided by the new wealth generated by the group as a whole.

Group

Information about the Safe and Sure group is very much more interesting than information about the parent company alone. That is why the preceding chapters have used the group information about Safe and Sure to explain the treatment of assets, liabilities and ownership interest. There are a few particular items of interest in respect of acquisitions of new subsidiaries and the use of the goodwill reserve. There is also some interesting information about the various segments of the business which contribute to the overall picture. This section summarises those particular features of the annual report.

14.4.3   Identifying segments

The IASB system requires the operating segments reported by an entity to be the organisational units for which information is reported regularly to the chief operating decision maker. The chief operating decision maker is likely to be the chief executive, working with the board of directors to use the information for evaluating past performance and making decisions about future allocation of resources. So the intention is that the segment reporting reflects the information that management is using in running the business.

14.4.4   Segmental information in Safe and Sure

As an illustration of the type of segmental information available, the note to the income statement (profit and loss account) of Safe and Sure plc is set out in Note 16 to the financial statements. It is one of the lengthiest notes provided by the company.

Note 16 Operating segments

For the purposes of reporting to the chief operating decision maker, the group is currently organised into two operating divisions, (1) disposal and recycling, (2) security and cleaning. Disposal and recycling includes all aspects of collection and safe disposal of industrial and commercial waste products. Security and cleaning is undertaken by renewable annual contract, predominantly for hospitals, other healthcare premises and local government organisations.

The group's disposal and recycling operation in North America was discontinued with effect from 30 April Year 7.

Business sector analysis

	Disposal and recycling		Security and cleaning		Total	
	Year 7 £m	Year 6 £m	Year 7 £m	Year 6 £m	Year 7 £m	Year 6 £m
REVENUES (all from external customers)						
Continuing	508.9	455.0	205.7	134.3	714.6	589.3
Discontinued	20.0	11.0			20.0	11.0
Total revenues	528.9	466.0	205.7	134.3	734.6	600.3
Operating profit (loss) by service						
Continuing	176.6	139.6	18.6	14.4	195.2	154.0
Discontinued	(20.5)	(10.0)			(20.5)	(10.0)
Total operating profit					174.7	144.0
Interest receivable (net)					2.3	3.0
Profit before tax					177.0	147.0
Taxation					(62.2)	(52.4)
Profit for the period					114.8	94.6

All costs of head office operations are allocated to divisions on an activity costing basis. The company does not allocate interest receivable or taxation paid to reportable segments.

Depreciation and amortisation included in the income statement are as follows:

	Disposal and recycling		Security and cleaning		Total	
	Year 7 £m	Year 6 £m	Year 7 £m	Year 6 £m	Year 7 £m	Year 6 £m
Depreciation	30.2	25.1	3.0	3.9	33.2	29.0
Impairment of goodwill	1.6	–	–	–	1.6	–

The segment assets and liabilities at the end of Years 7 and 6, with capital expenditure for each year are as follows:

	Disposal and recycling		Security and cleaning		Unallocated		Total	
	Year 7 £m	Year 6 £m	Year 7 £m	Year 6 £m	Year 7 £m	Year 6 £m	Year 7 £m	Year 6 £m
Total assets	498.5	370.9	68.7	132.7	120.1	112.3	687.3	615.9
Total liabilities	131.7	147.9	61.3	85.5	30.0	12.1	223.0	245.5
Capital expenditure	50.0	45.0	10.2	2.5	–	–	60.2	47.5

Information about geographical areas

The group's two business segments operate in four main geographical areas, even though they are managed on a worldwide basis. In the following analysis, revenue is based on the country in which the order is received. It would not be materially different if based on the country in which the customer is located. Total assets and capital expenditure are allocated based on where the assets are located.

	Revenues from external customers		Non-current assets	
	Year 7 £m	Year 6 £m	Year 7 £m	Year 6 £m
CONTINUING				
United Kingdom	323.4	246.7	174.2	148.7
Continental Europe	164.3	153.5	90.3	93.0
North America	104.5	80.1	85.9	49.2
Asia Pacific & Africa	122.4	109.0	56.1	75.0
	714.6	589.3	406.5	365.9
DISCONTINUED				
North America	20.0	11.0	–	0.5
Total	734.6	600.3	406.5	366.4

The information contained in Note 16 relates to a service business, so it might be expected that the non-current assets would be relatively low compared to the turnover and operating profit. Professional analysts would be particularly interested in the relationships and trends underlying these figures.

David and Leona have returned from their holiday and are again working on Leona's flat. In the middle of a less than successful attempt to fit a carpet, David pauses for coffee and explains how he looked at the segmental information presented by the company.

DAVID: *The first thing I did here was to feed all these tables of segmental information into our spreadsheet package. I asked for two printouts initially. The first calculated the sales (revenue) as a multiple of net assets and the operating profit as a percentage of sales, using continuing activities in each case because the assets remaining at the end of the period do not include the assets of the discontinued activity. [The results are shown in Table 14.1, panel (a).] The second printout shows the sales to non-current assets for each geographical area. [The results are shown in Table 14.1, panel (b).] From this the relative strengths and weaknesses within the organisation begin to emerge. The percentage changes (Table 14.2) also show some interesting differences. I need to ask why the total assets for security and cleaning have reduced so much when there was no disposal in this segment. Perhaps the assets were transferred into disposal and recycling to replace those that were discontinued.*

Table 14.1
Analysis

(a) Analysis of business segment revenues and operating profit (based on continuing activities)

	Revenues as a multiple of total assets		Operating profit as a % of sales	
	Year 7	Year 6	Year 7 %	Year 6 %
Segment				
Disposal and recycling	1.02	1.23	34.7	30.7
Security and cleaning	2.99	1.01	9.0	10.7

(b) Analysis of geographical segment sales compared to non-current assets

	Sales as a multiple of non-current assets	
	Year 7	Year 6
Geographical analysis		
United Kingdom	1.86	1.66
Continental Europe	1.82	1.65
North America	1.22	1.63
Asia Pacific and Africa	1.76	1.61

Table 14.2
Percentage changes on previous year

	Disposal and recycling Year 7 % on Year 6	Security and cleaning Year 7 % on Year 6	Total Year 7 % on Year 6
Sales (revenue)	+11.8	+53.0	+21.3
Operating profit	+26.5	+29.2	+25.0
Total assets	+34.4	negative	+11.6

Then I turned to the front of the annual report. The importance of segmental information becomes apparent as soon as you start to read the chairman's statement and it continues through the business reviews, presented on a segmental basis with some helpful illustrations to reinforce the message. The chief executive's review continues the segmental theme strongly and gives further information to augment the basic tables which I have already analysed. That attention to detail in their reports is a reflection of the thorough questioning which these people receive from the fund managers and analysts who follow the company closely. I know one analyst who would put Sherlock Holmes in the shade. She collects the accounts of each individual UK company in the group, and as many overseas subsidiary companies as she can get hold of. She puts them all together like a jigsaw and then starts to ask intensive questions based on what she has and what she can deduce about the missing pieces. Seasoned finance directors wilt visibly under her interrogation!

LEONA: *Segmental reporting is an area where you and your analyst friends probably put more pressures on the companies than we can as auditors. That's a good example of market forces at work, but it does assume that the information you prise out of the company is made available more widely. Companies make use of the business review or the operating and financial review to answer the questions which they know the investors ask on a regular basis.*

14.5 Off-balance-sheet finance

One major problem for UK accounting emerged in the 1980s in a period of business expansion. To finance expansion, companies were borrowing and therefore increasing their gearing ratios. Some companies looked for ways of avoiding disclosing in the statement of financial position (balance sheet) the full extent of the commitment on borrowed funds. Omitting the item from the statement of financial position (balance sheet) could not remove the commercial obligation but it could reduce the questions arising from those who would read the financial statements.

The accounting question is: How do you remove, or fail to include, a liability so that no one will notice? The answer, as with all accounting questions, starts in the accounting equation. To keep the equation in balance, any removal of a liability must be matched by removal of an asset of equal amount.

Many ingenious schemes emerged, but one of the least complex is the sale and leaseback of land and buildings.

14.5.1 Sale and leaseback of property

Consider the following scenario. A company has the following statement of financial position (balance sheet):

	£m
Land and buildings	20
Other assets, *less* current liabilities	15
	35
Less long-term loan	(20)
Net assets	15
Share capital	15

The company sells the land and buildings for £20m and repays the loan. The statement of financial position (balance sheet) now appears to contain no gearing:

	£m
Other assets, *less* current liabilities	15
Share capital	15

However, enquiry behind the scenes reveals a complex arrangement. The land and buildings were sold to a consortium of finance companies, but on the same day a lease was signed that allowed the company to continue occupying the property at a rental payment which would vary according to current rates of interest and would be calculated as a percentage of the £20m cash received. In five years' time the company would have the option to repurchase the land and buildings at £20m and the consortium of finance companies would have the option to force the company to repurchase at £20m. These options would mean that if the price rose over the next five years the company would wish to buy at £20m. If the price fell over the next five years the consortium would insist on repurchase.

Now ask yourself, where do the benefits and risks of this contract lie? The benefits of a rise in value and the risks of a decrease in value remain with the company, as they would if the company had remained the owner. The company will pay a rental which looks very much like an interest payment on a loan of £20m. If the company fails to meet its obligations, then the consortium will claim the asset. The commercial effect of this transaction is that of a loan based on the security of the asset of land and buildings.

14.5.2 UK response

In the absence of a standard to back up the argument, auditors felt unable to argue against the directors of companies who moved assets and liabilities off the statement of financial position (balance sheet). After some years of consultation and discussion with interested parties, the UK ASB decided that such transactions did not change the commercial substance of the transaction and it is the commercial substance which matters. A standard was introduced to require a transaction of this type to be reported on the statement of financial position (balance sheet)[10] in the form of an asset and matching liability. Not all countries shared this view because it involved making a judgement on the balance of risks and rewards. Making judgements leaves the company and the auditors open to challenge and so it could be argued that specific rules are preferable to general principles. In particular the US had a more rules-based approach to defining recognition on and off the statement of financial position (balance sheet).

14.5.3 Special purpose entities

The problems associated with off-balance-sheet finance received a high public profile at the end of 2001, running into 2002, with the failure of a large US company called Enron. Because of the size of the company and the political impact of its failure, hearings were called by the US Congress at which witnesses gave evidence on accounting practices, among other matters. One of the accounting issues discussed was the question of 'off-balance-sheet finance'. The Chief Accountant of the Securities and Exchange Commission described to the House of Representatives how money could be borrowed at advantageous rates of interest using a 'special purpose entity' which was not consolidated with the rest of the group accounts. Provided the assets of the special purpose entity retained sufficient value, the lender would be content with the arrangement. If the assets fell in value then the lender would look to the parent company for reimbursement. Shareholders in the parent would be unaware of the extent of such borrowing until the lenders demanded repayment. At the time of the failure of Enron the US standard-setting body (the Financial Accounting Standards Board) was still in the process of providing guidance on consolidation of such special purpose entities. The International Accounting Standards Board had no standard that directly addressed such entities.

Subsequently the US regulators and the IASB strengthened their rules relating to special purpose entities, to bring more of these entities into group financial statements.

Despite these efforts at improvement, the use of special purpose entities, to take transactions off the balance sheet, became a concern again during the financial crisis of 2007–08. Some of the problems experienced in the banking sector had remained out of sight in off-balance sheet arrangements. The leading world economies, through the G20, asked the standard setters to address the continuing problems associated with off-balance sheet finance. The IASB responded in 2011 with three new accounting standards, covering consolidated financial statements, joint arrangements and disclosures of interests in other entities. The IASB claimed these changes would provide a check on off-balance sheet activities and would give investors a much clearer picture of the nature and extent of a company's involvement with other entities. The detail is beyond the scope of a first-level textbook but this outline shows why annual reports are becoming ever more lengthy and detailed.

Activity 14.2

Off-balance-sheet finance is one example of information which would never come to the attention of the users of financial statements but for the concern of some auditors. Make a list of other types of information which may be evident to the auditors but which are unlikely to be conveyed to the readers. Consider this list in the light of the requirement that financial statements must show a true and fair view. To what extent is the reader of financial statements reliant on the directors and the auditors?

14.6 Corporate social responsibility

Corporate social responsibility means that entities report to stakeholders on the ways in which social and environmental concerns are integrated with their business operations.

Definition   **Corporate social responsibility** means that companies integrate social and environmental concerns in their business operations and in their interactions with stakeholders.

Companies disclose in their annual reports more information than is represented only in financial statements. Depending on social attitudes or pressures, companies may voluntarily disclose additional information intended to confirm the company's sense of social responsibility. In some instances, the provisions of law eventually catch up with the values of society and disclosures become mandatory. Section 14.2.5 explains that in the UK the OFR Regulation requires the OFR to include information about environmental matters and social and community issues.

Investors are increasingly asking questions about the corporate social responsibility of the companies in which they invest. Many investors want to be reassured that the businesses in which they have a stake adopt ethical business practices towards employees, the community and the environment. You will see increasing numbers of what are described as 'ethical investment funds' which make careful enquiry before buying shares. Some ethical investors feel that they are best placed to influence a company if they become shareholders; others feel that they should not become shareholders until the company has a sound policy.

14.6.1 Types of disclosure

Examples of social disclosure on mandatory topics include: information about pensions for employees, employees' share option schemes, policy regarding employment of disabled persons, donations to charity and consultation with employees. Social disclosure on a voluntary basis includes: information about employee matters, health and safety, community work, energy and the environment.

In terms of relative volume, the amount of information disclosed about employee-related matters exceeds other types of social and environmental disclosures, but the area where there is the fastest growth in interest is that of environmental issues. Many leading companies now have an 'environment' section in the annual report and some go even further in producing a separate environmental report.

Below are extracts from the 'environment' section of the report of the directors of Safe and Sure plc, the company used for illustration throughout this text.

Safe and Sure is committed to the provision of services and products which improve the quality of life, both for our customers and the community, using working practices designed to protect the environment.

Heightened awareness of environmental issues and increased legislation provide a focal point for developing greener techniques and solutions to problems, both in our more traditional businesses and also in offering opportunities to develop new businesses.

Antibacterial deep cleaning of premises, in particular high-risk areas such as washrooms, drains and food production and preparation areas, has been developed to meet increased legislation and concern as to health and food safety.

It is the responsibility of the company and all its employees to ensure that all services and products are procured, produced, packaged and delivered, and waste materials ultimately disposed of, in ways which are appropriate from an environmental viewpoint. It is the responsibility of our employees to carry out their work in a manner that will not cause damage to the environment.

14.6.2 Need for measurement

Social and environmental disclosures in annual reports have so far centred on narrative description in the directors' report or in the non-statutory part of the document. There is little evidence of impact on the accounting numbers but that may be the next step. Environmental obligations create liabilities. An oil rig in the North Sea will eventually have to be removed. The liability may be regarded as existing now because the event creating the obligation was the original act of positioning the rig in the oil field. But what will eventual removal cost? Will the rig be dismantled to a few hundred feet below the surface, out of the way of fishing nets? Will it be dismantled down to the sea bed with the debris left behind? Will the rig be towed away for dismantling elsewhere? Until these questions can be answered, the liability cannot be measured as a money amount and therefore cannot be recognised in the statement of financial position (balance sheet). Most oil companies make a provision each year towards the ultimate cost of removal of the rig and they accumulate the provision in the statement of financial position (balance sheet). They do not, in general, report the full liability at the outset.

14.6.3   The Global Reporting Initiative

The Global Reporting Initiative (GRI) is a venture that was started through a link between the United Nations Environmental Programme and a US body called the Coalition for Environmentally Responsible Economies. It has developed into a global institution that sets out a disclosure framework, called the GRI Guidelines, for sustainability reporting. Companies are increasingly referring to the GRI Guidelines in designing parts of their annual report. The recommendations include reporting on vision and strategy, the profile of the organisation, the governance structure and management system and performance indicators. These indicators should cover economic, environmental and social performance. This combination is sometimes referred to in the press as 'the triple bottom line'. The reason for this description is that for many years the earnings for equity holders has been described as 'the bottom line' (of the income statement): extending to three performance measures leads to a triple bottom line.

14.6.4   Climate change accounting

International agreements on supporting sustainable development have consequences for accounting. One example is seen in the Kyoto Protocol, an agreement resulting from a conference held in Kyoto, Japan in 1997 as an amendment to the United Nations Framework Convention on Climate Change. The Kyoto Protocol set out measures for dealing with problems of climate change by reducing greenhouse gas emissions. Some countries were more reluctant than others to ratify the agreement (confirm that they will make it operational) although gradually more countries have agreed. All member states of the EU have ratified the Protocol.

The Kyoto agreement requires action to be taken to reduce carbon-based emissions (particularly carbon dioxide) over a defined timescale. Countries are given limits of emissions of greenhouse gases. The countries then set limits on companies in specified industries.

One interesting feature of the Kyoto agreement is that companies are given 'allowances to emit'. The allowance, in the form of a licence, is capable of being transferred from one company to another. The entity that buys a licence to emit acquires an asset. This in turn creates new assets and liabilities for individual companies. The liabilities are easier to see: companies which do not reduce emissions will face penalties. However, there are also opportunities to take actions that prevent emissions and extract value from the new carbon market. If these actions meet the definition and recognition criteria, they are regarded as assets. The European Union Greenhouse Gas Emissions Trading Scheme began in January 2005. It establishes a market in carbon dioxide gas emissions for companies in specified industry sectors. Information on emissions trading is seen in annual reports published from 2005 onwards.

There is no international accounting standard dealing directly with accounting for the environment and sustainable development but there are interested groups working on the accounting issues in various countries.

A survey of accounting practices[11] observed in annual reports found that many companies report the asset of emissions allowances as an intangible asset measured at cost. If the allowances are granted by the government then the cost to the company is zero. Only when allowances are purchased does a cost appear. Fair value is an alternative method of measurement but is rarely used. The obligation to deliver up allowances to match emissions of the period is generally reported at the cost of the allowances granted, which is zero. In a cost-based system the obligation only has a measured value if there are excess emissions requiring the company to purchase additional allowances. Fair value could be used as an alternative but is rarely found.

Activity 14.3

Write down the accounting equation: Assets minus Liabilities equals Ownership interest. Suppose you are the accountant for an oil company and you have been asked to record the full liability for dismantling an oil rig in 20 years' time. How would you make the accounting equation balance?

14.7 Corporate governance

The term **corporate governance** is used to describe the way in which companies are directed and controlled. In Chapter 1 the idea of stewards and their agents was put forward briefly as a model of the relationship between shareholders and the directors of a company. It could be argued that these two groups could be left together to work out their fate, but a series of well-publicised corporate failures and financial scandals of the 1980s raised concern that such a system does not always work and the public interest may suffer as a result.

There has therefore been considerable interest in intervening to improve the quality of corporate governance. The issue has been high on the agenda in several of the English-speaking countries and the ideas have strong international interest although perhaps translated into different words and phrases.

14.7.1 The UK Corporate Governance Code

In the UK, the government has taken some action through legislation but has largely followed the traditional route of encouraging the self-regulatory approach. The self-regulatory approach is outlined in section 4.5.4 in Chapter 4. The origin of this self-regulatory approach was the 1992 report of what is usually referred to as the Cadbury Committee.[12]

The Cadbury Committee was set up by the Financial Reporting Council, the London Stock Exchange and the accountancy profession. It was asked to report on a range of issues concerned with the way directors run their companies and auditors monitor those companies, considering also the links between directors, auditors and shareholders. The recommendations of the Cadbury Committee were wide-ranging but included proposed improvements in financial reporting such as:

● more detail in the interim reports
● clearer information about directors' remuneration
● effective use of the operating and financial review
● the effectiveness of the internal control procedures used by the business
● reassurance that the business is a going concern
● a statement of the responsibilities of directors.

Although the report was issued in 1992 it took some time for further working parties to agree on the manner of reporting on internal controls and the going concern confirmation. By the end of 1995 these were in place and 1996 saw the start of a review of the first three years of implementing the Cadbury Report.

The review was chaired by Sir Ronald Hampel, so that the report which eventually appeared in 1998 was called 'The Hampel Report'.[13] It took as its starting point the view that good corporate governance was not merely a matter of complying with a number of hard and fast rules. There was seen to be a need for broad principles. It was important to take account of the diversity of circumstances and experience among companies, and within the same company over time. On this basis Hampel suggested that the true safeguard for good corporate governance lay in the application of informed and independent judgement by experienced and qualified individuals –

executive and non-executive directors, shareholders and auditors. Relatively little was said about financial reporting, beyond the assertion that the board of directors should present a balanced and understandable assessment of the company's position and prospects.

Following the Hampel Report, the Stock Exchange issued a Combined Code for listed companies containing recommendations on directors; directors' remuneration; relations with shareholders; and accountability and audit. The accountability section emphasised the responsibilities of directors in respect of financial reporting. They should present a balanced and understandable assessment of the company's position and prospects. In particular they should explain their responsibilities and they should also report that the business is a going concern.

The Combined Code was subsequently taken into the responsibility of the Financial Reporting Council. It is now called the UK Corporate Governance Code. Companies must report on how they have applied the code in their annual report and accounts.

The information provided by companies in their annual reports is based on the principle of 'comply or explain', first set out in the Cadbury Report. The **Listing Rules** of the London Stock Exchange require that companies should report whether they have followed the recommendations of the Code. If they have not done so, they should explain the reason. Companies with a Premium Listing (see section 4.5.5) must provide a 'comply or explain' statement in the annual report explaining how the company has applied the UK Corporate Governance Code.

Most companies have a separate 'Corporate Governance' section in their annual report. This section tends to grow longer each year as more headings are added. The detailed nature of most Corporate Governance sections suggests that companies are moving closer to a practice of 'comply *and* explain' rather than the principle of 'comply *or* explain'. The following typical list of headings is extracted from the Corporate Governance section of an annual report:

- Introduction
- Putting governance into practice
- The Board
- Non-executive Directors
- Board Committees
- Board meetings
- Attendance at meetings
- Induction, development and support
- Election of directors
- Board performance evaluation
- Relations with shareholders
- Internal control
- Performance reporting and information
- Review of effectiveness of internal control.

14.7.2 Directors' remuneration

There is a continuing interest in the subject of directors' remuneration, partly because it provides opportunities for newspaper headlines. Typically the interest of financial journalists focuses on the salary of the highest paid director and the amount that person is gaining through share option schemes. These schemes allow directors to obtain each year the option to buy shares at an agreed price. If the share price rises subsequently the directors exercise the option, buy the share at the agreed price and may sell immediately at a profit. Some companies offer such options to some or all of their employees by way of encouraging loyalty to the company and supplementing cash salaries. There are constant questions about whether remuneration is justified by meeting performance targets.

In response to well-publicised concerns about the need to disclose and control the level of directors' remuneration, a study group chaired by Sir Richard Greenbury (1995) produced a code of best practice on disclosure and remuneration policy.[14] These recommendations are now incorporated partly in the Companies Act 2006 and partly in the Corporate Governance Code. A typical annual report of a listed company contains several pages on the remuneration policy and the payments to directors. There is a particular focus on how performance targets are set and monitored.

Activity 14.4

Obtain the annual report of a listed company. Turn to the report on corporate governance. What does the company say about corporate governance and about compliance with the Corporate Governance Code? What do the auditors say about the report on corporate governance? What is disclosed about the remuneration committee? What information is given elsewhere in the annual report, relating to directors' remuneration?

14.8 Meaning of 'present fairly' and 'true and fair view'

The IASB system of accounting requires financial statements to *present fairly* the financial position, financial performance and cash flows of an entity.[15] In virtually all circumstances a fair presentation is achieved by compliance with the applicable IFRSs.[16] Entities cannot use notes or explanatory material to compensate for inappropriate accounting policies – the choice of policies must in itself achieve a fair presentation.[17] In the extremely rare circumstances where management considers that compliance with a requirement of an IFRS would conflict with the objective of a fair presentation, the entity will depart from the requirement and explain the reasons and consequences.[18]

The Companies Act 2006 requires that financial statements of companies should show *a true and fair view*.[19] In most situations a company will achieve a true and fair view by following the requirements of company law and UK accounting standards. In the rare circumstances where management considers that compliance with a requirement of law and standards would conflict with the true and fair view, the entity will depart from that requirement and explain the reasons and consequences.

14.8.1 Equivalence of meaning

The question arises as to whether 'present fairly' and 'a true and fair view' have different meanings. The Financial Reporting Council (FRC)[20] has obtained legal opinion that 'present fairly' and 'true and fair view' are not different requirements. They are different ways of expressing the same concept. The FRC has also pointed out that the IASB Framework equates 'true and fair view' and 'fair presentation' in asserting that the application of the principal qualitative characteristics and of appropriate accounting standards normally results in financial statements that convey what is generally understood as a true and fair view or a fair presentation of information.[21]

The remainder of this section discusses the meaning of 'true and fair view' because it has a longer history of debate and development in the UK. The phrase 'true and fair' was taken into European Directives when the UK joined as a member state but it has never found an exact equivalent in the underlying meaning. For example the French wording 'image fidèle' is closer to 'a faithful picture'.

The UK has traditionally taken the position that it may be necessary for individual companies to take action which contravenes legal rules, in the interest of presenting 'a true and fair view'. In other countries, including the US, the position taken is generally that the law prevails and any questions about fair presentation should be analysed within the legal framework. The US wording is 'faithful representation'.

14.8.2   Meaning of a true and fair view

The UK Companies Act provides no definition of the meaning of 'a true and fair view'. Consequently from time to time those who set accounting standards have sought the opinion of expert legal advisers. The lawyers have put forward the view that the requirement for a true and fair view is a dynamic concept which changes its nature as the general values of society change. Although the words stay the same, the meaning of the words changes because the opinions of society in general change.

What does that mean in practice? The lawyers have provided an example.[22] The Bill of Rights 1688 prohibited 'cruel and unusual punishments'. The dictionary definition of 'cruel' has changed little since that time but a judge today would characterise as 'cruel' some punishments which a judge of 1688 would not have regarded as cruel. The meaning of the word remains the same but the facts to which it is applied have changed. Based on reasoning of that type, the lawyers have argued that the words 'true and fair' may carry the same dictionary meaning from one time to another but the accounting principles and practice contributing to a true and fair view will change as circumstances change.

One very important issue is the question of whether society, and the public interest, would expect the application of accounting standards to be necessary as evidence of intent to apply a true and fair view. Legal advice provided to the ASB analysed the role of an accounting standard:

What is the purpose of an accounting standard? The initial purpose is to identify proper accounting practice for the benefit of preparers and auditors of accounts. However, because accounts commonly comply with accounting standards, the effect of the issue of standards has also been to create a common understanding between users and preparers of accounts as to how particular items should be treated in accounts and accordingly an expectation that, save where good reason exists, accounts will comply with applicable accounting standards.[23]

Accounting standards have, over a period of years, become regarded as an authoritative source of accounting practice. The legal opinion given to the ASB is that accounting standards provide very strong evidence of the proper practice which should be adopted. The 'true and fair view' is seen as a dynamic concept:

Thus what is required to show a true and fair view is subject to continuous rebirth and in determining whether the true and fair requirement is satisfied the Court will not in my view seek to find synonyms for the words 'true and fair' but will seek to apply the concepts which those words imply.[24]

14.8.3   Who is responsible for the true and fair view?

Under company law, it is the directors who are responsible for ensuring that the accounts are prepared in such a way as to show a true and fair view. The auditors state whether, in their opinion, the accounts show a true and fair view. If you turn back to Chapter 4 you will see an example of the statement of directors' responsibilities which now appears in many company reports and also a copy of the auditors' report. Both contain the phrase 'a true and fair view' and emphasise the different types of responsibility held by directors and auditors.

14.8.4   How specific is the 'true and fair' concept?

You should have gained an understanding, from various chapters of this book, that there is more than one accounting treatment for many transactions and events. It is a great puzzle to many people that companies could produce different accounting statements for one particular period of time, each of which would show a true and fair view. The answer lies in one very small word. The requirement of law is for 'a true and fair view' but not for 'the true and fair view'. Thus the directors do not have to find 'the very best true and fair view', which may surprise some users of financial statements. It also becomes very difficult for auditors to enter into dispute with directors where there are two acceptable alternatives, either of which could result in a true and fair view. To be successful in contradicting the directors, the auditors need to show that a particular practice does *not* show a true and fair view. If they can successfully argue that opinion then the company has the choice of revising the proposed treatment or facing a *qualified* audit opinion. Here is an example of a qualified audit opinion where the auditor and directors were in disagreement:

Qualified audit opinion
We found that the company has made no provision for doubtful debts, despite circumstances which indicate that such a provision is necessary.
In our opinion the accounts do not give a true and fair view . . .

It is therefore essential, in reading the annual report, to read the auditors' report at an early stage in order to be aware of any problems with the financial statements. It is also essential to realise that the meaning of 'true and fair' is highly subjective and changes over a period of time.

Activity 14.5	*Looking back through Chapters 8 to 12, identify matters of accounting practice where more than one accounting policy is permitted. If you were an auditor, how would you decide whether one or other of the permitted choices gave a true and fair view?*

14.9 Measurement of value

Throughout the majority of this financial accounting text the value of assets and liabilities has been measured at historical cost. That means the price paid, or the liability agreed, when the transaction was first undertaken. In times when prices are changing, that information about the cost at the date of the transaction will become less relevant to the needs of users (although it may be seen as a reliable measure). The IASB *Conceptual Framework* says relatively little about measurement,[25] perhaps because of the difficulties of obtaining international agreement. A useful overview is provided by the ICAEW.[26]

14.9.1 Stages of recognition and measurement

At the moment when the transaction takes place, the historical cost is also the current value, where current value is regarded as the value of the item at the accounting date. This is identified as the point of initial recognition. If an asset or a liability is involved, then there will be various points at which it may be appropriate to remeasure the amount at which the asset or liability is recorded. This is referred to as subsequent remeasurement. Finally there may come a point at which the asset or liability should be removed from the financial statements. This is referred to as derecognition.

The conditions to be applied in deciding on initial **recognition** have been explained in Chapter 2. **Derecognition** reverses the conditions so that an asset or a liability should cease to be recognised if there is no longer sufficient evidence that the entity has access to future economic benefits or an obligation to transfer economic benefits.[27]

14.9.2 Limitations of historical cost accounting

Throughout this text you have studied historical cost accounting where the acquisition of assets is recorded at the amount paid at the time of acquisition. The academic literature is bursting at the seams with criticisms of historical cost accounting, but the practice has proved hard to change. There were brief practical attempts in the UK to apply a different approach for a period from the mid-1970s to the mid-1980s but the rate of inflation then became less of a problem and interest waned.

Critics of historical cost accounting have said that in the statement of financial position (balance sheet) there is the addition of items bought at different times and with £s of different purchasing power. That is not a satisfactory procedure. In the income statement (profit and loss account) the costs are matched against revenue without regard for the fact that goods were bought and expenses paid for at an earlier point in time. Sales are therefore matched against outdated costs. The tax system takes the accounting profit as its starting point and therefore the tax payable is dictated by outdated accounting figures.

Supporters of historical cost accounting point to its reliability and objectivity because the monetary amount of the transaction is known. Verifiability is straightforward because documentation exists. The preference for historical cost values remains strong; if companies do decide to revalue fixed assets then both the IASB and UK ASB require them to keep the current values up to date in each year's statement of financial position (balance sheet).[28]

14.9.3 Subsequent remeasurement

Subsequent remeasurement poses more problems and is one of the more controversial aspects of setting accounting standards. Each standard sets relevant conditions, with a general principle that there should be a change in the amount at which an asset or liability is recorded if there is sufficient evidence that: (a) the amount has changed and (b) the new amount can be measured with sufficient reliability.[29] In times of inflation (when prices generally are increasing), the idea of remeasurement becomes particularly important. Even when inflation is not a major problem, there may be one particular asset whose value increases through scarcity of supply or decreases through lack of demand.

That leads into an extremely controversial question: 'How do you measure value?' Methods of valuation are listed in the *IASB Conceptual Framework*,[30] but without any firm preferences being expressed.

14.9.4 Entry price and exit price

Taking fixed assets and stocks as the main examples to begin with, it could be said that there are two different categories of measures of value. There is a price which the organisation will have to pay to acquire the asset and there is a price at which the organisation will be able to sell the asset to someone else. If you have ever tried buying and selling second-hand goods you will know that the buying price and the selling price are often quite different. The student who tries to sell an outdated personal computer through an advertisement on the college noticeboard knows that any enquirer will try to push the price downwards. The student attempting to enquire about a similar item of equipment knows that the seller will try to keep the price high. Somehow the price for which you are able to sell your second-hand possessions invariably appears to be lower than the price someone else is asking for their unwanted belongings.

The price paid by a business to acquire an asset is called in accounting the **entry price** and the price at which the business would be able to sell the asset is called the **exit price**. Academic authors will argue long and hard on both sides of the case and if you pursue the study of accounting further you will meet that academic debate. In the real world a decision has to be made. In the UK, that decision was made by the standard-setting body at the beginning of the 1980s, when SSAP 16 required companies to use the entry price approach and to measure the value of fixed assets and stocks at the cost of replacement at the date of the financial statements. That approach was used to provide additional information in annual reports of the UK for the first half of the 1980s, but gradually the enthusiasm of companies waned and by the late 1980s they had reverted to their traditional practice of using primarily historical cost for most aspects of measurement.

14.9.5 Current values[31]

In a current value system, changes in value are recorded as they occur. This idea, if accepted, puts quite a large hole in the concept of **realisation**, which is at the heart of traditional accounting practice. It has been the practice to record changes in ownership interest only when the change in an asset or liability is realised, in the form either of cash or of other assets the ultimate realisation of which can be assessed with reasonable certainty. That practice finds continuing support in the Companies Act 2006 which states that the income statement (profit and loss account) reported under the Act may report only those profits which are realised (although this requirement does not apply to companies reporting under full IFRS).

Chapter 12 has explained how some gains and losses on revaluation may be reported in Other Comprehensive Income. There is an unanswered question of how to measure current value.

The argument favoured by some commentators in the UK, is the one which leads to a measurement system based on **value to the business**. Those who support this idea start by asking: What is the worst that can happen to a person, or business, which owns a fixed asset or item of trading stock? The answer is that they may be deprived of the item, perhaps by theft, fire, obsolescence or similar cause. The next question is: What would the owners need in order to be returned to the position they enjoyed previously? The answer, in most cases, is that they need to be provided with the cost of replacement of a similar item so that they may continue with the activity of the business. In a few rare cases, where the owners may have decided to sell rather than continue using the asset, the selling price is the measure of deprival.

From this analysis it is argued that the value to the business of a fixed asset or an item of stock is usually the **replacement cost** at the accounting date. The replacement cost is that of a similar item in a similar state. Such a replacement cost might be found in a catalogue of prices of used equipment or it could be estimated by starting with the cost of a new item and applying an appropriate proportion of depreciation.

14.9.6 Fair value

The IASB standards have moved towards a fair value approach to valuation rather than a 'value to the business' approach. Several of the standards in the IASB system permit or require the use of **fair value**, which to based on exit price.

Definition | **Fair value** is the price that would be received to sell an asset or paid to transfer a liability in an orderly transaction between market participants at the measurement date.[32]

The definition of fair value has been agreed between the IASB and the US standard setter, the FASB (Financial Accounting Standards Board), taking effect from the start of 2013. Ideally the price should be found from an active market, in which transactions for the asset or liability take place with sufficient frequency and volume to provide pricing information on an ongoing basis. If the company operates in more than one market, then the price should be taken from the market that maximises the amount that would be received to sell the asset or minimises the amount that would be paid to transfer the liability, after taking into account transaction costs and transport costs.

In some cases there is no active market for an asset or a liability. The accounting standard then sets out a sequence of attempts (a 'hierarchy') to be followed in deciding on fair value. Companies must explain how they have applied this hierarchy. For property, plant and equipment[33] a company might use depreciated replacement cost where market-based evidence is not available. For biological assets a range of suggestions is given, such as market price of similar assets or discounted present value of future cash flows.[34]

14.9.7 Current practice

In annual reports of UK companies there is a general adherence to historical cost but some companies show evidence of using revaluation, which is permitted by the UK ASB as well as by the IASB system.

The International Accounting Standard IAS 16 permits entities to choose either the cost model or the revaluation model. Under the cost model, property, plant and equipment are carried at cost less accumulated depreciation. Under the revaluation model an item of property, plant and equipment may be carried at a revalued amount. The revalued amount is fair value less accumulated depreciation. Revaluations must be made regularly so that the carrying amount remains close to fair value at the date of the financial statements.

Activity 14.6

Look at the items you possess. These might include a house or a flat or a car, but equally well they could be a bicycle and some modest items of furniture. Whatever their nature, write down on a piece of paper a figure in £s which answers the question: What is the value of these possessions? Now think about how you arrived at that figure. Did you use the original cost because that was the amount you paid to acquire them? Did you use replacement cost because that is the amount you would have to pay to replace them? Did you use selling price because that is the amount you could collect in cash for conversion to other uses? Did you have some other method? What was the reason for the method you chose? Would you obtain the same answer using all the methods listed for this activity? Which answer is the most relevant for your information needs? Which is the most reliable? Is there any conflict here between relevance and reliability? Would other students answer these questions as you have done?

14.10 Risk reporting

One of the major causes of increasing disclosure in annual reports is the need to explain the risks that the business faces. For UK company reporting there are several sources of requirements for risk reporting in the notes to the accounts and in the narrative sections of the annual report. Many companies provide additional voluntary information about risks because they are aware of its importance to investors and other users of the annual report.

The Business Review regulations require companies to provide information on description of the principal risks and uncertainties facing the company. It is for companies to decide how to implement this requirement. The Financial Reporting Review Panel has repeatedly questioned whether companies meet this regulatory requirement. It suggests companies test their disclosures against the following questions:

1 Do the disclosures state clearly which are the principal risks and uncertainties facing the business?

2 Are those risks and uncertainties described as principal the main risks and uncertainties that currently face the business? For example, have the risks and uncertainties listed as principal been the subject of recent discussions at board or audit committee meetings? Are there risks which have been the subject of such discussions which should be considered as principal?

3 Is the description of each principal risk and uncertainty sufficient for shareholders to understand the nature of that risk or uncertainty and how it might affect the company?

4 Are the principal risks and uncertainties described in a manner consistent with the way in which they are discussed within the company?

5 Are the principal risks and uncertainties shown consistent with the rest of the report and accounts? Are there risks and uncertainties on the list which are not referred to elsewhere or are there significant risks and uncertainties discussed elsewhere which do not appear on the list?

6 Is there a description, in the directors' report, or elsewhere in the report and accounts and explicitly cross-referenced from the directors' report, of how the company manages each of the principal risks and uncertainties?

Researchers have found that risk information is important for analysts, professional and private investors. While the annual report is an important source of risk information for the private investor, the professional investors say they prefer one-to-one meetings with companies to explore risk information. There is a feeling that most of the information disclosed in the annual report is already known to the well informed professional investor before the report is published, because these investors keep in contact with the company on a regular basis. It seems that the information published is of greatest potential use to the private investor or to persons less closely familiar with the company.

14.11 Developing issues: how valid is the stakeholder model?

This book takes as its starting point the IASB's *Conceptual Framework*, and has constantly returned to that *Conceptual Framework* for explanation or discussion of the accounting practices explained in various chapters. The *Conceptual Framework* is, in its turn, built on a model which sees the objective of accounting as serving the needs of a wide range of users. Those users are sometimes referred to as **stakeholders** and the *Conceptual Framework* is regarded as an example of a stakeholder model of the process of regulating accounting.

There are, however, those who would argue that the stakeholder model is the wrong place to start and therefore the significant problems of accounting will not be solved using a statement of principles of this type. At the basic level of understanding existing accounting practice, which is the limit of this book, the validity of one model versus another may not be a critical issue, but you should be aware that there are views that more complex accounting problems may not be solved using a stakeholder approach.

Those who argue against the 'user needs' approach suggest that accounting regulation is a much more complex process of social interaction. Standard-setters producing accounting rules in a self-regulatory environment need to be sure of a consensus of opinion supporting the proposed rules. They will therefore seek out a range of opinions and will undoubtedly be subjected to lobbying (letters of comment and personal contact) by persons or organisations seeking to put forward a particular viewpoint. Indeed, part of the UK standard-setting process involves issuing an exposure draft for comment before a financial reporting standard is issued, although there is no way of knowing what lobbying occurs behind the scenes.

The process of standard-setting may therefore be regarded as one of negotiating and balancing various interests. There has been research after the event, both in the UK and in other countries, which has shown that the standard-setting bodies were influenced by one or more powerful forces. One particularly clear example may be seen in the development of an accounting standard to tighten up practices in reporting expenditure on research and development.[35] There is a significant amount of academic literature on factors influencing the process of setting accounting standards.

Those who have identified these 'political' pressures would suggest that the accounting standard-setting process should openly admit that there are influential factors such as: the relative balance of power among those who prepare and those who use accounting information; relative dependency of some on others; the balance of individual liberty against collective need; and the ideology observed in particular systems of social relations. (Ideology means that a group in society may hold strong beliefs which make it genuinely unable to appreciate different positions taken by others.)

Thus claims that the standard-setting process is neutral in its impact on the economy or on society may be unrealistic. This book does not seek to impose any particular view on its readers. It has used the *Conceptual Framework* as a consistent basis for explaining current practice, but it leaves to the reader the task of taking forward the knowledge of external financial reporting and the understanding of what influences the future development of external financial reporting.

14.12 Summary

- The **operating and financial review** (OFR) provides a balanced and comprehensive analysis of the business, its year-end position, the trends in performance during the year and factors likely to affect future position and performance. It is good practice for quoted UK companies.

- A **highlights statement** in the annual report shows what the company regards as important information for investors as the primary users of the annual report. A table of five-year trends is also useful in evaluating the position and performance of the business.

- **Segmental reporting** has developed as a means of supplementing the consolidated financial statements by providing more insight into the activities of the group. In particular it reports information about the different types of products and services that an entity produces and the different geographical areas in which it operates.

- **Off-balance-sheet finance** describes the situation where an asset and a liability are omitted from the financial statements of an entity. The UK ASB takes the view that such transactions should remain on the entity's statement of financial position (balance sheet) if the risks and rewards remain with the entity. The IASB has specific rules to deal with special purpose vehicles, which are one form of off-balance-sheet finance.

- **Corporate social responsibility** means that companies integrate social and environmental concerns in their business operations and in their interactions with stakeholders. Many companies include social and environmental disclosures in their annual reports. The Global Reporting Initiative provides a framework for such disclosures.

- Carbon trading, arising from the Kyoto Protocol, provides a new form of asset in the licence to emit carbon dioxide and a new form of liability in the obligation to reduce emissions.

● The term **corporate governance** is used to describe the way in which companies are directed and controlled. Listed companies in the UK are required to follow the Corporate Governance Code. In the annual report the directors must either confirm compliance with the Code or explain reasons for non-compliance.

● Directors' remuneration is one aspect of corporate governance that receives a great deal of attention. There are rules and guidance on the disclosure of remuneration (pay) policy and the amount due to each director. The information is usually contained in the report of the Remuneration Committee.

● The IASB system of accounting requires financial statements to **present fairly** the financial position, financial performance and cash flows of an entity. The Companies Act 2006 requires that financial statements of companies should show a **true and fair view**. The Financial Reporting Council has given an opinion that the two phrases are broadly equivalent.

● There is a continuing debate on the methods of measuring assets and liabilities. **Reliability** points towards historical cost accounting but **faithful representation** points towards current values.

● **Entry price** values are values that measure the cost of buying, acquiring or replacing an asset or liability. **Exit price** values represent the sale, disposal or other form of realisation of an asset.

● **Fair value** is the price that would be received to sell an asset or paid to transfer a liability in an orderly transaction between market participants at the measurement date.

● Finally, it should be noted that this entire book on financial accounting has been built on a **stakeholder** model of user needs which itself is the basis of the IASB's *Conceptual Framework*. That idea meets general acceptance in the accounting profession from those who set accounting standards, but you need to be aware that further study of the academic literature will encourage you to question the user needs model.

Further reading

The following reference materials are all available free of charge on the relevant web sites:

Abraham, S., Marston, C. and Darby, P. (2012), *Risk reporting: clarity, relevance and location.* The Institute of Chartered Accountants of Scotland.

Climate Disclosure Standards Board (2010), *Disclosure Framework*.

Crawford, L., Extance, H., Helliar, C. and Power, D. (2012), *Operating Segments: The usefulness of IFRS 8*. The Institute of Chartered Accountants of Scotland.

Financial Reporting Council (October 2010), *The UK Approach to Corporate Governance*.

Financial Reporting Council (July 2011), *True and Fair*.

Financial Reporting Review Panel Press notice FRRP PN 130 (Feb 2011), *The Financial Reporting Review Panel highlights challenges in the reporting of principal risks and uncertainties*.

ICAEW (2010), *Measurement in Financial Reporting*. The Institute of Chartered Accountants in England and Wales.

Lovell, H., Sales de Aguiar, T., Bebbington, J. and Larrinaga-Gonzalez, C. (2010), *Accounting for Carbon*. Association of Chartered Certified Accountants.

QUESTIONS

The Questions section of each chapter has three types of question. 'Test your understanding' questions to help you review your reading are in the 'A' series of questions. You will find the answers to these by reading and thinking about the material in the book. 'Application' questions to test your ability to apply technical skills are in the 'B' series of questions. Questions requiring you to show skills in problem solving and evaluation are in the 'C' series of questions. A letter [S] indicates that there is a solution at the end of the book.

A | Test your understanding

A14.1 What is the objective of the operating and financial review? (Section 14.2.1)

A14.2 Why is there no prescribed format for the OFR? (Section 14.2.2)

A14.3 What are the main principles set by the ASB for the OFR? (Section 14.2.2)

A14.4 What are the main elements of the disclosure framework for the OFR? (Section 14.2.3)

A14.5 What are key performance indicators (KPIs)? (Section 14.2.4)

A14.6 What are the particular requirements of the OFR Regulation that must be reported in an OFR? (Section 14.2.5)

A14.7 What are the responsibilities of the directors and auditors in relation to the OFR? (Section 14.2.6)

A14.8 What is the purpose of a highlights statement? (Section 14.3.1)

A14.9 How does a five-year summary of historical results help investors? (Section 14.3.2)

A14.10 How does segmental information help the users of financial statements? (Section 14.4.1)

A14.11 Which items are reported on a segmental basis? (Section 14.4.1)

A14.12 How are segments identified? (Section 14.4.3)

A14.13 Why is off-balance-sheet finance a problem in accounting? (Section 14.5)

A14.14 What principles are recommended by the UK ASB for determining whether assets and liabilities should be reported on the statement of financial position (balance sheet)? (Section 14.5.2)

A14.15 What is a special purpose entity? (Section 14.5.3)

A14.16 What is corporate social responsibility? (Section 14.6)

A14.17 What is the Global Reporting Initiative? (Section 14.6.3)

A14.18 What accounting issues arise in relation to carbon trading? (Section 14.6.4)

A14.19 What is meant by corporate governance? (Section 14.7)

A14.20 What is the Combined Code? (Section 14.7.1)

A14.21 How does financial reporting help to improve corporate governance? (Section 14.7)

A14.22 Why has it been found impossible to write a definitive guide on the meaning of 'a true and fair view'? (Section 14.8)

A14.23 What are the limitations of historical cost accounting? (Section 14.9.2)

A14.24 Why is it desirable to remeasure assets and liabilities subsequent to acquisition? (Section 14.9.3)

A14.25 Explain what is meant by entry price and exit price. (Section 14.9.4)

A14.26 Explain what is meant by fair value. (Section 14.9.6)

A14.27 Should accounting standards focus primarily on the needs of users? (Section 14.10)

B   Application

B14.1
Suggest, with reasons, three KPIs for each of the following types of business, and explain why it is unlikely that two businesses will choose identical KPIs.

(a) a private hospital
(b) a car repair garage
(c) a clothing manufacturer.

C   Problem solving and evaluation

C14.1 [S]
Carry out a trend analysis on Safe and Sure plc, using the historical summary set out in Appendix I. Write a short report on the key features emerging from the trends.

Activities for study groups

Case 14.1

Turn to the annual report of a listed company which you have used for activities throughout the previous chapters. Split the group to take two different roles: one half of the group should take the role of the finance director and the other half should take the role of the broker's analyst writing a report on the company.

Look through the annual report for any ratio calculations performed by the company and check these from the data in the financial statements, so far as you are able. Prepare your own calculations of ratios for analysis of all aspects of performance. Find the current share price from a current newspaper.

Once the data preparation is complete, the finance director subgroup should prepare a short report to a meeting with the analysts. The analysts should then respond with questions arising from the ratio analysis. The finance directors should seek to present answers to the questions using the annual report. Finally write a short report (250 words) on problems encountered in calculating and interpreting financial ratios.

Case 14.2

Turn to the annual report of a listed company which you have used for activities in previous chapters. Is this a group? How do you know? Where is the list of subsidiary companies?

If you do not have a group report, obtain another annual report which is for a group of companies (nearly all large listed companies operate in group form). As a group, imagine that you are a team of analysts seeking to break down the component segments of the group for analytical purposes. How much information can you find about the segments? What are the problems of defining segments in this group? If you can obtain the annual report for the previous year, compare the definitions of segments. Are they consistent from one year to the next?

Based on your analysis, prepare a short essay (250 words): 'The usefulness of segmental information in the analysis of group performance'.

Case 14.3

Divide the group into sections to take on four different roles: a private shareholder in a company; a financial journalist; a finance director of a company; and a broker's analyst providing an advisory service to clients.

In each section develop your opinion on the subject Taking the user needs perspective will solve all the problems of accounting.

Arrange a meeting to present all four opinions and then discuss the extent to which the International Accounting Standards Board will be able to obtain the co-operation of all parties in solving accounting problems.

Notes and references

1. ASB (1993, revised 2003), Statement, *Operating and Financial Review*, Accounting Standards Board.
2. Companies Act 2006, section 417; http://www.legislation.gov.uk/ukpga/2006/46/contents.
3. ASB (2006), *Reporting Statement 1: Operating and Financial Review*, issued January, 2006. Financial Reporting Council.
4. ASB (2006), RS 1 paras 75–7.
5. ASB (2006), RS 1 para. 1.
6. ASB (2006), RS 1 paras 4, 6, 8, 13, 16, 22 and 24.
7. ASB (2006), RS 1 para. 27.
8. IASB (2012), IFRS 8 *Operating Segments*, International Accounting Standards Board.
9. Crawford et al. (2012), *Operating Segments: The usefulness of IFRS 8*.
10. ASB (1994), Financial Reporting Standard (FRS 5), *Reporting the Substance of Transactions*, Accounting Standards Board.
11. Lovell et al. (2010), *Accounting for Carbon*.
12. The Committee on the Financial Aspects of Corporate Governance (1992) *The Financial Aspects of Corporate Governance* (The Cadbury Report), December. The Committee Chairman was Sir Adrian Cadbury.
13. *The Committee on Corporate Governance Final Report* (1998), Gee Publishing Ltd. (The Committee chairman was Sir Ronnie Hampel.)
14. *Report of a Study Group on Directors' Remuneration* (1995) (The Greenbury Report), Gee Publishing Ltd.
15. IASB (2012), IAS 1 *Presentation of financial statements*, para. 15.
16. IASB (2012), IAS 1 para. 15.
17. IASB (2012), IAS 1 para. 18.
18. IASB (2012), IAS 1 paras 19 and 20.
19. Companies Act 2006, section 393.
20. FRC (2011), *True and Fair*. Financial Reporting Council website, www.frc.org.uk.
21. IASB *Conceptual Framework*, para. BC 3.44.
22. Hoffman, L. and Arden, M. H. (1983), 'Legal opinion on "true and fair" ', *Accountancy*, November, pp. 154–6.
23. ASB (1993), *Foreword to Accounting Standards*, appendix, 'Accounting Standards Board: the true and fair requirement', para. 4. Opinion prepared by Mary Arden, barrister of Erskine Chambers, Lincoln's Inn, London.
24. *Ibid.*, para. 14.
25. IASB *Conceptual Framework* (2010), paras 4.37–4.53.
26. ICAEW (2006), *Measurement in Financial Reporting*.
27. Explained in various IFRS such as IFRS 9 *Financial Instruments*.
28. IASB (2012), IAS 16 *Property, Plant and Equipment*, para. 31; ASB (1999), Financial Reporting Standard (FRS 15), *Measurement of Tangible Fixed Assets*, Accounting Standards Board, paras 43–52.
29. E.g. IAS 16 *Property, Plant and Equipment*, para. 31.
30. IASB *Conceptual Framework* (2010), para. 4.55.
31. ICAEW (2006), *Measurement in Financial Reporting*. The Institute of Chartered Accountants in England and Wales.
32. IASB (2012), IFRS 13 *Fair Value Measurement*.
33. IASB (2012), IAS 16 *Property, Plant and Equipment*, para. 33.
34. IASB (2012), IAS 41 *Agriculture*, paras 13–25.
35. Hope, T. and Gray, R. (1982), 'Power and policy making: the development of an R&D standard', *Journal of Business Finance and Accounting*, 9(4): 531–58.

Chapter 15

Reporting cash flows

Amazon

One of the joys of Amazon's business model is that customers pay straight away while suppliers are paid later. When a company is growing quickly, this mismatch (that is, the difference between days receivable and days payable) feeds through to cash flows – though this working capital benefit declines with maturity.

Alamy Images/Pixelbully

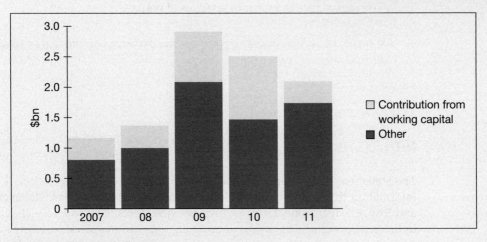

Amazon's free cash flow

Because Amazon pays its suppliers much more slowly than it is paid by its customers, in 2011 it averaged 90 days' worth of sales in payables (money due to be paid out) versus 16 days in receivables (money due to come in). Good inventory management also frees up cash. Over the past five years, these benefits (known as negative working capital) have accounted for almost a third of Amazon's free cash flow . . . this working capital benefit will decline when Amazon's growth slows. Working capital will not be a significant source of cash flow forever.

Source: Robert Armstrong and Stuart Kirk, at: http://www.ft.com/cms/s/0/f3a02a44-cb53-11e1-b896-00144feabdc0.html#axzz21o2gR2kd.

Discussion points

1 What items, other than working capital, may affect free cash flow (it is not defined in the article)?

2 Why will the working capital benefit for cash decline when growth slows?

Contents

Learning outcomes

After reading this chapter you should be able to:

- Explain why statements of cash flows are regarded as providing useful information.
- Explain the meaning of cash and cash equivalents.
- Explain the direct and the indirect forms of presentation of a statement of cash flows.
- Prepare a statement of cash flows using the direct and the indirect method.

15.1 Introduction

The statement of cash flows is one of the primary financial statements. It provides information that can not be seen in the balance sheet and income statement (profit and loss account) alone. Users of financial statements want to know about changes in financial position. This involves providing information about an entity's ability to generate cash flows and the entity's use of those cash flows.

Chapter 3 gives a very simple introduction to the statement of cash flows. In particular it shows why cash flow and profit differ because of the different timings of cash flow and profits. Chapter 9 indicates the working capital cycle through which inventories are acquired from suppliers on credit and sold to customers on credit. The cash eventually received from customers is used to pay suppliers and the cycle starts again. Chapter 13 illustrates a statement of cash flows prepared from the statements of financial position and income statement of the illustrative company used in that chapter. The case study of Safe and Sure plc runs throughout several chapters with outline discussion of the statement of cash flows in Chapter 4.

This chapter provides a more thorough explanation of a statement of cash flows as presented in the IASB system. It explains in sections 15.2 and 15.3 the nature of the two choices – the 'direct' and the 'indirect' methods. Section 15.4 explains the nature and purpose of each line item of a statement of cash flows prepared using the indirect system. Section 15.5 explains the nature and purpose of each line item of a statement of cash flows prepared using the direct system. Section 15.6 presents a worked example for those who wish to practise preparation of a statement of cash flows based on the IASB system.[1]

15.2 Cash and cash equivalents

The IASB system[2] presents a statement of cash flows that explains changes in **cash** and **cash equivalents**.

Definitions

> **Cash** comprises cash on hand and demand deposits.
>
> **Cash equivalents** are short-term, highly liquid investments that are readily convertible to known amounts of cash and which are subject to an insignificant risk of changes in value.[3]

Cash is relatively easy to understand – it is cash that is immediately available. Cash equivalents are investments that are held to meet short-term commitments. To qualify as a cash equivalent the investment must be readily convertible to a known amount of cash and there must be an insignificant risk of changes in value. An investment qualifies as a cash equivalent only when it has a short maturity of, say, three months or less from the date of acquisition.[4]

Bank borrowings are generally considered to be financing activities. However, bank overdrafts that are repayable on demand are part of the cash management of a business. The bank balance fluctuates from a positive balance to an overdrawn balance at different times of the year.[5]

15.3 The direct method and the indirect method

There are two approaches to presenting the cash flows arising from operations. The direct method presents cash inflows from customers and cash outflows to suppliers and employees, taken from the entity's accounting records of cash receipts and payments. The indirect method starts with the operating profit and makes a series of adjustments to convert profit to cash. The data in Table 15.1 and Table 15.2 are used to illustrate each method.

Table 15.1
Income statement (profit and loss account), Year 2

	£
Revenue	100
Cost of sales: materials	(40)
Wages	(20)
Depreciation	(10)
Operating profit	30

Table 15.2
Statements of financial position (balance sheets), end of Years 1 and 2

	Year 2	Year 1
	£	£
Non-current assets	90	100
Current assets		
Inventory (stock) of materials	55	40
Trade receivables (debtors)	12	15
Cash	35	10
Total current assets	102	65
Total assets	192	165
Current liabilities		
Trade payables (creditors)	(11)	(14)
Non-current liabilities		
Long-term loans	(100)	(100)
Total liabilities	(111)	(114)
Net assets	81	51
Ownership interest	81	51

15.3.1 Direct method

The direct method reports the cash inflows from customers and cash outflows to suppliers, employees and other aspects of operations. This information is contained in the cash book or in the cash receipts and cash payments records used as input to the bookkeeping records in the general ledger. The direct method calculation is presented in Table 15.3. It is followed by a comment on each line in the calculation.

Table 15.3
Direct method

Operating cash flow, Year 1	
	£
Cash received from customers	103
Cash paid to suppliers	(58)
Wages paid	(20)
Operating cash flow	25

General comment. In the direct method the cash flows are taken from the cash records. The cash records have to be analysed into categories suitable for the statement of cash flows. In Chapters 5 and 6 you have seen spreadsheets in which the cash record is the 'cash at bank' column. That column was used as the basis for the simple statement of cash flows on the direct method illustrated in those chapters (see sections 5.5.1 and 6.6.1). This chapter does not provide the detail of the cash records of receipts and payments but the following comments explain how the cash figures can be confirmed from the information in the balance sheet and the income statement (profit and loss account).

Cash received from customers. The cash inflows from customers may be confirmed by starting with the revenue earned in the period. Some of the revenue has been earned from selling to customers on credit. The amounts receivable from customers (debtors) at the start of the period will have been collected in cash during the period. The amounts shown as receivable from customers (debtors) at the end of the period are the revenue not yet collected in cash. This analysis is presented in the following calculation:

	£m
Revenue of the period	100
Add receivables at the start of the period	15
Less receivables at the end of the period	(12)
Cash received from customers	103

Cash paid to suppliers. The cash outflows to suppliers may be confirmed by starting with the materials purchased in the period. Some of the purchases have been obtained from suppliers on credit. The amounts payable to suppliers (creditors) at the start of the period will have been paid in cash during the period. The amounts shown as payable to suppliers (creditors) at the end of the period are the payments not yet made.

The next question is – how to confirm the figure for purchases?

The purchases of materials are needed to supply the goods sold and to provide an inventory at the end of the period. If there is an inventory (stock) at the start of the period this reduces the need to make purchases. This analysis is presented in the following calculation:

	£m
Cost of materials sold in the period	40
Add inventory at the end of the period	55
Less inventory at the start of the period	(40)
Purchases of materials	55

Then the payment to suppliers is calculated.

	£m
Purchases of the period	55
Add payables at the start of the period	14
Less payables at the end of the period	(11)
Cash paid to suppliers	58

Wages paid. Usually the wages are paid as soon as the work is done so the amount shown for wages in the income statement (profit and loss account) is the same as the cash payment. To confirm the wages payment, if any amount of wages remains unpaid at the start or end of the period then the wages cost must be adjusted for these unpaid amounts in a manner similar to the calculation of cash paid to suppliers.

15.3.2 Indirect method

The indirect method starts with the operating profit and makes adjustments to arrive at cash flow from operations. The indirect method calculation is presented in Table 15.4. It is followed by an explanation of each line in the calculation.

Table 15.4
Indirect method

Operating cash flow, Year 1	
	£
Operating profit	30
Add back depreciation	10
	40
(Increase) in inventory	(15)
Decrease in receivables	3
(Decrease) in payables	(3)
Operating cash flow	25

Operating profit. This figure is taken from the income statement in Table 15.1.

Add back depreciation. **Depreciation** is an accounting expense that does not involve any flow of cash. It is an **allocation** of the cost of the non-current (fixed) asset. So if we are looking for the cash generated by making profits, this depreciation needs to be excluded. It was deducted as an expense to calculate profit, so now it is added back to exclude it.

(Increase) in inventory. When a business acquires inventory it uses up cash. The cash is recovered when the inventory is sold. The greater the build-up of inventory, the greater the amount of cash that the business is waiting to recover. So an increase in inventory uses cash. A decrease in inventory releases cash and so is a source of cash.

Decrease in receivables. When a business sells goods or services to customers on credit it has to wait to collect the cash. The greater the increase in receivables (debtors) the greater is the amount of cash that the business is waiting to collect. So an increase in receivables has the effect of decreasing cash flow. A decrease in receivables releases cash and so is a source of cash.

(Decrease) in payables. When a business buys goods or services from suppliers on credit it delays payment of the cash. The greater the increase in payables (creditors) the greater is the amount of cash payment that the business is delaying. So an increase in payables has the effect of increasing cash flow by postponing payments. A decrease in payables means that suppliers are being paid sooner and so is equivalent to a use of cash.

Change in cash in the statement of financial position. Finally it is important to check that the cash flow matches the change in cash in the statement of financial position. Looking at the statements of financial position in Table 15.2 you will see that the cash has increased from £10m to £35m which equals the positive cash flow of £25m calculated by both the direct and the indirect method.

15.3.3   Which to choose – direct or indirect?

When students are asked at this point whether they prefer the direct or the indirect method they usually choose the direct method because it looks less cumbersome. In practice almost all companies choose the indirect method because it can be prepared from the opening and closing statements of financial position and the income statement (profit and loss account). Some supporters also argue that it is useful to highlight the effect of working capital on cash flows.

The direct method needs more work to identify all the operating flows from the cash records. Bookkeeping records, as illustrated in the supplements to previous chapters in this book, are based on ledger accounts which include non-cash items. The sales ledger account, for example, combines cash sales and credit sales. All expense accounts combine expenses paid in cash and expenses obtained on credit. In practice the direct method creates additional work in analysing the accounting records, because there are many aspects to operating cash flow. Supporters of cash flow reporting advocate the direct method because it gives a clearer picture of cash flows. It also provides information on details of cash flows that is not available under the indirect method.

The standard-setters recognise that there are valid arguments for and against each method and so continue to permit both. The IASB 'encourages' entities to report cash flow from operating activities using the direct method,[6] but this encouragement appears to have been ineffective in many cases.

15.4 Preparing a statement of cash flows: the indirect method

Most companies prepare their statement of cash flows using the **indirect method**. This means they start with the reported operating profit and then make adjustments to work back to the cash amounts that are incorporated in profit and in working capital. This section explains the indirect method. A format for a statement of cash flows is presented in Table 15.5. Line numbers have been added at the left-hand side. Each line is explained in the section following Table 15.5.

Line 1 Cash flows from operating activities

This line indicates the start of the first major section of the statement of cash flows, showing how cash flows are generated from the operations of the business.

Line 2 Profit before taxation

The indirect method always starts with the operating profit *before* deducting interest and taxation, taken from the income statement (profit and loss account). This is because interest is seen as a separate payment to reward lenders and taxation is seen as a separate outflow of cash to government which needs to be emphasised. If the operating profit includes any investment income or interest received this must also be

Table 15.5
Format for statement of cash flows, indirect method

Line		£m	£m
1	**Cash flows from operating activities**		
2	Profit before taxation		xx
3	Adjustment for items not involving a flow of cash:		
4	Depreciation, amortisation, gain or loss on disposal of non-current assets etc.		<u>xx</u>
5	*Adjusted profit*		xx
6	(Increase)/decrease in inventories	xx	
7	(Increase)/decrease in trade receivables	xx	
8	(Increase)/decrease in prepayments	<u>xx</u>	
9	Increase/*(decrease)* in cash due to (increases)/decreases in current assets	xx	
10	Increase/(decrease) in trade payables	xx	
11	Increase/(decrease) in accruals	<u>xx</u>	
12	Increase/(decrease) in cash due to increases/(decreases) in liabilities	xx	
13	Increase/(decrease) in cash due to working capital changes		<u>xx</u>
14	Cash generated from operations		xx
15	Interest paid		(xx)
16	Taxes paid		<u>(xx)</u>
17	*Net cash inflow from operating activities*		xx
18	**Cash flows from investing activities**		
19	Purchase of non-current assets	xx	
20	Proceeds from sale of non-current assets	xx	
21	Interest received	xx	
22	Dividends received	<u>xx</u>	
23	*Net cash used in investing activities*		xx
24	**Cash flows from financing activities**		
25	Proceeds from issue of share capital	xx	
26	Proceeds from long-term borrowing	xx	
27	Dividends paid	<u>xx</u>	
28	*Net cash used in financing activities*		xx
29	Increase/(decrease) in cash and cash equivalents		xx
30	**Cash and cash equivalents at the start of the period**		xx
31	**Cash and cash equivalents at the end of the period**		xx

removed because it is reported in the separate section for investing activities (see lines 21 and 22). So the following checklist should be used to ensure the correct starting point:

	£m
Operating profit before taxes	xx
Is there any interest expense included in this figure? If so add it back to	
arrive at:	xx
Operating profit before deducting interest payable and taxes	xx
Is there any interest received/receivable or any dividends received in	
this figure? If so deduct it to arrive at:	(xx)
Operating profit before deducting interest payable and taxes and before	
including interest receivable and dividends received.	xx

Line 3 Adjustment for items not involving a flow of cash

The finance director now looks at the profit figure and asks, 'Are there any items in here that do not involve a flow of cash? If so we want to remove these so that we can get closer to cash.' Most income statements (profit and loss accounts) contain depreciation and amortisation, which have no effect on cash. Other items to look out for are changes in provisions, unrealised gains and losses on foreign currency translation.

Line 4 Adding back depreciation, amortisation, gain or loss on disposal etc

So the depreciation and amortisation are 'added back' to remove them from the profit figure. This usually causes some problems for readers of a statement of cash flows. If it worries you, just ask yourself – how did the depreciation get in there in the first place? The answer is that it was deducted as an expense, so if we add it back we exclude the expense. Other items that could come under this heading of 'not involving a flow of cash' are changes in provisions charged through income statement and gains or losses calculated on disposal of a non-current (fixed) asset. The following table summarises the action to be taken in the statement of cash flows:

Item in calculation	Reason
Add back any **expenses** that do not involve a flow of cash (e.g. depreciation, amortisation, loss on disposal of non-current assets).	These expenses reduced the profit but they do not involve any flow of cash and so must be excluded by adding back.
Deduct any **revenue** that does not involve a flow of cash (e.g. gain on disposal of non-current assets).	These revenues increased the profit but they do not involve any flow of cash and so must be excluded by deducting.

Line 5 Adjusted profit

In some presentations of the statement of cash flows this line is not shown separately, but it is a useful subtotal to remind yourself that you have now removed all non-cash items and you are ready to think about how working capital changes affect cash flow from operations.

Line 6 (Increase)/decrease in inventories (stocks)

When a business buys inventories of raw materials or produces work in progress and finished goods, it uses up cash. The cash is only recovered when the inventories are sold. While the inventories are increasing the cash invested in them is increasing and there is a negative impact on cash flow.

The following table summarises the action to be taken in the statement of cash flows:

Item in calculation	Reason
Deduct increase in inventories	Allowing inventories to increase takes up more cash in paying for them, or prevents cash being obtained through sale.
Add decrease in inventories	Allowing inventories to decrease reduces the cash needed to pay for them, or allows cash to be obtained through sale.

Line 7 (Increase)/decrease in trade receivables (debtors)

When a business sells goods and services on credit to customers, these customers are given some time to pay. They become debtors of the business until they pay cash. Selling goods and services on credit encourages customers to buy from the business but it delays the flow of cash to the business. The longer the period of credit taken by customers, the longer the delay. The danger of allowing the period of credit to increase is that the customer may become increasingly reluctant to pay. Chapter 13 explains how to estimate the average period of credit taken by credit customers.

The following table summarises the action to be taken in the statement of cash flows:

Item in calculation	Reason
Deduct increase in receivables	Allowing amounts of receivables to increase means that cash is not being collected from credit customers.
Add decrease in receivables	Allowing amounts of receivables to decrease means that cash is being collected faster from credit customers.

Line 8 (Increase)/decrease in prepayments

When a business makes payments for expenses in advance of enjoying the benefit of the payment, there is an outflow of cash. Examples are rent in advance or insurance premiums in advance (see Chapter 9 for the accounting treatment of prepayments). If the business is making more prepayments, there is a greater outflow of cash. If the business reduces its prepayments the cash flow position improves.

The following table summarises the action to be taken in the statement of cash flows:

Item in calculation	Reason
Deduct increase in prepayments	If prepayments increase then more cash is being used to make payments in advance.
Add decrease in prepayments	If prepayments decrease then less cash is being used to make payments in advance.

Line 9 Increase/(decrease) in cash due to (increases)/decreases in current assets

This line adds all the increases in current assets and deducts all the decreases in current assets. If the current assets have increased in total then the cash flow has decreased. If the current assets have decreased in total then the cash flow has increased. It is good practice to delete the alternative words here that do not apply to the particular circumstances of the company. Some published statements of cash flows leave all the words in the statement but this can be very confusing to readers.

Line 10 Increase/(decrease) in trade payables (creditors)

When a business buys goods or services on credit, the supplier often allows a period of credit. This helps the cash flow of the business in the gap between buying inputs and selling outputs of goods or services. The longer the period of credit taken from the supplier, the better the effect on cash flow. The danger of delaying payment beyond an agreed date is that the supplier may refuse to supply more goods or services and may even begin legal action for recovery of amounts owing. Chapter 13 explains how to calculate the average period of credit taken from suppliers.

The following table summarises the action to be taken in the statement of cash flows:

Item in calculation	Reason
Deduct decrease in payables	Allowing amounts of payables to decrease means that more cash is being paid to suppliers and other creditors.
Add increase in payables	Allowing amounts of payables to increase means that less cash is being paid to suppliers and other creditors.

Line 11 Increase/(decrease) in accruals

Accruals is the general description for unpaid expenses. If a business delays paying expenses there is a benefit for cash flow. If the accruals increase then there is a greater benefit for cash flow. The danger of delaying payment beyond an agreed date is that the supplier may refuse to supply more goods or services and may even begin legal action for recovery of amounts owing.

The following table summarises the action to be taken in the statement of cash flows:

Item in calculation	Reason
Deduct decrease in accruals	Allowing amounts of unpaid expenses (accruals) to decrease means that more cash is being paid to settle these obligations.
Add increase in accruals	Allowing amounts of unpaid expenses (accruals) to increase means that less cash is being paid to settle these obligations.

Line 12 Increase/(decrease) in cash due to increases/(decreases) in liabilities

This line adds all the increases in current liabilities and deducts all the decreases in current liabilities. If the current liabilities have increased in total then the cash flow has benefited – less cash has been paid to settle current liabilities. If the current liabilities have decreased in total then the cash flow has suffered – more cash has been paid to settle liabilities. It is good practice to delete the alternative words here that do not apply to the particular circumstances of the company. Some published statements of cash flows leave all the words in the statement but this can be very confusing to readers.

Line 13 Increase/(decrease) in cash due to working capital changes

This line shows the result of comparing the change in current assets with the change in current liabilities. There are several combinations of increases and decreases in current assets and liabilities so the easiest way to think about the outcome is to ask 'what has happened to working capital (current assets less current liabilities) overall?'

If the working capital has *increased*, then cash flow has *decreased*.
If the working capital has *decreased*, then cash flow has *increased*.

Line 14 Cash generated from operations

This is a subtotal combining the cash flow effect of the adjusted profit and the cash flow effect of the changes in working capital.

Line 15 Interest paid

Interest must be paid on loans. If it is not paid on time the lender will take action to demand payment of the interest and might even demand immediate repayment of the loan in full, depending on the conditions of the loan agreement. The interest expense in the income statement represents the interest cost of the accounting period but if the payment dates fall outside the accounting period there may be an accrual of unpaid interest in the statement of financial position. A calculation is required to arrive at the amount of cash paid during the accounting period.

Item in calculation	Reason
Interest expense in income statement	We are starting with the expense in the income statement, to adjust it to a cash figure.
minus liability at end of period	This is the part of the expense that has not yet been paid in cash.
plus liability at start of period	During this period the liability at the start of the period has been paid.
equals cash paid to lenders	

Line 16 Taxes paid

There is a corporation tax expense in the income statement (profit and loss account). The due dates for payment depend on the size of the company, as explained in Chapter 10. Any unpaid taxation at the start or end of the period will appear as a liability in the statement of financial position. A calculation is required to arrive at the amount of tax paid in the accounting period.

Item in calculation	Reason
Taxation expense in income statement	We are starting with the expense in the income statement, to adjust it to a cash figure.
minus liability at end of period	This is the part of the expense that has not yet been paid in cash.
plus liability at start of period	During this period the liability at the start of the period has been paid.
equals cash paid to tax authorities	

Line 17 Net cash inflow from operating activities

This is a subtotal that indicates the end of the first major section of the statement of cash flows.

Line 18 Cash flows from investing activities

This line starts the second major section of the statement of cash flows showing how cash has been used for making new investment in non-current assets and also released from sales of existing investment in non-current assets.

Line 19 Purchase of non-current assets

In many cases the amount spent on non-current assets will be known from the accounting records. However, if you are preparing a statement of cash flows using only the statement of financial position and income statement plus some notes, you may find that you need to calculate the amount spent on non-current assets. The following table summarises the calculation of changes in non-current assets which includes the cash payment. It assumes that all assets of one type are recorded together as one category (e.g. vehicles, plant and machinery).

Item in calculation	Reason
Original cost of non-current assets in a specified category at start of period	Begin with the amount of the assets at the start of the period.
plus cash paid for additions	**Cash is spent during the period on additions to the assets.**
minus disposals at original cost	Assets are removed – see later calculation of gain or loss on disposal.
equals Non-current assets at end of period	The result is the amount of the assets at the end of the period.

Line 20 Proceeds from sale of non-current assets

This line reports the cash received from sale or disposal of non-current assets. It is important to use the cash received from the disposal of the asset and not the gain or loss on disposal recorded in the income statement (profit and loss account). Look back to Chapter 8 and you will see that the gain or loss on disposal arises only when the cash received is different from the book value. If the depreciation had been calculated with perfect foresight then the net book value would be equal to the cash received and there would be no gain or loss. A gain or loss on disposal is the result of estimating depreciation at the start of the asset's life when the proceeds on disposal have to be estimated.

The following table summarises the calculation relating to the sale or disposal of non-current assets which includes the cash received.

Item in calculation	Comment
Original cost of non-current asset at start of period	This item of information is shown as 'disposal' in the 'cost' section of the schedule of non-current assets.
minus accumulated depreciation of non-current asset at start of period	This item of information is shown as 'disposal' in the 'accumulated depreciation' section of the schedule of non-current assets.
minus cash received on disposal	**This is the amount of cash received for the asset sold.**
equals gain or loss on disposal	The gain or loss on disposal is reported in the income statement.

Line 21 Interest received

Interest received is a reward for investment and so it is regarded as part of the cash flows relating to investing activities. Look back to the calculations in the workings for line 2 and you will see the item:

Is there any interest received/receivable or any dividends received in this figure? If so deduct it.

The interest receivable is removed in calculating operating profit at line 2 so that interest received can be inserted at line 21. The following table summarises the action to be taken in the statement of cash flows:

Item in calculation	Reason
Interest receivable in the income statement	We are starting with the revenue reported in the income statement, to adjust it to a cash figure.
minus asset at end of period	This is the part of the revenue that has not yet been received in cash.
plus asset at start of period	During this period the asset at the start of the period has been received.
equals interest received in cash	

Line 22 Dividends received

The dividends received relate to equity investments held by the company. The calculation is very similar to that for interest received.

Item in calculation	Reason
Dividend receivable in the income statement	We are starting with the revenue reported in the income statement, to adjust it to a cash figure.
minus asset at end of period	This is the part of the revenue that has not yet been received in cash.
plus asset at start of period	During this period the asset at the start of the period has been received.
equals dividend received in cash	

Line 23 Net cash used in investing activities

This subtotal indicates the end of the second major section of the statement of cash flows. It will usually be a negative figure showing that the business is expanding through more investment in non-current assets. Less commonly, a business may be selling off existing investments to raise cash for future plans. Having the separate subtotal draws attention to the magnitude and direction of investing activities.

Line 24 Cash flows from financing activities

This line starts the third and final major section of the statement of cash flows showing how cash has been raised from financing activities. This usually means issuing new share capital and raising or repaying long-term loans.

Line 25 Proceeds from issue of share capital

Chapter 12 explains the process of issuing share capital, both when the business starts and when it looks for more finance some time later. In many cases the shares are issued at market price, which is higher than nominal value. The difference is called a share premium. The total cash raised is measured in terms of the market price but company law requires separate reporting of the change in nominal value and the changes in the share premium. The calculation required is as follows:

Item in calculation	Reason
Increase in nominal value of share capital *Increase* in share *plus* premium reserve *equals* cash received from issue of shares	The amount of cash raised by issuing shares at market price is the nominal value plus the share premium.

Line 26 Proceeds from long-term borrowings

The proceeds from long-term borrowings can be seen from the change in the statement of financial position figures for long-term borrowings, after allowing for any long-term borrowings that have changed category to short term in the accounting period.

Item in calculation	Reason
Long-term borrowing in balance sheet at the start of the period	We are starting with amount reported in the balance sheet at the start of the accounting period.
minus long-term reclassified as short-term during the period	This is the part of loan that is reclassified but remains in the balance sheet.
plus new loans taken up in cash	Cash received.
minus loans repaid	Cash paid out.
equals long-term borrowing in balance sheet at the end of the period	The amount reported in the balance sheet at the end of the accounting period.

Line 27 Dividends paid

The dividend paid during the period may be a combination of the dividend paid in respect of the previous year's profit plus an interim dividend for the current year.

Chapter 12 explains in more detail the accounting procedures for reporting dividends. The amount of dividend paid will appear in the statement of changes in equity.

Line 28 Net cash used in financing activities

This subtotal indicates the end of the third section of the statement of cash flows.

Line 29 Increase/(decrease) in cash and cash equivalents

This line is the arithmetic total of the three separate sections as reported in lines 17 + 23 + 28.

Lines 30 and 31 Cash and cash equivalents at the start and end of the period

This is the moment of truth where you find out whether you have made errors on the way through the statement of cash flows. Lines 30 and 31 are taken from the statement of financial position. If your statement of cash flows is correct then line 29 plus line 30 will equal line 31. The following table is used to record the information extracted from the statement of financial position.

	Start of period	End of period
Cash on hand and balances with banks	xx	xx
Short-term investments	xx	xx
Cash and cash equivalents	xx	xx

15.5 Preparing a statement of cash flows: the direct method

Line 1 Cash flows from operating activities

This line indicates the start of the first major section of the statement of cash flows, showing how cash flows are generated from the operations of the business.

Line 2 Cash receipts from customers

This line reports the total cash received from customers in the period. Some customers may have paid immediate cash for goods and services. Others may have taken credit and paid later.

Line 3 Cash paid to suppliers

This line reports the total cash paid to suppliers in the period. The business may have paid immediate cash for some goods and services. In other cases the suppliers may have allowed a period of credit to be paid later.

Line 4 Cash paid to employees

This line reports the total cash paid to employees in the period. Usually the employees are paid promptly each week or each month and so the cash payments are closely related to the wages expense.

Lines 14 to 31 have the same meaning as described for these lines in Section 15.4.

The alternative *direct method* is shown in Table 15.6 and explained as follows.

Table 15.6
Format for statement of cash flows, direct method

Line		£m	£m
1	**Cash flows from operating activities**		
2	Cash receipts from customers		xx
3	Cash paid to suppliers		xx
4	Cash paid to employees		xx
5–13	*(Lines not used)*		
14	Cash generated from operations		xx
15	Interest paid		(xx)
16	Taxes paid		(xx)
17	*Net cash inflow from operating activities*		xx
18	**Cash flows from investing activities**		
19	Purchase of non-current assets	xx	
20	Proceeds from sale of non-current assets	xx	
21	Interest received	xx	
22	Dividends received	xx	
23	*Net cash used in investing activities*		xx
24	**Cash flows from financing activities**		
25	Proceeds from issue of share capital	xx	
26	Proceeds from long-term borrowing	xx	
27	Dividends paid	xx	
28	*Net cash used in financing activities*		xx
29	Increase/(decrease) in cash and cash equivalents		xx
30	**Cash and cash equivalents at the start of the period**		xx
31	**Cash and cash equivalents at the end of the period**		xx

15.6 Interpretation of cash flow information

The cash flow information is useful in itself in showing trends in the company's cash resources. Some businesses operate on cycles lasting several years where the cash position moves from negative to positive. The industry position is often a useful starting point for understanding company cash flows. If the industry is cyclical and all companies in the sector have negative cash flow then we might expect any company in the sector to show the same trends. Equally, any company in the sector should be showing signs of improvement as the cycle moves upwards.

For the indirect method, which reports the cash flow effects of working capital, it may be useful to link the increases or decreases in working capital items to the number of days in the working capital cycle. The calculation of the working capital cycle appears in Chapter 13. For example, if there is an increase in cash invested in inventory there are two possible causes: one is a lengthening of the inventory holding period and the other is an increase in sales volume causing more inventory to be held. The inventory holding period helps to narrow down the possible cause. If the trade receivables increase there are two possible causes. One is that customers are taking longer to pay and the other is that credit sales are increasing. The period of credit given to customers helps to narrow down the cause here.

The amount of cash invested in capital expenditure is an important sign of the continuing development of the business. Ratios are used by analysts in comparing capital expenditure to depreciation and comparing capital expenditure to the existing asset base.

15.7 Illustration

The following information is used to illustrate the indirect method and then compare the direct method of preparing and presenting a statement of cash flows.

Income statement Year 2

	£m
Revenue	246
Cost of sales	(110)
Gross profit	136
Investment income – interest received	4
Gain on disposal of equipment	5
Depreciation	(30)
Administrative and selling expenses	(10)
Operating profit before interest	105
Interest expense	(15)
Profit after deducting interest	90
Taxation	(30)
Profit after tax	60

Statements of financial position (balance sheets) at 31 December

	Year 2 £m	Year 1 £m
Non-current assets		
Property, plant and equipment at cost	150	100
Accumulated depreciation 40 + 30 – 10	(60)	(40)
	90	60
Investments	100	100
Total non-current assets	190	160
Current assets		
Inventory (stock)	20	15
Trade receivables (debtors)	18	16
Cash and cash equivalents	32	5
Total current assets	70	36
Total assets	260	196
Current liabilities		
Trade payables (creditors)	(14)	(13)
Interest payable	(6)	(7)
Taxes payable	(8)	(7)
Total current liabilities	(28)	(27)
Non-current liabilities		
Long-term loans	(20)	(15)
Total liabilities	(48)	(42)
Net assets	212	154
Capital and reserves		
Share capital	140	130
Share premium	20	18
Retained earnings	52	6
	212	154

Further information

1 The dividend paid during Year 2 was £14m. The retained earnings increased by £60m profit of the period and decreased by the amount of the dividend £14m.
2 During Year 2 the company acquired property, plant and equipment costing £80m.
3 During Year 2 the company sold property, plant and equipment that had an original cost of £30m and accumulated depreciation of £10m. The proceeds of sale were £25m.

15.7.1 Indirect method

A statement of cash flows using the indirect method is presented in Table 15.7.

Table 15.7
Statement of cash flows using the indirect method

Notes		£m	£m
	Cash flows from operating activities		
1	Profit before taxation		101
	Adjustment for items not involving a flow of cash:		
2	Depreciation	30	
3	Gain on disposal of equipment	(5)	
			25
	Adjusted profit		126
4	(Increase) in inventories	(5)	
5	(Increase) in trade receivables	(2)	
6	Increase in trade payables	1	
	Increase/(decrease) in cash due to working capital changes		(6)
	Cash generated from operations		120
7	Interest paid		(16)
8	Taxes paid		(29)
	Net cash inflow from operating activities		75
	Cash flows from investing activities		
9	Purchase of non-current assets	(80)	
10	Proceeds from sale of non-current assets	25	
11	Interest received	4	
	Net cash used in investing activities		(51)
	Cash flows from financing activities		
12	Proceeds from issue of share capital	12	
13	Proceeds from long-term borrowing	5	
14	Dividends paid	(14)	
	Net cash used in financing activities		3
	Increase/(decrease) in cash and cash equivalents		27
15	**Cash and cash equivalents at the start of the period**		5
15	**Cash and cash equivalents at the end of the period**		32

Working note 1

	£m
Operating profit before taxes	90
Is there any interest expense included in this figure? If so add it back to arrive at:	15
Operating profit before deducting interest payable and taxes	105
Is there any interest received/receivable or any dividends received in this figure? If so deduct it to arrive at:	(4)
Operating profit before deducting interest payable and taxes and before including interest receivable and dividends received.	101

Working note 2

The depreciation is seen in the income statement (profit and loss account). It is added back to exclude the effect of a non-cash item.

Working note 3

The gain on disposal is seen in the income statement (profit and loss account). It is added back to exclude the effect of a non-cash item.

Working note 4

There is an increase in inventory seen by comparing the statements of financial position at the end of year 1 and year 2. This decreases the cash flow.

Working note 5

There is an increase in trade receivables (debtors) seen by comparing the statements of financial position at the end of year 1 and year 2. This decreases the cash flow.

Working note 6

There is an increase in trade payables (creditors) seen by comparing the statements of financial position at the end of year 1 and year 2. This has a positive effect on the cash flow by increasing the amount unpaid.

Working note 7

Interest paid is calculated from the income statement expense £15m plus the unpaid interest at the start of the year £7m minus the unpaid interest at the end of the year, £6m.

Working note 8

Taxes paid are calculated from the income statement charge £30m plus the unpaid liability at the start of the year £7m minus the unpaid liability at the end of the year £8m.

Working note 9

The purchase cost of non-current assets is given in the further information. It can be checked by taking the cost at the start of the year £100m, adding £80m and deducting the £30m cost of the disposal to leave £150m as shown in the statement of financial position at the end of the year.

Working note 10

The proceeds of sale £25m are given in the further information. This can be checked by taking the net book value of the asset sold (£30m − £10m = £20m) and adding the gain on disposal, the £5m shown in the income statement.

Working note 11

The interest received is taken from the income statement. There is no interest receivable shown in the statement of financial position so the income statement figure must be the same as the cash figure.

Working note 12

The proceeds from the share issue are the total of the increase in share capital £10m plus the increase in share premium £2m.

Working note 13

The proceeds from long-term borrowings are the increase in long-term loans calculated by comparing the opening and closing statements of financial position.

Working note 14

The dividend paid is given in the further information. It can be checked by taking the retained earnings at the start of the period, £6m, add the profit of the period, £60m, and deduct dividend £14m to arrive at the retained earnings at the end of the period, £52m.

Working note 15

The cash and cash equivalents at the start and end of the period are taken from the statement of financial position.

15.7.2 Direct method

A statement of cash flows presented by the direct method is presented in Table 15.8.

Table 15.8
Statement of cash flows using the direct method

Notes		£m	£m
	Cash flows from operating activities		
1	Cash receipts from customers		244
2	Cash paid to suppliers and employees		(114)
3	Cash paid for administrative and selling expenses		(10)
	Cash generated from operations		120
4	Interest paid		(16)
5	Taxes paid		(29)
	Net cash inflow from operating activities		75
	Cash flows from investing activities		
6	Purchase of non-current assets	(80)	
7	Proceeds from sale of non-current assets	25	
8	Interest received	4	
	Net cash used in investing activities		(51)
	Cash flows from financing activities		
9	Proceeds from issue of share capital	12	
10	Proceeds from long-term borrowing	5	
11	Dividends paid	(14)	
	Net cash used in financing activities		3
	Increase/(decrease) in cash and cash equivalents		27
12	**Cash and cash equivalents at the start of the period**		5
12	**Cash and cash equivalents at the end of the period**		32

In practice the cash receipts from customers and cash payments to suppliers and employees are taken from the records of cash received and paid, which requires analysis of the cash records. In this relatively straightforward situation the figures may be confirmed from the information in the statement of financial position and income statement.

Working note 1

The cash receipts from customers may be confirmed from revenue £246m, plus receivables at the start of the period £16m, minus receivables at the end of the period £18m, equals £244m.

Working note 2

There are two stages to the confirmation of cash paid to suppliers. First the purchases are calculated from cost of sales £110m plus inventory at the end £20m minus inventory at the start £15m = £115m. Next the payment to suppliers is confirmed from purchases: £115m plus liability at the start £13m minus liability at the end £14m equals £114m. It is assumed that the wages are all paid when the work is done so there is no accrual.

Working note 3

The administrative and selling expenses are seen in the income statement. There is no accrual indicated in the statement of financial position and so the cash figure equals the expense figure.

Working notes 4 to 12

See working notes 7 to 15 for the indirect method.

15.7.3 Comment on statement of cash flows

The cash flow from operating activities amounted to £75m. The purchase of non-current (fixed) assets cost £80m but this was offset by £25m proceeds of sale of non-current assets no longer required and was also helped by the £4m interest received from investments. The net outflow from investments was £51m. This left £24m of cash flow available to increase cash resources but £14m was required for dividend payments. The remaining £10m was added to the proceeds of a share issue, £12m and an increase in long-term loans, £5m, giving an overall cash inflow of £27m.

15.8 Summary

- The statement of cash flows provides information about changes in financial position that adds to the understanding of the business obtainable from the statement of financial position and income statement (profit and loss account).
- It explains changes in cash and cash equivalents arising from operating activities, investing activities and financing activities.
- **Cash** comprises cash on hand and demand deposits.
- **Cash equivalents** are short-term, highly liquid investments that are readily convertible to known amounts of cash and which are subject to an insignificant risk of changes in value.
- The **indirect method** and the **direct method** are alternative approaches to calculating the cash flow arising from operating activities.
- The **indirect method** starts with the profit from operations, eliminates non-cash expenses such as depreciation, and adds on or deducts the effects of changes in working capital to arrive at the cash flow arising from operating activities.
- The **direct method** takes each item of operating cash flow separately from the cash records to arrive at the cash flow arising from operating activities.
- The cash flow is useful in analysis when combined with ratio analysis that shows relationships of liquidity, working capital management, rates of investment in non-current assets and financial gearing.

Further reading

The following standard is too detailed for a first-level course, but the definitions section may be helpful and the Appendices give illustrations of statements of cash flows.

IASB (2012), IAS 7, *Statement of Cash Flows*, International Accounting Standards Board.

QUESTIONS

The Questions section of each chapter has three types of question. 'Test your understanding' questions to help you review your reading are in the 'A' series of questions. You will find the answers to these by reading and thinking about the material in the book. 'Application' questions to test your ability to apply technical skills are in the 'B' series of questions. Questions requiring you to show skills in problem solving and evaluation are in the 'C' series of questions. A letter [S] indicates that there is a solution at the end of the book.

A　Test your understanding

A15.1　What is the definition of 'cash'? (Section 15.2)

A15.2　What is the definition of 'cash equivalent'? (Section 15.2)

A15.3　What is meant by the 'direct method' of calculating operating cash flow? (Section 15.3.1)

A15.4　What is meant by the 'indirect method' of calculating operating cash flow? (Section 15.3.2)

A15.5　Why is depreciation 'added back' to operating profit in the indirect method of calculating operating cash flow? (Section 15.3.2)

A15.6　What is the effect on cash flow of an increase in inventory levels? (Section 15.3.2)

A15.7　What is the effect on cash flow of an increase in trade receivables (debtors)? (Section 15.3.2)

A15.8　What is the effect on cash flow of an increase in trade payables (creditors)? (Section 15.3.2)

A15.9　What are the relative benefits of the direct method compared to the indirect method? (Section 15.3.3)

A15.10　What are the three main sections of a statement of cash flows? (Section 15.4)

A15.11　What kinds of items in an income statement do not involve a flow of cash? (Section 15.4)

A15.12　What happens to cash flow when working capital increases? (Section 15.4)

A15.13　How is taxation paid calculated from the taxation payable and the taxation liability at the start and end of the period? (Section 15.4)

A15.14　How is the cash paid for additions to fixed assets if we know the opening and closing balances and there are no disposals? (Section 15.4)

A15.15　Explain how the proceeds of sale of a non-current asset differ from the net book value. (Section 15.4)

A15.16　Explain how the cash proceeds of a share issue are calculated from knowledge of the share capital and the share premium reserve. (Section 15.4)

A15.17　Explain how cash received from customers is calculated if we know the sales of the period and the receivables (debtors) at the start and end of the period. (Section 15.5)

A15.18　Explain how the purchases of goods or materials is calculated if we know the cost of goods sold and the inventory (stock) at the start and end of the period. (Section 15.5)

A15.19　Explain how the cash paid to suppliers is calculated if we know the purchases and the payables (creditors) at the start and end of the period. (Section 15.5)

B　Application

B15.1 [S]
Sales on credit during Year 2 amount to £120m. The trade receivables (debtors) at the start of Year 2 were £8. The trade receivables (debtors) at the end of Year 2 were £10. What is the amount of cash received from customers during Year 2?

B15.2 [S]
Purchases on credit during Year 3 amount to £20m. The trade payables (creditors) at the start of Year 3 were £6m. The trade payables (creditors) at the end of Year 3 were £4m. What is the amount of cash paid to suppliers during Year 3?

B15.3 [S]

The equipment at cost account at the start of Year 2 records a total of £34m. The equipment at cost account at the end of Year 2 records a total of £37m. An asset of original cost £5m was sold during the period. What was the amount spent on acquisition of equipment?

B15.4

A vehicle costing £20m and having accumulated depreciation of £12m was sold for £5m. How will this information be reported in the statement of cash flows?

B15.5

The share capital account increased by £40m during Year 4. The share premium reserve increased by £20m. What amount of cash was raised by the issue of shares?

B15.6

The corporation tax charge in the income statement (profit and loss account) for Year 2 was £30m. The tax liability in the statement of financial position at the start of Year 2 was £6m. The tax liability in the statement of financial position at the end of Year 2 was £10m. What was the amount of cash paid in taxation during Year 2?

B15.7

D Ltd has an operating profit of £12m, which includes a depreciation charge of £1m. During the year the trading stock has increased by £4m, trade debtors have increased by £3m and trade creditors have increased by £5m. Prepare a statement of cash flow from operations.

B15.8

E Ltd has an operating profit of £16m, which includes a depreciation charge of £2m. During the year the trading stock has increased by £1m, trade debtors have decreased by £3m and trade creditors have decreased by £2m. Prepare a statement of cash flow from operations.

C   Problem solving and evaluation

C15.1 [S]

The directors of Fruit Sales plc produced the following income statement (profit and loss account) for Year 2 and balance sheet at the end of Year 2.

Income statement for year 2

	£m
Revenue	320
Cost of sales	(143)
Gross profit	177
Investment income – interest received	5
Gain on disposal of equipment	7
Depreciation	(39)
Administrative and selling expenses	(13)
Operating profit before interest	137
Interest expense	(20)
Profit after deducting interest	117
Taxation	(35)
Profit after tax	82

Statements of financial position (balance sheets) at 31 December

	Year 2 £m	Year 1 £m
Non-current assets		
Vehicles at cost	195	130
Accumulated depreciation	(79)	(52)
	116	78
Investments	100	80
Total non-current assets	216	158
Current assets		
Inventory (stock)	26	20
Trade receivables (debtors)	23	21
Cash and cash equivalents	43	6
Total current assets	92	47
Total assets	308	205
Current liabilities		
Trade payables (creditors)	(18)	(13)
Interest payable	(8)	(7)
Taxes payable	(10)	(7)
Total current liabilities	(36)	(27)
Non-current liabilities		
Long-term loans	(26)	(18)
Total liabilities	(62)	(45)
Net assets	246	160
Capital and reserves		
Share capital	152	120
Share premium	26	23
Retained earnings	68	17
	246	160

Further information

1 The dividend paid during Year 2 was £31m. The retained earnings increased by £82m profit of the period and decreased by the amount of the dividend £31m.
2 During Year 2 the company acquired vehicles costing £90m.
3 During Year 2 the company sold vehicles that had an original cost of £25m and accumulated depreciation of £12m. The proceeds of sale were £20m.
4 Cost of sales consists entirely of purchases of fruit on credit from suppliers. Wages are included in administrative and selling expenses and are paid when incurred.

Required

1 Prepare a statement of cash flows using (a) the direct method and (b) the indirect method of calculating operating cash flow.
2 Write a comment on the cash flow of the period.

C15.2
Consider the following:

	£m
Revenue	320
Cost of sales	(143)
Gross profit	177
Investment income – interest received	5
Loss on disposal of equipment	(8)
Depreciation	(39)
Administrative and selling expenses	(13)
Operating profit before interest	122
Interest expense	(6)
Profit after deducting interest	116
Taxation	(39)
Profit after tax	77

Statements of financial position (balance sheets) at 31 December

	Year 2	Year 1
	£m	£m
Property, plant and equipment at cost	225	150
Accumulated depreciation	(90)	(60)
	135	90
Investment	70	100
Total non-current assets	205	190
Inventory (stock)	30	22
Trade receivables (debtors)	27	24
Cash and cash equivalents	48	8
Total current assets	105	54
Total assets	310	244
Trade payables (creditors)	(21)	(20)
Interest payable	(9)	(11)
Taxes payable	(12)	(9)
Total current liabilities	(42)	(40)
Long-term loans	(20)	(15)
Total liabilities	(62)	(55)
Net assets	248	189
Share capital	144	140
Share premium	26	23
Retained earnings	78	26
	248	189

Further information

1 The dividend paid during Year 2 was £25m. The retained earnings increased by £77m profit of the period and decreased by the amount of the dividend, £25m.
2 During Year 2 the company acquired property, plant and equipment costing £94m.
3 During Year 2 the company sold for scrap property, plant and equipment that had an original cost of £19m and accumulated depreciation of £9m. The proceeds of disposal were £2m.
4 Investments were sold during the year for cash proceeds of £30m. There were no purchases of investments.

Required

1 Prepare a statement of cash flows using (a) the direct method and (b) the indirect method of calculating operating cash flow.
2 Write a comment on the cash flow of the period.

Notes and references

1. Statements of cash flows in published financial statements are often prepared for a group as a whole. The details of group statements of cash flows are too complex for a first-level text, but in general appearance they are similar to those for individual companies.
2. IASB (2012), IAS 7 *Statement of Cash Flows*.
3. IAS 7 para. 6.
4. IAS 7 para. 7.
5. IAS 7 para. 8.
6. IAS 7 para. 19.

Financial accounting terms defined

The definition of one word or phrase may depend on understanding another word or phrase defined elsewhere in the reference list. Words in **bold** indicate that such a definition is available.

account payable An amount due for payment to a supplier of goods or services, also described as a **trade creditor**.

account receivable an amount due from a customer, also described as a **trade debtor**.

accountancy firm A business partnership (or possibly a limited company) in which the partners are qualified accountants. The firm undertakes work for clients in respect of audit, accounts preparation, tax and similar activities.

accountancy profession The collective body of persons qualified in accounting, and working in accounting-related areas. Usually they are members of a professional body, membership of which is attained by passing examinations.

accounting The process of identifying, measuring and communicating financial information about an entity to permit informed judgements and decisions by users of the information.

accounting equation The relationship between assets, liabilities and ownership interest.

accounting period Time period for which financial statements are prepared (e.g. month, quarter, year).

accounting policies Accounting methods which have been judged by business enterprises to be most appropriate to their circumstances and adopted by them for the purpose of preparing their financial statements.

accounting standards Definitive statements of best practice issued by a body having suitable authority.

Accounting Standards Board The authority in the UK which issued definitive statements of best accounting practice until 2012.

accruals basis The effects of transactions and other events are recognised when they occur (and not as cash or its equivalent is received or paid) and they are recorded in the accounting records and reported in the financial statements of the periods to which they relate (see also **matching**).

accumulated depreciation Total **depreciation** of a **non-current (fixed) asset**, deducted from original cost to give **net book value**.

acid test The ratio of liquid assets to current liabilities.

acquiree Company that becomes controlled by another.

acquirer Company that obtains control of another.

acquisition An acquisition takes place where one company – the **acquirer** – acquires control of another – the **acquiree** – usually through purchase of shares.

acquisition method Production of **consolidated financial statements** for an **acquisition**.

administrative expenses Costs of managing and running a business.

agency A relationship between a principal and an agent. In the case of a limited liability company, the shareholder is the principal and the director is the agent.

agency theory A theoretical model, developed by academics, to explain how the relationship between a principal and an agent may have economic consequences.

aggregate depreciation See **accumulated depreciation**.

allocate To assign a whole item of cost, or of revenue, to a simple cost centre, account or time period.

allocated, allocation See **allocate**.

amortisation Process similar to **depreciation**, usually applied to intangible fixed assets.

annual report A document produced each year by limited liability companies containing the accounting information required by law. Larger companies also provide information and pictures of the activities of the company.

articles of association Document setting out the relative rights of shareholders in a limited liability company.

articulation The term 'articulation' is used to refer to the impact of transactions on the balance sheet and profit and loss account through application of the accounting equation.

assets Rights or other access to future economic benefits controlled by an entity as a result of past transactions or events.

associated company One company exercises significant influence over another, falling short of complete control.

audit An audit is the independent examination of, and expression of opinion on, financial statements of an entity.

audit manager An employee of an accountancy firm, usually holding an accountancy qualification, given a significant level of responsibility in carrying out an audit assignment and responsible to the partner in charge of the audit.

bad debt It is known that a credit customer (**debtor**) is unable to pay the amount due.

balance sheet A statement of the financial position of an entity showing assets, liabilities and ownership interest. Under the **IASB system** the preferred title is **statement of financial position**.

bank facility An arrangement with a bank to borrow money as required up to an agreed limit.

bond The name sometimes given to loan finance (more commonly in the USA).

broker (stockbroker) Member of a stock exchange who arranges purchase and sale of shares and may also provide an information service giving buy/sell/hold recommendations.

broker's report Bulletin written by a stockbroking firm for circulation to its clients, providing analysis and guidance on companies as potential investments.

business combination A transaction in which one company acquires control of another.

business cycle Period (usually 12 months) during which the peaks and troughs of activity of a business form a pattern which is repeated on a regular basis.

business entity A business which exists independently of its owners.

business review A report by the directors giving a fair review of the company's business to inform members of the company and help them assess how the directors have performed their duty to promote the success of the company.

called up (share capital) The company has called upon the shareholders who first bought the shares, to make their payment in full.

capital An amount of finance provided to enable a business to acquire assets and sustain its operations.

capital expenditure Spending on **non-current (fixed)** assets of a business.

capitalisation issue Issue of shares to existing shareholders in proportion to shares already held. Raises no new finance but changes the mix of share capital and reserves.

cash Cash on hand (such as money held in a cash box or a safe) and deposits in a bank that may be withdrawn on demand.

cash equivalents Short-term, highly liquid investments that are readily convertible to known amounts of cash and which are subject to an insignificant risk of changes in value.

cash flow projections Statements of cash expected to flow into the business and cash expected to flow out over a particular period.

chairman The person who chairs the meetings of the board of directors of a company (preferably not the chief executive).

charge In relation to interest or taxes, describes the reduction in ownership interest reported in the income statement (profit and loss account) due to the cost of interest and tax payable.

chief executive The director in charge of the day-to-day running of a company.

close season Period during which those who are 'insiders' to a listed company should not buy or sell shares.

commercial paper A method of borrowing money from commercial institutions such as banks.

Companies Act The Companies Act 1985 as modified by the Companies Act 1989. Legislation to control the activities of limited liability companies.

comparability Qualitative characteristic expected in financial statements, comparable within company and between companies.

completeness Qualitative characteristic expected in financial statements.

conceptual framework A statement of principles providing generally accepted guidance for the development of new reporting practices and for challenging and evaluating the existing practices.

conservatism See **prudence**. Sometimes used with a stronger meaning of understating assets and overstating liabilities.

consistency The measurement and display of similar transactions and other events is carried out in a consistent way throughout an entity within each accounting period and from one period to the next, and also in a consistent way by different entities.

consolidated financial statements Present financial information about the group as a single reporting entity.

consolidation Consolidation is a process that aggregates the total assets, liabilities and results of the parent and its subsidiaries (the group) in the **consolidated financial statements**.

contingent liabilities Obligations that are not recognised in the balance sheet because they depend upon some future event happening.

control The power to govern the financial and operating policies of an entity so as to obtain benefits from its activities.

convertible loan Loan finance for a business that is later converted into **share capital**.

corporate governance The system by which companies are directed and controlled. Boards of directors are responsible for the governance of their companies.

corporate recovery department Part of an accountancy firm which specialises in assisting companies to recover from financial problems.

corporate social responsibility Companies integrate social and environmental concerns in their business operations and in their interactions with stakeholders.

corporation tax Tax payable by companies, based on the taxable profits of the period.

cost of a non-current asset is the cost of making it ready for use, cost of finished goods is cost of bringing them to the present condition and location.

cost of goods sold Materials, labour and other costs directly related to the goods or services provided.

cost of sales See **cost of goods sold**.

coupon Rate of interest payable on a loan.

credit (bookkeeping system) Entries in the credit column of a ledger account represent increases in liabilities, increases in ownership interest, revenue, or decreases in assets.

credit (terms of business) The supplier agrees to allow the customer to make payment some time after the delivery of the goods or services. Typical trade credit periods range from 30 to 60 days but each agreement is different.

credit note A document sent to a customer of a business cancelling the customer's debt to the business, usually because the customer has returned defective goods or has received inadequate service.

credit purchase A business **entity** takes delivery of goods or services and is allowed to make payment at a later date.

credit sale A business **entity** sells goods or services and allows the customer to make payment at a later date.

creditor A person or organisation to whom money is owed by the entity.

critical event The point in the business cycle at which **revenue** may be recognised.

current asset An asset that is expected to be converted into cash within the trading cycle.

current liability A liability which satisfies any of the following criteria: (a) it is expected to be settled in the entity's normal operating cycle; (b) it is held primarily for the purpose of being traded; (c) it is due to be settled within 12 months after the balance sheet date.

current value A method of valuing assets and liabilities which takes account of changing prices, as an alternative to historical cost.

customers' collection period Average number of days credit taken by customers.

cut-off procedures Procedures applied to the accounting records at the end of an accounting period to ensure that all transactions for the period are recorded and any transactions not relevant to the period are excluded.

debenture A written acknowledgement of a debt – a name used for loan financing taken up by a company.

debtor A person or organisation that owes money to the entity.

deep discount bond A loan issued at a relatively low price compared to its nominal value.

default Failure to meet obligations as they fall due for payment.

deferred asset An asset whose benefit is delayed beyond the period expected for a current asset, but which does not meet the definition of a fixed asset.

deferred income Revenue, such as a government grant, is received in advance of performing the related activity. The deferred income is held in the balance sheet as a type of liability until performance is achieved and is then released to the income statement.

deferred taxation The obligation to pay tax is deferred (postponed) under tax law beyond the normal date of payment.

depreciable amount Cost of a **non-current (fixed) asset** minus **residual value**.

depreciation The systematic allocation of the **depreciable amount** of an asset over its useful life. The depreciable amount is cost less **residual value**.

derecognition The act of removing an item from the financial statements because the item no longer satisfies the conditions for **recognition**.

difference on consolidation Difference between **fair value** of the payment for a **subsidiary** and the **fair value** of **net assets** acquired, more commonly called **goodwill**.

direct method (of operating cash flow) Presents cash inflows and cash outflows.

Directive A document issued by the European Union requiring all member states to adapt their national law to be consistent with the Directive.

director(s) Person(s) appointed by shareholders of a limited liability company to manage the affairs of the company.

disclosed, disclosure An item which is reported in the notes to the accounts is said to be disclosed but not **recognised**.

discount received A supplier of goods or services allows a business to deduct an amount called a discount, for prompt payment of an invoiced amount. The discount is often expressed a percentage of the invoiced amount.

dividend Amount paid to a shareholder, usually in the form of cash, as a reward for investment in the company. The amount of dividend paid is proportionate to the number of shares held.

dividend cover Earnings per share divided by dividend per share.

dividend yield Dividend per share divided by current market price.

doubtful debts Amounts due from credit customers where there is concern that the customer may be unable to pay.

drawings Cash taken for personal use, in **sole trader** or **partnership** business, treated as a reduction of **ownership interest**.

earnings for ordinary shareholders Profit after deducting interest charges and taxation and after deducting preference dividends (but before deducting extraordinary items).

earnings per share calculated as **earnings for ordinary shareholders** divided by the number of shares which have been issued by the company.

effective interest rate The rate that exactly discounts estimated future cash payments or receipts through the expected life of the financial instrument.

efficient markets hypothesis Share prices in a stock market react immediately to the announcement of new information.

endorsed International financial reporting standards approved for use in member states of the European Union through a formal process of **endorsement**.

endorsement See **endorsed**.

enterprise A business activity or a commercial project.

entity, entities Something that exists independently, such as a business which exists independently of the owner.

entry price The value of entering into acquisition of an asset or liability, usually **replacement cost**.

equities analyst A person who investigates and writes reports on ordinary share investments in companies (usually for the benefit of investors in shares).

equity A description applied to the **ordinary share** capital of an entity.

equity accounting Reports in the **balance sheet** the parent or group's share of the investment in the **share capital** and **reserves** of an **associated company**.

equity holders Those who own ordinary shares in the **entity**.

equity interest See **ownership interest**.

equity portfolio A collection of **equity shares**.

equity shares/share capital Shares in a company which participate in sharing dividends and in sharing any surplus on winding up, after all liabilities have been met.

eurobond market A market in which bonds are issued in the capital market of one country to a non-resident borrower from another country.

exit price See **exit value**.

exit value A method of valuing assets and liabilities based on selling prices, as an alternative to **historical cost**.

expense An expense is caused by a transaction or event arising during the ordinary activities of the business which causes a decrease in the ownership interest.

external reporting Reporting financial information to those users with a valid claim to receive it, but who are not allowed access to the day-to-day records of the business.

external users (of financial statements) Users of financial statements who have a valid interest but are not permitted access to the day-to-day records of the company.

fair value The price that would be received to sell an asset or paid to transfer a liability in an orderly transaction between market participants at the measurement date.

faithful presentation Qualitive characteristic, information represents what it purports to represent.

financial accounting A term usually applied to *external reporting* by a business where that reporting is presented in financial terms.

financial adaptability The ability of the company to respond to unexpected needs or opportunities.

financial gearing Ratio of loan finance to equity capital and reserves.

financial information Information which may be reported in money terms.

Financial Reporting Standard Title of an accounting standard issued by the UK *Accounting Standards Board* as a definitive statement of best practice (issued from 1990 onwards – predecessor documents are Statements of Standard Accounting Practice, many of which remain valid).

financial risk Exists where a company has loan finance, especially long-term loan finance where the company cannot relinquish its commitment. The risk relates to being unable to meet payments of interest or repayment of capital as they fall due.

financial statements Documents presenting accounting information which is expected to have a useful purpose.

financial viability The ability to survive on an ongoing basis.

financing activities Activities that result in changes in the size and composition of the contributed equity and borrowings of the entity.

fixed asset An asset that is held by an enterprise for use in the production or supply of goods or services, for rental to others, or for administrative purposes on a continuing basis in the reporting entity's activities.

fixed assets See **non-current assets**.

fixed assets usage Revenue divided by **net book value** of **fixed assets**.

fixed capital Finance provided to support the acquisition of fixed assets.

fixed cost One which is not affected by changes in the level of output over a defined period of time.

floating charge Security taken by lender which floats over all the assets and crystallises over particular assets if the security is required.

forecast estimate of future performance and position based on stated assumptions and usually including a quantified amount.

format A list of items which may appear in a financial statement, setting out the order in which they are to appear.

forward exchange contract An agreement to buy foreign currency at a fixed future date and at an agreed price.

fully paid Shares on which the amount of share capital has been paid in full to the company.

fund manager A person who manages a collection (portfolio) of investments, usually for an insurance company, a pension fund business or a professional fund management business which invests money on behalf of clients.

gearing (financial) The ratio of debt capital to ownership claim.

general purpose financial statements Documents containing accounting information which would be expected to be of interest to a wide range of user groups. For a limited liability company there would be: a balance sheet, a profit and loss account, a statement of recognised gains and losses and a cash flow statement.

going concern basis The assumption that the business will continue operating into the foreseeable future.

goodwill Goodwill on **acquisition** is the difference between the **fair** value of the amount paid for an investment in a **subsidiary** and the **fair value** of the **net assets** acquired.

gross Before making deductions.

gross margin Sales minus cost of sales before deducting administration and selling expenses (another name for **gross profit**). Usually applied when discussing a particular line of activity.

gross margin ratio Gross profit as a percentage of sales.

gross profit Sales minus cost of sales before deducting administration and selling expenses (see also **gross margin**).

group Economic **entity** formed by **parent** and one or more **subsidiaries**.

highlights statement A page at the start of the annual report setting out key measures of performance during the reporting period.

historical cost Method of valuing assets and liabilities based on their original cost without adjustment for changing prices.

HM Revenue and Customs (HMRC) The UK government's tax-gathering organisation (previously called the Inland Revenue).

IAS International Accounting Standard, issued by the IASB's predecessor body.

IASB International Accounting Standards Board, an independent body that sets accounting standards accepted as a basis for accounting in many countries, including all Member States of the European Union.

IASB system The accounting standards and guidance issued by the **IASB**.

IFRS International Financial Reporting Standard, issued by the **IASB**.

impairment A reduction in the carrying value of an **asset**, beyond the expected **depreciation**, which must be reflected by reducing the amount recorded in the **balance sheet**.

impairment review Testing assets for evidence of any **impairment**.

impairment test Test that the business can expect to recover the carrying value of the intangible asset, through either using it or selling.

improvement A change in, or addition to, a **non-current (fixed) asset** that extends its useful life or increases the expected future benefit. Contrast with repair which restores the existing useful life or existing expected future benefit.

income statement Financial statement presenting revenues, expenses, and profit. Also called **profit and loss account**.

incorporation, date of The date on which a company comes into existence.

indirect method (of operating cash flow) Calculates operating cash flow by adjusting operating profit for non-cash items and for changes in working capital.

insider information Information gained by someone inside, or close to, a listed company which could confer a financial advantage if used to buy or sell shares. It is illegal for a person who is in possession of inside information to buy or sell shares on the basis of that information.

institutional investor An organisation whose business includes regular investment in shares of companies, examples being an insurance company, a pension fund, a charity, an investment trust, a unit trust, a merchant bank.

intangible Without shape or form, cannot be touched.

interest (on loans) The percentage return on **capital** required by the lender (usually expressed as a percentage per annum).

interim reports Financial statements issued in the period between annual reports, usually half-yearly or quarterly.

internal reporting Reporting financial information to those users inside a business, at various levels of management, at a level of detail appropriate to the recipient.

inventory Stocks of goods held for manufacture or for resale.

investing activities The acquisition and disposal of long-term assets and other investments not included in cash equivalents.

investors Persons or organisations which have provided money to a business in exchange for a share of ownership.

invoices When a sale is made on credit terms the invoice is the document sent to the customer showing the quantities sold and the amount due to be paid.

joint and several liability (in a partnership) The partnership liabilities are shared jointly but each person is responsible for the whole of the partnership.

key performance indicators (KPIs) Quantified measures of factors that help to measure the performance of the business effectively.

leasing Acquiring the use of an **asset** through a rental agreement.

legal form Representing a transaction to reflect its legal status, which might not be the same as its economic form.

leverage Alternative term for **gearing**, commonly used in the USA.

liabilities Obligations of an entity to transfer economic benefits as a result of past transactions or events.

limited liability A phrase used to indicate that those having liability in respect of some amount due may be able to invoke some agreed limit on that liability.

limited liability company Company where the liability of the owners is limited to the amount of capital they have agreed to contribute.

liquidity The extent to which a business has access to cash or items which can readily be exchanged for cash.

listed company A company whose shares are listed by the Stock Exchange as being available for buying and selling under the rules and safeguards of the Exchange.

listing requirements Rules imposed by the Stock Exchange on companies whose shares are listed for buying and selling.

Listing Rules Issued by the UK Listing Authority of the Financial Services Authority to regulate companies listed on the UK Stock Exchange. Includes rules on accounting information in annual reports.

loan covenants Agreement made by the company with a lender of long-term finance, protecting the loan by imposing conditions on the company, usually to restrict further borrowing.

loan notes A method of borrowing from commercial institutions such as banks.

loan stock Loan finance traded on a stock exchange.

long-term finance, long-term liabilities Money lent to a business for a fixed period, giving that business a commitment to pay interest for the period specified and to repay the loan at the end of the period Also called **non-current liabilities** information in the financial statements should show the commercial substance of the situation.

management Collective term for those persons responsible for the day-to-day running of a business.

management accounting Reporting accounting information within a business, for management use only.

market value (of a share) The price for which a share could be transferred between a willing buyer and a willing seller.

marking to market Valuing a marketable **asset** at its current market price.

margin Profit, seen as the 'margin' between revenue and expense.

matching Expenses are matched against revenues in the period they are incurred (see also **accruals basis**).

material See **materiality**.

materiality Information is **material** if its omission or misstatement could influence the economic decisions of users taken on the basis of the financial statements.

maturity The date on which a liability is due for repayment.

maturity profile of debt The timing of loan repayments by a company in the future.

memorandum (for a company) Document setting out main objects of the company and its powers to act.

merger Two organisations agree to work together in a situation where neither can be regarded as having acquired the other.

minority interest The **ownership interest** in a company held by persons other than the **parent company** and its **subsidiary** undertakings. Also called a **non-controlling interest**.

net After making deductions.

net assets Assets minus **liabilities** (equals **ownership interest**).

net book value Cost of **non-current (fixed) asset** minus **accumulated depreciation**.

net debt Borrowings minus cash balances.

net profit Sales minus cost of sales minus all administrative and selling costs.

net realisable value The proceeds of selling an item, less the costs of selling.

neutral Qualitative characteristic of freedom from bias.

nominal value (of a share) The amount stated on the face of a share certificate as the named value of the share when issued.

non-controlling interest See **minority interest**.

non-current assets Any asset that does not meet the definition of a current asset. Also described as **fixed assets**.

non-current liabilities Any liability that does not meet the definition of a **current liability**. Also described as **long-term liabilities**.

notes to the accounts Information in financial statements that gives more detail about items in the **financial statements**.

off-balance-sheet finance An arrangement to keep matching assets and liabilities away from the entity's balance sheet.

offer for sale A company makes a general offer of its shares to the public.

operating activities The principal revenue-producing activities of the entity and other activities that are not investing or financing activities.

operating and financial review Section of the annual report of many companies which explains the main features of the financial statements.

operating gearing The ratio of fixed operating costs to variable operating costs.

operating margin Operating profit as a percentage of sales.

operating risk Exists where there are factors, such as a high level of fixed operating costs, which would cause profits to fluctuate through changes in operating conditions.

ordinary shares Shares in a company which entitle the holder to a share of the dividend declared and a share in net assets on closing down the business.

ownership interest The residual amount found by deducting all of the entity's liabilities from all of the entity's assets. (Also called **equity interest**.)

par value See **nominal value**.

parent company Company which controls one or more subsidiaries in a group.

partnership Two or more persons in business together with the aim of making a profit.

partnership deed A document setting out the agreement of the partners on how the partnership is to be conducted (including the arrangements for sharing profits and losses).

partnership law Legislation which governs the conduct of a partnership and which should be used where no partnership deed has been written.

portfolio (of investment) A collection of investments.

portfolio of shares A collection of shares held by an investor.

preference shares Shares in a company which give the holder a preference (although not an automatic right) to receive a dividend before any ordinary share dividend is declared.

preliminary announcement The first announcement by a listed company of its profit for the most recent accounting period. Precedes the publication of the full annual report. The announcement is made to the entire stock market so that all investors receive information at the same time.

premium An amount paid in addition, or extra.

prepaid expense An expense paid in advance of the benefit being received, e.g. rentals paid in advance.

prepayment An amount paid for in advance for an benefit to the business, such as insurance premiums or rent in advance. Initially recognised as an asset, then transferred to expense in the period when the benefit is enjoyed. (Also called a **prepaid expense**.)

present fairly A condition of the **IASB system**, equivalent to **true and fair view** in the **UK ASB system**.

price–earnings ratio Market price of a share divided by earnings per share.

price-sensitive information Information which, if known to the market, would affect the price of a share.

primary financial statements The balance sheet, profit and loss account, statement of total recognised gains and losses and cash flow statement.

principal (sum) The agreed amount of a loan, on which interest will be charged during the period of the loan.

private limited company (Ltd) A company which has **limited liability** but is not permitted to offer its shares to the public.

production overhead costs Costs of production that are spread across all output, rather than being identified with specific goods or services.

profit Calculated as revenue minus expenses.

profit and loss account Financial statement presenting revenues, expenses, and profit. Also called **income statement**.

prospective investor An investor who is considering whether to invest in a company.

prospectus Financial statements and supporting detailed descriptions published when a company is offering shares for sale to the public.

provision A liability of uncertain timing or amount.

provision for doubtful debts An estimate of the risk of not collecting full payment from credit customers, reported as a deduction from **trade receivables (debtors)** in the **balance sheet**.

prudence A degree of caution in the exercise of the judgements needed in making the estimates required under conditions of uncertainty, such that gains and assets are not overstated and losses and liabilities are not understated.

public limited company (plc) A company which has **limited liability** and offers its shares to the public.

purchase method Method of producing consolidated financial statements (see **acquisition method**).

purchases Total of goods and services bought in a period.

qualified audit opinion An audit opinion to the effect that: the accounts do *not* show a true and fair view; or the accounts show a true and fair view *except for* particular matters.

quality of earnings Opinion of investors on reliability of earnings (profit) as a basis for their forecasts.

quoted company Defined in section 262 of the Companies Act 1985 as a company that has been included in the official list in accordance with the provisions of Part VI of the Financial Services and Markets Act 2000, or is officially listed in an EEA state, or is admitted to dealing on either the New York Stock Exchange or the exchange known as Nasdaq.

realised profit, realisation A profit arising from revenue which has been earned by the entity and for which there is a reasonable prospect of cash being collected in the near future.

recognised An item is recognised when it is included by means of words and amount within the main financial statements of an entity.

recognition See **recognised**.

Registrar of Companies An official authorised by the government to maintain a record of all annual reports and other documents issued by a company.

relevance Qualitative characteristic of influencing the economic decisions of users.

replacement cost A measure of **current value** which estimates the cost of replacing an asset or liability at the date of the balance sheet. Justified by reference to **value to the business**.

reserves The claim which owners have on the *assets* of a company because the company has created new wealth for them over the period since it began.

residual value The estimated amount that an entity would currently obtain from disposal of the asset, after deducting the estimated cost of disposal, if the asset were already of the age and in the condition expected at the end of its useful life.

retained earnings Accumulated past profits, not distributed in dividends, available to finance investment in assets.

retained profit Profit of the period remaining after **dividend** has been deducted.

return The yield or reward from an investment.

return on capital employed (ROCE) Operating profit before deducting interest and taxation, divided by share capital plus reserves plus long-term loans.

return on shareholders' equity Profit for shareholders divided by share capital plus reserves.

return on total assets Operating profit before deducting interest and taxation, divided by total assets.

return (in relation to investment) The reward earned for investing money in a business. Return may appear in the form of regular cash payments (dividends) to the investor, or in a growth in the value of the amount invested.

revaluation reserve The claim which owners have on the **assets** of the business because the balance sheet records a market value for an asset that is greater than its historical cost.

revenue Created by a transaction or event arising during the ordinary activities of the business which causes an increase in the ownership interest.

rights issue A company gives its existing shareholders the right to buy more shares in proportion to those already held.

risk (in relation to investment) Factors that may cause the profit or cash flows of the business to fluctuate.

sales See **revenue, turnover**.

sales invoice Document sent to customers recording a sale on credit and requesting payment.

secured loan Loan where the lender has taken a special claim on particular assets or revenues of the company.

segmental reporting Reporting revenue, profit, cash flow assets, liabilities for each geographical and business segment within a business, identifying segments by the way the organisation is managed.

share capital Name given to the total amount of cash which the shareholders have contributed to the company.

share certificate A document providing evidence of share ownership.

share premium The claim which owners have on the assets of a company because shares have been purchased from the company at a price greater than the nominal value.

shareholders Owners of a **limited liability company**.

shareholders' funds Name given to total of **share capital** and **reserves** in a company balance sheet.

shares The amount of share capital held by any shareholder is measured in terms of a number of shares in the total capital of the company.

short-term finance Money lent to a business for a short period of time, usually repayable on demand and also repayable at the choice of the business if surplus to requirements.

sole trader An individual owning and operating a business alone.

specific purpose financial statements Documents containing accounting information which is prepared for a particular purpose and is not normally available to a wider audience.

stakeholders A general term devised to indicate all those who might have a legitimate interest in receiving financial information about a business because they have a 'stake' in it.

statement of cash flows Provides information about changes in financial position.

statement of changes in equity A financial statement reporting all items causing changes to the ownership interest during the financial period, under the **IASB system**.

statement of comprehensive income Provides information on all gains and losses causing a change in **ownership interest** during a period, other than contributions and withdrawals made by the owners.

statement of financial position Provides information on assets, liabilities and equity at a specified reporting date. It is the preferred title under the **IASB system** for the document that is also called a **balance sheet**.

statement of principles A document issued by the Accounting Standards Board in the United Kingdom setting out key principles to be applied in the process of setting accounting standards.

statement of recognised income and expense A financial statement reporting **realised** and **unrealised** income and expense as part of a **statement of changes in equity** under the **IASB system**.

statement of total recognised gains and losses A financial statement reporting changes in equity under the UK ASB system.

stepped bond Loan finance that starts with a relatively low rate of interest which then increases in steps.

stewardship Taking care of resources owned by another person and using those resources to the benefit of that person.

stock A word with two different meanings. It may be used to describe an **inventory** of goods held for resale or for use in business. It may also be used to describe **shares** in the ownership of a company. The meaning will usually be obvious from the way in which the word is used.

stock exchange (also called **stock market**). An organisation which has the authority to set rules for persons buying and selling shares. The term 'stock' is used loosely with a meaning similar to that of 'shares'.

stock holding period Average number of days for which inventory (stock) is held before use or sale.

stock market See **stock exchange**.

subsidiary company Company in a group which is controlled by another (the parent company). (*See* Chapter 7 for full definition.) Sometimes called subsidiary undertaking.

substance (economic) Information in the financial statements should show the economic or commercial substance of the situation.

subtotal Totals of similar items grouped together within a financial statement.

suppliers' payment period Average number of days credit taken from suppliers.

tangible fixed assets A **fixed asset** (also called a **non-current asset**) which has a physical existence.

timeliness Qualitative characteristic that potentially conflicts with **relevance**.

total assets usage Sales divided by total assets.

trade creditors Persons who supply goods or services to a business in the normal course of trade and allow a period of credit before payment must be made.

trade debtors Persons who buy goods or services from a business in the normal course of trade and are allowed a period of credit before payment is due.

trade payables Amounts due to suppliers (**trade creditors**), also called **accounts payable**.

trade receivables Amounts due from customers (**trade debtors**), also called **accounts receivable**.

treasury shares Shares which a company has repurchased from its own shareholders and is holding with the intention of reselling the shares in the future.

true and fair view Requirement of UK company law for UK companies not using **IASB system**.

turnover The sales of a business or other form of revenue from operations of the business.

understandability Qualitative characteristic of financial statements, understandable by users.

unlisted (company) Limited liability company whose shares are not **listed** on any stock exchange.

unrealised Gains and losses representing changes in values of assets and liabilities that are not **realised** through sale or use.

unsecured creditors Those who have no claim against particular assets when a company is wound up, but must take their turn for any share of what remains.

unsecured loan Loan in respect of which the lender has taken no special claim against any assets.

value to the business An idea used in deciding on a measure of **current value**.

variance The difference between a planned, budgeted or standard cost and the actual cost incurred. An adverse variance arises when the actual cost is greater than the standard cost. A favourable variance arises when the actual cost is less than the standard cost.

working capital Finance provided to support the short-term assets of the business (stocks and debtors) to the extent that these are not financed by short-term creditors. It is calculated as current assets minus current liabilities.

working capital cycle Total of stock holding period plus customers collection period minus suppliers payment period.

work in progress Cost of partly completed goods or services, intended for completion and recorded as an asset.

written down value See **net book value**.

Information extracted from annual report of Safe and Sure Group plc, used throughout Financial Accounting

Safe and Sure Group plc
Consolidated statement of financial position (balance sheet)
at 31 December

	Notes	Year 7 £m	Year 6 £m
Non-current assets			
Property, plant and equipment	1	137.5	121.9
Intangible assets	2	260.3	237.6
Investments	3	2.8	2.0
Taxation recoverable	4	5.9	4.9
Total non-current assets		406.5	366.4
Current assets			
Inventories (stocks)	5	26.6	24.3
Amounts receivable (debtors)	6	146.9	134.7
Six-month deposits		2.0	–
Cash and cash equivalents		105.3	90.5
Total current assets		280.8	249.5
Total assets		687.3	615.9
Current liabilities			
Amounts payable (creditors)	7	(159.8)	(157.5)
Bank overdraft	8	(40.1)	(62.6)
Total current liabilities		(199.9)	(220.1)
Non-current liabilities			
Amounts payable (creditors)	9	(2.7)	(2.6)
Bank and other borrowings	10	(0.2)	(0.6)
Provisions	11	(20.2)	(22.2)
Total non-current liabilities		(23.1)	(25.4)
Total liabilities		(223.0)	(245.5)
Net assets		464.3	370.4
Capital and reserves			
Called-up share capital	12	19.6	19.5
Share premium account	13	8.5	5.5
Revaluation reserve	14	4.6	4.6
Retained earnings	15	431.6	340.8
Equity holders' funds		464.3	370.4

Safe and Sure Group plc
Consolidated income statement (profit and loss account)
for the year ended 31 December Year 7

	Notes	Year 7 £m	Year 6 £m
Continuing operations			
Revenue	16	714.6	589.3
Cost of sales	16	(491.0)	(406.3)
Gross profit		223.6	183.0
Distribution costs		(2.2)	(2.5)
Administrative expenses	17	(26.2)	(26.5)
Profit from operations		195.2	154.0
Interest receivable (net)	18	2.3	3.0
Profit before tax	19	197.5	157.0
Tax	20	(62.2)	(52.4)
Profit for the period from continuing operations		135.3	104.6
Discontinued operations			
Loss for the period from discontinued operations	21	(20.5)	(10.0)
Profit for the period attributable to equity holders		114.8	94.6

Safe and Sure plc
Consolidated statement of comprehensive income
for the year ended 31 December Year 7

	Year 7 £m	Year 6 £m
Profit for the period	114.8	94.6
Other comprehensive income:		
Exchange rate adjustments	5.5	(6.0)
Total comprehensive income for the year	120.3	88.6
Earnings per share	22 11.74	9.71

Safe and Sure plc
Consolidated statement of changes in equity for the year ended 31 December Year 7

	Share capital	Share premium	Revaluation reserve	Retained earnings (including exchange rate adjustments)	Total
	£m	£m	£m	£m	£m
Balance at 1 Jan Year 6	19.4	3.6	4.6	276.6	304.2
Share capital issued	0.1	1.9			2.0
Total comprehensive income				88.6	88.6
Less dividend				(24.4)	(24.4)
Balance at 1 Jan Year 7	19.5	5.5	4.6	340.8	370.4
Share capital issued	0.1	3.0			3.1
Total comprehensive income				120.3	120.3
Less dividend				(29.5)	(29.5)
Balance at 31 Dec Year 7	19.6	8.5	4.6	431.6	464.3

Safe and Sure Group plc
Consolidated statement of cash flows for the years ended 31 December

	Notes	Year 7 £m	Year 6 £m
Cash flows from operating activities			
Cash generated from operations	23	196.7	163.5
Interest paid		(3.1)	(2.4)
UK corporation tax paid		(20.1)	(18.3)
Overseas tax paid		(30.5)	(26.5)
Net cash from operating activities		**143.0**	**116.3**
Cash flows from investing activities			
Purchase of property, plant and equipment		(60.0)	(47.5)
Sale of property, plant and equipment		12.0	10.1
Purchase of companies and businesses	25	(27.7)	(90.1)
Sale of a company		3.1	–
Movement in short-term deposits		(30.7)	36.3
Interest received		5.0	5.9
Net cash used in investing activities		**(98.3)**	**(85.3)**
Cash flows from financing activities			
Issue of ordinary share capital		3.1	2.0
Dividends paid to equity holders		(29.5)	(24.4)
Net loan movement (excluding overdraft)		16.2	(24.0)
Net cash used in financing activities		**(10.2)**	**(46.4)**
Net increase/(decrease) in cash and cash equivalents*		**34.5**	**(15.4)**
Cash and cash equivalents at the beginning of the year		27.9	45.3
Exchange adjustments		2.8	(2.0)
Cash and cash equivalents at the end of the year	28	65.2	27.9

* Cash on demand and deposits of maturity less than 3 months, net of overdrafts.

Accounting policies (extracts)

Intangible non-current (fixed) assets

Purchased goodwill is calculated as the difference between the fair value of the consideration paid for an acquired entity and the aggregate of the fair values of that entity's identifiable assets and liabilities. An impairment review has been undertaken at the balance sheet date.

Freehold and leasehold property

Freehold and leasehold land and buildings are stated either at cost (Security and Cleaning) or at their revalued amounts less depreciation (Disposal and Recycling). Full revaluations are made at five-year intervals with interim valuations in the intervening years, the most recent full revaluation being in year 5.

Provision for depreciation of freehold land and buildings is made at the annual rate of 1% of cost or the revalued amounts. Leasehold land and buildings are amortised in equal annual instalments over the periods of the leases subject to a minimum annual provision of 1% of cost or the revalued amounts. When properties are sold the difference between sales proceeds and net book value is dealt with in the income statement (profit and loss account).

Plant and equipment

Plant and equipment are stated at cost less depreciation. Provision for depreciation is made mainly in equal annual instalments over the estimated useful lives of the assets as follows:

4 to 5 years   vehicles
5 to 10 years   plant, machinery and equipment

Inventories (stocks and work in progress)

Inventories (stocks and work in progress) are stated at the lower of cost and net realisable value, using the first in first out principle. Cost includes all direct expenditure and related overheads incurred in bringing the inventories to their present condition and location.

Deferred tax

The provision for deferred tax recognises a future liability arising from past transactions and events. Tax legislation allows the company to defer settlement of the liability for several years.

Warranties

Some service work is carried out under warranty. The cost of claims under warranty is charged against the profit and loss account of the year in which the claims are settled.

Deferred consideration

For acquisitions involving deferred consideration, estimated deferred payments are accrued in the balance sheet. Interest due to vendors on deferred payments is charged to the profit and loss account as it accrues.

Notes to accounts

Note 1 Property, plant and equipment

	Land and buildings £m	Plant and equipment £m	Vehicles £m	Total £m
Cost or valuation				
At 1 January Year 7	28.3	96.4	104.8	229.5
Additions at cost	3.9	18.5	37.8	60.2
On acquisitions	0.3	1.0	0.7	2.0
Disposals	(0.6)	(3.1)	(24.7)	(28.4)
At 31 December Year 7	31.9	112.8	118.6	263.3
Aggregate depreciation				
At 1 January Year 7	2.2	58.8	46.6	107.6
Depreciation for the year	0.5	13.5	19.2	33.2
On acquisitions	0.1	0.7	0.6	1.4
Disposals	(0.2)	(2.8)	(13.4)	(16.4)
At 31 December Year 7	2.6	70.2	53.0	125.8
Net book value at 31 December Year 7	29.3	42.6	65.6	137.5
Net book value at 31 December Year 6	26.1	37.6	58.2	121.9

Analysis of land and buildings at cost or valuation

	Year 7 £m	Year 6 £m
At cost	10.4	7.1
At valuation	21.5	21.2
	31.9	28.3

The group's freehold and long-term leasehold properties in the Disposal and Recycling division were revalued during Year 5 by independent valuers. Valuations were made on the basis of the market value for existing use. The book values of the properties were adjusted to the revaluations and the resultant net surplus was credited to the revaluation reserve.

Analysis of net book value of land and buildings

	Year 7 £m	Year 6 £m
Freehold	24.5	21.0
Leasehold:		
Over 50 years unexpired	2.1	2.4
Under 50 years unexpired	2.7	2.7
	29.3	26.1

If the revalued assets were stated on the historical cost basis the amounts would be:

	Year 7 £m	Year 6 £m
Land and buildings at cost	15.7	14.5
Aggregate depreciation	(2.2)	(1.9)
	13.5	12.6

Note 2 Intangible non-current assets

	Year 7 £m	Year 6 £m
Goodwill at 1 January	237.6	139.1
Additions in year	24.3	98.5
Reduction in year	(1.6)	–
Goodwill at 31 December	260.3	237.6

The reduction of £1.6m results from the annual impairment review.

Note 3

Relates to investments in subsidiary companies and is not reproduced here.

Note 4

Explains the nature of taxation recoverable after more than 12 months from the balance sheet date. The detail is not reproduced here.

Note 5 Inventories (stocks)

	Year 7 £m	Year 6 £m
Raw materials	6.2	5.4
Work in progress	1.9	1.0
Finished products	18.5	17.9
	26.6	24.3

The value of inventories of finished products is stated after impairment of £0.6m (Year 6 – £0.4m), due to obsolescence.

Note 6 Amounts receivable (debtors)

	Year 7 £m	Year 6 £m
Trade receivables (trade debtors)	133.3	121.8
Less: provision for impairment of receivables	(5.2)	(4.8)
Trade receivables, net	128.1	117.0
Other receivables (debtors)	10.9	9.8
Prepayments and accrued income	7.9	7.9
	146.9	134.7

The ageing of the Group's year-end overdue receivables, against which no provision has been made, is as follows:

	Year 7 £m	Year 6 £m
Not impaired		
Less than 3 months	19.4	12.1
3 to 6 months	0.3	0.3
Over 6 months	0.1	–
	19.8	12.4

The individually impaired receivables relate to customers in unexpectedly difficult circumstances. The overdue receivables against which no provision has been made relate to a number of customers for whom there is no recent history of default and no other indication that settlement will not be forthcoming.

The carrying amounts of the Group's receivables are denominated in the following currencies:

	Year 7 £m	Year 6 £m
Sterling	80.8	79.4
US Dollar	33.6	29.1
Euro	27.2	25.5
Other	5.3	3.4
	146.9	137.4

Movements in the Group's provision for impairment of trade receivables are as follows:

	Year 7 £m	Year 6 £m
At 1 January	4.8	4.9
(Released)/charged to income statement	0.3	(0.1)
Net write off of uncollectible receivables	0.1	–
At 31 December	5.2	4.8

Amounts charged to the income statement are included within administrative expenses. The other classes of receivables do not contain impaired assets.

Note 7 Current liabilities: amounts payable

	Year 7	Year 6
	£m	£m
Deferred consideration on acquisition	1.1	4.3
Trade payables (trade creditors)	23.6	20.4
Corporation tax	31.5	26.5
Other tax and social security payable	24.5	21.2
Other payables (creditors)	30.7	23.8
Accruals and deferred income	48.4	61.3
	159.8	157.5

Trade payables (trade creditors) comprise amounts outstanding for trade purchases. The average credit period taken for trade purchases is 27 days. Most suppliers charge no interest on the trade payables for the first 30 days from the date of the invoice. Thereafter, interest is charged on the outstanding balances at various interest rates. The Group has financial risk management policies in place to ensure that all payables are paid within the agreed credit terms.

Note 8 Bank borrowings: current liabilities

	Year 7	Year 6
	£m	£m
Bank overdrafts due on demand:	40.1	62.6

Interest on overdrafts is payable at normal commercial rates appropriate to the country where the borrowing is made.

Note 9 Non-current liabilities: payables (creditors)

	Year 7	Year 6
	£m	£m
Deferred consideration on acquisition	0.6	–
Other payables (creditors)	2.1	2.6
	2.7	2.6

Note 10 Non-current liabilities: bank and other borrowings

	Year 7	Year 6
	£m	£m
Secured loans	–	0.3
Unsecured loans	0.2	0.3
	0.2	0.6
Loans are repayable by instalments:		
Between one and two years	0.1	0.2
Between two and five years	0.1	0.4
	0.2	0.6

Interest on long-term loans, which are denominated in a number of currencies, is payable at normal commercial rates appropriate to the country in which the borrowing is made. The last repayment falls due in Year 11.

Note 11 Provisions

	Year 7 £m	Year 6 £m
Provisions for treating contaminated site:		
At 1 January	14.2	14.5
Utilised in the year	(2.2)	(0.3)
At 31 December	12.0	14.2
Provisions for restructuring costs:		
At 1 January	4.2	–
Created in year	1.0	4.3
Utilised in year	(1.0)	(0.1)
At 31 December	4.2	4.2
Provision for deferred tax:		
At 1 January	3.8	2.7
Transfer to income statement	0.5	1.2
Other movements	(0.3)	(0.1)
At 31 December	4.0	3.8
Total provision	20.2	22.2

Note 12 Share capital

	Year 7 £m	Year 6 £m
Ordinary shares of 2 pence each		
Authorised: 1,050,000,000 shares		
(Year 6: 1,000,000,000)	21.0	20.0
Issued and fully paid: 978,147,487 shares	19.6	19.5

Certain senior executives hold options to subscribe for shares in the company at prices ranging from 33.40p to 244.33p under schemes approved by equity holders at various dates. Options on 3,479,507 shares were exercised during Year 7 and 66,970 options lapsed. The number of shares subject to options, the years in which they were purchased and the years in which they will expire are:

Options granted	Exercisable	Option price (pence)	Numbers
	Year 8	33.40	13,750
All granted	Year 9	53.55	110,000
10 years before	Year 10	75.42	542,500
exercisable	Year 11	100.22	1,429,000
	Year 12	120.33	2,826,600
	Year 13/14	150.45	3,539,942
	Year 15	195.20	3,690,950
	Year 16	201.50	2,279,270
	Year 17	244.33	3,279,363
			17,711,375

Note 13 Share premium account

	Year 7 £m	Year 6 £m
At 1 January	5.5	3.6
Premium on shares issued during the year under the share option schemes	3.0	1.9
At 31 December	8.5	5.5

Note 14 Revaluation reserve

	Year 7 £m	Year 6 £m
At 1 January	4.6	4.6
At 31 December	4.6	4.6

Note 15 Retained earnings

	Year 7 £m	Year 6 £m
At 1 January	340.8	276.6
Exchange adjustments	5.5	(6.0)
Profit for the year	114.8	94.6
Dividend paid	(29.5)	(24.4)
At 31 December	431.6	340.8

Note 16 Operating segments

For the purposes of reporting to the chief operating decision maker, the group is currently organised into two operating divisions, (1) disposal and recycling, (2) security and cleaning. Disposal and recycling includes all aspects of collection and safe disposal of industrial and commercial waste products. Security and cleaning is undertaken by renewable annual contract, predominantly for hospitals, other healthcare premises and local government organisations.

The group's disposal and recycling operation in North America was discontinued with effect from 30 April Year 7.

Business sector analysis

	Disposal and recycling		Security and cleaning		Total	
	Year 7 £m	Year 6 £m	Year 7 £m	Year 6 £m	Year 7 £m	Year 6 £m
REVENUES (all from external customers)						
Continuing	508.9	455.0	205.7	134.3	714.6	589.3
Discontinued	20.0	11.0			20.0	11.0
Total revenues	528.9	466.0	205.7	134.3	734.6	600.3
Operating profit (loss) by service						
Continuing	176.6	139.6	18.6	14.4	195.2	154.0
Discontinued	(20.5)	(10.0)			(20.5)	(10.0)
Total operating profit					174.7	144.0
Interest receivable (net)					2.3	3.0
Profit before tax					177.0	147.0
Taxation					(62.2)	(52.4)
Profit for the period					114.8	94.6

All costs of head office operations are allocated to divisions on an activity costing basis. The company does not allocate interest receivable or taxation paid to reportable segments.

Depreciation and amortisation included in the income statement are as follows:

	Disposal and recycling		Security and cleaning		Total	
	Year 7 £m	Year 6 £m	Year 7 £m	Year 6 £m	Year 7 £m	Year 6 £m
Depreciation	30.2	25.1	3.0	3.9	33.2	29.0
Impairment of goodwill	1.6	–	–	–	1.6	–

The segment assets and liabilities at the end of Years 7 and 6 are as follows:

	Disposal and recycling		Security and cleaning		Unallocated		Total	
	Year 7 £m	Year 6 £m	Year 7 £m	Year 6 £m	Year 7 £m	Year 6 £m	Year 7 £m	Year 6 £m
Total assets	498.5	370.9	68.7	132.7	120.1	112.3	687.3	615.9
Total liabilities	131.7	147.9	61.3	85.5	30.0	12.1	223.0	245.5

Information about geographical areas

The group's two business segments operate in four main geographical areas, even though they are managed on a worldwide basis. In the following analysis, revenue is based on the country in which the order is received. It would not be materially different if based on the country in which the customer is located. Total assets and capital expenditure are allocated based on where the assets are located.

	Revenues from external customers		Non-current assets	
	Year 7 £m	Year 6 £m	Year 7 £m	Year 6 £m
CONTINUING				
United Kingdom	323.4	246.7	174.2	148.7
Continental Europe	164.3	153.5	90.3	93.0
North America	104.5	80.1	85.9	49.2
Asia Pacific & Africa	122.4	109.0	56.1	75.0
	714.6	589.3	406.5	365.9
DISCONTINUED				
North America	20.0	11.0	–	0.5
Total	734.6	600.3	406.5	366.4

Notes 17–20

Contain supporting details for the profit and loss account and are not reproduced here.

Note 21 Discontinued operations

On 31 March Year 7, the Group entered into a sale agreement to dispose of Carers Inc., its recycling business in North America. The purpose of the disposal was to prevent further loss-making activity. The disposal was completed on 30 April Year 7, on which date control of Carers Inc. passed to the acquirer.

The results of the discontinued operations which have been included in the consolidated income statement, were as follows:

	Year 7 £m	Year 6 £m
Revenue	20.0	11.0
Expenses	(40.5)	(21.0)
Loss attributable to discontinued operations	(20.5)	**(10.0)**

Note 22

Contains supporting details for earnings per share and is not reproduced here.

Note 23 Cash flow from operating activities

Reconciliation of operating profit to net cash flow from operating activities

	Year 7 £m	Year 6 £m
Profit before tax from continuing operations	195.2	154.0
Loss from discontinued operations	(20.5)	(10.0)
Profit from operations	174.7	144.0
Depreciation charge	33.2	30.1
Increase in inventories (stocks)*	(1.9)	(1.1)
Increase in trade receivables (debtors)*	(7.4)	(5.3)
Decrease in trade payables (creditors)*	(0.4)	(3.6)
Net cash inflow from continuing activities	198.2	164.1
Cash outflow in respect of discontinued item	(1.5)	(0.6)
Net cash inflow from operating activities	196.7	163.5

* *Note*: It is not possible to reconcile these figures with the balance sheet information because of the effect of acquisitions during the year.

Note 24 Information on acquisitions (extract)

The group purchased 20 companies and businesses during the year for a total consideration of £25m. The adjustments required to the balance sheet figures of companies and businesses acquired, in order to present the net assets at fair value, are shown below:

	£m
Net assets of subsidiaries acquired, as shown in their balance sheets	4.1
Adjustments made by directors of Safe and Sure plc	(3.4)
Fair value of net assets acquired (**a**)	0.7
Cash paid for subsidiaries (**b**)	25.0
Goodwill (**b** − **a**)	24.3

From the dates of acquisition to 31 December Year 7, the acquisitions contributed £13.5m to revenue, £2.7m to profit before interest and £2.2m to profit after interest.

If the acquisitions had been completed on the first day of the financial year, they would have contributed £30m to group revenues for the year and £5m to group profit attributable to equity holders of the parent.

Notes 25–27

Contain supporting detail for the cash flow statement and are not reproduced here.

Note 28 Cash and cash equivalents

Reconciliation of cash flow for the year to the balance sheet items

	Year 7 £m	Year 6 £m
Balance sheet items		
Cash and cash equivalents	105.3	90.5
Bank overdraft	(40.1)	(62.6)
Net	65.2	27.9

Notes 29–32

Contain various other items of information required by company law and are not reproduced here.

Note 33 Contingent liabilities

The company has guaranteed bank and other borrowings of subsidiaries amounting to £3.0m (Year 6: £15.2m). The group has commitments, amounting to approximately £41.9m (Year 6: £28.5m), under forward exchange contracts entered into in the ordinary course of business.

Certain subsidiaries have given warranties for service work. These are explained in the statement on accounting policies. There are contingent liabilities in respect of litigation. None of the actions is expected to give rise to any material loss.

Note 34

Contains commitments for capital expenditure and is not reproduced here.

Five-year summary

(Continuing and discontinued operations combined)

	Year 3	Year 4	Year 5	Year 6	Year 7
	£m	£m	£m	£m	£m
Group revenue	309.1	389.0	474.1	600.3	734.6
Group profit before tax	74.4	90.4	114.5	147.0	177.0
Tax	(27.2)	(33.9)	(44.3)	(52.4)	(62.2)
Group profit after tax	47.2	56.5	70.2	94.6	114.8
Earnings per share	4.88p	6.23p	8.02p	9.71p	11.74p
Dividends per share	1.32p	1.69p	2.17p	2.50p	3.02p
	£m	£m	£m	£m	£m
Share capital	19.4	19.4	19.4	19.5	19.6
Reserves	160.8	195.3	284.8	350.9	444.7
Total equity	180.2	214.7	304.2	370.4	464.3

Operating and financial review (extract)

The Directors' Report explains that the requirement to prepare a business review is satisfied by the production of the operating and financial review, extracts of which are presented here.

CHIEF EXECUTIVE'S REVIEW OF OPERATIONS

Group results

Group revenue from continuing operations in Year 7 increased by 21.3% to £714.6m, while continuing profits before tax increased by 25.8% to £197.5m. Earnings per share increased by 20.9% to 11.74 pence. These results show the benefits of our geographic diversification across the major economies of the world. We have achieved excellent growth in the UK, together with continued good growth in North America. Growth in Europe continued to be constrained by depressed economies, while excellent results in Australia were held back by disappointing growth in South East Asia. Segmental results are set out in detail in Note 16 to the financial statements.

In Disposal and Recycling, revenue improved by 13.4% and profits improved by 20.4%. Revenue in Security and Cleaning improved by 53.2% and profits improved by 29.2%.

Organisation

We continue to be organised into four geographic regions, each headed by a regional managing director. Group services are provided for finance, legal, research and development, corporate affairs, business development and management development. These costs are allocated to divisions on the basis of activity costing.

Strategy

Our ultimate objective is to achieve for our equity holders a high rate of growth in earnings and dividends per share each year. Our strategies are to provide customers with the highest standards of service and to maintain quality of service as we enter new fields. We also operate a prudent financial policy of managing our businesses to generate a strong operating cash flow.

Disposal and recycling

Disposal and recycling includes all aspects of collection and safe disposal of industrial and commercial waste products. During Year 7 all our operational landfill sites gained certification to the international environment management standard. Organic waste deposited in landfill sites degrades naturally and gives off a gas rich in methane which has to be controlled for environmental reasons. However, landfill sites can also be a cheap, clean and highly efficient source of renewable energy. Through strategic long-term contracts we are generating 64MW of electricity each year from landfill waste to energy schemes. New waste transfer and recycling centres in Germany and France were added to the Group's network during Year 7.

Security and cleaning

Security and cleaning is undertaken by renewable annual contract, predominantly for hospitals, other healthcare premises and local government organisations. During Year 7 we acquired a security company in the UK and some smaller operations in Switzerland and Spain. Improved margins in contract cleaning reflected continued demands for improved hygiene standards and our introduction of new techniques to meet this need.

FINANCE DIRECTOR'S REVIEW OF THE POSITION OF THE BUSINESS

Profits

Operating profits, including the effect of discontinued operations, rose to £174.7m in Year 7, up from £144.0m in Year 6. Interest income fell £0.7m to £2.3m in Year 7, as a result of the cash spent on acquisitions towards the end of Year 6. At constant average Year 6 exchange rates, the Year 7 profit before tax, including the effect of discontinued operations, would have been £0.6m higher at £177.6m, an increase of 20.8% over the reported Year 6 figures.

Cash flow

The Group's businesses are structured to utilise as little fixed and working capital as is consistent with the profit and earnings growth objective in order to produce a high cash flow. The impact of working capital on cash flow was held to an increase in Year 7 of £9.7m (Year 6: £10.0m).

A net cash flow of £196.7m was generated from operating activities. That was boosted by other amounts of cash from interest received. After paying interest and tax, the Group had £143.0m remaining. Fixed assets required £48.0m after allowing for the proceeds of selling some of our vehicle fleet in the routine replacement programme. That left £95m from which £24.6m was required to pay for acquisitions. The remaining £70.4m covered dividends of £29.5m leaving £40.9m. We received £5m interest on investments and raised £3.1m in ordinary share capital to give a net inflow of liquid funds in the year of £49.0m. Out of that amount, short-term deposits have increased by £14.5m, leaving an increase in cash of £34.5m.

Foreign currency

We borrowed £35.2m of foreign currency bank borrowings to fund overseas acquisitions. The main borrowings were £26.8m in US dollars and £8.4m in yen (to fund our Japanese associate investment). The borrowings are mainly from banks on a short-term basis with a maturity of up to one year. We have fixed the interest rate on $20m of the US dollar loans through to November Year 8 at an overall cost of 4.5%.

All material foreign currency transactions are matched back into the currency of the Group company undertaking the transaction. It is not the Group's current practice to hedge the translation of overseas profits or assets back into sterling, although overseas acquisitions may be financed by foreign currency borrowings.

Capital expenditure

The major items of capital expenditure are vehicles, equipment used on customers' premises and office equipment, particularly computers. Disposals during the year were mainly of vehicles being replaced on a rolling programme.

Taxation

The overall Group taxation charge comprises tax at 30% on UK profits and an average rate of 38% on overseas profits, reflecting the underlying rates in the various countries in which the Group operates.

Future development and performance

Once again, in Year 7 Safe and Sure met its declared objective of increasing its pre-tax profits and earnings per share by at least 20% per annum. The board expects a return to much better growth in Europe and a substantially improved performance in the USA to underpin good Group growth for the year.

Principal risks and uncertainties

The group operates through a wide range of activities across many countries. The principal risks and uncertainties identified by the directors relate to the market conditions in which we operate and to management's capability to deliver the large number of change programmes and recovery strategies currently underway across the businesses.

The principal risks we face may be summarised as: (1) a weakening of the economies in which we operate; and (2) the number, scope, complexity and interdependencies of many initiatives – risk of management stretch and overlapping priorities.

We outline below the principal risks we have identified and the actions we take to mitigate these risks.

Description of risk	Management action
Operating costs	
In the Disposal and Recycling Division across France, Belgium and Germany we have experienced rising wages and increasing employment costs such as taxes. Such costs are determined by the governments of those countries and not under our own control.	Actions to mitigate these risks include passing on price increases to customers to counter cost inflation and pricing contracts appropriately to remain competitive.
State of the economy	
The group is exposed to the economic environments in more than 20 countries across the world. Whilst the UK represents a large proportion of the group's businesses our international diversification means that our economic and geopolitical risks are spread widely. Current unrest in two African countries has caused us to suspend security and cleaning contracts.	Divisional managers monitor economic activity in their respective geographical areas. In relation to areas of unrest, we take advice from the Foreign and Commonwealth Office, having particular regard to the safety of personnel and long-term security of contracts.
Market demand and competition	
In France, Belgium and the Netherlands we experienced competitive pricing pressure in the Disposal and Recycling Division. This resulted in a number of contract losses earlier in the year and also affected the division's ability to win new contracts.	In those circumstances where our competitors are engaging in aggressive price discounting and where we believe that to offer similar prices would compromise service levels, our only mitigating course of action is to ensure that contract losses do not directly result from poor customer care, service or relationships. Further mitigating actions include improving the competitiveness of the business through significant restructuring programmes in Belgium and France and through extensive cost-savings programmes across all businesses.
Regulation	
The Disposal and Recycling Division is vulnerable to increased costs due to changing national regulations regarding hazardous waste and safe disposal in the countries where we operate.	We monitor national initiatives on regulation of disposal and recycling in the countries where we operate. Anticipated increased costs are built into contract negotiations. We also include flexible clauses in contracts to reflect the impact of regulatory change.

Description of risk	Management action

Currency and interest rates

The group is exposed to market risk primarily related to foreign exchange and interest rate risk. The group's objective is to reduce, where it is deemed appropriate to do so, fluctuations in earnings and cash flows associated with changes in interest rates, foreign currency rates and the exposure of certain net investments in foreign subsidiaries.

Management actively monitors these exposures and the group enters into currency and interest rate swaps, forward rate agreements and forward foreign exchange contracts to manage the volatility relating to these.

The majority of sales and purchases are local, limiting transaction risk. The policy is therefore to accept the risk, except where significant acquisitions or disposals are to be undertaken, where the transaction may be hedged to give certainty of pricing.

People

The company's current management team is implementing a five-year recovery plan based on operational excellence which itself is built around five key strategies, namely: to deliver outstanding customer service, to develop capability, to drive operational excellence, to operate at lowest cost and to generate profitable growth. The principal risk for the group is that management has the capacity and capability to deliver the key strategies.

Within each of the five key strategies there are a large number of improvement initiatives which individually are managed through a proper risk control process. The Nominations Committee scrutinises all appointments to senior management posts, The Remuneration Committee sets strict targets for performance rewards.

Directors' report (extract)

The Business Review, including a description of the principal risks and uncertainties facing the group, is provided under the heading of Operating and Financial Review on pages nn to nn.

The directors recommend a final dividend of 3.54 pence per ordinary share to be paid to shareholders on the register on 31 March Year 8. The proposed dividend for Year 8 of 3.02 pence per share was paid on 31 March Year 7. There is no interim dividend in either Year 6 or Year 7.

Solutions to numerical and technical questions in Financial Accounting

Note that solutions are provided only for numerical and technical material since other matters are covered either in the book or in the further reading indicated.

Chapter 1 has no solutions given in this Appendix because there are no numerical questions.

Chapter 2

Application **B2.1**

Classify each of the items in the following list as: asset; liability; neither an asset nor a liability:

Cash at bank	Asset
Loan from the bank	Liability
Letter from the bank promising an overdraft facility at any time in the next three months	Neither
Trade debtor (a customer who has promised to pay later)	Asset
Trade debtor (a customer who has promised to pay later but has apparently disappeared without leaving a forwarding address)	Neither
Supplier of goods who has not yet received payment from the business	Liability
Inventory (stock) of finished goods (fashion clothing stored ahead of the spring sales)	Asset
Inventory (stock) of finished goods (fashion clothing left over after the spring sales)	Neither, unless value remains
Investment in shares of another company where the share price is rising	Asset
Investment in shares of another company where the share price is falling	Asset while there is still some benefit expected
Lender of five-year loan to the business	Liability
Customer to whom the business has offered a 12-month warranty to repair goods free of charge	Liability
A motor vehicle owned by the business	Asset
A motor vehicle rented by the business for one year	Neither
An office building owned by the business	Asset
An office building rented by the business on a 99-year lease, with 60 years' lease period remaining	Asset, but may not be shown

B2.2

Yes to all, except the rented building where risks and benefits are mainly for the owners, not the users.

B2.3

A letter from the owner of the business, guarantee the bank overdraft of the business.	Transaction is between owner and bank, not addressed to the bank manager, promising to with business
A list of the customers of the business.	Has benefit for the future but no event, also not measurable with reliability.
An order received from a customer.	Future benefit expected but insufficient evidence that it will be obtained.
The benefit of employing a development engineer with a high level of 'know-how' specifically relevant to the business.	Future benefit exists but not measurable with sufficient reliability.
Money spent on an advertising campaign to boost sales.	Future benefit exists but not measurable with sufficient reliability.
Structural repairs to a building.	Repairs put right the problems of the past – do not create future benefits.

Chapter 3

Application **B3.1**

Sunshine Wholesale Traders
Statement of financial position (balance sheet) at 30 June Year 2

	£	£
Non-current (fixed) assets		
Fleet of delivery vehicles		35,880
Furniture and fittings		18,800
Total fixed assets		54,680
Current assets		
Receivables (debtors)		34,000
Bank deposit		19,000
Total current assets		53,000
Total assets		107,680
Current liabilities		
Trade payables (trade creditors)		(8,300)
Net assets		99,380
Ownership interest at the start of the year		56,000
Profit of the year		43,380
Ownership interest at end of year		99,380

Note that ownership interest at the start of the year is entered as the missing item.

Sunshine Wholesale Traders
Income statement (profit and loss account) for the year ended 30 June Year 2

	£	£
Revenues		
Sales		294,500
Expenses		
Cost of goods sold		(188,520)
Gross profit		105,980
Wages and salaries	(46,000)	
Transport costs	(14,200)	
Administration costs	(1,300)	
Depreciation	(1,100)	
Total expenses		(62,600)
Net profit of the year		43,380

B3.2

Statement of financial position (balance sheet) at . . .

	£	£
Non-current (fixed) assets		
Land and buildings		95,000
Vehicles		8,000
Total fixed assets		103,000
Current assets		
Inventory (stock) of goods for resale		35,000
Cash at bank		9,000
Total current assets		44,000
Total assets		147,000
Current liabilities		
Trade payables (trade creditors)		(43,000)
Wages due		(2,000)
		(45,000)
Liabilities due after one year		(20,000)
Total liabilities		65,000
Net assets		82,000
Ownership interest		82,000

(a) Decrease liability to employees £2,000, decrease asset of cash £2,000.
(b) Decrease ownership interest by £8,750, decrease asset of inventory (stock) by £8,750.
(c) Increase asset of inventory (stock) £5,000, increase liability of trade creditors £5,000.

Test your understanding **S3.1**
(a) Debit liability to employees £2,000, credit asset of cash £2,000.
(b) Debit ownership interest £8,750, credit asset of inventory (stock) £8,750.
(c) Debit asset of inventory (stock) £5,000, credit liability of trade creditors £5,000.

Chapter 4

Application **B4.1**
This requires a narrative answer based on sections 4.5.1, 4.5.3 and 4.5.5.

B4.2
This requires a narrative answer based on section 4.3. The more difficult aspect of this question is explaining how each convention affects current accounting practice. One example of each would be:

● *Going concern*: In historical cost accounting the fixed assets of an enterprise are recorded in the statement of financial position (balance sheet) at the historical cost, after deducting depreciation, rather than at estimated selling price, because the enterprise is a going concern and it is expected that the fixed assets will be held for long-term use.

- *Accruals*: The expense of electricity consumed during a period includes all units of electricity used, irrespective of whether an invoice has been paid.
- *Consistency*: It would be inconsistent, in a statement of financial position (balance sheet), to measure inventory (trading stock) at selling price at one point of time and at cost at another point of time.
- *Prudence*: It is prudent to measure inventory (stock of goods) at cost, rather than at selling price, because to value at selling price would anticipate a sale which may not take place.

B4.3

This is an essay which shows the student's understanding of the issues in the chapter and the ability to think about them in the context of a variety of users' needs. It requires the student to link the information in Chapter 4 with the ideas set out in section 1.5.

Chapter 5

Test your understanding

A5.1

Transaction		Asset	Liability	Ownership interest
(a)	Owner puts cash into the business	Increase[†]		Increase
(b)	Buy a vehicle for cash	Increase and decrease[†]		
(c)	Receive a bill for electricity consumed		Increase	Decrease*
(d)	Purchase stationery for office use, paying cash	Increase and decrease[†]		
(e)	Pay the electricity bill in cash	Decrease[†]	Decrease	
(f)	Pay rental for a computer, used for customer records	Decrease[†]		Decrease*
(g)	Buy spare parts for cash, to use in repairs	Increase and decrease[†]		
(h)	Buy spare parts on credit terms	Increase	Increase	
(i)	Pay garage service bills for van, using cash	Decrease[†]		Decrease*
(j)	Fill van with petrol, using credit account at local garage, to be paid at the start of next month		Increase	Decrease*
(k)	Carry out repairs for cash	Increase[†]		Increase*
(l)	Carry out repairs on credit terms	Increase		Increase*
(m)	Pay wages to an employee	Decrease[†]		Decrease*
(n)	Owner takes cash for personal use	Decrease[†]		Decrease

A5.2

Symbol * shows items which will have an effect on an income statement (profit and loss account).

A5.3

Symbol [†] shows items which will have an effect on a statement of cash flows.

A5.4

All items other than those asterisked will have a direct effect on a statement of financial position (balance sheet). The asterisked items will collectively change the accumulated profit which will increase the ownership interest reported in the statement of financial position (balance sheet).

A5.5

Transactions analysed to show the two aspects of the transaction:

	£		
Apr. 1	60,000	Increase asset of cash	Increase ownership interest
Apr. 1	800	Decrease asset of cash	Decrease ownership interest (expense)
Apr. 2	35,000	Increase asset of equipment	Decrease asset of cash
Apr. 3	5,000	Increase asset of supplies	Increase liability to trade creditor
Apr. 4	1,200	Increase asset of cash	Increase ownership interest (revenue)
Apr. 15	700	Decrease asset of cash	Decrease ownership interest (expense)
Apr. 20	500	Decrease asset of cash	Decrease ownership interest (voluntary)
Apr. 21	2,400	Increase asset of cash	Increase ownership interest (revenue)
Apr. 29	700	Decrease asset of cash	Decrease ownership interest (expense)
Apr. 29	1,900	Increase asset of debtor	Increase ownership interest (revenue)
Apr. 30	80	Decrease asset of cash	Decrease ownership interest (expense)
Apr. 30	*1,500	Decrease asset of supplies	Decrease ownership interest (expense)

* Inventory (stock) acquired £5,000, less amount remaining £3,500 = £1,500 asset used in period.

Application   B5.1

		Cash and bank	Other assets	Liabilities	Capital contributed or withdrawn	Revenue	Expenses
		£	£	£	£	£	£
April 1	Jane Gate commenced her dental practice on April 1 by depositing £60,000 in a business bank account.	60,000			60,000		
April 1	Rent for a surgery was paid, £800, for the month of April.	(800)					800
April 2	Dental equipment was purchased for £35,000, paying in cash.	(35,000)	35,000				
April 3	Dental supplies were purchased for £5,000, taking 30 days' credit from a supplier.		5,000	5,000			
April 4	Fees of £1,200 were collected in cash from patients and paid into the bank account.	1,200				1,200	
April 15	Dental assistant was paid wages for two weeks, £700.	(700)					700
April 20	Jane Gate withdrew £500 cash for personal use.	(500)			(500)		
April 21	Fees of £2,400 were collected in cash from patients and paid into the bank.	2,400				2,400	
April 29	Dental assistant was paid wages for two weeks, £700.	(700)					700
April 29	Invoices were sent to patients who are allowed 20 days' credit, for work done during April amounting to £1,900.		1,900			1,900	
April 30	Telephone bill for April was paid, £80.	(80)					80
April 30	Dental supplies unused were counted and found to be worth £3,500, measured at cost price (i.e. inventory [stock] decreased by £1,500).		(1,500)				1,500
	Totals	25,820	40,400	5,000	59,500	5,500	3,780

Accounting equation:

Cash	plus	other assets	less	liabilities		
25,820	+	40,400	–	5,000	=	61,220
Capital contributed or withdrawn	plus	revenue	less	expenses		
59,500	+	5,500	–	3,780	=	61,220

B5.2

Dental Practice of Jane Gate
Statement of cash flows for the month of April Year XX

Operating activities	£
Inflow from fees	3,600
Outflow: rent paid	(800)
wages	(1,400)
telephone	(80)
Net inflow from operations	1,320
Investing activities	
Payment for equipment	(35,000)
Net outflow for investing activities	(35,000)
Financing activities	
Capital contributed by owner	60,000
Capital withdrawn as drawings	(500)
Net inflow from financing activities	59,500
Increase in cash at bank over period	25,820

Dental Practice of Jane Gate
Income statement (profit and loss account) for the month of April Year XX

	£	£
Fees charged		5,500
Dental supplies used	1,500	
Wages	1,400	
Rent	800	
Telephone	80	
		3,780
Profit		1,720

Dental Practice of Jane Gate
Statement of financial position (balance sheet) at 30 April Year XX

	£
Non-current (fixed) assets	
Dental equipment at cost	35,000
Current assets	
Dental supplies	3,500
Receivables (debtors)	1,900
Cash at bank	25,820
Total current assets	31,220
Total assets	66,220
Current liabilities	
Trade payables (trade creditors)	(5,000)
Net assets	61,220
Capital at start	60,000
Add profit	1,720
Less drawings	(500)
Total ownership interest	61,220

Chapter 6

A6.1

(a) Profit is only reported when there is a sale. The number of items sold is 60. Each one gives a profit of £5 so the total profit is £300.

(b) When the 200 items are purchased there is an increase of £4,000 in the asset of inventory (stock) of spare parts and a decrease of £4,000 in the asset of cash. When the 60 items are sold for £1,500 there is an increase in the asset of cash and an increase in the ownership interest reported as revenue. The 60 items cost £1,200 to purchase and so at the date of sale there is a reduction in the asset of inventory (stock) amounting to £1,200 and a decrease in the ownership interest due to the expense of cost of goods sold £1,200.

A6.2

(a) Transactions summarised by spreadsheet

	Cash	Inventory (stock)	Revenue	Expense
	£	£	£	£
Purchase 200 items @ £20 each	(4,000)	4,000		
Sell 60 items @ £25	1,500		1,500	
Cost of goods sold 60 @ £20		(1,200)		1,200
Totals	(2,500)	2,800	1,500	1,200

(b) Inventory (stock) increases by £2,800 while cash decreases by £2,500, overall increase in assets amounting to £300. Ownership interest increases by £300 when expenses of £1,200 are set against revenue of £1,500.

A6.3

(a) Calculation of profit on sale:

	£
Sale of 50 trays for £8 each	400
Cost of 50 trays at £5.50 each	275
Profit on sale	125

(b) Analysis of transactions using the accounting equation

	£		
June 1	300	Increase asset of inventory (stock) of raw materials.	Decrease asset of cash.
June 3	210	Decrease asset of inventory (stock) of raw materials.	Increase asset of work in progress.
June 5	175	Decrease asset of cash.	Increase asset of work in progress.
June 6	385	Increase asset of finished goods.	Decrease asset of work in progress.
June 11	275	Decrease ownership interest: expense of cost of goods sold.	Decrease asset of finished goods.
June 14	400	Increase asset of cash.	Increase ownership interest: revenue.

A6.4

Date	Amount		
	£		
Apr. 1	60,000	Increase asset of cash.	Increase ownership interest.
Apr. 2	20,000	Increase asset of buildings.	Decrease asset of cash.
Apr. 4	12,000	Increase asset of equipment.	Decrease asset of cash.
Apr. 6	8,500	Increase asset of inventory (stock).	Decrease asset of cash.
Apr. 7	7,000	Increase asset of inventory (stock).	Increase liability to supplier.
Apr. 11	7,000	Decrease liability to supplier.	Decrease asset of cash.
Apr. 14	400	Decrease ownership claim (expense).	Decrease asset of cash.
Apr. 17	5,500	Decrease ownership claim (expense).	Decrease asset of inventory (stock).
Apr. 17	6,000	Increase asset of cash.	Increase ownership claim (revenue).
Apr. 17	4,200	Increase asset of debtor.	Increase ownership claim (revenue).
Apr. 24	4,200	Increase asset of cash.	Decrease asset of debtor.
Apr. 28	2,700	Decrease ownership claim (voluntary withdrawal).	Decrease asset of cash.
Apr. 30	2,800	Decrease ownership claim (expense).	Decrease asset of cash.
Apr. 30	550	Decrease ownership claim (expense of depreciation).	Decrease asset of equipment.

Application B6.1 (a)

		Cash at bank	Fixed assets and debtors	Inventory (stock) of goods	Trade creditor	Capital contributed or withdrawn	Revenue	Expenses
		£	£	£	£	£	£	£
Apr. 1	The owner pays cash into a bank account for the business.	60,000				60,000		
Apr. 2	The business acquires buildings for cash.	(20,000)	20,000					
Apr. 4	The business acquires equipment for cash.	(12,000)	12,000					
Apr. 6	The business purchases an inventory (stock) of goods for cash.	(8,500)		8,500				
Apr. 7	The business purchases goods on credit from R. Green and receives an invoice.			7,000	7,000			
Apr. 11	The business pays R. Green in cash for the goods it acquired on credit.	(7,000)			(7,000)			
Apr. 14	The business pays a gas bill in cash.	(400)						400
Apr. 17	Some of the goods purchased for resale (items costing £5,500) are removed from the store because sales have been agreed with customers for this date.			(5,500)				5,500
Apr. 17	The business sells goods for cash.	6,000					6,000	
Apr. 17	The business sells goods on credit to P. Weatherall and sends an invoice.		4,200				4,200	
Apr. 24	P. Weatherall pays in cash for the goods obtained on credit.	4,200	(4,200)					
Apr. 28	The owner draws cash from the business for personal use.	(2,700)				(2,700)		
Apr. 30	The business pays wages to employees, in cash.	(2,800)						2,800
Apr. 30	The business discovers that its equipment has fallen in value over the month.		(550)					550
	Totals	16,800	31,450	10,000	nil	57,300	10,200	9,250

(b) Accounting equation:

Assets	–	Liabilities	=	Ownership interest
16,800 + 31,450 + 10,000		nil	=	57,300 + 10,200 – 9,250
58,250				58,250

B6.2

Peter Gold, furniture supplier
Statement of cash flows for the month of April Year XX

	£
Operating activities	
Cash from customers	10,200
Outflow: payment for goods	(8,500)
payment to supplier (R. Green)	(7,000)
Wages	(2,800)
Gas	(400)
Net outflow from operations	(8,500)
Investing activities	
Payment for buildings	(20,000)
Payment for equipment	(12,000)
Net outflow for investing activities	(32,000)
Financing activities	
Capital contributed by owner	60,000
Capital withdrawn as drawings	(2,700)
Net inflow from financing activities	57,300
Increase in cash at bank over period	16,800

Peter Gold, furniture supplier
Income statement (profit and loss account) for the month of April Year XX

	£	£
Revenue		10,200
Cost of goods sold		(5,500)
Gross profit		4,700
Other expenses		
Wages	(2,800)	
Gas	(400)	
Depreciation	(550)	
		(3,750)
Net profit		950

Peter Gold, furniture supplier
Statement of financial position (balance sheet) at 30 April Year XX

	£
Non-current (fixed) assets	
Buildings	20,000
Equipment	12,000
	32,000
Depreciation	(550)
Depreciated cost of fixed assets	31,450
Current assets	
Inventory (stocks)	10,000
Cash at bank	16,800
	26,800
Net assets	58,250
Capital at start	60,000
Add profit	950
Less drawings	(2,700)
Total ownership interest	58,250

Chapter 7

Application **B7.1 to B7.4**

The questions at the end of Chapter 7 provide opportunities for writing about accounting information. An outline for an answer could be developed from the chapter and it could be illustrated by using annual reports obtained from companies or their websites.

To write a short essay for question B7.1 or question B7.3 the IASB *Conceptual Framework* would be very helpful.

Problem solving and evaluation Question C7.1 requires you to show that you have thought about all the material in the first seven chapters of the book. A reader of your essay might expect to find some or all of the following questions addressed:

(a) This is a listed company and so shares are bought and sold through the stock market. Does your answer show that you have thought about this active market process?
(b) In giving advice on principles have you made use of the IASB *Conceptual Framework*?
(c) Have you given examples of the kind of information which would be relevant to the *Conceptual Framework*? Furthermore, have you carried out some research on company annual reports so that you can provide first-hand examples or illustrations?

Chapter 8

Test your understanding **A8.14**

Judgement on value, amount and future economic benefit.

Application **B8.1**

(a) The amount of £8,000 has been reported as an asset. Since this is a repair it must be removed from the assets. Removing an asset causes a decrease in the ownership interest through an additional expense of £8,000 in the income statement (profit and loss account).

Problem solving and evaluation **C8.1 The Biscuit Manufacturing Company**

(a) Depreciation calculated on a straight-line basis: $\dfrac{22,000 - 2,000}{4} = £5,000$ per annum

	Transaction or event	Assets			Ownership interest	
		Machine at cost	Accumulated depreciation of van	Cash	Capital contributed or withdrawn	Profit = revenue minus expenses
Year 1		£	£	£	£	£
1 Jan.	Owner contributes cash			22,000	22,000	
1 Jan.	Purchase biscuit machine	22,000		(22,000)		
All year	Collected cash from customers			40,000		40,000
All year	Paid for wages, other costs			(17,000)		(17,000)
31 Dec.	Calculate annual depreciation		(5,000)			(5,000)
	Totals	22,000	(5,000)	23,000	22,000	18,000

		Assets			Ownership interest		
	Transaction or event	Machine at cost	Accumulated depreciation of machine	Cash	Ownership interest at start of year	Capital contributed or withdrawn	Profit = revenue minus expenses
Year 2		£	£	£	£	£	£
1 Jan.	Amounts brought forward at start of year	22,000	(5,000)	23,000	40,000		
All year	Collected cash from customers			40,000			40,000
All year	Paid for wages, fuel, etc.			(17,000)			(17,000)
31 Dec.	Calculate annual depreciation		(5,000)				(5,000)
	Totals	22,000	(10,000)	46,000	40,000		18,000

		Assets			Ownership interest		
	Transaction or event	Machine at cost	Accumulated depreciation of machine	Cash	Ownership interest at start of year	Capital contributed or withdrawn	Profit = revenue minus expenses
Year 3		£	£	£	£	£	£
1 Jan.	Amounts brought forward at start of year	22,000	(10,000)	46,000	58,000		
All year	Collected cash from customers			40,000			40,000
All year	Paid for wages, fuel, etc.			(17,000)			(17,000)
31 Dec.	Calculate annual depreciation		(5,000)				(5,000)
	Totals	22,000	(15,000)	69,000	58,000		18,000

		Assets			Ownership interest		
	Transaction or event	Machine at cost	Accumulated depreciation of machine	Cash	Ownership interest at start of year	Capital contributed or withdrawn	Profit = revenue minus expenses
Year 4		£	£	£	£	£	£
1 Jan.	Amounts brought forward at start of year	22,000	(15,000)	69,000	76,000		
All year	Collected cash from customers			40,000			40,000
All year	Paid for wages, fuel, etc.			(17,000)			(17,000)
31 Dec.	Calculate annual depreciation		(5,000)				(5,000)
	Totals	22,000	(20,000)	92,000	76,000		18,000

(b)

Biscuit Manufacturing Company
Statement of financial position (balance sheet) at 31 December Year 3

	£
Non-current (fixed) assets	
Machine at cost	22,000
Accumulated depreciation	(15,000)
Net book value	7,000
Current assets	
Cash	69,000
Total assets	76,000
Ownership interest	
Ownership interest at the start of the year	58,000
Profit of the year	18,000
	76,000

Biscuit Manufacturing Company
Income statement (profit and loss account) for the year ended
31 December Year 3

	£	£
Revenue		
Sale of biscuits		40,000
Expenses		
Wages, ingredients and running costs	(17,000)	
Depreciation	(5,000)	
		(22,000)
Net profit		18,000

C8.2

(a)

		Assets			Ownership interest		
	Transaction or event	Machine at cost	Accumulated depreciation of machine	Cash	Ownership interest at start of year	Capital contributed or withdrawn	Profit = revenue minus expenses
Year 4		£	£	£	£	£	£
1 Jan.	Amounts brought forward at start of year	22,000	(15,000)	69,000	76,000		
All year	Collected cash from customers			40,000			40,000
All year	Paid for wages, fuel, etc.			(17,000)			(17,000)
31 Dec.	Calculate annual depreciation		(5,000)				(5,000)
31 Dec.	Machine disposal	(22,000)	20,000	3,000			1,000
	Totals	nil	nil	95,000	76,000		19,000

Note that at the end of Year 4 the net book value is £2,000 (cost £22,000 less accumulated depreciation £20,000). The cash received £3,000 is therefore £1,000 more than expected. The amount of £1,000 is recorded as an increase in the ownership interest.

(b)
Biscuit Manufacturing Company
Statement of financial position (balance sheet) at 31 December Year 4

	£
Non-current (fixed) assets	
Machine at cost	nil
Current assets	
Cash	95,000
Total assets	95,000
Ownership interest	
Ownership interest at the start of the year	76,000
Profit of the year	19,000
	95,000

Biscuit Manufacturing Company
Income statement (profit and loss account) for the year ended 31 December Year 4

	£	£
Revenue		
Sale of biscuits		40,000
Expenses		
Wages, ingredients and running costs	(17,000)	
Depreciation less gain on disposal	(4,000)	
		(21,000)
Net profit		19,000

(c) There is apparently a gain on disposal because the cash collected is greater than the net book value of the asset. In reality, all that has happened is that the estimate of depreciation over the asset life is, with the benefit of hindsight, a marginally incorrect estimate. Perfect foresight at the outset would have used £3,000 as a residual value, rather than £2,000, in calculating the annual depreciation charge. However, it is known that accounting involves estimates so it would be inappropriate in most cases to attempt to rewrite the income statements (profit and loss accounts) of the past. Accordingly all of the 'gain' is reported in Year 4, as a deduction from annual depreciation.

C8.3 Souvenir Company
(a) Straight-line depreciation

Machine cost £16,000, estimated residual value £1,000, so depreciate the difference, £15,000, over five-year life to give annual depreciation of £3,000.

End of Year	Depreciation of the year (b) £	Total depreciation (c) £	Net book value of the asset (£16,000 – (c)) £
1	3,000	3,000	13,000
2	3,000	6,000	10,000
3	3,000	9,000	7,000
4	3,000	12,000	4,000
5	3,000	15,000	1,000

(b) Guess a rate which is at least twice the percentage applied on a straight-line basis (i.e. in this case guess 20% × 2 = 40%).
   Calculation of reducing balance depreciation (as in Table 8.2):

Year	Net book value at start of year (a) £	Annual depreciation (b) = 40% of (a) £	Net book value at end of year (a – b) £
1	16,000	6,400	9,600
2	9,600	3,840	5,760
3	5,760	2,304	3,456
4	3,456	1,382	2,074
5	2,074	830	1,244

(The residual value at the end of Year 5 should ideally be £1,000, so a first estimate which arrives at £1,244 is quite reasonable.)

(c) The net book value at the end of Year 5 is £1,000 and therefore disposal at £2,500 gives an apparent gain of £1,500 which is best described as caused by over-depreciation of earlier years. The effect on the accounting equation is that the asset of machine decreases by £1,000 while the asset of cash increases by £2,500 so that overall the ownership interest increases by £1,500.

(d) The net book value at the end of Year 5 is £1,000 and therefore disposal at nil scrap value gives an apparent loss of £1,000 which is best described as caused by underdepreciation of earlier years. The effect on the accounting equation is that the asset of machine decreases by £1,000 with no increase in any other asset so that overall the ownership interest decreases by £1,000.

Chapter 9

Test your understanding

A9.10

Use lower of cost and net realisable value on each category separately:

Description	Basis	Stock value £
Engine	Cost	6,500
Chassis	Net realisable value	1,600
Frame	Net realisable value	4,600

A9.11

The recorded inventory (stock) will increase by £18,000 and the ownership interest will increase by £18,000 (reported as a reduction in the cost of goods sold).

A9.12

The asset of debtor (trade receivable) will be reduced by £154,000 and the ownership interest will decrease by £154,000 (reported as an expense of cost of bad debts).

Application

B9.1

(a) The FIFO approach to the issue of units for sale, where:
  (i) the calculation is carried out at the date of sale; and
  (ii) the calculation is carried out at the end of the month without regard for the date of sale.

Date	Number of units purchased	Unit cost	Number of units sold	Cost of goods sold (i) £	Cost of goods sold (ii) £	Inventory (stock) (i)	Inventory (stock) (ii)
Jan. 5	100	£1.00					
Jan. 10			50	50			
Jan. 15	200	£1.10					
Jan. 17			150	50 110			
Jan. 24	300	£1.15					
Jan. 30			200	110 115	100 220 115		
	600		400	435	435	230	230

	£
Sales 400 × £2	800
Cost of goods sold	435
Profit	365

Inventory (stock) = 200 × £1.15 = £230

(b) The LIFO approach to the issue of units for sale, where:
   (i) the calculation is carried out at the date of sale; and
   (ii) the calculation is carried out at the end of the month without regard for the date of sale; and

Date	Number of units purchased	Unit cost	Number of units sold	Cost of goods sold (i) £	Cost of goods sold (ii) £	Inventory (stock) (i)	Inventory (stock) (ii)
Jan. 5	100	£1.00					
Jan. 10			50	50		50	
Jan. 15	200	£1.10					
Jan. 17			150	165		55	
Jan. 24	300	£1.15					
Jan. 30			200	230	345	115	100
					110		110
	600		400	345	455	220	210

either (i):

	£
Sales 400 × £2	800
Cost of goods sold	345
Profit	455

Inventory (stock) = (50 × £1.00) + (50 × £1.10) + (100 × £1.15)
= 50 + 55 + 115 = 220

or (ii):

	£
Sales 400 × £2	800
Cost of goods sold	455
Profit	345

Inventory (stock) = (100 × £1) + (100 × £1.10)
= 100 + 110 = £210

Note that in all cases the Cost of goods sold plus the unsold Inventory (stock) = £665.

(c) The average-cost approach to the issue of units for sale, making the calculation at the end of the month without regard for the date of sale.

Date	Number of units purchased	Unit cost	£
Jan. 5	100	£1.00	100
Jan. 10			
Jan. 15	200	£1.10	220
Jan. 17			
Jan. 24	300	£1.15	345
Jan. 30			
	600		665

Average cost = £665/500 = £1.108

	£
Sales 400 × £2	800
Cost of goods sold 400 × £1.108	443
Profit	357

Inventory (stock) 200 × £1.108 = £222

B9.2

Group of items	Basis	Inventory (stock) value £
A	Cost	1,000
B	Net realisable value	800
C	Net realisable value	1,900
D	Cost	3,000
Total inventory (stock)		6,700

Chapter 10

A10.9

The liability to the supplier will increase and the ownership interest will decrease (recorded as an increase in the cost of goods sold).

A10.10

The recorded asset of cash will decrease and the recorded liability to the supplier will decrease.

A10.11

First the original incorrect entry must be reversed. When the entry was made, it was treated as an increase in the ownership interest and an increase in the asset of debtor. This error must be reversed by decreasing the ownership interest and decreasing the asset of debtor.

Then the correct entry must be made which is a decrease in the ownership interest and an increase in a liability to the landlord.

B10.1

The aim of the calculation is to show the cost of telephone used during the year.

	£
Cash paid	3,500
Less rental in advance for July, one-third of £660	(220)
Add calls for May and June, two-thirds of £900	600
Expense of the period	3,880

The rental paid in advance will be shown as a prepayment of £220 in the statement of financial position (balance sheet) and the calls made during May and June will be shown as an accrual of £600 in the statement of financial position (balance sheet).

B10.2

		Asset	Liability	Ownership interest profit of the period
Date	Transactions with security company	Cash	Security company	Security expense
Year 1		£	£	£
Mar. 31	Invoice received £800		800	(800)
Apr. 5	Security company paid £800	(800)	(800)	
June 30	Invoice received £800		800	(800)
July 5	Security company paid £800	(800)	(800)	
Sept. 30	Invoice received £800		800	(800)
Oct. 5	Security company paid £800	(800)	(800)	
Dec. 31	Invoice received £800		800	(800)
	Totals	(2,400)	800	(3,200)

B10.3

The tax charge reduces the ownership interest and is shown as an expense of £8,000 in the income statement (profit and loss account). The accounting equation remains in balance because there is a matching liability of £8,000 recorded. However, the liability is split as £6,000 current liability and £2,000 deferred liability to reflect different patterns of payment of the overall liability.

Problem solving and evaluation **C10.1**

The year-end is 31 December Year 1.

Item	Description	Amount £		
1	Invoice dated 23 December for goods received 21 December.	260	Increase asset of inventory (stock).	Increase liability to supplier.
2	Invoice dated 23 December for goods to be delivered on 3 January Year 2.	310	Nothing recorded – this will be an asset and a liability of the following year.	
3	Foreman's note of electricity consumption for month of December – no invoice yet received from electricity supply company.	100	Decrease ownership interest (expense of electricity).	Increase liability to electricity supplier.
4	Letter from employee claiming overtime payment for work on 1 December and note from personnel office denying entitlement to payment.	58	Nothing recorded in the financial statements because it is not yet clear that there is an obligation (might be a contingent liability note).	
5	Telephone bill dated 26 December showing calls for October to December.	290	Decrease ownership interest (expense of telephone calls).	Increase liability to phone company.
6	Telephone bill dated 26 December showing rent due in advance for period January to March Year 2.	90	Nothing recorded – this will be an expense of the following year.	
7	Note of payment due to cleaners for final week of December (to be paid on 3 January under usual pattern of payment one week in arrears).	48	Usually nothing recorded if payment in arrears is normal, since the corresponding payment from January Year 1 will be included in the year's expense.	
8	Invoice from supplier for promotional calendars received 1 December (only one-third have yet been sent to customers).	300	Decrease ownership interest £300 (expense of calendars).	Increase liability to calendar supplier £300.
			Increase inventory (stock) of calendars by £200.	Reduce expense by £200.
9	Letter dated 21 December Year 1 to customer promising a cheque to reimburse damage caused by faulty product – cheque to be sent on 4 January Year 2.	280	Decrease ownership interest (expense of damage).	Increase liability to customer.
10	Letter dated 23 December promising donation to local charity – amount not yet paid.	60	Decrease ownership interest (expense of donation).	Increase liability to charity.

Chapter 11

Test your understanding **A11.6**

Reduce revenue by £40,000 (two-thirds of £60,000) and increase statement of financial position (balance sheet) deferred income by £40,000. Effect on income statement (profit and loss account) is to reduce reported profit. Reason is application of the matching concept. The £40,000 deferred income will be transferred to income statement (profit and loss account) over the next two years.

A11.7

Increase expense of provision for repairs by £50,000 (reporting as an expense in the income statement (profit and loss account)) and create a liability under the 'provisions' heading. Effect on income statement (profit and loss account) is to reduce reported profit.

Application **B11.1**

The income statement (profit and loss account) would show an expense of £8,000 provision in Year 1 and an expense of £9,000 provision in Year 2. The actual amount of expenditure as shown in the question would be set against the provision in the statement of financial position (balance sheet).

Date of repair	Profit and loss expense	Statement of financial position (balance sheet) provision in total before expense charged	Actual expense matched against provision	Provision remaining in statement of financial position (balance sheet)
Year	£	£	£	£
1	8,000	8,000	4,500	3,500
2	9,000	12,500	8,000	4,500
3	*500	4,500	*4,500	nil

* The actual cost in Year 3 is £5,000 but there is only £4,500 provision remaining, so the extra £500 must be charged to income statement (profit and loss account) as an unexpected expense.

Note that the total amount charged to income statement (profit and loss account) is £17,500 and the total amount paid out for repair work is also £17,500. The accounting entries in the income statement (profit and loss account) are an attempt to spread the expense on the basis of matching with revenue, but the total must be the same over the three-year period, whatever matching approach is taken.

Date of repair	Profit and loss expense using provision approach	Profit and loss expense using actual repair amount paid
	£	£
1	8,000	4,500
2	9,000	8,000
3	*500	5,000
Total	17,500	17,500

B11.2

The grant will initially be recorded as an increase in the asset of cash and an increase in the statement of financial position (balance sheet) liability item headed 'deferred income'. The deferred income is transferred from the liability to revenue over three years (so that the ownership interest increases evenly over the three-year period).

Chapter 12

Application **B12.1**

(a) Increase the asset of cash by £50,000. Increase the ownership interest by the nominal value of shares, £50,000.
(b) Increase the asset of cash by £75,000. Increase the ownership interest by (i) nominal value of shares £25,000 and (ii) share premium £50,000.
(c) Increase asset of property by £20,000. Increase ownership interest by revaluation reserve £20,000.

B12.2

(a) Decrease asset of cash by £20,000. Decrease ownership interest by £20,000 as a reduction in the owners' claim on the business.
(b) Record a note in the directors' report. There is no liability at the date of the financial statements.

B12.3 Nithsdale Ltd

	£000s	(a) £000s	(b) £000s	(c) £000s
Cash	20	70.0	20	260
Other assets less liabilities	320	320.0	320	320
	340	390.0	340	580
Ordinary shares (400,000 of 25 pence each)	100	112.5	125	120
Share premium	40	77.5	40	260
Reserves of retained profit	200	200.0	175	200
	340	390.0	340	580

B12.4

If the directors decide that they wish to incorporate the revaluation in the statement of financial position (balance sheet), then the asset will be reported at £380,000. The difference between the previous recorded book value £250,000 and the new value £380,000 is £130,000. This is an increase in the ownership interest and will be reported as a revaluation reserve as part of the total ownership interest.

B12.5

In this case the value has decreased by £10,000. This is a reduction in the value of the asset and a decrease in the ownership claim. On grounds of prudence the loss should be reported in the income statement (profit and loss account) immediately and the recorded book value of the asset should be reduced.

Chapter 13

Application **B13.1**

(a) Hope plc

(i) Liquidity

		Hope plc	
Ratio	Definition in words	Workings	Result
Current ratio	Current assets:Current liabilities	2,360:1,240	1.90:1
Acid test	(Current assets – Inventory (stock)): Current liabilities	(2,360 – 620):1,240	1.40:1
Inventory (stock) holding period*	$\dfrac{\text{Average inventory held}}{\text{Cost of sales}} \times 365$	$\dfrac{620}{2,750} \times 365$	82.3 days
Customers collection period	$\dfrac{\text{Trade receivables (debtors)}}{\text{Credit sales}} \times 365$	$\dfrac{1,540}{6,200} \times 365$	90.7 days
Suppliers payment period[†]	$\dfrac{\text{Trade payables (creditors)}}{\text{Credit purchases}} \times 365$	$\dfrac{300}{2,750} \times 365$	39.8 days

* Assuming the opening inventory (stock) is the same as the closing inventory (stock).
[†] Assuming purchases = cost of goods sold.

(a) 50,000 × 25p = £12,500; 50,000 × £0.75 = £37,500.
(b) Transfer £25,000 from reserves to share capital.
(c) 80,000 × £3 = £240,000; 80,000 × 25p = £20,000; 80,000 × £2.75 = £220,000.

(ii) Analysis of management performance

		Hope plc	
Ratio	Definition in words	Workings	Result
Return on shareholders' equity	$\dfrac{\text{Profit after tax}}{\text{Share capital + Reserves}} \times 100\%$	$\dfrac{692}{1,470} \times 100$	47.1%
Return on capital employed	$\dfrac{\text{Profit before interest and tax}}{\text{Total assets – Current liabilities}} \times 100\%$	$\dfrac{1,256}{2,870} \times 100$	43.8%
Net profit on sales	$\dfrac{\text{Profit before interest and taxes}}{\text{Sales}} \times 100$	$\dfrac{1,256}{6,200} \times 100$	20.3%
Gross profit percentage	$\dfrac{\text{Gross profit}}{\text{Sales}} \times 100$	$\dfrac{3,450}{6,200} \times 100\%$	55.6%
Total assets usage	$\dfrac{\text{Sales}}{\text{Total assets}}$	$\dfrac{6,200}{1,750 + 2,360}$	1.5 times
Fixed assets usage	$\dfrac{\text{Sales}}{\text{Non-current (fixed) assets}}$	$\dfrac{6,200}{1,750}$	3.5 times

(iii) Gearing (leverage)

		Hope plc	
Ratio	Definition in words	Workings	Result
Debt/equity ratio	$\dfrac{\text{Debt + Preference share capital}}{\text{Ordinary share capital reserves}} + 100\%$	$\dfrac{1,400}{1,470} + 100$	95.2%
Interest cover	$\dfrac{\text{Profit before interest and tax}}{\text{Interest}}$	$\dfrac{1,256}{84}$	15.0 times

(c) Investor ratios

		Hope plc	
Ratio	Definition in words	Workings	Result
Earnings per share	$\dfrac{\text{Profit after for ordinary shareholders}}{\text{Number of ordinary shares}}$	$\dfrac{692}{900}$	76.9 pence
Price/earnings ratio	$\dfrac{\text{Share price}}{\text{Earnings per share}}$	$\dfrac{1,100}{76.9}$	14
Dividend cover (payout ratio)	$\dfrac{\text{Earning per share}}{\text{Dividend per share}}$	$\dfrac{76.9}{36.7}$	2.1 times
Dividend yield	$\dfrac{\text{Dividend per share}}{\text{Share price}} \times 100\%$	$\dfrac{36.7}{1,100} \times 100\%$	3.34%

Chapter 14

Problem solving and evaluation

C14.1 Trend analysis: Safe and Sure

	Year 3	Year 4	Year 5	Year 6	Year 7
Group revenue	309.1	389.0	474.1	600.3	734.6
Group profit before tax	74.4	90.4	114.5	147.0	177.0
Tax	(27.2)	(33.9)	(44.3)	(52.4)	(62.2)
Group profit after tax	47.2	56.5	70.2	94.6	114.8
Earnings per share	4.88	6.23	8.02	9.71	11.74
Dividends per share	1.32	1.69	2.17	2.50	3.02
Share capital	19.4	19.4	19.4	19.5	19.6
Reserves	160.8	195.3	265.4	350.9	444.7
Total equity	180.2	214.7	284.8	370.4	464.3
Ratios					
Pre-tax profit to sales	24.1%	23.2%	24.2%	24.5%	24.1%
Tax charge as % of pre-tax profit	36.6%	37.5%	38.7%	35.6%	35.1%
Dividend cover	3.70	3.70	3.70	3.88	3.89
Growth in revenue	n/a	25.9%	21.9%	26.6%	22.4%
Growth in eps	n/a	27.7%	28.7%	21.1%	20.9%
Growth in dividend per share	n/a	28.0%	28.4%	15.2%	20.8%
Return on shareholders' equity	26.2%	26.3%	24.7%	25.5%	25.3%

Commentary. The company has exceeded its annual earnings growth target of 20% in each year for which calculations can be made. The dividend cover is relatively high, indicating a policy of retaining new wealth to finance expansion. In Year 6 the dividend cover increased because the dividend growth decreased. In Year 7 the cover remains higher and the dividend growth improved. With the expansion the company has maintained its rate of return on shareholders' equity. The company is likely to be attractive to investors if future prospects are similar to the historical trend.

Chapter 15

Application

B15.1
£120m + £8m − £10m = £118m

B15.2
£20m + £6m − £4m = £22m

B15.3
£34m − £5m + ? = £37m Missing number is £8m acquisition.

Problem solving **C15.1**
and evaluation **Fruit Sales plc – indirect method**

Notes		£m	£m
	Cash flows from operating activities		
1	Profit before taxation		132
	Adjustment for items not involving a flow of cash:		
	Depreciation	39	
	Gain on disposal of equipment	(7)	
			32
	Adjusted profit		164
	(Increase) in inventories	(6)	
	(Increase) in trade receivables	(2)	
	Increase in trade payables	5	
	Increase/(decrease) in cash due to working capital changes		(3)
	Cash generated from operations		161
2	Interest paid		(19)
3	Taxes paid		(32)
	Net cash inflow from operating activities		110
	Cash flows from investing activities		
4	Purchase of vehicles	(90)	
5	Proceeds from sale of vehicles	20	
6	Investments acquired	(20)	
	Interest received	5	
	Net cash used in investing activities		(85)
	Cash flows from financing activities		
7	Proceeds from issue of share capital	35	
8	Proceeds from long-term borrowing	8	
	Dividends paid	(31)	
	Net cash raised from financing activities		12
	Increase/(decrease) in cash and cash equivalents		37
9	**Cash and cash equivalents at the start of the period**		6
9	**Cash and cash equivalents at the end of the period**		43

Working note 1

	£m
Operating profit before taxes	117
Is there any interest expense included in this figure? If so add it back to arrive at:	20
Operating profit before deducting interest payable and taxes	137
Is there any interest received/receivable or any dividends received in this figure? If so deduct it to arrive at:	(5)
Operating profit before deducting interest payable and taxes and before including interest receivable and dividends received.	132

Working note 2
Interest paid = expense £20m plus liability at the start £7m minus liability at the end £8m.

Working note 3
Taxes paid = tax charge of the period £35m plus liability at the start £7m minus liability at the end £10m.

Working note 4

The vehicles at cost start with a balance of £130m. Additions are £90m and disposals cost £25m originally, leaving a balance of £195m.

Vehicles at cost – ledger account

	Debit	Credit	Balance
	£m	£m	£m
Balance at start	130		130
Additions	90		220
Disposals		25	195

Working note 5

The accumulated depreciation starts with a balance of £52m. This increases by the expense of the period £39m and decreases by the accumulated depreciation of the vehicles sold £12m, leaving a balance of £79m. The net book value of the vehicles sold was £13m (£25m – £12m). Deduct this from the proceeds of sale £20m to calculate the gain on disposal of £7m shown in the income statement.

Vehicles accumulated depreciation – ledger account

	Debit	Credit	Balance
	£m	£m	£m
Balance at start		52	(52)
Depreciation expense for the period		39	(91)
Accumulated depreciation on vehicles sold	12		(79)

Vehicles disposal – ledger account

	Debit	Credit	Balance
	£m	£m	£m
Asset at cost	25		25
Accumulated depreciation		12	13
Proceeds of sale		20	(7)
Transfer to income statement, gain on disposal	7		nil

Working note 6

The statement of financial position (balance sheet) investments increase by £20m. Assume no sales.

Working note 7

Increase in share capital £32m plus increase in share premium £3m.

Working note 8
Increase in borrowings £8m. Assume no repayments.

Fruit sales plc – direct method

Notes		£m	£m
	Cash flows from operating activities		
1	Cash receipts from customers		318
2	Cash paid to suppliers and employees		(144)
	Cash paid for administrative and selling expenses		(13)
	Cash generated from operations		161
	Interest paid		(19)
	Taxes paid		(32)
	Net cash inflow from operating activities		110
	Cash flows from investing activities		
	Purchase of vehicles	(90)	
	Proceeds from sale of vehicles	20	
	Investments acquired	(20)	
	Interest received	5	
	Net cash used in investing activities		(85)
	Cash flows from financing activities		
	Proceeds from issue of share capital	35	
	Proceeds from long-term borrowing	8	
	Dividends paid	(31)	
	Net cash used in financing activities		12
	Increase/(decrease) in cash and cash equivalents		37
	Cash and cash equivalents at the start of the period		6
	Cash and cash equivalents at the end of the period		43

Working note 1
Revenue in income statement £320m plus receivables at start of period £21m minus receivables at the end of the period £23m.

Accounts receivable – ledger account

	Debit	Credit	Balance
	£m	£m	£m
Balance at start	21		21
Revenue – sales	320		341
Cash received		318	23

Working note 2
Purchases = cost of goods sold £143m plus inventory at the end £26m less inventory at the start £20m = £149m.

Purchases – ledger account

	Debit	Credit	Balance
	£m	£m	£m
Balance of inventory at start	20		(20)
Purchases of supplies	149		(169)
Cash paid		144	26

Payment to suppliers = £149m plus payables at the start £13m less payables at the end £18m.

Accounts payable – suppliers

	Debit	Credit	Balance
	£m	£m	£m
Balance of payables at start		13	(13)
Purchases		149	(162)
Cash paid	144		(18)

Index